STR... 5

Cumbria

First published in 2004 by

Philip's, a division of
Octopus Publishing Group Ltd
2-4 Heron Quays, London E14 4JP

First edition 2004
Third impression 2006
CAMAA

ISBN-10   0-540-08500-6 (pocket)
ISBN-13   978-0-540-08500-2 (pocket)

© Philip's 2004

Ordnance Survey®

This product includes mapping data licensed from
Ordnance Survey® with the permission of the
Controller of Her Majesty's Stationery Office.
© Crown copyright 2004. All rights reserved.
Licence number 100011710.

Contents

III **Key to map symbols**

IV **Key to map pages**

VI **Route planning**

X **Administrative and Postcode boundaries**

1 **Street maps** at 1⅓ inches to 1 mile

172 **Street maps** at 2⅔ inches to 1 mile

214 **Street map of Carlisle city centre**
at 5⅓ inches to 1 mile

215 **Town maps with indexes** of Dumfries and
Morecambe

217 **Index** of towns and villages

219 **Index** of streets, hospitals, industrial estates, railway
stations, schools, shopping centres, universities
and places of interest

Digital Data

The exceptionally high-quality mapping found in this atlas is available as digital data in TIFF
format, which is easily convertible to other bitmapped (raster) image formats.

The index is also available in digital form as a standard database table. It contains all the details
found in the printed index together with the National Grid reference for the map square in which
each entry is named.

For further information and to discuss your requirements, please contact Philip's on
020 7644 6932 or james.mann@philips-maps.co.uk

	Motorway with junction number			**Ambulance station**
	Primary route – dual/single carriageway			**Coastguard station**
	A road – dual/single carriageway			**Fire station**
	B road – dual/single carriageway			**Police station**
	Minor road – dual/single carriageway			**Accident and Emergency entrance to hospital**
	Other minor road – dual/single carriageway			**Hospital**
	Road under construction			**Place of worship**
	Tunnel, covered road			**Information Centre** (open all year)
	Rural track, private road or narrow road in urban area			**Parking**
	Gate or obstruction to traffic (restrictions may not apply at all times or to all vehicles)			**Park and Ride**
	Path, bridleway, byway open to all traffic, road used as a public path			**Post Office**
	Pedestrianised area			**Camping site**
	Postcode boundaries			**Caravan site**
	County and unitary authority boundaries			**Golf course**
	Railway, tunnel, railway under construction			**Picnic site**
	Tramway, tramway under construction		Prim Sch	**Important buildings, schools, colleges, universities and hospitals**
	Miniature railway		River Medway	**Water name**
Walsall	**Railway station**			**River, weir, stream**
	Private railway station			**Canal, lock, tunnel**
South Shields	**Metro station**			**Water**
	Tram stop, tram stop under construction			**Tidal water**
	Bus, coach station			**Woods**

Acad	**Academy**	Inst	**Institute**	Recn Gd	**Recreation Ground**

Built up area / Non-Roman antiquity / Roman antiquity / Adjoining page indicators

Acad	**Academy**	Inst	**Institute**	Recn Gd	**Recreation Ground**
Allot Gdns	**Allotments**	Ct	**Law Court**		
Cemy	**Cemetery**	L Ctr	**Leisure Centre**	Resr	**Reservoir**
C Ctr	**Civic Centre**	LC	**Level Crossing**	Ret Pk	**Retail Park**
CH	**Club House**	Liby	**Library**	Sch	**School**
Coll	**College**	Mkt	**Market**	Sh Ctr	**Shopping Centre**
Crem	**Crematorium**	Meml	**Memorial**	TH	**Town Hall/House**
Ent	**Enterprise**	Mon	**Monument**	Trad Est	**Trading Estate**
Ex H	**Exhibition Hall**	Mus	**Museum**	Univ	**University**
Ind Est	**Industrial Estate**	Obsy	**Observatory**	W Twr	**Water Tower**
IRB Sta	**Inshore Rescue**	Pal	**Royal Palace**	Wks	**Works**
	Boat Station	PH	**Public House**	YH	**Youth Hostel**

Church — **Non-Roman antiquity**

ROMAN FORT — **Roman antiquity**

87 / **228** **Adjoining page indicators and overlap bands**
The colour of the arrow and the band indicates the scale of the adjoining or overlapping page (see scales below)

■ The small numbers around the edges of the maps identify the 1 kilometre National Grid lines

■ The dark grey border on the inside edge of some pages indicates that the mapping does not continue onto the adjacent page

The scale of the maps on the pages numbered in blue is 4.2 cm to 1 km • 2⅔ inches to 1 mile • 1: 23810

0 ¼ ½ ¾ 1 mile
0 250 m 500 m 750 m 1 kilometre

The scale of the maps on pages numbered in green is 2.1 cm to 1 km • 1⅓ inches to 1 mile • 1: 47620

0 ¼ ½ ¾ 1 mile
0 250m 500m 750m 1 kilometre

The scale of the maps on pages numbered in red is 8.4 cm to 1 km • 5⅓ inches to 1 mile • 1: 11900

0 220 yards 440 yards 660 yards ½ mile
0 125m 250m 375m ½ kilometre

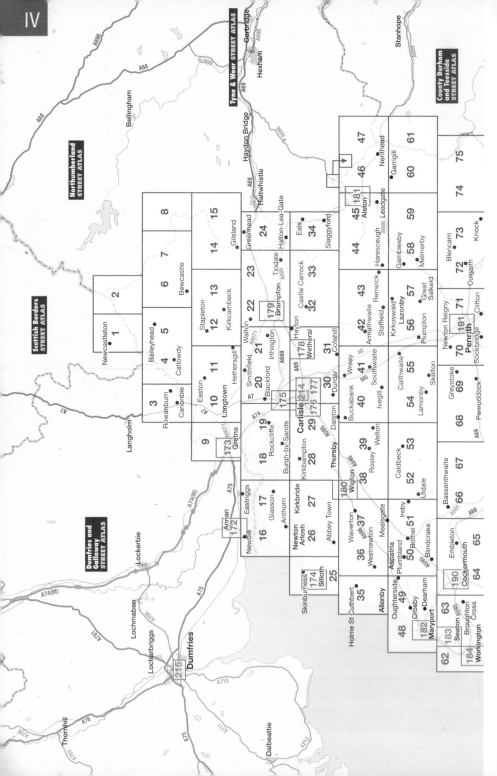

IV

Tyne & Wear STREET ATLAS

County Durham and Teesside STREET ATLAS

Northumberland STREET ATLAS

Scottish Borders STREET ATLAS

Dumfries and Galloway STREET ATLAS

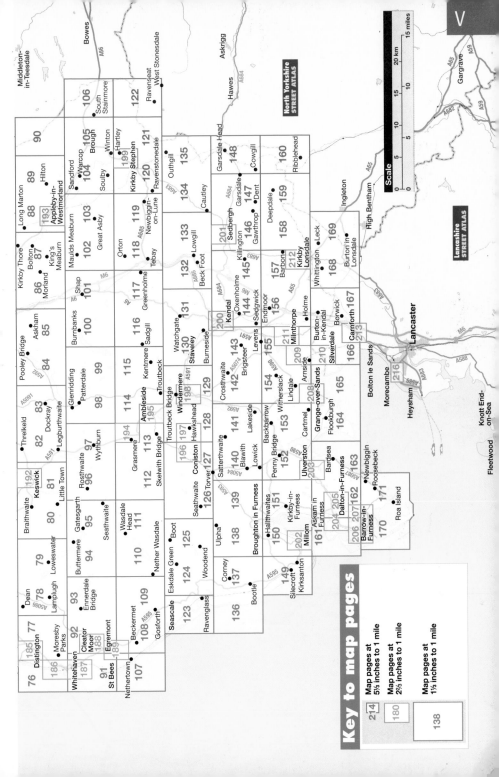

V

North Yorkshire STREET ATLAS

Lancashire STREET ATLAS

Scale

0 5 10 15 20 km

0 5 10 15 miles

Key to map pages

Map pages at
5½ inches to 1 mile — 214

Map pages at
2⅔ inches to 1 mile — 180

Map pages at
1⅓ inches to 1 mile — 138

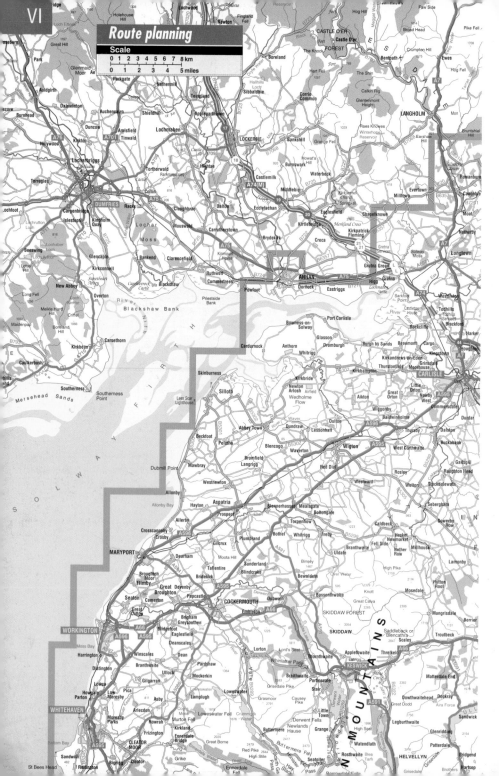

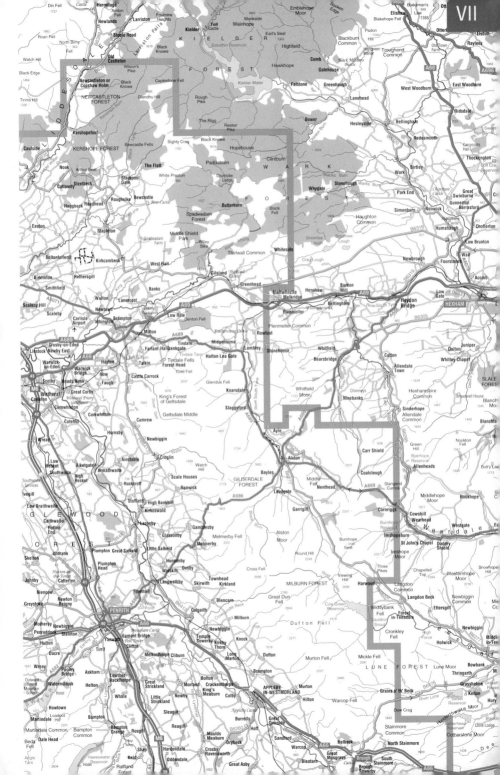

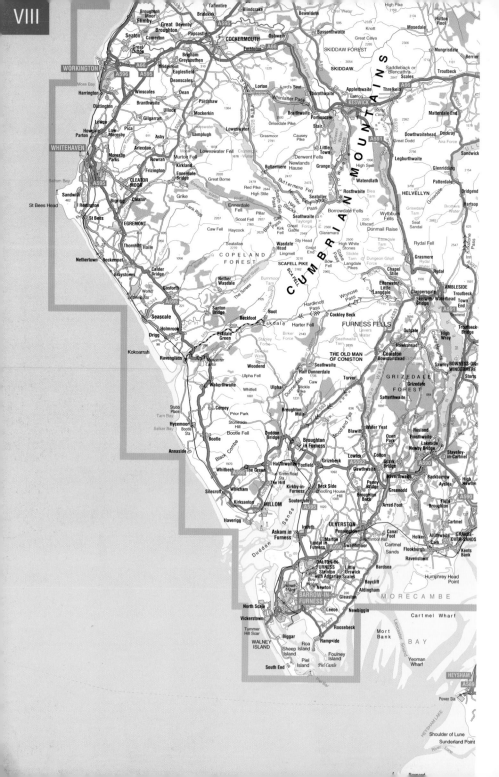

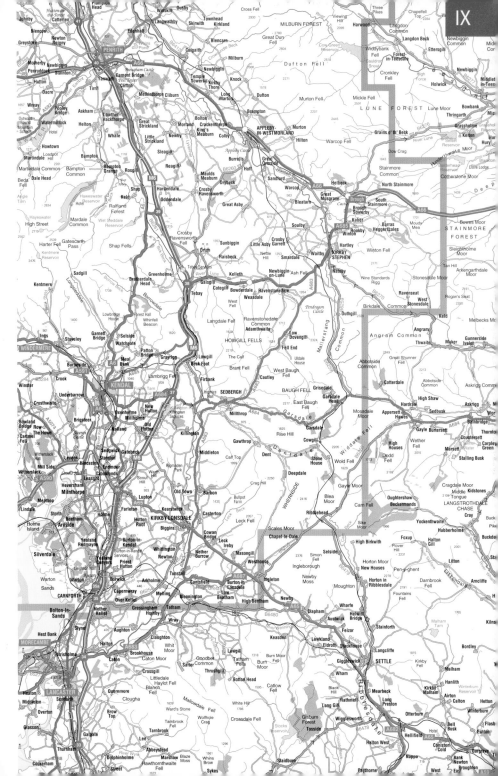

Major administrative and Postcode boundaries

County and unitary authority boundaries
District boundaries
Postcode boundaries
Area covered by this atlas

Scale
0   5   10   15 km
0   5   10 miles

NT
NY

Dumfries and Galloway

Scottish Borders

Northumberland

NX NY

Newcastleton or Copshaw Holm
TD9
NE48

DG11
DG14
Canonbie
DG11
DG16 Longtown
CA6
Annan DG12 Gretna
Carlisle
CA8
Bowness-on-Solway
Brampton
NE49
Burgh by Sands
CA3
CA2 Carlisle
Silloth
CA5
Wetheral
CA1
Abbey Town
Wigton
CA4
Alston
NE47
CA7
Renwick
CA9
DL13
Allonby
Aspatria
Melmerby
Durham
Maryport CA15
Allerdale
CA11
Penrith
Culgaith
DL12
Seaton Cockermouth
Greystoke
Eden
Workington
CA13
Keswick
Cumbria CA10
CA14 Ullock
CA12
CA16
Appleby-in-Westmorland
Whitehaven CA28 CA26
Glenridding
Warcop
Brough
CA24 CA25 Frizington
Rosthwaite
Shap
CA17
St Bees Cleator Moor
CA23
CA27 Egremont
Kirkby Stephen
CA22
Grasmere LA22
DL11
CA21 CA20
Copeland Gosforth
Ambleside
Seascale
LA23
NX NY
Drigg
CA19
Tebay
SC SD
CA18
Coniston
Windermere LA8
LA20 LA21
South Lakeland
Kendal
Bootle
Broughton in Furness
LA9
Sedbergh
LA18
LA12
LA10
Millom
LA17
DL8
Ulverston
LA11 LA7 Milnthorpe
BD23
LA16 LA15
Grange-over-Sands
LA6
Flookburgh
Kirkby Lonsdale
BD24
Barrow-in-Furness LA14
Arnside
Dalton-in-Furness
Silverdale
North Yorkshire
Barrow-in Furness
Carnforth LA5
LA13
LA2
Lancashire

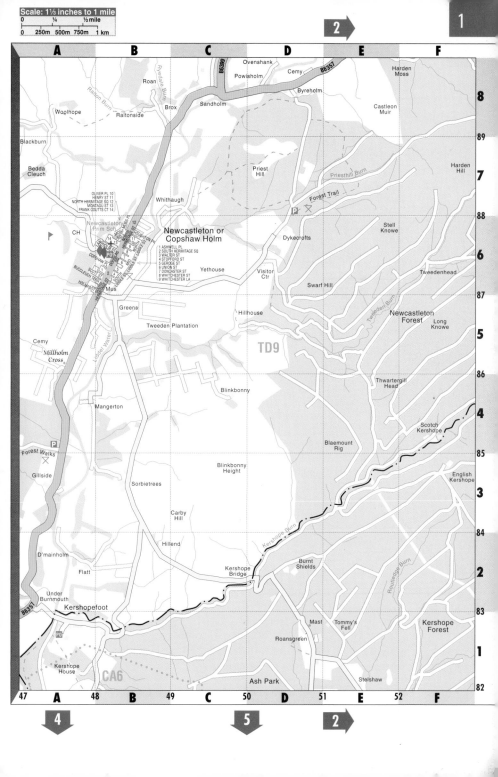

Scale: 1½ inches to 1 mile

0   ¼   ½ mile
0 250m 500m 750m 1 km

1

2

4

5

2

Ryedale Burn

B6399

Ovenshank

Powisholm

Cemy

B6357

Harden Moss

Roan

Ralton Burn

Brox

Sandholm

Byreholm

Castleon Muir

Woolhope

Raltonside

Blackburn

Priest Hill

Priesthill Burn

Harden Hill

Bedda Cleuch

Whithaugh

Forest Trail

P

Newcastleton Prim Sch

CH

Newcastleton or Copshaw Holm

Dykecrofts

Stell Knowe

OLIVER PL 10
HENRY ST 11
NORTH HERMITAGE SQ 12
MONTAGU ST 13
FRANK COLITTS CT 14

CHURCH PL
BROUGHTON PL

12

13

14

Tweedenhead

CH

PO

1 ASHWELL PL
2 SOUTH HERMITAGE SQ
3 WALTER ST
4 STOPFORD ST
5 GEROGE ST
6 UNION ST
7 DONCASTER ST
8 WHITCHESTER ST
9 WHITCHESTER LA

Visitor Ctr

Swarf Hill

Newcastleton Forest

COPSHAW PL

SCOTT ST

BUCCLEUCH TERR

HOLM-PORT RD

Yethouse

Long Knowe

Mus

Greens

Hillhouse

TD9

Tweeden Plantation

Cemy

Millholm Cross

Liddel Water

Blinkbonny

Thwartergill Head

Mangerton

Blinkbonny Height

Scotch Kershope

Forest Walks

P

Blaemount Rig

English Kershope

Gillside

Sorbietrees

Carby Hill

Kershope Burn

D'mainholm

Hillend

Burnt Shields

Rootledge Burn

Flatt

Kershope Bridge

Kershope Forest

Under Burnmouth

B6357

Kershopefoot

Mast

Tommy's Fell

Roansgreen

PO

CA6

Kershope House

Ash Park

Stelshaw

47   A   48   B   49   C   50   D   51   E   52   F   82

8
89
7
88
6
87
5
86
4
85
3
84
2
83
1
82

A   B   C   D   E   F

Tyne & Wear and Northumberland STREET ATLAS

Tyne & Wear and Northumberland STREET ATLAS

Watch Knowe

Wilson's Pike

Clark's Sike

Whiteside Rig

Deep Sike

Neale Burn

Dinmontlair Knowe

Scotch Knowe

Newcastleton Forest

Lazy Knowe

Caplestone Fell

Black Knowe

Yearning Flow

Marven's Pike

Kershope Burn

Kaim Brae

Glendhu Hill

NE48

Kershopehead

Dove Crags

Greens' Gear

Lewis Burn

TD9

Glen Dhu

Long Rigg

Tod Crag

Black Hill

Mon

Davy's Round

Robbie's Rigg

Currick

Caldwell Sike

Reamy Rigg

Skelton Pike

Beckhead Crag

Kershope Forest

The Back

CA6

Black Knowe

Blacklyne Common

Christianbury Crag

53   A   54   B   55   C   56   D   57   E   58   F

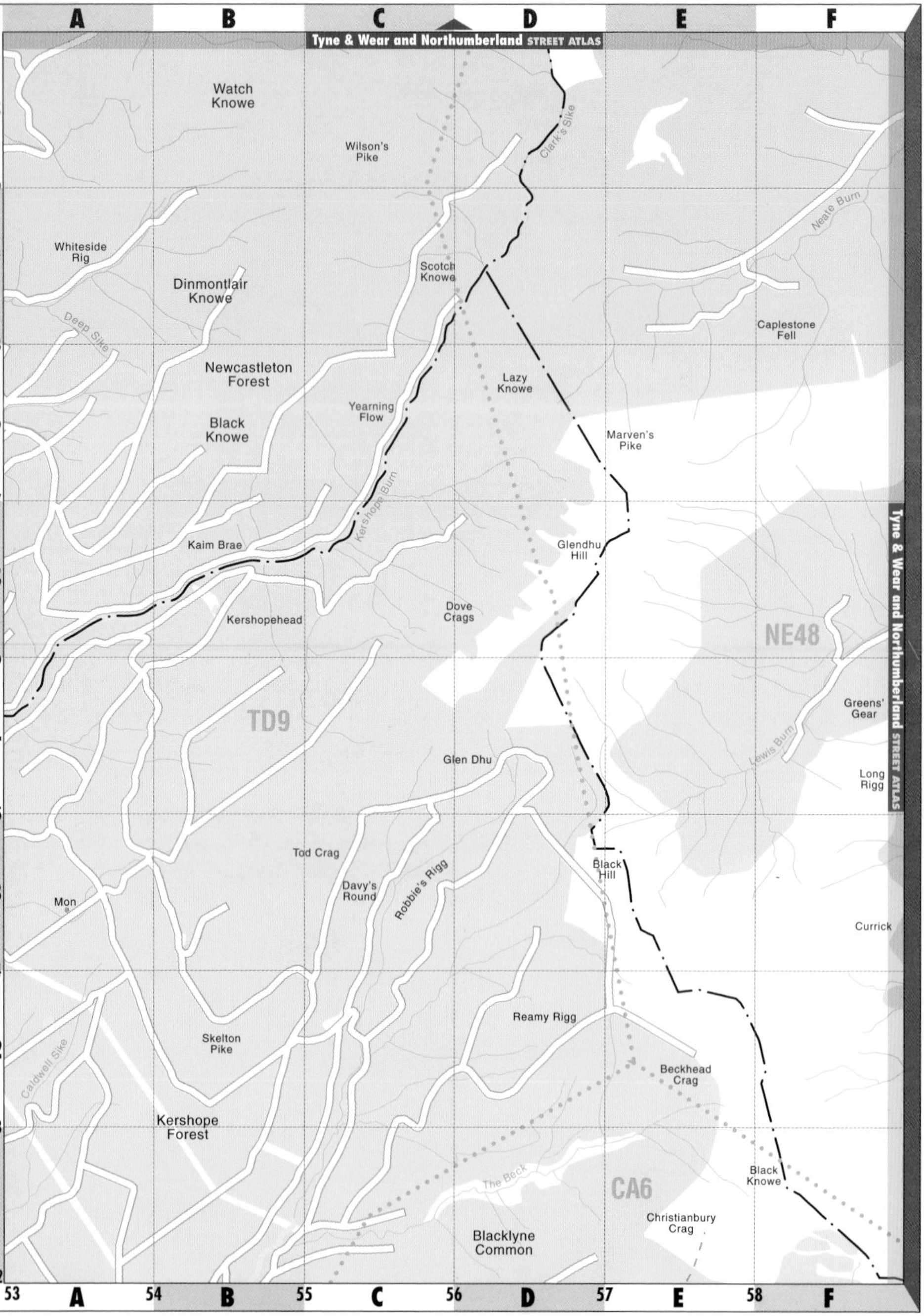

8
89
7
88
6
87
5
86
4
85
3
84
2
83
1
82

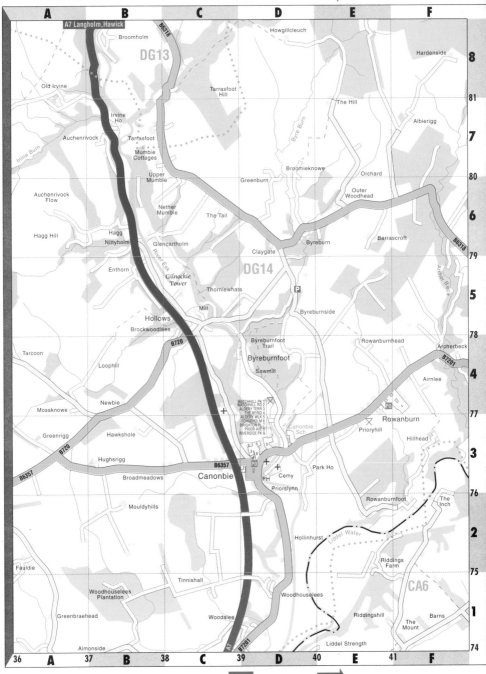

Scale: 1½ inches to 1 mile

0   ¼   ½ mile

0   250m 500m 750m 1 km

A7 Langholm, Hawick

A   B   C   D   E   F

Broomholm

DG13

Hardenside

Howgillcleuch

Old Irvine

Tarrasfoot Hill

The Hill

Albierigg

Irvine Ho

Byre Burn

Auchenrivock

Tarrasfoot

Mumbie Cottages

Broomieknowe

Orchard

Outer Woodhead

Auchenrivock Flow

Upper Mumbie

Greenburn

Irvine Burn

Nether Mumble

Hagg Hill

Hagg

The Tail

Byreburn

Barrascroft

Nittyholm

River Esk

Glencartholm

Claygate

DG14

Enthorn

Gilnockie Tower

Thornlewhats

Arden Beck

Mill

Byreburnside

P

Hollows

Byreburnfoot Trail

Rowanburnhead

Brockwoodlees

Archerbeck

Tarcoon

Byreburnfoot

B720

Loophill

Sawmill

Airnlee

PO

B7201

Mossknowe

Newbie

WATCHILL PK 1
WATCHILL RD 2
ALDERY TERR 3
THE WYND 4
ALDERY WLK 5
FORGEHOLM 6
BRIGHTON PL 7
PRIOR AVE 8
RIVERSIDE PK 9

Rowanburn

Greenrigg

Hawkshole

Canonbie Sch

Prioryhill

Hillhead

B6357

Hughsrigg

B6357

PO

Broadmeadows

Canonbie

PH

Cemy

Park Ho

Rowanburnfoot

Priorslynn

The Inch

Mouldyhills

Hollinhurst

Liddel Water

Fauldie

Riddings Farm

CA6

Woodhouselees Plantation

Tinnishall

Woodhouselees

Riddingshill

Barns

Greenbraehead

Woodslee

A7

B7201

Liddel Strength

The Mount

36   A   37   B   38   C   39   D   40   E   41   F

8
81
7
80
6
79
5
78
4
77
3
76
2
75
1
74

4

10   4

B6318

B6318

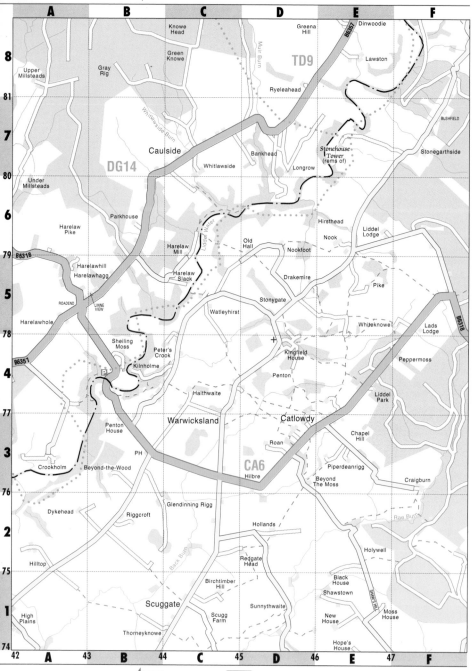

8

81

7

80

6

79

5

78

4

77

3

76

2

75

1

74

A   B   C   D   E   F

Upper Millsteads

Gray Rig

Knowe Head

Green Knowe

Greena Hill

Dinwoodie

Lawston

TD9

B6357

Ryeleahead

Whitlawside Burn

Caulside

DG14

Whitlawside

Bankhead

Longrow

Stonehouse Tower (rems of)

Stonegarthside

BUSHFIELD

Under Millsteads

Parkhouse

Hirsthead

Liddel Lodge

Nook

Harelaw Pike

B6318

Harelawhill

Harelawhagg

Harelaw Mill

Harelaw Slack

Liddel Water

Old Hall

Nookfoot

Drakemire

Pike

ROADEND

LINNE VIEW

Watleyhirst

Stonygate

Whiteknowe

Lads Lodge

B6318

Harelawhole

Sheiling Moss

Peter's Crook

Kilnholme

Kingfield House

Penton

Peppermoss

B6351

Liddel Park

Haithwaite

Warwicksland

Catlowdy

Chapel Hill

Roan

Penton House

PH

CA6

Piperdeanrigg

Craigburn

Crookholm

Beyond-the-Wood

Hilbre

Beyond The Moss

Dykehead

Riggcroft

Glendinning Rigg

Black Burn

Hollands

Rae Burn

Holywell

Hilltop

Redgate Head

Birchtimber Hill

Black House

Shaw's Hill

Scuggate

Scugg Farm

Sunnythwaite

Shawstown

Moss House

High Plains

Thorneyknowe

New House

Hope's House

42   43   44   45   46   47

A   B   C   D   E   F

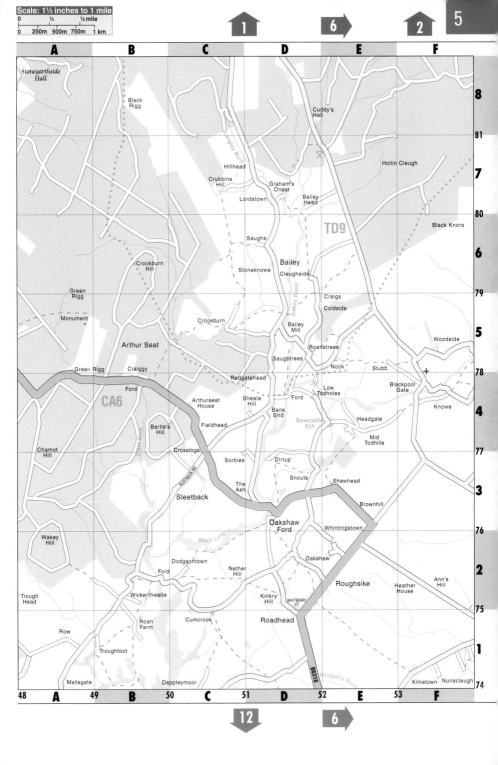

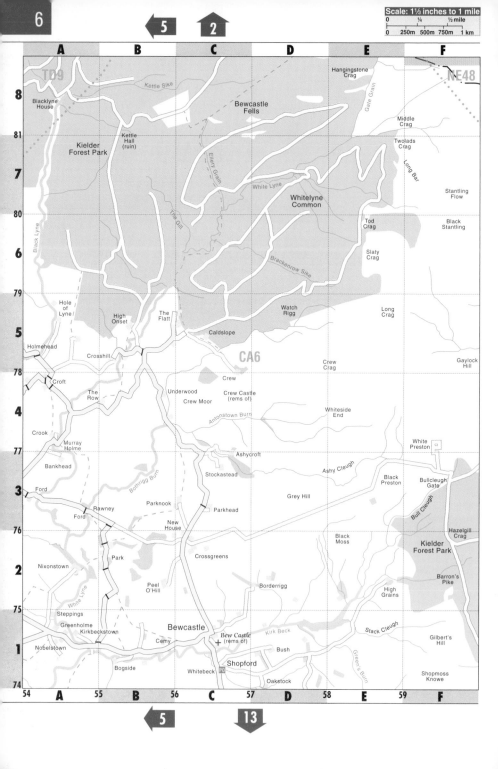

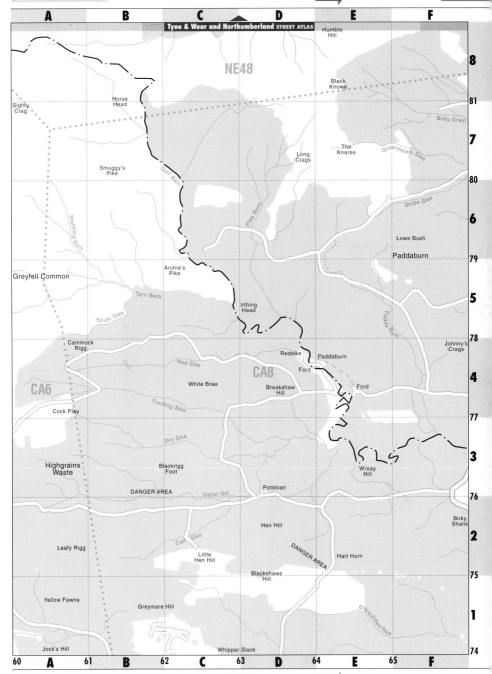

Tyne & Wear and Northumberland STREET ATLAS

| A | B | C | D | E | F |

NE48

Humble
Hill

8

Sighty
Crag

Horse
Head

Black
Knowe

81

Birky Grain

Startling Burn

Smuggy's
Pike

Gair Burn

Long
Crags

The
Knares

Greenmeath Sike

7

80

Pike Burn

Stripe Sike

6

Greyfell Common

Tarn Beck

Archie's
Pike

Lowe Bush

Paddaburn

79

South Sike

Irthing
Head

Padda Burn

Johnny's
Crags

5

78

Cammock
Rigg

Red Sike

Redsike

Paddaburn

CA8

Ford

Ford

4

CA6

White Brae

Breakshaw
Hill

77

Cock Play

Foulbog Sike

Dry Sike

Wreay
Hill

3

Highgrains
Waste

Blackrigg
Foot

Potsloan

76

DANGER AREA

Hazel Gill

Birky
Shank

Leafy Rigg

Calf Sike

Hen Hill

DANGER AREA

Hart Horn

2

Little
Hen Hill

Blackshaws
Hill

75

Yellow Fawns

Greymare Hill

Blackshaws Sike

1

Jock's Hill

Whipper Slack

74

A   B   C   D   E   F

8

Memorial
Rushy Knowe
Bolts Law
Mast
Whickhope Nick
Chirdonhead
Chirdonhead

81

Black Cleugh

7

Hopehouse

NE48

Chirdon Burn

80

6

The Shanks

Clintburn

Muckle Dodd Hill

79

Muckle Samuel's Crags

5

Blind Sike

Whitehill

Little Dodd Hill

78

Churn Sike

CA8

4

Whitehill

Thross Burn

Coal Burn

Great Tongue Rigg

77

Churnsike Lodge

Round Top

NE48

3

Shrank End (ruin)

The Flothers

Lawrence Burn

Long Rigg

Greenlee Cleugh

Butterburn Flow

Spy Rigg

Rushy Rigg

76

2

Gowany Knowe

River Irthing

Great Watch Hill

75

Stourcleugh Gair

Butter Burn

1

Butterburn

Lampert

Linen Sike

NE49

74

66   A   67   B   68   C   69   D   70   E   71   F

Tyne & Wear and Northumberland STREET ATLAS

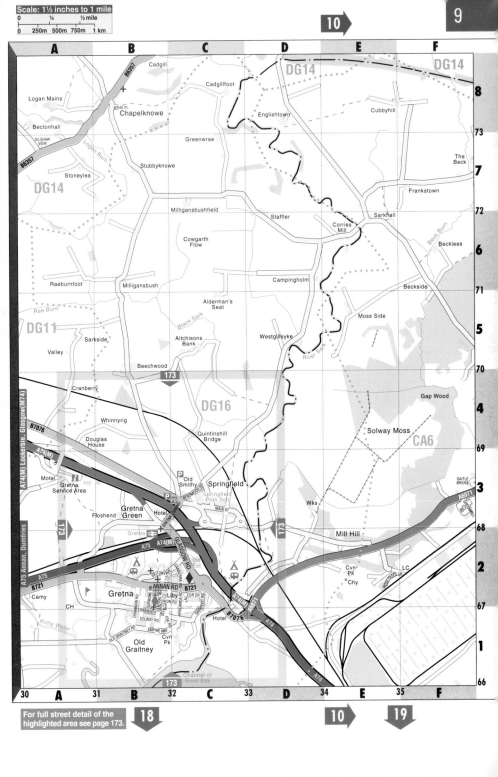

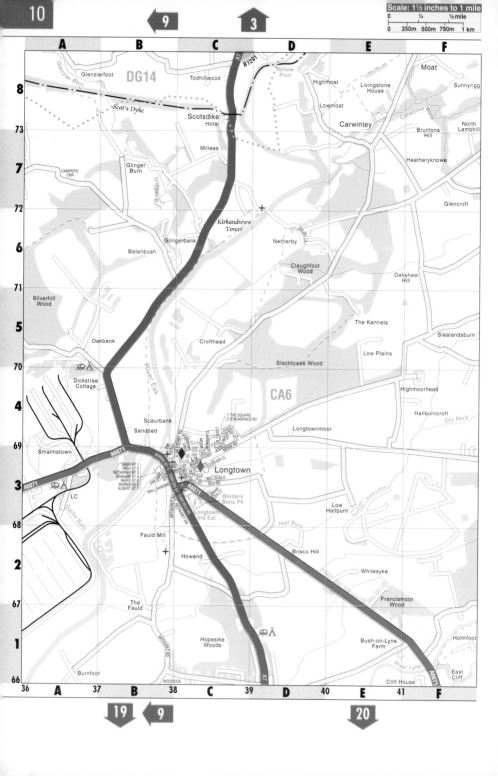

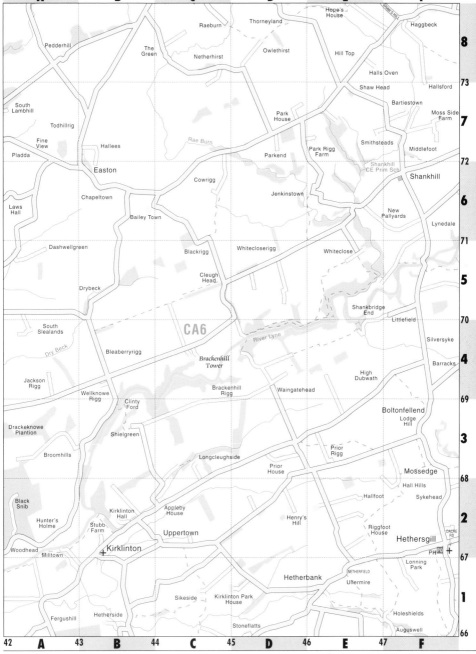

CA6

A   **B**   **C**   **D**   **E**   **F**

8
73
7
72
6
71
5
70
4
69
3
68
2
67
1
66

Pedderhill
Raeburn
Thorneyland
Hope's House
Haggbeck
The Green
Netherhirst
Owlethirst
Hill Top
Halls Oven
Hallsford
South Lambhill
Shaw Head
Bartiestown
Moss Side Farm
Todhillrig
Park House
Smithsteads
Middlefoot
Fine View
Hallees
Rae Burn
Parkend
Park Rigg Farm
Shankhill CE Prim Sch
Shankhill
Pladda
Easton
Cowrigg
Jenkinstown
New Pallyards
Laws Hall
Chapeltown
Lynedale
Bailey Town
Dashwellgreen
Blackrigg
Whitecloserigg
Whiteclose
Drybeck
Cleugh Head
Shankbridge End
Littlefield
South Slealands
River Lyne
Silversyke
Dry Beck
Bleaberryrigg
Brackenhill Tower
Barracks
Jackson Rigg
Brackenhill Rigg
Waingatehead
High Dubwath
Wellknowe Rigg
Clinty Ford
Boltonfellend
Lodge Hill
Drackeknowe Plantion
Shielgreen
Prior Rigg
Broomhills
Longcleughside
Prior House
Mossedge
Hall Hills
Sykehead
Black Snib
Hallfoot
Hunter's Holme
Kirklinton Hall
Appleby House
Henry's Hill
Riggfoot House
Hethersgill
DACRE RD
Stubb Farm
Uppertown
PH
Woodhead
Milltown
Kirklinton
Lonning Park
NETHERFIELD
Hetherbank
Uffermire
Fergushill
Hetherside
Sikeside
Kirklinton Park House
Holeshields
Stoneflatts
Auguswell

42   **A**   43   **B**   44   **C**   45   **D**   46   **E**   47   **F**   66

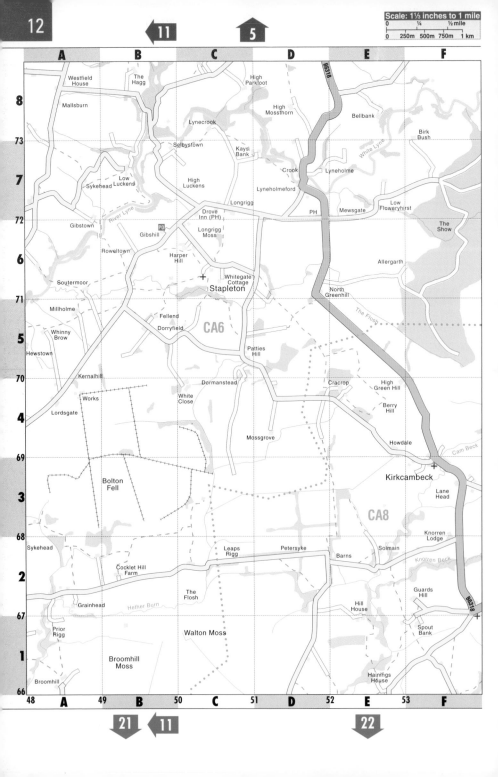

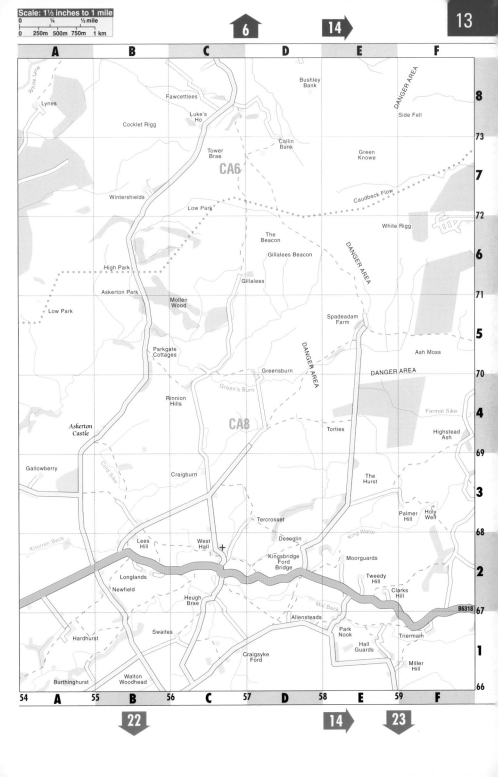

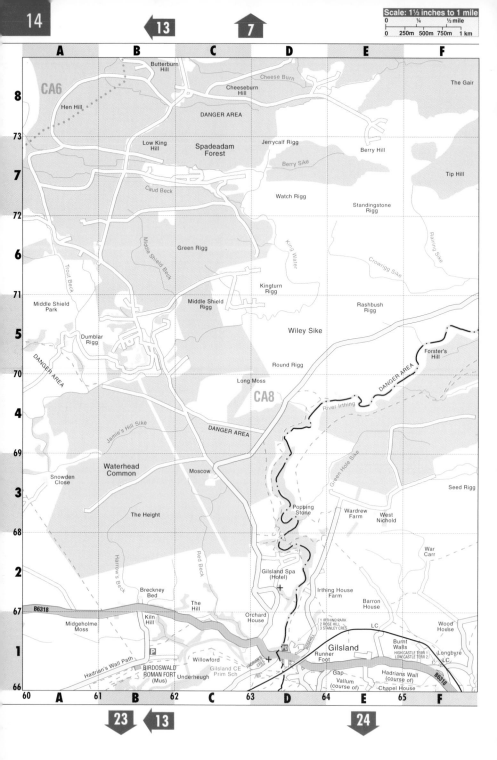

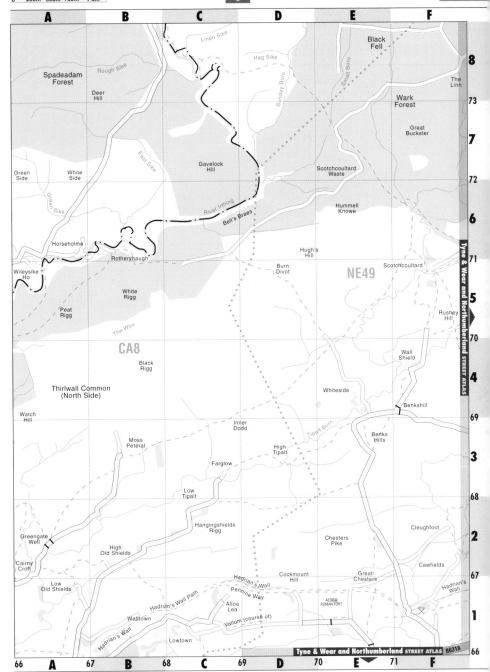

Black Fell

Spadeadam Forest

Linen Sike

Hag Sike

Deer Hill

Sunday Burn

Small Burn

The Linn

Wark Forest

Great Buckster

Green Side

White Side

East Sike

Gavelock Hill

Scotchcoultard Waste

Green Sike

River Irthing

Bell's Braes

Hummell Knowe

Horseholme

Rotheryhaugh

Hugh's Hill

Burn Divot

NE49

Scotchcoultard

Wileysike Ho

Peat Rigg

White Rigg

The Wou

Rushey Hill

CA8

Black Rigg

Wall Shield

Thirlwall Common (North Side)

Whiteside

Benkshill

Watch Hill

Inner Dodd

Tipalt Burn

Benks Hills

Moss Peteral

High Tipalt

Farglow

Low Tipalt

Hangingshields Rigg

Cleughfoot

Chesters Pike

Greengate Well

High Old Shields

Cawfields

Cairny Croft

Low Old Shields

Cockmount Hill

Great Chesters

Hadrian's Wall

Hadrian's Wall

Hadrian's Wall Path

Pennine Way

Alloa Lea

AESICA ROMAN FORT

Walltown

Vallum (course of)

Lowtown

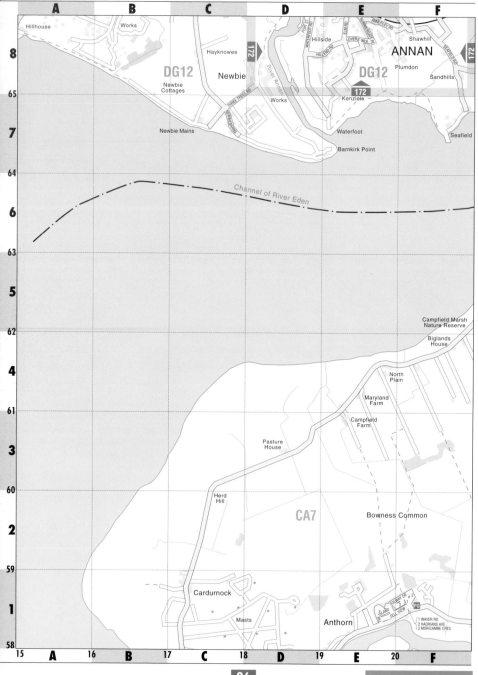

Scale: 1½ inches to 1 mile

For full street detail of the highlighted area see page 172.

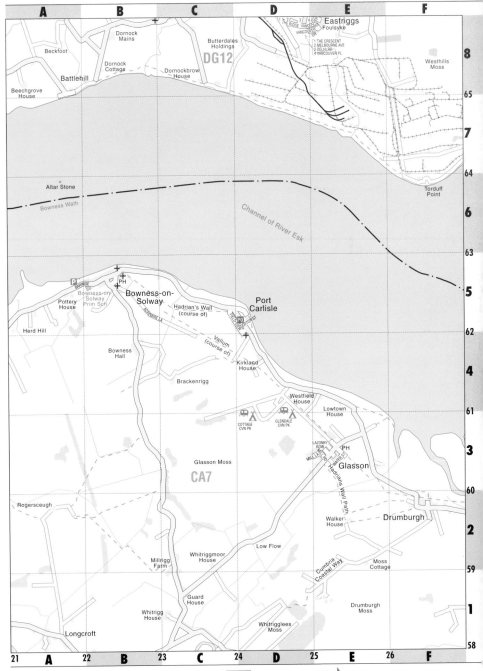

Dornock Mains

Beckfoot

Butterdales Holdings

DG12

Battlehill

Dornock Cottage

Dornockbrow House

Beechgrove House

THE BRIDGE

Eastriggs
Foulsyke

1 THE CRESCENT
2 MELBOURNE AVE
3 DELHI RD
4 VANCOUVER PL

Westhills Moss

8

65

7

64

Altar Stone

Bowness Wath

Channel of River Esk

Torduff Point

6

63

P
BOWNESS
PH
Bowness-on-Solway Prim Scn

Pottery House

Bowness-on-Solway

Hadrian's Wall (course of)

ACREMIRE LA

Port Carlisle

5

62

Herd Hill

Bowness Hall

Brackenrigg

Vallum (course of)

Kirkland House

Westfield House

Lowtown House

4

61

COTTAGE CVN PK

GLENDALE CVN PK

LAZONBY ROW

MILL LA

PH

Glasson

3

60

Glasson Moss

CA7

Hadrians Wall Path

Walker House

Drumburgh

Rogersceugh

Whitriggmoor House

Low Flow

Cumbria Coastal Way

Moss Cottage

2

59

Millrigg Farm

Guard House

Drumburgh Moss

1

Whitrigg House

Whitrigglees Moss

Longcroft

58

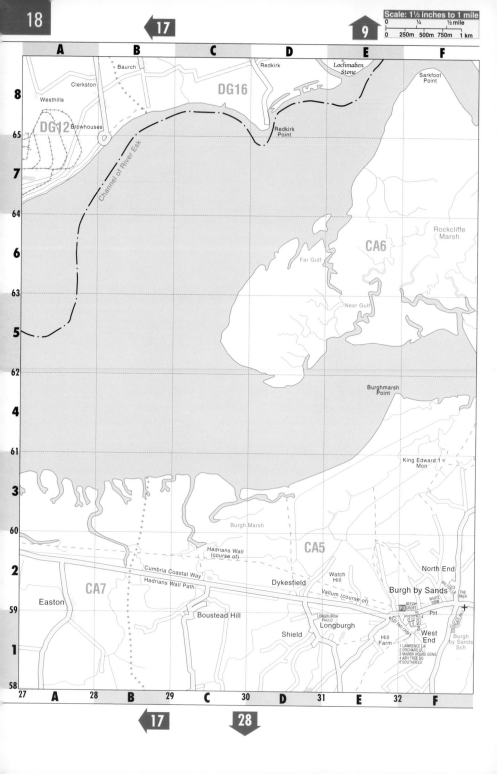

17

9

Scale: 1⅓ inches to 1 mile

0   ¼   ½ mile

0   250m 500m 750m 1 km

A   B   C   D   E   F

Baurch

Clerkston

Redkirk

DG16

Lochmaben
Stone

Sarkfoot
Point

8

Westhills

DG12 Browhouses

65

Redkirk
Point

7

Channel of River Esk

64

Rockcliffe
Marsh

6

CA6

Far Gulf

63

Near Gulf

5

62

Burghmarsh
Point

4

61

King Edward 1
Mon

3

Burgh Marsh

60

Hadrians Wall
(course of)

CA5

Cumbria Coastal Way

North End

2

Watch
Hill

Burgh by Sands

Hadrians Wall Path

Dykesfield

Vallum (course of)

CA7

Easton

Boustead Hill

BEECH
CROFT

PO
PH

59

LONGBURGH
FAULD

Longburgh

West
End

Burgh
by Sands
Sch

Shield

Hill
Farm

1 LAWRENCE LA
2 ORCHARD CL
3 MARSH HOUSE GDNS
4 ASH TREE SQ
5 SOUTHFIELD

1

58

27   A   28   B   29   C   30   D   31   E   32   F

17

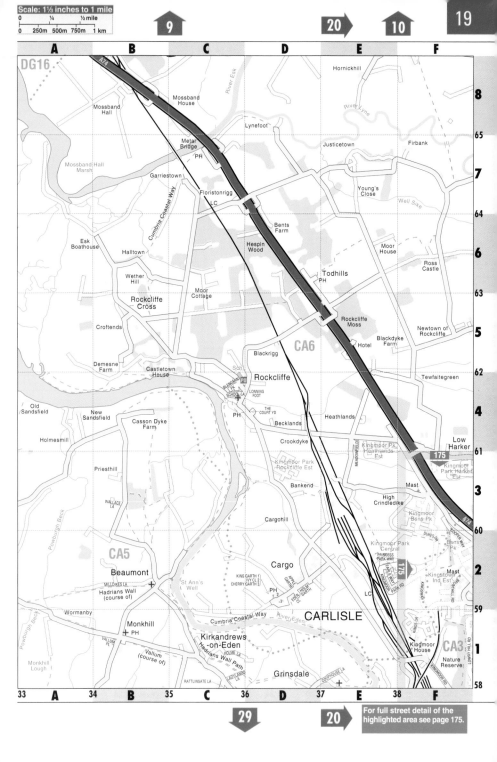

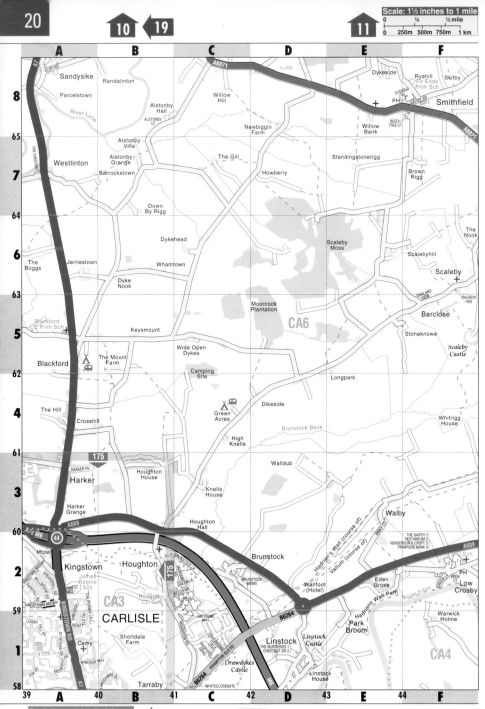

10   19

11

Scale: 1⅓ inches to 1 mile

0   ¼   ½ mile

0   250m 500m 750m 1 km

A   **B**   **C**   **D**   **E**   **F**

8

CLIFF RD
Sandysike
Randalinton
Parcelstown
Willow Hill
Alstonby Hall
ALSTONBY CT
River Lyne
Dykeside
Ryehill Fir Ends Prim Sch
Skitby
RYEHILL
PH
OAKTREE RD
BEECH TREE CT
Smithfield
A6071

65

Westlinton
Alstonby Villa
Alstonby Grange
Barrockstown
THE CHESTNUTS
Newbiggin Farm
The Gill
Howberry
Standingstonerigg
Willow Bank
Brown Rigg

7

64

Down By Rigg
Dykehead

6

The Boggs
Jerriestown
Whamtown
Dyke Nook
Scaleby Moss
Scalebyhill
Scaleby
The Nook

63

Moorcock Plantation
CA6
Barclose
OAKLAND VIEW
CHURCH HOS

5

Blackford CE Prim Sch
Keysmount
Wide Open Dykes
Stoneknowe
Scaleby Castle

62

Blackford
The Mount Farm
Camping Site
Longpark

4

The Hill
Crosshill
Green Acres
Dikeside
Brunstock Beck
Whitrigg House
High Knells

61

175
HARKER PK
Harker
Houghton House
Walldub
Knells House

3

Harker Grange
Houghton Hall
Hadrian's Wall (course of)
Vallum (course of)
Walby
THE GARTH 1
VESTANEUM 2
HENDERSON'S CROFT 3
PRIMROSE BANK 4
A689
Sch

60

A74
A689
M6
44
Motel
Houghton
Brunstock
BRUNSTOCK MEWS
Wallfoot (Hotel)
Eden Grove
EDEN CT
PH
Low Crosby
River Eden
BRIER

2

Kingstown
James Rennie Sch
PO
175
GREEN LA
BEECH LA
Hadrians Wall Path
Warwick Holme

59

CA3
Houghton CE Sch
CARLISLE
ANTOINE WAY
Shortdale Farm
B6264
Linstock
THE NURSERIES 1
CHESTNUT GR 2
Linstock Castle
Park Broom
River Eden
CA4

1

Cemy
Drawdykes Castle
Linstock House

58

Tarraby
WHITECLOSEGATE
M6

39   **A**   **40**   **B**   **41**   **C**   **42**   **D**   **43**   **E**   **44**   **F**

For full street detail of the highlighted area see page 175.

19   30

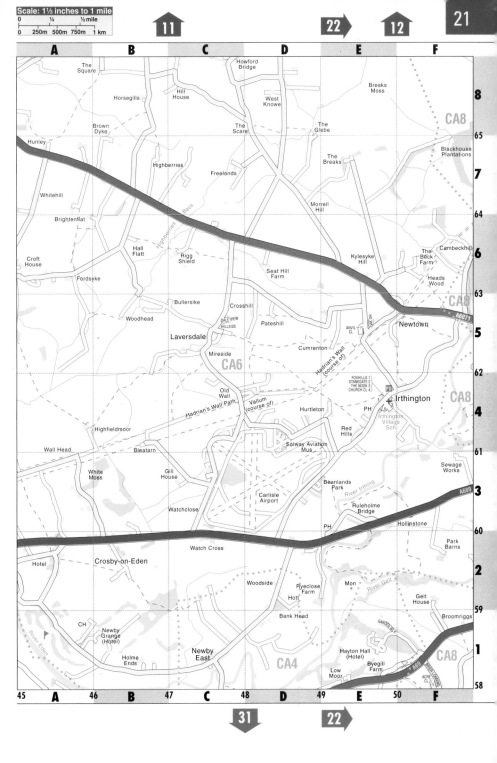

A B C D E F

8

The Square

Horsegills

Hill House

Howford Bridge

West Knowe

Breaks Moss

CA8

Brown Dyke

The Scare

The Glebe

65

Blackhouse Plantations

Hunley

Highberries

Freelands

The Breaks

7

Whitehill

Morrell Hill

64

Brightenflat

Highberries Beck

Kylesyke Hill

Cambeckhill

The Beck Farm

6

Croft House

Hall Flatt

Rigg Shield

Seat Hill Farm

Heads Wood

CA8

Fordsyke

Bullersike

Crosshill

A6071

63

Woodhead

DALE VIEW
HILLSIDE

Pateshill

ANVIL CL

TAYLOR DR

Newtown

5

Laversdale

Mireside

Cumrenton

Hadrian's Wall (course of)

62

CA6

FOXHILLS 1
STANEGATE 2
THE NOOK 3
CHURCH CL 4

PO

CA8

Old Wall

Hurtleton

Irthington

4

Hadrian's Wall Path

Vallum (course of)

PH

Irthington Village Sch

Highfieldmoor

Red Hills

61

Wall Head

Bleatarn

Solway Aviation Mus

Sewage Works

White Moss

Gill House

Beanlands Park

River Irthing

A689

3

Watchclose

Carlisle Airport

Ruleholme Bridge

Hollinstone

60

PH

Park Barns

Hotel

Crosby-on-Eden

Watch Cross

2

Woodside

Ryeclose Farm

Mon

River Gelt

Gelt House

59

Hott

CH

Bank Head

Broomriggs

Newby Grange (Hotel)

Newby East

GARDEN VILLAS

CA4

Hayton Hall (Hotel)

A69

CA8

1

Holme Ends

Low Moor

Byegill Farm

ACRE CL

River Eden

58

45 A 46 B 47 C 48 D 49 E 50 F

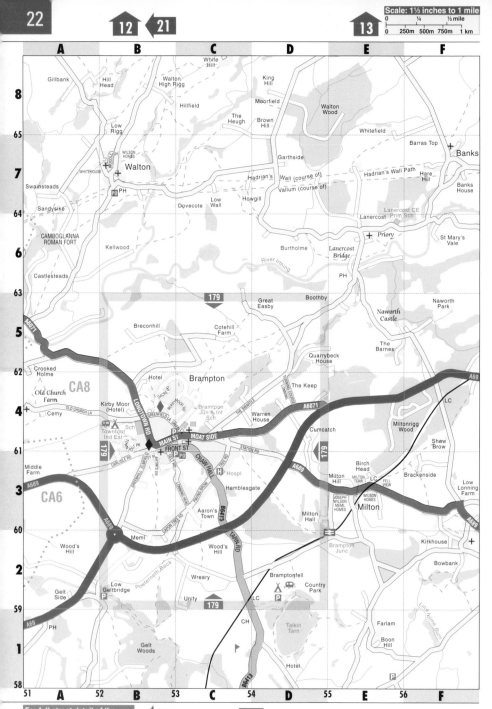

Scale: 1⅓ inches to 1 mile

0   ¼   ½ mile
0 250m 500m 750m 1 km

A B C D E F

8

Gillbank

Hill Head

Walton High Rigg

White Hill

King Hill

Moorfield

Walton Wood

65

Low Rigg

WILSON HOMES

Hillfield

The Heugh

Brown Hill

Whitefield

Barras Top

Banks

7

WHITEHOUSE

Walton

PO PH

Swainsteads

Hadrian's Wall (course of)

Vallum (course of)

Hadrian's Wall Path

Hare Hill

Banks House

64

Sandysike

Dovecote

Low Wall

Howgill

Garthside

Lanercost

Lanercost CE Prim Sch

St Mary's Vale

CAMBOGLANNA ROMAN FORT

Kellwood

Priory

6

Castlesteads

Burtholme

River Irthing

Lanercost Bridge

PH

Naworth Park

63

179

Great Easby

Boothby

Naworth Castle

5

A6071

Breconhill

Cotehill Farm

The Barnes

Crooked Holme

Quarryback House

62

CA8

Hotel

Brampton

The Keep

A69

LC

Old Church Farm

Cemy

Old Church La

Kirby Moor (Hotel)

DACRE RD

BERRY MOOR RD

GREENFIELD LA

Brampton Jun & Int Sch

The Brattle

A6071

Cumcatch

Miltonrigg Wood

Shaw Brow

4

Townfoot Ind Est

Sch

Warren House

Birch Head

Brackenside

61

LONGTOWN RD

CARLISLE RD

GREENFIELD RD

DACRE RD

ANTINE'S DR

MAIN ST

MOAT SIDE

FRONT ST

CRAW HALL

STATION RD

179

A689

Milton Hill

MILTON TERR

LC

FELL VIEW

Low Lonning Farm

Middle Farm

A689

H

Hospl

Hemblesgate

JOSEPH WILSON MEML HOMES

WILSON HOMES

Milton

3

CA6

B6413

PETERS BRYDGE

CAROON TREE RD

Aaron's Town

Milton Hall

60

A689

Meml

Wood's Hill

Brampton Junc

Kirkhouse

2

Wood's Hill

Powtermeth Beck

Wreary

Bramptonfell

Country Park

Bowbank

Line-home Burn

Gelt Side

Low Geltbridge

Unity

179

LC

P

Farlam

59

A69

PH

CH

Talkin Tarn

Boon Hill

1

Gelt Woods

B6413

Hotel

P

58

51 **A** 52 **B** 53 **C** 54 **D** 55 **E** 56 **F**

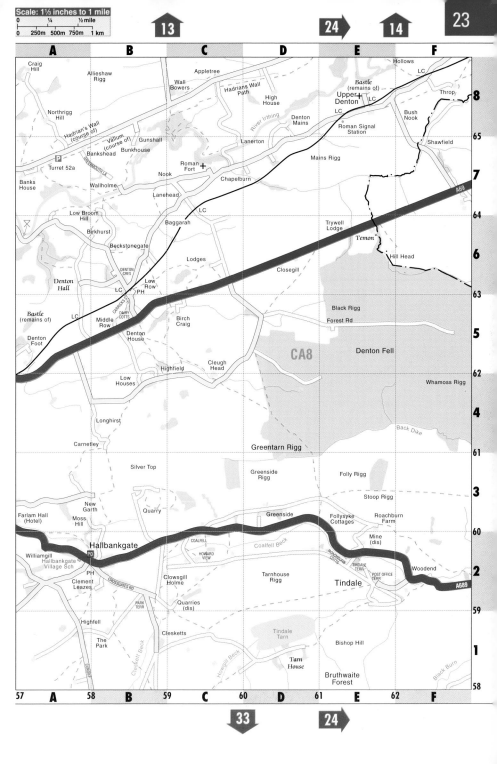

A   B   C   D   E   F

Craig Hill
Northrigg Hill
Allieshaw Rigg
Appletree
Wall Bowers
Hadrians Wall Path
High House
Hollows
LC
Bastle (remains of)
Upper Denton
Throp
Bush Nook
Shawfield
8

Hadrian's Wall (course of)
Vallum (course of)
Gunshall
Bunkhouse
Bankshead
Turret 52a
GREENMOUTH LN
Nook
Roman Fort
Chapelburn
Lanerton
Denton Mains
River Irthing
Roman Signal Station
LC
65

Banks House
Wallholme
Lanehead
LC
Mains Rigg
7

Low Broom Hill
Birkhurst
Baggarah
Beckstonegate
Trywell Lodge
Temon
Hill Head
64

DENTON CRES
Lodges
Low Row
PH
Closegill
Black Rigg
Forest Rd
6

Denton Hall
LC
CARROCKS LN
DAIRY COTTS
Middle Row
Birch Craig
Denton House
Bastle (remains of)
LC
63

Denton Foot
Highfield
Cleugh Head
Denton Fell
CA8
5

Low Houses
Whamoss Rigg
62

Longhirst
Greentarn Rigg
Back Dike
4

Carnetley
Silver Top
Greenside Rigg
Folly Rigg
Stoop Rigg
61

New Garth
Quarry
Greenside
Follysyke Cottages
Roachburn Farm
3

Farlam Hall (Hotel)
Moss Hill
COALFELL
Coalfell Beck
Mine (dis)
ROACHBURN COTTS
60

Williamgill
Hallbankgate
PO
HOWARD VIEW
Hallbankgate Village Sch
PH
CROSSGATES RD
Clowsgill Holme
Tarnhouse Rigg
TINDALE TERR
POST OFFICE TERR
Tindale
Woodend
A689
2

Clement Leazes
PARK TERR
Quarries (dis)
59

Highfell
The Park
Clesketts
Tindale Tarn
Bishop Hill
Cleskett Beck
GILBOURN
Howgill Beck
Tarn House
Bruthwaite Forest
Black Burn
1

A69

A689

A B C D E F

Lawn Top
Vallum (course 0f)
CH
MILLBURN TERR
B6318
Carvoran
MAGNIS ROMAN FORT
Mus
Walks
Peatsteel Crags
Fell End
B6318

Wardoughan
Banktop
GREENHEAD BANK
YH
PH
GLENWHELT BANK
Greenhead
Greenhead CE Fst Sch
Hardriggs

Gapshield
BYRON TERR
Bankfoot
BLENKINSOPP TERR
College Farm
Wrytree
Mine (dis)
Painsdale Burn
Blenkinsopp Hall

A69
Reaygarth
Blenkinsopp Castle (PH)
OLD ROW
BLENKINSOPP CASTLE HOME PK
Darlees
Blenkinsopp Hall

Todholes
Mast
Mast
Wydoncleughside
LC
The Spittal

Thirlwall Common (South Side)
Blenkinsopp Common
Waterloo
Hole House
REDPETH
Redpeth

Hot Moss
Snell Burn

Wain Rigg
Pennine Way
Featherstone Common
Glencune Burn
Mast
Wydon Eals
Park Burnfoot

CA8
Cross Rigg
Hartleyburn Common (North Side)
Highside
Bridge End
NE49
Park Village
Park Burn

Whamoss Rigg
Ash Cleugh
Peat Gate
Kellah
Meml
Maiden Way
Horse Close

Cocklit Hill
Kellah Burn
Batey Shield
Burnfoot
Cross Dike
Featherstone Castle
PH
Featherstone Rowfoot

Byers/Hall
Hartley Burn
River South Tyne
Watch Trees

Haining House
Foul Potts
Haining Burn
Doubledyes
Greenriggs
Hillis Close
Wood Houses

A689
Hill House
Lambley Farm
HIGH RIDLEY
Lane Head
Moss House

Midgeholme
Halton Lea
Clover Hill
Mine (dis)
Herdley Bank Fst Sch
Coanwood

Halton-Lea-Gate
LANE TERR
Black Burn
PENNINE RD
Lambley
Hag Wood
A689

Waughold Holme
Ashholme

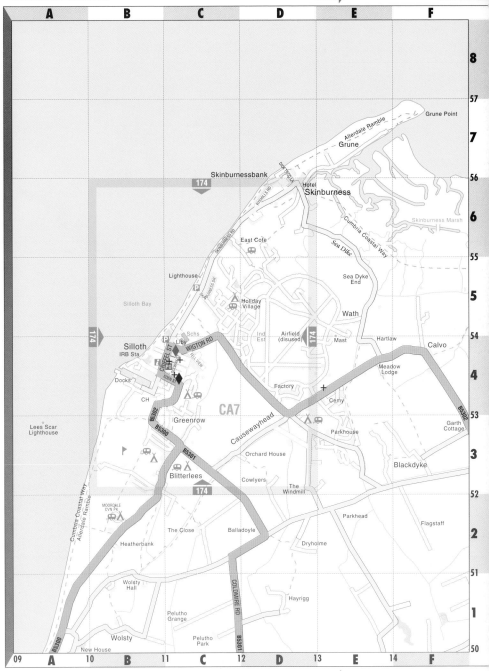

26

8

57

Grune Point

Allerdale Ramble

Grune

7

Skinburnessbank

Hotel
Skinburness

56

Cumbria Coastal Way

Skinburness Marsh

6

174

East Cote

55

Sea Dike

Lighthouse

Sea Dyke
End

Holiday
Village

Wath

5

174

Silloth Bay

Ind
Est

Airfield
(disused)

174

Mast

Hartlaw

Calvo

54

Silloth

Schs

WIGTON RD

Lby

FELL VIEW

IRB Sta

Meadow
Lodge

B5302

4

Docks

CH

EDEN ST

CRIFFEL ST

Factory

Cemy

53

Lees Scar
Lighthouse

Greenrow

Causewayhead

Parkhouse

Garth
Cottage

B5300

CA7

B5302

B5301

Orchard House

Blackdyke

3

Blitterlees

174

Cowlyers

The
Windmill

52

Cumbria Coastal Way

MOORDALE
CVN Pk

The Close

Balladoyle

Parkhead

Flagstaff

2

Allerdale Ramble

Heatherbank

Dryholme

51

Wolsty
Hall

COLDMIRE RD

Hayrigg

1

B5300

Pelutho
Grange

Wolsty

Pelutho
Park

B5301

New House

50

For full street detail of the
highlighted area see page 174.

26   36

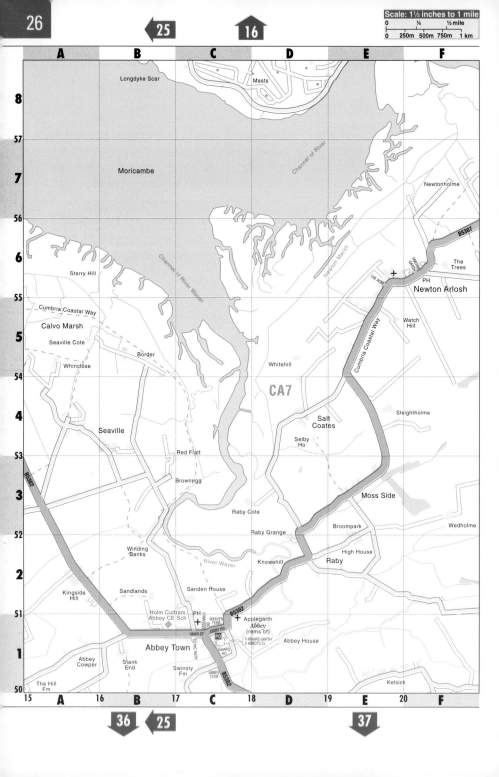

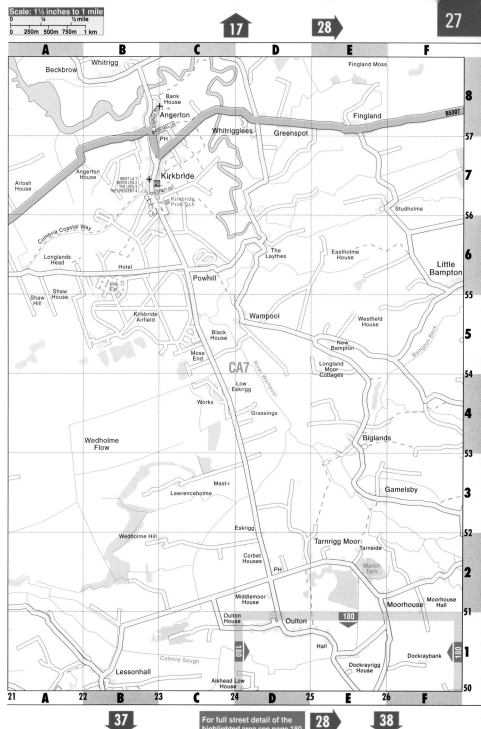

Scale: 1⅓ inches to 1 mile

0 ¼ ½ mile
0 250m 500m 750m 1 km

Beckbrow
Whitrigg
Fingland Moss

Bank House
Angerton
B5307
Fingland
Whitrigglees
Greenspot

8

57

Angerton House

Arlosh House

WEST LA 1
BEECH LA 2
THE LEES 3
THE CRESCENT 4

Kirkbride
CHURCH RD
HIGH HILL LA
PH
CHESTNUT GR

Kirkbride Prim Sch

Studholme

7

56

Cumbria Coastal Way

Longlands Head

Hotel

The Laythes

Eastholme House

Little Bampton

6

55

Shaw Hill
Shaw House

Ind Est

Kirkbride Airfield

Powhill

Wampool

Westfield House

New Bampton

Bampton Beck

5

54

Black House

Moss End

CA7

River Wampool

Longland Moor Cottages

Low Eskrigg

Works

Grassings

Biglands

4

53

Wedholme Flow

Mast

Lawrenceholme

Gamelsby

3

52

Wedholme Hill

Eskrigg

Tarnrigg Moor
Tarnside

Corbet Houses
PH

Martin Tarn

2

51

Middlemoor House

Moorhouse
Moorhouse Hall

Oulton House
Oulton
180

Lessonhall

Colmire Sough

180

Hall

Dockrayrigg House

Dockraybank

180

1

50

Aikhead Low House

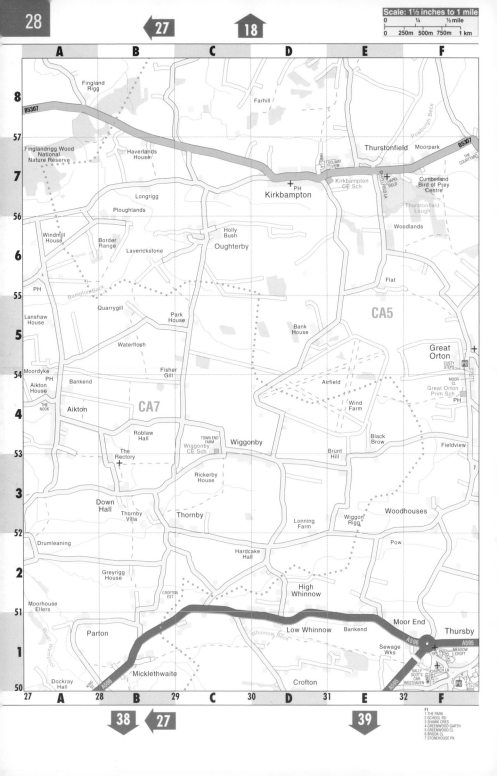

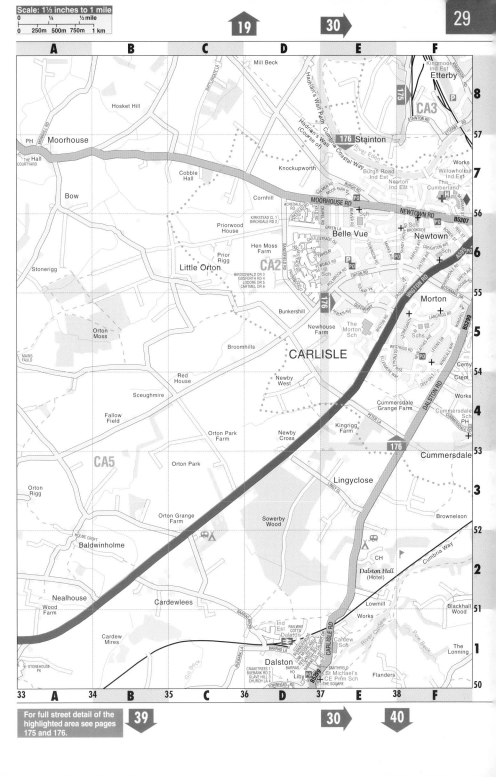

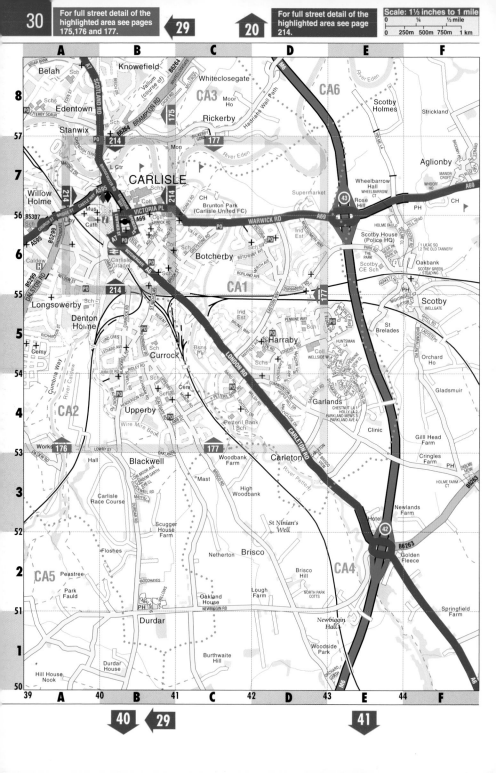

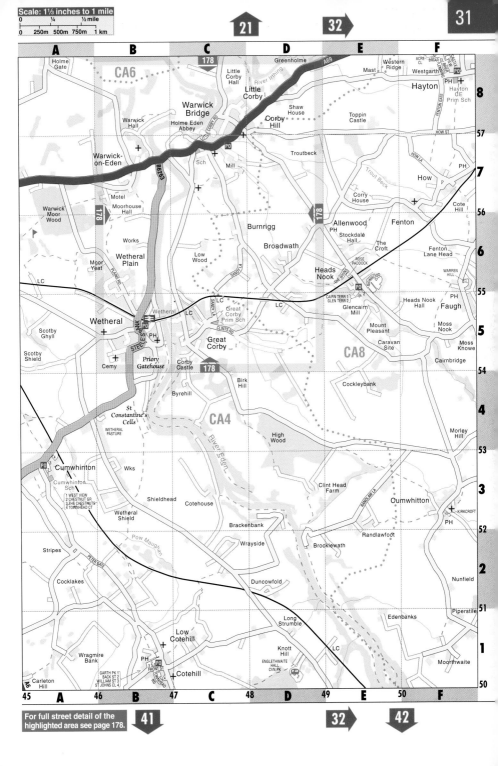

A   B   C   D   E   F

Holme Gate

CA6

178

Little Corby Hall

Greenholme

A69

Mast

Western Ridge

Westgarth

ACRE CL

CASTLE VIEW

BRIAR CL

CASTLE HILL

DRIVE

PO

PH

Hayton

Hayton CE Prim Sch

8

Warwick Bridge

Warwick Hall

Little Corby

Shaw House

Corby Hill

Toppin Castle

HOW ST

FENTON GATE

57

Holme Eden Abbey

VAL CORBY RD

PO

HOW LA

PH

Warwick-on-Eden

Sch

Mill

Troutbeck

How

P

7

B6263

Motel

Corry House

Cote Hill

Moorhouse Hall

178

178

Allenwood

Fenton

56

Warwick Moor Wood

PH

Stockdale Hall

Fenton Lane Head

Burnrigg

The Croft

WARREN HILL

6

Works

Broadwath

ROSE PADDOCK

Wetheral Plain

Low Wood

SANDY LA

Heads Nook

THE BANKS

BSL

55

Moor Yeat

FLAING RD

LC

LC

CAIRN TERR 1
GLEN TERR 2

AUGHWOOD

PO

Heads Nook Hall

PH

Faugh

Wetheral

SANDY LA

Great Corby Prim Sch

LC

Glencairn Mill

Moss Nook

5

Scotby Ghyll

STEEL'S BANK

PO

PH

CLINTS RD

Mount Pleasant

Moss Knowe

Scotby Shield

Cemy

Priory Gatehouse

Great Corby

Corby Castle

178

Caravan Site

CA8

Cairnbridge

54

Birk Hill

Byrehill

CA4

St Constantine's Cells

WETHERAL PASTURE

High Wood

Morley Hill

4

River Eden

53

PO

Cumwhinton

Wks

Clint Head Farm

Cumwhitton

KIRKCROFT

PH

3

Cumwhinton Sch

1 WEST VIEW
2 CHESTNUT GR
3 THE CHESTNUTS
4 TOWNHEAD CT

Shieldhead

Cotehouse

RANDLAW LA

Wetheral Shield

Brackenbank

Randlawfoot

52

Pow Maughan

Wrayside

Brocklewath

Stripes

PETER GATE

Nunfield

2

Cocklakes

Duncowfold

Piperstile

51

Long Strumble

Edenbanks

Low Cotehill

Knott Hill

LC

Moorthwaite

1

Wragmire Bank

PH

GARTH PK 1
BACK ST 2
WILLIAM ST 3
ST JOHNS CL 4

PO

FRONT ST

TOWNHEAD RD

Cotehill

ENGLETHWAITE HALL CVN PK

A6

Carleton Hill

50

45   A   46   B   47   C   48   D   49   E   50   F

For full street detail of the highlighted area see page 178.

41   32   42

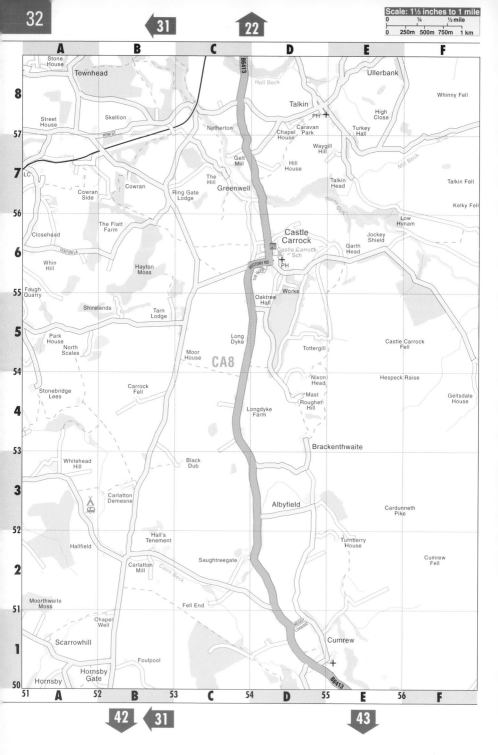

Scale: 1½ inches to 1 mile

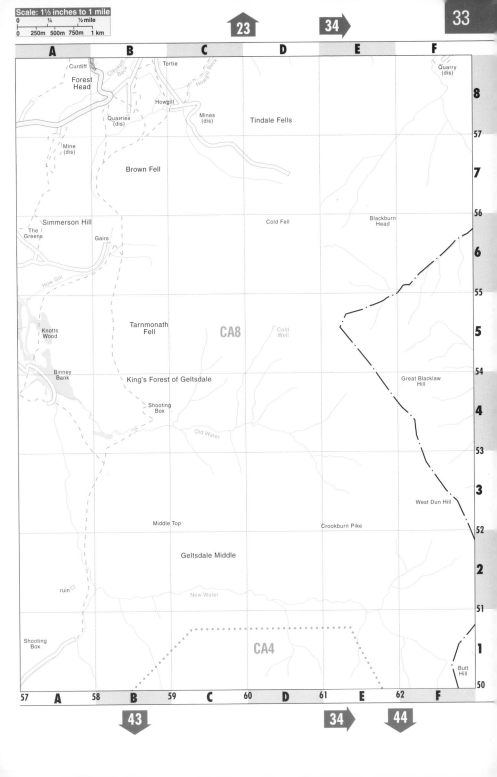

A   B   C   D   E   F

Curdiff
Tortie
Forest Head
Cleskett Beck
Howgill Beck
Quarry (dis)

8

Howgill
Quarries (dis)
Mines (dis)
Tindale Fells

57

Mine (dis)
Brown Fell

7

56

Simmerson Hill
Cold Fell
Blackburn Head

The Greens
Gairs

6

How Gill

55

Tarnmonath Fell
CA8
Cold Well

Knotts Wood

5

54

Binney Bank
King's Forest of Geltsdale
Great Blacklaw Hill

Shooting Box

4

Old Water

53

3

Middle Top
Crookburn Pike
West Dun Hill

52

Geltsdale Middle

2

ruin
New Water

51

Shooting Box
CA4

1

Butt Hill

50

57   A   58   B   59   C   60   D   61   E   62   F

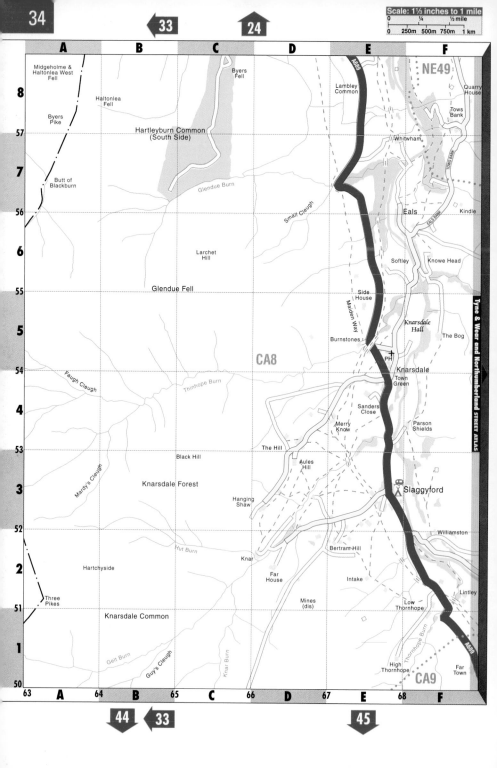

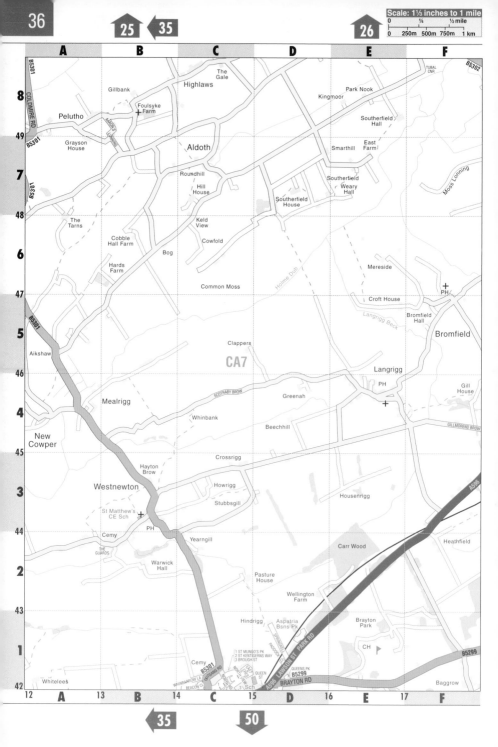

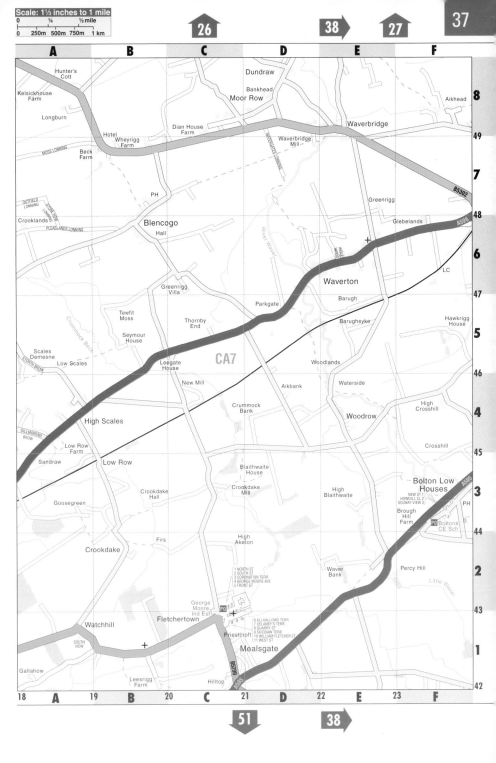

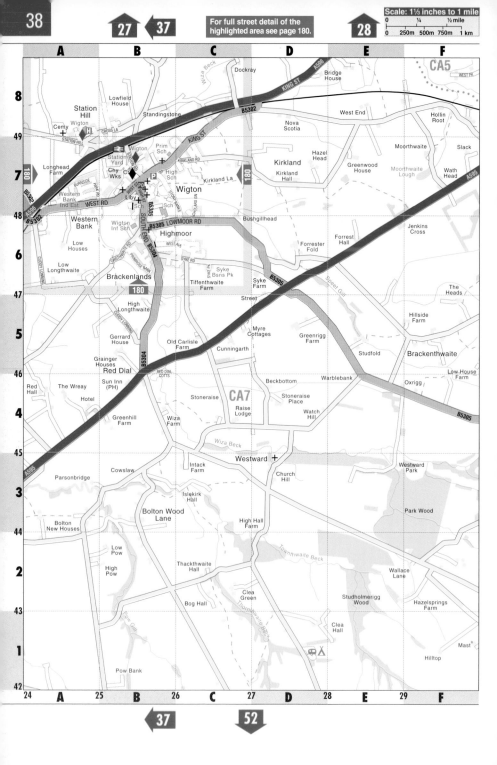

38

27 37

For full street detail of the
highlighted area see page 180.

28

Scale: 1⅓ inches to 1 mile
0   ¼   ½ mile
0   250m 500m 750m   1 km

A B C D E F

CA5
WEST PK

Dockray
Bridge House
KING ST
B5302
West End
Hollin Root
Lowfield House
Standingstone
Nova Scotia
Moorthwaite
Slack
Station Hill
Wigton
Cemy
CROSS LA
Hazel Head
Moorthwaite Lough
Wath Head
STATION HILL
KING ST
Prim Sch
Wigton
Station Yard
Chy Wks
Kirkland
Kirkland Hall
Greenwood House
A595
KIRKLAND RD
High Sch
Kirkland La
Longhead Farm
BURNSIDE
Wigton
P
Sch
Wigton
Jenkins Cross
Western Bank Ind Est
WEST RD
Liby Sch
Sch
Bushgillhead
Forrest Hall
Western Bank
Wigton Inf Sch
B5305 LOWMOOR RD
Highmoor
WEST AVE
Forrester Fold
The Heads
Low Houses
SYKE RD
Syke Bsns Pk
Syke Farm
B5305
Hillside Farm
Low Longthwaite
Brackenlands
180
Tiffenthwaite Farm
Street
Speet Gill
High Longthwaite
Myre Cottages
Greenrigg Farm
Gerrard House
Old Carlisle Farm
Cunningarth
Studfold
Brackenthwaite
Grainger Houses
B5304
Red Dial
RED DIAL COTTS
Beckbottom
Warblebank
Oxrigg
Low House Farm
Red Hall
The Wreay
Sun Inn (PH)
Stoneraise
CA7
Stoneraise Place
Watch Hill
Hotel
Raise Lodge
Greenhill Farm
Wiza Farm
B5305
Wiza Beck
Westward Park
Parsonbridge
Cowslaw
Intack Farm
Westward
Church Hill
Park Wood
Islekirk Hall
Bolton Wood Lane
High Hall Farm
Bolton New Houses
Low Pow
Thackthwaite Hall
Townthwaite Beck
High Pow
Wallace Lane
Clea Green
Studholmerigg Wood
Hazelsprings Farm
Pow Gill
Bog Hall
Thornthwaite Beck
Clea Hall
Mast
Hilltop
Pow Bank

24 A 25 B 26 C 27 D 28 E 29 F

8 49 7 48 6 47 5 46 4 45 3 44 2 43 1 42

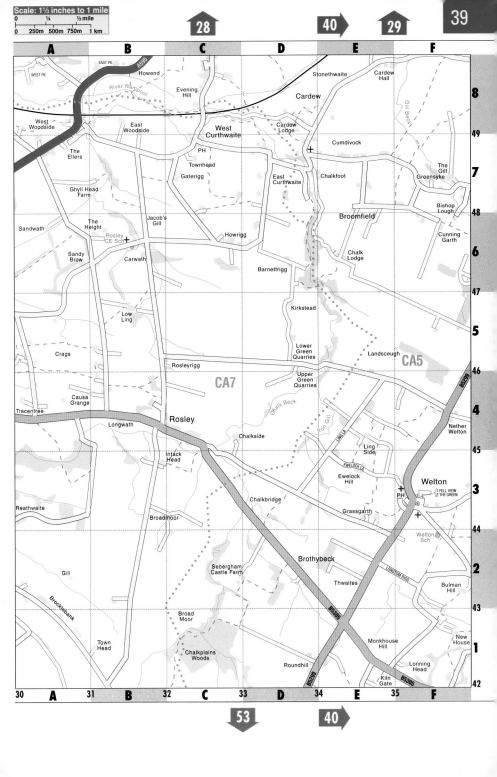

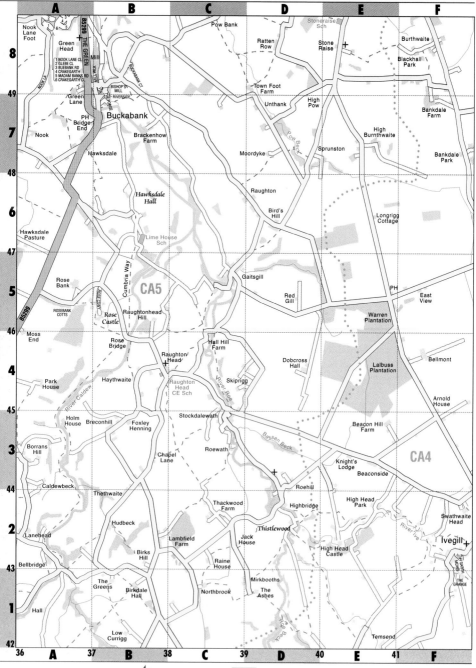

Scale: 1⅓ inches to 1 mile

0   ¼   ½ mile

0 250m 500m 750m 1 km

8

Nook Lane Foot

Green Head

1 NOOK LANE CL
2 GLEBE CL
3 BUEBANK RD
4 CRAKEGARTH
5 MADAM BANKS RD
6 CRAKEGARTH CL

Mill

THE GREEN

B5299

CROBANK CT

Pow Bank

Ratten Row

Stoneraise Sch

Stone Raise

Burthwaite

Blackhall Park

49

Town Foot Farm

BISHOP'S MILL

RIVERSIDE

PYBE

Unthank

High Pow

Bankdale Farm

7

Green Lane

PH Bridge End

Buckabank

Brackenhow Farm

Moordyke

Pow Beck

Sprunston

High Burnthwaite

Nook

Hawksdale

Raughton

Bankdale Park

48

Hawksdale Hall

Bird's Hill

Longrigg Cottage

6

Hawksdale Pasture

Lime House Sch

47

5

Rose Bank

Cumbria Way

CA5

Gaitsgill

Red Gill

PH

East View

B5299

ROSEBANK COTTS

ROSE CRES

Rose Castle

Raughtonhead Hill

Warren Plantation

46

Moss End

Rose Bridge

Hall Hill Farm

Dobcross Hall

Lalbuss Plantation

Bellmont

4

Park House

Haythwaite

River Caldew

Raughton Head

Raughton Head CE Sch

River Roe

Skiprigg

Arnold House

45

Holm House

Breconhill

Foxley Henning

Stockdalewath

Beacon Hill Farm

CA4

3

Borrans Hill

Chapel Lane

Roewath

Bassen Beck

Knight's Lodge

Beaconside

Caldewbeck

Thethwaite

Roehill

44

Thackwood Farm

Highbridge

High Head Park

Swathwaite Head

2

Lanehead

Hudbeck

Lambfield Farm

Jack House

Thistlewood

River Ive

High Head Castle

Ivegill

43

Bellbridge

Birks Hill

Raine House

Mirkbooths

GARTH MEWS

THE GRANGE

1

Hall

The Greens

Birkdale Hall

Northbrook

The Ashes

42

Low Currigg

Roe Beck

Temsend

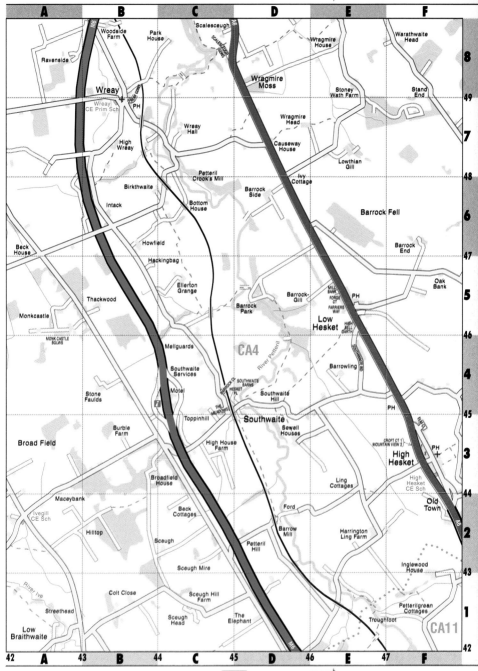

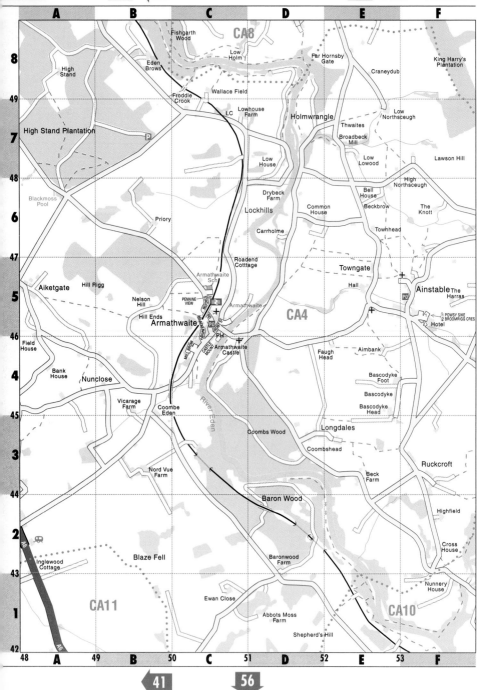

CA8

High Stand

Eden Brows

Fishgarth Wood

Low Holm

Far Hornsby Gate

Craneydub

King Harry's Plantation

Froddle Crook

Wallace Field

High Stand Plantation

LC

Lowhouse Farm

Holmwrangle

Low Northsceugh

Thwaites

Broadbeck Mill

Lawson Hill

Low House

Low Lowood

High Northsceugh

Blackmoss Pool

Priory

Drybeck Farm

Lockhills

Common House

Bell House

Beckbrow

The Knott

Carrholme

Townhead

Roadend Cotttage

Aiketgate

Hill Rigg

Armathwaite Sch

Towngate

Hall

Ainstable

The Harras

Nelson Hill

PENNINE VIEW

Armathwaite

CA4

Hotel

1 POWSY SIKE
2 BROOMRIGG CRES

Hill Ends

Armathwaite

Field House

PH

Armathwaite Castle

Faugh Head

Aimbank

Bank House

Nunclose

Bascodyke Foot

Bascodyke

Vicarage Farm

Coombe Eden

River Eden

Coombs Wood

Longdales

Bascodyke Head

Coombshead

Ruckcroft

Nord Vue Farm

Beck Farm

Baron Wood

Highfield

Blaze Fell

Cross House

Inglewood Cottage

CA11

Ewan Close

Baronwood Farm

Nunnery House

Abbots Moss Farm

CA10

Shepherd's Hill

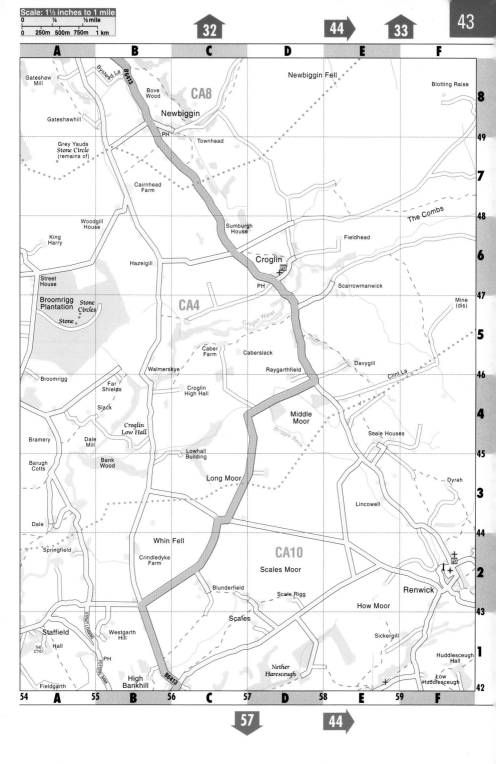

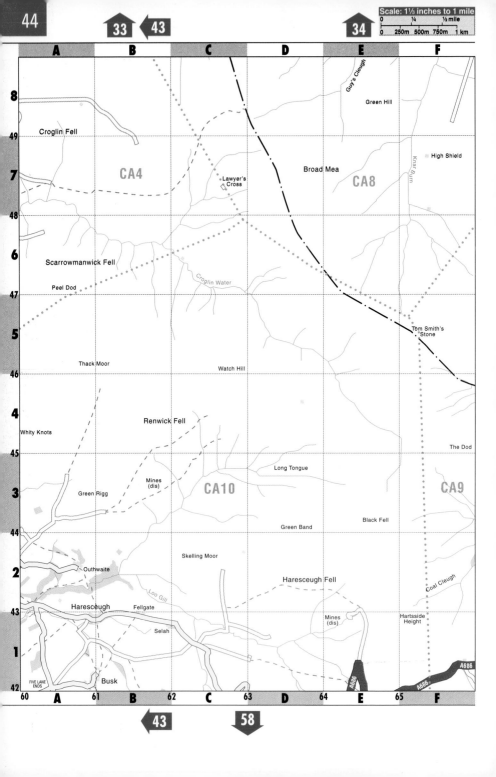

Guy's Cleugh

Green Hill

Croglin Fell

49

CA4

High Shield

Broad Mea

7

Lawyer's Cross

CA8

Knar Burn

48

6

Scarrowmanwick Fell

Peel Dod

Croglin Water

47

5

Tom Smith's Stone

Thack Moor

Watch Hill

46

4

Renwick Fell

Whity Knots

The Dod

45

Long Tongue

Mines (dis)

3

Green Rigg

CA10

CA9

Black Fell

44

Green Band

Skelling Moor

2

Outhwaite

Haresceugh Fell

Loo Gill

Harsside Height

43

Haresceugh

Fellgate

Mines (dis)

Selah

Coal Cleugh

1

A686

A686

FIVE LANE ENDS

Busk

A686

42

60   A   61   B   62   C   63   D   64   E   65   F

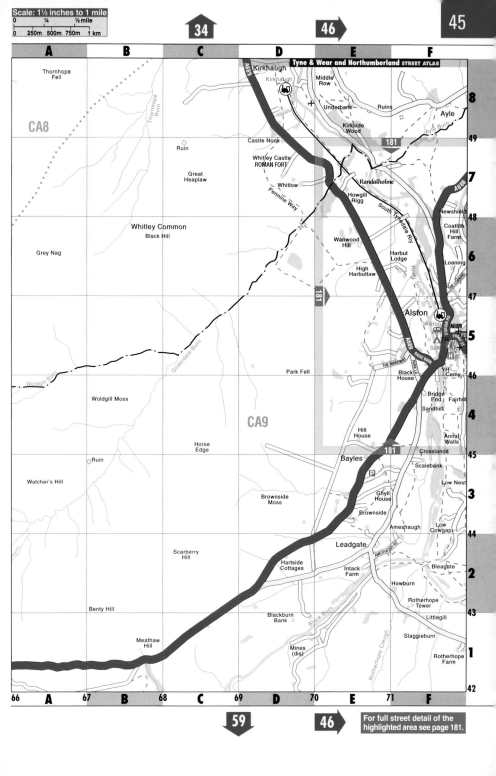

Tyne & Wear and Northumberland STREET ATLAS

A   B   C   D   E   F

Thornhope
Fell

CA8

Thornhope Burn

Kirkhaugh
Kirkhaugh
Middle
Row
Underbank
Ruins
Ayle
Ayle Burn

8

Ruin

Castle Nook
Kirkside
Wood

181

49

Whitley Castle
ROMAN FORT

Great
Heaplaw

Whitlow

Randalholme

7

Pennine Way
Howgill
Rigg
South Tynedale Rly

Newshield

Whitley Common
Black Hill

Coatlith
Hill
Farm

48

Grey Nag

Wanwood
Hill

Harbut
Lodge

Loaning

6

High
Harbutlaw

THE LOANING

River South Tyne

181

47

Alston
Alston

Gilderdale Burn

A689

Park Fell

THE WARDWAY

Black
House

PARK LA

RAISE BANK

YH
Cemy

46

CA9

Woldgill Burn
Woldgill Moss

Bridge
End
Sandhill

Fairhill

4

Horse
Edge

Hill
House

Annat
Walls

Watcher's Hill

Ruin

Bayles

181

Crosslands

Scalebank

45

Brownside
Moss

Ghyll
House

Low Nest

3

Brownside

Ameshaugh

Low
Cowgap

44

Scarberry
Hill

Leadgate

AMESHAUGH RD

Benty Hill

Hartside
Cottages

Intack
Farm

Howburn

Bleagate

Rotherhope
Tower

2

Blackburn
Bank

Black Burn

Littlegill

43

Meathaw
Hill

Mines
(dis)

Rotherhope Cleugh

Slaggieburn

Rotherhope
Farm

1

42

A   B   C   D   E   F
66   67   68   69   70   71

59   46

For full street detail of the
highlighted area see page 181.

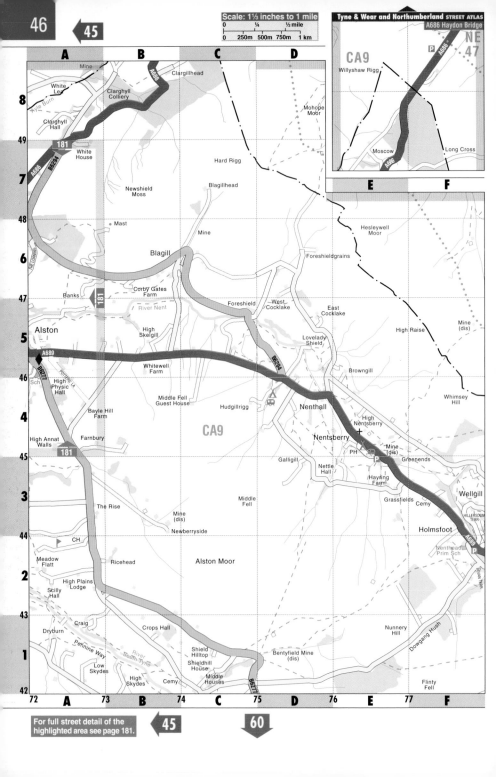

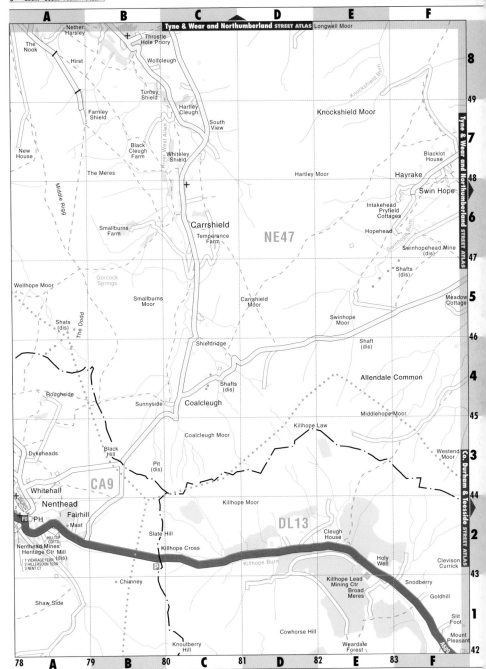

The Nook
Nether Harsley
Hirst
Throstle Hole Priory
Wolfcleugh
Longwell Moor

Turney Shield
Farnley Shield
Hartley Cleugh
South View

Black Cleugh Farm
Whiteley Shield
New House
The Meres

Knockshield Moor

Hartley Moor

Blacklot House
Hayrake
Swin Hope

Smallburns Farm
Carrshield
Temperance Farm

NE47

Intakehead
Pryfield Cottages
Hopehead

Swinhopehead Mine (dis)

Gorcock Springs

Wellhope Moor

Smallburns Moor
Carrshield Moor

Swinhope Moor

Shafts (dis)

Meadow Cottage

Shats (dis)
The Dodd

Shieldridge

Shaft (dis)

Roughside

Shafts (dis)

Allendale Common

Sunnyside
Coalcleugh

Coalcleugh Moor

Killhope Law

Middlehope Moor

Dykeheads

Black Hill

Pit (dis)

Westend Moor

Whitehall
Nenthead

CA9

Killhope Moor

Fairhill
Mast

Slate Hill

Cleugh House

DL13

Hilltop Cotts
Nenthead Mines Heritage Ctr Mill (dis)
1 VICARAGE TERR
2 HILLERSDON TERR
3 NENT CT

Killhope Cross

Killhope Burn

Holy Well

Clevison Currick

Chimney

Killhope Lead Mining Ctr
Broad Meres

Snodberry

Goldhill

Shaw Side

Slit Foot

Mount Pleasant

Knoutberry Hill

Cowhorse Hill

Weardale Forest

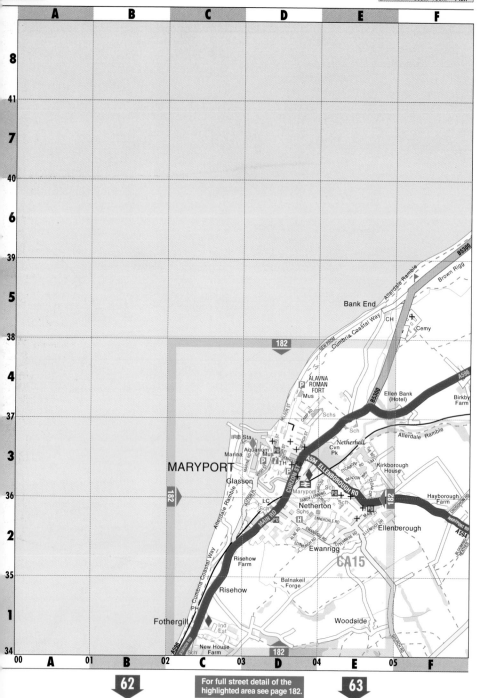

A   **B**   **C**   **D**   **E**   **F**

8

41

7

40

6

39

5

38

4

37

3

36

2

35

1

34

Bank End

CH   Cemy

Brown Rigg

B5300

Cumbria Coastal Way

Allerdale Ramble

NEW PROM

A596

ALAVNA ROMAN FORT
Mus

Ellen Bank (Hotel)

Birkby Farm

Schs

Sch

Netherfall
Cvn Pk

Allerdale Ramble

IRB Sta

Aquarium
Mus

Marina

TH

MARYPORT

Glasson

Maryport

Netherton

Sch

Kirkborough House

Hayborough Farm

Ellenborough

LC
Sch

H

ENNERDALE RD

Ewanrigg

CA15

Balnakeil Forge

Woodside

Risehow Farm

Cumbria Coastal Way

Allerdale Ramble

Risehow

PH

Fothergill

Ind Est

New House Farm

A594

ELLENBOROUGH RD

CURZON ST

MAIN RD

A596

182

182

182

182

00   **A**   **01**   **B**   **02**   **C**   **03**   **D**   **04**   **E**   **05**   **F**

62

For full street detail of the highlighted area see page 182.

63

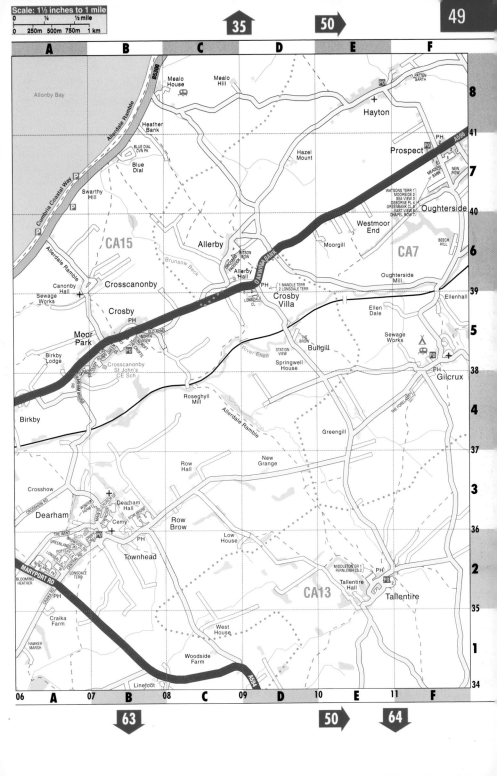

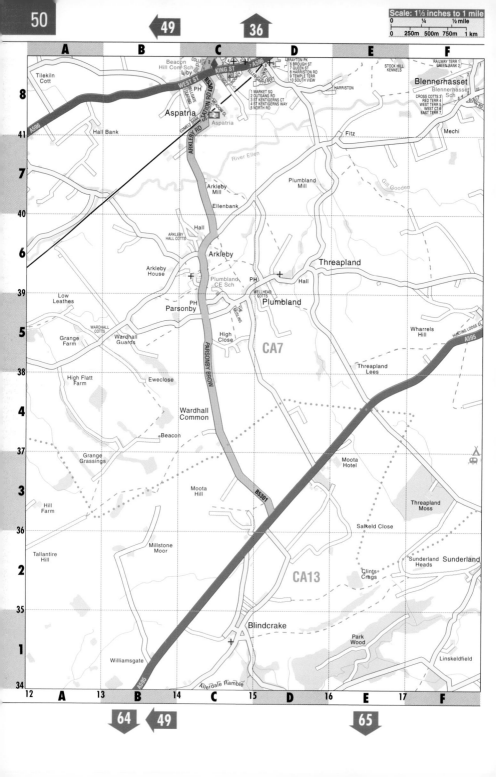

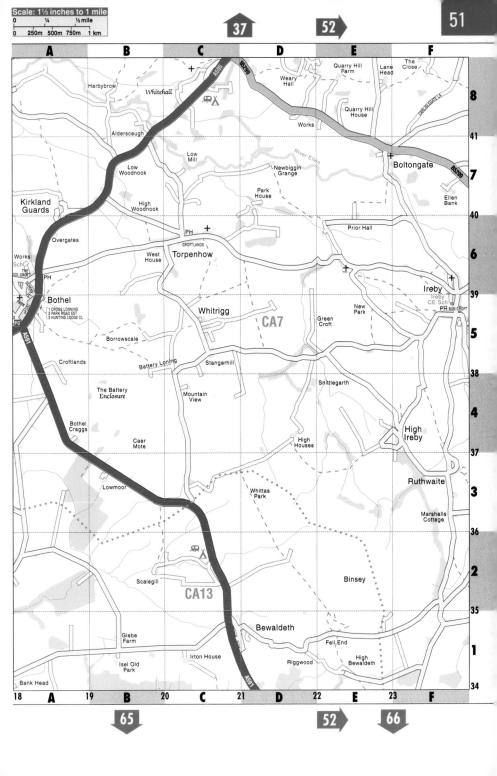

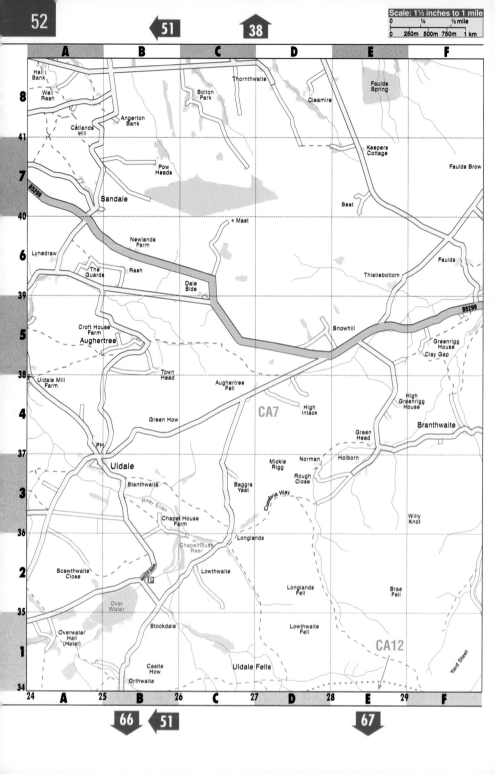

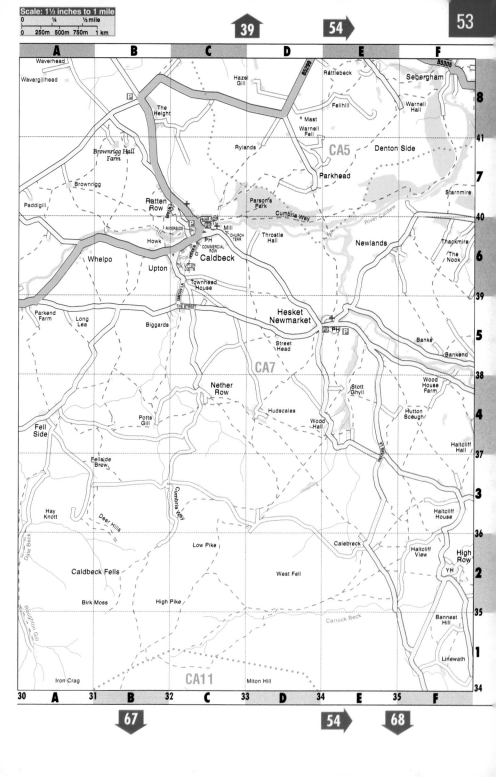

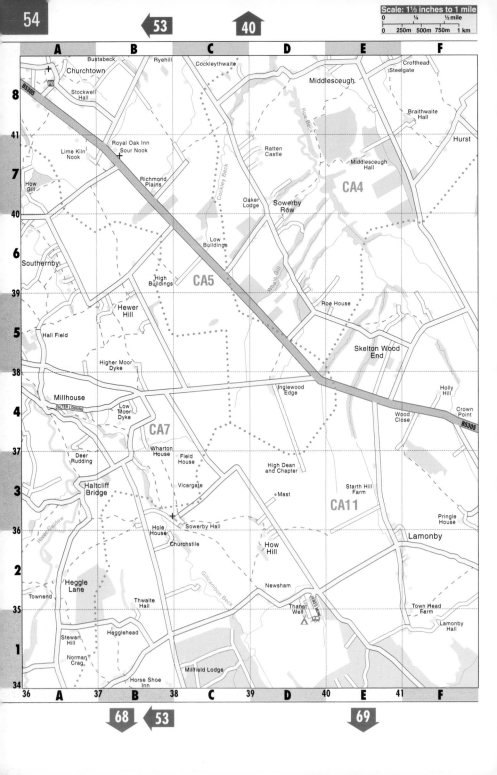

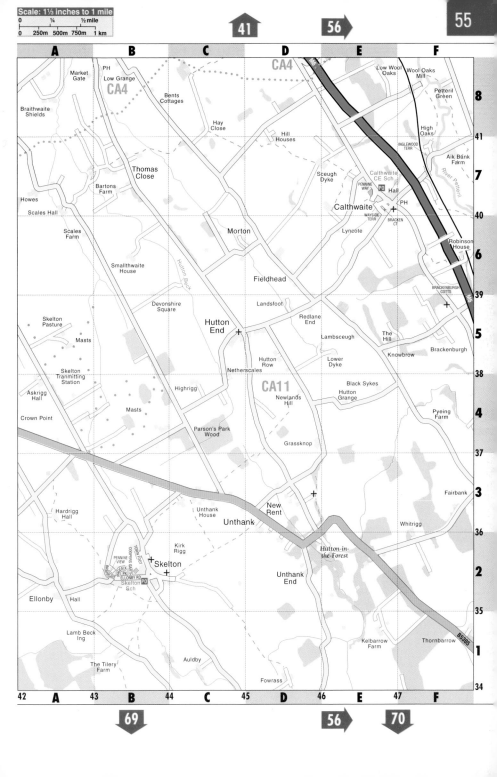

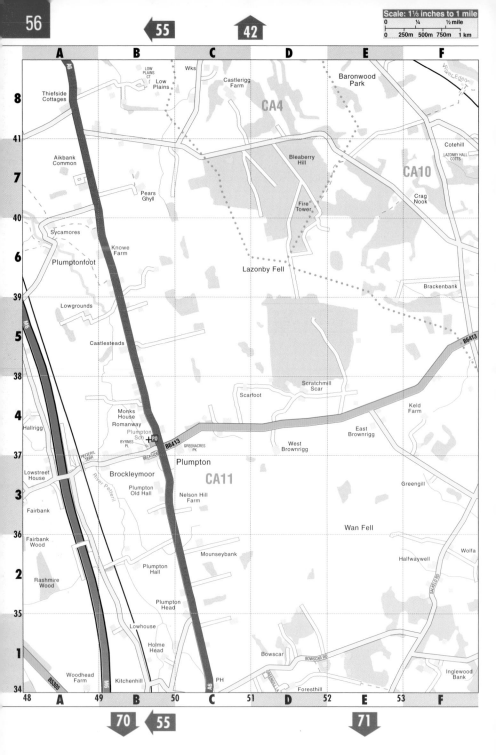

55
42

Scale: 1½ inches to 1 mile

0   ¼   ½ mile
0 250m 500m 750m 1 km

A **B** **C** **D** **E** **F**

A6

Thiefside
Cottages

LOW
PLAINS
CT

Low
Plains

Wks

Castlerigg
Farm

Baronwood
Park

CA4

VALE of EDEN

8

41

Aikbank
Common

Bleaberry
Hill

Cotehill

LAZONBY HALL
COTTS

CA10

7

Pears
Ghyll

Fire
Tower

Crag
Nook

40

Sycamores

Knowe
Farm

Plumptonfoot

Lazonby Fell

Brackenbank

6

39

Lowgrounds

B6413

M6

5

Castlesteads

38

Scratchmill
Scar

Scarfoot

Keld
Farm

4

Hallrigg

Monks
House
Romanway

Plumpton
Sch

BYRNES
PL

PO

B6413

BECK CLOSE

GREENACRES
PK

West
Brownrigg

East
Brownrigg

37

PETERIL
TERR

Lowstreet
House

Brockleymoor

Plumpton

CA11

Greengill

3

River Petteril

Fairbank

Plumpton
Old Hall

Nelson Hill
Farm

36

Fairbank
Wood

Wan Fell

Wolfa

Halfwaywell

2

Rashmire
Wood

Plumpton
Hall

Mounseybank

SALKELD RD

35

Plumpton
Head

Lowhouse

1

M6

Holme
Head

Woodhead
Farm

B5305

Kitchenhill

A6

PH

Bowscar

BOWSCAR RD

Foresthill

GREENHILL LA

Inglewood
Bank

34

48   **A**   49   **B**   50   **C**   51   **D**   52   **E**   53   **F**

70
55
71

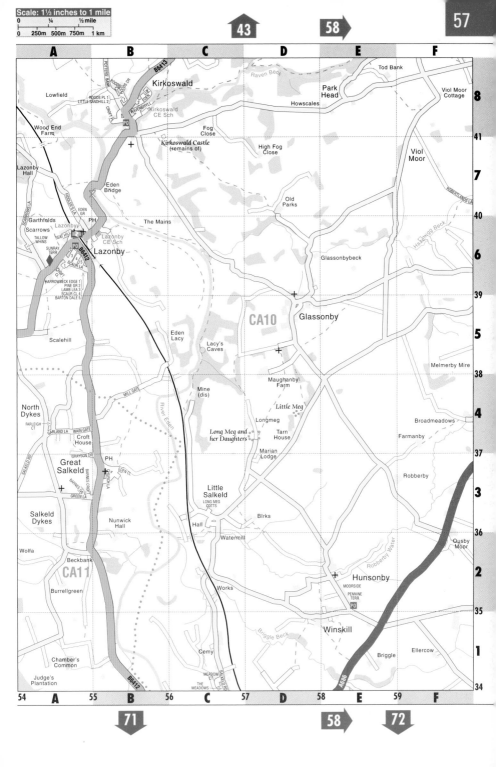

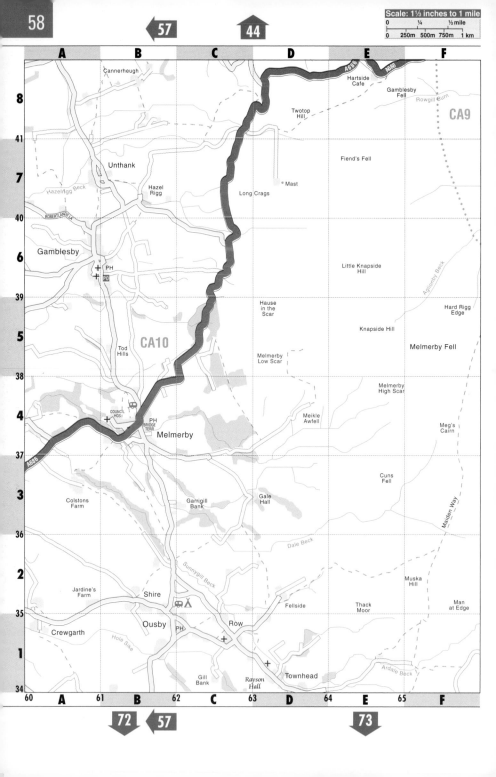

Scale: 1½ inches to 1 mile

0   ¼   ½ mile
0   250m 500m 750m   1 km

A   B   C   D   E   F

8

41

Cannerheugh

A686   A686

Hartside
Cafe

Gamblesby
Fell

Rowgill Burn

CA9

Twotop
Hill

Unthank

7

Hazelrigg Beck

Hazel
Rigg

Long Crags

° Mast

Fiend's Fell

40

ROBERTLAND LA.

Gamblesby

6

PH

Little Knapside
Hill

Aglionby Beck

39

Hause
in the
Scar

Hard Rigg
Edge

Knapside Hill

5

Tod
Hills

CA10

Melmerby
Low Scar

Knapside Hill

Melmerby Fell

38

Melmerby
High Scar

4

COUNCIL
HOS?

PH
BRIDGE
TERR.

Melmerby

Meikle
Awfell

Meg's
Cairn

37

A686

3

Colstons
Farm

Garrigill
Bank

Gale
Hall

Cuns
Fell

Maiden Way

36

Dale Beck

2

Jardine's
Farm

Sunnygill Beck

Shire

Muska
Hill

Man
at Edge

35

Crewgarth

Ousby

Hole Sike

PH

Row

Fellside

Thack
Moor

1

Gill
Bank

Rayson
Hall

Townhead

Ardale Beck

34

60   A   61   B   62   C   63   D   64   E   65   F

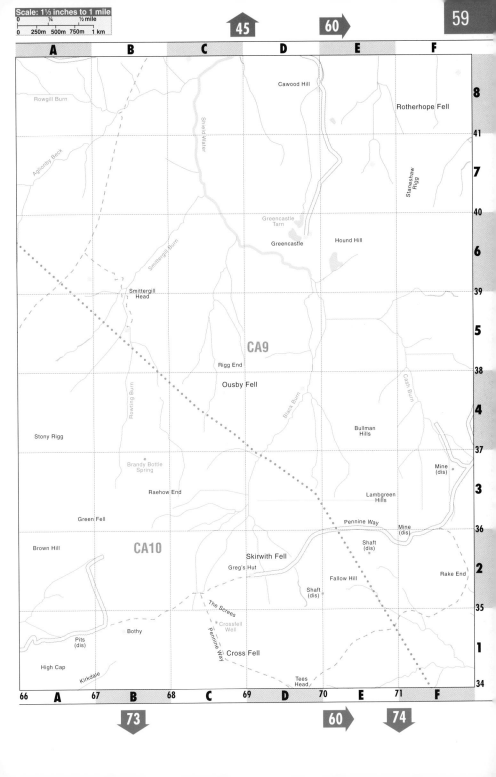

A B C D E F

8

Rowgill Burn

Cawood Hill

Rotherhope Fell

41

Aglionby Beck

Shield Water

7

Staneshaw Rigg

40

Greencastle Tarn

6

Smittergill Burn

Greencastle

Hound Hill

39

Smittergill Head

Rowling Burn

5

CA9

Rigg End

38

Ousby Fell

Black Burn

Cash Burn

4

Stony Rigg

Bullman Hills

37

Brandy Bottle Spring

Mine (dis)

3

Raehow End

Lambgreen Hills

Green Fell

Pennine Way

Mine (dis)

36

Brown Hill

CA10

Skirwith Fell

Shaft (dis)

2

Greg's Hut

Rake End

Fallow Hill

The Screes

Shaft (dis)

35

Crossfell Well

Bothy

Pennine Way

1

Pits (dis)

Pennine Way

Cross Fell

High Cap

Kirkdale

Tees Head

34

66 A 67 B 68 C 69 D 70 E 71 F

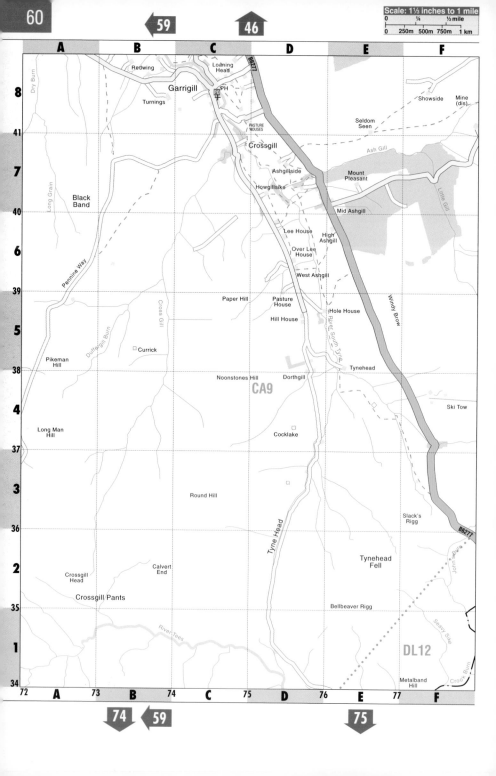

59
46

Scale: 1⅓ inches to 1 mile

0   ¼   ½ mile
0   250m   500m   750m   1 km

B6277

Dry Burn

Redwing
Loaning Head
Garrigill
PH
Turnings

PASTURE HOUSES

Showside
Mine (dis.)
Seldom Seen

Crossgill

Ash Gill

Long Grain

Black Band

Ashgillside

Howgillsike

Mount Pleasant

Little Gill

Mid Ashgill

Pennine Way

Lee House

High Ashgill

Over Lee House

West Ashgill

Cross Gill

Paper Hill

Pasture House

Hill House

Hole House

River South Tyne

Windy Brow

Duffergill Burn

Currick

Pikeman Hill

Noonstones Hill

Dorthgill

Tynehead

CA9

Ski Tow

Long Man Hill

Cocklake

Round Hill

Tyne Head

Slack's Rigg

B6277

Crossgill Head

Calvert End

Tynehead Fell

John's Burn

Crossgill Pants

Bellbeaver Rigg

DL12

Selah Syke

River Tees

Metalband Hill

Crook Burn

74
59
75

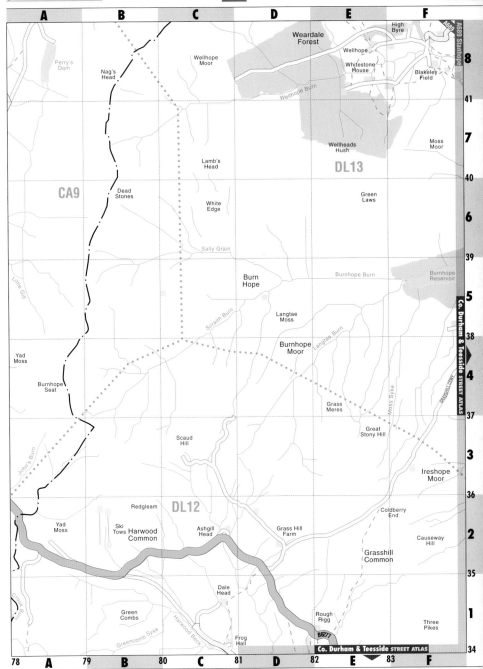

Perry's Dam

Nag's Head

Wellhope Moor

Weardale Forest

Wellhope

High Byre

Whitestone House

Blakeley Field

A689

A689 Stanhope

Moss Moor

Wellheads Hush

DL13

Lamb's Head

CA9

Dead Stones

White Edge

Green Laws

Sally Grain

Little Gill

Burn Hope

Burnhope Burn

Burnhope Reservoir

Langtae Moss

Scraith Burn

Langtae Burn

Burnhope Moor

Yad Moss

Burnhope Seat

Grass Meres

Moss Syke

Great Stony Hill

GRASSHILL ROAD

Co. Durham & Teesside STREET ATLAS

John's Burn

Scaud Hill

Ireshope Moor

DL12

Redgleam

Yad Moss

Ski Tows

Harwood Common

Ashgill Head

Grass Hill Farm

Coldberry End

Grasshill Common

Causeway Hill

Crook Burn

Green Combs

Dale Head

Rough Rigg

Three Pikes

Greencomb Syke

Harwood Beck

Frog Hall

B6277

Co. Durham & Teesside STREET ATLAS

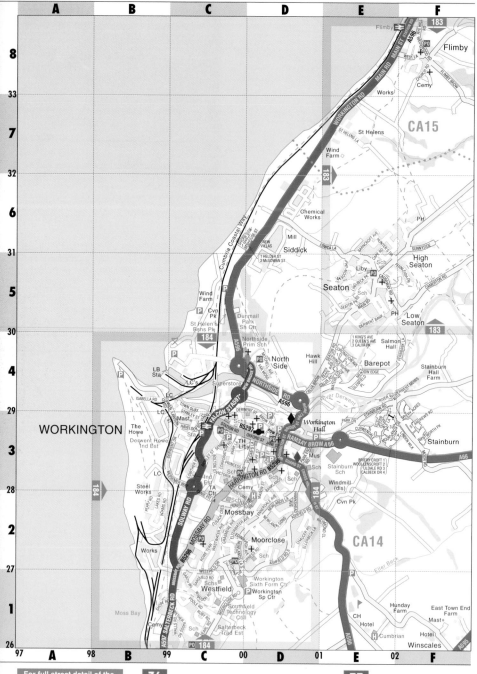

Flimby

183

Flimby

CA15

Works

St Helens

Wind
Farm

183

Chemical
Works

Mill

Cumbria Coastal Way

NEW
VILLAS

1 HELDER ST
2 McGOWAN ST

Siddick

LYNICA LA

Liby

High
Seaton

Sch

Seaton

PH

Low
Seaton

183

Wind
Farm

Cvn
Pk

St Helen's &
Bshs Pk

Dunmail
Park
Sh Ctr

184

Northside
Prim Sch

North
Side

Hawk
Hill

1 KING'S AVE
2 QUEEN'S AVE
3 CALVA PK

Salmon
Hall

Barepot

Stainburn
Hall
Farm

LB
Sta

LC's

Superstore

NORTHSIDE RD

A596

River Derwent

ISABELLA RD

LC

TOWN QUAY

Mast

HAVELOCK

FALCON ST

DERWENT ST

Sch

Workington
Hall

PARK RD

STAINBURN RD

Stainburn

WORKINGTON

The Howe

Derwent Howe
Ind Est

A596

B5297

STATION RD

OXFORD ST

TH
Liby

Mus

RAMSAY BROW A66

A66

LC

HARRINGTON RD B5296

GUARD ST

Sch

Stainburn
Sch

BREEZY CROFT 1
WOOLLENSCROFT 2
OLDALE RD 3
CALBECK DR 4

Steel
Works

Ind
Est

TA
Ctr

PRINCESS

VICTORIA RD

SOLWAY RD

MOSSBAY RD

Cemy

184

Windmill
(dis)

Cvn Pk

184

Mossbay

Moorclose

Sch

CA14

Works

B5296

Sch

Eller Beck

SALTERBECK RD

A597

Westfield

Schs

Workington
Sixth Form Ctr

Workington
Sp Ctr

Southfield
Technology
Coll

Moss Bay

Cemy

Sch

Salterbeck
Trad Est

184

Hunday
Farm

East Town End
Farm

CH
Hotel

Mast

Hotel

Cumbrian

Winscales

A596

A595

For full street detail of the highlighted area see pages 183 and 184.

76

77

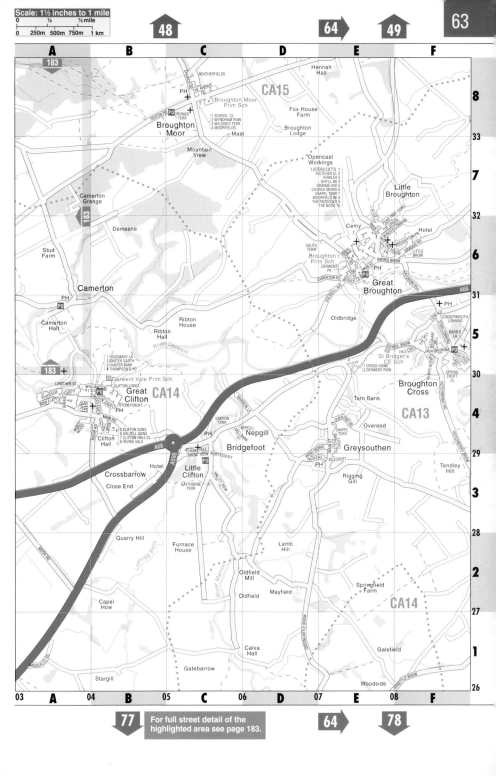

CA15

Broughton Moor

Heatherfields
PH
THE AVENUE
2
Broughton Moor Prim Sch
SEATON RD PO
IRVINGS TERR
1 SCHOOL CL
2 WYNDHAM ROW
3 WILSON'S TERR
4 MOORFIELDS
Mast
Mountain View

Hennah Hall
Fox House Farm
Broughton Lodge

Opencast Workings

LISTERS COTTS 1
FLETCHER CL 2
KIRKLEA 3
GHYLL BK 4
GRANGE AVE 5
CHURCH MDWS 6
CHAPEL TERR 7
MOORFIELD BK 8
THE PADDOCK'S 9
THE NOOK 10

Little Broughton

Cemy

Hotel

183

Camerton Grange
Demesne
Stud Farm

Camerton

PH
PO

Camerton Hall

Ribton House
Ribton Hall
River Derwent

SOUTH TERR
Broughton Prim Sch
DERWENT PK
PH
CAMERTON RD
COLDGILL AVE
EAST END

Great Broughton
PO
A66

Oldbridge

COCKERMOUTH LONNING
PH
BARR'S LA
School Brow
Hill Cres
St Bridget's CE Sch
SPRING CROFT CL

1 ROSEMARY LA
2 CARTER GARTH
3 HUNTER BANK
4 THOMPSON'S YD

183

Derwent Vale Prim Sch

CLIFTON LODGE
Great Clifton
STONEYCROFT
PH
MAIN RD

CA14

A66

Clifton Hall
1 RIVERSIDE
BOW FLAT
LOWTHER ST
WILLIAMS

5 CLIFTON GDNS
6 DALZELL GDNS
7 CLIFTON HALL CL
8 IRVING VALE

STATION TERR
NEPGILL
MILL BANK
PH
Nepgill
Bridgefoot
MARTIN LA
SCOTS CROFT

Tarn Bank
Overend
CHAPEL TERR
Broughton Cross

CA13

Tendley Hill

Crossbarrow
Hotel
CHAPEL BROW
GAYTHORNE TERR
Little Clifton
PO
VALE VIEW

Greysouthen
WENT MEWS
FAIRFIELD
PH
SILECROFT
Rigging Gill

Close End

Quarry Hill

Furnace House

Oldfield Mill
Oldfield

Lamb Hill

Mayfield

Springfield Farm

CA14

Capel How

Calva Hall

Gatebarrow

Galefield

Stargill

Woodside

For full street detail of the highlighted area see page 183.

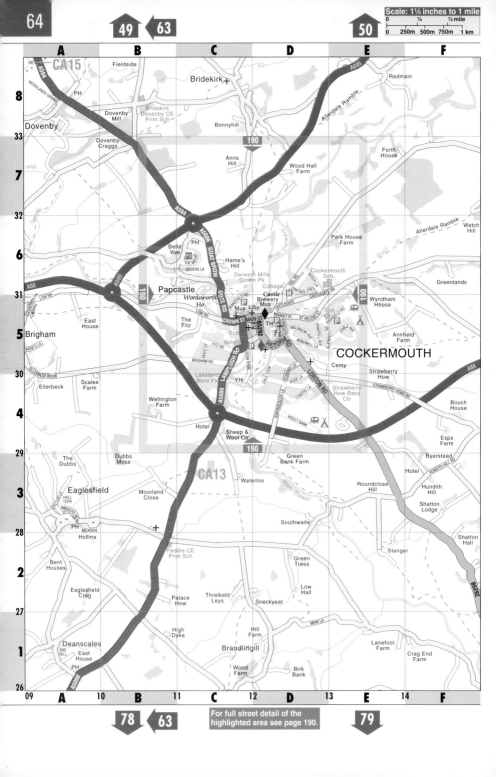

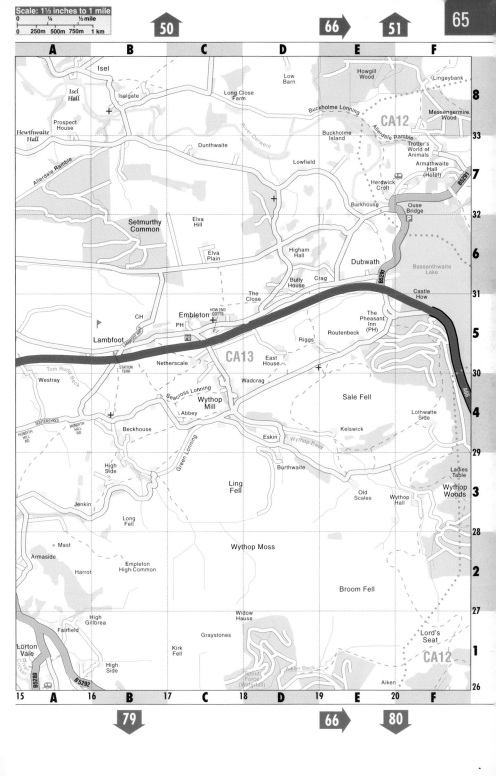

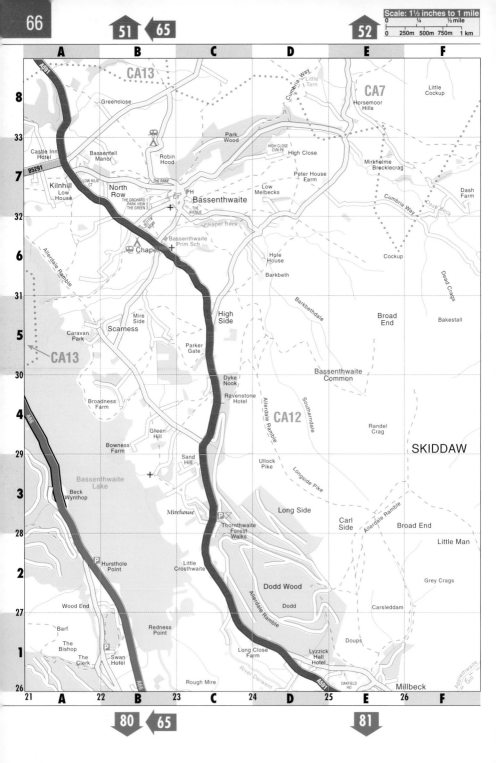

Scale: 1⅓ inches to 1 mile

0 ¼ ½ mile

0 250m 500m 750m 1 km

A **B** **C** **D** **E** **F**

A591

CA13

8

Greenclose

33

Park Wood

Cumbria Way

Little Tarn

CA7

Horsemoor Hills

Little Cockup

Castle Inn Hotel

Bassenfell Manor

Robin Hood

HIGH CLOSE CVN PK

High Close

Mirkholme Brecklecrag

7

B5291

Kilnhill

Low House

LOW KILN CT

North Row

THE RAKE

PH

Peter House Farm

Dash Farm

Cumbria Way

Dash Beck

Low Melbecks

32

THE ORCHARD 1
PARK VIEW 2
THE GREEN 3

Bassenthwaite

THE AVENUE

Chapel Beck

Cumbria Way

6

Chapel

Bassenthwaite Prim Sch

Hole House

Cockup

Dead Crags

Allerdale Ramble

Barkbeth

31

Barkbethdale

Broad End

Bakestall

Mire Side

5

Caravan Park

Scarness

Parker Gate

Bassenthwaite Common

CA13

30

Dyke Nook

Ravenstone Hotel

CA12

Randel Crag

SKIDDAW

Broadness Farm

4

A66

Green Hill

Allerdale Ramble

Southerndale

Bowness Farm

Sand Hill

Ullock Pike

Longside Pike

Allerdale Ramble

29

Bassenthwaite Lake

Long Side

Carl Side

Broad End

3

Beck Wynthop

Mirehouse

Little Man

28

Thornthwaite Forest Walks

Grey Crags

2

Hursthole Point

Little Crosthwaite

Dodd Wood

Allerdale Ramble

Dodd

Carsleddam

27

Wood End

Redness Point

Doups

1

Barf

The Bishop

Long Close Farm

Lyzzick Hall Hotel

Applethwaite Gill

The Clerk

Swan Hotel

River Derwent

A591

OAKFIELD HO

Millbeck

26

Rough Mire

A591

21 **A** 22 **B** 23 **C** 24 **D** 25 **E** 26 **F**

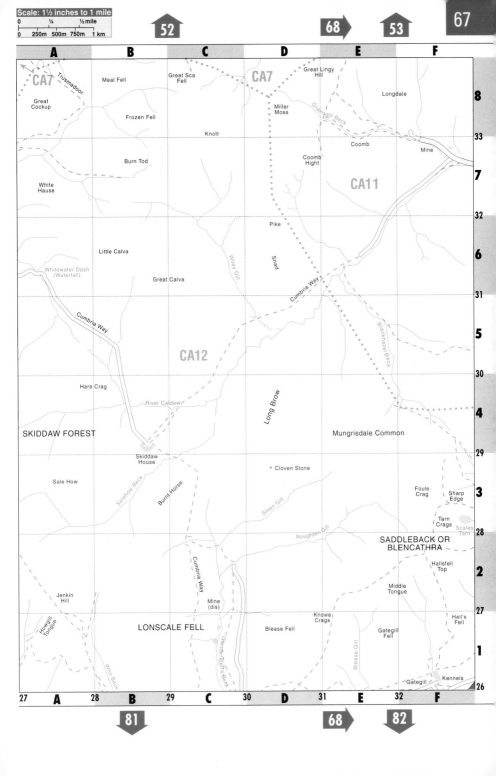

A   B   C   D   E   F

8
Round Knott
Carrock Fell
CA7
Stone Ends
Bank House
Scales

33
Crook-a-Fleet

7
Swineside
Roundhouse
Mosedale
Low Mill

32
River Caldew
Murrah Hall

6
Bowscale Tarn
Bowscale
Moss Dyke
Murrah

Tarn Crags

31
Raven Crags
Bowscale Fell
Undercrag

5
The Tongue
PO
Mungrisdale
CA11
PH

30
Low Beckside
Redmire

4
Bannerdale
Bannerdale Crags
Hazelhurst
Barrow Beck
Naddles Crags
Eycott Hill

29
River Glenderamackin
Near Howe
Naddles Beck

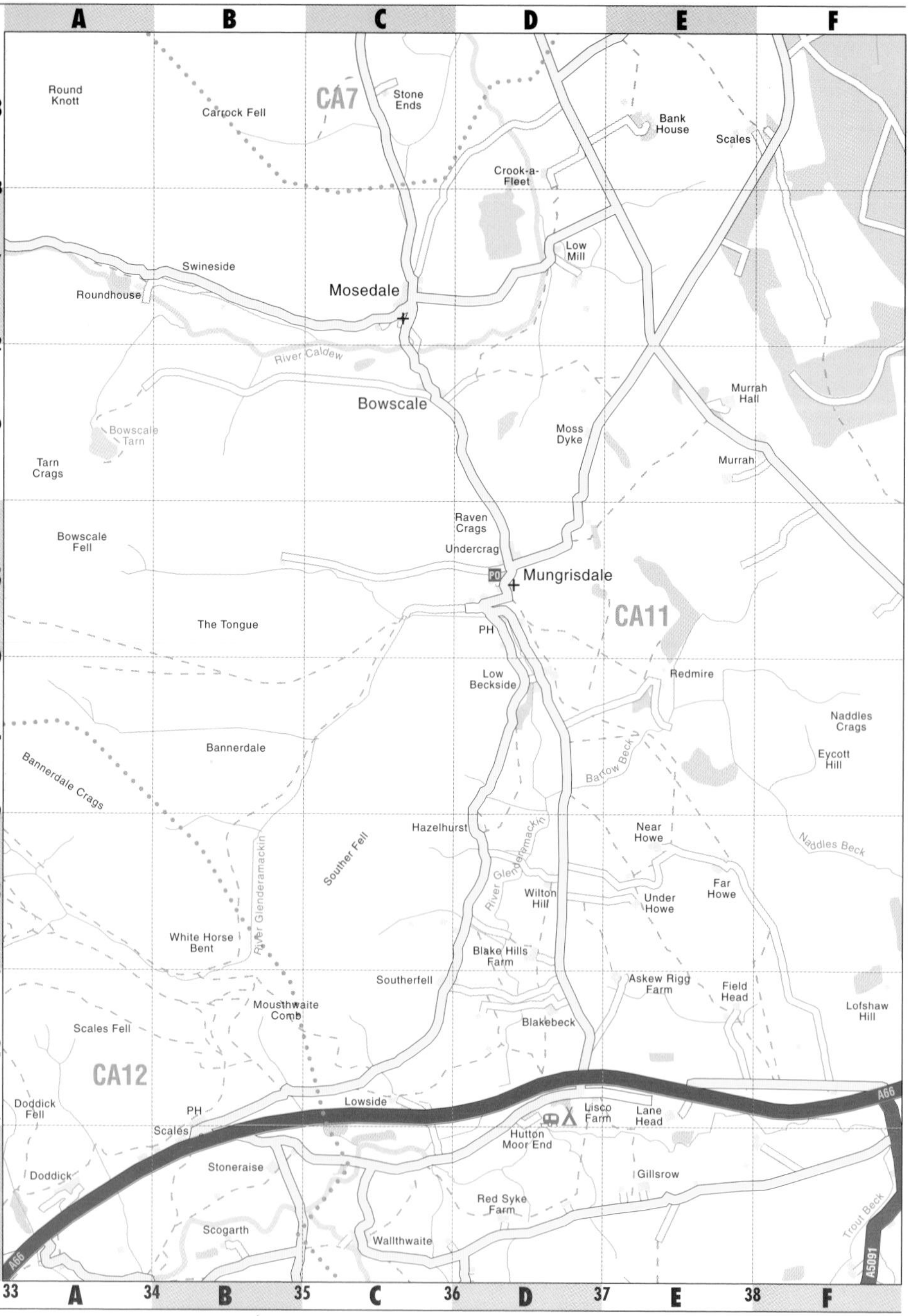

3
Southerfell
Wilton Hill
Under Howe
Far Howe

White Horse Bent

28
Southerfell
Blake Hills Farm
Askew Rigg Farm
Field Head
Lofshaw Hill

Mousthwaite Comb

2
Scales Fell
CA12
Blakebeck
Lisco Farm
Lane Head

Doddick Fell
PH
Lowside
Hutton Moor End
A66

27
Scales
Gillsrow
Trout Beck

Doddick
Stoneraise
Red Syke Farm

1
Scogarth
Wallthwaite
A5091

A66

26
33   A   34   B   35   C   36   D   37   E   38   F

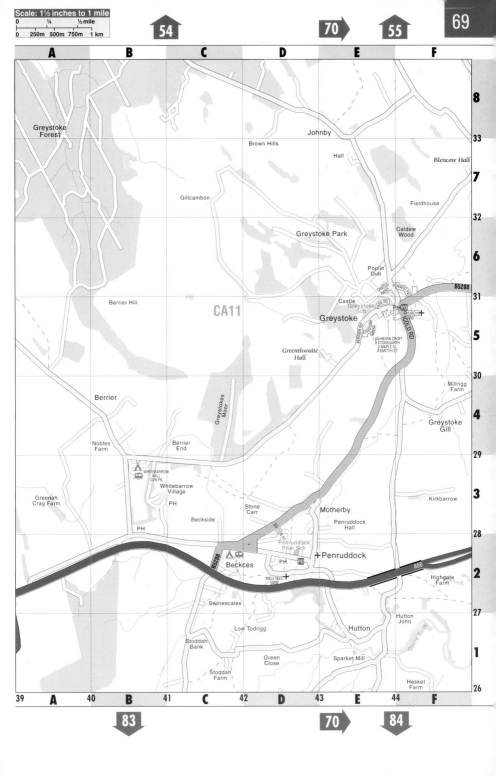

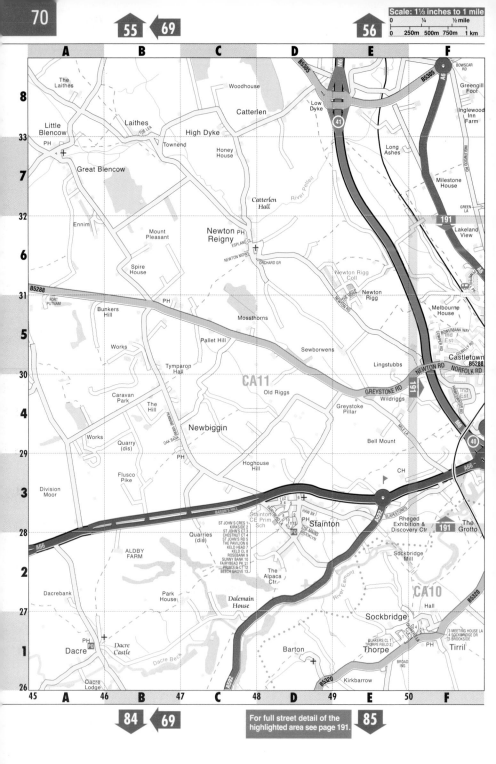

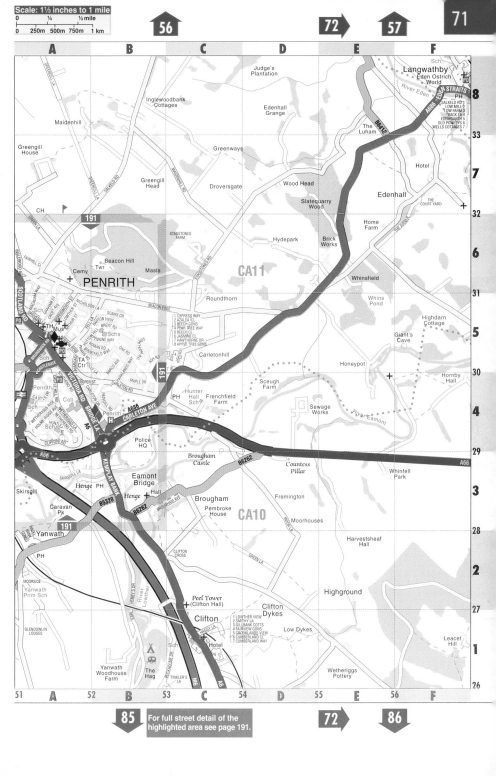

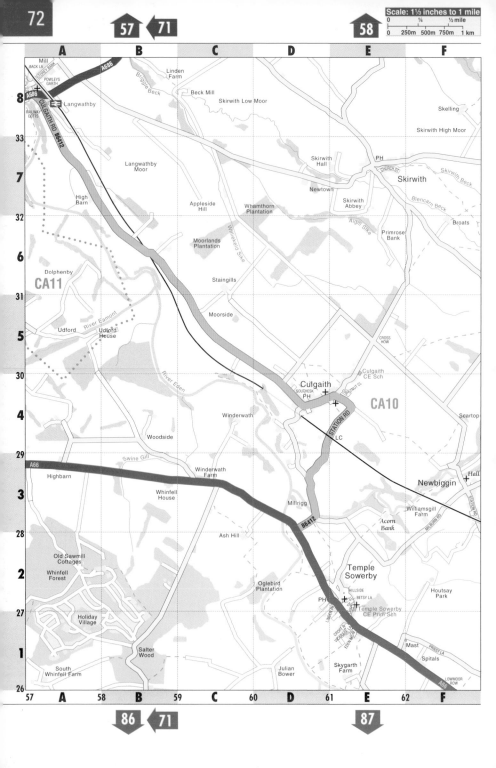

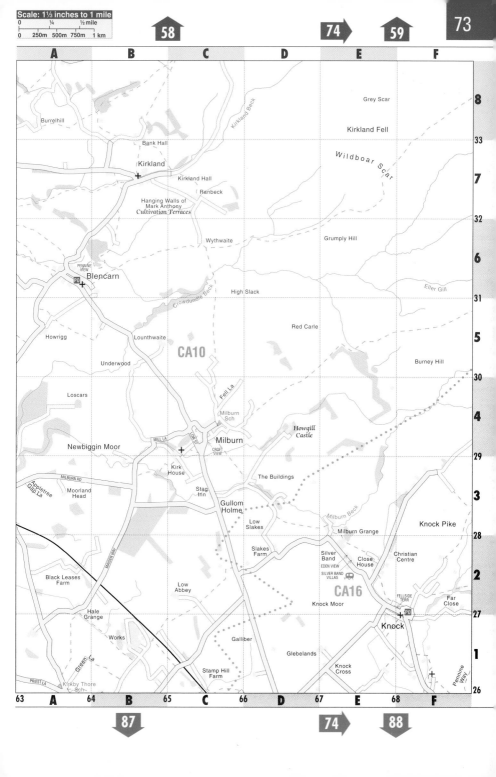

	A	B	C	D	E	F

Tees Head

Swah Beck

Moor House
National Nature Reserve

Hard Hill

8

Little Dun Fell

Mine (dis)

33

MILBURN FOREST

Middle Tongue

Pennine Way

CA9

7

CA10

Great Dun Fell

Mineworkings (dis)

Trout Beck

Mast

32

Moss Burn

Iron Howe

Silverband Mine

6

Green Castle

31

Knock Fell

Knock Ore Gill

5

DL12

Knock Old Man

30

Green Fell

Shafts (dis)

4

CA16

Sink Beck

Pennine Way

29

High Scald Fell

Wool Beck

Swindale Beck

Stake Beck

3

Mine (dis)

Great Rundale Tarn

28

Brownber Hill

Threlkeld Side

Seamore Tarn

2

Great Rundale Beck

Little Rundale Tarn

27

Huning Lane

Bluethwaite Hill

Little Rundale Beck

Backstone Edge

Pennine Way

High Cup Plain

1

Dufton Pike

High Cup Nick

Narrowgate Beacon

26

69	A	70	B	71	C	72	D	73	E	74	F

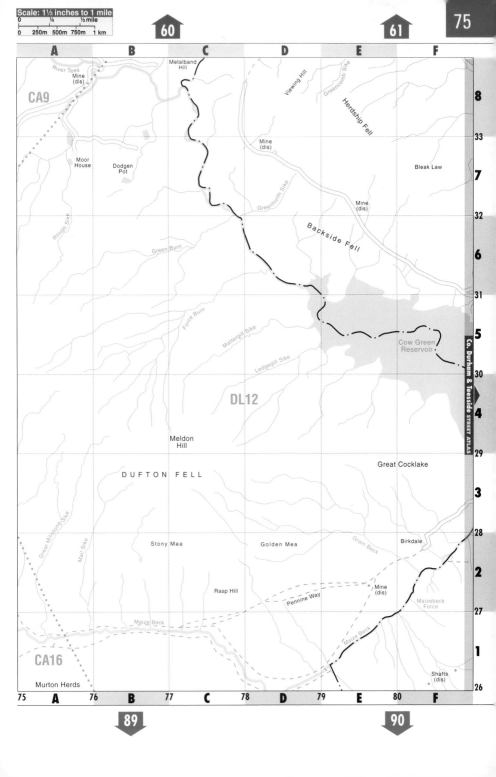

Scale: 1⅓ inches to 1 mile

0   ¼   ½ mile

0   250m   500m   750m   1 km

60

61

River Tees

Mine
(dis)

CA9

Moor
House

Dodgen
Pot

Metalband
Hill

Viewing Hill

Greencomb Sike

Herdship Fell

Mine
(dis)

Bleak Law

Greenhurth Sike

Mine
(dis)

Backside Fell

Rough Sike

Green Burn

Force Burn

Mattergill Sike

Ledgegill Sike

Cow Green
Reservoir

DL12

Meldon
Hill

DUFTON FELL

Great Cocklake

Great Millstone Sike

Mail Sike

Stony Mea

Golden Mea

Grain Beck

Birkdale

Rasp Hill

Pennine Way

Mine
(dis)

Maizebeck
Force

Maize Beck

Maize Beck

CA16

Shafts
(dis)

Murton Herds

Co. Durham & Teesside STREET ATLAS

8

33

7

32

6

31

5

30

4

29

3

28

2

27

1

26

75   A   76   B   77   C   78   D   79   E   80   F

89

90

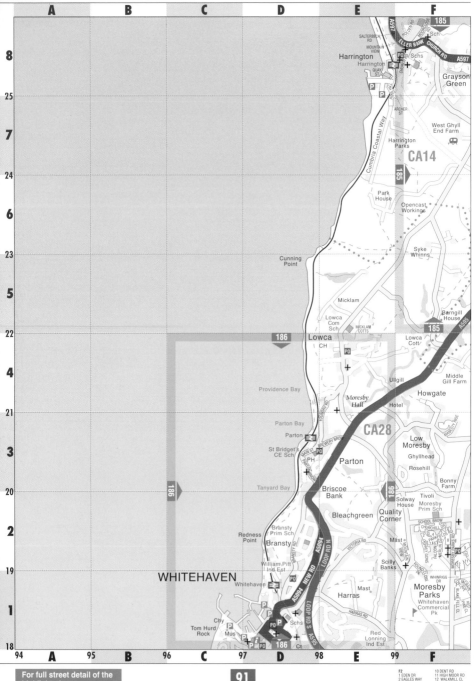

Scale: 1½ inches to 1 mile

62

For full street detail of the highlighted area see pages 185 and 186.

91

F2
1 EDEN DR
2 EAGLES WAY
3 PEREGRINE CL
4 HAWK PL
5 KESTREL GR
6 ROUND CL
7 HARRIER CT
8 ROWNTREE CRES
9 SOLWAY RD
10 DENT RD
11 HIGH MOOR RD
12 WALKMILL CL

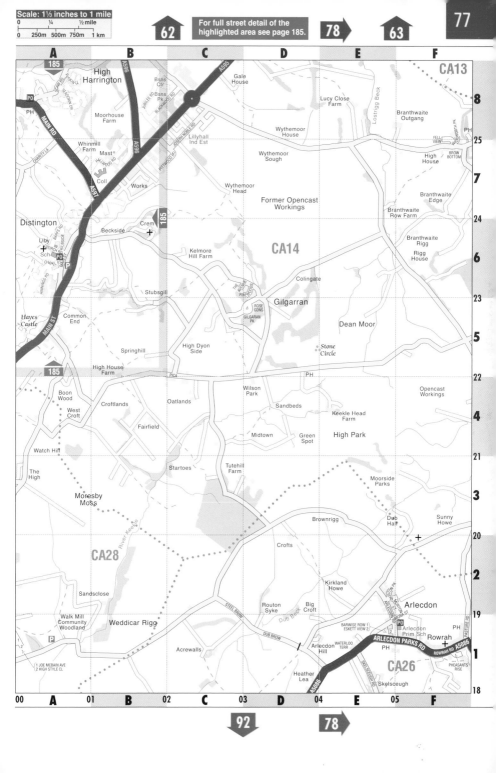

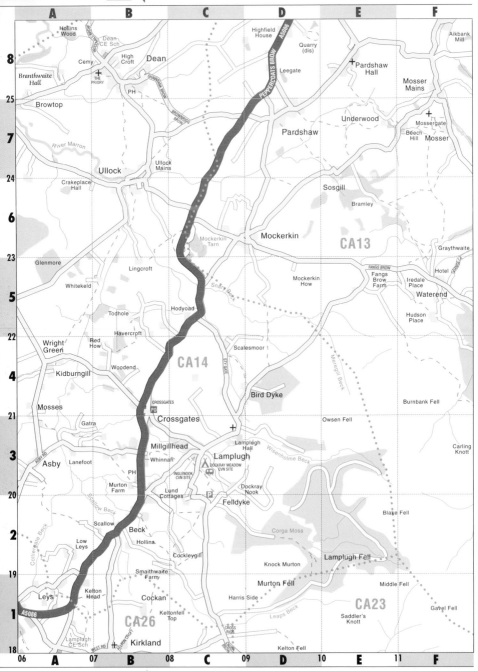

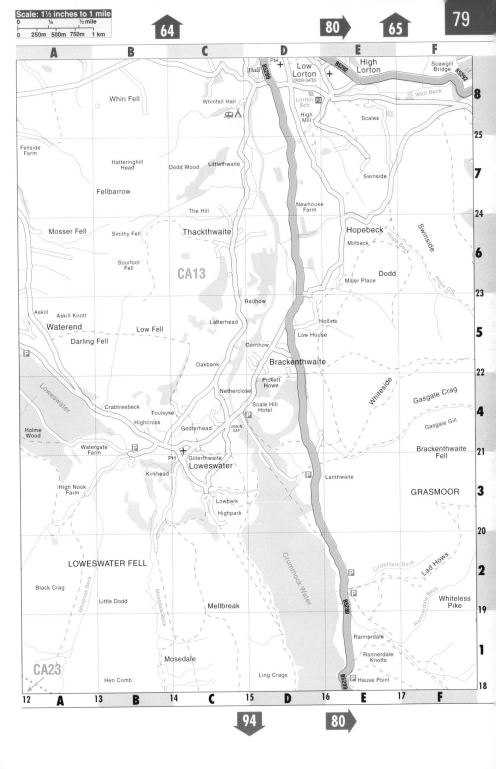

A B C D E F

Scawgill
Bridge
B5292
High
Lorton
B5292
Low
Lorton
CROSS GATES
PH
Hall
B5289
Whit Beck

8

Whinfell Hall
Whin Fell
Lorton
Sch
PO
High
Mill
Scales

25

Fellside
Farm

Hatteringhill
Head
Dodd Wood
Littlethwaite
Swinside

7

Fellbarrow
Newhouse
Farm

The Hill

24

Mosser Fell
Smithy Fell
Thackthwaite
Hopebeck
Swinside

6

Millbeck
Hope Beck

Sourfoot
Fell
CA13
Dodd
Miller Place
Hope Gill

23

Askill
Redhow
Hollins

Askill Knott
Latterhead
Low House

5

Waterend
Low Fell
Cornhow

Darling Fell
Brackenthwaite

22

Loweswater
Oakbank
Pickett
Howe
Whiteside
Gasgale Crag

4

Crabtreebeck
Netherclose
Scale Hill
Hotel
Gasgale Gill

Highcross
Foulsyke

Holme
Wood
Godferhead
JENKIN
GAP
Brackenthwaite
Fell

21

Watergate
Farm
PH
Gillerthwaite
Loweswater
Lanthwaite
GRASMOOR

3

Kirkhead

High Nook
Farm
Lowpark
Highpark

20

LOWESWATER FELL
Lad Hows

Cinderdale Beck

2

Black Crag
Little Dodd
Mellbreak
Crummock Water
B5289
Whiteless
Pike

19

CA23
Mosedale
Rannerdale

1

Hen Comb
Ling Crags
Rannerdale
Knotts
Hause Point
B5289

18

12 A 13 B 14 C 15 D 16 E 17 F

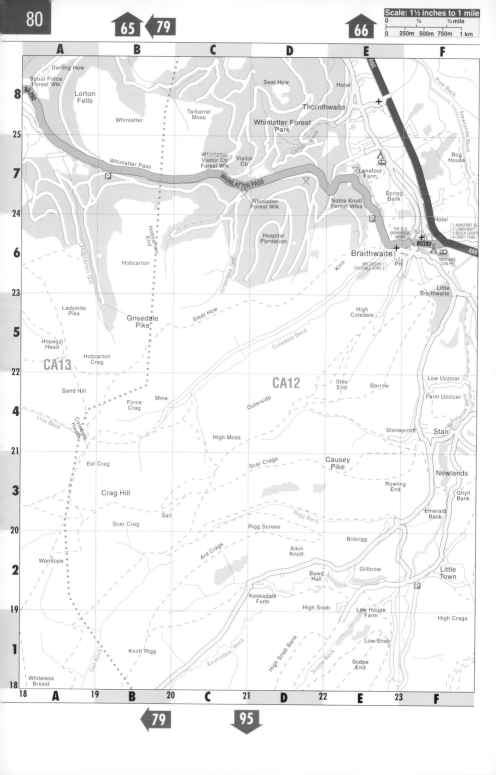

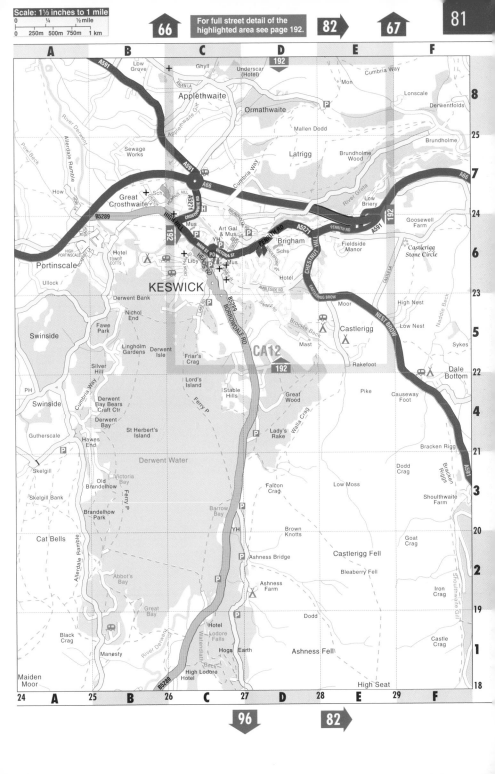

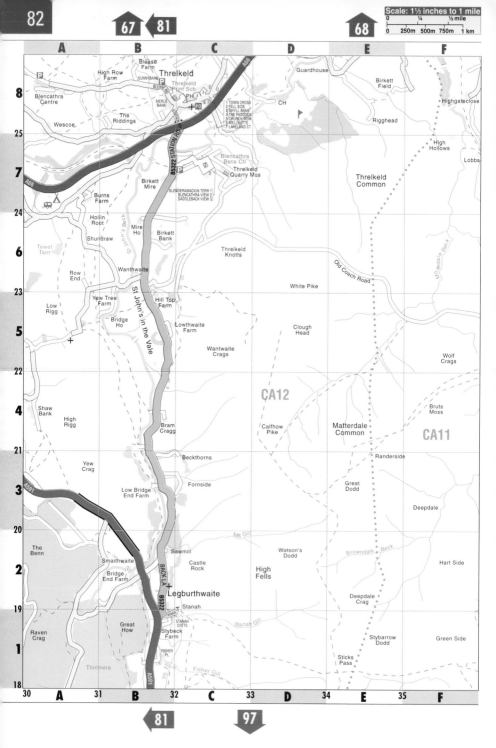

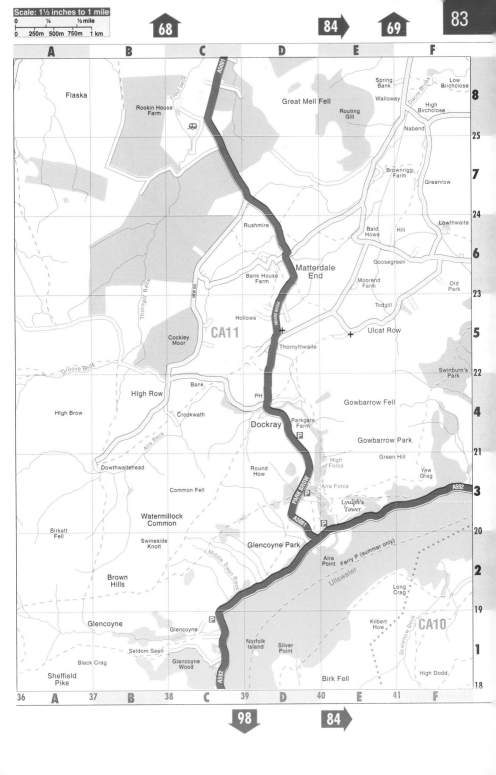

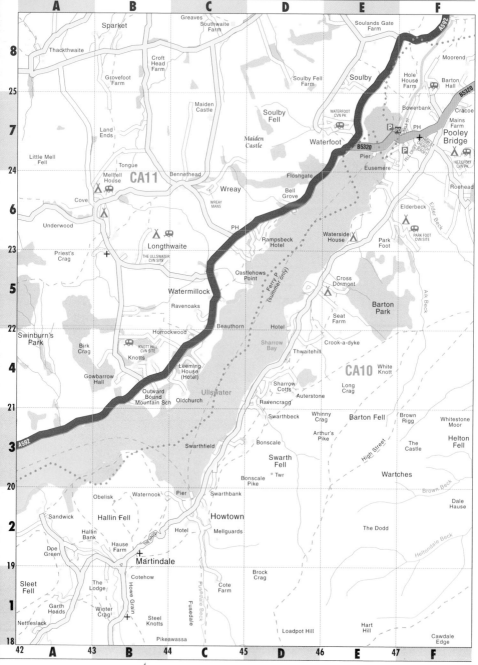

69 83

70

Scale: 1½ inches to 1 mile

0   ¼   ½ mile
0   250m   500m   750m   1 km

A B C D E F

Sparket

Greaves
Southwaite
Farm

Soulands Gate
Farm

Moorend

Thackthwaite

Croft
Head
Farm

Maiden
Castle

Soulby Fell
Farm

Soulby

Hole
House
Farm

Barton
Hall

8

Grovefoot
Farm

B5320

Cracoe

25

Land
Ends

Soulby
Fell

WATERFOOT
CVN PK

Bowerbank

Mains
Farm

Pooley
Bridge

7

Little Mell
Fell

Maiden
Castle

Waterfoot

P PO

PH

HIGH ST

FELL CROFT CVN SITE

HELCROFT
CVN SITE

Tongue

CA11

Bennethead

Wreay

B5320

Pier

Eusemere

P

Roehead

24

Melfell
House

WREAY
MANS

Floshgate

Cove

Bell
Grove

Elderbeck

PARK FOOT
CVN SITE

6

Underwood

PH

Rampsbeck
Hotel

Waterside
House

Park
Foot

Elder Beck

Priest's
Crag

Longthwaite

THE ULLSWATER
CVN SITE

Castlehows
Point

Cross
Dormont

23

Watermillock

Ferry P
(summer only)

Barton
Park

5

Ravenoaks

Seat
Farm

Aik Beck

Swinburn's
Park

Horrockwood

Beauthorn

Hotel

Crook-a-dyke

CA10

White
Knott

22

Birk
Crag

KNOTT HILL
CVN SITE

Knotts

Sharrow
Bay

Thwaitehill

Long
Crag

Brown
Rigg

Whitestone
Moor

4

Gowbarrow
Hall

Leeming
House
(Hotel)

Ullswater

Sharrow
Cotts

Auterstone

Barton Fell

Arthur's
Pike

High Street

The
Castle

Helton
Fell

Outward
Bound
Mountain Sch

Oldchurch

Ravencragg

Whinny
Crag

21

Swarthbeck

Brown Beck

Dale
Hause

A592

Swarthfield

Bonscale

Swarth
Fell

Wartches

3

Bonscale
Pike

Twr

Heltondale Beck

20

Obelisk

Waternook

Pier

Swarthbank

The Dodd

Sandwick

Hallin Fell

Hotel

Mellguards

2

Doe
Green

Hallin
Bank

Hause
Farm

THE CRAG

Brock
Crag

19

Martindale

Cotehow

Cote
Farm

Sleet
Fell

The
Lodge

Howe Grain

Fusedale Beck

Hart
Hill

1

Garth
Heads

Winter
Crag

Steel
Knotts

Loadpot Hill

Cawdale
Edge

Nettleslack

Pikeawassa

18

42   A   43   B   44   C   45   D   46   E   47   F

Howtown

83

99

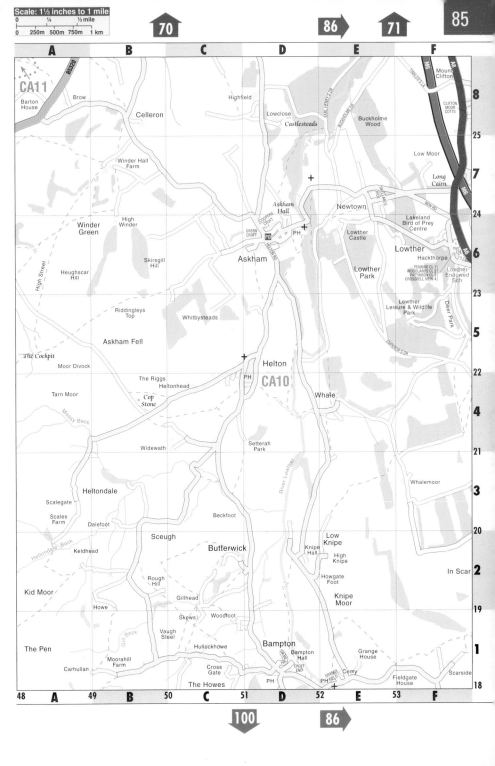

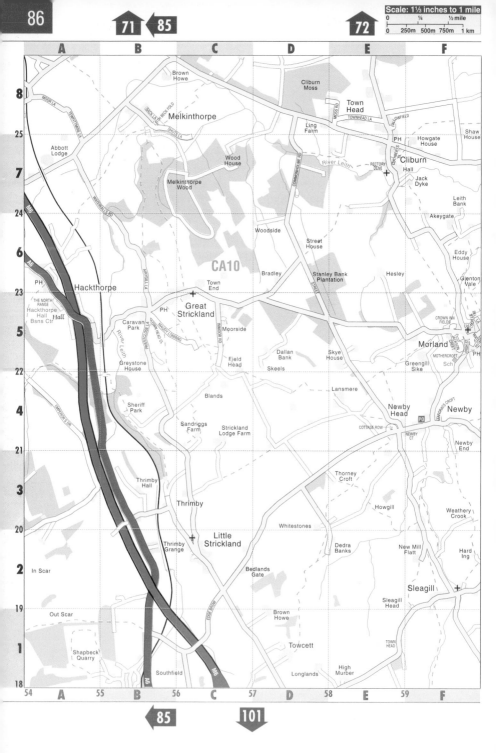

71 85
72

Scale: 1⅓ inches to 1 mile

0   ¼   ½ mile
0   250m   500m   750m   1 km

Brown Howe
Cliburn Moss
Town Head
TOWNHEAD LA
Shaw House

Melkinthorpe
Ling Farm
PH
Howgate House
Cliburn
Hall
Jack Dyke

MOOR LA
TWITTERING LA
BACK LA
BECK FOLD
SHUTE LA
MOSS RD
CHOWFIELD
CHARITY'S

Abbott Lodge

Wood House
RECTORY DENE

River Leith

Leith Bank

Melkinthorpe Wood
Akeygate

M6
WATERFALL'S RD
COMMONMIRE RD

Woodside
Street House
Eddy House

CA10
Bradley
Stanley Bank Plantation
Hesley
Glenton Vale

Hackthorpe
PH
Town End
Great Strickland
PH
STREET

THE NORTH RANGE
Hackthorpe Hall Bsns Ctr   Hall
Caravan Park
Moorside
CROWN INN FIELDS

ASKRIGG LA
TOWN HEAD CL
BOLTON'S LONNING
Morland

Greystone House
River Leith
Field Head
Dallan Bank
Skye House
MOTHERCROFT
Sch
PH

Greengill Sike

Skeels

Lansmere

Sheriff Park
Blands

EAMONT DR
Sandriggs Farm
Strickland Lodge Farm
Newby Head
PO
Newby

COTTAGE ROW
NEWBY CT
Newby End

MARGARET'S CROFT

Thrimby Hall
Thorney Croft

Thrimby
Howgill
Weathery Crook

Whitestones

In Scar
Thrimby Grange
Little Strickland
Dedra Banks
New Mill Flatt
Hard Ing

Bedlands Gate
Sleagill

Sleagill Head
Out Scar
Brown Howe

ESKE DENN

Shapbeck Quarry
Towcett
TOWN HEAD

A6
M6
Southfield
Longlands
High Murber

54   55   56   57   58   59

85
101

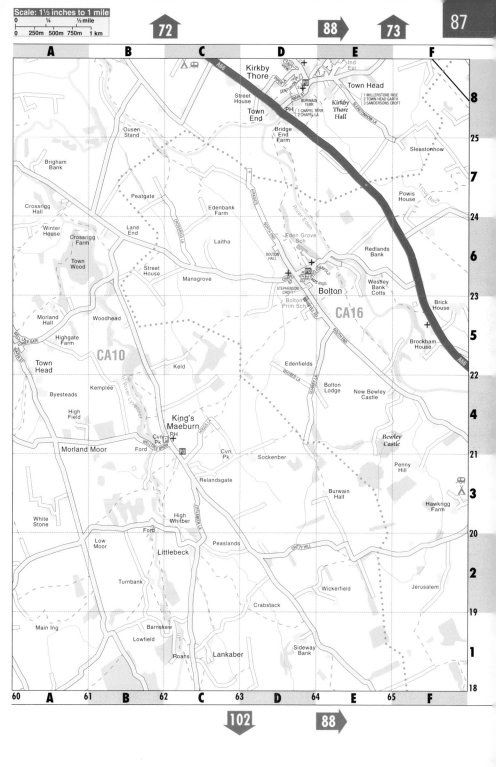

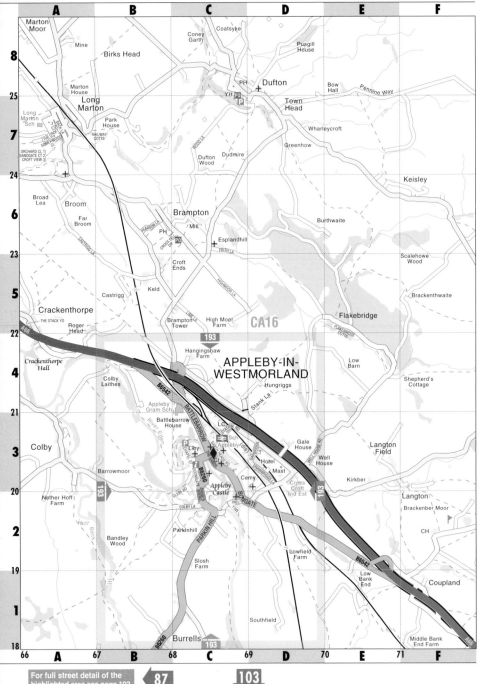

Scale: 1⅓ inches to 1 mile

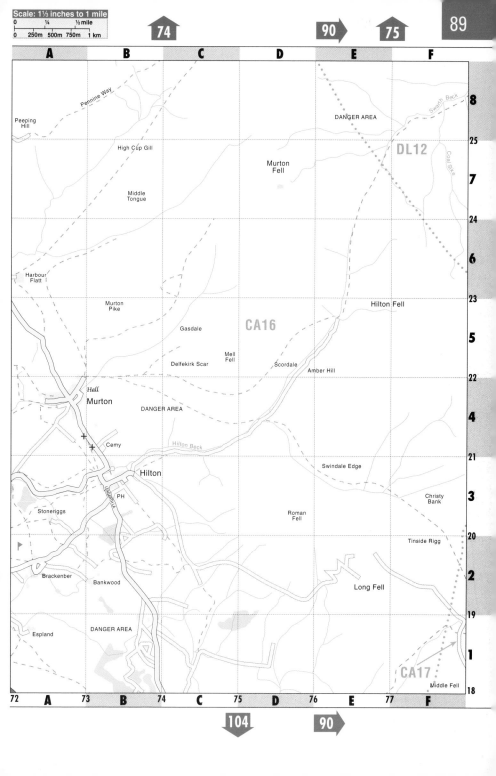

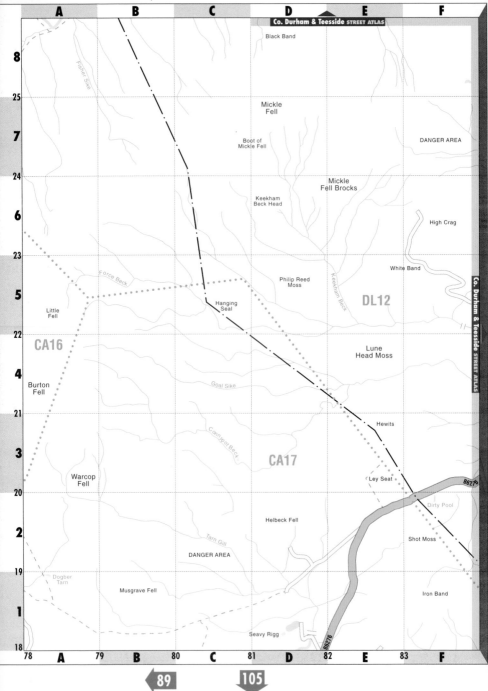

Black Band

Mickle Fell

Boot of Mickle Fell

DANGER AREA

Mickle Fell Brocks

Keekham Beck Head

High Crag

Fisher Sike

Philip Reed Moss

White Band

Force Beck

Keekham Beck

DL12

Hanging Seal

Little Fell

Lune Head Moss

CA16

Burton Fell

Goal Sike

Hewits

Conypor Beck

CA17

Ley Seat

B6276

Warcop Fell

Dirty Pool

Helbeck Fell

Shot Moss

Tarn Gill

DANGER AREA

Dogber Tarn

Musgrave Fell

Iron Band

Seavy Rigg

B6276

Co. Durham & Teesside STREET ATLAS

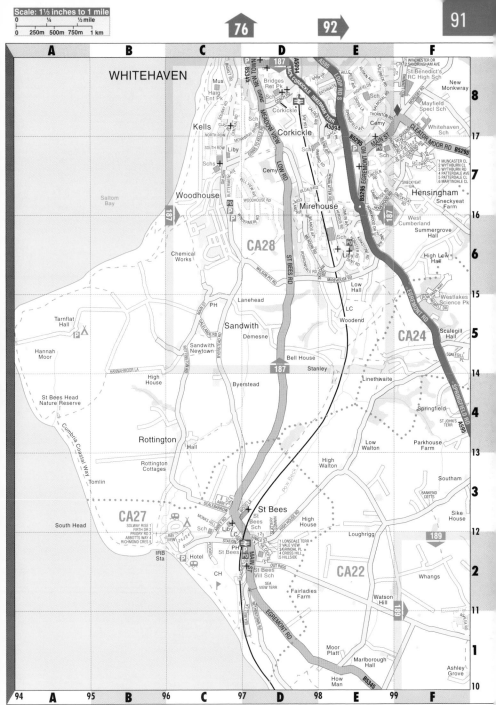

WHITEHAVEN

Kells

Woodhouse

Corkickle

Mirehouse

Hensingham

West Cumberland

Summergrove Hall

High Low Hall

Westlakes Science Pk

Scalegill Hall

CA28

CA24

Chemical Works

Lanehead

Sandwith

Demesne

Woodend

Low Hall

Stanley

Linethwaite

Springfield

Tarnflat Hall

Sandwith Newtown

High House

Byerstead

Bell House

Hannah Moor

Saltom Bay

St Bees Head Nature Reserve

Cumbria Coastal Way

Rottington

Rottington Cottages

Hall

Tomlin

High Walton

Low Walton

Parkhouse Farm

Southam

Sike House

CA27

South Head

St Bees

St Bees Sch

High House

Loughrigg

CA22

Whangs

Moor Platt

Marlborough Hall

How Man

Ashley Grove

Watson Hill

Fairladies Farm

IRB Sta

St Bees Vill Sch

1 LONSDALE TERR
2 VALE VIEW
3 GRINDAL PL
4 CROSS HILL
5 HILLSIDE

1 MUNCASTER CL
2 WYTHBURN CL
3 WYTHBURN RD
4 PATTERDALE AVE
5 PATTERDALE CL
6 MARTINGALE CL

For full street detail of the highlighted area see pages 187 and 189.

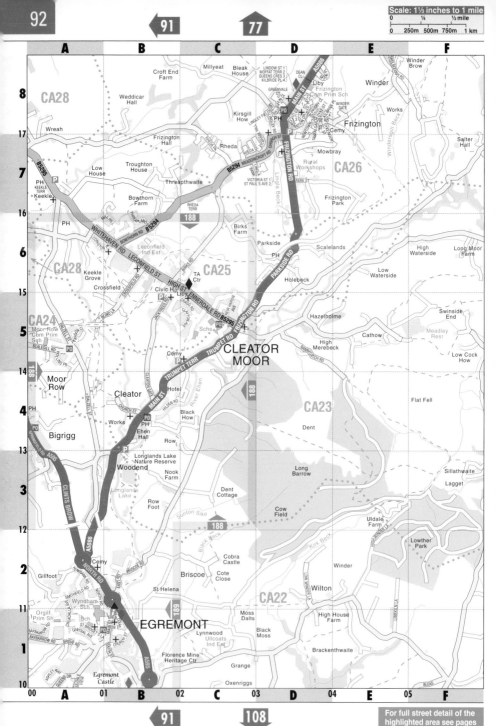

91
77

Scale: 1⅓ inches to 1 mile

0   ¼   ½ mile
0   250m   500m   750m   1 km

A   **B**   **C**   **D**   **E**   **F**

8

CA28

Croft End Farm
Millyeat
Bleak House

LINDOW ST 1
MOFFAT TERR 2
QUEENS CRES 3
KILBRIDE PL 4

Libby
Frizington Com Prim Sch

Winder

Winder Brow

Weddicar Hall

GREENVALE
PH

Works

17

Wreah

Kirsgill How

Frizington Hall

Rheda

Cemy

Frizington

Salter Hall

7

B5295

Low House

Troughton House

Threapthwaite

B5294 MEADOWCROFT RD

Mowbray

Rural Workshops

CA26

PH
KEEKLE TERR
Keekle
P

Frizington Park

PARK ST

Bowthorn Farm

VICTORIA ST 1
ST PAUL'S AVE 2

FRIZINGTON RD

Lingla Beck

16

PH

WHITEHAVEN RD

BOWTHORN RD

MILL HILL

THRELKELD

RHEDA TERR

188

Birks Farm

Parkside

PH

6

CA28

Keekle Grove

LECONFIELD ST

Leconfield Ind Est

CONISTON

CROSSFIELD RD

HIGH ST

CA25

PARKSIDE RD

Scalelands

Holebeck

High Waterside

Long Moor Farm

15

Crossfield

TA Ctr
Civic Hall Libby

ENNERDALE RD

B5295

Low Waterside

Hazelholme

Swinside End

5

CA24

Moor Row Com Prim Sch

SCALEGILL RD

LINS PK

DALZELL ST

BOUND LA

JACKTREES RD

Schs
P

TRUMPET RD

FRIZINGTON RD

High Merebeck

Cathow

Meadley Resr

Low Cock How

14

188

Moor Row

Cemy
P

TRUMPET TERR

CLEATOR MOOR

River Ehen

188

CA23

Flat Fell

4

PH
P

Cleator

DAZELL ST

CHURCH ST

Works

MAIN ST

CLEATOR GATE RD

HILDEN RD

Hotel

Black How

188

Dent

13

CLINTS BROW

A5086

P
Ehen Hall
PH

Row

Longlands Lake Nature Reserve

3

Woodend

Longlands Lake

Nook Farm

Dent Cottage

Long Barrow

Sillathwaite

Lagget

12

A5086

Row Foot

Sunton Sike

188

Black Beck

Cow Field

Uldale Farm

Lowther Park

2

Gillfoot

NORTH RD

Cemy
P

EAST RD

HOWBANK RD

BRISCOE RD

Briscoe

Cobra Castle

Cote Close

St Helena

Winder

Wilton

Kirk Beck

LOW RD

LIMEKILN LA

11

Orgill Prim Sch

BAYBARROW RD

GROVE RD

Wyndham Sch

ST BRIDGET'S

189

CA22

Moss Dalts

Black Moss

High House Farm

1

ASPLEY WAY

ADAMS DR

CENTRAL AVE

CHURCH ST

EGREMONT

A595

Lynnwood Ullcoats Ind Est

Florence Mine Heritage Ctr

Grange

Brackenthwaite

BLEAS

10

Egremont Castle

Oxenriggs

00   **A**   **01**   **B**   **02**   **C**   **03**   **D**   **04**   **E**   **05**   **F**

91
108

For full street detail of the highlighted area see pages 188 and 189.

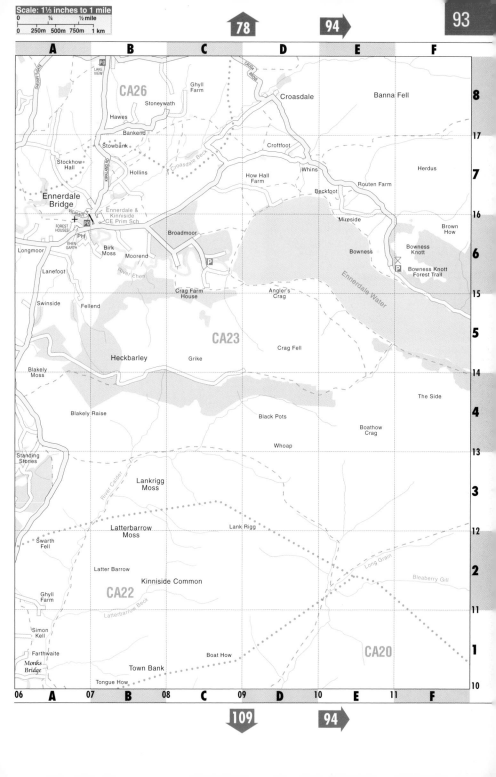

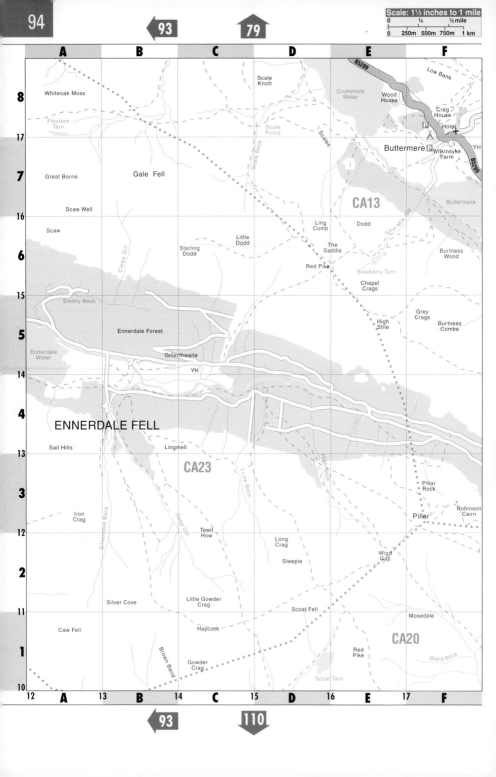

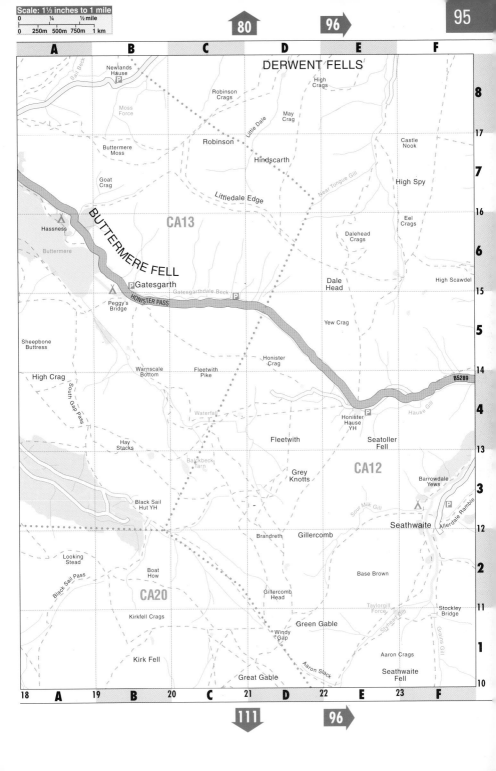

DERWENT FELLS

Newlands
Hause

Robinson
Crags

High
Crags

Moss
Force

May
Crag

Little Dale

Buttermere
Moss

Robinson

Hindscarth

Castle
Nook

Goat
Crag

High Spy

Near Tongue Gill

Littledale Edge

CA13

Hassness

BUTTERMERE FELL

Dalehead
Crags

Eel
Crags

Buttermere

High Scawdel

Gatesgarth

Gatesgarthdale Beck

Dale
Head

Peggy's
Bridge

HONISTER PASS

Yew Crag

Sheepbone
Buttress

Honister
Crag

Warnscale
Bottom

Fleetwith
Pike

Honister
Hause YH

Hause Gill

B5289

High Crag

South Gap Pass

Waterfall

Seatoller
Fell

Fleetwith

Hay
Stacks

Blackbeck
Tarn

Grey
Knotts

CA12

Barrowdale
Yews

Black Sail
Hut YH

Brandreth

Gillercomb

Sour Milk Gill

Seathwaite

Allerdale Ramble

Looking
Stead

Boat
How

CA20

Gillercomb
Head

Base Brown

Black Sail Pass

Taylorgill
Force

Styhead Gill

Stockley
Bridge

Kirkfell Crags

Green Gable

Grains Gill

Kirk Fell

Windy
Gap

Aaron Crags

Aaron Slack

Seathwaite
Fell

Great Gable

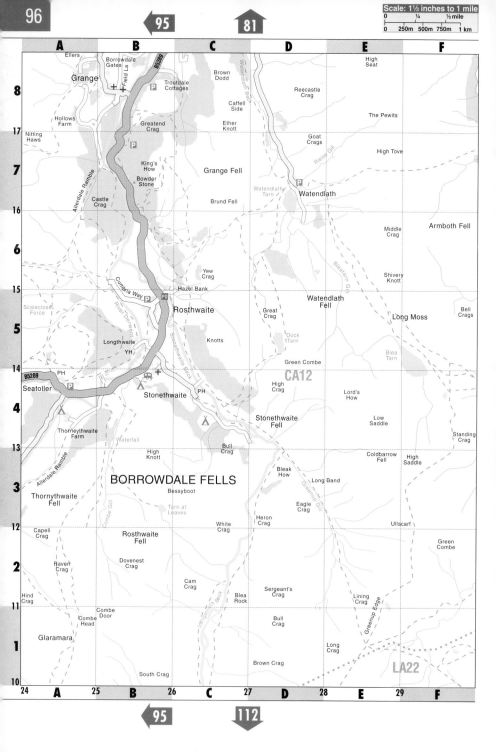

Scale: 1⅓ inches to 1 mile

0   ¼   ½ mile
0   250m 500m 750m 1 km

A **B** **C** **D** **E** **F**

Ellers

Borrowdale Gates

High Seat

Grange

Brown Dodd

Reecastle Crag

Troutdale Cottages

Caffell Side

8

Hollows Farm

Greatend Crag

Ether Knott

The Pewits

17

Nitting Haws

Goat Crags

High Tove

King's How

Grange Fell

Raise Gill

7

Bowder Stone

Watendlath Tarn

Watendlath

Castle Crag

Brund Fell

16

Middle Crag

Armboth Fell

6

Yew Crag

Bleaberry Gill

Shivery Knott

Cumbria Way

Hazel Bank

15

Scaleclose Force

River Derwent

Rosthwaite

Great Crag

Watendlath Fell

Long Moss

Bell Crags

5

Longthwaite YH

Knotts

Dock Tarn

Green Combe

Blea Tarn

14

B5289 PH

Stonethwaite Beck

High Crag

CA12

Lord's How

Low Saddle

Seatoller

Stonethwaite

PH

Stonethwaite Fell

4

Standing Crag

Thorneythwaite Farm

Waterfall

Bull Crag

Coldbarrow Fell

High Saddle

13

High Knott

Bleak How

Long Band

BORROWDALE FELLS

Bessyboot

Greenup Gill

Eagle Crag

3

Thornythwaite Fell

Tarn at Leaves

Ullscarf

12

Capell Crag

Rosthwaite Fell

White Crag

Heron Crag

Green Combe

2

Raven Crag

Dovenest Crag

Cam Crag

Blea Rock

Sergeant's Crag

Lining Crag

Hind Crag

Combe Door

Bull Crag

Greenup Edge

11

Combe Head

Combe Gill

Langstrath Beck

1

Glaramara

Long Crag

LA22

South Crag

Brown Crag

10

24 **A** 25 **B** 26 **C** 27 **D** 28 **E** 29 **F**

95
81
95
112

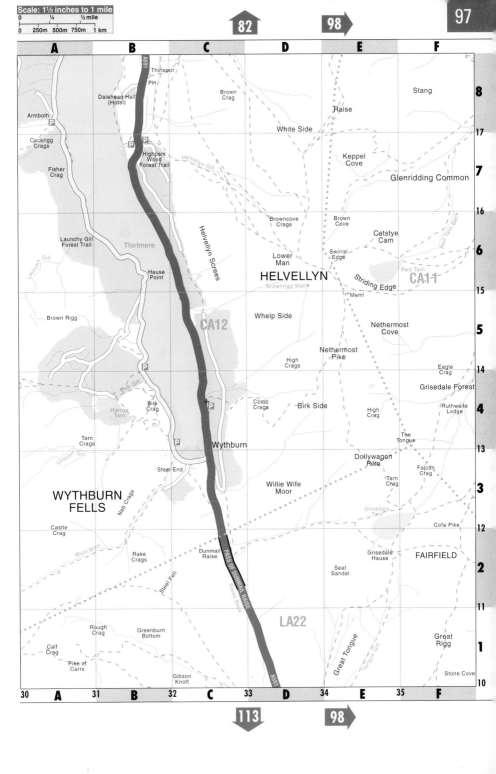

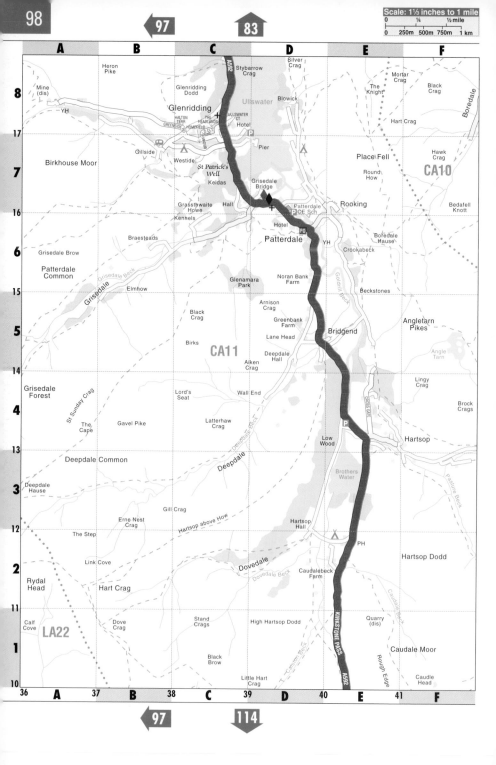

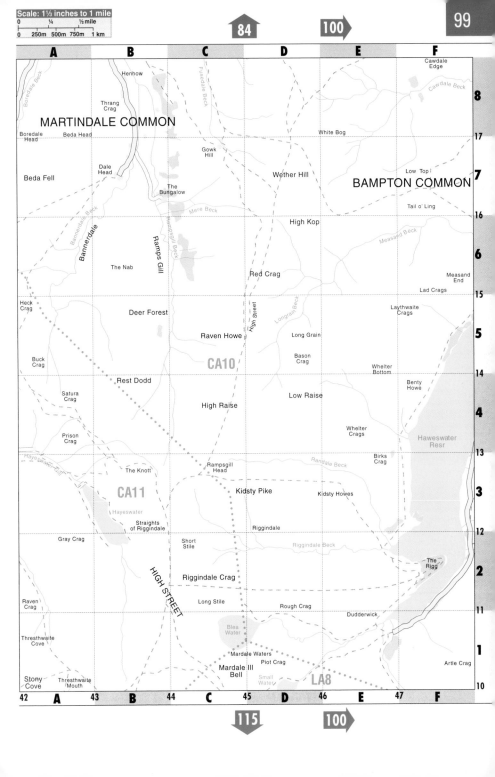

Scale: 1⅓ inches to 1 mile

0 — ¼ — ½ mile

0 — 250m — 500m — 750m — 1 km

A   B   C   D   E   F

84   100

Cawdale Edge

Cawdale Beck

8

Henhow

Thrang Crag

MARTINDALE COMMON

White Bog

Boredale Head

Beda Head   Beda Head

17

Gowk Hill

Wether Hill

Low Top

BAMPTON COMMON

7

Beda Fell

Dale Head

The Bungalow

Tail o' Ling

Mere Beck

Bannerdale Beck

Bannerdale

Ramps Gill

Rampsgill Beck

High Kop

16

Measand Beck

6

The Nab

Red Crag

Measand End

Lad Crags

15

Heck Crag

Deer Forest

High Street

Long Grain

Laythwaite Crags

5

Raven Howe

Longrain Beck

Bason Crag

CA10

Whelter Bottom

Benty Howe

14

Buck Crag

Rest Dodd

High Raise

Low Raise

Satura Crag

Whelter Crags

Haweswater Resr

4

Prison Crag

Hayeswater Gill

The Knott

Rampsgill Head

Randale Beck

Birks Crag

13

CA11

Kidsty Pike

Kidsty Howes

3

Hayeswater

Straights of Riggindale

Riggindale

The Rigg

12

Gray Crag

Short Stile

Riggindale Beck

HIGH STREET

Riggindale Crag

2

Long Stile

Rough Crag

Dudderwick

Raven Crag

11

Thresthwaite Cove

Blea Water

Artle Crag

1

Stony Cove

Thresthwaite Mouth

Mardale Waters

Piot Crag

Mardale Ill Bell

Small Water

LA8

10

42   A   43   B   44   C   45   D   46   E   47   F

115   100

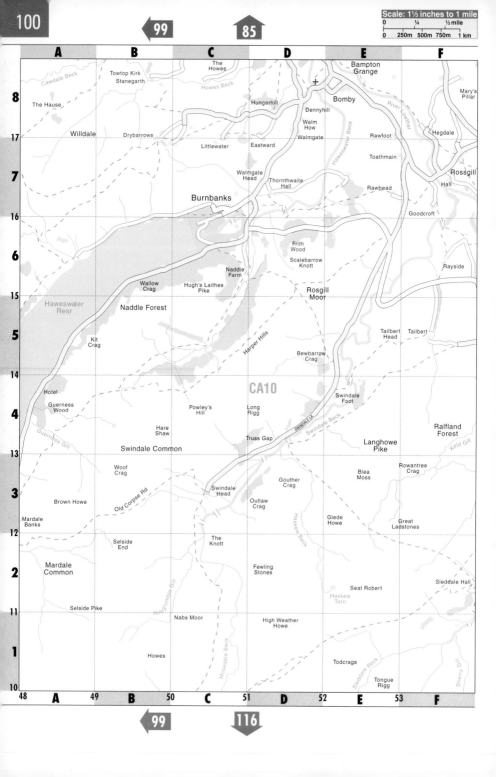

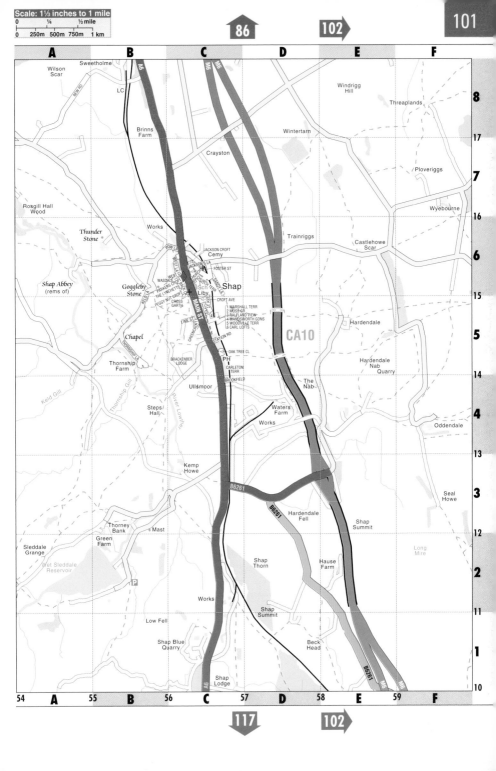

Wilson Scar

Sweetholme

LC

Brinns Farm

Crayston

Windrigg Hill

Threaplands

Wintertarn

Ploveriggs

Rosgill Hall Wood

Wyebourne

Thunder Stone

Works

Castlehowe Scar

Trainriggs

Shap Abbey (rems of)

Goggleby Stone

JACKSON CROFT

Cemy

FOSTER ST

Shap

CA10

Hardendale

POW L

JACKSON LA

WEST LA

WEST ST

WASDALE GR

PARKERS GR

THE LYNCHETTS

PEGGY NUT CROFT

CROSS GARTH

CROFT AVE

1 MARSHALL TERR
2 MOSS GR
3 RALFLAND VIEW
4 WANDSWORTH GDNS
5 WOODVILLE TERR
6 CARL LOFTS

Hardendale Nab Quarry

Chapel

LIME ST

GREENCROFT

STATION RD

Lily

MAIN ST

Thornship Farm

BRACKENBER LODGE

OAK TREE CL

PH

CARLETON TERR

BROOKFIELD

The Nab

Keld Gill

Thornship Gill

Ullsmoor

Steps Hall

River Lowther

Waters Farm

Works

Oddendale

Kemp Howe

B6261

Seal Howe

Thorney Bank

Green Farm

Mast

B6261

Hardendale Fell

Shap Summit

Sleddale Grange

Wet Sleddale Reservoir

P

Shap Thorn

Hause Farm

Long Mire

Works

Shap Summit

Low Fell

Shap Blue Quarry

Beck Head

Shap Lodge

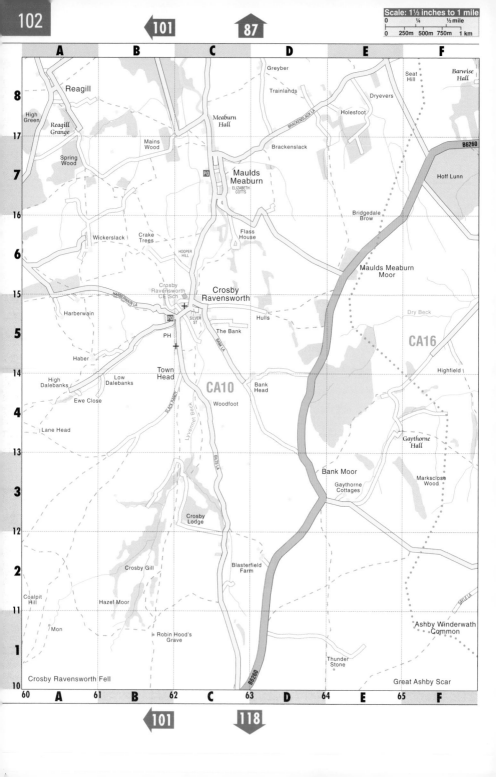

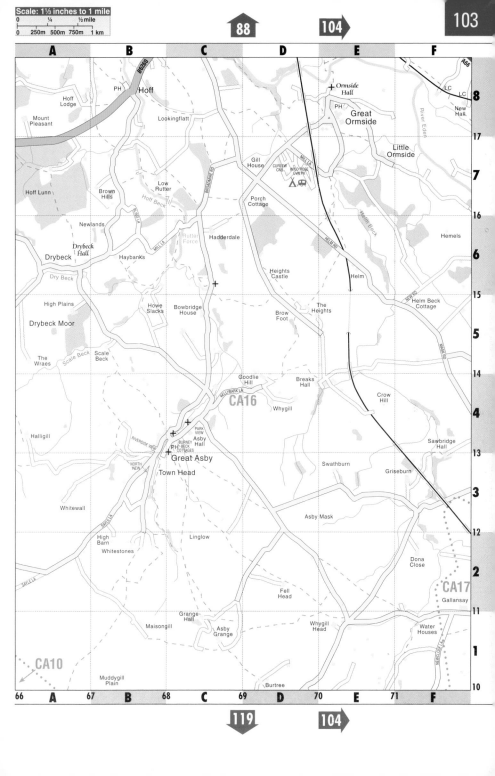

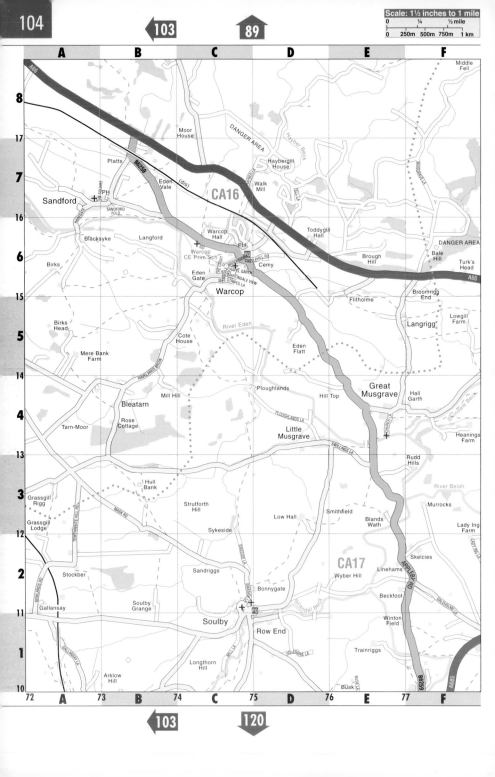

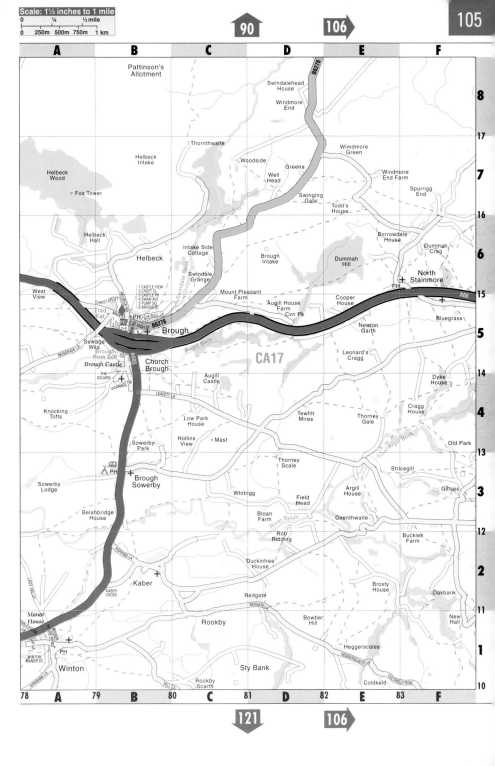

Pattinson's Allotment

Swindalehead House

Windmore End

B6276

Thornthwaite

Woodside

Well Head

Greena

Wimdmore Green

Windmore End Farm

Spurrigg End

Helbeck Wood

Helbeck Intake

Fox Tower

Swinging Gate

Todd's House

Borrowdale House

Dummah Crag

Helbeck Hall

Intake Side Cottage

Brough Intake

Dummah Hill

North Stainmore
PH

Helbeck

Swindale Grange

Swindale Beck

Mount Pleasant Farm

Augill House Farm
Cvn Pk

Cooper House

Newton Garth

A66

Bluegrass

West View

CHRIST CROFT
HELBECK RD
1 CASTLE VIEW
2 CROFT CL
3 CASTLE PK
4 SWAN AVE
5 PUMP SQ
6 BRIDGE ST
Trad Est
MAIN ST
PO
PH
HIGH ST
CH BULL LA
B6276
Brough

Augill Beck

CA17

Leonard's Cragg

Sewage Wks

Brough Prim Sch

MUSGRAVE LA

Church Brough

Brough Castle

THE SQUARE

VICARAGE DR

Augill Castle

Dyke House

Knocking Tofts

LEACETT LA

Low Park House

Tewfitt Mires

Thorney Gale

Cragg House

Hollins View

Mast

Thorney Scale

Old Park

Sowerby Park

Stricegill

PH

Brough Sowerby

Whitrigg

Field Head

Argill House

Gillses

Sowerby Lodge

Argill Beck

Belahbridge House

Bloan Farm

River Belah

Oxenthwaite

Buckles Farm

Rob Ridding

POPPING LA

Duckintree House

Kaber

KABER CROSS

Redgate

Broxty House

Oakbank

Redgate
REDGATE LA

Bowber Hill

New Hall

Manor House

Rookby

Heggerscales

PH

Winton
WINTON MANOR CT
KIRKBANK LA

Sty Bank

Rookby Scarth

HEGGERSCALES LA

COLDKELD RIGG

Coldkeld

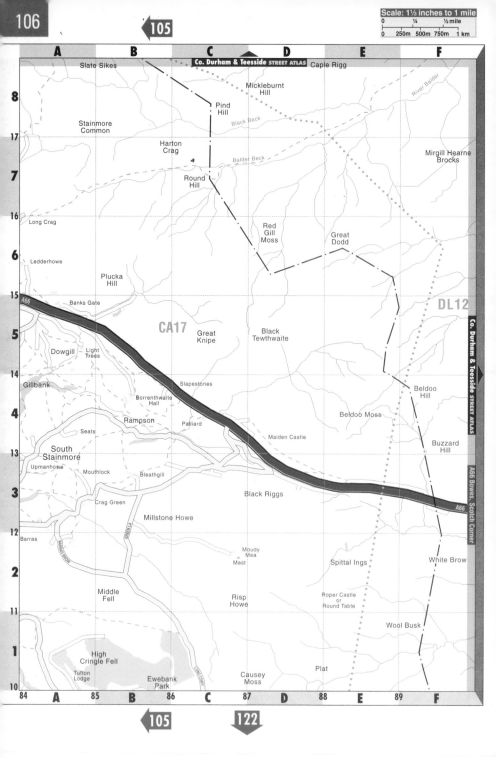

Scale: 1⅓ inches to 1 mile

0   ¼   ½ mile
0 250m 500m 750m 1 km

A   B   C   D   E   F

Co. Durham & Teesside STREET ATLAS

Slate Sikes

Caple Rigg

Mickleburnt
Hill

River Balder

8

Pind
Hill

Stainmore
Common

Black Beck

17

Harton
Crag

Mirgill Hearne
Brocks

Balder Beck

7

Round
Hill

16

Long Crag

Red
Gill
Moss

Great
Dodd

6

Ledderhowe

Plucka
Hill

15

A66

Banks Gate

DL12

Great
Knipe

Black
Tewthwaite

CA17

5

Dowgill

Light
Trees

14

Beldoo
Hill

Gillbank

Slapestones

Borrenthwaite
Hall

4

Rampson

Palliard

Beldoo Moss

Seats

Maiden Castle

South
Stainmore

Mouthlock

Bleathgill

Buzzard
Hill

Upmanhowe

13

Black Riggs

3

Crag Green

Millstone Howe

Barras

12

Moudy
Mea

Spittal Ings

White Brow

Mast

2

Middle
Fell

Risp
Howe

Roper Castle
or
Round Table

Wool Busk

11

High
Cringle Fell

1

Tufton
Lodge

Ewebank
Park

Causey
Moss

Plat

10

84   A   85   B   86   C   87   D   88   E   89   F

Co. Durham & Teesside STREET ATLAS

A66 Bowes, Scotch Corner

Scale: 1⅓ inches to 1 mile

0   ¼   ½ mile
0   250m   500m   750m   1 km

For full street detail of the highlighted area see page 189.

91

108

Ghyll Farm

B5345

BLACK LING COTTS

QUEENS DR

Coneyside Farm

189

Coulderton

CA22

Snellings

Middletown

B5345

189

Nethertown

PH

P

Nethertown

CA21

Cumbria Coastal Way

For full street detail of the highlighted area see page 189.

Scale: 1⅓ inches to 1 mile
0   ¼   ½ mile
0   250m 500m 750m 1 km

How Hills
Great Wood
Tortolocate
Cold Fell
Pickett How
Catgill Hall
Carleton
Whitehow Head
Brayshaw
PH
Winscales
Haile Hall
Head of Haile
Thornhill
Sch
CA22
Haile
Rothersyke Farm
COP LA
B5345
B5345
Town End
Strudda Bank
Cemy
Yeortoh Hall Farm
Sheepfields
Beckcote Farm
River Ehen
YEORTON BROW A595
Broad Leys
Abbey Flats
Ehenside Farm
Beckermet
FLEMING DR
Blackbeck
Moor House Farm
Low Ehenside
Sch
PH
PO
Godderthwaite
CA21
BRAYSTONE RD
CALDER VIEW
KIRKBECK
Stephney
Calder Abbey
1 HOLYOAKE TERR
2 BROOKSIDE
3 RIFLE TERR
4 CROFT TERR
River Calder
Calder Bridge
ABBEY GARTH
PO
PH
LOW CROFT
Braystones
COTTAGE ROW
TARNSIDE CVN PK
BECK CL
Petersburgh
NORTH DR
Ponsonby
Braystones
Middlebank
Greenmoor Side
Pelham House
Church House Farm
Ponsonby Old Hall
LANTERN MOSS CVN PK
Sella Park House
BNFL Vst Ctr
Yottenfews
CA20
New Mill
Sally Hill
Starling Castle
Works
Lingbank
High Sellafield
Longlands
Calder Hall
Newton Manor
A595
PH
Sellafield
Calder
Fleming Hall
Works
Newmill Beck
Stone Circle
Seascale Hall
How Farm
Bleawath
TARN HOW LA
B5344
Brownbank
B5344
B5344

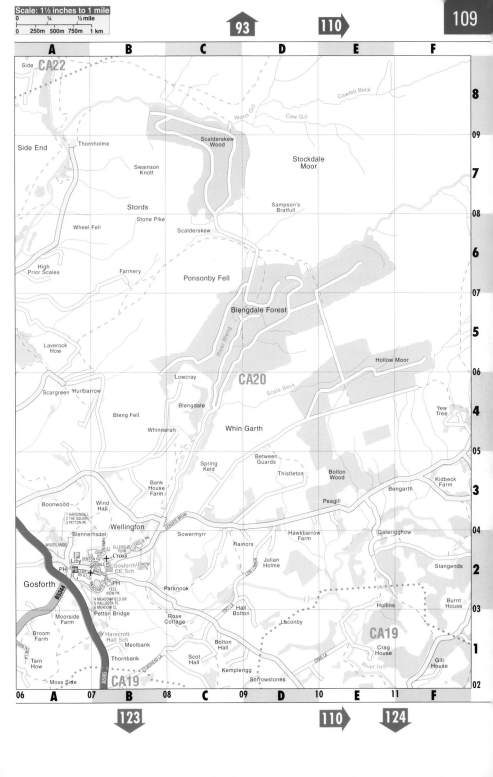

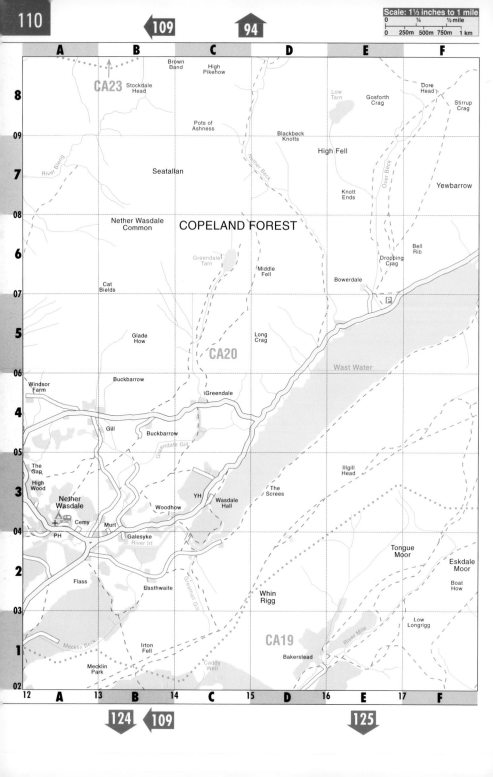

109
94

Scale: 1⅓ inches to 1 mile

0   ¼   ½ mile

0   250m   500m   750m   1 km

A   B   C   D   E   F

Brown
Band

High
Pikehow

CA23

Stockdale
Head

Low
Tarn

Gosforth
Crag

Dore
Head

8

Pots of
Ashness

Stirrup
Crag

09

Blackbeck
Knotts

High Fell

River Bleng

Seatallan

Nether Beck

Knott
Ends

Over Beck

Yewbarrow

7

08

Nether Wasdale
Common

COPELAND FOREST

6

Greendale
Tarn

Middle
Fell

Bell
Rib

Dropping
Crag

Bowerdale

Cat
Bields

07

P

5

Glade
How

Long
Crag

CA20

Wast Water

06

Windsor
Farm

Buckbarrow

Greendale

4

Gill

Buckbarrow

Greendale Gill

05

The
Gap

Illgill
Head

High
Wood

3

YH

The
Screes

Nether
Wasdale

Woodhow

Wasdale
Hall

Cemy

Murt

PH

Galesyke

River Irt

04

Tongue
Moor

Eskdale
Moor

2

Flass

Easthwaite

Greathall Gill

Whin
Rigg

Boat
How

03

Mecklin Beck

Irton
Fell

CA19

River Mite

Low
Longrigg

1

Bakerstead

Mecklin
Park

Caddy
Well

02

12   A   13   B   14   C   15   D   16   E   17   F

124
109
125

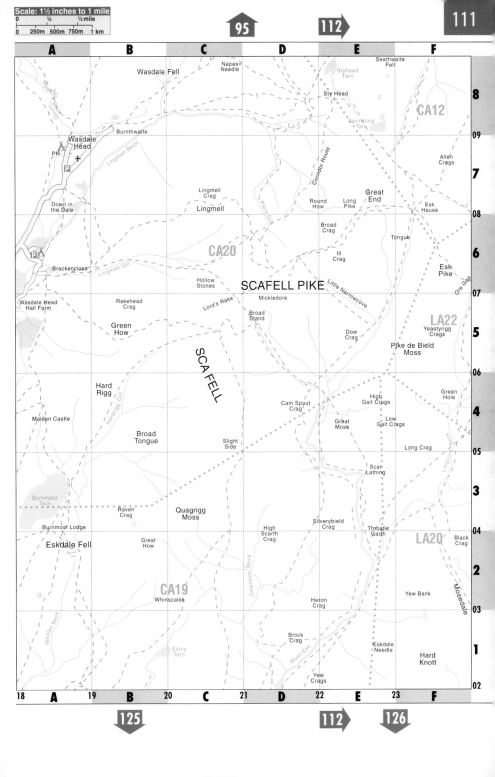

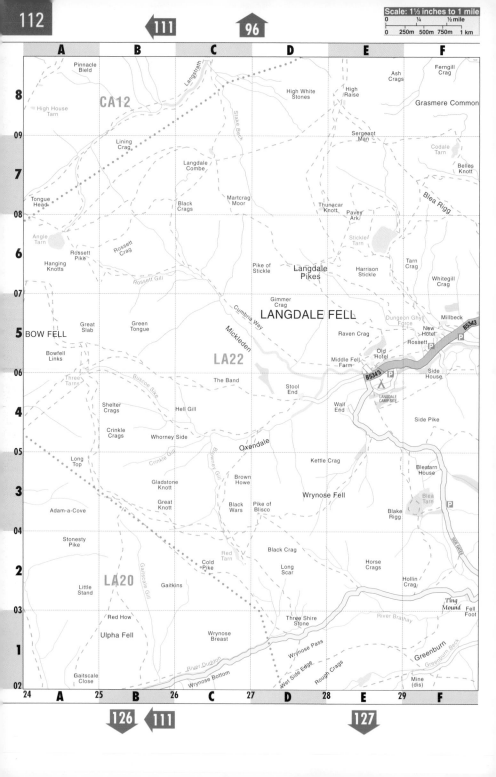

111
96

Scale: 1½ inches to 1 mile

0   ¼   ½ mile
0 250m 500m 750m 1 km

A   **B**   **C**   **D**   **E**   **F**

Pinnacle
Bield

CA12

High House
Tarn

Langstrath

Stake Beck

High White
Stones

High
Raise

Ash
Crags

Ferngill
Crag

Grasmere Common

8

09

Lining
Crag

Sergeant
Man

Codale
Tarn

Belles
Knott

7

Langdale
Combe

Martcrag
Moor

Thunacar
Knott

Pavey
Ark

Blea Rigg

Black
Crags

08

Tongue
Head

Angle
Tarn

Rossett
Pike

Rossett
Crag

Rossett Gill

Pike of
Stickle

Langdale
Pikes

Stickle
Tarn

Harrison
Stickle

Tarn
Crag

Whitegill
Crag

6

Hanging
Knotts

07

Gimmer
Crag

Dungeon Ghyll
Force

Millbeck

B5343

BOW FELL

Great
Slab

Green
Tongue

Cumbria Way

LANGDALE FELL

Raven Crag

New
Hotel

Rossett

P

P

5

Bowfell
Links

Mickleden

LA22

Middle Fell
Farm

Old
Hotel

Side
House

06

Three
Tarns

Buscoe Sike

The Band

Stool
End

B5343

P

4

Shelter
Crags

Hell Gill

Wall
End

LANGDALE
CAMP SITE

Side Pike

Crinkle
Crags

Whorney Side

Crinkle Gill

Oxendale

Kettle Crag

Bleatarn
House

05

Long
Top

Browney Gill

Brown
Howe

Blea
Tarn

P

3

Gladstone
Knott

Great
Knott

Black
Wars

Pike of
Blisco

Wrynose Fell

Blake
Rigg

Adam-a-Cove

04

Stonesty
Pike

Red
Tarn

Black Crag

Long
Scar

Horse
Crags

Hollin
Crag

Side End

Ting
Mound

Fell
Foot

2

LA20

Gaitscale Gill

Gaitkins

Cold
Pike

River Brathay

03

Little
Stand

Red How

Wrynose
Breast

Three Shire
Stone

Greenburn

Greenburn Beck

1

Ulpha Fell

River Duddon

Wrynose Pass

Wet Side Edge

Rough Crags

Mine
(dis)

02

Gaitscale
Close

Wrynose Bottom

24 **A** **25** **B** **26** **C** **27** **D** **28** **E** **29** **F**

126 111   127

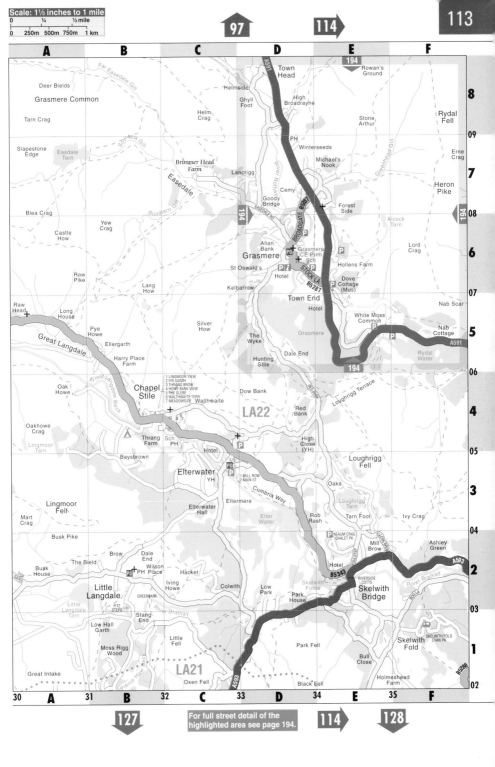

Scale: 1⅓ inches to 1 mile

0   ¼   ½ mile

0   250m   500m   750m   1 km

97
114

A   B   C   D   E   F

8

Deer Bields

Grasmere Common

Tarn Crag

Far Easedale Gill

Helmside

Ghyll Foot

Helm Crag

Helmside

Town Head

A591

High Broadrayhe

194

Rowan's Ground

Stone Arthur

Rydal Fell

09

Slapestone Edge

Easdale Tarn

Sour Milk Gill

Brimmer Head Farm

Lancrigg

PH

Winterseeds

Michael's Nook

Erne Crag

7

Easedale

Blindtarn Gill

River Rothay

Cemy

Goody Bridge

194

EASEDALE RD

B5287

BROADGATE

Forest Side

Greenhead Gill

Alcock Tarn

Heron Pike

194

08

Blea Crag

Yew Crag

Allan Bank

Grasmere

St Oswald's

PO

P

P i

Grasmere CE Prim Sch

Hotel

STOCK LA

B5287

Hollens Farm

P

Dove Cottage (Mus)

Lord Crag

6

Castle How

Raw Pike

Lang How

Kelbarrow

Town End

Hotel

White Moss Common

P

P

Nab Scar

Nab Cottage

07

Raw Head

Long House

Pye Howe

Ellergarth

Great Langdale

Silver How

The Wyke

Hunting Stile

Dale End

Grasmere

194

A591

Rydal Water

5

Harry Place Farm

Oak Howe

Great Langdale Beck

Chapel Stile

Thrang Farm

Dow Bank

Walthwaite

1 LINGMOOR VIEW
2 FIR GARPH
3 THRANG BROW
4 HOWE BANK VIEW
5 THE GLEBE
6 WALTHWAITE TERR
7 MEADOWSIDE

LA22

Red Bank

RED BANK

Loughrigg Terrace

06

Oakhowe Crag

Lingmoor Tarn

Sch PH

Hotel

Baysbrown

PO
P

Elterwater YH

1 MILL ROW
2 MAIN ST

Eltermere

High Close (YH)

Oaks

Loughrigg Fell

Loughrigg Tarn

Ivy Crag

4

05

Lingmoor Fell

Mart Crag

Busk Pike

Brow

Dale End

Wilson Place

Elterwater Hall

Cumbria Way

Elter Water

Rob Rash

Tarn Foot

3

Busk House

The Bield

PO PH

Hacket

Iving Howe

Colwith

Low Park

NEAUM CRAG CHALET PK

POLSTER

STANG ENO

Mill Brow

Ashley Green

A593

04

Little Langdale

GREENBANK

FITZ STEPS

Stang End

River Brathay

Little Fell

Park House

Skelwith Force

B5343

RIVERSIDE COTTS

Skelwith Bridge

River Brathay

B5414

2

Little Langdale Tarn

Low Hall Garth

Moss Rigg Wood

Pierce How Beck

LA21

Oxen Fell

A593

Park Fell

Black Fell

Bull Close

Skelwith Fold

SKELWITH FOLD CVAN PK

Holmeshead Farm

B5286

1

Great Intake

Great Intake

02

30   A   31   B   32   C   33   D   34   E   35   F

127

For full street detail of the highlighted area see page 194.

114
128

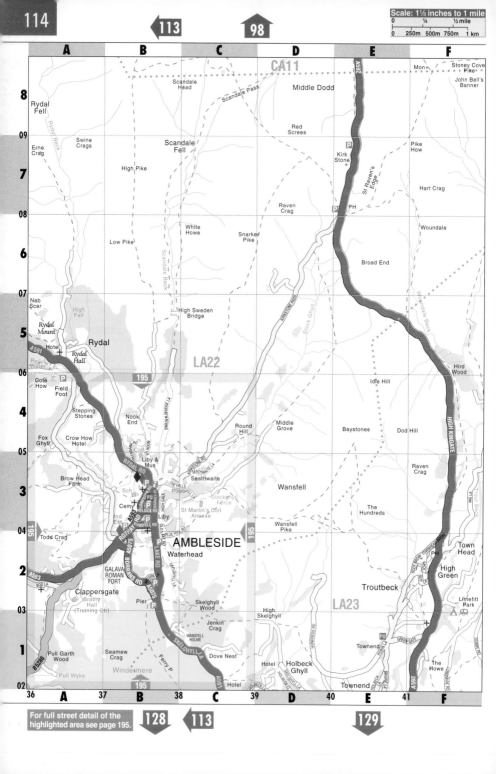

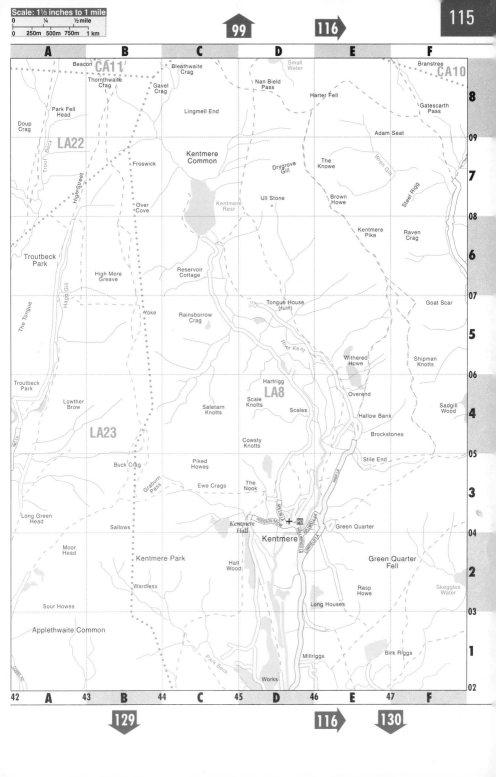

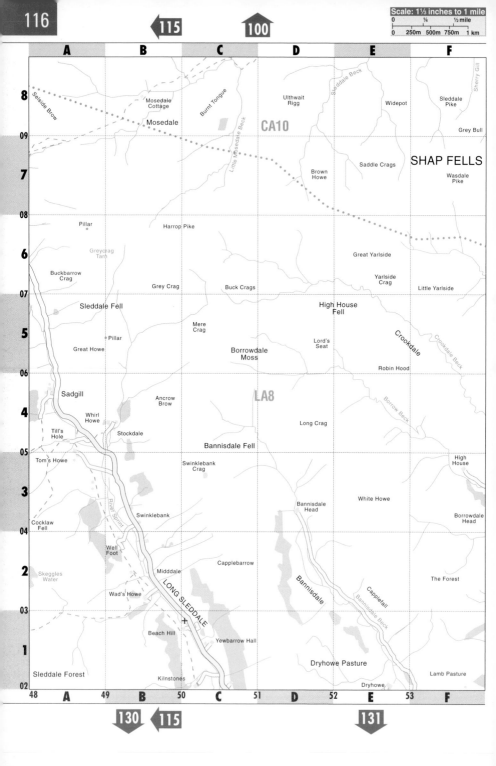

Scale: 1⅓ inches to 1 mile

0   ¼   ½ mile
0   250m 500m 750m 1 km

A   **B**   **C**   **D**   **E**   **F**

8

Selside Brow

Mosedale Cottage

Burnt Tongue

Ulthwait Rigg

Little Mosedale Beck

Sleddale Beck

Widepot

Sleddale Pike

Sherry Gill

09   Mosedale   **CA10**   Grey Bull

7

Brown Howe

Saddle Crags

SHAP FELLS

Wasdale Pike

08

Pillar

Harrop Pike

Great Yarlside

6

Greycrag Tarn

Buckbarrow Crag

Grey Crag

Buck Crags

Yarlside Crag

Little Yarlside

07

Sleddale Fell

High House Fell

5

Mere Crag

Lord's Seat

Crookdale

Crookdale Beck

Pillar

Great Howe

Borrowdale Moss

Robin Hood

06

Sadgill

Ancrow Brow

LA8

Borrow Beck

4

Whirl Howe

Stockdale

Long Crag

Till's Hole

05

Tom's Howe

Bannisdale Fell

High House

Swinklebank Crag

3

White Howe

Borrowdale Head

Cocklaw Fell

Swinklebank

Bannisdale Head

04

River Sprint

Well Foot

Bannisdale

Cipplefall

2

Skeggles Water

Midddale

Capplebarrow

The Forest

Wad's Howe

LONG SLEDDALE

Bannisdale Beck

03

Beach Hill

Yewbarrow Hall

1

Dryhowe Pasture

Lamb Pasture

Sleddale Forest

Kilnstones

Dryhowe

02

48   **A**   49   **B**   50   **C**   51   **D**   52   **E**   53   **F**

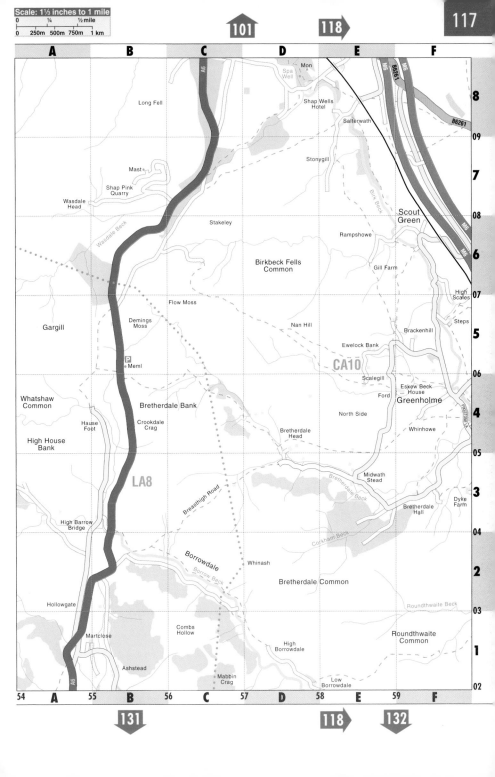

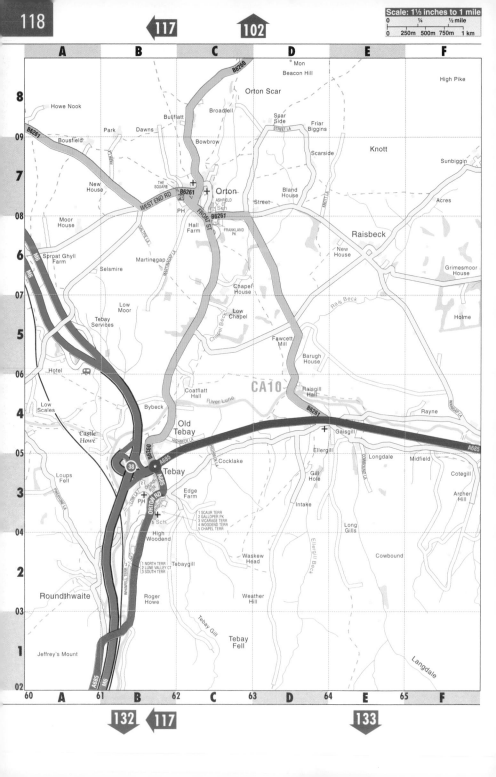

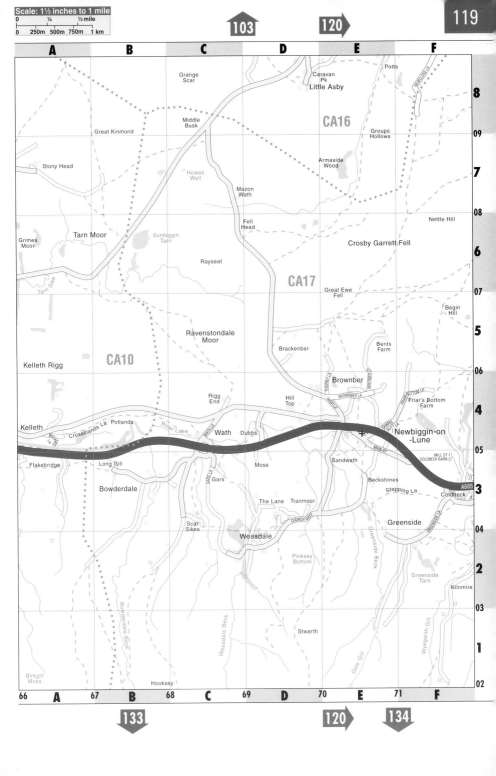

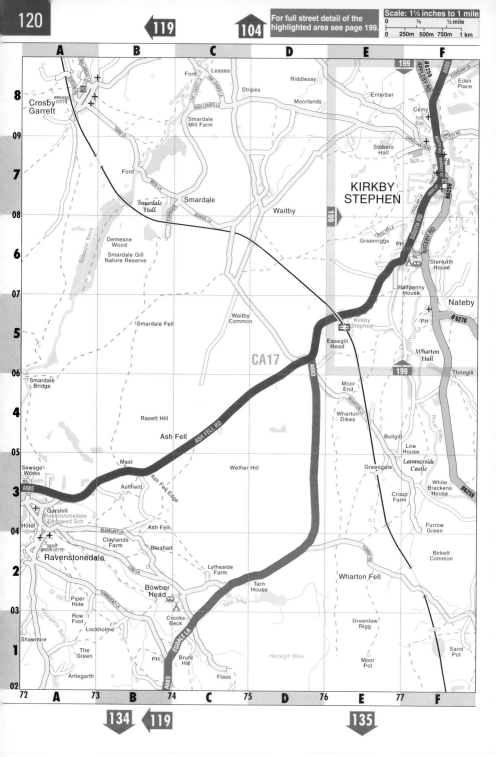

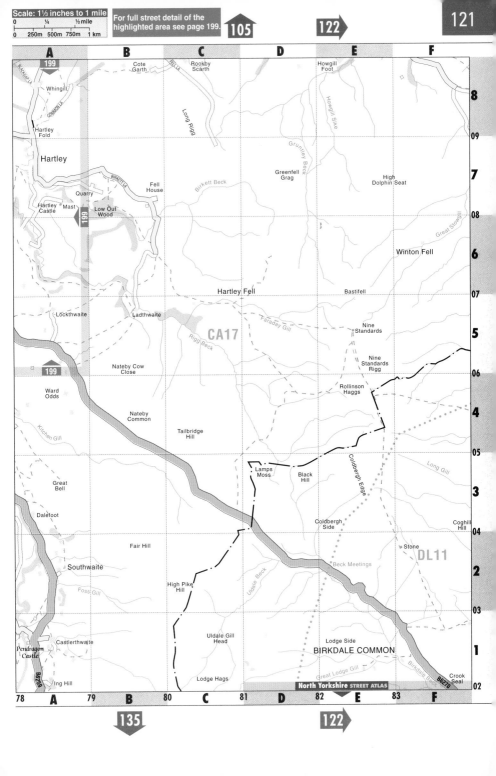

Scale: 1⅓ inches to 1 mile

0   ¼   ½ mile
0   250m 500m 750m 1 km

For full street detail of the highlighted area see page 199.

105

122

A   B   C   D   E   F

199

Cote Garth

Rookby Scarth

FELL

Long Rigg

Howgill Foot

Howgill Sike

Whingill

COMMON LA

BLACKBAR LA

8

09

Hartley Fold

Grunhey Beck

Greenfell Grag

High Dolphin Seat

7

Hartley

Birkett Beck

Fell House

08

Quarry

Hartley Castle   Mast

Low Out Wood

BIRKETT LA

199

Winton Fell

6

07

Lockthwaite

Ladlthwaite

Hartley Fell

Bastifell

Faraday Gill

Nine Standards

5

CA17

Rigg Beck

Nine Standards Rigg

Nateby Cow Close

199

06

Rollinson Haggs

4

Ward Odds

Nateby Common

Kitchen Gill

Tailbridge Hill

Coldbergh Edge

Long Gill

05

Lamps Moss

Black Hill

3

Great Bell

Coldbergh Side

Coghill Hill

Dalefoot

04

Fair Hill

Beck Meetings

Stone

DL11

2

Southwaite

Foss Gill

High Pike Hill

Uldale Beck

03

Uldale Gill Head

Lodge Side

BIRKDALE COMMON

Pendragon Castle

Castlerthwaite

1

B6259

Ing Hill

Lodge Hags

Great Lodge Gill

Birkdale Beck

B6270

Crook Seal

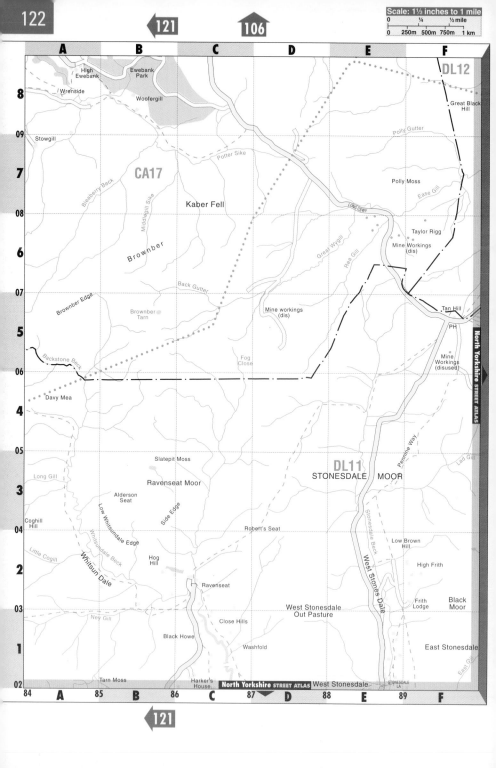

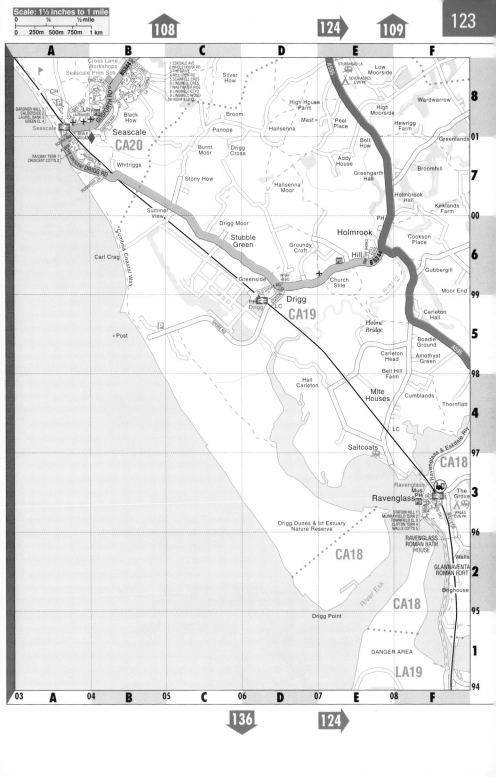

Scale: 1½ inches to 1 mile

0	¼	½ mile
0	250m 500m 750m	1 km

A **B** **C** **D** **E** **F**

CA20 ←

Santon

Gatesgarth
Seed Hill
PH

8

Irton
Pike

Ain
House

Miterdale
Forest

Great
Bank

Santon
Bridge

P

Greenlands

Hall
Santon

Mill Place

Cubben

01

Low
Holme

P

7

Irton Cross

Parkgate
Tarn

Irton Park

Plumgarth

St Bega's
CE Prim
Sch

Eskdale
Green
Forest Walks

Eskdale
Green

Gate House
Outward Bound
Ctr

Aikbank
Farm

Irton
Hall

Parkgate

Sleathwaite

KEYHOW

PO

Eskdale
Green

00

Mainsgate

Crag
Farm

Mill House
Farm

PH

Irton Road

LC

PH

6

Kitchen
Ground

Hollowstones

CA19

Forge
House

Sword
House

Wood End

Ravenglass & Eskdale Rly

Muncaster
Head

99

Moorgate

River Mite

Muncaster
Fell

Gasketh

5

Hooker
Crag

Ross's Camp

Linbeck

Miteside

High
Eskholme

Linbeck Gill

98

Chapel
Hill

River Esk

Muncaster

Muncaster
Water Mill

Mon

Cropple
How

Knott
End

4

Cragg
Farm

CA18

Low
Eskholme

Hinning
House

Branken
Wall

P

Raven Crag

97

Muncaster
Castle

Howbank

Birkby Fell

3

Cumbria Coastal Way

Ellerbeck

Black Beck

Newtown

Rougholme

Graymains

Barnécar

LA20 →

2

Nether
Stainton

Tower

The Knott

Hall
Waberthwaite

Dyke

95

Cross

Broad
Oak

Stainton

Stainton Beck

The Intake

Stainton Fell

1

Woodgate
Row

Woodside

Bengill

Samgarth Beck

LA19

NEWBIGGIN
COTTS

Glebe
House

Grange

94

Newbiggin

09 **A** **10** **B** **11** **C** **12** **D** **13** **E** **14** **F**

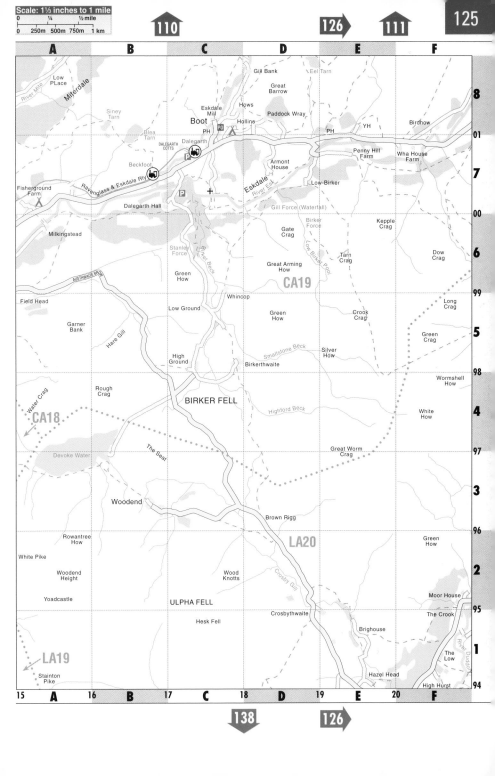

111 125

112

Scale: 1½ inches to 1 mile

0   ¼   ½ mile
0   250m   500m   750m   1 km

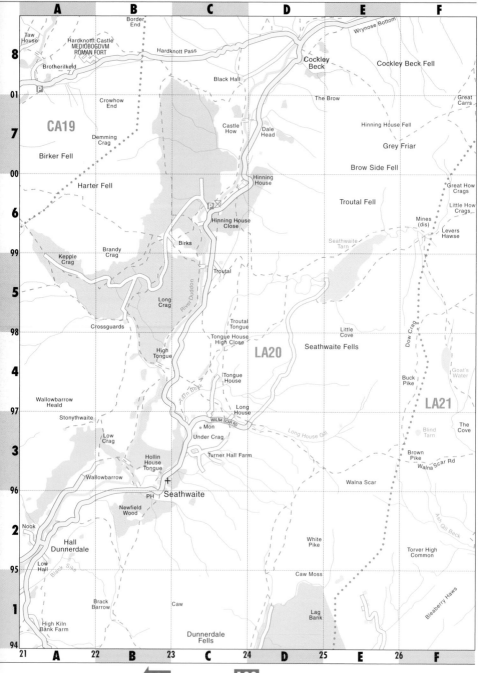

A | B | C | D | E | F

8

Taw House
Hardknott Castle
MEDIOBOGDVM
ROMAN FORT
Brotherilkeld
P
Border End
Hardknott Pass
Black Hall
Cockley Beck
Wrynose Bottom
Cockley Beck Fell

01

Crowhow End
The Brow
Great Carrs

CA19

7

Demming Crag
Castle How
Dale Head
Hinning House Fell
Grey Friar

Birker Fell

00

Harter Fell
Hinning House
Brow Side Fell
Great How Crags
Little How Crags

6

P
Hinning House Close
Troutal Fell
Mines (dis)
Levers Hawse

Kepple Crag
Brandy Crag
Birks
Seathwaite Tarn

99

5

Long Crag
Troutal
Dow Crag
Great How Crags

River Duddon

Crossguards

98

High Tongue
Troutal Tongue
Tongue House High Close
Little Cove
Seathwaite Fells
Goat's Water

4

LA20
Tongue House
LA21

Wallowbarrow Heald
Long House
Buck Pike

97

Stonythwaite
WALNA SCAR RD
Long House Gill
Blind Tarn
The Cove

Low Crag
Mon
Under Crag
Brown Pike
Walna Scar Rd

3

Hollin House Tongue
Turner Hall Farm
Walna Scar
Torver High Common

Wallowbarrow
+
PH   Seathwaite

96

Newfield Wood

Nook

2

Hall Dunnerdale
White Pike

Low Hall
Caw Moss
Ash Gill Beck

95

Black Sike

1

High Kiln Bank Farm
Brack Barrow
Caw
Lag Bank
Bleaberry Haws

94

Dunnerdale Fells

21 | A | 22 | B | 23 | C | 24 | D | 25 | E | 26 | F

125

139

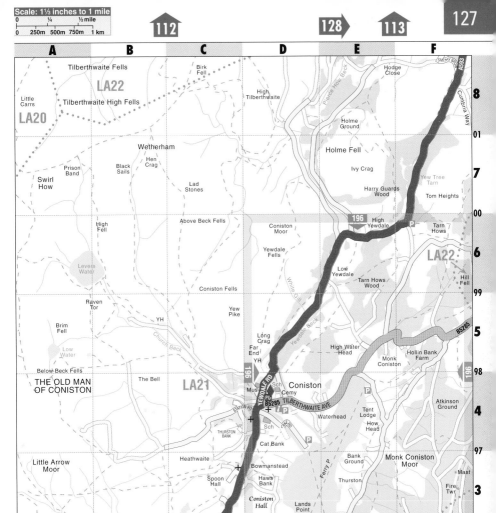

Scale: 1⅓ inches to 1 mile

0	¼	½ mile
0	250m	500m	750m	1 km

112

128

113

127

Tilberthwaite Fells

LA22

Birk Fell

High Tilberthwaite

Piece How Beck

Hodge Close

Cumbria Way

Tilberthwaite High Fells

Little Carrs

LA20

8

Holme Ground

01

Wetherham

Hen Crag

Holme Fell

Yew Tree Tarn

Tom Heights

7

Black Sails

Holme Ground

Ivy Crag

Swirl How

Prison Band

Lad Stones

Harry Guards Wood

High Fell

Above Beck Fells

Coniston Moor

196

High Yewdale

00

Tarn Hows

LA22

6

Leves Water

Yewdale Fells

Low Yewdale

Tarn Hows Wood

Hill Fell

Coniston Fells

White Gill

99

Raven Tor

Yew Pike

High Water Head

Monk Coniston

Hollin Bank Farm

B5285

5

Brim Fell

YH

Church Beck

Long Crag

Far End YH

Yewdale Beck

High Water Head

196

98

Low Water

The Bell

LA21

196

YEWDALE RD

Mus

Coniston

Atkinson Ground

Below Beck Fells

THE OLD MAN OF CONISTON

Sch Cemy PO

Tilberthwaite Ave

Tent Lodge

How Head

4

STATION RD

B5285

Waterhead

Little Arrow Moor

THURSTON BANK

Heathwaite

Sch

Cat Bank

Bowmanstead

Haws Bank

Ferry P

Bank Ground

Thurston

Monk Coniston Moor

Mast

97

Spoon Hall

Fire Twr

3

Coniston Hall

Lands Point

196

96

Tranearth

Bleathwaite Pasture

High Ground

Park Coppice

Brantwood

LA22

2

Little Arrow

Cumbria Way

Lawson Park

95

Hare Crags

Scarr Head

Hoathwaite Farm

Torver Common Wood

Park Plantation

Bull Haw

Brackenbarrow Farm

Coniston Water

1

Under Crag

Torver

GREEN COTTS

PH

A593

A5084

Ferry P (Summer only)

Heald Brow Pasture

94

27 A 28 B 29 C 30 D 31 E 32 F

140

128

For full street detail of the highlighted area see page 196.

Scale: 1½ inches to 1 mile

0   ¼   ½ mile
0   250m 500m 750m 1 km

A   B   C   D   E   F

LA21

Arnside

Arnside
Intake

Iron
Keld

Cumbria Way

Renny
Park
Coppice

Drunken
Duck
(PH)

Pull
Woods

Huyton
Hill

Camping
Site

Low Wood
Water Sport
& Activity Centre
SKELGHYLL LA

Low Wray
Water Sport

LA23

Ecclerigg
House

High
Crag

Randy
Pike

Low
Wray

Low Wray
Bay

Wray
Castle

Windermere

Sunny
Brow

Dan
Becks

High Wray
Bay

Balla
Wray

Rose
Castle

Field Head
House

197

Knipe
Fold

Yewfield

Sand
Ground

Sawrey
Ground

Hole
House

Bleham
Tarn

Outgate

Birkwray

Belmount

Loanthwaite

High
Wray

Arthur
Wood

Red
Nab

Belle
Grange

Courthouse
(Mus)

Highfield
House

Hawkshead
Hill

Hawkshead

Colthouse

Latterbarrow
Mon

Gillbank

LA22

Long
Height

Heald
Wood

Slape
Scar

B5285

LA21

Hawkshead Hall
Park

Town
End

Roger
Ground

Hannakin

TH
Mus
Sch

Priest
Pot

Colthouse
Heights

Wise Ben
Tarn

Three
Dubs
Crags

Claife
Heights

Mast

Caravan
Site

Howe
Farm

Water Side
Woods

Three Dubs
Tarn

Belt Ash
Coppice

Cycle
Trails

Esthwaite
Water

Esthwaite
Lodge
(YH)

Fold
Gate

Moss Ecoles
Tarn

Lake
Bank

Cuckoo
Brow
Wood

Harrow
Slack

Hawkshead
Moor

197

Great
Coppice

Esthwaite
Hall

Near
Sawrey

PH

Claife
Nature
Trail

B5286

Jack Gap
Plantation

Mast

Grizedale Beck

Hill Top

PH

Far
Sawrey

Town
End

Bryers
Fold

Grizedale
Forest Park

Devil's
Gallop

Out Dubs
Tarn

Dub How
Farm

High
Cunsey

Fellborough

Grizedale
Visitor
Centre

Grizedale

Grizedale
Visitor
Centre
Forest
Walks

Grizedale
Tarn

Cycle
Trails

Cunsey Beck

LA12

Bishop
Woods

LA23

Ferry P

For full street detail of the
highlighted area see page 197.

127   141

33   34   35   36   37   38

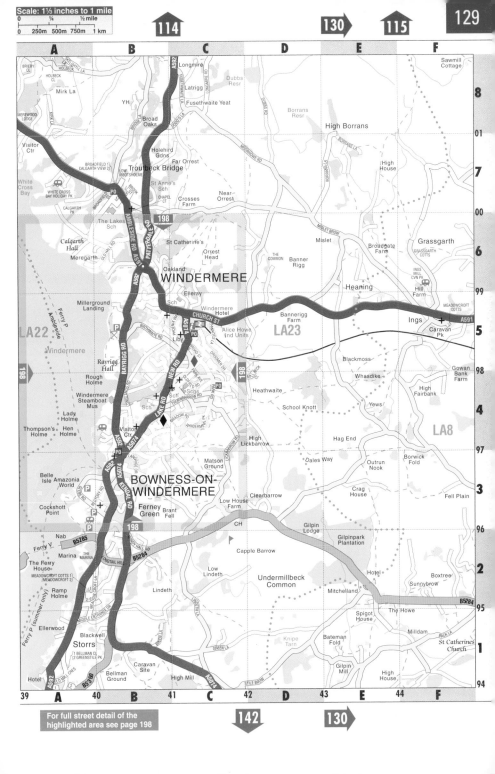

Scale: 1⅓ inches to 1 mile
0 ¼ ½ mile
0 250m 500m 750m 1 km

8

Sawmill Cottage
Croft Head
Staveley Head Fell
High House
Docker Nook

01

Millrigg Knott
Park House
Browfoot

7

Williamson's Monument
High House
Low Fold
Ghyll Bank
Brunt Knott
Brunt Knott Farm

00

The Heights
Fellfoot
Elfhowe
Hugill Hall
Hugill Fell
Scroggs Farm

6

Low House
Raw Ghyll
Littlewood Farm
Birk Field
Gurnal Dubs
Potter Fell

99

Reston
Reston Cotts
Staveley
Haw Lane Cnr
1 GOWAN TERR
2 FAIRFIELD CL
3 THE BANKS
4 GOWAN CRES
5 MILLFIELD TERR
6 CRAG VIEW
7 SILVER ST
8 KENT DR
9 CHURCH VIEW
Piked Howe
Frost Hole
Potter Tarn

5

River Gowan
Scroggs Cl
The Green 2
Gowan Cl 3
Danes Rd
Ind Est
Chapel
Staveley Park
Spring Hag
Side House
Godmond Hall

98

Fairbank Farm
Brownspring Coppice
Station La
River Kent
Sandyhill
Dales Way
Hundhow
Potter Fell Rd
Gilpin Bank

4

Field Close
Staveley Crossing
LA8
Cragg Farm
Hagg Foot
Capplebarrow
Artlecrag
Carbank La
Braban House

97

New Hall
Ashes
Broadfold
Cowan Head
Bowston
Laithwaite Farm
Bannisdale
Mill Cotts

3

The Glen
Fell Plain
Waingap
Plantation Bridge
Winter La
Winstanley Pl
Burneside

96

Crook End
Beckside
Hollin Hall
Tarn Close
Rather Heath
Garnett House
Holme Houses
Roger Row
Burneside
Brow Foot

2

Yew Tree Farm
Crook
Oakbank
Barn Farm
Ratherheath Lane Camping & Cvn Site
Moss Side
Bonning Gate
Tolson Hall
Hollins
Steele's Row 1
Howgill Houses
LA9

95

B5284
Crook Brow
Pound Farm
Brundrigg
Crook Rd
Halhead Brow
Crook Rd
Bannel Head
Toadpool
Mon
Madgegill
200

1

Crook Hall
Ellerbeck Farm
Capplerigg
Fell Gate
Halhead Hall
Plumgarths
Cunswick Scar
Lane Foot

94

Crag
Ash Spring

45 A 46 B 47 C 48 D 49 E 50 F

For full street detail of the highlighted area see page 200.

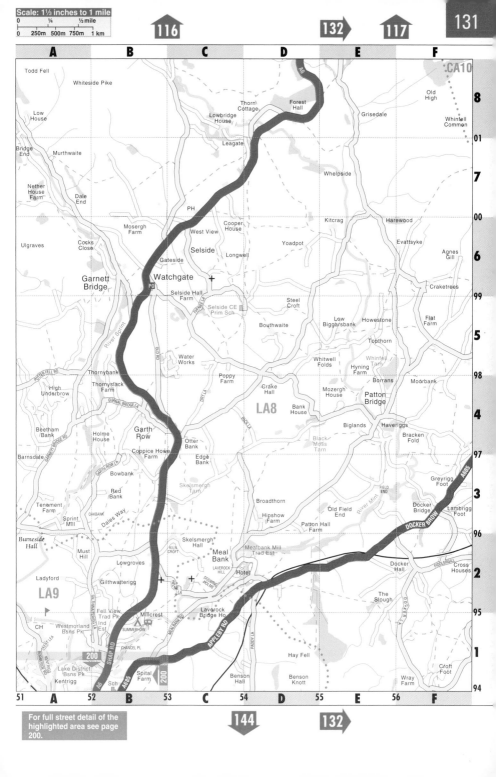

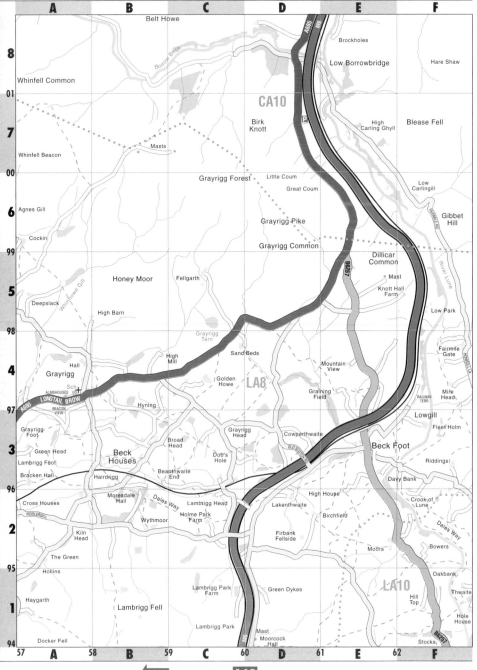

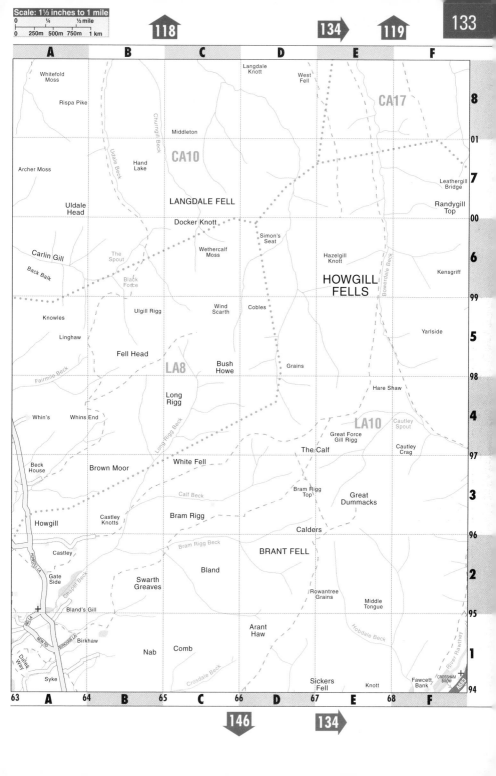

Scale: 1⅓ inches to 1 mile

0   ¼   ½ mile
0 250m 500m 750m 1 km

A   **B**   **C**   **D**   **E**   **F**

Whitefold Moss

Rispa Pike

Langdale Knott

West Fell

CA17

8

Churngill Beck

Middleton

01

Uldale Beck

Hand Lake

CA10

Archer Moss

7

Leathergill Bridge

LANGDALE FELL

Uldale Head

Randygill Top

00

Docker Knott

Simon's Seat

Carlin Gill

The Spout

Wethercalf Moss

Hazelgill Knott

HOWGILL FELLS

6

Back Balk

Black Force

Bowerdale Beck

Kensgriff

99

Knowles

Ulgill Rigg

Wind Scarth

Cobles

Linghaw

Yarlside

5

Fell Head

LA8

Bush Howe

Grains

Fairmile Beck

Hare Shaw

98

Long Rigg

Whin's   Whins End

Long Rigg Beck

LA10

Cautley Spout

4

Great Force Gill Rigg

Cautley Crag

Beck House

Brown Moor

White Fell

The Calf

97

Calf Beck

Bram Rigg Top

Great Dummacks

3

Howgill

Castley Knotts

Bram Rigg

Calders

96

Castley

Bram Rigg Beck

BRANT FELL

2

Gate Side

Chapel Beck

Swarth Greaves

Bland

Rowantree Grains

Middle Tongue

95

Bland's Gill

Birkhaw

Arant Haw

Hobdale Beck

River Rawthey

Dales Way

Nab

Comb

CROSSHAM BROW

1

Syke

Crosdale Beck

Sickers Fell

Knott

Fawcett Bank

94

63   **A**   64   **B**   65   **C**   66   **D**   67   **E**   68   **F**

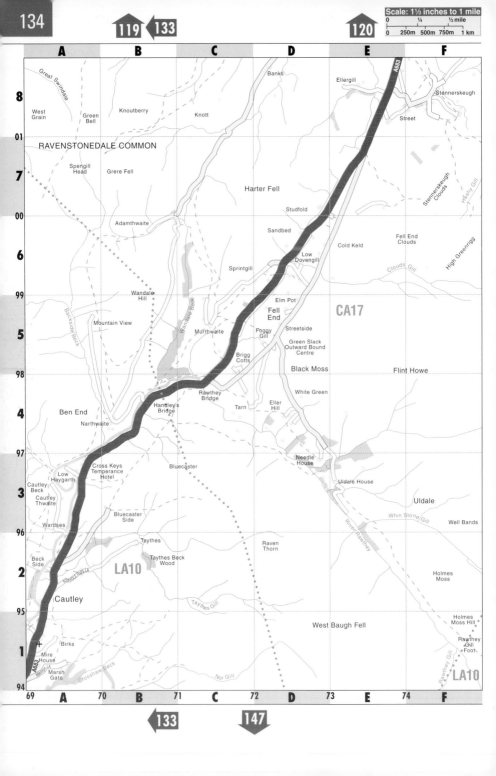

119 133

120

Scale: 1⅓ inches to 1 mile

0   ¼   ½ mile
0   250m 500m 750m 1 km

A   B   C   D   E   F

Great Swindale

Banks

Ellergill

Stennerskeugh

8

West
Grain

Green
Bell

Knoutberry

Knott

Street

01

RAVENSTONEDALE COMMON

Stennerskeugh
Clouds

Hazby Gill

Spengill
Head

Grere Fell

7

Harter Fell

Studfold

Fell End
Clouds

High Greenrigg

00

Adamthwaite

Sandbed

Cold Keld

6

Low
Dovengill

Springgill

Clouds Gill

99

Wandale
Hill

Elm Pot

CA17

Fell
End

5

Mountain View

Murthwaite

Foggy
Gill

Streetside

Green Slack
Outward Bound
Centre

Brigg
Cotts

Black Moss

Flint Howe

98

Rawthey
Bridge

White Green

Handley's
Bridge

Tarn

Eller
Hill

4

Ben End

Northwaite

Backside Beck

Wandale Beck

Cross Keys
Temperance
Hotel

Bluecaster

Needle
House

97

Low
Haygarth

Uldale House

Uldale

Cautley
Beck

Cautley
Thwaite

Wardses

Bluecaster
Side

Whin Stone Gill

Well Bands

River Rawthey

3

96

Beck
Side

Taythes

Taythes Beck
Wood

Raven
Thorn

Holmes
Moss

LA10

Knott Lane

2

Cautley

Taythes Gill

Holmes
Moss Hill

95

West Baugh Fell

Rawthey
Gill
Foot

Birks

Rawthey Gill

1

A683

Mire
House

A683

Marsh
Gate

Crosshaw Beck

Nor Gill

LA10

94

69   A   70   B   71   C   72   D   73   E   74   F

133

147

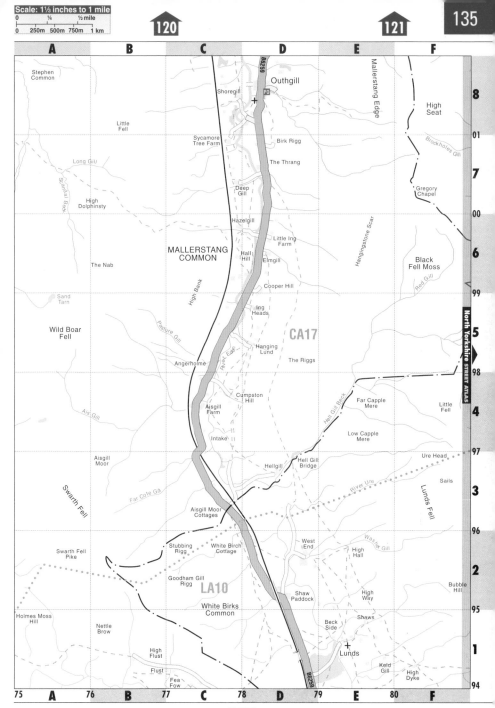

Scale: 1⅓ inches to 1 mile

0   ¼   ½ mile
0 250m 500m 750m 1 km

120

121

135

North Yorkshire STREET ATLAS

A B C D E F

8

Stephen Common

Outhgill

Shoregill

Mallerstang Edge

High Seat

01

Little Fell

Sycamore Tree Farm

Birk Rigg

Brockholes Gill

Long Gill

The Thrang

7

Scandal Back

Deep Gill

Gregory Chapel

High Dolphinsty

Hazelgill

00

Hangingstone Scar

The Nab

MALLERSTANG COMMON

Little Ing Farm

Black Fell Moss

6

Hall Hill

Elmgill

Red Gill

Sand Tarn

High Bank

Cooper Hill

99

Ing Heads

Wild Boar Fell

Pasture Gill

CA17

5

River Eden

Hanging Lund

The Riggs

Angerholme

Far Capple Mere

98

Ais Gill

Cumpston Hill

Hell Gill Beck

Little Fell

Aisgill Farm

Low Capple Mere

4

Intake

Aisgill Moor

Hellgill

Hell Gill Bridge

Ure Head

97

Far Cote Gill

Sails

River Ure

Swarth Fell

Lunds Fell

3

Aisgill Moor Cottages

96

Stubbing Rigg

White Birch Cottage

West End

Washer Gill

Swarth Fell Pike

Goodham Gill Rigg

LA10

High Hall

Bubble Hill

2

Holmes Moss Hill

Nettle Brow

White Birks Common

Shaw Paddock

High Way

95

Beck Side

Shaws

High Flust

Lunds

Keld Gill

High Dyke

1

Flust

Fea Fow

B6259

94

75 A 76 B 77 C 78 D 79 E 80 F

148

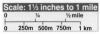

Scale: 1½ inches to 1 mile

| 0 | ¼ | ½ mile |

| 0 | 250m | 500m | 750m | 1 km |

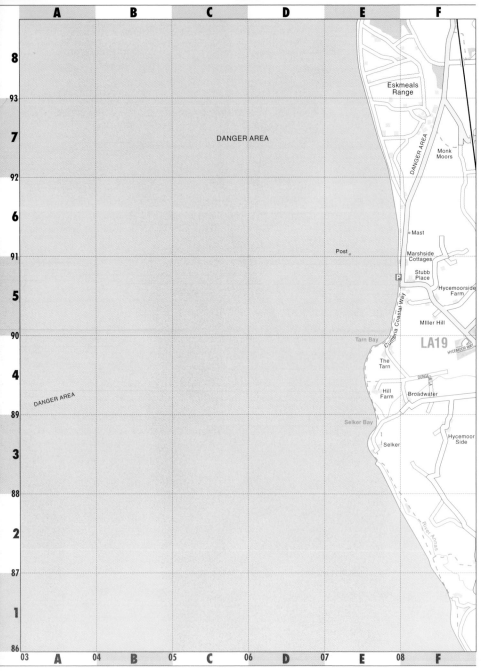

Eskmeals
Range

DANGER AREA

DANGER AREA

Monk
Moors

Mast

Post

Marshside
Cottages

Stubb
Place

Hycemoorside
Farm

Cumbria Coastal Way

Miller Hill

Tarn Bay

LA19

HYCEMOOR WAY

The
Tarn

DUNGEON LA

Hill
Farm

Broadwater

DANGER AREA

Selker Bay

Hycemoor
Side

Selker

River A1083

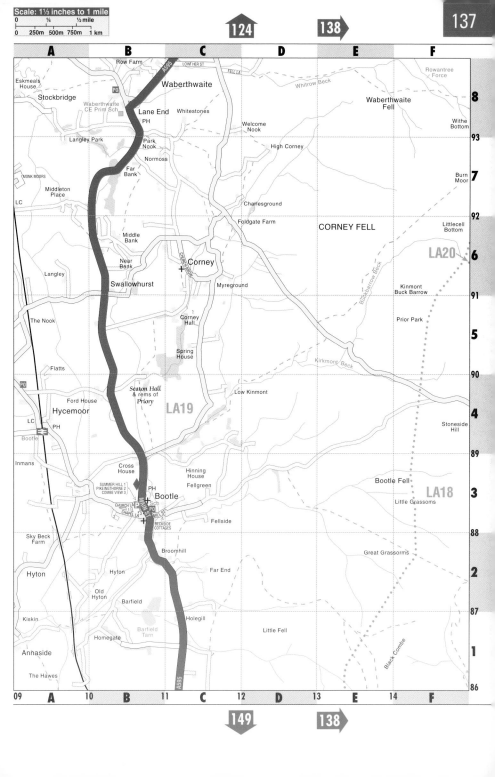

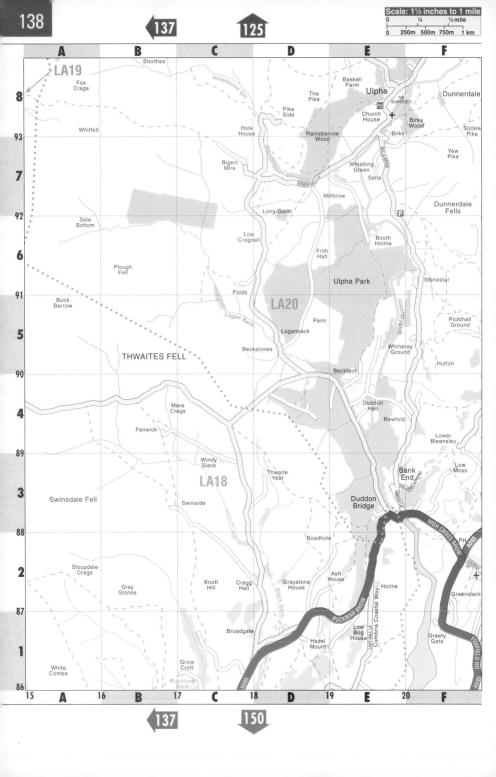

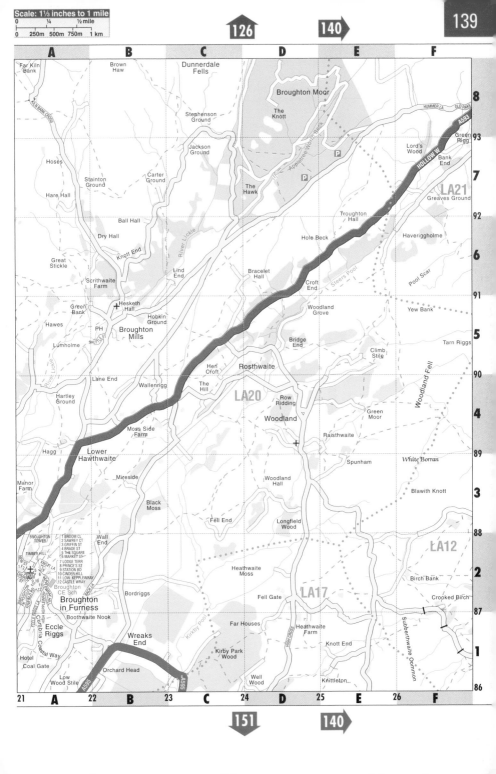

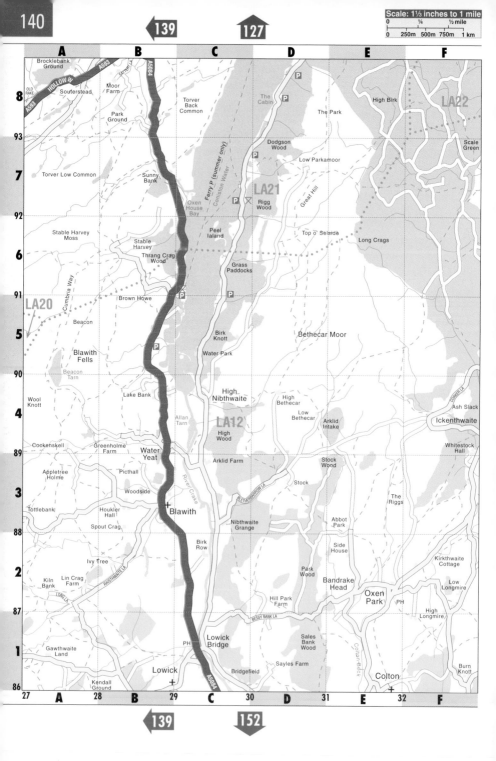

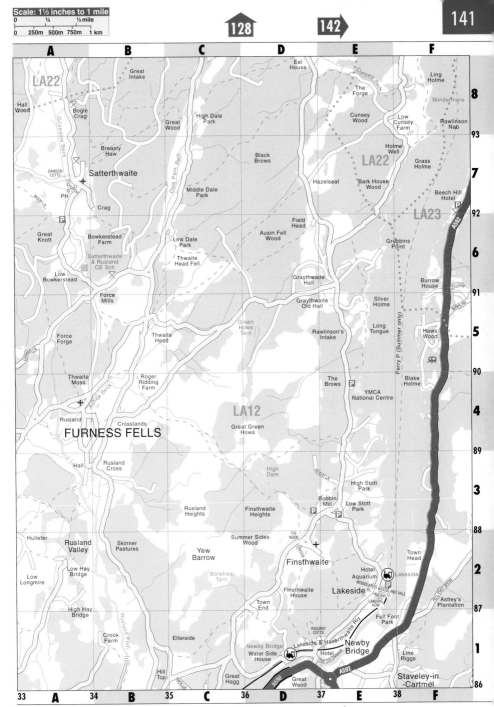

Scale: 1⅓ inches to 1 mile

0   ¼   ½ mile

0   250m 500m 750m 1 km

128

142

141

A   B   C   D   E   F

LA22

8

Hall
Wood

Bogle
Crag

Great
Intake

Eel
House

Ling
Holme

Windermere

93

Breasty
Haw

Great
Wood

High Dale
Park

The
Forge

Cunsey
Wood

Low
Cunsey
Farm

Rawlinson
Nab

DAMSON
COTTS

Satterthwaite

Black
Brows

Hazelseat

LA22

Holme
Well

Grass
Holme

7

MOOR LA

PH

Crag

Middle Dale
Park

Bark House
Wood

Beech Hill
Hotel

92

Great
Knott

Bowkerstead
Farm

Low Dale
Park

Field
Head

LA23

FELLSIDE

Low
Bowkerstead

Satterthwaite
& Rusland
CE Sch

Thwaite
Head Fell

Ausin Fell
Wood

Grubbins
Point

Burrow
House

6

Force
Mills

Graythwaite
Hall

Silver
Holme

91

Force
Forge

Thwaite
Head

Graythwaite
Old Hall

Long
Tongue

Haws
Wood

5

Thwaite
Moss

Roger
Ridding
Farm

Green
Hows
Tarn

Rawlinson's
Intake

Ferry P (Summer only)

Blake
Holme

90

Rusland

Crosslands

LA12

The
Brows

YMCA
National Centre

4

FURNESS FELLS

Great Green
Hows

89

Hall

Rusland
Cross

High
Dam

High Stott
Park

3

Hulleter

Rusland
Valley

Skinner
Pastures

Rusland
Heights

Finsthwaite
Heights

Bobbin
Mill

Low Stott
Park

88

Low
Longmire

Low Hay
Bridge

Yew
Barrow

Summer Sides
Wood

THE
NOOK

Finsthwaite

Hotel
Aquarium

Lakeside

Town
Head

2

High Hay
Bridge

Boretree
Tarn

Finsthwaite
House

Lakeside

WOODLANDS CL

WOODLAND AND VALE

Astley's
Plantation

87

Crook
Farm

Town
End

RAILWAY
COTTS

Lakeside & Haverthwaite Rly

LANDING
HOW

Fell Foot
Park

FELL FOOT BROW

Ellerside

Newby Bridge
Water Side
House

Hotel

Newby
Bridge

Line
Riggs

1

Hill
Top

Great
Hagg

BACK LA

THE COLONNADE

Great
Wood

A592

Staveley-in
-Cartmel

86

33   A   34   B   35   C   36   D   37   E   38   F

153

142

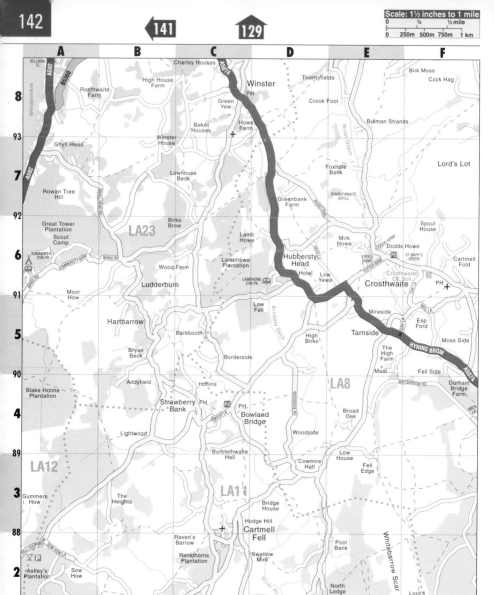

141

129

Scale: 1⅓ inches to 1 mile

0   ¼   ½ mile
0   250m 500m 750m 1 km

A   B   C   D   E   F

BELLMAN
CL.

Charley Houses

Winster
PH

Thornyfields

Birk Moss

Cock Hag

8

Rosthwaite
Farm

High House
Farm

Green
Yew

Crook Foot

Bulman Strands

Ghyll Head

Birket
Houses

Howe
Farm

93

Winster
House

River Gilpin

Lord's Lot

7

Rowan Tree
Hill

Lowhouse
Beck

Greenbank
Farm

Foxhole
Bank

STARNTHWAITE
GHYLL

92

Great Tower
Plantation

Birks
Brow

LA23

Lamb
Howe

Mirk
Howe

Dodds Howe

Spout
House

Scout
Camp

SUMMERHILL
CVN PK.

Lambhowe
Plantation

Hubbersty
Head

LOOP'S HOWE

CROSS
HOWE

ST MARY'S
GREEN

Cartmell
Fold

6

Moor
How

Wood Farm

LAMBHOWE
CVN PK

Hotel

Low
Yews

Crosthwaite
C E Sch

OTTER BANK

Crosthwaite

PH

91

Ludderburn

Low
Fell

Mireside

Esp
Ford

Moss Side

MILL LA.

Hartbarrow

Barkbooth

Arndale Beck

High
Birks

Tarnside

HYNING BROW

The
High
Farm

5

Bryan
Beck

Borderside

Mast

Fell Side

Durham
Bridge
Farm

90

Blake Holme
Plantation

Addyfield

Hollins

LA8

WHITBARROW RD.

BACK LA.

4

Strawberry
Bank

PH

PO

PH

Bowland
Bridge

WOODSIDE RD

Broad
Oak

Lightwood

Woodside

89

LA12

Burblethwaite
Hall

Cowmire
Hall

Low
House

Fell
Edge

3

Gummers
How

The
Heights

LA11

Bridge
House

FELL FOOT BROW

HOW TOW LA.

Raven's
Barrow

Hodge Hill
Cartmell
Fell

Pool
Bank

Whitebarrow Scar

2

Astley's
Plantation

Sow
How

Rankthorns
Plantation

Swallow
Mire

North
Lodge

Hervey
Nature
Reserve

Lord's
Seat

Wakebarrow

Foxfield

River Winster

Park
Wood

Whitebarrow

87

The
Ashes

HOG HOUSE LA.

1

Simpson Ground
Resr

SIMPSON
GROUND
RD.

Simpson
Ground

High
Loft
Wood

Thorphinsty
Hall

TARN GREEN
RD.

Middle
Low
Wood

Witherslack Hall
Sch

86

A   40   **B**   41   **C**   42   **D**   43   **E**   44   **F**
39

141

154

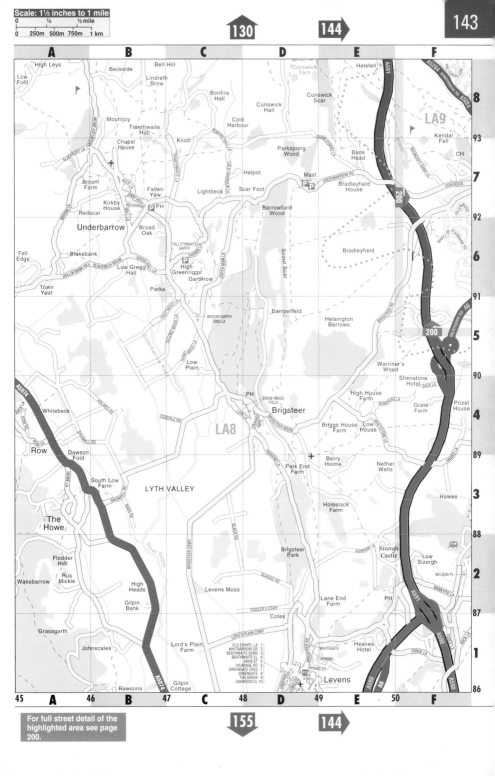

High Leys
Low Fold
Beckside
Bell Hill
Lindreth Brow
Bonfire Hall
Cunswick Tarn
Helsfell
LA9
Kendal Fell
CH

Mountjoy
Tranthwaite Hall
Cunswick Hall
Cunswick Scar

Chapel House
Knott
Cold Harbour
Parkspring Wood
Bank Head
Bradleyfield House

Broom Farm
Fallen Yew
Helpot
Lightbeck
Scar Foot
Mast
P P

Kirkby House
PH
Barrowfield Wood

Redscar
Underbarrow
Broad Oak
Bradleyfield

Fell Edge
Blakebank
Tallythwaite Garth
Low Gregg Hall
High Greenriggs
Garthrow

Town Yeat
Parks
Barrowfield

Broom Garth End La
Helsington Barrows

Low Plain
Scout Scar

Whitebeck
Holmes Rd
Crow Wood Field
PH
Brigsteer
Warriner's Wood
Shenstone Hotel
Prizet House

Row
Dawson Fold
LA8
Brigsteer Brow
High House Farm
Grate Farm

South Low Farm
Briggs House Farm
Low House

The Howe
LYTH VALLEY
Park End Farm
Berry Holme
Nether Wells
Hawes

Flodder Hall
Black Rd
Holeslack Farm

Rus Mickle
Wakebarrow
High Heads
Brigsteer Park
Sizergh Castle
Low Sizergh

Gilpin Bank
Levens Moss
Lane End Farm
PH

Grassgarth
Johnscales
Cotes
Fiddler's Cswy
Heaves Hotel

Lord's Plain Farm
Lord's Plain Cswy
Whitegate
Hyning

OLD CHAPEL LA   1
WHITBARROW GR   2
BEATHWAITE GDNS 3
BEATHWAITE CL   4
MAIN ST   5
VICARAGE RD   6
GREENGATE CRES   7
GREENGATE   8
THE GREEN   9
OAKWOOD CL   10

Rawsons
Gilpin Cottage
Levens

For full street detail of the highlighted area see page 200.

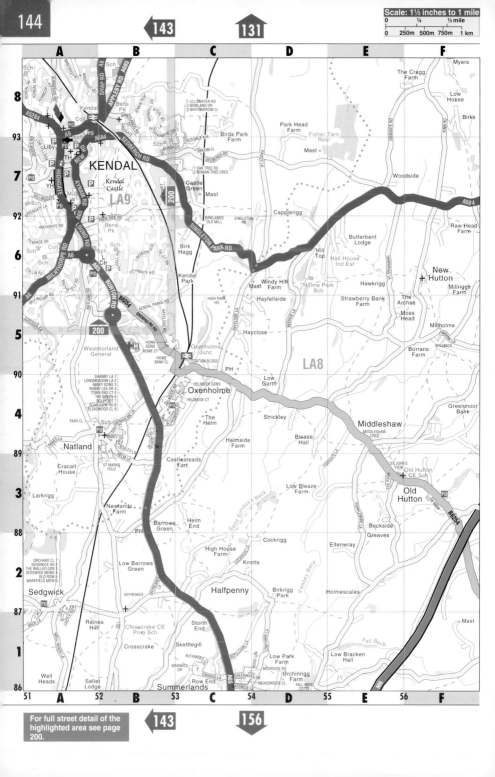

144

143

131

Scale: 1½ inches to 1 mile
0   ¼   ½ mile
0   250m 500m 750m 1 km

A   B   C   D   E   F

Myers

The Cragg
Farm

Low
House

Birks

MINEFELL RD

SHAP RD A6

APPLEBY RD A685

Sch

8

1 ULLSWATER RD
2 BOWLAND DR
3 WHITBARROW CL

Park Head
Farm

Fisher Tarn
Resr

DOCKER RD

KIRK RD

Kendal
Coll

SANDYGATE

KENT RYDAL RD

GRASMERE CRES

PEAT LA

93

Libry

SEDBERGH RD

Birds Park
Farm

BROOM CL

GRIZEDALE AVE

Mast

Woodside

TH

NEW

A684

1 OAK TREE RD
2 ROWAN TREE CRES

SEDBERGH RD

KENDAL

HIGHGATE

AYNAM RD

7

YH

Kendal
Castle

Castle
Green

Mast

LA9

CApplerigg

Raw Head
Farm

A684

PARK SIDE RD

SINGLETON PARK RD

92

Bsns
Pk

BIRKLANDS
OLD MILL

SINGLETON
LA

Butterbent
Lodge

Birk
Hagg

Hill
Top

Hall House
Ind Est

New
Hutton

MILNTHORPE RD

A6

Coll

Sch

Sch

LINGMOOR CL

FLETT DR

Kendal
Park

Hawkrigg

Millrigg's
Farm

6

BURTON RD

A65

LES HOWAITE AVE

Mast

Windy Hill
Farm

Holme Park
Sch

Strawberry Bank
Farm

The
Arches

Moss
Head

Millholme

B6254

High park
Ho

Hayfellside

91

KENDAL PARKS RD

HAYCLOSE RD

OXENHOLME RD

Hayclose

Borrans
Farm

MILLBECK

5

200

Westmorland
General

HOWE
GDNS HOWE CT

Oxenholme
Junc

LA8

Greenmoor
Bank

HOWE
BANK LA

STATION BLDGS

PH

90

SHANNY LA 1
LONGMEADOW LA 2
ABBEY GDNS 3
ROBBY LEA DR 4
TOWN END CT 5
THE GREEN 6
BOLDFOOT 7
SCAR VIEW RD 8
BLEASWOOD CL 9

HELMSIDE GDNS

Oxenholme

HELMSIDE CT

Low
Garth

4

Sch

OXENHOLME LA

The
Helm

Strickley

Middleshaw

MIDDLESHAW
CRES

Park Cl

ABBEY DR

Helmside
Farm

Bleaze
Hall

Natland

ST MARKS
FOLD

Castlesteads
Fort

89

Cracalt
House

St JOHN'S
VIEW

Old Hutton
CE Sch

Old
Hutton

B6254

3

Larkrigg

Low Bleaze
Farm

THE PARK

LOW MDW

Newlands
Farm

Barrows
Green

Helm
End

Beckside
Greaves

PEPPER HALL LA

88

PH

High House
Farm

Cockrigg

Ellenway

Low Barrows
Green

Knotts

Holmescales

2

ORCHARD CL 1
SEDGWICK HO 2
THE WALLED GDN 3
SEDGWICK MEWS 4
OLD ROW 5
WAKEFIELD MDW 6

SHYREAKES

Birkrigg
Park

Sedgwick

Halfpenny

87

Raines
Hall

Crosscrake CE
Prim Sch

Storth
End

Mast

Crosscrake

Skettlegill

Fall Beck

1

Well
Heads

WARWICK
DR

ALEXANDRA

Low Park
Farm

MOORSIDE RD

Low Bracken
Hall

A65

Sellet
Lodge

Row End

Summerlands

MEADOWSIDE CL

Urchinrigg
Farm

FALL BECK
COTTS

A6

86

51   A   52   B   53   C   54   D   55   E   56   F

For full street detail of the
highlighted area see page
200.

143

156

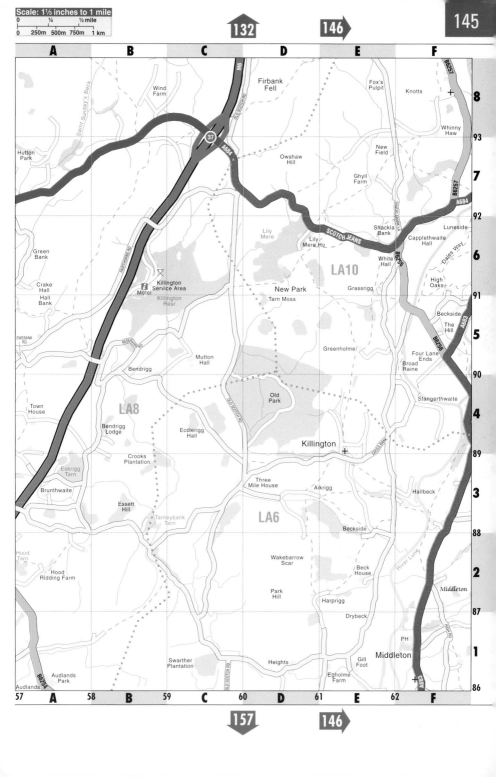

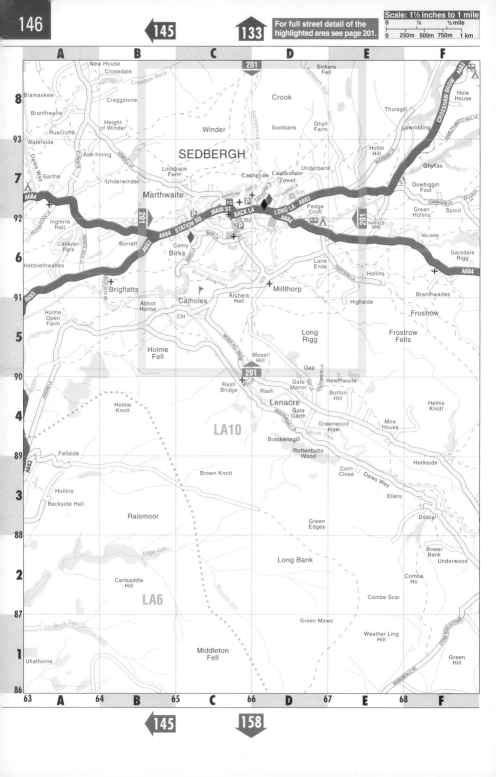

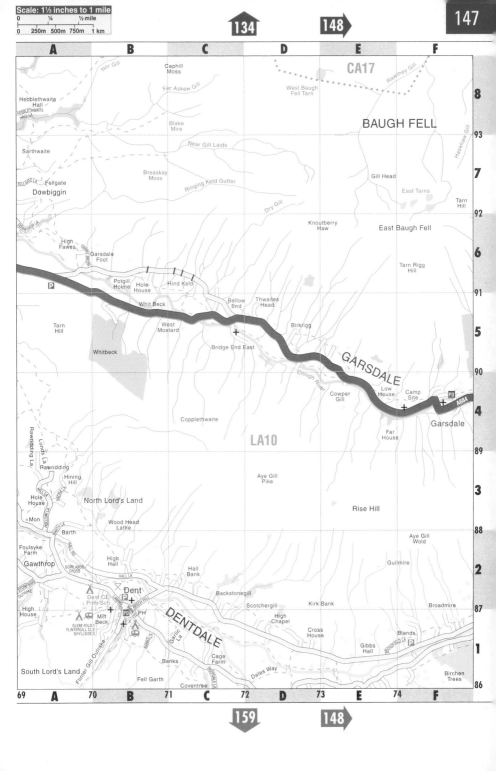

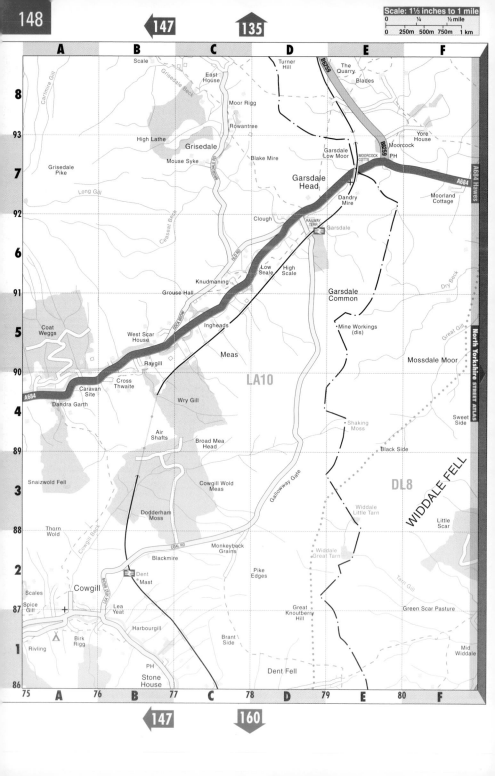

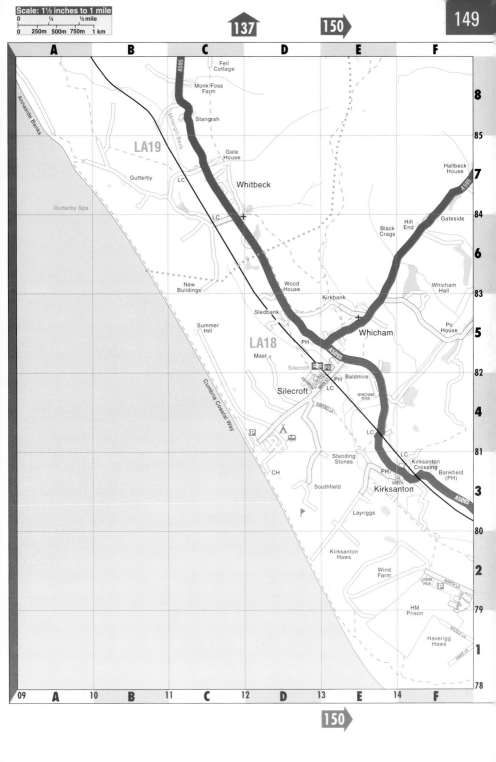

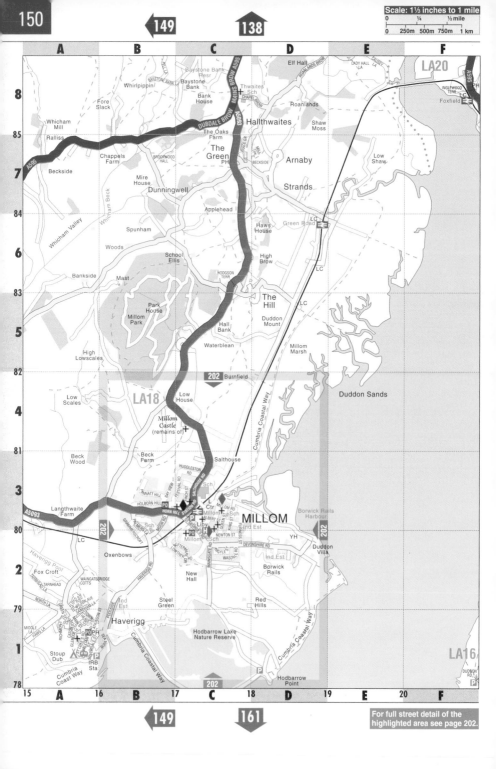

Scale: 1⅓ inches to 1 mile

| 0 | ¼ | ½ mile |
| 0 | 250m | 500m | 750m | 1 km |

A B C D E F

8

Elf Hall

LADY HALL LA

LA20

Baystone Bank Resr

INGLEWOOD TERR

Baystone Bank

Foxfield

Whirlpippin

Thwaites Sch

Roanlands

Fore Slack

Bank House

Hallthwaites

Shaw Moss

Whicham Mill

85

The Oaks Farm

Ralliss

Chappels Farm

BROOKWOOD HALL

The Green PH

Arnaby

Low Shaw

Beckside

7

Mire House

Dunningwell

Strands

84

Applehead

Haws House

Green Road

Whicham Valley

Spunham

6

Woods

School Ellis

High Brow

Bankside

Mast

HODGSON TERR

83

Park House

The Hill

Millom Park

Duddon Mount

5

Hall Bank

Waterblean

Millom Marsh

High Lowscales

82

202 Burnfield

Duddon Sands

4

Low Scales

LA18

Low House

Millom Castle (remains of)

81

Beck Wood

Beck Farm

Salthouse

3

Langthwaite Farm

A5093

HUDDLESTON RD

202

HOLBORN HILL

HORN HILL

MILLOM

Borwick Rails Harbour

80

Oxenbows

Millom Sch

YH

Duddon Villa

2

Fox Croft

Tarnhead

WAINGATEBRIDGE COTTS

New Hall

Borwick Rails

79

Steel Green

Red Hills

Haverigg

1

Stoup Dub

Hodbarrow Lake Nature Reserve

Cumbria Coast Way

Cumbria Coastal Way

Hodbarrow Point

LA16

DUDDON RD

78

202

15 A 16 B 17 C 18 D 19 E 20 F

For full street detail of the highlighted area see page 202.

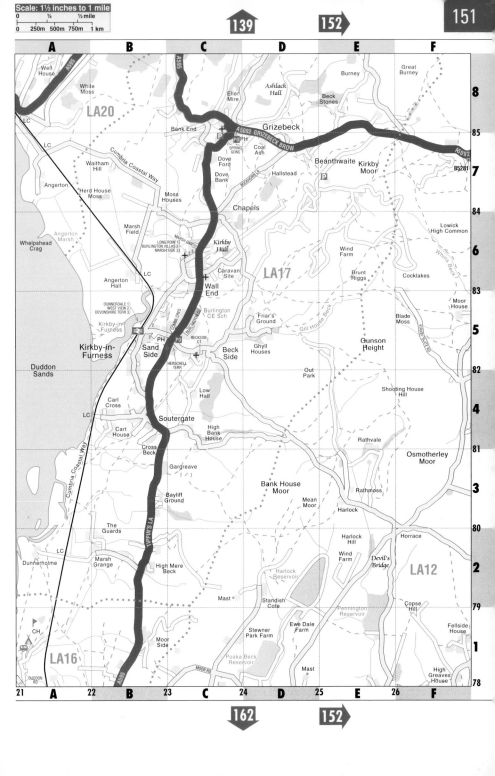

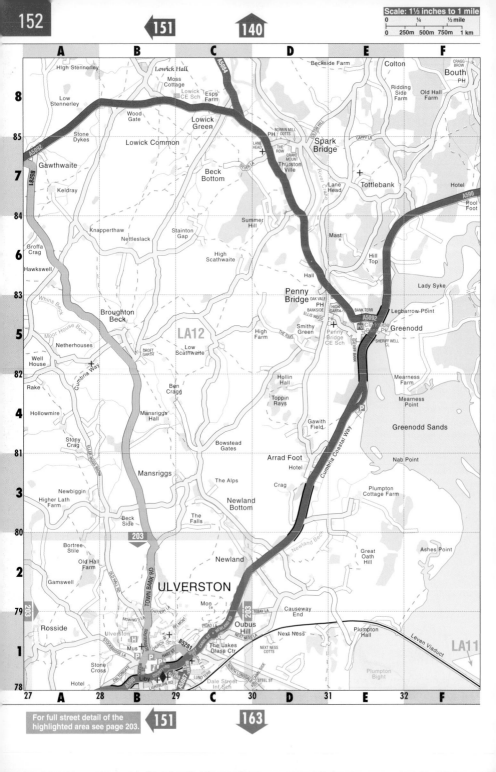

151
140

Scale: 1⅓ inches to 1 mile
0   ¼   ½ mile
0   250m   500m   750m   1 km

A   **B**   **C**   **D**   **E**   **F**

High Stennerley

Lowick Hall
Moss Cottage
Lowick CE Sch
Esps Farm

Beckside Farm

Colton

Bouth
PH

CRAGG BROW

Low Stennerley

Wood Gate

Lowick Green

Ridding Side Farm

Old Hall Farm

8

Stone Dykes

Lowick Common

BOBBIN MILL COTTS
PH

Spark Bridge

CAPPY LA

85

Gawthwaite

LANE HEAD
THE ROW

DRAKE MOUNT
Thurston Ville

Lane Head

Tottlebank

Hotel

A590

7

B5281

Keldray

Beck Bottom

Pool Foot

84

Knapperthaw
Nettleslack

Stainton Gap

Summer Hill

Mast

A5092

Groffa Crag

Hawkswell

High Scathwaite

Hill Top

Lady Syke

6

Whins Beck

Broughton Beck

Hall

Penny Bridge

OAK VALE PH

BANK TERR

Legbarrow Point

Greenodd

83

Moor House Beck

LA12

BANKSIDE
ELLIS WOOD

HIGH GARTH

Penny Bridge CE Sch

SHERIFF WELL CL

5

Netherhouses

Low Scathwaite

High Farm

Smithy Green

THE RAKE

SHERIFF BANK

82

Well House

Cumbria Way

DROFT GARTH

Mearness Farm

Rake

Ben Cragg

Hollin Hall

Mearness Point

4

Hollowmire

Mansrigg's Hall

Toppin Rays

Greenodd Sands

81

Stony Crag

Mansriggs

Bowstead Gates

Gawith Field

Cumbria Coastal Way

Nab Point

3

Newbiggin
Higher Lath Farm

The Alps

Arrad Foot

Crag

Hotel

Plumpton Cottage Farm

Ashes Point

Gamswell

Old Hall Farm

Beck Side

The Falls

Newland Bottom

Newland Beck

Great Oath Hill

80

203

TOWN BANK RD

2

Bortree Stile

Newland

ULVERSTON

Mon

TEBAY LA

Causeway End

Plumpton Hall

Leven Viaduct

LA11

203

Rosside

MOWING LA

Ulverston

Mus

H

P

CHURCH RD
BELMONT

B5281

ROAD LA

NEW LA

Oubus Hill

Next Ness

NEXT NESS COTTS

1

Stone Cross

Liby

The Lakes Glass Ctr

HART ST
HOAD ST

LUND ST

Dale Street Inf Sch

NORTH LONSDALE RD

STEEL ST

Plumpton Bight

Hotel

78

27   **A**   **28**   **B**   **29**   **C**   **30**   **D**   **31**   **E**   **32**   **F**

151
163

For full street detail of the highlighted area see page 203.

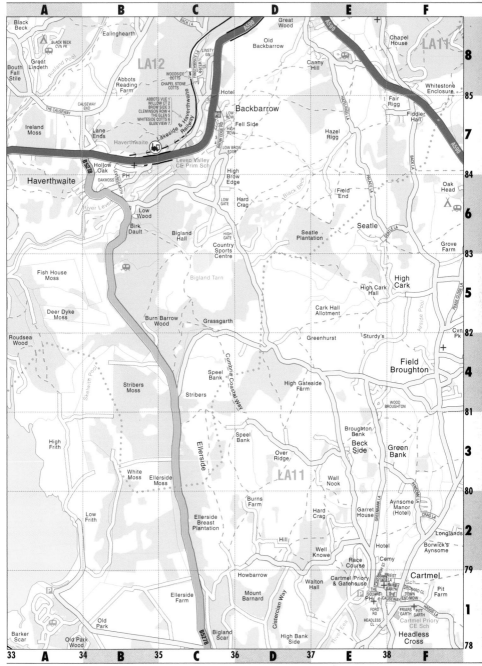

A   B   C   D   E   F

Black Beck
Bouth Fall Stile
Great Lindeth
BLACK BECK CVN PK
Ealinghearth
Ireland Moss
LA12
Abbots Reading Farm
CAUSEWAY END
THE CAUSEWAY
Lane Ends
Haverthwaite
Lakeside & Haverthwaite Railway
Woodside Cotts
Chapel Stone Cotts
Abbots Vue 1
Willow Ct 2
Brow Side 3
Cleminson Row 4
The Glen 5
Whiteside Cotts 6
Glenview 7
BACK LA
LINSTY CL
Hotel
Fell Side
High Row
Low Row
Backbarrow
Great Wood
Old Backbarrow
A590
Chapel House
LA11
Whitestone Enclosure
Canny Hill
Fair Rigg
Fiddler Hall
Hazel Rigg
MATHER LA
Hollow Oak
OAKMOSS
PH
High Brow Edge
Leven Valley CE Prim Sch
Low Brow Edge
LOW GATE
High Brow Edge
Hard Crag
Field End
PAGET LA
Oak Head
Haverthwaite
River Leven
Low Wood
Birk Dault
Bigland Hall
HIGH GATE
Country Sports Centre
Black Beck
Seatle Plantation
Seatle
SEATLE LA
Grove Farm
B5278
Fish House Moss
Bigland Tarn
High Cark Hall
High Cark
Ayside Pool
Deer Dyke Moss
Burn Barrow Wood
Grassgarth
Cark Hall Allotment
Sturdy's
FELL CLOSE LA
Cvn Pk
Roudsea Wood
Stelwith Pool
Greenhurst
Field Broughton
Stribers Moss
Speel Bank
Stribers
Cumbria Coastal Way
High Gateside Farm
Wood Broughton
High Frith
Speel Bank
Broughton Bank
Beck Side
Green Bank
White Moss
Ellerside Moss
Ellerside
Over Ridge
LA11
Wall Nook
GREENBANK LA
Low Frith
Burns Farm
Hard Crag
Garret House
Aynsome Manor (Hotel)
CRAG LA
Longlands
A590
Borwick's Aynsome
Hill
Well Knowe
Hotel
Cemy
Cartmel
Ellerside Breast Plantation
Race Course
Cartmel Priory & Gatehouse
Sch
THE SQUARE
PRIEST LA
BANK GARTH
TOWN END MDW
Pit Farm
ORCHARD CL
Barker Scar
Old Park
Ellerside Farm
Howbarrow
Mount Barnard
Cistercian Way
Walton Hall
River Eea
PH
FORD RD
HEADLESS CL
THE CAUSEWAY
FRIARS GARTH
PRIT GARTH
HAGGS LA
Cartmel Priory CE Sch
Old Park Wood
Bigland Scar
High Bank Side
Headless Cross

8
85
7
84
6
83
5
82
4
81
3
80
2
79
1
78

A   B   C   D   E   F
33   34   35   36   37   38

A   B   C   D   E   F

8

High Crag Wood

High Tarn Green
Askew Green
Lawns

Hare Hill
Low Tarn Green
Strickland Hill
Low Crag Wood

85

Helton Tarn

The Height

7

Barrow Hollin
Key Moss
Nether Hall
Mill Side
Beck Head

84

Hotel
Dean Barwick Sch
Witherslack

Holme
BLEACRAG BRIDGE
Slate Hill
Halecat House
Town End

6

Ayside
Bowes Lodge
High Fell End
Latterbarrow Farm
Longhowe End

Hill Top
Tow Top Plantation
The Grove
PH

83

Barber Green
PH
Newton Fell
FOUR LANE ENDS
High Newton

5

Greaves Farm
Low Green
Nichols Wood

Head House Farm
Low Newton
Sunny Green

82

Buck Crag

Broughton House
Ellerhow House
Meathop Moss

4

Stony Date
FOUR LANE ENDS
THE LEVEL OLD TOWN HILL
Burnbank Farm
Wilson House
B5277

COACH HO
BROUGHTON LODGE
81

Hampsfield
PH

3

Hampsfield Hall
1 HILLSIDE COTTS
2 CORONATION COTTS
3 SCHOOL HILL
4 SMITHY HILL
5 NEW COTTS
6 STONEBECK COTTS
7 THE ORCHARD
Meathop

Longlands Farm
Lindale
Low Meathop Farm
MEATHOP GRANGE

80

Brocka
Castle Head Field Ctr
208

2

Twr
Merlewood
Low Meathop Marsh
Sunnyside Farm

Hospice

Hampsfell
Holme Farm

79

208
Cistercian Way
The Slack
Cumbrian Coastal Way

1

GRANGE-OVER-SANDS
High Farm
Eggerslack Wood
Hotel
CH
LC
River Kent

Fell End
CHARNEY WELL LA
HAMPSFELL RD
Eden Mount
B5277
Blawith Point
Grange-over-Sands
Holme Island
NEW BARNS RD
BEACHWOOD
LA5

78

39 A 40 B 41 C 42 D 43 E 44 F

For full street detail of the highlighted area see page 208.

153   165

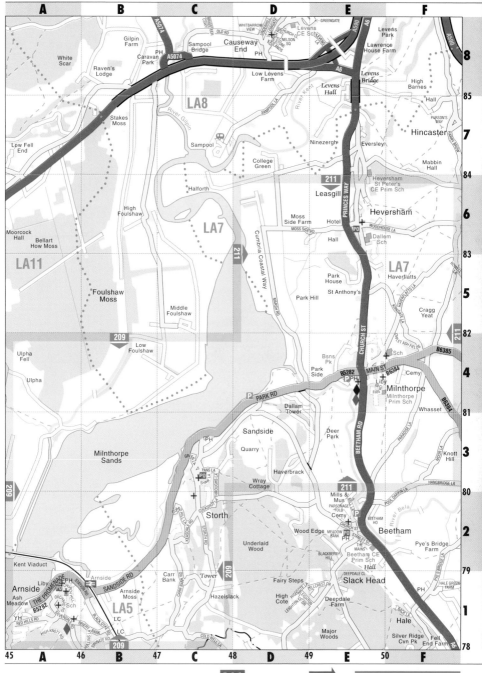

166   156   For full street detail of the
highlighted area see pages
209 and 211.

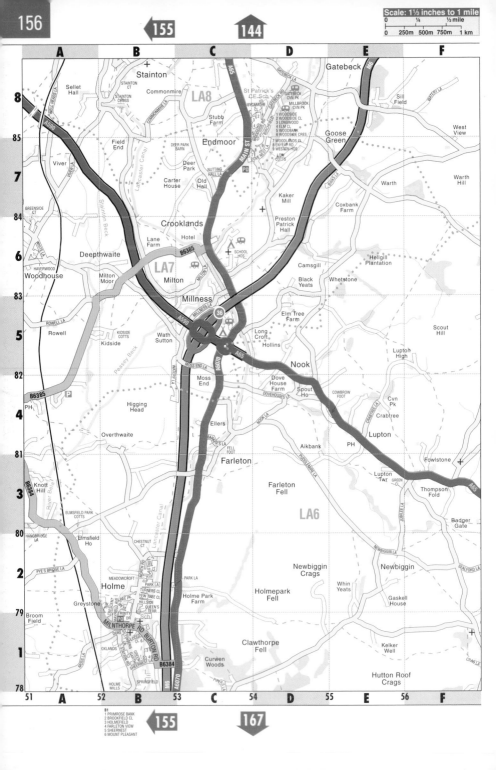

155

144

Scale: 1⅓ inches to 1 mile

| 0 | ¼ | ½ mile |
| 0 | 250m | 500m 750m | 1 km |

8

Sellet Hall

Stainton

Commonmire

STAINTON CT
STAINTON CROSS

LA8

St Patrick's C.E.Sch

Gatebeck

GATEBECK LA

Sill Field

WATERY LA

85

A590

WELL HEADS LA

Field End

DEER PARK BARN

Stubb Farm

SYCAMORE CL
GATEBECK LA
MILLBROOK CVN PK

1 WOODSIDE
2 WOODSIDE CL
3 LONGWOOD
4 ELM CL
5 WOODBANK
6 WOODSIDE CRES
7 WOODLANDS CL
8 ENYEAT RD
9 WESTON HO

Goose Green

West View

7

VIVER LA

Viver

Deer Park

Carter House

Old Hall

NUTTING HALL LA

MAIN ST

A65

DOVY LA

LOW COTTS

HINES

Warth

Warth Hill

84

GREENSIDE CT

Lancaster Canal

Stainton Beck

Crooklands

Hotel

Kaker Mill

Preston Patrick Hall

Coxbank Farm

6

WHITE LA

HAVERWOOD LA

Woodhouse

Deepthwaite

Lane Farm

Milton Moor

LA7

B6385

Milton

MILTON LA

Camsgill

Black Yeats

Whetstone

Hellgill Plantation

83

Millness

A590

MILLNESS LA

36

Elm Tree Farm

Scout Hill

5

ROWELL LA

Rowell

KIDSIDE COTTS

Kidside

Peasey Beck

Wath Sutton

MOSS END LA

WATER LA

A5070

A65

Long Croft

Hollins

Nook

Lupton High

82

B6385

P

Higging Head

Moss End

Dove House Farm

DOVEHOUSE LA

Spout Ho

COWBROW FOOT

Cvn Pk

Crabtree

GRABREE LA

4

PH

Overthwaite

Ellers

BACK'S LA

FELL FOOT

NOOK LA

Aikbank

PH

Lupton

81

Farleton

Lupton Twr

GREEN CL

Fowlstone

Thompson Fold

A65

3

B6384

Knott Hill

River Bela

ELMSFIELD PARK COTTS

Farleton Fell

LA6

Badger Gate

JUBILEE LA

80

HANGBRIDGE LA

Elmsfield Ho

CHESTNUT CT

NEWBIGGIN LA

2

PYE'S BRIDGE LA

MEADOWCROFT

PARK LA

TURNERS CL
YEW TREE CL
HILLSIDE
QUEEN'S TERR

PARK LA

Newbiggin Crags

Newbiggin

Whin Yeats

Gaskell House

BEALFORD LA

Holme

Greystone

TRINITY DR

Sch

Holme Park Farm

Holmepark Fell

79

Broom Field

MILNTHORPE

DUKE S LA

BURTON RD

OXLANDS

Clawthorpe Fell

Kelker Well

1

HOLME MILLS

SPRINGFIELD

SHEERNEST LA

B6384

M6

A5070

PU

Curwen Woods

Hutton Roof Crags

CRAG LA

| 51 | A | 52 | B | 53 | C | 54 | D | 55 | E | 56 | F |

155

167

Scale: 1⅓ inches to 1 mile

0 ¼ ½ mile
0 250m 500m 750m 1 km

145

158

157

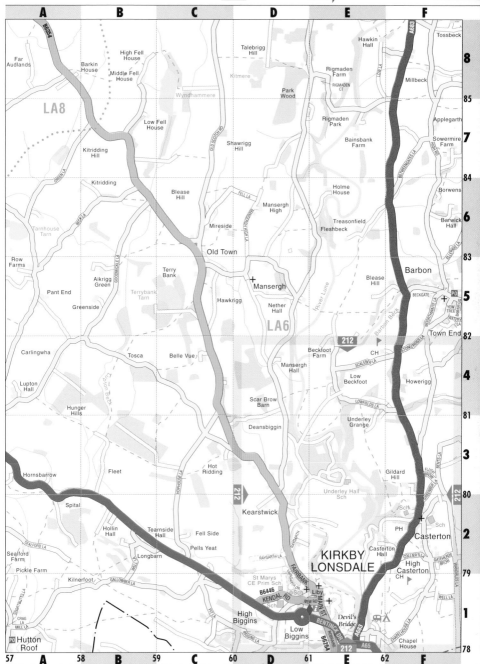

168

158

For full street detail of the
highlighted area see page 212.

157
146

Scale: 1½ inches to 1 mile

0   ¼   ½ mile
0   250m 500m 750m 1 km

A   **B**   **C**   **D**   **E**   **F**

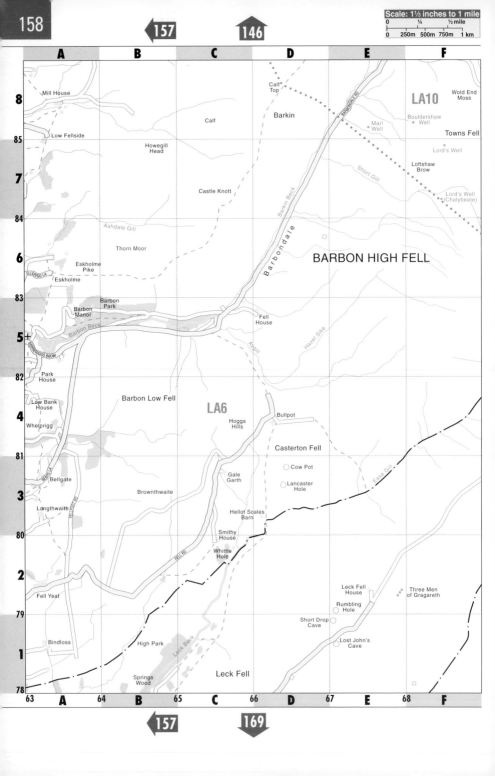

8
Mill House

LA10   Wold End Moss

Calf Top

Barkin   Bouldershaw Well

Calf

85
Low Fellside   Marl Well   Towns Fell

Howegill Head   Lord's Well

7
Loftshaw Brow

Castle Knott   Short Gill

84
Ashdale Gill   Lord's Well (Chalybeate)

Thorn Moor

6
Eskholme Pike

Eskholme

ELLERGG LA

83
Barbon Park

Barbon Manor   Fell House

BARBON HIGH FELL

Barbon Beck   Barbondale

Hazel Sike

5
Barbon Beck

Park House

82

Low Bank House

Barbon Low Fell   **LA6**

4
Whelprigg   Hoggs Hills   Bullpot

Casterton Fell   Ease Gill

81
Cow Pot

Bellgate   Gale Garth   Lancaster Hole

3
Langthwaite   Brownthwaite

Hellot Scales Barn

80
Smithy House

Whittle Hole

2
Fell Yeat   Leck Fell House   Three Men of Gragareth

Rumbling Hole

79
Short Drop Cave

Bindloss   Lost John's Cave

1
High Park   Leck Fell

Springs Wood

78

63 **A** **64** **B** **65** **C** **66** **D** **67** **E** **68** **F**

FELL RD

Leck Beck

157
169

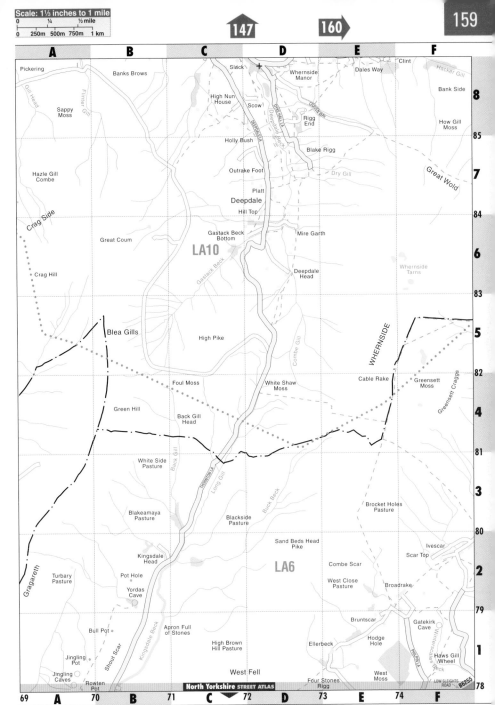

Scale: 1½ inches to 1 mile

0   ¼   ½ mile
0 250m 500m 750m 1 km

147

160

159

A   B   C   D   E   F

8

Pickering

Banks Brows

Slack

Whernside Manor

Dales Way

Clint

Hacker Gill

Bank Side

High Nun House

Scow

Gill Head

Flinter Gill

Sappy Moss

DEEPDALE LA

Dyke Hall

Rigg End

How Gill Moss

COTA WA

Deepdale Beck

Holly Bush

Blake Rigg

85

Hazle Gill Combe

Outrake Foot

Dry Gill

Great Wold

7

Platt

Deepdale

Crag Side

Hill Top

84

Gastack Beck Bottom

Mire Garth

Great Coum

LA10

Gastack Beck

Deepdale Head

Whernside Tarns

6

Crag Hill

83

Blea Gills

High Pike

Combe Gill

WHERNSIDE

5

Foul Moss

White Shaw Moss

Cable Rake

Greensett Moss

82

Greensett Craggs

Green Hill

Back Gill Head

4

White Side Pasture

Back Gill

THORNTON LA

Long Gill

Buck Beck

Brocket Holes Pasture

81

Blakeamaya Pasture

Blackside Pasture

3

Sand Beds Head Pike

80

Kingsdale Head

LA6

Combe Scar

Ivescar

Scar Top

Gragareth

Turbary Pasture

Pot Hole

West Close Pasture

Broadrake

2

Yordas Cave

Kingsdale Beck

79

Bull Pot

Apron Full of Stones

Bruntscar

Gatekirk Cave

Jingling Pot

Shout Scar

High Brown Hill Pasture

Ellerbeck

Hodge Hole

Wintersoales Beck

DALE LA

Haws Gill Wheel

B6255

1

Jingling Caves

West Fell

West Moss

LOW SLEIGHTS ROAD

Rowten Pot

Four Stones Rigg

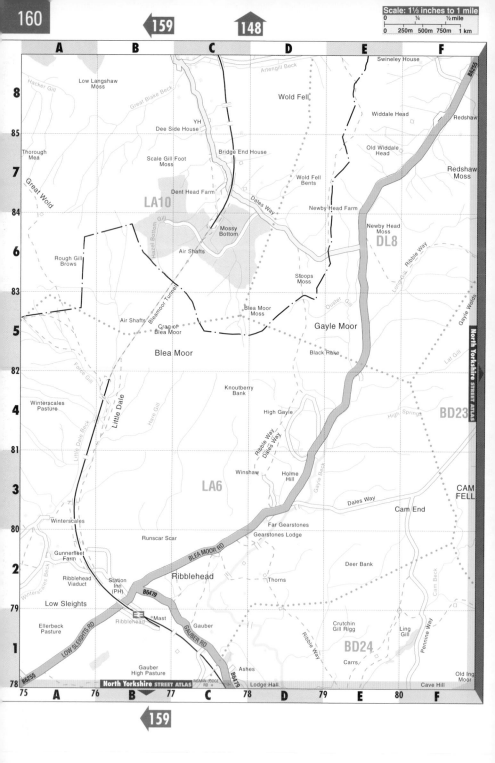

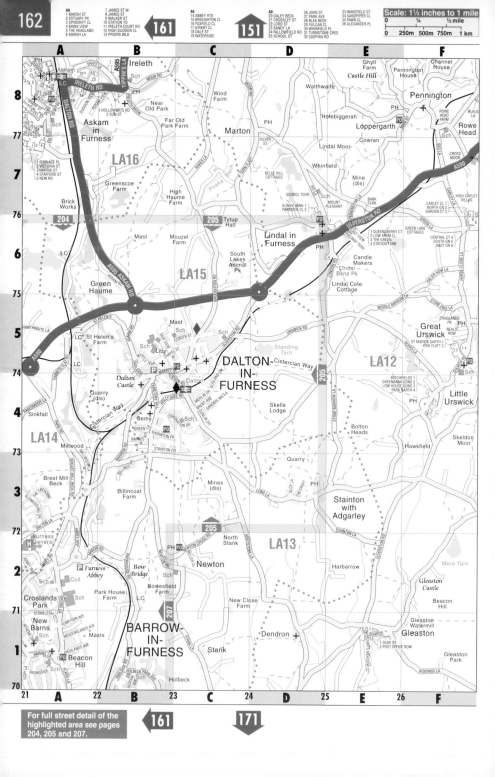

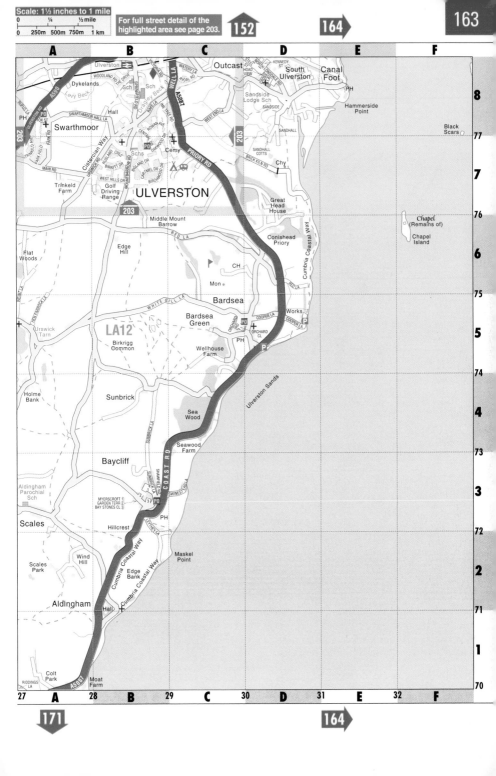

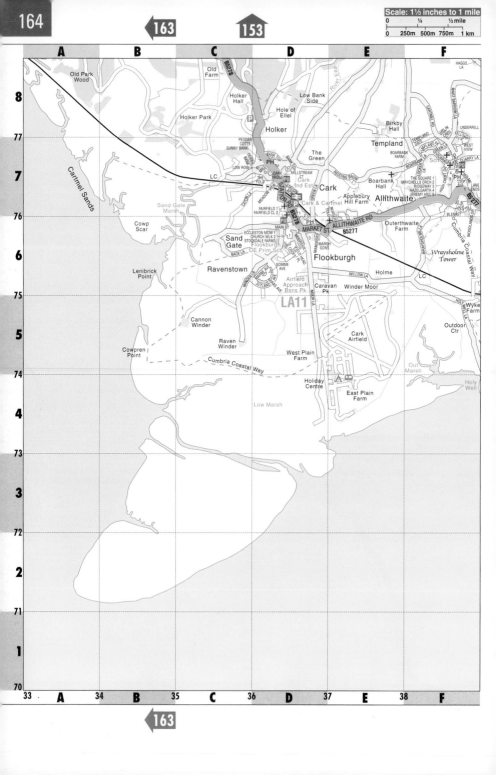

Scale: 1⅓ inches to 1 mile

0   ¼   ½ mile
0 250m 500m 750m 1 km

154

166

165

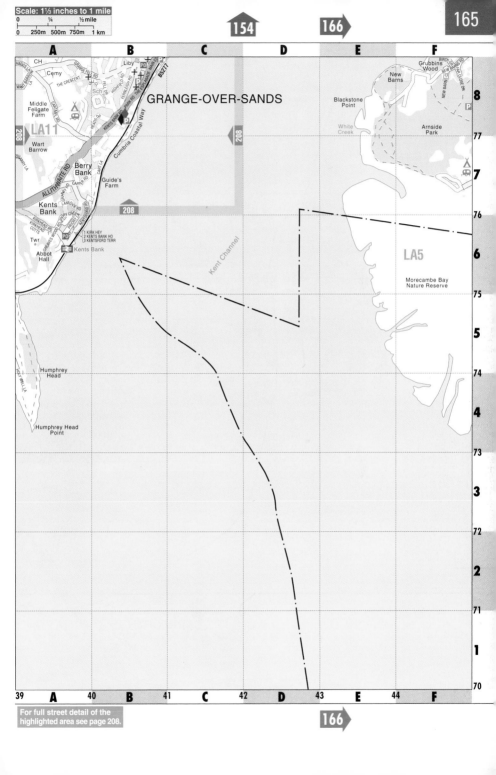

| | A | B | C | D | E | F | |

CH
Cemy
THE CRESCENT
Libby
Sch
Middle Feligate Farm
LA11
208
Wart Barrow
GRANGE-OVER-SANDS
208
B5277
Cumbria Coastal Way
Berry Bank
Guide's Farm
208
Kents Bank
1 KIRK HEY
2 KENTS BANK HO
3 KENTSFORD TERR
Twr
Abbot Hall
Kents Bank

Grubbins Wood
New Barns
Blackstone Point
White Creek
Arnside Park
P

LA5
Morecambe Bay Nature Reserve

Kent Channel

Humphrey Head
Humphrey Head Point

8
77
7
76
6
75
5
74
4
73
3
72
2
71
1
70

| 39 | A | 40 | B | 41 | C | 42 | D | 43 | E | 44 | F |

For full street detail of the highlighted area see page 208.

166

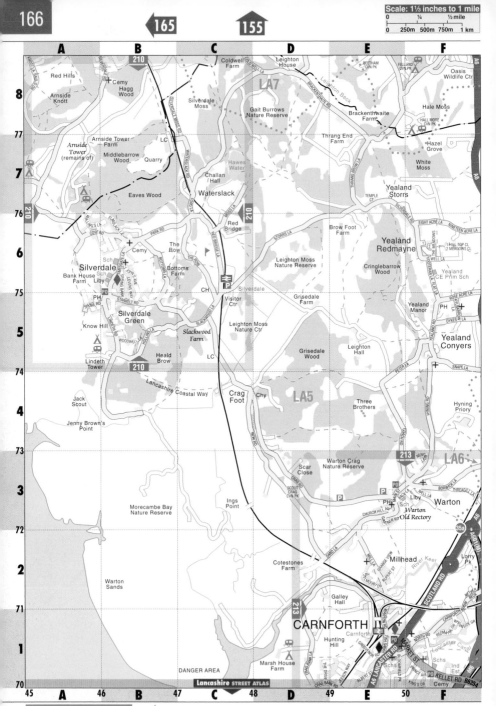

165

155

Scale: 1⅓ inches to 1 mile

0   ¼   ½ mile

0 250m 500m 750m 1 km

A   **B**   **C**   **D**   **E**   **F**

8

Red Hills

Arnside Knott

Cemy Hagg Wood

Silverdale Moss

Coldwell Farm

Leighton House

LA7

BESTHAM CVN PK

FELL END CVN PK

Oasis Wildlife Ctr

Gait Burrows Nature Reserve

Brackenthwaite Farm

Hale Moss

HALL MORE CVN PK

77

Arnside Tower Farm

Middlebarrow Wood

Quarry

LC

Thrang End Farm

Hazel Grove

White Moss

Arnside Tower (remains of)

7

Eaves Wood

Challan Hall

Hawes Water

Temple Ct

Yealand Storrs

210

Waterslack

210

Red Bridge

Brow Foot Farm

EIGHT ACRE LA

NINETEEN ACRE LA

Yealand Redmayne

ROSE ACRE LA

76

STORRS LA

Leighton Moss Nature Reserve

Cringlebarrow Wood

Yealand CE Prim Sch

The Row

Cemy

Park Rd

Bottoms Farm

6

Silverdale

Sch

Liby

Bank House Farm

PH

Shore Rd

CH

Silverdale

Visitor Ctr

Grisedale Farm

Yealand Manor

PH

DYKES LA

75

Silverdale Green

Slackwood Farm

Leighton Moss Nature Ctr

Grisedale Wood

Leighton Hall

Yealand Conyers

5

Know Hill

Woodwell

Heald Brow

LC

SNAPE LA

Lindeth Tower

210

Lancashire Coastal Way

Crag Foot

Chy

LA5

Three Brothers

Hyning Priory

74

4

Jack Scout

Jenny Brown's Point

New Rd

213

NEWS

LA6

73

Morecambe Bay Nature Reserve

Ings Point

Scar Close

Warton Crag Nature Reserve

SCOUT CRAG CVN PK

P

PO

Liby

Warton

3

PH

Sch

Warton Old Rectory

CHURCH HILL

BORWICK LA

THREAGILL LA

P

35a

72

Warton Sands

Cotestones Farm

Millhead

Lorry Pk

River Keer

2

SCOTLAND RD

71

Galley Hall

213

CARNFORTH

Carnforth

PO

SCOTLAND RD

KELLET RD

B6254

1

DANGER AREA

Hunting Hill

Marsh House Farm

Schs

Ind Est

Cemy

70

45 **A** **46** **B** **47** **C** **48** **D** **49** **E** **50** **F**

Lancashire STREET ATLAS

For full street detail of the highlighted area see pages 210 and 213.

165

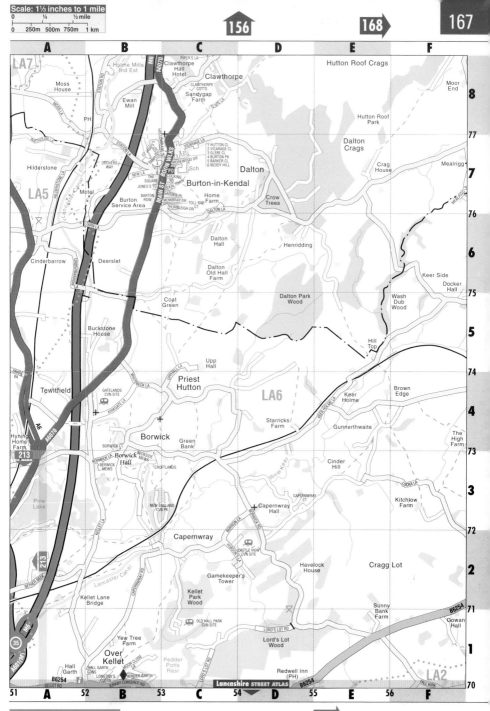

Scale: 1½ inches to 1 mile

0 ¼ ½ mile
0 250m 500m 750m 1 km

For full street detail of the highlighted area see page 213.

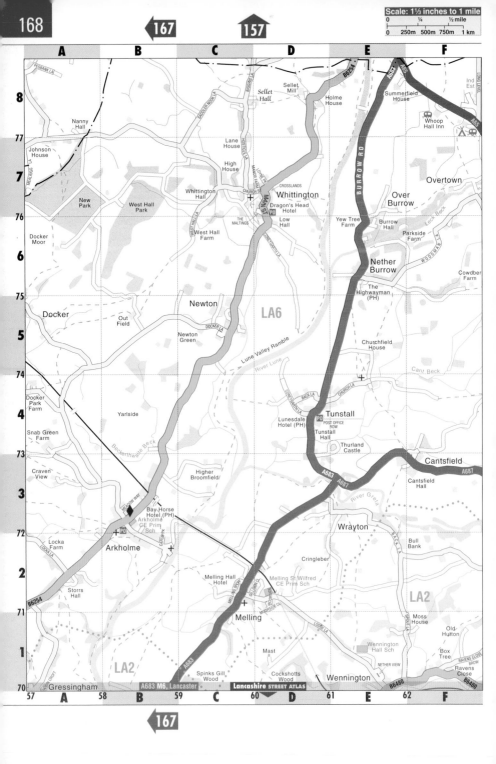

Scale: 1⅓ inches to 1 mile

0   ¼   ½ mile

0   250m   500m   750m   1 km

A   B   C   D   E   F

8

Nanny Hall

Johnson House

77

Sellet Hall

Sellet Mill

Holme House

Summerfield House

Ind Est

Whoop Hall Inn

Lane House

High House

7

New Park

West Hall Park

Whittington Hall

CROSSLANDS

Whittington

Dragon's Head Hotel

Over Burrow

Overtown

Docker Moor

THE MALTINGS

Low Hall

Yew Tree Farm

Burrow Hall

Parkside Farm

Cowdber Farm

76

West Hall Farm

Nether Burrow

6

Docker

Out Field

Newton

LA6

The Highwayman (PH)

75

Newton Green

Churchfield House

5

Lune Valley Ramble

River Lune

74

Docker Park Farm

Yarlside

Lunesdale Hotel (PH)

Tunstall

POST OFFICE ROW

4

Snab Green Farm

Tunstall Hall

Thurland Castle

73

Craven View

Higher Broomfield

Cantsfield

Cantsfield Hall

3

Bay Horse Hotel (PH)

Arkholme CE Prim Sch

Wrayton

Bull Bank

River Greta

Locka Farm

2

Arkholme

Melling Hall Hotel

Melling St Wilfred CE Prim Sch

Cringleber

LA2

Moss House

Old Hutton

Storrs Hall

71

Melling

Box Tree

Ravens Close

1

Mast

Wennington Hall Sch

NETHER VIEW

LA2

Spinks Gill Wood

Cockshotts Wood

Wennington

70

Gressingham

A683 M6, Lancaster

Lancashire STREET ATLAS

57   A   58   B   59   C   60   D   61   E   62   F

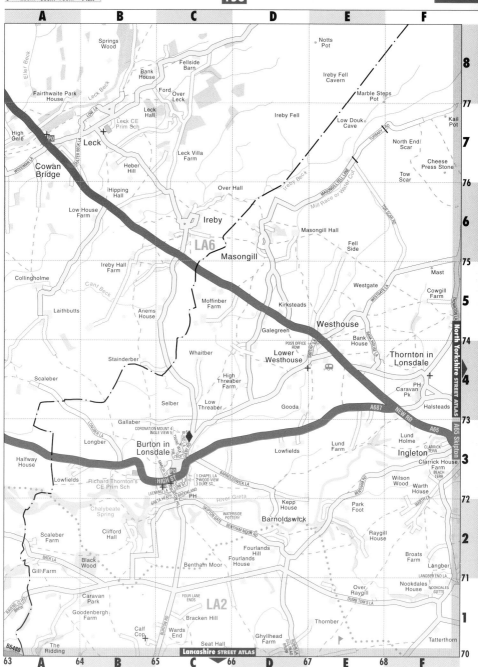

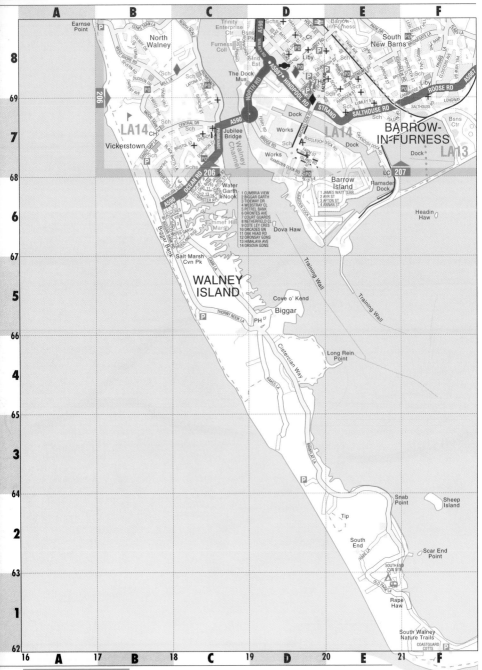

8

69

7

68

6

67

5

66

4

65

3

64

2

63

1

62

A   B   C   D   E   F

16   A   17   B   18   C   19   D   20   E   21   F

Earnse Point

North Walney

Trinity Enterprise Ctr

Furness Coll

Barrow-in-Furness

South New Barns

The Dock Mus

BARROW-IN-FURNESS

LA14

LA14

LA13

Vickerstown

Jubilee Bridge

Walney Channel

Dock

Works

Dock

Dock

Barrow Island

Ramsden Dock

1 CUMBRIA VIEW
2 BIGGAR GARTH
3 TIDEWAY DR
4 WEBSTRAY CL
5 PETREL BANK
6 ORONTES AVE
7 COURT GUARDS
8 NETHERFIELD CL
9 COTE LEY CRES
10 ORCADES GN
11 OAK HEAD RD
12 ORONSAY GDNS
13 HIMALAYA AVE
14 ORSOVA GDNS

1 JAMES WATT TERR
2 AYR ST
3 AFTON ST
4 ANNAN ST

Water Garth Nook

Dova Haw

Salt Marsh Cvn Pk

WALNEY ISLAND

Cove o' Kend

Biggar

Headin Haw

Long Rein Point

Training Wall

Training Wall

Cistercian Way

Snab Point

Sheep Island

Tip

South End

Scar End Point

SOUTH END CVN SITE

Rape Haw

South Walney Nature Trails

COASTGUARD COTTS

For full street detail of the highlighted area see pages 206 and 207.

Scale: 1⅓ inches to 1 mile

| 0 | | ¼ | | ½ mile |
| 0 | 250m | 500m | 750m | 1 km |

162

163

171

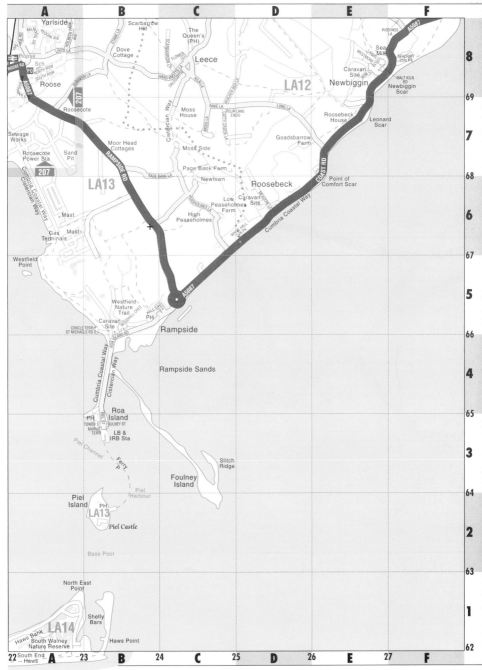

A5087

Yarlside

Scarbarrow Hill

The Queen's (PH)

Leece

Dove Cottage

LA12

Caravan Site
Newbiggin

Sea Mill

RIDDINGS LA

WESTMORL CL
LAND CL

SEACROFT CVN PK

MALT KILN RD

Newbiggin Scar

Roose

Sch
PO

NORTH ROW
SOUTH ROW

Roosecote

DUNNERDALE LA

RAMPSIDE RD

207

A5087

LEECE LA

Moss House

RAKE LA
FATTY CROOK LA

FOUR LANE ENDS

Roosebeck House

Leonard Scar

LONG LA

Sewage Works

Moor Head Cottages

Moss Side

Goadsbarrow Farm

Roosecote Power Sta

Sand Pit

207

PAGE BANK LA

Page Bank Farm

Newtown

Roosebeck

COAST RD

Point of Comfort Scar

LA13

Cistercian Way

Mast

Gas Mast
Terminals

Low Peaseholmes Farm

High Peaseholmes

PEASHOLMES LA

Caravan Site

WHITE HALL CVN PK

MEADOW LA

Cumbria Coastal Way

+

Westfield Point

A5087

Westfield Nature Trail

PH

HALL GARTH

WOODMILL DRIVE

HALL SAND RD

Caravan Site

CONCLE TERR
ST MICHAELS RD

Rampside

Cumbria Coastal Way

Cistercian Way

Rampside Sands

PH

Roa Island

TOWER ST
MARINE TERR

FOULNEY ST

LB & IRB Sta

Piel Channel

Ferry P

Slitch Ridge

Piel Harbour

Foulney Island

Piel Island

PH

LA13

Piel Castle

Bass Pool

North East Point

LA14

Shelly Bars

Haws Bank

South Walney Nature Reserve

Haws Point

South End Haws

22   A   23   B   24   C   25   D   26   E   27   F

62 63 64 65 66 67 68 69 7 8

For full street detail of the highlighted area see page 207.

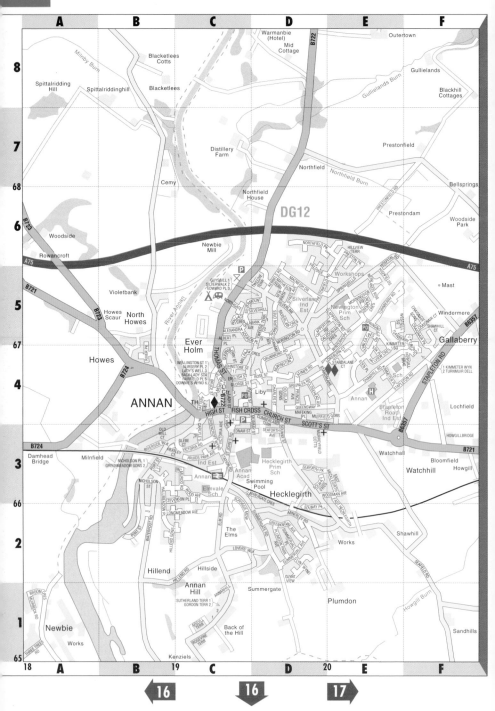

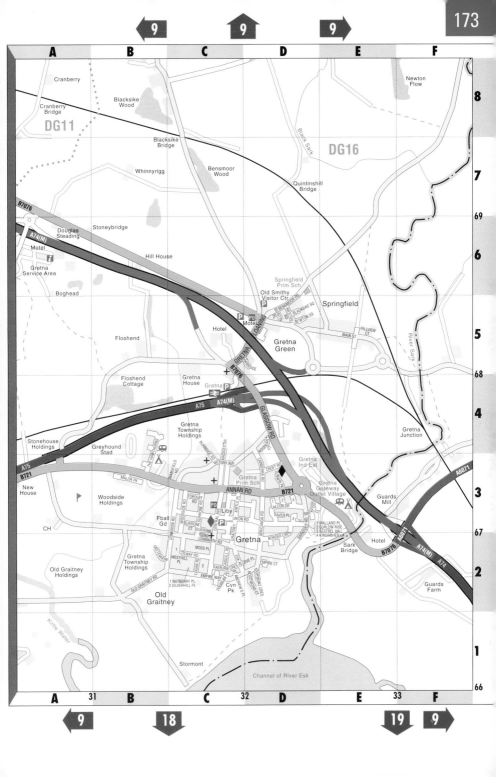

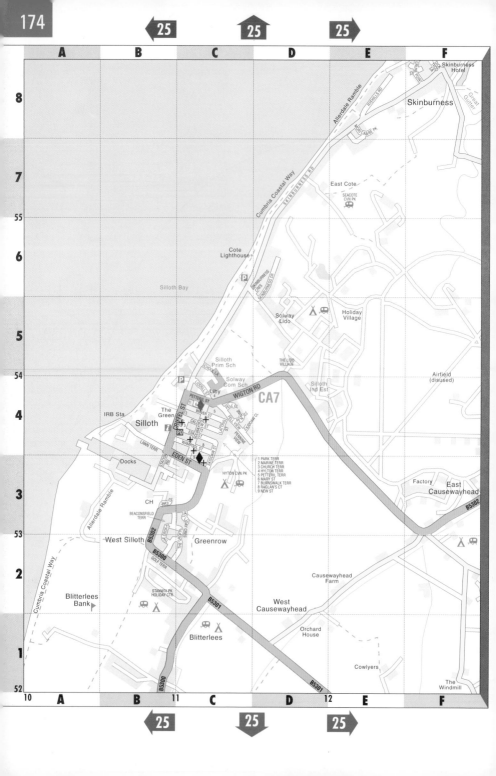

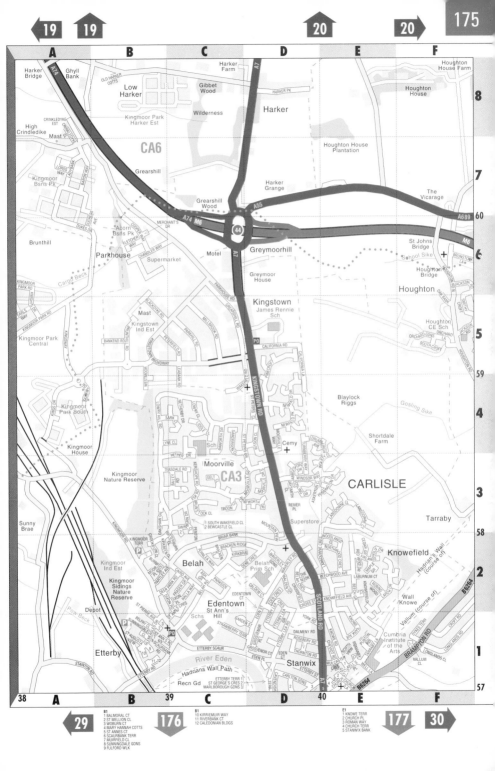

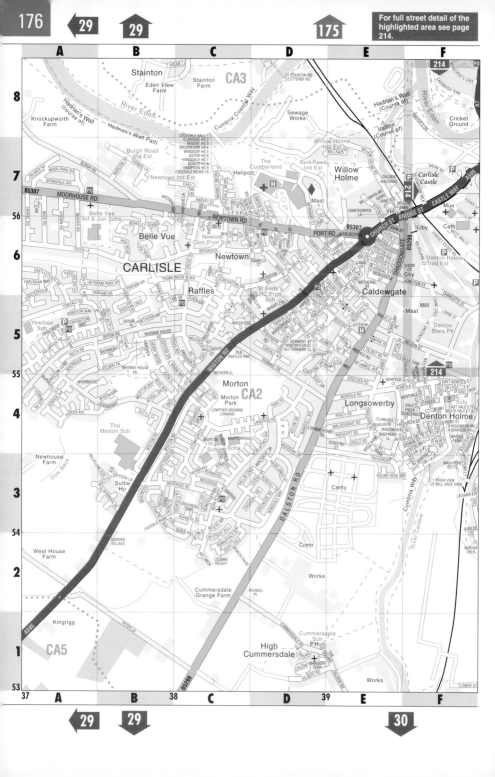

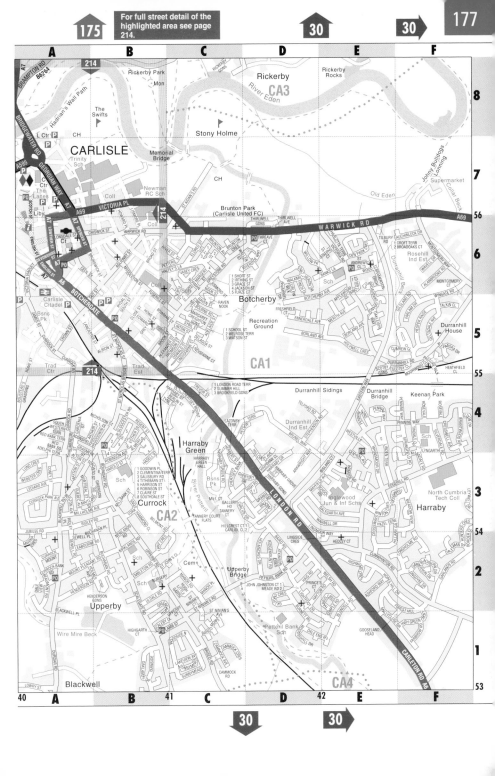

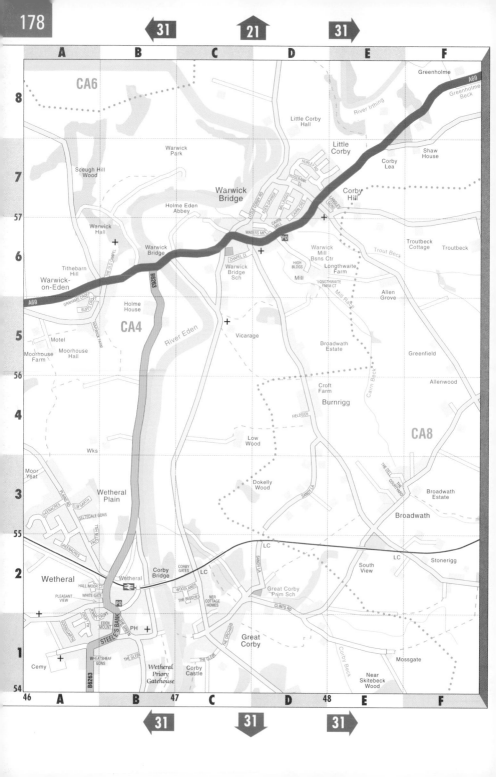

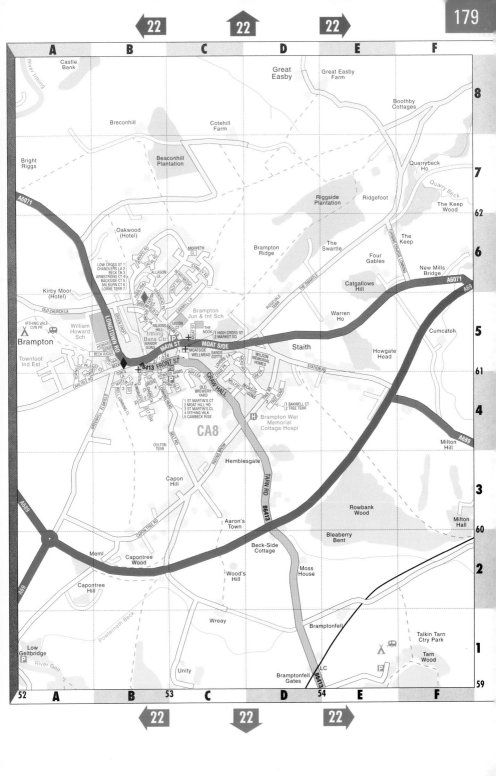

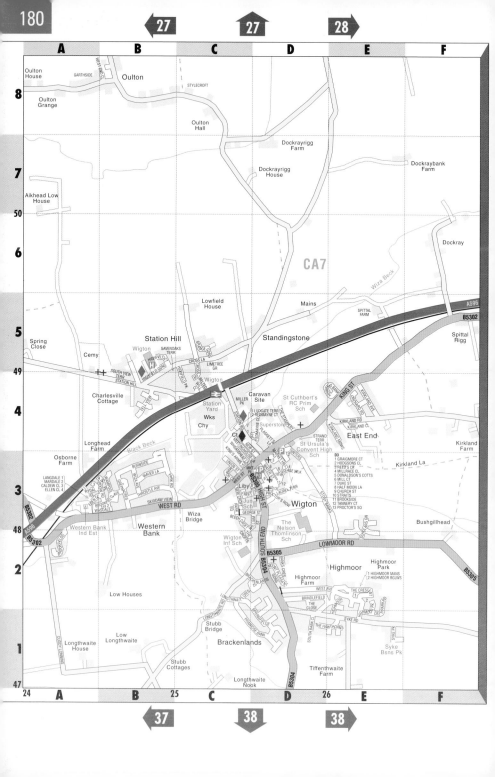

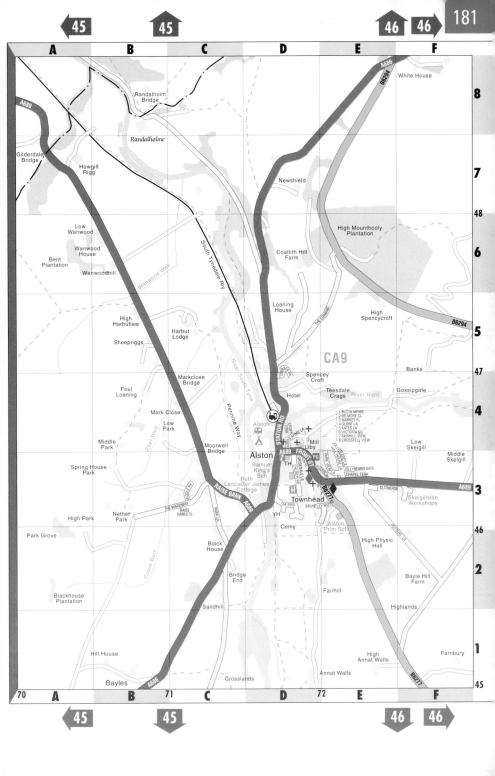

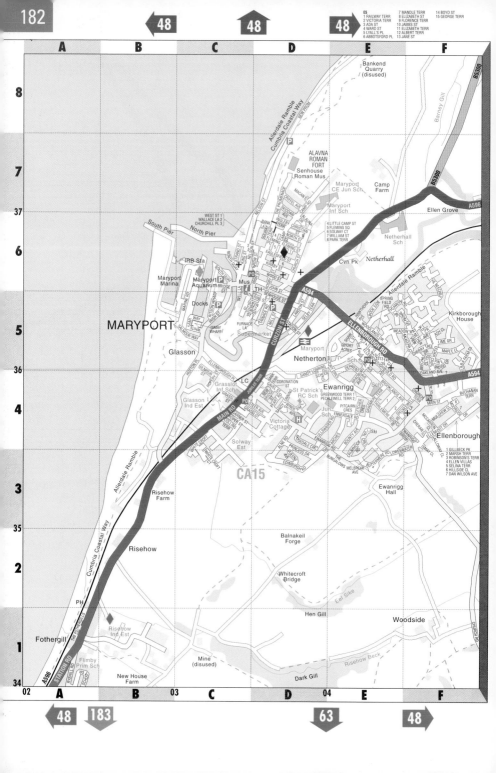

48   48   48

E5
1 RAILWAY TERR
2 VICTORIA TERR
3 ADA ST
4 WARD ST
5 LYALL'S PL
6 ABBOTSFORD PL

7 MANDLE TERR
8 ELIZABETH ST
9 FLORENCE TERR
10 JAMES ST
11 ELIZABETH TERR
12 ALBERT TERR
13 JANE ST

14 BOYD ST
15 GEORGE TERR

Bankend
Quarry
(disused)

ALAVNA
ROMAN
FORT
Senhouse
Roman Mus

Camp
Farm

Maryport
CE Jun Sch

Ellen Grove

Maryport
Inf Sch

Netherhall
Sch

South Pier
North Pier

WEST ST 1
WALLACE LA 2
CHURCHILL PL 3

4 LITTLE CAMP ST
5 FLEMING SQ
6 SOLWAY CT
7 WILLIAM ST
8 PARK TERR

Cvn Pk   Netherhall

IRB Sta

Maryport
Marina

Maryport
Aquarium

Kirkborough
House

Docks

MARYPORT

FURNACE

Supermarket

Maryport

Glasson

Netherton

Allerdale Ramble

SPRING
FIELD

SHORT
ACRES

Ellenborough

St Patrick's
RC Sch

Coronation
St

GREENWOOD TERR 1
PECKLEWELL TERR 2

Ewanrigg

Victoria
Cottage

Solway
Est

PITCAIRN
CRES

1 GILLBECK PK
2 MARSH TERR
3 ROBINSON'S TERR
4 ELLEN VILLAS
5 SELINA TERR
6 HILLSIDE CL
7 DAN WILSON AVE

THE
BUNGALOWS
MELBREAK
AVE

Ewanrigg
Hall

CA15

Risehow
Farm

Balnakeil
Forge

Whitecroft
Bridge

Hen Gill

Woodside

Risehow

Fothergill

PH

Risehow
Ind Est

Flimby
Prim Sch

New House
Farm

Mine
(disused)

Dark Gill

Risehow Beck

48   183   63   48

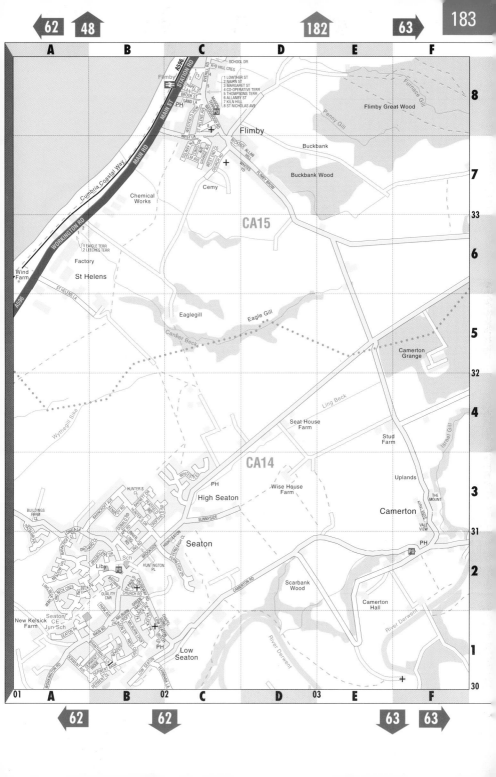

A B C D E F

8

Flimby Great Wood

Penny Gill

Furnace Gill

SCHOOL DR
RYE HILL CRES
WYTHBURN

Flimby

STATION RD
A596
MAIN ST
MAIN RD
PH
SAND LA
BROOK ST
CHAPEL LA
WEST LA

1 LOWTHER ST
2 NAIRN ST
3 MARGARET ST
4 CO-OPERATIVE TERR
5 THOMPSONS TERR
6 ALLANBY ST
7 KILN HILL
8 ST NICHOLAS AVE

Flimby

Buckbank

7

Cumbria Coastal Way

WORKINGTON RD

WEST LA
WEST END CL

BECKSIDE
ALLAN HILL
WYTES TO
TUMBY BROW
CHURCH LA
Cemy

Buckbank Wood

CA15

33

6

1 EAGLE TERR
2 LEECHS TERR

Factory

A596

Chemical
Works

Wind
Farm

St Helens

ST HELENS LA

Eaglegill

Eagle Gill

Canker Beck

Camerton
Grange

5

32

Wythegill She

Ling Beck

4

Seat House
Farm

Stud
Farm

Israel Gill

CA14

Uplands

THE
MOUNT
KIRKLANDS

3

HUNTER'S
CL
BARNGROVE AVE

PH

Wise House
Farm

Camerton

31

BUILDINGS
FARM
CL

HAVERIGG

LINGLA LA

SUNNYSIDE

High Seaton

VALE
VIEW

PH

PO

2

Liby

PO

Sch

HUNTINGTON
PL
HIGH SEATON

Seaton

CAMERTON RD

Scarbank
Wood

Camerton
Hall

River Derwent

New Kelsick
Farm

Seaton
CE
Jun·Sch

QUALITY
CNR
CHURCH RD

PH
Low
Seaton

LOW SEATON
FERNDALE CL

River Derwent

1

WORKINGTON RD
DERWENT BROW
DERWENT CL

MAIN RD

30

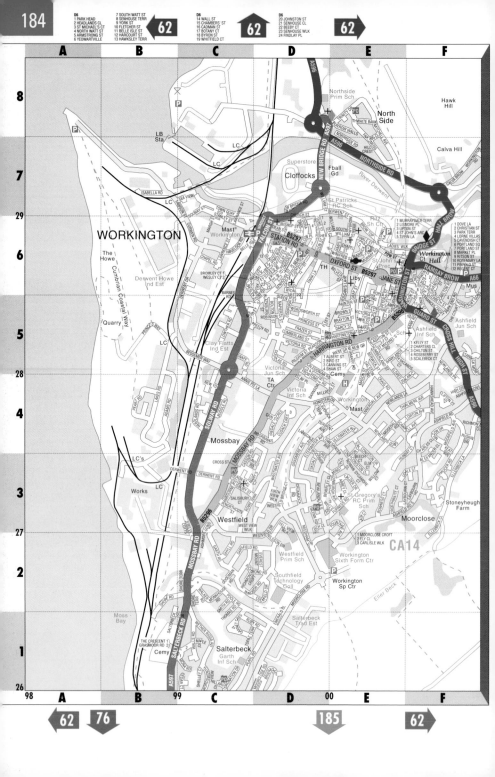

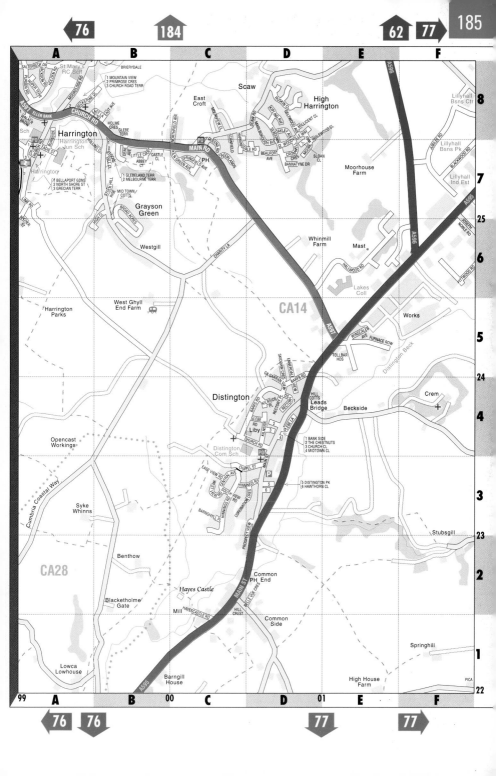

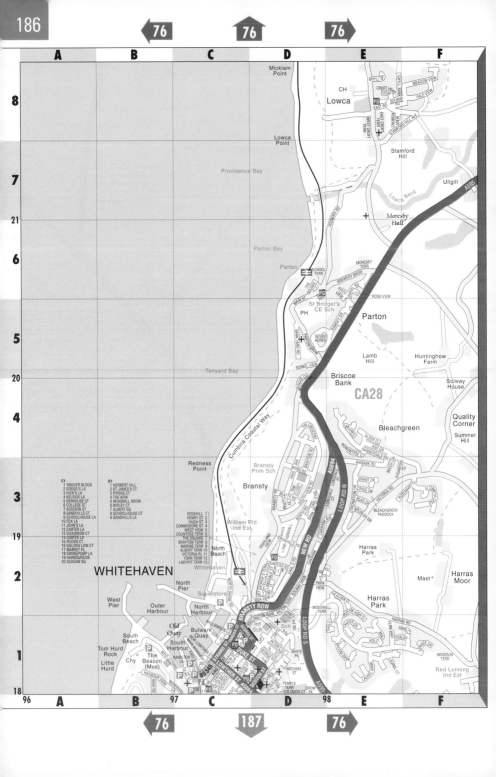

8
7
21
6
5
20
4
3
19
2
1
18

A B C D E F

Micklam
Point

CH
Lowca

GHYLL G
CROFT HEAD
VIEW
EAST CROFT
PO
SOLWAY
WEST DROFT
TERR
WORTHY
STAMFORD HILL AVE
OPYLL BANK VIEW
MEADOW VIEW
VALE VIEW

Stamford
Hill

Lowca
Point

Providence Bay

Lowca Beck

Ullgill

A595

21

Moresby
Hall

Parton Bay

Parton

SCHOOL
TERR

MORESBY
TERR

Brewery Brow

ROSS VIEW

Parton

St Bridget's
CE Sch

PH

SEVEN
ACRES

Lamb
Hill

Huntinghow
Farm

Tanyard Bay

SCREEL VIEW

Briscoe
Bank

Solway
House

CA28

Quality
Corner

Bleachgreen

Summer
Hill

Cumbria Coastal Way

Redness
Point

Bransty
Prim Sch

Bransty

THE CRESCENT

OAK CREST
ASH GR
HANNERDALE DR
ROWANTREE LA
AIKBANK RD
GRANT DR
CRAIG LN

A5094

LOOP RD N

BLEACHGREEN
PADDOCK

William Pitt
Ind Est

North
Beach

Harras
Park

WHITEHAVEN

North
Pier

Superstore

Whitehaven

Mast

Harras
Moor

West
Pier

Outer
Harbour

North
Harbour

Harras
Park

MOSSWELL
TERR

LOOP RD S

South
Beach

Old
Quay

Bulwark
Quay

BRANSTY ROW

Tom Hurd
Rock

Chy

The
Beacon
(Mus)

South
Harbour

Little
Hurd

WINDSOR
TERR

Red Lonning
Ind Est

B5345

MICHAEL
ST

TEMPLE
TERR
SOLOMON CT

CROW
PK

96 A B 97 C D 98 E F

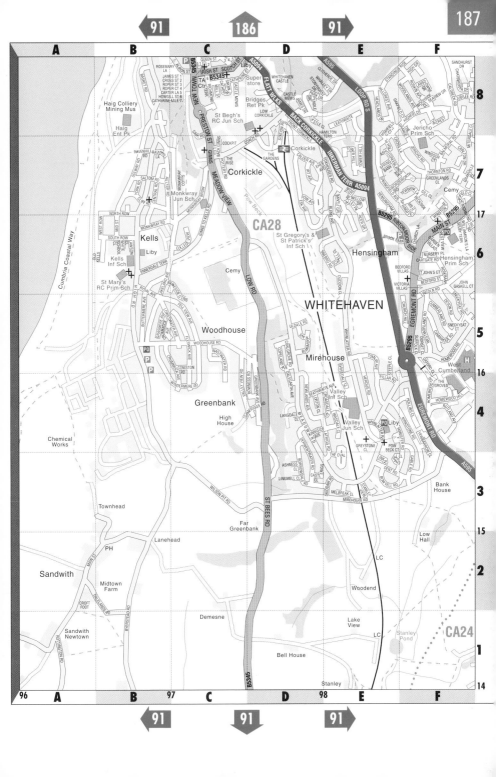

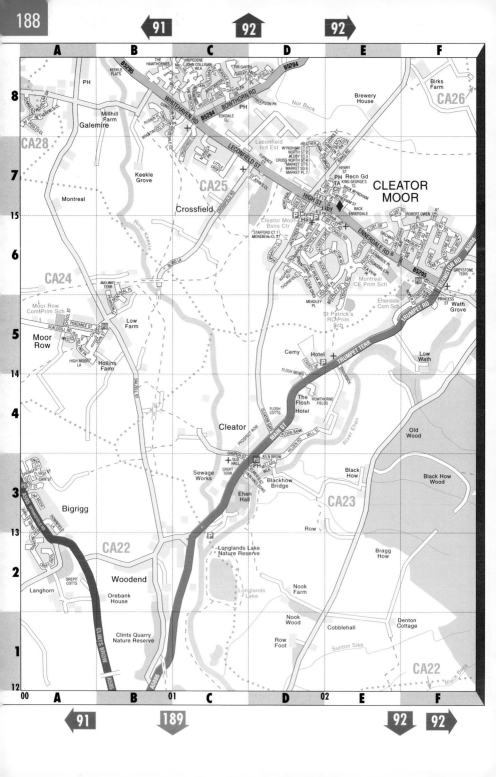

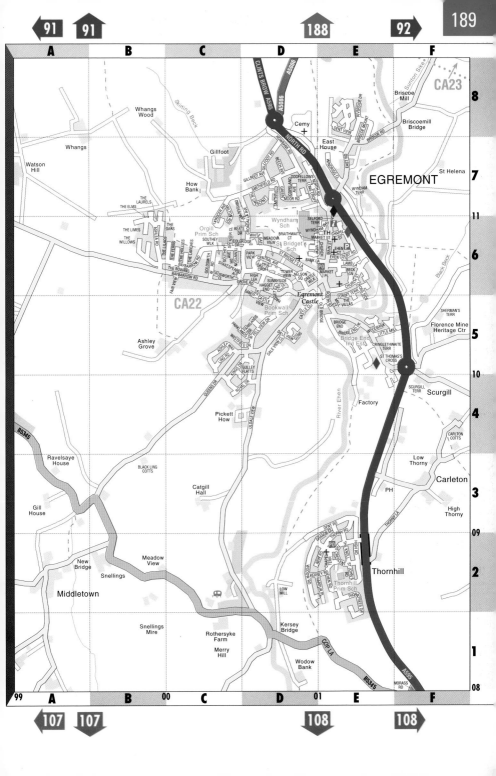

A B C D E F

CLINTS BROW
A595
A5086
NORTH RD

Whangs Wood
Skirting Beck
Whangs
Watson Hill
How Bank
Gillfoot
GILLFOOT AVE
BEECK AVE
HORMAN RD
SMITHFIELD
SMITHFIELD RD
COPELAND AVE
MOOR RD
ODDFELLOWS LA
GREEN AVE

Cemy
East House
EGREMONT
St Helena
DENT VIEW
BRISCOE RD
BRISCOE MOUNT
PARKSIDE DR
BRISCOE RD
WINDSOR RD
EAST RD
WYNDAM TERR

Briscoe Mill
Briscoemill Bridge
CA23

THE LAURELS
THE ELMS
THE LIMES
THE OAKS
THE WILLOWS
THE ROWANS
THE BEECHES
THE LARCHES
THE FIRS
THE HOLLIES
ASHLAR RD
BRIDGE VIEW
FAIR VIEW
BAYBARROW RD
BAYBARROW RD
GOLDSMITH RD
SHAKESPEARE AVE
WORDSWORTH RD
GROVE RD
CASTLE VIEW
SANDS LA
CASTLE
HAGGET END
SUNNYSIDE
HIGH SEA
TOWER VIEW
CASTLE CROFT
HIGH END
PARK VIEW
CENTRAL AVE
MEADOW VIEW
SPENCER CL
LANCASTER AVE
KEATS DR
WHITE CROFT
COLERIDGE
SOUTHEY WLK
Orgill Prim Sch
Wyndham Sch
BRAITHWAITE CT
St Bridget's Sch
BANK LA
NELSON ST
MARKET ST
SELFORD TERR
WYNDHAM ST
MARKET PL
ST BRIDGE'S T
EHEN COURT RD
LAMB LA
BECK GN
St Bridget's Sch
CHAPEL ST
CHURCH
Egremont Castle
Bookwall Prim Sch
WYDNAM
CROFT TERR
THE VILLAS
BRIDGE END
BRIDGE END
Bridge End Ind Est
WOODHAM
LITTLE MILL
CRINGLETHWAITE TERR
St Thomas's Cross
SHERMAN'S TERR
Florence Mine Heritage Ctr

CA22

Ashley Grove
ASHLEY WAY
WESTFIELD DR
KINGS ST
BOXDALE DR
GULLEY FLATTS
QUEENS DR
DALE VIEW
ULCOAT VIEW
LAIG RD
PARK LANCASTER DR
HOWGILLS
EDGEHILL
CASTLE RD
Pickett How
ULDALE VIEW

River Ehen
Factory
Scurgill
SCURGILL TERR
Low Thorny
Carleton
PH
High Thorny
CARLTON COTTS

B5345
Ravelsaye House
BLACK LING COTTS
Catgill Hall
Gill House
New Bridge
Meadow View
Snellings
Middletown
Snellings Mire
Rothersyke Farm
Merry Hill
Kersey Bridge
Wodow Bank
Low Mill

DENT RD
THORNY RD
GRAHAM RD
NEW RD
KERBY RD
CHERRY RD
WOODOW
KELK RD
HARPER RD
THE KNOTT
TARN RD
HIGH HILL
THORNY LA
THORNHILL
Thornhill Prim Sch
COP LA
A595
B5345
MORASS RD

09
08

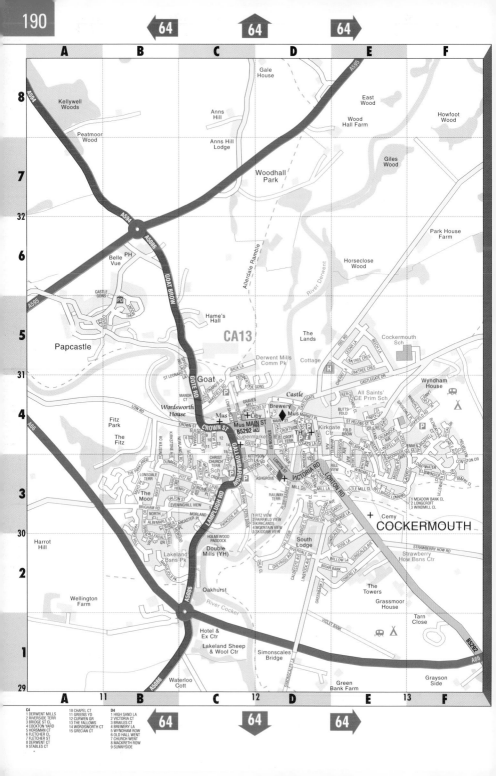

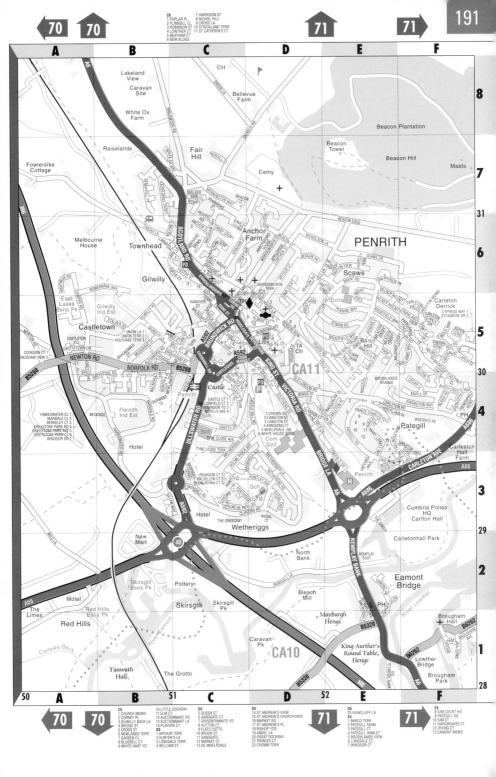

C6
1 POPLAR PL
2 PLIMSOLL CL
3 ROBINSON ST
4 LOWTHER CT
5 BEATHAM CT
6 NEW BLDGS
7 HARRISON ST
8 NICHOL HILL
9 CROSS LA
10 STRICKLAND TERR
11 ST CATHERIN'S CT

PENRITH

CA11

CA10

C5
1 CHURCH MEWS
2 CORNEY PL
3 GILWILLY BACK LA
4 BRIDGE ST
5 CROSS ST
6 NEWLANDS TERR
7 GARDEN CL
8 BLUEBELL CT
9 WHITE HART YD
10 LITTLE DOCKRAY
11 ELM CT
12 AUCTIONMART RD
13 AUCTIONMART LA
14 PLAYERS CT

D5
1 ARTHUR TERR
2 HUNTER'S LA
3 LONSDALE ST
4 WILLIAM ST

D5
5 QUEEN ST
6 SANDGATE CT
7 GROSENTHWAITE YD
8 HUTTON CT
9 FLATS COTTS
10 BROOK ST
11 SANDGATE
12 MARKET CT
13 DE WHELPDALE

D5
14 ST ANDREW'S VIEW
15 ST ANDREW'S CHURCHYARD
16 MARKET SQ
17 ST ANDREW'S PL
18 BISHOP YDS
19 ANGEL LA
20 GREAT DOCKRAY
21 PRINCES CT
22 CROWN TERR

D5
23 ROWCLIFFE LA

E4
1 BARCO TERR
2 PATEGILL FARM
3 PATEGILL CT
4 PATEGILL HAMLET
5 BROOKLANDS VIEW
6 LONSDALE CT
7 WINDSOR CT

E4
8 SIM COURT HO
9 PATEGILL SQ
10 SIM CT
11 HARGREAVES CT
12 IRVING CT
13 EAMONT MEWS

C4
1 CROWN SQ
2 LANGTON ST
3 LANGTON CT
4 ARNISONS CT
5 WHELPDALE HO
6 WHITE HOUSE GDNS

C4
CASTLE CT 1
FALLOWFIELD CT 2
ROBINSON YD 3
NEVILLE AVE 4

A5
UNION LA 1
UNION TERR 2
HOLYOAKE TERR 3

A4
COOKSON CT 1
SKIDDAW VIEW 2

A4
HAWESWATER CL 1
MARDALE CL 2
BERKELEY CT 3
GREYSTOKE PARK RD 4
GREYSTOKE PARK AVE 5
GREYSTOKE PARK CL 6
WINDSOR DR 7

C3
PEARSON CT 1
HALVELLYN CT 2
BLENCATHRA CT 3

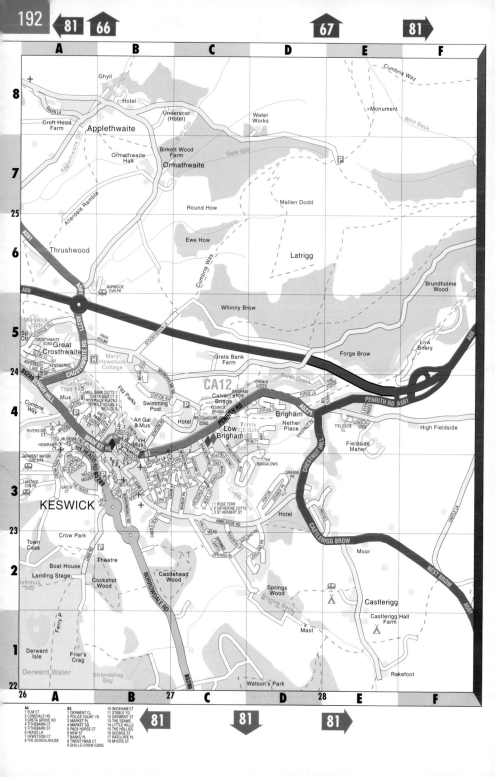

KESWICK

CA12

A4
1 ELM CT
2 LONSDALE HO
3 GRETA GROVE HO
4 TITHEBARN CT
5 TITHEBARN ST
6 HEADS LA
7 HEWETSON CT
8 THE SCHOOLHOUSE

B3
1 DERWENT CL
2 POLICE COURT YD
3 MARKET PL
4 MARKET SQ
5 PACK HORSE CT
6 NEW ST
7 BANKS PL
8 TWENTYMAN CT
9 SHU-LE-CROW GDNS

10 WICKHAM CT
11 STABLE YD
12 DERWENT ST
13 THE SEAMS
14 LITTLE HILLS
15 THE HOLLIES
16 GEORGE ST
17 RATCLIFFE PL
18 MYERS ST

1 ROSE TERR
2 CATHERINE COTTS
3 ST HERBERT ST

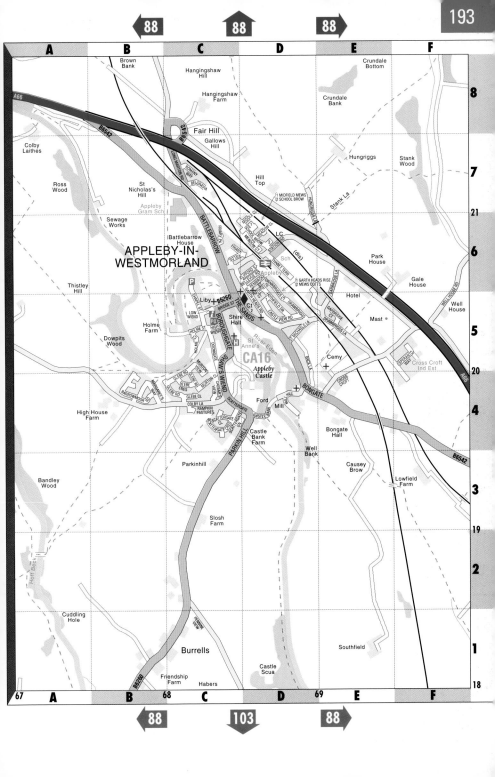

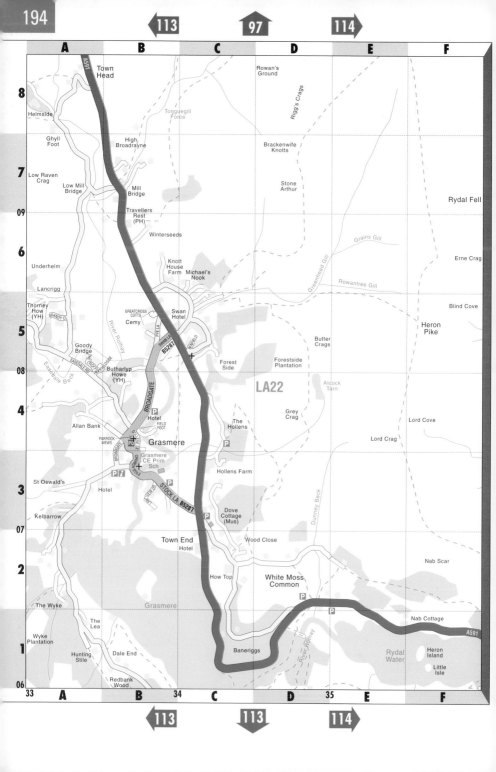

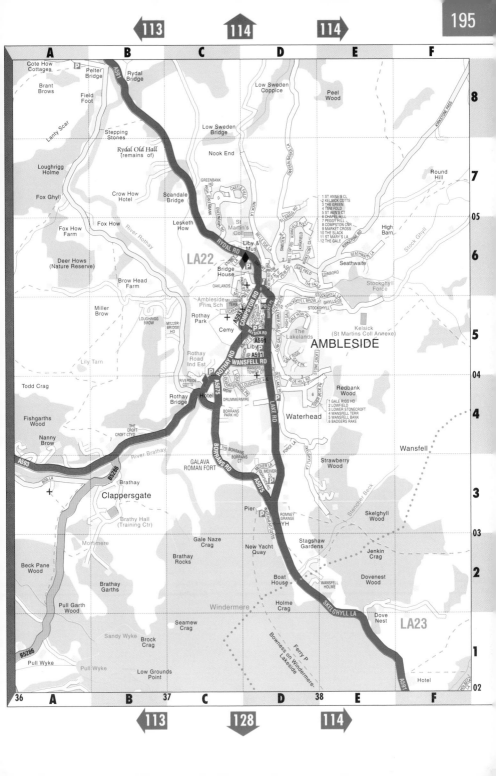

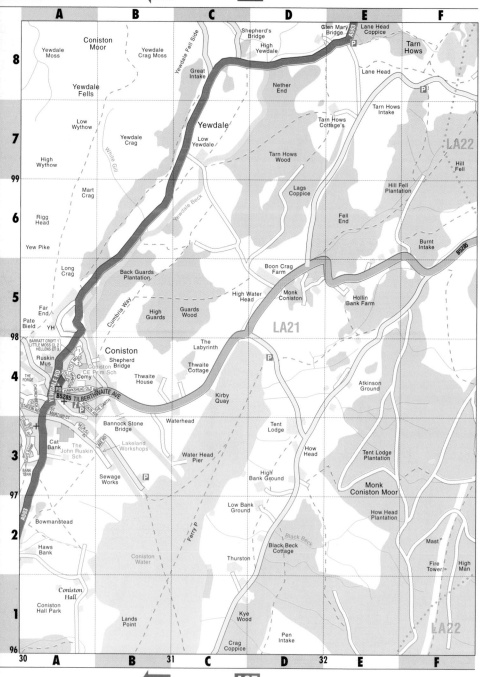

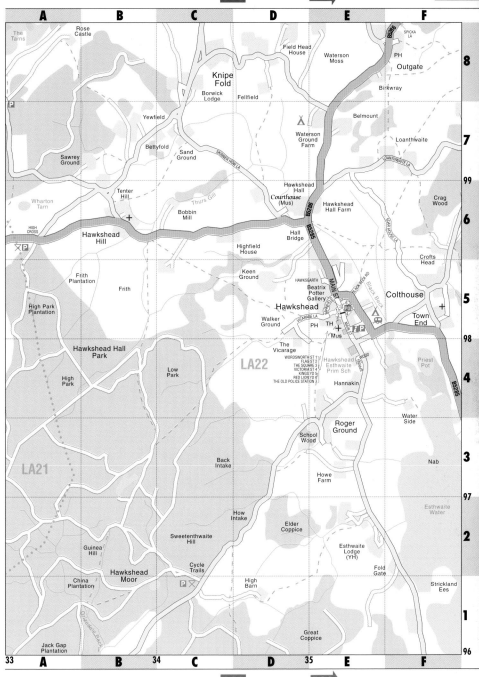

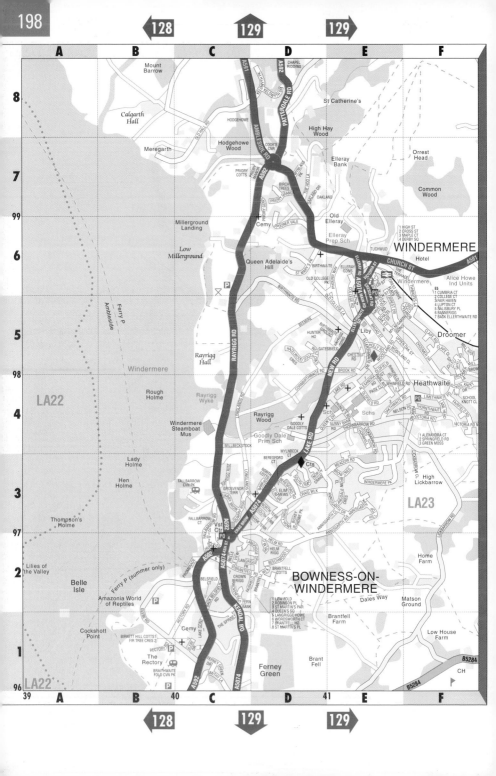

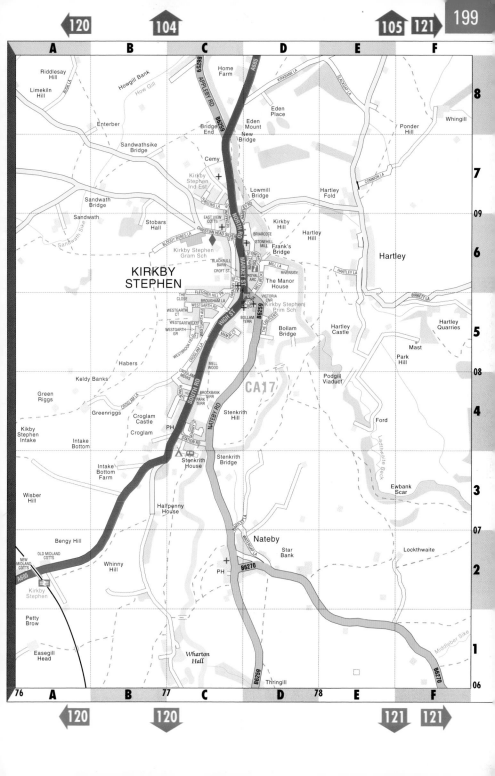

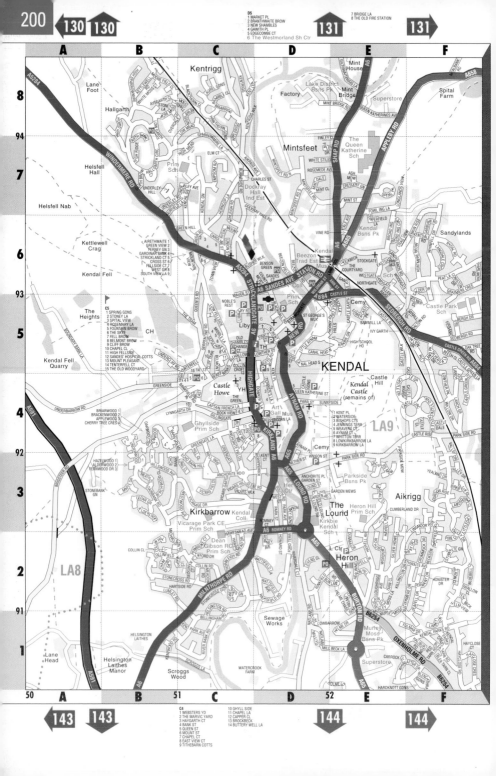

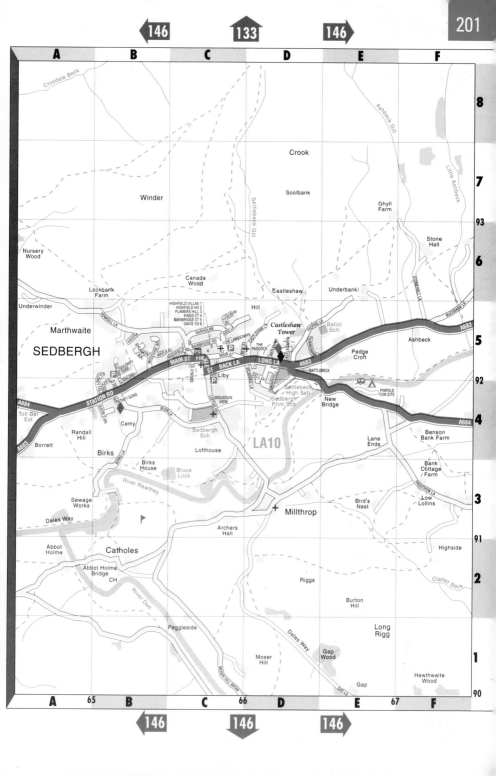

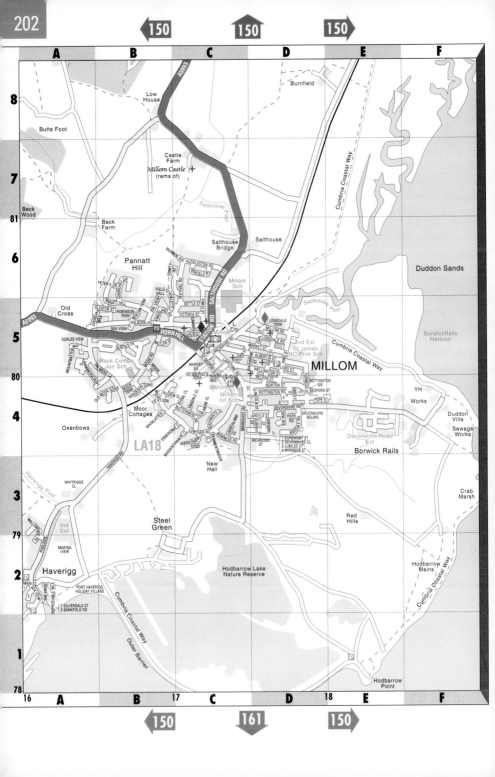

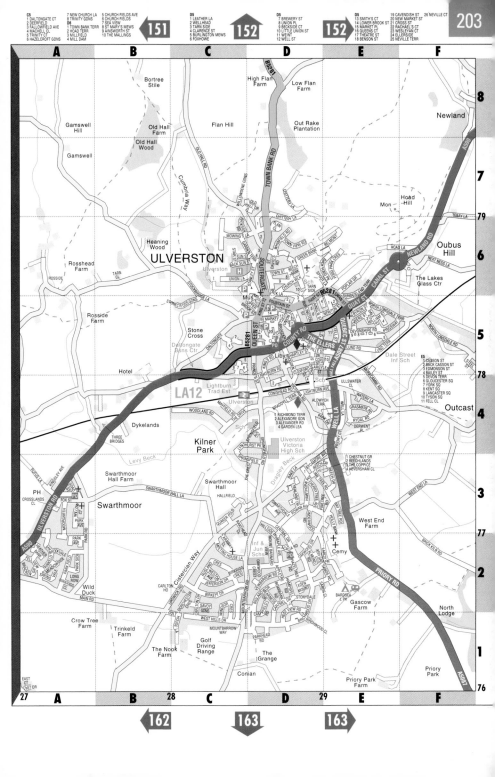

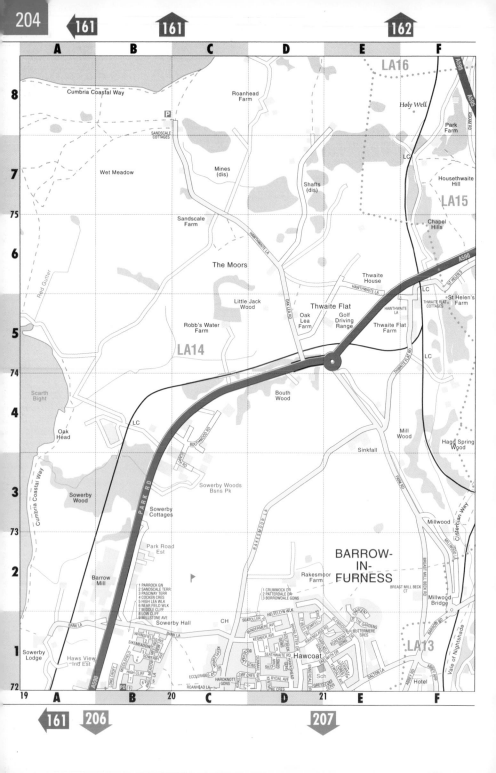

C5
1 HOPE ST
2 LANCASTER ST
3 ASHWORTH ST
4 JAMES TERR
5 BRIDGE HOUSE
6 CAMBRIDGE CT
7 WESLEY CT
8 DEVONSHIRE ST
9 PORTER ST
10 BROUGHTON LODGE
11 FELL CROFT
12 TUDOR SQ
13 CROWN MEWS
14 VICTORIA TERR
15 STOREY SQ

162
162

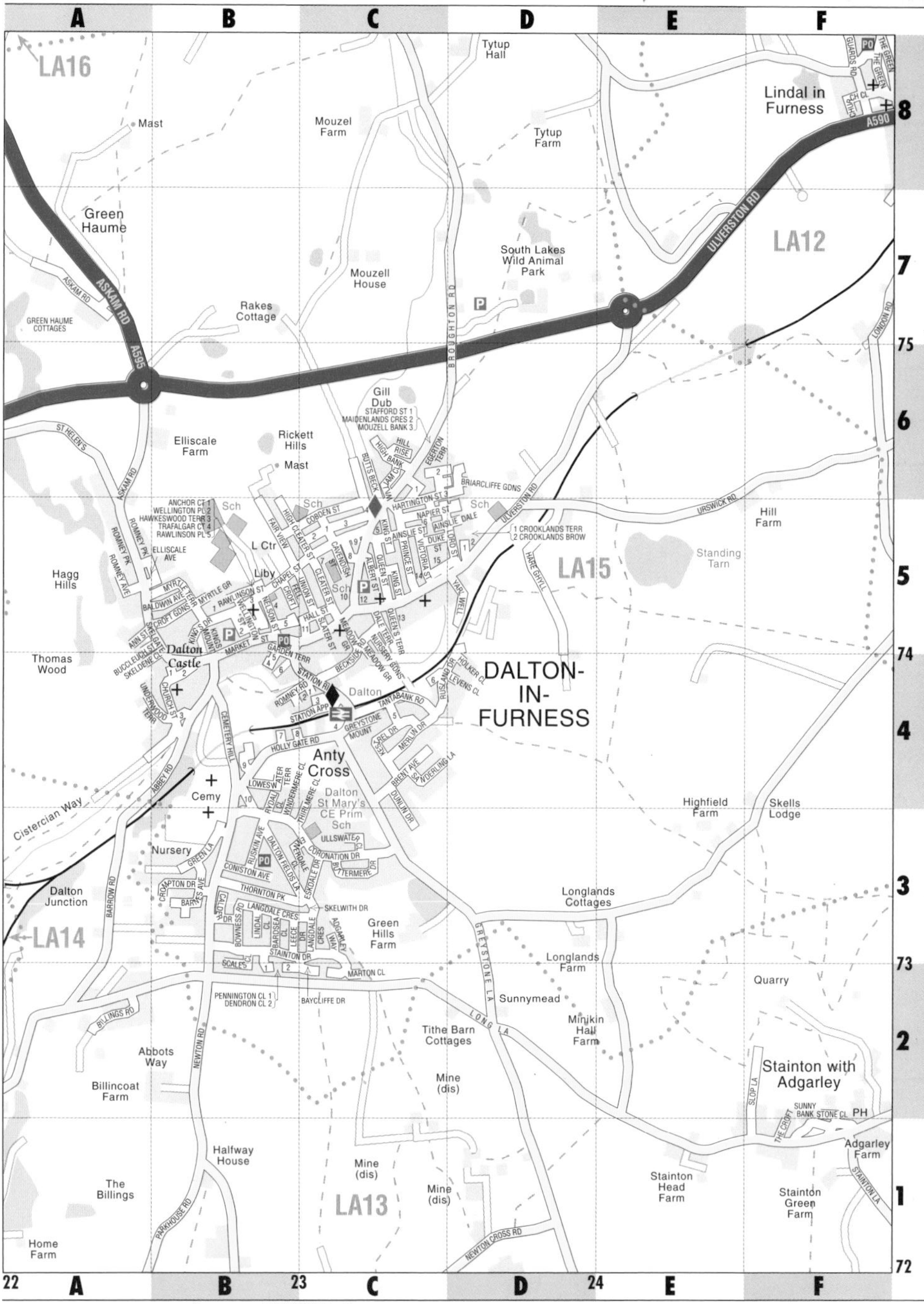
A
B
C
D
E
F
LA16
Mast
Tytup Hall
Mouzel Farm
Tytup Farm
Lindal in Furness
A590
Green Haume
ULVERSTON RD
LA12
South Lakes Wild Animal Park
Mouzell House
BROUGHTON RD
Rakes Cottage
ASKAM RD
A595
GREEN HAUME COTTAGES
Gill Dub
Ellisscale Farm
Rickett Hills
Mast
Sch
L Ctr
Liby
Hagg Hills
Hill Farm
Standing Tarn
LA15
Thomas Wood
Dalton Castle
Dalton
DALTON-IN-FURNESS
Anty Cross
Cemy
Cistercian Way
Dalton St Mary's CE Prim Sch
Nursery
Highfield Farm
Skells Lodge
Dalton Junction
LA14
Longlands Cottages
Green Hills Farm
Longlands Farm
Quarry
Sunnymead
Minjkin Hall Farm
Tithe Barn Cottages
Abbots Way
Billincoat Farm
Mine (dis)
Stainton with Adgarley
Halfway House
Mine (dis)
Mine (dis)
LA13
Stainton Head Farm
Stainton Green Farm
Adgarley Farm
The Billings
Home Farm
NEWTON CROSS RD
LONG LA
GREYSTONE LA
NEWTON RD
PARKHOUSE RD
BILLINGS RD
BARROW RD
URSWICK RD
22
23
24
72
73
74
75
1
2
3
4
5
6
7
8

B4
1 CASTLE ST
2 MARKET PL
3 GOOSE GREEN
4 GLENFIELD RD
5 HAMILTON TERR
6 GARDEN LEA
7 OLIVE CL
8 JUNIPER CL
9 DEVOKE WATER GDNS
10 DALTON FIELDS LA

C4
1 STATION TERR
2 GROVE ST
3 STATION CL
4 RAILWAY TERR
5 SISKIN AVE
6 GRAYTHWAITE CL

207
162
162

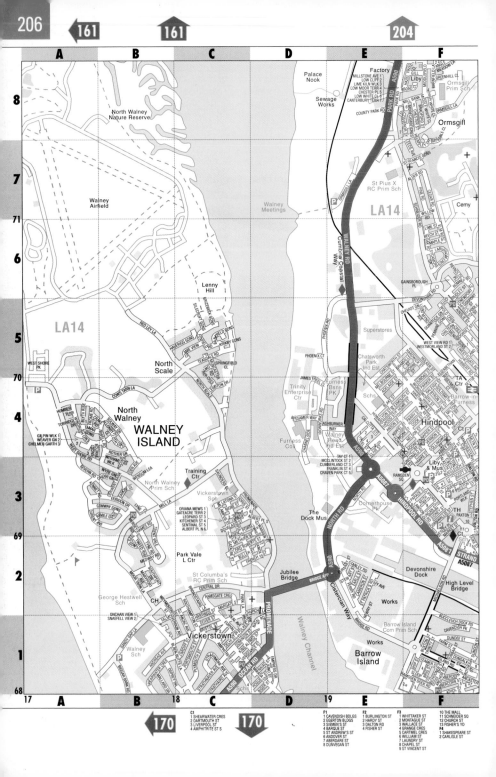

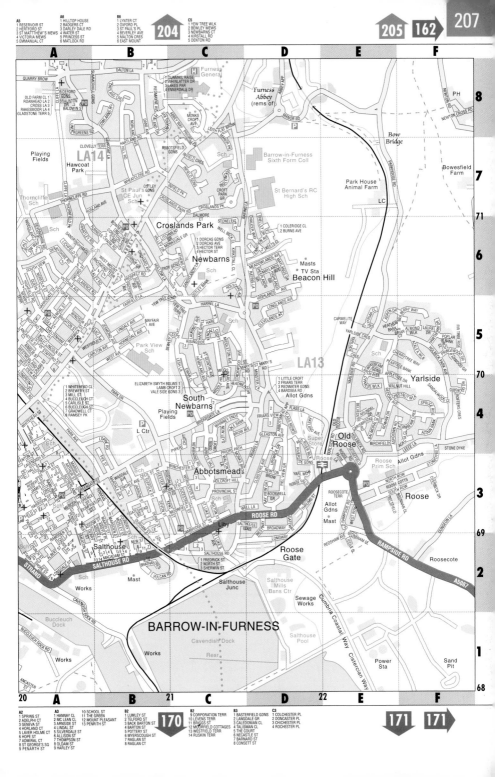

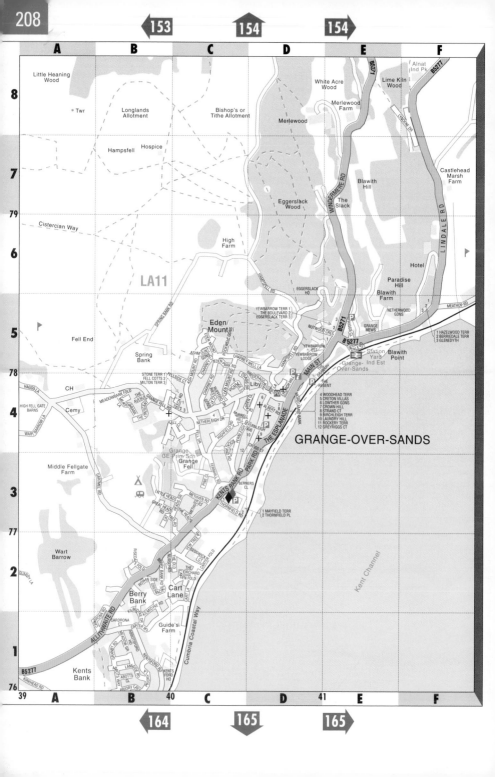

153 154 154

A **B** **C** **D** **E** **F**

8

Little Heaning
Wood

Twr

Longlands
Allotment

Bishop's or
Tithe Allotment

White Acre
Wood

Merlewood
Farm

Lime Kiln
Wood

Alnat
Ind Pk

Merlewood

7

Hampsfell Hospice

WINDERMERE RD

Blawith
Hill

Castlehead
Marsh
Farm

LINDALE RD

79

Cistercian Way

Eggerslack
Wood

The
Slack

6

High
Farm

Hotel

LA11

Paradise
Hill

Blawith
Farm

NETHERWOOD
GDNS

MEATHOP RD

5

Fell End

Eden
Mount

YEWBARROW TERR 1
THE BOULEVARD 2
EGGERSLACK TERR 3

NUTWOOD CRES

B5277

GRANGE
MEWS

B 5277

1 HAZELWOOD TERR
2 BERRIEDALE TERR
3 GLENEDYTH

Spring
Bank

YEWBARROW
LODGE

Station
Ind Est

Blawith
Point

78

CH

STONE TERR 1
FELL COTTS 2
MILTON TERR 3

Liby

MAIN ST

Grange-
Over-Sands

THE
REGENT

Cemy

MEADOWBANK FOLD

NETHERLEIGH CT

PO

4 WOODHEAD TERR
5 CRETON VILLAS
6 LOWTHER GDNS
7 CROWN HILL
8 STRAND CT
9 BIRCHLEIGH TERR
10 LAUNDRY HILL
11 ROCKERY TERR
12 GREYRIGGS CT

4

HIGH FELL GATE
BARNS

HAGGS LA

WA?L

THE ESPLANADE

GRANGE-OVER-SANDS

Grange
GE Prim Sch

Grange
Fell

3

Middle Fellgate
Farm

KENTS BANK RD

PARK RD

BERNERS
CL

1 MAYFIELD TERR
2 THORNFIELD PL

77

Wart
Barrow

Kent Channel

2

QUARRY LA

Berry
Bank

Cart
Lane

THE
ORCHARD

OVEN FOLD

ALLITHWAITE RD

Guide's
Farm

Cumbria Coastal Way

1

B5277

Kents
Bank

KENTS
FORD RD

76

KIRKHEAD RD

A **B** **C** **D** **E** **F**

39 40 41

164 165 165

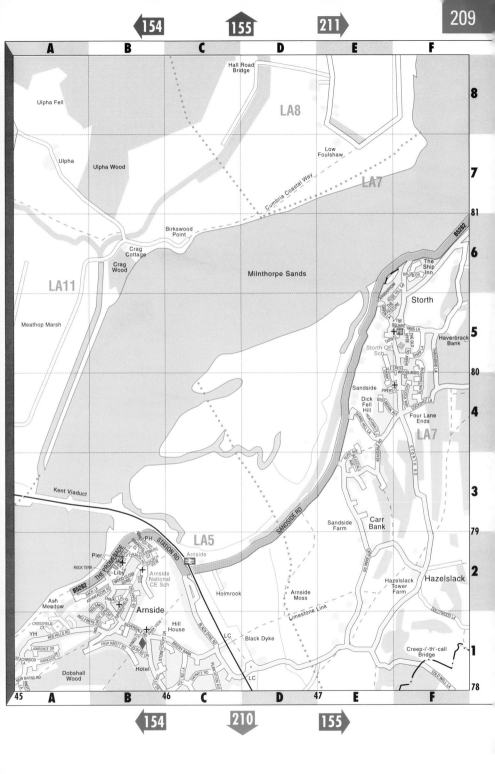

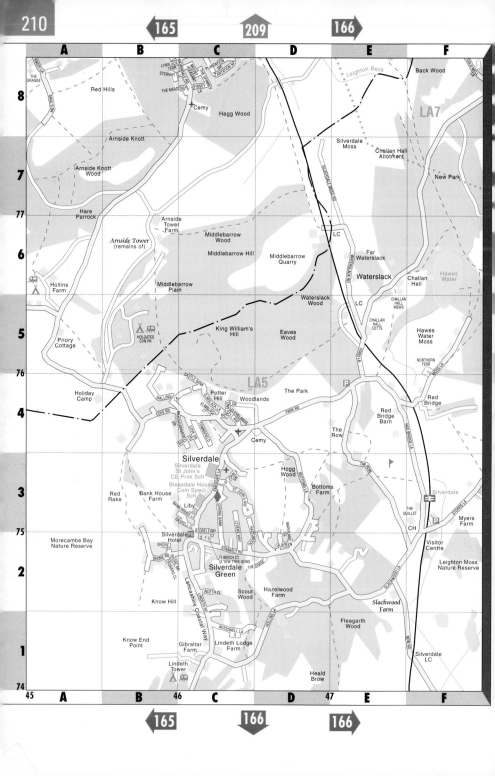

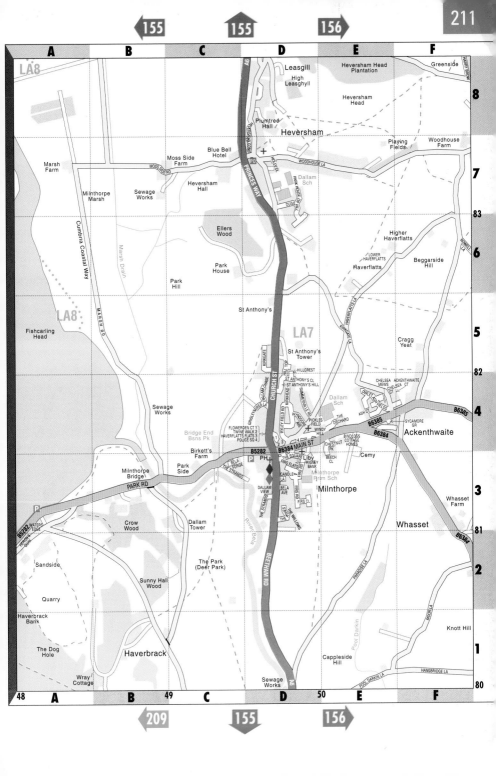

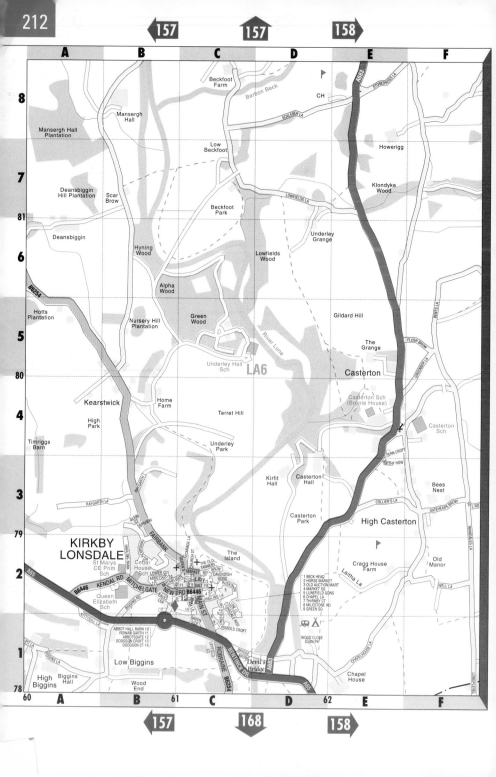

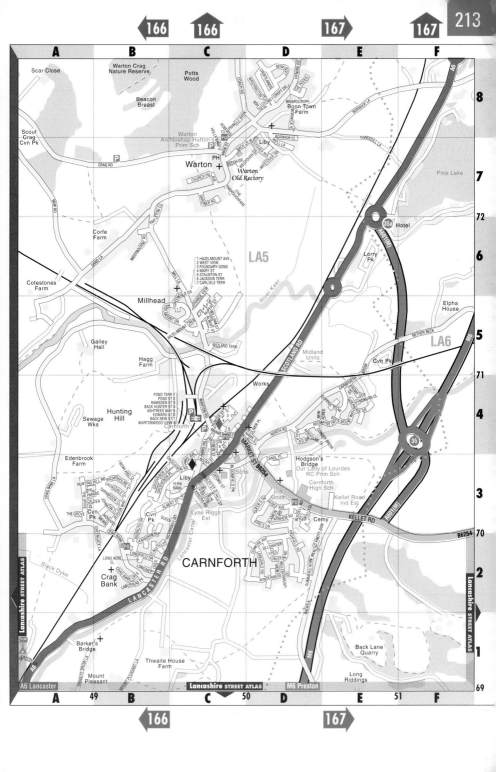

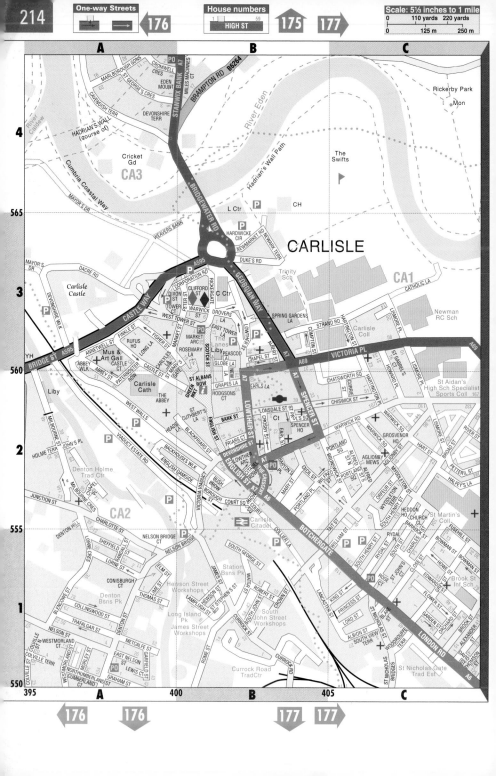

B3	C1	C2	6 WESTPARK TERR	D2
1 GORDON ST	1 HEYWOOD PL	1 ASSEMBLY ST	7 FRANKLIN PL	1 CUMBERLAND ST
2 MEWS LA	2 WOODSIDE TERR	2 SOUTH & TOWNHEAD HO	8 WALLDALE PK	2 MURRAY PL
3 WELL ST	3 ROSELAND TERR	3 BURNS CT	9 LINDEN GR	3 ST MICHAEL'S TERR
4 MARKET SQ		4 CLERKHILL	10 SWANS VENNEL	4 PARK TERR
5 HIGH ST		5 NITH ST	11 OCTOCENTENARY WLK	5 NITHSDALE MILLS

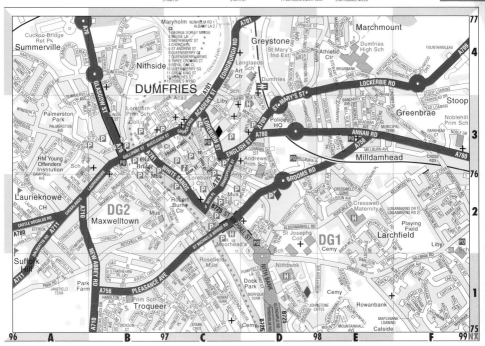

Dumfries

Academy St	C3	Burns House Mus*	C2
Airds Ave	F2	Burns St	C2
Airds Dr	F2	Caledonian Pl	F1
Albany La	C4	Calside Rd	F1
Albert Rd	A2	Campbell Ave	E3
Alder Ct	F1	Cardoness St	E3
Aldermanhill Rd	D2	Cargen Ave	E3
Alexandra Dr	A3	Carnegie Dr	D4
Annan Rd	E3	Cartha Pl	F1
Ardwall Rd	D3	Cartha Rd	F1
Armour Dr	A3	Cassalands	A2
Arnott Terr	C1	Castle Douglas Rd	A1
Art Ctr	C4	Castle St	C3
Ashfield Dr	A3	Catherine St	C3
Aspen Cres	E1	Caul View	B2
Assembly St 1	C2	Charlotte St	C3
Athletic Ctr	B1	Charnwood Gdns	E3
Atkinson Rd	B1	Charnwood Rd	D3
Averill Cres	B1	Church Cres	C3
Babbington Gdns	A4	Church Pl 4	C3
Ballater Ave	E4	Church St	C3
Balliol Ave	B1	Clerkhill 4	C2
Balmoral Ave	E4	College Ct	E3
Balmoral Rd	E4	College Rd	A4
Banchory Ave	E3	College St	A4
Banc Loaning	E4	Corbelly Hill	B2
Bankend Rd	D1	Corberry Ave	B2
Bank St	C3	Corberry Mews	B2
Barkerland Ave	E2	Corberry Pk	B2
Barn Slaps	D2	Corberry Terr	C2
Barnton Dr	F2	Cornwall Mount	D3
Barnton Pl	F2	Craigs Dr	F1
Barnton Rd	F2	Craigs Loaning	E1
Barrie Ave	D2	Craigs Rd	F1
Beech Ave	A4	Crathie Ave	E1
Bell Vue St	E2	Cresswell Ave	D2
Birch Wlk	E2	Cresswell Gdns	D2
Birchwood Ave	F4	Cresswell Hill	D2
Birchwood Cres	F4	Cresswell Maternity	
Birchwood Pl	E4	Hosp	E2
Birchwood Rd	F4	Cross Rds	F3
Braemar Ave	E3	Cuckoo Bridge	A1
Brewery St	B3	Cumberland St 1	D2
Briarbank	E4	Dalbeattie Rd	A1
Brodie Ave	C1	Darlison Ave	E1
Brooke St	C3	David St	D2
Broomlands Dr	B1	Dickson Ct	A2
Brooms Rd	C3	Dobie's Wynd 13	C2
Buccleuch St	B3	Dockhead	C2
Burns St 3	C2	Dock Park	D1

Doon Terr	A3	HM Young Offenders'	
Dumfries High Sch	E4	Institution	A3
Dumfries Mus*	B2	Holm Ave	C1
Dumfries Station	C3	Hoods Loaning	C1
Eastfield Rd	C2	Howat Terr	C1
Edinburgh Rd	C4	Howgate St	B3
Elderbank Pl	C1	Huntingdon Ave	D4
Ellisland Dr	A3	Huntingdon Rd	D4
Elmbank Dr	A3	Huntingdon Sq	D4
English St	C3	Ingleston Pl	D4
Essex Park Dr	C1	Innerkip Dr	C1
Essex Park Meuse	C1	Irish St	C3
Ettric Ct	F2	Irving St	C3
Fairfield Cres	F2	James Ave	A3
Forsyth St	B4	Janefield Av	A1
Fountainbleau	A1	Janefield Gdns	A1
Franklin Pl 7	C2	Janefield Terr	A1
Friars Vennel	C3	Johnstone Cotts	D1
Galloway St	B3	Johnstone Pk	D1
George Douglas Dr	B1	Kellwood Pl	F2
George St	B3	Kellwood Rd	F2
George Street		Kingholm Rd	D1
Meuse 1	B2	King St	B3
Georgetown Rd	F3	Kirkland Ct	F1
Gillbrae	E3	Kirkland Pl	F1
Gillbrae Rd	F1	Kirkland Rd	F1
Glasgow St	B4	Kirkowens St	E3
Glebe St	D2	Kirkpatrick Ct	C1
Glebe Terr	D2	Kirkpatrick Meuse	C1
Glencaple Rd	D2	Langlands	C4
Gloucester Ave	A4	Langlands St	D3
Goldie Ave	A4	Larchbank Pl	F1
Goldie Cres	B4	Larchfield Rd	C2
Golf Ave	A2	Laurieknowe	B2
Gordon St 1	B3	Laurieston Ave	A2
Grant Ct	D1	Leafield Gdns	D3
Great King St 11	C3	Leafield Rd	D3
Greenacre Dr	D1	LibyAirds Ct	F2
Greenbrae Loaning	E3	Liby Dobie's	
Greenbrae Pl	E3	Wynd 13	C3
Greyfriars' St 3	C3	Lime Tree Wlk	C3
Greystone Ave	D4	Linden Gr 9	E2
Greystone Cres	D4	Lindsey Pl	E4
Hamilton Ave	E2	Lochar Dr	E2
Hardthorn Ave	B1	Lochfield Rd	A1
Hardthorn Cres	B1	Loch Rd	A4
Henry St	D2	Lochvale Dr	E2
Hermitage Ave	A2	Lockerbie Rd	E3
Hermitage Dr	A2	Loreburn Ctr	C2
Heywood Pl 1	C2	Loreburn St	C3
High St 5	C3	Loreburn Prim Sch	B3
Hill Ave	B1	Lovers' Wlk	C3
Hill St	B2	McAughtrie Ct	B2

McKenzie Terr	C1	Palmerston Ave	A3
McKie Ave	E2	Palmerston Dr	A3
McLellan St	D2	Palmerston Park	A3
Makbrar Rd	F1	Park Farm	A1
Maplebank		Parkhead Ct	A1
Loaning	E1	Parkhead Dr	F3
Marchmount Ave	E4	Parkhead Loaning	F3
Marchmount Dr	E4	Park La	B3
Marchmount Rd	E4	Park Rd	A3
Market Sq 4	B3	Park St	A2
Martin Ave	B3	Park Terr 4	B2
Maxwell St	B2	Picket Cross	D1
Meuse La 2	B3	Pleasance Ave	A3
Mews La 2	B3	Pleasance Cotts	A3
Millbrae St	A2	Pleasance Pk	A3
Millburn Ave	E3	Police HQ	D3
Millburn Pl	D3	Portland Dr	B4
Mill Rd	D3	Priestlands Dr	A1
Moat Rd	C1	Primrose St	B2
Moffat Rd	D4	Pumpfield La	C1
Montague St	D3	Queensberry Ct 6	C3
Moorhead's	C2	Queensberry	
Mossgiel Ave	A3	Mews 7	C3
Mountainhall Ave	E1	Queensberry Sq 10	C3
Mountainhall Ct	E1	Queensberry St	C3
Mountainhall Pk	E1	Queensberry View	C3
Mountainhall St	E1	Queen St	C3
Munches St 12	C3	Rae St	C3
Municipal Terr	C3	Retail Pk	C4
Murray Pl 2	D2	Richmond Ave	B1
Nellieville Terr	C1	Riverside Ct	B3
Nelson St	A3	Robert Burns Ctr*	B2
New Abbey Rd	B2	Robertson Ave	D1
Newall Terr	C3	Robison Dr	B3
Nith Ave	B3	Rosefield Mills	C1
Nithbank	D1	Rosefield Rd	C1
Nith Bank	D1	Rosemount St	C1
Nithbank Ave	B4	Rosevale Rd	C1
Nith Pl	C2	Rosevale St	C1
Nithsdale Mills 5	B4	Rotchell Gdns	B2
Nithside Ave	B4	Rotchell Pk	B2
Nith St 5	C2	Rotchell Rd	B2
Noble Gr	F3	Rowanbank	E1
Noblehill Prim Sch	D1	Rowanbank Ave	E1
Norfolk Terr	D1	Rowanbank Cres	E1
North		Rowanbank Pl	E1
Laurieknowe Pl	C4	Royal Oak Cl 9	C2
Nunholm Rd	C4	Ryedale Ct	C1
Nutberry Pl	C1	Ryedale Rd	C1
Octocentenary		Ryedale Terr	C1
Wlk 11	C2	Ryedale Villas	B1
Old Bridge	B2		
Old Bridge House			
Mus*	B3		

St Andrew's Prim		
Sch	D3	
St Andrew St 5	C2
St Cuthbert's Ave	C2
St Josephs Coll	D2
St Mary's Ind Est	D3
St Mary's St	D3
St Michael's	
Bridge Rd	C2
St Michael St	C2
St Michael's	
Terr 3	D2
School La	A2
Shakespeare St	C2
Solway Dr	C1
South & Townhead	
Ho 2	C2
Stakeford St	B4
Stark Cres	C1
Station Rd	C3
Steel Ave B	B3
Stewart Hall Gdns	C4
Stoop Loaning	F3
Strathear 1	B1
Suffolkhill Ave	A4
Summerville Ave	A4
Summerville Cres	A4
Sunderries Ave	B4
Sunderries Rd	B4
Suspension Brae	C2
Swans Vennel 10	C2
Terregles Rd	A3
Terregles St	A3
The Carruthers'	
Cotts	E1
The Lane	D1
Three Crowns	
Ct 8	C3
Troqueer Rd	C1
Union St	B3
Verdun Sq	C1
Victoria Rd	A2
Victoria Terr	D4
Watling St	C3
Welldale	C1
Well St 3	B3
Westfield Rd	C2
Westpark Cotts	A1
Westpark Terr 6	C2
White Sands	C3
Windsor Pl	A3
Woodside Terr 2	C2

A1	A2	C3	7 WHITMOOR CL	E2	F2	F4
1 ALEXANDRA RD	1 SPRINGFIELD ST	1 BK QUEEN ST		1 KENTMERE GR	1 STAINTON GR	1 HOME BREEZE GR
2 BK AVONDALE RD E	2 LANCASHIRE ST	2 BK LINES ST		2 BUTTERMERE AVE	2 BRAEMAR CT	2 TUDOR GR
3 CLEVELANDS WLK	3 YORKSHIRE ST E	3 WASHINGTON AVE		3 BLEA TARN PL	3 HAWESWATER PL	3 PALMER GR
4 LIMES AVE	4 BK MARINE RD	4 RABY ST		4 HAWESWATER RD	4 WASTWATER DR	4 SEABORN GR
5 MYRTLE GR	5 CLAREMONT CRES	5 RIBBLESDALE CT		5 LOWESWATER DR	5 OLD PENNY GDNS	5 LODGES CT
	6 CLARENDON RD W	6 PRIMROSE ST				6 LAISTER CT

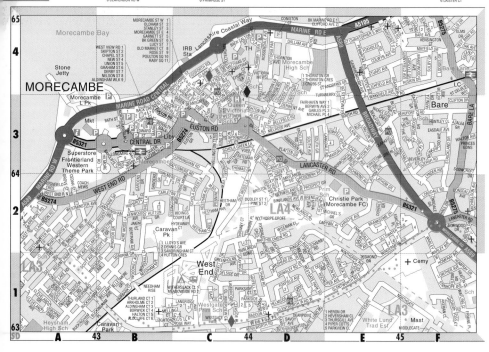

Morecambe

Acre Moss La B2
Akeman Cl F1
Albany Rd A2
Albert Rd A2
Aldcliffe Ct C1
Aldingham Wlk B3
Alexandra Rd 1 .. A1
Alice St C3
Altham Rd C3
Altham Wlk C3
Anstable Rd E2
Arkholme Ct E3
Arnside Cres D2
Ashton Rd A2
Audenshaw Rd ... D2
Azalea Gr F3
Back Avondale
Rd E 2 .... A1
Back Calton St C4
Back Crescent St . B3
Back Green St C4
Back Lines St 2 .. C3
Back Marine Rd 4 A2
Back Morecambe
St A2
Back Queen St 1 . C3
Back West End
Rd N A2
Baddon Cl A1
Balmoral Rd A2
Banbury Rd D1
Bare Ave F4
Bare La F4
Bare Lane Station . F4
Bartholomew Rd ... C2
Bateman Gr C1
Bateman St A2
Battismore Rd B3
Baxtergate C3
Baycliffe Cres C3
Beach St A1
Beaufort Gr A1
Beaufort Rd A1
Beecham St C1
Bellamy Ave B1
Bellfield Rd C3
Benson Ave E3
Bertram Ave E2

Berwyn Ave E3
Beulah Ave E3
Beverley Ct E3
Birkett's Pl D3
Birklands Ave C3
Borrowdale Gr E3
Borwick Ct C1
Bowfell Ave C1
Braemar Ct 2 .... F2
Branksome Dr E2
Brantwood Ave ... E3
Brendjean Rd D2
Bridge Rd D3
Bristol St D2
Broadway E2
Brook Ave A1
Brook Gr A1
Brook Rd A1
Broughton Gr D1
Buckingham Gr .. A1
Buckingham Pl ... A1
Buckingham St ... A1
Burlington Ave ... E3
Burlington Gr E3
Burneside Cl D2
Buttermere Ave 2 E2
Buxton St D2
Carleton St C1
Carlyle St F4
Carrington Gr C1
Cartmel Pl D2
Cedar St A2
Central Dr B3
Chapel St B3
Charles St C3
Chatsworth Av .. E2
Christie Ave E2
Christie Park
(Morecambe FC) . D4
Church Av D4
Church St C3
Claremont Cres 5 C2
Claremont Rd ... A2
Clarence St A2
Clarendon Rd E .. E1
Clarendon Rd W 6 E1
Clarkfield Dr E3
Clevelands Ave .. A1
Clevelands Gr ... A1

Clevelands Wlk 3 . A1
Clifford Ave E4
Clifton Dr F3
Coach Mews A2
Colwyn Ave E4
Coniston Ct D3
Coniston Rd D3
Corringham Rd ... C3
Croft St C3
Cross St C3
Dallam Ave D4
Deanpoint C1
Deansgate C2
Dennis Gr C2
Derby St B3
Derwent Ave D3
Devonshire Rd .. C1
Downes Rd E2
Dudley St C2
Easdale Ave F3
East St A2
Edward St B3
Eidsforth Rd ... C4
Elkin Rd C3
Ellesmere Gr ... B1
Ellesmere Rd ... C3
Ellis Dr F4
Elms Dr F4
Endcliffe Rd D3
Ennerdale Ave .. E2
Ermine Pl F1
Eskdale Pl F1
Essington Ave .. B2
Euston Gr C3
Euston Rd B3/C3
Fairbank Gr C1
Fairhaven Way . C1
Farnlea Dr F1
Filton Gr F1
Foss Ct C1
Foxfield Ave ... D1
Foxholes Rd ... C4
Gables Pl E1
Gainsborough Rd E1
Gais Gill Ave ... C1
Gardens Ct C3
Garnett St D3
George St D3
Gleneagles Dr .. E4
Glentworth Rd E . E1
Glentworth Rd W . E1
Graham St B3
Grange St C4
Grasmere Rd .. E4

Grayrigg Dr C1
Greenholme Ave . C1
Greenlea Dr E3
Green St C4
Gringley Rd C1
Grove St C4
Hadrian Rd F1
Hall Dr C1
Hall St C4
Halton Ct C3
Hampsfell Dr ... C1
Hanover St C3
Hawarden Ave .. C3
Hawkshead Dr .. D1
Hayfell Ave D1
Heaton Ct F1
Helmside Ave .. D1
Heron Dr C1
Hest Bank Rd .. F4
Hestham Ave ... C2
Hestham Cres .. C2
Hestham Dr C2
Hestham Par ... C2
Heversham Cl .. D1
Heysham High Sch A4
Hidings Court La . C2
Highfield Cres .. A2
Highgrove Cl ... B2
Hilmore Rd D3
Home Breeze
Ho 1 .... F4
Homfray Av F1
Homfray Gr F1
Hope St C3
Hornby Terr D4
Huntley Ct C1
Hutton Cres ... B2
Hutton Gr B2
Hydeaway Ct .. F4
James St D3
Janine Ct D3
Jesmond Gr ... E1
Kenilworth Rd .. B3
Kensington Ct .. F1
Kensington Rd .. F1
Kentmere Gr 1 . E2
Kenwood Ave .. B2
Kilnbank Ave .. C3
King St C3
Kirkstone Dr .. C3
Laister Ct 6 .. F4
Lake Av A1
Lake Gr A1
Lake Rd A1
Lambridge Cl . C1

Lancashire St 2 .. A2
Lancaster Rd D3
Langdale Rd D3
Langridge Way ... C1
Lathom Ave E2
Lathom Gr E2
Leamington Rd .. E1
Leighton Ct D3
Leyster St D3
Library B3
Lichfield Ave ... E4
Limes Ave 4 ... A1
Lincoln Cl C3
Lines St C3
Lloyd's Ave ... B2
Lodges Ct 5 ... F4
Lodges Gr F4
Longmire Way .. E3
Longton Dr C1
Lonsdale Cres .. C4
Lonsdale Gr ... C4
Lonsdale Rd ... C2
Lord St C4
Loupsfell Dr .. C2
Loweswater Dr 5 E2
Lowlands Rd ... C2
Lowther Ave ... C1
Lucy St C4
Lynden Ave ... C1
Mardale Ave .. E3
Marine Rd E ... D4
Marine Rd W .. A2
Marine Road
Central A3
Market A3
Market St B3
Matthias Ct ... C3
Matthias St ... C4
Mayfield Dr ... F4
Maylands Sq .. C1
Meadow Court Rd D2
Meadowside Rd . C1
Melling Dr ... B1
Melrose Ave .. C3
Michael Pl ... C3
Michaelson Ave . E3
Middlegate ... F3
Monkswood Ave . F3
Morecambe
High Sch D4
Morecambe
Leisure Pk* ... B3
Morecambe
Station B3
Morecambe St E . C4

Morecambe St W . C4
Myra Ave D2
Myrtle Gr 5 .... A1
Needham Ave .. B1
Needham Rise .. B1
Needham Rd ... B1
Nelson St B3
Netherlands Rd . D2
Newlands Rd ... D2
New St C3
Nicholson Cres .. E3
Northgate E1
North St C3
Northumberland St . E3
Norwood Dr ... F2
Oak Ave C2
Oldham St C3
Old Market Ct .. C4
Old Penny Gdns 5 F2
Osborne Cres .. A1
Osborne Rd ... A1
Out Moss La .. C2
Oxford St C4
Palmer Gr 3 .. F4
Parkside C1
Parkside Ct ... C1
Park St C4
Parkview Cl .. D1
Pedder St ... A3
Pembroke Ave . E4
Pennine View .. C2
Pine St C2
Piper Cotts ... D1
Platten Gr ... C3
Poulton Rd .. C3
Poulton Sq .. C3
Primrose St 4 . C3
Primrose St ... C3
Princes Gdns .. C2
Prospect Gr .. D2
Queen Elizabeth Ct B3
Queens Dr ... C3
Queen St ... C3
Queen Victoria
Hospital C3
Raby Sq C3
Raby St 4 ... C3
Redwood Dr .. A3
Regent Park Gr . B2
Regent Rd ... B3
Ribblesdale Ct 5 . C3
Richmond Ave . C1
Riverview Ct .. C1
Rochester Ave . D1
Rosebery Ave . D1
Rose St C4

Rossendale Ave .. D4
Royal Rd D4
Royalty Mall B3
Ruskin Dr D4
Ruslands Gdns .. C2
Rysdale Cres D2
St Andrews Gr .. C3
St Celia's Way .. C3
St Christopher's
Way E4
St Margaret's Rd . C4
St Michael's Gr . D2
St Ogg's Rd ... D1
Sanders Gr ... C4
Sandringham Ct . B2
Sandringham Rd . B2
Sandside Dr ... D1
Savoy Ave D1
Scafell Ave ... E3
Schola Green
La C2/C3
Scott Ave A1
Scott Gr B2
Scott Rd A1
Scowcroft Dr .. D1
Seaborn Gr 4 . F4
Seaborn Rd ... C1
Selside Dr ... C1
Sizergh Rd .. D2
Skipton St .. B3
Somerby Rd .. D2
South Ave ... D3
South Gr ... D3
South Rd ... D3
Springfield St 1 . A2
Stainton Gr 1 . F2
Stanhope Ave .. C1
Stanley St C3
Station Rd .. C3
Strickland Dr .. F3
Stuart Ave ... C4
Sulby Gr F4
Sunnyfield Ave . F4
The Coppice .. F3
The Glade ... F3
The Mews .. F3
Thirlmere Gr .. B3
Thirlmere Gr .. E4
Thomas Gr .. C3
Thonock Rd .. E1
Thornton Ave .. D4
Thornton Cres .. D3
Thornton La .. D3
Thornton Rd .. D3
Thrimby Ct .. C2

Index

Church Rd 🄶 **Beckenham BR2.........53** C6

Place name	Location number	Locality, town or village	Postcode district	Page and grid square
May be abbreviated on the map	Present when a number indicates the place's position in a crowded area of mapping	Shown when more than one place has the same name	District for the indexed place	Page number and grid reference for the standard mapping

Public and commercial buildings are highlighted in magenta. Places of interest are highlighted in blue with a star ★

Abbreviations used in the index

Acad	Academy	Comm	Common	Gd	Ground	L	Leisure	Prom	Promenade
App	Approach	Cott	Cottage	Gdn	Garden	La	Lane	Rd	Road
Arc	Arcade	Cres	Crescent	Gn	Green	Liby	Library	Recn	Recreation
Ave	Avenue	Cswy	Causeway	Gr	Grove	Mdw	Meadow	Ret	Retail
Bglw	Bungalow	Ct	Court	H	Hall	Meml	Memorial	Sh	Shopping
Bldg	Building	Ctr	Centre	Ho	House	Mkt	Market	Sq	Square
Bsns, Bus	Business	Ctry	Country	Hospl	Hospital	Mus	Museum	St	Street
Bvd	Boulevard	Cty	County	HQ	Headquarters	Orch	Orchard	Sta	Station
Cath	Cathedral	Dr	Drive	Hts	Heights	Pal	Palace	Terr	Terrace
Cir	Circus	Dro	Drove	Ind	Industrial	Par	Parade	TH	Town Hall
Cl	Close	Ed	Education	Inst	Institute	Pas	Passage	Univ	University
Cnr	Corner	Emb	Embankment	Int	International	Pk	Park	Wk, Wlk	Walk
Coll	College	Est	Estate	Intc	Interchange	Pl	Place	Wr	Water
Com	Community	Ex	Exhibition	Junc	Junction	Prec	Precinct	Yd	Yard

Thrimby Pl C2
Thurland Ct B1
Thursgill Ave D1
Townley St C4
Tudor Gr 🄶 F4
Tunstall St B3
Turnberry Cl E4
Ullswater Ave E2
Union St B3
Victor Ave F3
Victoria Mews D4
Victoria Par D4
Victoria St B3
Wakefield Ave E3
Walton Ave F3
Warley Ave F2
Warley Dr F2
Washington Ave 🄸 ..C3
Wastwater Dr 🄳 ...F2
Waterside Pl C1
Watling Cl F1
Wellington Terr ..C3
West End Rd A2
Westfield Gr B2
Westgate D1
Westgate Ave C1
Westgate Park Rd ..D1
Westgate Prim Sch ..C1
Westminster Ave ..A2
Westminster Rd ...A2
Westover St C3
West View Rd B3
Whinsfell View ...C3
Whitby Rd D3
Whitegate E1
White Lund Rd D1
White Lund
 Trading Est E1
Whitmoor Cl 🄷 ...C3
Winchester Ave ...E4
Windermere Ave ..E2
Windermere Ct 🄴 ..E2
Windsor Ave A1
Windsor Gr B2
Windsor Rd A1
Wingate Ave D2
Winthorpe Ave ...E2
Wiseman Cl D2
Witherslack Cl ...C1
Woodhill Ave B1
Woodhill Cl B1
Woodhill La B2
Wythorpe Croft ..C2
York Pl C3
Yorkshire St E 🄳 ..A2

Index of localities, towns and villages

A

Abbey Town 26 B1
Aglionby 30 F7
Ainstable 42 F5
Allerby 49 C6
Allithwaite ...164 E7
Allonby 35 C2
Alston 124 E5
Alston 45 F5
Ambleside 114 C2
Ambleside 195 E5
Annan 172 B4
Anthorn 16 E1
Appleby-in-
 Westmorland .193 B6
Appleby-in-
 Westmorland ..88 C4
Applethwaite ..192 B8
Arkholme 168 B2
Arlecdon 77 F2
Armathwaite ...42 B5
Arnside 155 A1
Arnside 209 B2
Asby 78 A3
Askam-in-
 Furness 162 A8
Askham 85 D6
Aspatria 50 C8

B

Backbarrow ...153 D7
Bampton
 Grange 100 E8
Barbon 157 F5
Bardsea 163 C5
Barepot 62 E4
Barnoldswick ..169 D2
Barrow-in-
 Furness 170 F7
Barrow-in-
 Furness 207 C1
Bassenthwaite ..66 C7
Baycliff 163 B3
Beckermet 108 B5
Beck Foot 132 E3
Beck Houses ...132 B3
Beetham 155 F2
Bewcastle 6 C1

Bigrigg 188 A3
Blackford 20 A5
Bladwith 140 C3
Blencarn 73 B6
Blencogo 37 B6
Blennerhasset ..50 F8
Bolton 87 E6
Bolton Low
 Houses 37 F3
Boot 125 C8
Bootle 137 B3
Borwick 167 B4
Bothel 51 A5
Bouth 152 F8
Bowland
 Bridge 142 D4
Bowness-on-
 Solway 17 B5
Bowness-on-
 Windermere ..129 B3
Bowness-on-
 Windermere ..198 D2
Bowston 130 E3
Braithwaite 80 E6
Brampton 179 A5
Brampton 22 C4
Bransty 186 D3
Braystones 108 A4
Bridekirk 64 C8
Bridgefoot 63 C4
Brigham 64 A5
Brigsteer 143 D4
Brisco 30 C2
Broadwath 178 F3
Brough 105 C5
Brougham 71 C3
Broughton Cross 63 F4
Broughton-in-
 Furness 139 A2
Broughton Moor 63 C8
Bullgill 78 A7
Burgh-by-
 Sands 18 F2
Burnbanks 100 C7
Burneside 130 F3
Burnrigg 178 E4
Burton-in-
 Lonsdale 169 B3
Buttermere 94 E7

C

Caldbeck 53 C6
Calder Bridge .108 D5
Caldewgate 176 E6
Calthwaite 55 E7
Camerton 183 F3
Canonbie 3 C3
Cargo 19 D2
Cark 164 D7
Carlisle 177 B7
Carlisle 214 B3
Carlisle 30 B7
Carnforth 213 C2
Cartmel 153 F1
Cartmell Fell ..142 D3
Casterton 158 F2
Casterton 212 E5
Castle
 Carrock 32 D6
Cautley 134 A2
Chapel Stile ..113 B4
Cleator 188 C4
Cleator Moor ..188 E7
Cleator Moor ...92 C5
Cliburn 92 B1
Clifton 71 C1
Coanwood 21 A3
Cockermouth ..190 F3
Cockermouth ...64 C5
Coniston 127 D4
Coniston 196 B4
Corney 137 C6
Cotehill 31 C1
Cowan Head ...130 D4
Cowgill 148 A2
Crofton 39 D1
Crook 130 B2
Crooklands 162 C6
Crosby 49 B5
Crosby
 Garrett 120 A8
Crosby-on-
 Eden 21 B2
Crosby
 Ravensworth .102 C5
Crosby Villa ...49 D5
Crosthwaite ..142 E6
Culgaith 72 D4
Cumwhinton ...31 A3
Cumwhitton ...31 F3

D

Dalston 29 D1
Dalton-in-
 Furness 162 C5
Dalton-in-
 Furness 205 D4
Dean 78 B8
Dearham 49 A3
Dent 147 B2
Distington 185 C4
Dockray 83 D4
Drigg 123 D5
Droomer 198 F5
Durdar 30 B1

E

Eaglesfield 64 A3
Eals 34 F7
Eamont Bridge .191 F2
Eastriggs 17 E7
Edenhall 71 E7
Egremont 189 E7
Egremont 92 B1
Elterwater 113 C3
Embleton 65 C5
Endmoor 156 C7
Ennerdale
 Bridge 93 A7
Eskdale Green .124 F7

F

Farleton 156 C3
Faugh 31 F5
Field
 Broughton ...153 F4
Finsthwaite ...141 D2
Flimby 183 D8
Flookburgh ...164 D6
Frizington 92 E8

G

Gamblesby 58 A6
Garrigill 60 C8
Garsdale Head .148 D7

Gatesgarth 95 B6
Gawthrop 147 A2
Gilcrux 49 F4
Gilgarran 77 D5
Gilsland 14 E1
Glasson 17 E3
Gleaston 162 F1
Glenridding ...98 C8
Gosforth 109 A2
Grange-over-
 Sands 154 A1
Grange-over-
 Sands 208 E4
Grasmere 113 D6
Grasmere 194 B4
Great Asby ...103 C3
Great
 Broughton ...63 E6
Great Clifton ..63 E6
Great Corby ..178 C1
Great Corby ...31 C5
Great
 Langdale 112 A5
Great Ormside 103 E8
Great Salkeld ..57 A3
Great
 Strickland ...86 C5
Great Urswick .162 F5
Greenhead 24 D8
Gressingham ..168 A1
Gretna 173 D2
Gretna 9 B2
Greysouthen ...63 E4
Greystoke 69 C5

H

Hackthorpe 86 A6
Haile 108 D7
Hallbankgate ..23 B2
Hallthwaites ..150 D8
Halton-Lea-
 Gate 24 D1
Harrington ...185 A8
Harrington 76 B2
Hartley 121 A7
Hartley 199 E6
Havering 98 F4
Haverigg 150 B1
Haverigg 202 A4
Haverthwaite .153 A6

Hawkshead ...128 B5
Hawkshead ...197 D5
Hayton 31 F8
Heads Nook 31 E6
Hensingham ..187 E6
Hensingham ...91 F7
Hesket
  Newmarket ...53 D5
Hethersgill 11 F2
Heversham ...155 E6
Heversham ...211 D8
High
  Casterton 212 E3
High
  Cummersdale 176 D1
High
  Harrington ..185 D8
High
  Harrington 77 B8
High Hesket ...41 F3
High Lorton ...79 E8
High Newton ..154 B5
Hilton 89 B3
Hincaster 155 F7
Holme 156 B2
Holme St
  Cuthbert 35 E6
Holmrook 123 E6
Houghton 175 F6
Houghton 20 B2
Howes 172 B4
Hunsonby 57 E2
Hutton Roof ..157 A1

I
Ickenthwaite ..140 F4
Ingleton 169 F3
Ireby 11 F6
Ireleth 162 B8
Ireshope Moor ..61 F3
Irthington 21 F4
Ivegill 42 F2

K
Kendal 144 B7
Kendal 200 E5
Kentmere ....11¹ S D2
Keswick 1⁵ A3
Keswick 81 C6
Killington 145 D4
Kilnhill 66 A7

King's
  Meaburn 87 C4
Kirkandrews-
  on-Eden 19 C1
Kirkbampton ...28 D7
Kirkbride 27 C7
Kirkby-in-
  Furness 151 B5
Kirkby
  Lonsdale 157 E2
Kirkby
  Lonsdale 212 A2
Kirkby
  Stephen 120 E7
Kirkby
  Stephen 199 B6
Kirkby Thore ...87 D8
Kirkland 78 B1
Kirkoswald 57 B8
Kirksanton ...149 E3
Knock 73 E1

L
Lakeside 141 E2
Lamonby 54 F2
Lamplugh 78 C3
Langwathby 71 F8
Laversdale 21 C5
Lazonby 57 B6
Leck 169 B7
Leece 171 C8
Legburthwaite .82 C2
Levens 143 E1
Lindal 154 D3
Lindal in
  Furness 162 D6
Lindal in
  Furness 205 F8
Lindsey 51 F6
Linstock 20 D1
Little Clifton ...63 C3
Little Langdale .113 B2
Little Salkeld ...57 C3
Little Strickland .86 C2
Little Urswick ..162 F4
Long Marton ...88 A2
Longthwaite ...84 B6
Longtown 10 C3
Lowca 186 E8
Lowca 76 E4
Loweswater 79 C3
Low Hesket 41 E5
Lowick 140 B1
Lowick Bridge .140 C1
Low Lorton 79 D8

Low Moresby ...76 F3
Lowther 85 F6
Lupton 156 E4

M
Martindale 84 B2
Marton 162 C8
Maryport 182 B5
Matterdale End .83 D6
Maulds
  Meaburn 102 C7
Mealsgate 37 D1
Melkinthorpe ..86 C8
Melling 168 C1
Melmerby 58 B4
Middleton 145 E1
Milburn 73 C4
Millbeck 66 F1
Millhouse 54 A4
Millness 156 C5
Millom 202 E5
Milnthorpe ...211 E3
Milton 22 E3
Moorhouse 29 A7
Moor Row 188 A5
Moresby Parks ..76 F1
Morland 86 F5

N
Natland 144 A4
Nenthead 47 A2
Newbie 16 C8
Newbie 172 A1
Newbiggin 171 E8
Newbiggin-
  on-Lune 119 F4
Newby Bridge .141 E1
Newcastleton ...1 C6
Newton 162 C2
Newton Arlosh .26 F6
Newton Reigny .70 C6
Newton Rigg ...70 E6
Nook 156 D5

O
Old Hutton ...144 F3
Old Town 157 C6
Orton 118 C7
Oughterside ...49 F7
Oulton 180 B8

Over Burrow ..168 E7
Over Kellet ...167 B1
Oxenholme ...144 C4

P
Parton 186 E5
Patterdale 98 D6
Pennington ...162 F8
Penny Bridge .152 D6
Penrith 191 E6
Penrith 71 B6
Penruddock 69 E2
Piel Island ...171 B2
Plantation
  Bridge 130 C3
Plumbland 50 D5
Plumpton 56 C3
Pooley Bridge ..84 F7
Port Carlisle ...17 D5
Portinscale 81 A6
Prospect 49 F7

R
Rampside 171 C5
Ravenglass ...123 F3
Ravenstonedale
  ....120 A2
Redhills 191 A1
Renwick 43 F2
Ribblehead ...160 C2
Roa Island ...171 B4
Rockcliffe 19 D4
Roosebeck ...171 D6
Rosley 39 C4
Rosthwaite 96 C5
Row 143 A4
Rowanburn 3 F3

S
St Bees 91 D3
St Helens 183 A6
Salterbeck 184 C1
Sandford 104 A7
Sandwith 187 A2
Sandwith 91 C5
Satterthwaite .141 B7
Scotby 30 F5
Seascale 123 B8
Seathwaite ...126 C2
Seatle 153 E6

Seaton 183 C2
Seaton 62 E5
Sedbergh 146 C7
Sedbergh 201 A5
Sedgwick 144 A2
Shap 101 C6
Silecroft 149 D4
Silloth 174 B4
Silloth 25 B4
Silverdale 166 A6
Silverdale 210 C3
Skelton 55 B2
Skelwith
  Bridge 113 E2
Skinburness ..174 F8
Skinburness ...25 E6
Skirsgill 191 C2
Slack Head ...155 E1
Sleagill 86 F2
Smithfield 20 F8
Sockbridge 70 E1
Soulby 104 C1
South
  Stainmore ..106 A3
Southwaite 41 D3
Spark Bridge .152 D7
Staffield 43 A1
Stainburn 62 F3
Stainton 70 D3
Stainton with
  Adgarley 162 E3
Stainton with
  Adgarley 205 F2
Staveley 130 B5
Storth 209 F5
Swarthmoor ..203 B3

T
Tallentire 49 F2
Tebay 118 B3
Temple Sowerby 72 E2
The Green 150 C7
Thornhill 189 E2
Thornton in
  Lonsdale ...169 F4
Thorpe 70 E1
Threlkeld 82 B8
Thursby 28 F1
Thurstonfield ..28 E7
Tindale 23 E2
Tirril 70 F1
Torver 127 B1
Town End 157 F5
Troutbeck 114 E2

Troutbeck
  Bridge 129 B7
Tunstall 168 E4

U
Uldale 52 B3
Ulpha 138 E8
Ulverston 163 B7
Ulverston 203 C6
Underbarrow ..143 B6

W
Waberthwaite .137 C8
Walney Island .170 C5
Walney Island .206 B4
Walton 22 B7
Warcop 104 C6
Warton 166 F3
Warton 213 C7
Warwick Bridge178 C7
Warwick-on-
  Eden 178 A6
Waverton 37 E6
Welton 39 F3
Westhouse ...169 E5
Westnewton ...36 B3
West
  Stonesdale ..122 E1
Wetheral 178 A2
Whitehaven ..186 B2
Whitehaven ...76 C1
Whittington ..168 D7
Wigton 180 D3
Wigton 38 C7
Windermere ..129 C6
Windermere ..198 F6
Winton 105 A1
Witherslack ..154 E6
Workington ..184 B6
Workington ...62 A3
Wrayton 168 E3
Wreay 41 B8
Wythburn 97 C4

Y
Yanwath 71 A2
Yealand
  Conyers 166 F5
Yealand
  Redmayne ..166 E6

A

Aaron's Lonning CA7 ....36 B8
Abbey App LA13 .....207 D8
Abbey Cl CA14 ......184 E3
Abbey Ct CA14 ....185 B7
Abbey Dr LA9 ....144 B4
Abbey Garth CA20 ...108 E5
Abbey Gdns LA9 .....144 B4
Abbey Hts 14 LA16 ...162 A8
Abbey Rd Abbey Town CA7 ..26 C1
  Barrow-In-F LA13,LA14 ...207 B6
  Dalton-In-F LA15 ...205 B4
  St Bees CA27 ....91 C3
Abbey St CA3 ....214 A2
Abbey Vale CA27 ......91 C3
Abbey Way LA14 .....207 C8
Abbey Wlk CA3 ......214 A3
Abbot Hall Art Gallery*
  LA9 ....200 D4
Abbot Hall Barn LA6 ...212 B2
Abbot Wood CA14 .....63 A4
Abbots Dr CA7 ....26 C1
Abbots Rd CA2 ....176 E5
Abbots Vale LA13 ....207 C3
Abbots Vue LA12 .....153 C7
Abbots Way LA11 ....208 B1
Abbotsfield Gdns LA13 .207 C7
Abbotsford Dr CA3 ...175 D3
Abbotsford Ho
  Grange-Over-S LA11 ...208 B1
  Penrith CA11 ....191 D6
Abbotsford Pl 6 CA15 ...182 E5
Abbotsgate LA6 .....212 B2
Abbotsmead App LA13 ...207 D4
Abbotts Way CA27 ....91 C2
Abercorn St LA14 ....206 F1
Aberdare St 7 LA14 ..206 F1
Aberdeen St LA14 ....206 F1
Abotts Cl LA11 ......208 B1
Acacia Cl LA13 ......207 F4
Acacia Rd LA12 ......203 D2
Acer Cl CA28 ....187 E6
Ackenthwaite Ct LA7 ...211 F4
Acorn Bank
  Barrow-In-F LA13 ...207 F4
  Cleator CA23 ....188 D4
Acorn Bank Garden & Water
  Mill* CA10 ....72 E3
Acorn Bsns Pk CA3 ...175 B6
Acorn St CA12 ....192 B3
Acre Cl CA8 ....31 F8
Acre Dales CA7 ......26 C1
Acre Moss La LA9 ....200 B8
Acre The CA7 ....26 A6
Acredale Rd CA2 .....29 D7
Acremire La CA7 .....17 B5
Ada St 3 CA15 ......182 E5
Adams Rd CA14 ......184 B4
Addison Pl DG12 ....172 C5
Addison St 7 CA28 ...186 C1
Adelaide St
  Barrow-In-F LA14 ...206 E4
  Carlisle CA1 ....177 C5
Adelphi Ct LA14 ....207 A2
Adelphi Terr CA2 ....177 A4
Adgarley Way LA15 ..205 C3
Admiral Ct 7 LA14 ...207 A2
Africanda Rd DG16 ...173 D3
Afton St LA14 ....170 D6
Agilonby St CA1 .....207 C3
Aikbank Rd CA28 ....186 E3
Aikrigg Ave LA9 .....200 C7
Ainslie Dale LA15 ...205 C5
Ainslie St
  Barrow-In-F LA14 ...206 F5
  Dalton-In-F LA15 ...205 C5
  Ulverston LA12 .....203 D5
Ainsworth St 3 LA12 ..203 D6
Aira Force* CA11 .....83 D3
Airethwaite LA9 .....200 C6
Airfield Approach Bsns Pk
  LA11 ....164 D6
Airygill La CA10 .....86 B6
Alamein Rd LA5 .....213 D3
Alan Ct CA14 ....184 F5
Alanbrooke Rd CA1 ..177 F6
Alauna Dr CA15 .....192 B8
Albemarle St CA13 ...190 B3
Albert Pl DG12 ......172 C5
Albert Pl N LA14 .....206 C3
Albert Pl S LA14 .....206 D3
Albert Rd LA11 ......208 D4
Albert Sq 7 CA28 ....186 D1
Albert St
  Barrow-In-F LA14 ...207 A2
  Carlisle CA1 ....214 B3
  Carnforth LA5 ......213 C3
  Carnforth,Millhead LA5 ..213 C5
  Dalton-In-F LA15 ...205 C5
  Longtown CA6 ......10 C3
  Millom LA18 ....202 D5
  Penrith CA11 ....191 D5
  Seascale CA20 .....123 A7
  Workington CA14 ...184 D5
Albert Terr
  12 Maryport CA15 ..182 E5
  Whitehaven CA28 ...186 D2
Albion St Carlisle CA1 ..214 C1
  Whitehaven CA28 ...186 D2
Aldby Ct CA25 ......188 E6
Aldby Farm CA11 .....70 B2
Aldby Gr CA25 ....188 E6
Aldby Pl CA25 ......188 F7
Aldby St CA25 ......188 E7
Alder Ave CA15 ......182 F5
Alder Cl CA28 ....186 E4

Alder Rd
  Barrow-In-F LA14 ...206 F7
  Penrith CA11 ....191 F4
Aldercroft LA9 ......200 B3
Alderwood LA9 ......200 B3
Aldery Terr LA12 .....3 D3
Aldingham Parochial Sch
  LA12 ....163 A3
Aldwych Terr LA12 ...203 E4
Alexander Cl CA14 ...184 F3
Alexander Dr LA8 ...164 C1
Alexander Pl 33 LA16 ..162 A8
Alexander Rd LA12 ...203 D4
Alexander St CA1 ....214 C1
Alexandra Cl CA3 ...198 E4
Alexandra Dr CA1 ...177 F5
Alexandra Rd DG12 ..172 C5
Alexandra Rd
  Carnforth LA5 ......213 C3
  Penrith CA11 ....191 B5
  Windermere LA23 ...198 E4
Alexandre Gdn LA12 ..203 D4
Alfred Barrow Sch The
  LA14 ....206 F2
Alfred St N CA1 .....214 C2
Alfred St S CA1 .....214 C2
Alice Howe Ind Units
  LA23 ....198 F6
Alice La LA13 ....63 E6
All Saints' CE Prim Sch
  CA13 ....190 E4
Allan Hill CA15 .....183 D7
Allanby St CA15 .....183 C8
Allandale Rd CA1 ....177 F3
Allason Cl CA8 ......179 B6
Allerdale Gr CA13 ...190 B2
Allhallows La LA9 ...200 C5
Allhallows Terr CA7 ..37 C1
Allison St 6 LA14 ...207 A3
Allithwaite CE Prim Sch
  LA11 ....164 F7
Allithwaite Rd
  Flookburgh LA11 ...164 E6
  Grange-Over-S LA11 ..208 B1
Allonby Cl LA14 .....206 B4
Allonby Prim Sch CA15 ..35 C2
Almery Dr LA12 ......204 A1
Almhouses The LA20 ..138 E8
Almond Rd LA12 .....203 D2
Almond Wlk LA13 ...207 F5
Almshouses LA8 .....132 A4
Alnat Ind Pk LA11 ...208 F8
Alne Rd CA15 ....182 D4
Alpaca Ctr The* CA11 ...70 D2
Alston Prim Sch CA9 ..181 E3
Alston Sta CA9 .....181 D4
Alston Watermill* CA9 181 D4
Alstonby Ct CA6 .....20 B8
Alton St CA2 ....177 A3
Amazonia World of
  Reptiles* LA12 .....198 B2
Ambleside Prim Sch
  LA22 ....195 C5
Ambleside Rd
  Keswick CA12 ......192 C3
  Windermere LA23 ...198 D7
Ameshaugh Rd CA9 ..45 E2
Amphitrite St LA14 ..206 C1
Amphitrite St S 4 LA14 ..206 C1
Ancaster St LA14 ....206 F6
Anchor Cl LA11 .....191 C6
Anchor Ct CA13 .....205 B5
Anchorite Fields LA9 ..200 C4
Anchorite Pl LA9 ....200 D3
Anchorite Rd LA9 ...200 D3
Andover Cl CA2 .....176 C5
Andover St 6 LA14 ..207 A3
Andreas Ave LA14 ...206 B1
Angel La LA19 ......191 D5
Angle Meadow La LA14 ..209 B1
Ann St Carlisle CA2 ..176 D6
  Dalton-In-F LA15 ...205 A5
  Kendal LA9 ....200 E6
Annan Acad DG12 ...172 C3
Annan Hospl DG12 ...172 C3
Annan Rd DG16 .....173 C3
Annan St LA14 ......206 F6
Annan Sta DG12 ....172 C3
Annanhill DG12 .....172 C1
Annerley Rd DG12 ...172 C2
Annetwell St CA3 ...214 A3
Annie Pit La CA14 ...184 C4
Annisgarth Ave LA23 ..198 E3
Annisgarth Cl LA23 ..198 E3
Annisgarth Dr LA23 ..198 E3
Annisgarth Pk LA23 ..198 E3
Anson St LA14 ......206 E4
Antonine Way CA3 ...20 C1
Anvil Cl CA8 ....21 E5
Anzac Ave LA14 ....206 C1
Apple Garth CA6 ....19 D2
Apple Tree Gdns CA11 ..71 C5
Appleby Castle* CA16 193 D4
Appleby Gram Sch
  CA16 ....193 C4
Appleby Prim Sch LA13 ..193 D6
Appleby Rd Kendal LA9 ..131 C1
  Kirkby Stephen CA17 ..104 F2
Appleby Sta CA16 ...193 D6
Applerigg Kendal LA9 ..200 E5
  Penrith CA11 ....191 D6
Applethwaite Ct LA9 ..200 E5
Appletree Rd LA12 ...203 E4
Applewood LA9 .....200 B4
Applewood Cl LA12 ..200 B4
Aquarium of the Lakes*
  LA12 ....141 E2

Archer St CA14 .....185 A7
Archers Garth CA2 ..176 C7
Archers Mdw LA9 ...200 E3
Arches The CA15 ....182 E4
Argyle Pl LA14 ......207 B3
Argyle St
  Barrow-In-F LA14 ...207 B3
  Millom LA18 ....202 D4
  Ulverston LA12 .....203 E5
Argyll Terr DG12 ....172 C1
Arkholme CE Prim Sch
  LA6 ....168 B3
Arkholme Cl LA14 ...213 D4
Arkley Hall Cotts CA7 ..50 C6
Arkley Rd CA7 ......50 C7
Arkwright Way CA1 ..177 D3
Arlecdon Parks Rd CA26 ..77 F1
Arlecdon Prim Sch CA26 ..77 F1
Arlecdon Rd CA26 ...77 E2
Armathwaite Sch LA4 ..42 C5
Armathwaite Sta CA4 ..42 C5
Armitt Liby & Mus The*
  LA22 ....195 D6
Armstrong Ct LA9 ...200 E3
Armstrong S 5 CA14 ..184 D6
Arnbarrow LA7 ......200 E4
Arnhem Rd LA5 .....213 D3
Arnisons Ct CA11 ...191 D4
Arnside National CE Sch
  LA5 ....209 B2
Arnside Rd CA1 .....177 E3
Arnside St 3 LA14 ..207 A3
Arnside Sta LA5 ....209 C2
Arras Ave LA11 .....164 D6
Arthur St
  Barrow-In-F LA14 ...207 A3
  Carlisle CA2 ....177 A4
  Penrith CA11 ....191 D6
Arthur Terr 1 CA11 ..191 D5
Arthuret Dr CA6 ....10 C3
Arthuret Rd CA6 ....10 B3
Artlecrag LA8 ......130 E4
Arundel Dr LA13 ....207 E4
Asby Rd CA14 ......78 A3
Ash Bank LA18 .....149 D4
Ash Cl CA15 ....182 F5
Ash Ct LA7 ....211 E4
Ash Dr LA6 ....213 D8
Ash Fell Rd CA17 ...120 C4
Ash Gr Carlisle CA3 ..175 C2
  Ulverston LA12 .....203 D2
  Whitehaven CA28 ..186 E4
Ash Lea CA8 ....179 C5
Ash Mdw LA9 ......200 E2
Ash Mount Rd LA11 ..208 C5
Ash Rd CA11 ....191 F5
Ash St LA23 ....198 C2
Ash Tree Sq CA5 ....18 F1
Ashbank La LA8 ....143 E2
Ashburn Croft LA11 ..69 E5
Ashburner Way LA14 ..206 F4
Ashby St CA1 ....182 E5
Ashcroft Cl CA12 ...80 F6
Ashdown Rd LA13 ..207 E4
Ashes La LA8 ......130 C3
Ashes The LA7 .....211 D3
Ashfield Ct CA10 ...118 C7
Ashfield Gdns CA14 ..184 F4
Ashfield Inf Sch CA14 ..184 F5
Ashfield Jun Sch CA14 ..184 F4
Ashfield Rd S CA14 ..184 E3
Ashford Way CA1 ...177 E2
Ashgrove CA13 .....190 D3
Ashlea Rd CA22 ....189 B6
Ashleigh Pl CA28 ...187 E7
Ashleigh Rd Arnside LA5 ..209 B2
  Kendal LA9 ....200 E2
Ashley St CA2 ......176 E6
Ashley Way CA22 ..189 C5
Ashman Cl CA2 .....177 A4
Ashmeadow Rd LA5 ..209 B2
Ashmore Gdns CA14 ..184 C3
Ashmount Gdns LA11 ..208 C5
Ashness Cl CA28 ...187 D3
Ashness Dr CA2 ....176 C3
Ashton St CA14 .....184 E5
Ashtrees Way LA5 ..213 C4
Ashwell Pl TD9 .....1 B6
Ashworth St 3 LA15 ..205 C5
Askam Rd
  Dalton-In-F LA15 ..204 F8
  Dalton-In-F LA15 ..205 A8
Askam Sta LA16 ....162 A8
Askam Village Sch
  LA16 ....162 A8
Askerton Cl CA2 ...175 D3
Askham Cres CA11 ..191 E5
Aspatria Bsns Pk CA7 ..36 D1
Aspatria Richmond Hill Sch
  CA7 ....36 D1
Aspatria Sta CA7 ...36 D8
Aspen Dr LA13 .....207 E5
Aspen Gdns CA11 ..191 F5
Assembly Sq CA7 ...26 C1
Astor Ho CA2 ......176 D4
Athens Dr LA13 ....207 C3
Athol St LA14 ......206 F1
Atholl Gr CA2 ......176 B4
Atkinson Cres CA7 ..177 D2
Atkinson St LA8 ....130 E4
Auchinleck Dr CA14 ..177 D6
Auctionmart La 13
  ....191 C5

Auctionmart Rd 12
  ....191 C5
Austhwaite Brow CA19 ..125 A6
Austin Friars Sch CA3 ..175 C1
Avenue The
  Bassenthwaite CA12 ..66 C7
  Broughton Moor CA15 ..63 C8
  Edenhall CA11 ......71 F6
  Gilgarran CA14 .....77 C6
  Grange-Over-S LA11 ..208 C5
Avocet Cres LA16 ...161 F8
Avon Cl CA2 ....176 B4
Avon St LA14 ....170 C6
Aynam Cl LA9 ......200 D4
Aynam Pl LA9 ......200 D4
Aynam Rd LA9 .....200 D4
Aynsome La LA11 ...153 F2
Ayr St LA14 ....170 D6
Aysgarth Cl LA9 ...200 B8
Azalea Wlk LA13 ....207 F5

B

Back Barton St 3 LA14 ..207 B2
Back Belsfield Rd LA23 ..198 C2
Back Casson St 2 LA12 ..203 E5
Back Corkickle CA28 ..187 D8
Back Ellerthwaite Rd 7
  ....198 E5
Back Ennerdale CA25 ..188 E7
Back Ford Pk LA12 ..203 D6
Back Ginns CA28 ...187 C7
Back Hunter St LA5 ..213 C4
Back La
  Appleby-In-W CA16 ..193 D5
  Arnside LA5 ....209 B2
  Backbarrow LA12 ...153 C8
  Beetham LA7 ......155 F1
  Bowness-On-W LA8 ..129 F1
  Brampton CA8 .....179 B5
  Brigsteer LA8 .....143 F7
  Broughton-In-F LA20 ..139 A2
  Carnforth LA5 .....213 D2
  Cockermouth CA13 ..190 C5
  Flookburgh LA11 ...164 C6
  Great Broughton CA13 ..63 E6
  Kendal LA9 ....200 E5
  Langwathby CA10 ...62 B3
  Legburthwaite CA12 ..82 B1
  Levens LA8 ....143 F1
  Lindale LA11 ......154 C3
  Long Marton CA16 ..88 A7
  Melkinthorpe CA10 ..86 B8
  Newby Bridge LA11,LA12 ..153 F7
  Penrith CA11 ......191 C6
  Row LA8 ....142 C6
  Sedbergh LA10 ....201 C5
  Sedgwick LA8 .....144 A1
  Shap CA10 ....101 C6
  Staveley LA8 ......130 C5
  Troutbeck LA23 ....114 F2
  Tunstall LA6 ......168 D4
  Wrayton LA2,LA6 ...63 F5
Back Lady St DG12 ..172 C4
Back New St LA5 ...213 C4
Back O'Th' Fell Rd
  LA11 ....154 C5
Back Rd LA11 ......154 C3
Back St Annan DG12 ..172 C4
  Carlisle CA3 ....214 B2
  4 Keswick CA12 ...192 B4
  Keswick CA12 .....192 B4
Back Wyndham St CA25 ..188 E7
Backhouses Wlk CA2 ..214 B2
Backside Ct CA8 ...179 B5
Baden Powell St LA14 ..206 C3
Badgers Ct 2 LA14 ..207 A6
Badgers Rake LA22 ..195 D4
Bailey Rd CA3 ......175 C3
Bailey St 4 LA12 ...203 E5
Bainbridge Ct LA10 ..201 C5
Bainbridge Rd LA10 ..201 C5
Baird Rd CA1 ....177 D2
Bakewell Ct CA8 ...179 D4
Baldwin Ave LA15 ..205 B5
Baldwin St LA14 ....207 A8
Balfour Rd CA2 ....176 C5
Balsil Sch LA10 ....201 C5
Balmoral Cl CA11 ..191 B4
Balmoral Ct 1 CA3 ..175 B1
Balmoral Dr LA13 ...207 E4
Balmoral Rd CA28 ..187 F7
Bank Head St 12
  ....149 F2
Bank House La
  Silverdale LA5 .....210 C3
  Westhouse LA6 ....169 E4
Bank La
  Barrow-In-F LA14 ...204 A1
  Crosby Ravensworth CA10 ..102 C5
  Egremont CA22 ...189 E6
  Maryport CA15 ....182 D6
Bank Rd
  Bransty CA28 ......186 D3
  Windermere LA23 ..198 D3
  Workington CA14 ..184 F5
Bank Side CA14 ....185 D4
Bank St Annan DG12 ..172 C4
  Carlisle CA1 ....214 B2
  4 Keswick CA12 ...192 B4
  Keswick CA12 .....192 B4
Bank Terr
  Bowness-On-W LA23 ..198 D3
  Coniston LA21 .....196 A3
  Lindal in F LA12 ...162 E2
  Maryport CA15 ....182 D4

Bank Terr continued
  Penny Bridge LA12 ..152 E5
Bank Top LA11 ......164 D7
Bank Top Cl LA11 ..164 D7
Bank Yard Rd CA28 ..186 D5
Bankend Cotts CA24 ..91 F3
Bankend Rd CA3 ...175 B5
Bankend View CA22 ..188 A2
Bankfield CA21 .....108 B6
Bankfield Gdns LA14 ..206 C5
Bankfield Rd
  Haverigg LA18 .....202 A2
  Kendal LA9 ....200 C4
Bankhead La LA8 ...143 E4
Banklands CA14 ....184 E5
Banklands Ct LA14 ..184 E5
Banks Cres CA7 ....180 D2
Banks Hill Turret 52a*
  CA8 ....23 A7
Banks La Carlisle CA1 ..177 E6
  Dent LA10 ....147 B1
Banks Pl 8 CA12 ...130 C5
Banks The LA8 .....130 C5
Bankside La LA12 ..152 D5
Bannatyne Dr CA14 ..185 D7
Bannerigg LA23 ....198 E5
Banneriggs Brow LA6 ..158 A5
Bannisdale LA8 ....130 E4
Bannisdale Way LA12 ..176 C2
Barbondale Rd LA10 ..158 E8
Barco Ave CA11 ...191 E5
Barco Cl CA11 .....191 E5
Barco Terr 1 CA11 ..191 E4
Bardsea Cl LA13 ...205 B3
Bardsea L Pk LA12 ..203 E2
Bardsea Rd LA13 ...207 D4
Bardsley St CA2 ...176 C6
Barfs Rd CA14 .....185 A6
Barker Cl LA6 ......167 B7
Barker's La LA6 ....156 C4
Barkers Mdw CA13 ..64 A3
Barkhouse Cl CA11 ..191 E4
Barn Garth LA13 ...153 F1
Barn Holme LA9 ...200 B4
Barnard St 7 LA13 ..207 B3
Barncroft Ave CA14 ..183 A2
Barncroft Ct LA12 ..183 A2
Barnes Ave LA15 ...205 B3
Barnes Croft CA11 ..57 A3
Barnes Gn CA11 ....57 A3
Barnes Rd CA14 ...184 C5
Barnett Dr CA14 ...183 B3
Barnfield LA22 .....197 E5
Barnfield La LA14 ..206 E4
Barnghyll Pl CA14 ..185 C3
Barnoldswick La LA6 ..169 D3
Barnrigg LA6 ......157 F5
Barnsdale Rd CA14 ..184 D4
Baron Way CA6 ....175 A7
Baron's Hill CA11 ..70 C3
Barque St 4 LA14 ..206 F1
Barr's La Brigham CA13 ..64 A5
  Broughton Cross CA13 ..63 F5
Barras Brow Dalston CA5 ..29 D1
  South Stainmore CA17 ..106 A2
Barras Ct Carlisle CA2 ..176 C3
  Dalston CA5 ....29 D1
Barras Ho CA5 .....29 D1
Barras La CA5 .....29 D1
Barratt Croft LA21 ..196 A4
Barrock Cl CA4 ....41 C4
Barrock St CA1 ....214 C2
Barrow Island Com Prim Sch
  LA14 ....206 F1
Barrow Rd
  Barrow-In-F LA13 ..204 F1
  Dalton-In-F LA13 ..205 A3
Barrow-in-Furness Sixth
  Form Coll LA13 ...207 D7
Barrow-in-Furness Sta
  LA14 ....206 F4
Barrowmoor Rd CA16 ..193 B4
Bartha LA10 ....147 A3
Barton Dale CA6 ...57 A6
Barton Row LA6 ...167 B7
Barton St 4 LA14 ..207 B2
Barton View CA11 ..191 E6
Barton's Pl CA1 ...214 B2
Barwise Brow CA7 ..17 A5
Barwise Row CA26 ..77 E1
Barwood Gr LA13 ..207 F5
Basket Rd CA28 ....187 B8
Bassenthwaite Cl LA8 ..202 C4
Bassenthwaite Prim Sch
  CA12 ....66 B6
Bassenthwaite St CA2 ..176 D5
Basterfield Gdns 1
  LA13 ....207 B3
Bath St LA14 ....206 E4
Battery St DG12 ...172 C4
Battlebarrow CA16 ..193 C6
Bay Stones Cl LA12 ..163 B3
Bay Tree Rd LA12 ..203 E3
Bay View Millom LA18 ..202 B5
  St Bees CA27 ......91 C2
Bay View Gr LA13 ..207 D3
Baybarrow Rd CA22 ..189 C6
Baycliffe Pl LA15 ...205 C2
Baysdale Cl LA14 ..207 F4
Baystone Bank La LA18 ..150 B8
Beach Cres LA14 ..206 F7
Beach St
  Askam-In-F LA16 ...162 A8
  Workington CA14 ..184 C3

Beach Terr LA6 ....**169** F3
Beachwood La LA5 ....**209** A1
Beacon Cl Aspatria CA7 ..**36** C1
Penrith CA11 ....**191** C7
Beacon Edge CA11 ....**191** E6
Beacon Hill Com Sch
CA7 ....**50** C8
Beacon Pk CA11 ....**191** D6
Beacon Sq CA11 ....**191** D6
Beacon St CA11 ....**191** D6
Beacon The (Museum)*
CA28 ....**186** B1
Beacon View LA8 .....**132** A4
Beaconsfield St CA2 ...**177** A4
Beaconsfield Terr CA7 ..**174** B3
Beaconside CE Inf Sch
CA11 ....**191** E6
Beaconside CE Jun Sch
CA11 ....**191** E5
Beast Banks LA9 ......**200** C5
Beatham Ct [S] CA11 ...**191** C6
Beathwaite Cl LA8 .....**143** D1
Beathwaite Gdns LA8 ..**143** D1
Beatrix Potter Gallery*
LA22 ....**197** E5
Beatty Cl CA28 ....**186** D3
Beatty Rd CA28 ....**186** D3
Beaufort Ave LA14 ....**185** D7
Beaumont Rd CA2 .....**177** A2
Beaver Rd CA2 ....**176** A6
Beck Cl Brayotones CA21 ..**108** A5
Carlisle CA2 ....**176** A7
Beck Gn CA22 ....**189** E6
Beck Head LA6 ....**212** C2
Beck La Brampton CA8 ..**179** E5
Crosby Garrett CA17 ....**120** B7
Old Town LA6 ....**157** A6
Beck Nook LA8 ....**130** B5
Beck Rd CA2 ....**176** A6
Beck Riggs CA8 ....**179** B5
Beck Rise CA21 ....**108** B5
Beck Yeat LA21 ....**105** A5
Beckermet CE Sch
CA21 ....**108** B5
Beckermet Gdns LA14 ..**204** C1
Beckfoot Sta* CA19 ....**125** B7
Beckgate LA6 ....**157** F5
Beckside Eaglesfield CA13 ..**64** A3
Flimby CA15 ....**163** C7
Hallthwaites LA18 ....**150** C7
Kendal LA9 ....**200** F2
Penrith CA11 ....**191** B4
Penrith,Scaws CA11 .....**191** F5
Plumpton CA11 ....**56** B3
Beckside CA28 ....**187** F7
Beckside Cl CA13 .....**190** E4
Beckside Cotts LA19 ...**137** B3
Beckside Ct
Kirkby-in-F LA17 ....**151** C5
[S] Ulverston LA12 ......**203** D5
Beckside Gdns CA8 ...**179** D4
Beckside Mews LA6 ...**167** B3
Beckside Rd
Dalton-In-F LA15 ....**205** C4
Ulverston LA12 ....**203** C6
Beckstone Cl CA14 ....**185** A8
Bective Rd LA6 ....**212** C2
Bedford Rd
Barrow-In-F LA14 ....**207** A5
Carlisle CA2 ....**176** E5
Bedford St
Hensingham CA28 ....**187** F6
Millom LA18 ....**202** D4
Bedford Villas CA28 ...**187** F6
Beeby Ct [S] CA14 ....**184** D6
Beeby St CA14 ....**184** D6
Beech Ave CA22 ....**189** D7
Beech Bank LA12 ......**203** D6
Beech Cl Clifton CA11 ..**71** C5
Kendal LA9 ....**200** F5
Milnthorpe LA7 ....**211** E3
Beech Croft
Braithwaite CA12 ....**80** F6
Burgh-By-S CA5 ....**18** F2
Wigton CA7 ....**180** C3
Beech Ct CA14 ....**184** B8
Beech Gdns CA11 .....**71** C5
Beech Gr Carlisle CA3 ..**175** E2
Houghton CA3 ....**20** C2
Seaton CA14 ....**183** B1
Stainton CA11 ....**70** D3
Warton LA5 ....**213** C7
Whitehaven CA28 ....**186** E3
Beech Hill Dent LA10 ..**147** B2
Oughterside CA7 ....**49** F6
Beech La CA13 ....**190** E5
Milnthorpe LA7 ....**211** E5
Beech Lea CA7 ....**27** B7
Beech Rd LA11 ....**208** C4
Beech St
Barrow-In-F LA14 ....**206** F6
Windermere LA23 ....**198** E6
Beech Tree Cl CA6 ....**20** F8
Beeches The
Great Corby CA4 ....**178** C2
Maryport CA15 ....**182** F6
Beechfields LA12 .....**162** F4
Beechlands LA12 ......**203** D6
Beechwood Ave CA3 ...**175** E2
Beechwood Cl
Bowness-On-W LA23 ...**197** D8
Maryport CA15 ....**182** D6
Beehive La LA8 ....**144** D5
Beemire LA23 ....**198** D5

Beetham CE Prim Sch
LA7 ....**155** E2
Beetham Cvn Pk LA7 ..**166** E8
Beetham Hall LA7 .....**155** E2
Beetham Rd LA7 ......**211** D2
Beezon Fields LA9 ....**200** D6
Beezon Rd LA9 ....**200** D6
Beezon Trad Est LA9 ..**200** D6
Beggars La CA10 .....**119** A4
Bela Ave LA7 ....**211** D3
Bela Forge LA7 ....**211** C3
Belah Cres CA3 ....**175** D2
Belah Prim Sch CA3 ...**175** D2
Belah Rd CA3 ....**175** C2
Belfry Cl CA3 ....**175** B1
Belgravia CA16 ....**193** C7
Bell Cl CA12 ....**192** B4
Bell Hill LA11 ....**154** C3
Bell Hill Pk LA11 ......**154** C3
Bell La CA10 ....**86** F5
Bellaport Gdns CA14 ..**185** A7
Bellbrigg Lonning CA13 ..**190** E3
Belle Hill Cotts LA12 ..**162** D7
Belle Isle Cl CA14 ....**184** C6
Belle Isle View LA23 ..**198** D2
Belle Vue Cres CA14 ..**184** D6
Belle Vue La LA22 ....**195** D6
Bellevue Rd LA16 .....**193** D6
Bellgarth Rd CA2 .....**176** C7
Bellgate Steading CA7 ..**50** C8
Bellingham Rd LA9 ....**200** C5
Bellman Cl LA23 ......**29** A1
Bellsfield CA6 ....**10** C3
Belmont Kendal LA9 ...**200** C5
Ulverston LA12 ....**203** E6
Belmont Brow [B] LA9 ..**9** A7
Belmont Rd CA2 ......**177** B3
Belsfield LA13 ....**207** E3
Belsfield Ct LA23 .....**198** C2
Belted Will Cl CA7 ....**180** C4
Belvedere Rd LA13 ...**190** E4
Belvedere St CA14 ...**184** E6
Benfield LA22 ....**194** C5
Bensmoor Rd DG16 ...**173** D5
Benson Gn LA9 ....**200** D6
Benson La CA11 ......**124** C1
Benson Row CA11 ....**191** D5
Benson St [S] LA12 ...**203** D5
Bentham Moor Rd LA2,
LA6 ....**169** D2
Bentham Rd LA2,LA6 ..**169** E3
Bents La LA6 ....**158** A3
Beresford Ct LA23 ....**198** D3
Beresford Rd LA23 ...**198** D3
Berkeley Ct CA11 .....**191** D5
Berkeley Grange CA2 ..**176** B6
Berlin St CA1 ....**177** C4
Bermuda Cres LA14 ...**170** C6
Berners Cl LA11 ......**208** C3
Berriedale Terr LA11 ..**208** F5
Berrier Rd CA11 ......**69** E5
Berry Bank Rd LA11 ...**208** B2
Berrymoor Rd CA8 ....**179** C3
Berwick St CA14 .....**184** E5
Bessamer Way LA14 ..**206** D4
Bessy Bank La LA12 ..**140** D1
Betsy La CA10 ....**72** E2
Betweengates La LA6 ..**157** F7
Bevan Terr CA9 ....**46** F2
Beveridge Rd CA2 ....**176** B7
Beverley Ave [4] LA14 ..**207** B6
Beverley Cl CA14 .....**184** D3
Beverley Rise CA1 ....**30** E5
Bewcastle Cl CA3 .....**175** C3
Bewcastle Sch CA6 ....**5** E4
Bewley Mews [2] LA13 ..**207** C5
Bewley Stps LA13 ....**207** C5
Bideford Gdns LA14 ...**204** C1
Biggar Bank Rd LA14 ..**170** B6
Biggar Garth LA14 ....**170** C6
Biggins La LA6 ....**212** A1
Biggins Rd LA6 ....**212** B2
Bigland Dr LA12 ......**203** D2
Billings Rd LA13 .....**205** A2
Bindloss Cottage Homes
LA7 ....**211** E4
Binfold Croft LA6 .....**212** C1
Birch Cl Barrow-In-F LA14 ..**207** F5
Workington CA14 ....**184** D3
Birch Cres CA11 ......**191** F4
Birch Dr LA5 ....**210** C4
Birch Gr LA5 ....**165** F8
Birch Hill La CA7 .....**27** C8
Birch Rd LA23 ....**198** E5
Birch Trees LA23 .....**198** D7
Birchdale Rd CA2 .....**29** D6
Birchfield LA8 ....**156** D8
Birchfields LA13 ......**207** E4
Birchleigh Terr LA11 ..**208** D4
Birchwood Cl
Kendal LA9 ....**200** B3
Ulverston LA12 ....**203** D1
Birchwood Dr LA12 ...**203** D1
Bird St CA14 ....**184** D5
Birdcage Wlk CA7 ....**180** D3
Birdoswald Dr CA2 ...**29** D6
Birdoswald Roman Fort
(mus)* LA8 ....**14** B1
Birkett Cl LA12 ....**200** F3
Birkett Dr LA12 ......**203** C2
Birkett Hill Cotts LA12 ..**198** C1
Birkett La Hartley CA17 ..**121** B7
Kirkby Stephen CA17 ....**199** F5

Birkfield Rd LA23 .....**198** E4
Birkhaw La LA10 .....**133** A1
Birkigg Cl LA12 ....**203** A2
Birkrigg Cres LA12 ...**203** C2
Birks La Endmoor LA7 ..**156** E7
Sedbergh LA10 ....**201** B4
Birks Rd
Cleator Moor CA25 .....**188** E7
Windermere LA23 ....**142** A6
Windermere LA23 ....**142** B6
Birky La CA6 ....**20** E3
Birley Cl [6] CA28 ....**186** D1
Birthwaite Dr LA23 ...**198** D6
Birthwaite Ground LA23 ..**198** E5
Birthwaite Rd LA23 ...**198** D6
Bishop Harvey Goodwin Sch
The CA2 ....**177** B3
Bishop Yds [5] CA11 ..**191** D5
Bishop's Mill CA5 .....**40** B8
Bishops Cl CA2 ....**176** E6
Bishops Cts LA5 ......**200** D4
Biskey Howe Pk LA23 ..**198** D3
Biskey Howe Rd LA23 ..**198** D3
Bisland Ct CA1 ....**177** E3
Black Beck Cvn Pk
LA12 ....**153** A8
Black Beck Rd LA12 ..**197** E5
Black Bull La CA17 ...**105** B5
Black Butts La CA14 ..**206** C1
Black Combe Jun Sch
LA18 ....**202** B5
Black Dyke Rd LA5 ...**209** C1
Black Ling Cotts CA22 ..**189** B3
Black Sail Cl LA14 ....**143** C3
Black Sail Hut YH* LA13 ..**95** B3
Blackbeck Brow LA8 ..**143** B6
Blackberry Hill LA7 ...**155** E2
Blackbull Barn CA17 ..**199** C6
Blackburn Dr CA1 ....**177** F2
Blackburn St CA14 ...**184** D5
Blackdyke Rd CA3 ....**175** B5
Blackford CE Prim Sch
CA6 ....**20** A5
Blackfriars St CA3 ...**214** B2
Blackhall Rd LA9 .....**200** D5
Blacksike Sq DG16 ...**173** D5
Blackthorn Cl LA9 ....**200** C8
Blackwell Pl CA2 .....**177** B3
Blackwell Rd CA2 ....**177** A3
Blackwood Rd LA14 ..**185** F7
Blake Fell Cl CA28 ....**76** F1
Blake St
Barrow-In-F LA14 ....**206** E4
Carlisle CA1 ....**214** C1
Blea Beck [2B] LA16 ..**162** A8
Blea Moor Rd LA6 ....**160** C2
Blea Tarn Cl LA9 .....**200** F1
Blea Tarn Rd LA4 ....**200** F1
Bleachgreen Paddock
CA28 ....**186** B3
Bleacrag Bridge LA11 ..**154** D6
Bleacrag Rd LA11 ....**154** D7
Bleaflatt La CA17 .....**120** B3
Bleas Egremont CA22 ..**92** F1
Haile CA22 ....**92** F2
Bleasdale House Com Specl
Sch LA5 ....**210** C3
Blease Rd CA2 ....**82** B8
Bleaswood Cl LA9 ....**144** B4
Bleaswood Rd LA9 ...**144** B4
Blencarn Pk CA6 .....**19** C4
Blencathra Bsns Ctr
CA12 ....**82** C7
Blencathra Cl
Cockermouth CA13 .....**190** F4
Penrith CA11 ....**191** C3
Blencathra Gdns LA9 ..**200** F1
Blencathra St CA2 ....**192** C3
Blencathra View LA12 ..**82** C7
Blencowe St CA2 .....**192** C3
Bleng Ave CA20 ......**187** E6
Blenket Cl LA11 ......**208** E5
Blenkinsopp Castle Home Pk
CA8 ....**24** D7
Blenkinsopp Terr CA8 ..**24** D7
Blenhasset Sch CA7 ..**50** F8
Bletherbarrow La LA12 ..**140** C3
Blind La Burton in L LA6 ..**159** E6
Cleator Moor CA24,CA25 ..**188** C6
Great Asby CA16 ....**103** B7
Bloody Bones La CA17 ..**199** C6
Bloomfield Pk LA5 ....**213** C3
Blooming Heather CA15 ..**49** A2
Blue Dial Cvn Pk CA15 ..**49** B7
Blue Hill Rd LA22 ....**195** D4
Bluebell Cl LA9 ....**200** F2
Bluebell Ct [8] CA15 ..**191** A5
Bluebell La CA11 .....**191** C5
Blundell Rd CA1 ......**177** E2
Blunt St CA2 ....**176** F4
Blyth Rise LA14 ......**206** A4
BNFL Vst Ctr* CA20 ...**108** D4
Boarbank Farm LA11 ..**164** F7
Boarbank La LA11 ....**164** F7
Boarbank Rd LA12 ...**203** D2
Bobbin Mill Cotts LA12 ..**152** D7
Bobbin Mill La CA20 ..**138** D7
Bog La Ambleside LA22 ..**195** A3
Skelwith Bridge LA22 ..**113** F2
Bogle Crag Forest Wlk*
LA12 ....**141** A8
Bolefoot LA9 ....**144** B4
Bollam Terr CA17 ....**199** D5
Bolton Hall LA16 .....**87** D6
Bolton Prim Sch CA16 ..**87** D5

Bolton St
Barrow-In-F LA13 ....**207** C3
Workington CA14 ....**144** D5
Boltons CE Sch CA7 ..**37** F3
Bonfire Hall La LA8 ...**143** C7
Bongate CA16 ....**193** D4
Bookwall Prim Sch
CA22 ....**189** D5
Boon Town LA6 ......**167** C7
Boon Wlks LA6 ......**167** C7
Boonwell Gr LA13 ...**207** D3
Booth St LA5 ....**213** C3
Bootle Sta LA19 .....**137** A4
Border Ave CA25 ....**188** C8
Border Cl CA1 ....**177** F2
Border Cres DG16 ...**173** D2
Borders Bsns Pk CA6 ..**10** C3
Borland Ave Carlisle CA1 ..**177** D5
Borough St CA3 ......**214** B2
Boroughgate CA16 ...**193** C5
Borrans Cl LA22 .....**195** C3
Borrans La LA23 .....**129** E7
Borrans Park Ho LA22 ..**195** C4
Borrans Rd LA22 .....**195** C3
Borrans The LA22 ....**195** C4
Borrans The LA22 ....**167** C3
Borrowdale Gdns
Barrow-In-F LA14 ....**204** D1
Carlisle CA2 ....**176** D5
Borrowdale Rd
Carlisle CA2 ....**176** D5
Keswick CA12 ....**192** B2
Whitehaven CA28 ....**187** D3
Borrowdale YH* CA12 ..**96** B5
Borwick Ave LA5 .....**213** D8
Borwick Cl LA5 ....**213** D8
Borwick Ct LA6 ......**167** B4
Warton LA5 ....**213** E8
Borwick La Borwick LA6 ..**167** B3
Warton LA5 ....**167** D3
Borwick Mews LA6 ...**167** D3
Boston Ave CA2 ......**177** A3
Botany Cl [F] CA14 ..**184** D6
Botcherby Ave CA1 ...**177** D5
Botchergate CA1 .....**214** B1
Bottoms La LA5 ......**209** A5
Boulevard The LA11 ..**208** E5
Boundary Bank La LA9 ..**200** A5
Boundary Rd CA2 ....**177** B3
Bourne Ave CA5 .....**182** E4
Bourne Gdns LA14 ...**206** A4
Boustead's Grassing
CA2 ....**159** F4
Bouthwood Rd LA14 ..**204** C4
Bow Bridge* LA13 .....**207** E7
Bow Fell Rd CA28 ....**187** E3
Bow Flatts CA14 .....**63** A4
Bowder Stone* CA12 ..**96** B7
Bower St CA2 ....**176** D6
Bowerbank Way CA11 ..**191** B6
Bowerhouse Bank CA19 ..**124** D7
Bowes Ho CA2 ....**176** C1
Bowfell Cres
Barrow-In-F LA14 ....**204** D1
Windermere LA23 ....**198** F5
Bowland Cl LA5 ......**213** B3
Bowland Dr LA4 .....**144** C8
Bowman St CA1 ......**214** C1
Bowness Ct LA14 ....**204** D1
Bowness Knott Forest Trail*
CA23 ....**93** F6
Bowness Rd
Barrow-In-F LA14 ....**207** B6
Dalton-In-F LA15 ....**205** B3
Millom LA18 ....**202** C4
Whitehaven CA28 ....**187** D4
Bowness-on-Solway Prim
Sch CA7 ....**17** B5
Bowscar Rd Penrith CA11 ..**70** F8
Plumpton CA11 ....**56** D1
Bowthorn Rd CA25 ...**188** C8
Boyd St [S] CA15 ....**182** E5
Bracken Bed La LA12 ..**171** C8
Bracken Cl CA3 ......**175** C2
Bracken Ct LA11 .....**55** E7
Bracken Gr LA12 ....**203** A2
Bracken Ridge CA3 ..**175** C2
Brackenber Ct CA11 ..**191** B5
Brackenber Lodge
CA10 ....**101** C5
Brackenburgh Cotts
CA11 ....**55** F6
Brackenfield LA23 ...**198** C2
Brackenhill La LA10 ..**190** B3
Brackenlands CA7 ...**180** D2
Brackenrigg Dr CA12 ..**42** C5
Brackenrigg Dr LA12 ..**192** C3
Brackensgill La LA10 ..**207** C5
Brackenslack La LA10 ..**102** D8
Brackenthaite Rd LA5,
LA7 ....**166** D8
Brackenwood LA9 ...**200** B4
Bradbury Ave CA15 ..**182** D4
Braddyll Terr LA12 ...**203** D4
Brade St LA12 ....**139** A2
Bradford St LA14 ....**206** F8
Bradshawgate Dr LA5 ..**210** C4
Braeside CA14 ....**144** D3
Brailes Ct [3] CA13 ..**190** D4
Braisgate CA11 ......**191** B2
Braithwaite CE Prim Sch
CA12 ....**80** F6
Braithwaite Ct CA22 ..**189** C6
Braithwaite Fold Cvn Pk
LA23 ....**198** B1
Brakeside Gdns CA28 ..**187** C6
Bramble Cl LA9 ......**200** C8

Bramerton Orch CA1 ..**177** E6
Brampton Jun & Inf Sch
CA8 ....**179** C5
Brampton Junc Sta CA8 ..**22** E2
Brampton Old Rd CA3,
CA6 ....**20** C1
Brampton Rd CA3 ....**175** F1
Brampton War Meml Cottage
Hospl CA8 ....**179** D4
Brandlehow Cres CA12 ..**192** C3
Bransty Prim Sch CA28 ..**186** D3
Bransty Rd CA28 .....**186** D3
Bransty Sta CA28 ....**186** D3
Bransty Row CA28 ...**186** C2
Brantfell Cotts CA28 ..**198** D2
Brantfell Ho LA23 ....**198** C2
Brantfell Rd LA23 ....**198** C2
Brantfell Wlk LA23 ...**198** C2
Branthwaite Brow [2]
LA9 ....**200** D5
Branthwaite La LA23 ..**198** B1
Brantwood* LA21 .....**127** E2
Brantwood Ave CA1 ..**177** F4
Brantwood La CA25 ..**188** B8
Brathay Cres LA14 ...**204** B2
Brathy Hall (Training Ctr)
LA22 ....**195** B3
Braunton Dr LA14 ...**207** A8
Braystones Rd CA2 ..**108** B5
Braystones Sta CA21 ..**108** A5
Brayton Pk CA7 ......**50** C8
Brayton Rd Aspatria CA7 ..**36** D1
Bransty CA28 ....**189** D2
Brayton St CA14 .....**184** E5
Brayton Terr CA28 ...**186** D2
Breast Mill Beck Ct
LA14 ....**204** F2
Breast Mill Beck Rd
LA14 ....**204** F2
Breen La LA23 ....**129** B1
Brennan Cl LA13 ....**207** F3
Brent Ave LA15 .....**205** C4
Brent Cl CA1 ....**191** D5
Brent Rd CA11 ......**191** C6
Brentfield Way CA11 ..**191** E5
Brewery Brow CA28 ..**186** E6
Brewery La [4] CA28 ..**190** D4
Brewery St Allonby CA15 ..**35** C1
Barrow-In-F LA14 ....**207** A4
[7] Ulverston LA12 .....**203** D5
Brewery Terr LA15 ...**35** C1
Briar Bank Carlisle CA3 ..**175** C2
Cockermouth CA13 .....**190** E2
Briar Cl CA8 ....**31** F8
Briar Ct LA13 ....**207** F5
Briar Lea Ct CA6 ....**10** C3
Briar Rigg CA12 .....**192** B5
Briarcliffe Gdns LA15 ..**205** C4
Briarcote CA17 ......**199** D6
Briarcote LA5 ....**213** D8
Briarscroft LA5 ......**213** D8
Briarwood LA9 ......**200** B4
Brick Kiln Rd LA12 ...**203** F2
Bridekirk Dovenby CE Prim
Sch LA13 ....**64** B8
Bridge Age LA14 ....**206** D2
Bridge Brow LA4 ....**212** C1
Bridge End Bsns Pk
LA7 ....**211** C4
Bridge End Ind Est
CA22 ....**189** C5
Bridge End Pk CA22 ..**189** E5
Bridge Ho*
Ambleside LA22 ....**195** D6
[3] Dalton-In-F LA15 ..**205** C5
Bridge La Carlisle CA2 ..**176** E7
[7] Kendal LA9 ....**200** D5
Penrith CA11 ....**191** E3
Bridge Rd
Barrow-In-F LA14 ....**206** E1
Carlisle CA2 ....**176** C7
Bridge St
Appleby-In-W CA16 ...**193** C5
Brough CA17 ....**105** B5
Burneside LA9 ....**130** F2
Caldewgate CA2,CA3 ..**214** A3
Cockermouth CA13 .....**190** C4
Kendal LA9 ....**200** D5
Longtown CA6 ....**10** B3
Maryport CA15 ....**182** C6
[4] Penrith CA11 ....**191** C5
Workington CA14 ....**184** F6
Bridge St [3] LA12 ..**203** D5
Bridge Terr Carlisle CA2 ..**176** F4
Keswick CA12 ....**192** B5
Melmerby CA10 ....**63** F5
Bridge Way LA13 ....**207** C4
Bridges Rest Pk CA28 ..**187** D8
Bridgewater Rd CA1,
CA3 ....**214** B4
Brier Lonning CA8 ...**21** F1
Brierley Rd CA25 ....**188** C6
Briery Acres CA14 ...**62** F3
Briery Bank LA5 .....**209** C1
Briery Cl LA23 ....**129** A8
Briery Croft CA14 ...**62** F3
Briery Gdr CA2 ......**30** C3
Brieryddale LA14 ....**184** D1
Brieryfield La CA14 ..**62** F3
Brig St LA14 ....**206** F1
Brigbourne Dr CA14 ..**183** B2
Brigflatts La LA10 ...**201** A6
Brigflatts Mdw [5] LA9 ..**207** B2
Brigham Hall LA13 ...**63** F5
Brigham Rd CA13 ...**190** B3
Brigham Row CA12 ..**192** C4

Bright St CA2 . . . . 176 D6
Brighton Pl DG14 . . . . 3 D3
Brighton St LA14 . . . . 207 A5
Brigsteer Brow LA8 . . . . . . 143 D4
Brigsteer Cswy LA8 . . . . . . 143 C2
Brigsteer Rd Kendal LA8 . . 143 E5
Levens LA8 . . . . 143 D1
Brindlefield CA7 . . . . 180 D2
Brisbane Park Inf Sch
LA14 . . . . 206 E4
Brisco Mdws CA2 . . . . 177 C1
Brisco Rd CA2 CA14 . . . . . 177 B3
Brisco View CA1 . . . . 30 D3
Briscoe Cres CA28 . . . . . . 186 D4
Briscoe Mount CA22 . . . . . 189 E8
Briscoe Rd CA28 . . . . 189 E8
Brisedale Rd LA10 . . . . . . 148 C7
Bristol St LA14 . . . . 206 C1
Broad Acres CA14 . . . . 185 B7
Broad Cl LA14 . . . . 206 C1
Broad Ing Kendal LA9 . . . . 200 E6
Thorpe CA10 . . . . 70 E1
Broad Ing Cres LA9 . . . . . 200 E6
Broad St Carlisle CA1 . . . . 214 C2
Windermere LA23 . . . . . . 198 E5
Broadfield LA23 . . . . 129 B7
Broadfield Cl LA23 . . . . . . 129 B7
Broadfield La LA10 . . . . . . 147 C1
Broadgate LA22 . . . . 194 B4
Broadguards CA2 . . . . 176 E6
Broadmire Rd CA6 . . . . . . 103 C7
Broadoaks Ct CA1 . . . . . . 177 E6
Broadoaks Grange CA1 . . 177 E5
Broadstairs La LA14 . . . . . 206 C2
Broadway LA13 . . . . 207 D3
Brockbank Terr CA7 . . . . . 199 C4
Brockbeck **5** LA9 . . . . . . 200 D4
Brockleymoor CA11 . . . . . . 56 B3
Brockwood Hall LA18 . . . . 150 B7
Brogden St LA12 . . . . 203 D5
Bromley Ct CA14 . . . . 184 C6
Bromley St CA14 . . . . 184 D6
Brook Bank CA28 . . . . 187 A6
Brook Cl **1** CA5 . . . . 28 F1
Brook Rd LA23 . . . . 198 E5
Brook Side CA15 . . . . 182 E5
Brook St
Barrow-in-F LA13 . . . . . . 207 C3
Carlisle CA2 . . . . 214 C1
Flimby CA15 . . . . 183 C8
10 Penrith CA11 . . . . . . 191 D5
Windermere LA23 . . . . . . 129 B7
Workington CA14 . . . . . . 184 D6
Brook St Inf Sch CA1 . . . . 214 C1
Brookfield CA14 . . . . 101 C4
Brookfield Ave CA7 . . . . . . 180 B3
Brookfield Cl **2** LA6 . . . . 156 B1
Brookfield Gdns CA1 . . . . 177 C4
Brookfields CA7 . . . . 180 A2
Brookland LA9 . . . . 169 C3
Brooklands Ave CA15 . . . . 182 E4
Brooklands Grange
CA11 . . . . 191 E4
Brooklands View **5**
CA11 . . . . 191 E4
Brooklyn CA11 . . . . 70 D3
Brookside
Beckermet CA21 . . . . . . 108 C5
Carlisle CA2 . . . . 176 C6
Cleator CA23 . . . . 188 E5
Seaton CA14 . . . . 183 B2
Sockbridge CA10 . . . . 70 F1
Warcop CA16 . . . . 104 C6
11 Wigton CA7 . . . . . . 180 D3
Brookside Pl CA2 . . . . 176 D6
Brookvale LA12 . . . . 203 A2
Broom Bank CA28 . . . . . . 186 E1
Broom Cl
Broughton-In-F LA20 . . . 139 A2
Kendal LA9 . . . . 144 C7
Broom Cres DG12 . . . . 172 A1
Broom Garth CA2 . . . . 30 B3
Broom Garth End La
LA8 . . . . 143 C5
Broom La LA8 . . . . 143 A7
Broome Ct CA1 . . . . 177 D3
Broomfallen Rd CA4 . . . . . . 30 F5
Broomrigg Cres CA4 . . . . . . 42 F5
Broomy Hill LA9 . . . . 30 F7
Brough Castle* CA17 . . . 105 B5
Brough Prim Sch CA17 . . 105 B5
Brough St CA7 . . . . 58 C8
Brougham Ave CA10 . . . . . . 71 C3
Brougham Castle* CA11 . 72 D3
Brougham Hall* LA10 . . 191 F1
Brougham Hall Gdns
CA10 . . . . 191 F1
Brougham La CA7 . . . . 199 C5
Brougham St LA11 . . . . . . 145 C5
Broughton CE Sch LA20 . . 139 A2
Broughton Cl **15** LA14 . . 162 A8
Broughton Lodge
10 Dalton-In-F LA15 . . 205 C5
Grange-Over-S LA11 . . . . 154 A3
Broughton Moor Prim Sch
CA15 . . . . 63 C8
Broughton Pk
Broughton-In-F LA20 . . . 139 A2
Broughton Prim Sch
CA13 . . . . 63 E6
Broughton Rd LA15 . . . . . 205 D2
Broughton Twr LA20 . . . . 139 A2
Broughton Way LA14 . . . . 207 D4
Brow Bottom CA14 . . . . . . 77 F7
Brow Cl LA23 . . . . 198 E3
Brow Cres LA23 . . . . 198 E3
Brow Edge Rd LA12 . . . . . 153 C7

Brow Foot La LA8 . . . . . . 130 B7
Brow La LA8 . . . . 130 B5
Brow Side La11 . . . . 153 C7
Brow St CA15 . . . . 182 D6
Brow The CA5 . . . . 49 D5
Brow Top CA14 . . . . 184 E6
Browfield Cl CA11 . . . . 98 C7
Browfoot Cl LA14 . . . . . . 213 E4
Brown St
Barrow-In-F LA14 . . . . . 207 A2
Workington CA14 . . . . . . 184 E5
Brown's Pl CA14 . . . . 183 D2
Brownber La CA17 . . . . . . 119 E4
Brownrigg Brow CA14 . . . . 78 C7
Brownrigg Dr CA2 . . . . . . 176 E6
Browsholme Cl LA5 . . . . . 213 B3
Browside Rd CA15 . . . . . . 49 A2
Bruce St DG12 . . . . 172 C4
Brundholme Gdns CA12 . . 192 C4
Brundholme Rd CA12 . . . . 192 B4
Brunel Way CA1 . . . . 177 D4
Brunlea Dr CA28 . . . . 186 E3
Brunstock Cl CA3 . . . . . . 175 C3
Brunstock La CA3,CA6 . . . 175 F6
Brunstock Mews CA6 . . . . 20 C2
Brunswick Rd CA11 . . . . . 191 C5
Brunswick Sch CA11 . . . . 191 C5
Brunswick Sq CA11 . . . . . 191 C5
Brunswick St LA1 . . . . . . 214 C2
Brunswick Terr CA11 . . . . 191 C5
Brunthill Rd CA3 . . . . 175 B5
Bruntley Mdws CA9 . . . . . 181 B3
Brunton Ave CA1 . . . . 177 C6
Brunton Cres CA1 . . . . . . 177 C6
Brunton Park (Carlisle United
FC) CA1 . . . . 177 C7
Buccleuch Ct LA14 . . . . . 207 A4
Buccleuch Dock Rd
LA14 . . . . 206 F1
Buccleuch St
Barrow-In-F LA14 . . . . . 206 F3
Dalton-In-F LA15 . . . . . 205 B5
Buccleuch Terr TD9 . . . . . . 1 B6
Buchanan Pl **E** CA2 . . . . 177 B2
Buchanan Rd CA2 . . . . . . 177 B2
Buchanan Terr CA15 . . . . 182 F4
Buckabank Ct CA5 . . . . . . 40 B8
Buckbank La LA10 . . . . . . 146 E2
Buckholme Dr
Askham CA10 . . . . 85 E8
Clifton CA10 . . . . 71 C1
Buckhorn La LA17 . . . . . . 151 D7
Buckle Ave CA25 . . . . 188 D6
Buckman Brow LA18,
LA20 . . . . 138 E1
Buddle Rd CA14 . . . . 184 C4
Buebank La CA5 . . . . 29 C1
Buebank Rd CA5 . . . . 40 A8
Buffs Croft CA4 . . . . 178 A5
Buildings Farm Cl CA14 . 183 A3
Buller St LA14 . . . . 206 C2
Bungalows The
Eamont Bridge CA10 . . . 191 E1
Keswick CA12 . . . . 192 D4
Maryport CA15 . . . . 28 A7
Burgh by Sands Sch CA5 . 18 F1
Burgh Rd CA2 . . . . 175 F6
Burgh Road Ind Est CA2 . 176 B7
Burland Gr LA9 . . . . 200 E2
Burlington CE Sch LA17 . 151 C5
Burlington St LA17 . . . . . 151 C5
Burlington Mews **5**
LA12 . . . . 203 D5
Burlington St
1 Barrow-In-F LA14 . . 206 F2
Ulverston LA12 . . . . 203 D5
Burlington Villas LA17 . . 151 C6
Burn St CA6 . . . . 10 C3
Burnaby St LA14 . . . . 206 E2
Burnbanks CA10 . . . . 100 C7
Burneside Rd LA9 . . . . . . 200 C7
Burneside Sta LA9 . . . . . 130 F2
Burnet Rd CA11 . . . . 191 D5
Burney Beck Cotts
CA16 . . . . 103 C4
Burnfoot Gr CA14 . . . . . . 184 C4
Burnmoor Ave CA28 . . . . 187 D5
Burnrigg CA2 . . . . 176 C3
Burns Ave LA13 . . . . 207 D6
Burnsall Cl CA2 . . . . 176 A4
Burnside
Harrington CA14 . . . . . . 185 A8
Longtown CA6 . . . . 10 C3
Wigton CA7 . . . . 180 B3
Burnside Cvn Pk CA12 . . . 192 B6
Burnside Rd DG16 . . . . . . 173 C3
Burnswalk Terr CA7 . . . . . 174 C4
Burntbarrow LA7 . . . . . . 154 F4
Burrow Rd LA6 . . . . 156 B2
Burrow Walls LA14 . . . . . 184 B4
Burrowgate CA11 . . . . . . 191 D5
Burton High Cl CA28 . . . . 186 E2
Burton Hill LA6 . . . . 169 C3
Burton Morewood CE Prim
Sch LA6 . . . . 167 C7
Burton Pk LA6 . . . . 167 B7
Burton Rd
Burton in L LA2 . . . . . . 169 C1
Holme LA6 . . . . 167 A3
Kendal LA9 . . . . 200 E2
Oxenholme LA9 . . . . . . 144 B4
Burwain Terr CA10 . . . . . . 87 D8
Bush Brow CA3 . . . . 214 B2
Busher Wlk LA9 . . . . 200 C6
Bushfield CA6 . . . . 4 F7
Busk La
Kirkby Stephen CA17 . . 199 A8
Sedbergh LA10 . . . . 201 B4

Butler St LA18 . . . . 202 B5
Butter Well La LA9 . . . . . 200 C4
Butterburn Cl CA3 . . . . . . 175 C2
Butterflies Cvn Pk LA18 . 150 A1
Buttermere Ave CA28 . . . 187 B5
Buttermere Cl
Carlisle CA2 . . . . 176 D5
Cockermouth CA13 . . . . 190 F3
Buttermere Cres LA14 . . . 204 E1
Buttermere Dr
Dalton-In-F LA15 . . . . . 205 C3
Kendal LA9 . . . . 200 F2
Millom LA18 . . . . 202 C4
Buttermere Rd LA13 . . . . 182 E3
Buttery Well La **14** LA9 . 200 C4
Buttery Well Rd LA9 . . . . 200 C4
Butts Beck LA15 . . . . 205 C6
Butts Fold CA13 . . . . 190 E4
Butts Mdw LA12 . . . . 66 B6
Butts Mews CA9 . . . . 181 D4
Butts St DG12 . . . . 172 C4
Buxton St LA14 . . . . 206 C1
Byerstead Rd CA28 . . . . . 187 B1
Byreburnfoot CA6 . . . . 3 C4
Byreburnfoot Trail*
DG14 . . . . 3 D4
Byrnes Pl CA11 . . . . 56 B4
Byron St
Barrow-In-F LA14 . . . . . 206 F4
Carlisle CA2 . . . . 176 E7
Ulverston LA12 . . . . 203 E5
10 Workington CA14 . . 184 D6
Byron Terr CA8 . . . . 24 D7

C

Cadgill Rd DG16 . . . . 173 C2
Cadman St **16** LA14 . . . . 184 D6
Caesar's View CA16 . . . . . 193 C4
Cain St Bigrigg CA22 . . . . 188 A3
Workington CA14 . . . . . . 184 D6
Caird Ave CA3 . . . . 175 C2
Cairn Cres CA14 . . . . 184 B6
Cairn Mist CA4 . . . . 178 D6
Cairn Terr CA8 . . . . 31 E6
Cairnwood CA8 . . . . 31 E6
Calbeck Dr CA14 . . . . 62 F3
Calcutta St LA14 . . . . 206 F4
Caldbeck Rd
Carlisle CA2 . . . . 176 D6
Whitehaven CA28 . . . . . 187 F8
Caldcotes CA2 . . . . 176 E6
Caldcote Ave CA14 . . . . . 190 D2
Calder Ave CA28 . . . . 187 A7
Calder Cl LA15 . . . . 213 A3
Calder Cres CA25 . . . . . . 188 D6
Calder Dr
Dalton-In-F LA15 . . . . . 205 B3
Kendal LA9 . . . . 200 F2
Workington CA14 . . . . . . 184 E3
Calder Gn LA14 . . . . 206 B3
Calder View CA11 . . . . . . 108 B5
Calderside CA20 . . . . 123 A8
Caldew Cl CA7 . . . . 180 A3
Caldew Cl CA3 . . . . 175 D2
Caldew Dr CA5 . . . . 29 D1
Caldew La LA14 . . . . 206 B3
Caldew Lea Prim Sch
CA2 . . . . 176 C6
Caldew Maltings CA2 . . . 176 B7
Caldew Rd CA2 . . . . 29 E1
Caldew St Carlisle CA2 . . 176 C7
Silloth CA7 . . . . 174 C4
Caldron Hill CA13 . . . . . . 89 A2
Caledonian Bldgs **12**
CA3 . . . . 175 B1
Caledonian Cl **3** LA14 . 207 B3
Caledonian Cres DG12 . . 172 C5
Caledonian Rd CA14 . . . . 184 D5
Calgarth Pk LA23 . . . . . . 129 A7
Calgarth View LA23 . . . . . 129 A7
California La LA9 . . . . 175 D5
California Rd LA9 . . . . . . 175 D5
Calthwaite CE Sch CA11 . 55 E7
Calva Brow CA14 . . . . . . 184 F7
Calva Pk CA14 . . . . 184 E7
Calva Rd CA14 . . . . 62 E4
Cambeck Cl CA8 . . . . 179 B4
Cambeck Rise CA8 . . . . . 179 B4
Camborne Ave CA14 . . . . 183 B2
Cambridge Ct **6** LA15 . . 205 C5
Cambridge Prim Sch
LA13 . . . . 207 C3
Cambridge Rd CA28 . . . . 187 F5
Cambridge St
Barrow-In-F LA13 . . . . . 207 C3
11 Millom LA18 . . . . . 202 C5
Cameron St LA14 . . . . . . 206 E2
Camerton Rd
Great Broughton CA13 . . 63 D4
Seaton CA14 . . . . 183 D2
Cammock Ave CA2 . . . . . 177 C1
Cammock Cres CA2 . . . . . 177 C1
Cammock Rd CA2 . . . . . . 177 C1
Camp Rd CA13 . . . . 207 A4
Camp St CA15 . . . . 182 D6
Campers' Cnr CA6 . . . . . . 10 A7
Campfield Marsh Nature
Reserve* CA7 . . . . 16 F5
Campfield Rd LA12 . . . . . 203 D2
Canal Cl CA7 . . . . 174 D4
Canal Head N LA9 . . . . . 200 D5
Canal Head S LA9 . . . . . 200 D5
Canal Pl LA9 . . . . 200 D5
Canal Side LA1 . . . . 152 D1
Canal St Carlisle CA2 . . . 176 E6

Canal St continued
Ulverston LA12 . . . . 203 E6
Canberra Rd DG16 . . . . . 173 D3
Candle La LA7 . . . . 211 D3
Canning St LA14 . . . . 184 D5
Canny Croft CA11 . . . . . . 191 C6
Canonbie Sch DG14 . . . . . 3 D3
Cant Cres CA2 . . . . 177 B2
Canterbury Terr LA14 . . . 206 B8
Cape Rd LA14 . . . . 183 B3
Capernwray Ct LA6 . . . . . 167 D3
Capernwray Rd LA6 . . . . . 167 D3
Capon Tree Rd CA8 . . . . . 179 B3
Capper Cl **15** LA9 . . . . . 200 C4
Capplebarrow LA8 . . . . . . 130 E4
Capplerigg La LA8 . . . . . . 130 C5
Cappy La LA12 . . . . 152 E7
Captain French La LA9 . . 200 C4
Captain Shaw's CE Sch
LA8 . . . . 137 B3
Caraway Cl LA12 . . . . 203 C2
Cardiff St LA14 . . . . 206 C1
Carding Mill La CA12 . . . 192 A4
Cardrona Rd LA11 . . . . . . 208 B1
Cardrona Rd LA11 . . . . . . 208 B1
Carisbrooke Cres LA13 . . 207 C4
Cark & Cartmel Sta
LA11 . . . . 164 D7
Cark Bridge LA11 . . . . . . 164 D7
Cark Ind Est LA11 . . . . . . 164 D7
Carl Lofts CA10 . . . . 101 C5
Carleton Ave CA10 . . . . . 191 C5
Carleton Cl CA1 . . . . 30 D3
Carleton Derrick Dr
CA11 . . . . 191 F5
Carleton Dr CA11 . . . . . . 191 E6
Carleton Fields CA11 . . . 191 F5
Carleton Hall Gdns
CA10 . . . . 191 F5
Carleton Hall Rd CA10,
CA11 . . . . 191 E3
Carleton Hall Wlk CA11 . 191 F5
Carleton Mdws CA11 . . . 191 F5
Carleton Pl CA11 . . . . . . 191 E4
Carleton Rd Carlisle CA1 . 177 C1
Penrith CA11 . . . . 191 E4
Carleton Terr CA10 . . . . . 101 C5
Carley Cl LA12 . . . . 162 F7
Carley La LA12 . . . . 162 F7
Carlingdale LA9 . . . . 130 F2
Cariiol Cl CA1 . . . . 30 D3
Cariiol St CA1 . . . . 177 C3
Carlisle Airport CA6 . . . . . 21 D3
Carlisle Castle* CA3 . . . 214 A3
Carlisle Cath* CA3 . . . . . 214 A2
Carlisle Citadel Sta CA1 . 214 B2
Carlisle Coll CA1 . . . . . . 214 C3
Carlisle Race Course
CA2 . . . . 30 B3
Carlisle Rd
Brampton CA8 . . . . 179 A4
Dalston CA5 . . . . 29 E1
Longtown CA6 . . . . 10 C3
Carlisle St **2** LA14 . . . . 206 F4
Carlisle St Tait LA5 . . . . . 213 C5
Carlislegate La CA7 . . . . . 51 F8
Carlton Ave LA13 . . . . . . 207 B5
Carlton Cotts CA22 . . . . . 189 F4
Carlton Dr
Ulverston LA12 . . . . 203 C2
Whitehaven CA28 . . . . . 187 F7
Carlton Rd CA11 . . . . 175 D1
Carlton Rd CA14 . . . . 184 F6
Carlyle's Pl DG12 . . . . . . 172 C3
Carlyles La CA3 . . . . 214 A3
Carmelite Way LA13 . . . . 207 E5
Carnforth Brow LA5 . . . . 213 C4
Carnforth Christ Church CE
Prim Sch LA5 . . . . 213 C3
Carnforth High Sch LA5 . 213 C4
Carnforth Sta LA5 . . . . . 213 C4
Caroline St LA9 . . . . 200 C6
Carr Bank Rd LA7 . . . . . . 209 E2
Carr La Torver LA12 . . . . 127 B1
Walney Island LA14 . . . . 170 C5
Carricks Ct CA8 . . . . 23 B5
Cars of the Stars Motor
Mus* CA12 . . . . 192 B3
Cart La LA11 . . . . 208 C2
Cart Rd CA28 . . . . 187 C7
Carter Fold LA11 . . . . . . 208 B1
Carter Garth LA14 . . . . . . 63 B4
Carter La **12** CA28 . . . . 186 C1
Carter Rd CA11 . . . . 208 B1
Carter Rd CA14 . . . . 187 F6
Cartmel CE Prim Sch
LA11 . . . . 153 F1
Cartmel Dr
10 Ulverston LA12 . . . 203 D5
Workington CA14 . . . . . . 184 F6
Cartmel Grange LA11 . . . 154 A4
Cartmel La LA11 . . . . 154 B4
Cartmel Priory &
Gatehouse LA11 . . . . . 153 E1
Cartmel Rd
Allithwaite LA7 . . . . 164 F8
Grange-Over-S LA11 . . . 208 B3
Carus Rk LA6 . . . . 156 A2
Carvoran Roman Army Mus*
CA8 . . . . 24 D8
Carvoran Way CA2 . . . . . 176 A6
Caspian Rd **12** LA14 . . 207 B3
Casson Rd CA14 . . . . 184 C3
Casson St **1** LA12 . . . . 203 E5
Casterton Sch LA6 . . . . . 212 F4

Castle Bank
Appleby-In-W CA16 . . . . 193 D4
Silverdale LA5 . . . . 210 C4
Castle Carrock Sch CA8 . 32 D6
Castle Circ LA9 . . . . 200 F4
Castle Cl Egremont CA22 . 189 D5
High Harrington CA14 . . 185 B7
Kendal LA9 . . . . 200 F4
Whitehaven CA28 . . . . . 187 D8
Castle Cres LA9 . . . . 200 E5
Castle Croft CA22 . . . . . 189 D6
Castle Ct Carlisle CA3 . . . 214 A3
Penrith CA11 . . . . 191 C4
Castle Dale LA9 . . . . 200 F4
Castle Dr Kendal LA9 . . . 200 E4
Penrith CA11 . . . . 191 C4
Castle Field LA22 . . . . . . 195 C7
Castle Garth LA9 . . . . . . 200 E5
Castle Gdns
Cockermouth CA13 . . . . 190 B5
Greystoke CA11 . . . . 69 E6
Kendal LA9 . . . . 200 D6
Castle Gr LA9 . . . . 200 F4
Castle Green CA14 . . . . . 200 F4
Castle Green La LA9 . . . . 200 F5
Castle Green Rd LA9 . . . . 200 F5
Castle Hill Rd CA11 . . . . 191 D4
Castle La LA12 . . . . 192 F3
Castle Mdws CA28 . . . . . 187 C8
Castle Mews CA28 . . . . . 187 D8
Castle Mount CA4 . . . . . . 42 C4
Castle Oval LA9 . . . . 200 F4
Castle Park Sch LA9 . . . . 200 F5
Castle Pk CA9 . . . . 105 B5
Castle Riggs LA9 . . . . . . 200 E5
Castle Rise LA9 . . . . 200 F4
Castle St Carlisle CA3 . . . 214 A3
1 Dalton-In-F LA15 . . 205 B4
Kendal LA9 . . . . 200 E5
Millom LA18 . . . . 202 D4
Castle Terr LA11 . . . . 191 C4
Castle View Brough CA17 . 105 B5
Egremont CA22 . . . . 189 D5
Hayton CA8 . . . . 31 F8
Sedgwick LA8 . . . . 144 A2
Walney Island LA14 . . . . 170 C6
Castle View Cvn Site
LA14 . . . . 167 D2
Castle View Rd CA16 . . . . 193 D5
Castle Way CA3 . . . . 214 A3
Castle Wlk
Egremont CA22 . . . . . . 189 D6
Kendal LA9 . . . . 200 E5
Castle Wray LA12 . . . . . . 139 A2
Castlegarth La LA11 . . . . 201 D5
Castlegate
Cockermouth CA13 . . . . 190 D4
Penrith CA11 . . . . 191 C5
Castlegate Dr CA13 . . . . 190 E4
Castlehaw La LA10 . . . . . 201 D5
Castlehaw La LA10 . . . . . 201 D5
Castlehead Cl LA12 . . . . 192 B3
Castlerigg Cl CA28 . . . . . 187 D3
Castlerigg Dr CA12 . . . . . 192 B3
Castlerigg Stone Circ*
CA12 . . . . 81 F6
Castlesteads Dr CA2 . . . . 176 A6
Castleton Cl CA11 . . . . . . 191 A5
Castletown Dr LA14 . . . . 170 B5
Castrigg La CA10 . . . . . . 88 A6
Cat Tree Rd LA11 . . . . . . 208 C3
Catherine Cotts CA12 . . . 192 C4
Catherine Mews CA28 . . . 187 C8
Catherine Mill CA28 . . . . 187 C8
Catherine St
Maryport CA15 . . . . 182 D5
Whitehaven CA28 . . . . . 186 D1
1 Workington CA14 . . 184 D6
Catholic La CA1 . . . . 214 C3
Caton La LA11 . . . . 164 C7
Caton St LA18 . . . . 150 A1
Catty Crook La LA12 . . . . 171 C7
Cauda Brow CA26 . . . . . . 93 D8
Causeway End LA12 . . . . 153 A7
Causeway Rd LA14 . . . . . 183 B2
Causeway The
Cartmel LA11 . . . . 153 F1
Haverthwaite LA12 . . . . 153 F1
Causey La LA14 . . . . 150 E8
Cautley Spout* LA10 . . 133 F4
Cavendish Bldgs **1**
LA14 . . . . 206 F1
Cavendish Ct LA14 . . . . . 184 F6
Cavendish Dock Rd
LA14 . . . . 207 A2
Cavendish Gdns LA6 . . . 212 C2
Cavendish Pk LA14 . . . . 206 F1
Cavendish St
Barrow-In-F LA14 . . . . . 206 F3
Barrow-In-F LA14 . . . . . 207 A3
Dalton-In-F LA15 . . . . . 153 E1
Dalton-In-F LA15 . . . . . 205 C5
10 Ulverston LA12 . . . 203 D5
Workington CA14 . . . . . . 184 F6
Cavendish Terr CA3 . . . . 214 A4
Cawflands CA2 . . . . 30 B2
Cawthorpes La CA2 . . . . . 30 B2
Caxton Rd CA2 . . . . 176 C7
Cecil St Barrow-In-F LA13 . 207 B3
Carlisle CA1 . . . . 214 B2
Cedar Cl CA14 . . . . 191 F4
Cedar Cres CA15 . . . . . . 182 F5

Cedar Ct CA14 ....184 C1
Cedar Gr Carlisle CA3 ...175 E2
Kendal LA9 ....200 B3
Cedar House Sch LA6 ..212 B2
Cedar La CA13 ....190 E5
Cedar Rd LA14 ....206 F7
Cemetery Hill LA15 .....205 B4
Central Ave Carlisle CA4 .177 E3
Distington CA14 ....185 C3
Egremont CA22 ....189 D6
Gretna DG16 ....173 C3
Central Ct LA12 ....162 F6
Central Dr
Ulverston LA12 ....203 D2
Walney Island LA14 ....206 C2
Central Rd Dearham CA15 .49 A2
Whitehaven CA28 ......187 D5
Centurion Pk CA10 .....87 D8
Centurions Wlk CA3 ....20 C1
Challan Hall Cotts LA5 .210 E5
Challan Hall Mews LA5 .210 E5
Challoner Ct LA14 ......190 D4
Challoner St CA13 ......190 D4
Chambers Cl LA9 ......200 B2
Chambers' St 13 LA14 .184 D6
Chancel Pl LA9 ....131 B1
Chandler Way CA3 .....175 B6
Chandlers La CA8 ......179 B5
Channelside LA14 ......206 D4
Chapel Brow
Hallthwaites LA18 .....150 D8
Bridgefoot CA14 ....63 C4
Chapel Butt La CA27 ...119 E4
Chapel Cl 10 Kendal LA9 .200 C5
Warwick Bridge CA4 ...178 C6
Whitehaven CA28 ......187 E3
Chapel Ct
10 Cockermouth CA13 .190 C4
7 Kendal LA9 ....200 C4
Windermere LA23 ......129 B7
Chapel Field
Burneside LA9 ....130 F2
Thurstonfield CA5 ....28 E7
Chapel Garth CA16 ....104 C6
Chapel Gdns CA14 .....183 B1
Chapel Hill LA22 ......195 D6
Chapel La Arnside LA5 .209 B2
Bootle LA19 ....137 B3
Burton in L LA6 ....169 C3
11 Kendal LA9 ....200 C4
Kirkby Lonsdale LA6 ...212 C2
Kirkby Thore CA10 ......87 D8
Chapel Pl CA2 ....214 A2
Chapel Rd CA14 ....184 C6
Chapel Ridding CA23 ..198 D8
Chapel Row CA7 ....49 F7
Chapel St
Appleby-In-W CA16 ....193 C5
8 Barrow-In-F LA14 ...206 F3
Bigrigg CA22 ....188 A3
Bolton CA16 ....87 D6
Carlisle CA1 ....214 B3
Dalton-In-F LA15 ......205 B5
Distington CA14 ....185 D3
Egremont CA22 ....189 C6
Flimby CA15 ....183 C8
Temple Sowerby CA10 ..72 E2
Ulverston LA12 ....203 D5
Whitehaven CA28 ......186 C1
Workington CA14 ......184 E6
Chapel St Inf Sch LA15 .205 C5
Chapel Stone Cotts
LA12 ....153 C8
Chapel Terr Alston CA9 .181 E3
Great Broughton CA13 ..63 E6
Greysouthen CA13 ....63 E4
Kirkby Thore CA10 ......87 D8
Tebay CA10 ....118 B3
Thornhill CA22 ....189 E7
Chapelbield CA5 ....28 E7
Chapelhouse La LA6 ...212 E1
Charity La CA14 ....185 C6
Charles Cl CA14 ....184 F4
Charles Ct LA9 ....130 F2
Charles St Annan DG12 .172 D4
Carlisle CA1 ....214 C1
Kendal LA9 ....200 C7
Charlotte St CA2 ......214 A2
Charlotte Terr CA1 .....177 E6
Charney Ct LA11 ......208 C5
Charney Rd LA11 ......208 C4
Charney Well La LA11 .208 C5
Charters Cl CA14 ......184 E5
Chase The LA5 ....210 A2
Chatsworth Dr CA28 ..187 F8
Chatsworth Park Ind Est
LA14 ....186 D4
Chatsworth Sq CA1 ....214 C2
Chatsworth St LA14 ...206 E5
Chaucer Ave CA22 ....189 C7
Chaucer Rd CA14 .....184 F3
Chaucer Way LA13 ....207 D6
Cheapside LA22 ......195 D5
Chelmer Garth LA14 ..206 A4
Chelsea Cl LA7 ....211 E4
Chelsea Mews LA7 ....211 E4
Cheltenham St LA14 ...207 A5
Cherry Brow CA2 ......176 E5
Cherry Garth CA6 ......19 C2
Cherry Gdns CA11 ....175 E5
Cherry La Carlisle CA1 ..30 E4
Cockermouth CA13 ....190 E5
Cherry Tree Cres LA9 ..200 B2
Cherry Tree Dr CA15 ..182 F5
Cherrytree Ave LA12 ..203 D3

Cherrytree Way LA13 ..207 F5
Chertsey Bank CA1 ....177 C3
Chertsey Gr CA1 ......177 D3
Chertsey Mount CA1 ..177 C4
Chester Pl LA14 ....206 F8
Chester St LA14 ....206 F8
Chesterholm CA2 ......176 A6
Chestnut Cl Culgaith CA10 .72 E4
Holme LA6 ....156 B2
Penrith CA11 ....191 F4
Chestnut Ct Holme LA6 .156 B2
Stainton CA11 ....70 D3
Chestnut Gr
Cumwhinton CA4 ....31 A3
Kirkbride CA7 ....27 B7
Linstock CA6 ....20 D1
Ulverston LA12 ....203 D3
Chestnut Hill
Carlisle CA2 ....176 C2
Keswick CA12 ....192 D3
Chestnut La CA14 ......30 E4
Chestnut Pk
Keswick CA12 ....192 D4
Milnthorpe LA7 ....211 E4
Chestnut Rd LA23 .....198 E5
Chestnut Wlk LA13 ....207 F4
Chestnuts The
Cumwhinton CA4 ....31 A3
Distington CA14 ....185 D4
Longtown CA6 ....20 A7
Cheviot Gn LA14 ......206 F5
Cheviot Rd CA3 ....175 E1
Chichester Pl 3 LA13 ..207 C3
Chiltern Cres LA14 ....206 F5
Chilton St CA14 ....184 E5
Chiswick St CA1 ......214 C2
Chittery La LA12 ......203 D7
Chitty Hill CA10 ....87 D2
Christ Church Terr
CA13 ....190 C3
Christ Croft CA17 ......105 B5
Christian Head CA17 ..199 C6
Christian St
Maryport CA15 ....182 D6
Workington LA14 .....184 F6
Chrysler Gr CA25 .....188 C8
Church Brow LA19 ....137 C6
Church Cl Carlisle CA1 .214 C2
Distington CA14 ......185 D4
Irthington CA6 ....21 E4
Levens LA8 ....155 D8
Lindal in F LA12 ......205 F8
Satterthwaite LA12 ....141 A7
Church Croft CA10 .....84 F7
Church Fields 6 LA12 .203 D6
Church Fields Ave 5
LA1 ....203 D6
Church Gate CA17 ....119 D3
Church Hill Arnside LA5 .209 B2
Grange-Over-S LA11 ..208 D4
Hensingham CA28 ....187 F5
Church Hill Ave LA5 ..213 C7
Church Hos CA6 ....20 F6
Church La Bootle LA19 .137 B3
Brampton CA8 ....179 B5
Carlisle CA3 ....175 E1
Great Salkeld CA11 ...57 B3
Keswick CA12 ....81 B7
Morland CA10 ....86 F5
Nenthead CA9 ....47 A2
Thursby CA5 ....28 F1
Tunstall LA6 ....168 E4
Walney Island LA14 ..206 D1
Warcop CA17 ....104 E4
Whitehaven CA28 .....187 E6
Church Mdws CA13 ...48 B1
Church Mews 1 LA14 .191 C5
Church Pl 2 CA3 ......175 E1
Church Rd
Allithwaite LA11 ....164 F7
Alston CA9 ....181 D3
Broughton Moor CA15 ..63 C8
Distington CA14 ......185 D3
Flimby CA15 ....183 C7
Great Urswick LA12 ..162 F5
Greystoke CA11 ....69 F5
Harrington CA14 .....185 A4
Kirkbride CA7 ....27 B8
Levens LA8 ....155 D8
Seaton CA14 ....155 D8
Witherslack LA11 .....154 E6
Church Rise CA10 ....118 B3
Church Road Terr CA14 .185 A8
Church Row LA12 .....82 C8
Church St
Ambleside LA22 .....195 D5
Annan DG12 ....172 D4
Barrow-In-F LA14 ....207 A2
Beetham LA7 ....55 F2
Bowness-On-W LA23 ..198 C2
Broughton-In-F LA20 .138 F2
Caldewgate CA2 .....176 E6
Carlisle CA3 ....175 E1
Cleator CA23 ....188 C3
Dalton-In-F LA15 .....205 B4
Egremont CA22 ......189 E6
Frizington CA26 ....90 D7
Keswick CA12 ....192 B3
Kirkby Lonsdale LA6 ..212 C2
Langwathby CA10 .....72 E7
Maryport CA15 ....182 D6
Milnthorpe LA7 ....211 D4
Moor Row CA24 .....188 D5
Whitehaven CA28 .....186 C1
Whittington LA6 ......168 C7
9 Wigton CA7 ....180 D3

Church St continued
Windermere LA23 ....198 E6
Workington LA14 .....184 D7
Church Stile LA22 .....194 B3
Church Terr Caldbeck CA7 .53 C6
4 Carlisle CA3 ....175 E1
Maryport CA15 ......182 F4
Shap CA10 ....101 C6
Silloth CA7 ....174 C4
Church View Arnside LA5 .209 B2
Egremont CA22 ......189 D6
Lowca CA28 ....186 E8
Staveley LA8 ....130 C5
Church Went 7 CA13 .190 D4
Church Wlk
Flookburgh LA11 ....164 D6
Millom LA18 ....202 A5
Ulverston LA12 ......203 D6
Churchbeck Cl LA21 ..196 A4
Churchill Ct LA9 ......152 D8
Churchill Dr Millom LA18 .202 B6
Moresby Parks CA28 ..76 F2
Churchill Pl CA15 ....182 C6
Cinder Hill LA20 .....139 A2
Cinderbarrow La LA5,
LA6 ....167 A6
Citadel Row CA3 .....214 B2
Claife Ave LA23 ......198 F5
Claife Cl LA23 ....198 F5
Claife Nature Trail*
LA22 ....128 F2
Claire St CA2 ....177 B3
Clairmont Dr CA6 .....10 C3
Clapperton Rd DG12 .172 D5
Clarence Rd LA14 ....207 A6
Clarence St Carlisle CA2 .176 E4
8 Ulverston LA12 ....203 D5
Claridge Ho CA2 .....176 C7
Clarkside Bsns Pk LA12 .152 E5
Clarrick Terr LA6 .....169 F3
Clawthorpe Cotts LA6 .167 C8
Clay Flatts Ind Est CA14 .184 C5
Clay St CA14 ....184 D6
Clayton Ave CA25 ....188 E6
Cleater St LA15 ......205 C5
Cleator Gate CA23 ...188 D4
Cleator Moor Bsns Ctr
CA25 ....188 D6
Cleator Moor Rd CA28 .91 F7
Cleator St LA18 ......202 B5
Clementina Terr CA2 .177 B4
Cleminson Row LA12 .153 C7
Clevelands Ave
Barrow-In-F LA13 ....207 D5
Silverdale LA5 ......210 C4
Cliff Brow 9 LA9 ....200 C5
Cliff Dr Longtown CA6 ..20 A8
Whitehaven CA28 ....187 B7
Cliff Terr LA9 ....200 C5
Cliffe La
Barrow-In-F LA14 ....207 A7
Barrow-In-F LA14 ....207 A8
Clifford Cl CA11 .....191 C3
Clifford Ct CA11 .....191 D3
Clifford Dr LA9 ......200 C2
Clifford Rd CA11 ....191 D3
Clifford St
Appleby-In-W CA16 ..193 D6
Barrow-In-F LA14 ...206 F3
Carlisle CA3 ....214 B3
Clift St CA2 ....176 D7
Clifton Cross CA10 ...71 C2
Clifton Ct CA14 .....184 F4
Clifton Gdns CA14 ....63 B4
Clifton Hill Cl CA14 ..63 B4
Clifton Lodge CA14 ...63 B4
Clifton Moor Cotts CA10 .85 F8
Clifton Prim Sch CA10 .71 C1
Clifton St CA2 ....176 E5
Clifton Terr CA18 ....123 F3
Clints Brow Bigrigg CA22 .188 B1
Egremont CA22 .....189 D8
Clints Quarry Nature
Reserve* CA22 .....188 B1
Clints Rd LA14 ......178 D2
Clitheroe CA9 ....181 E3
Clitheroe Dr CA28 ...187 E8
Clive St LA14 ....206 E4
Cloisters Ave LA13 ...207 D3
Close St CA1 ....214 C1
Close The Bransty CA28 .186 D3
Kirkby Stephen CA17 .199 C5
Wigton CA7 ....180 D2
Closehead Ave DG12 .172 D4
Clovelly Terr LA14 ...207 B7
Co-operative Terr CA15 .183 C8
Coach Ho LA11 .....154 A3
Coach Rd Warton CA5 .213 C8
Whitehaven CA28 ...186 C3
Coal Rd LA10 ....148 C2
Coalfell CA8 ....23 C2
Coalfell Ave CA2 ....176 A6
Coalgrove Rd CA28 ..187 D5
Coast Rd Baycliff LA12 .163 B3
Newbiggin LA12,LA13 .171 E7
Coastguard Cotts LA14 .178 C1
Coates La 14 CA28 ..186 C1
Cobden St LA15 .....205 C5
Cock Brow LA10 ....148 C5
Cocken Cres LA14 ...204 B1
Cocker La CA13 .....190 D4
Cockermouth Lonning
CA13 ....63 F5
Cockermouth Sch CA13 .190 B6
Cockfield Dr LA14 ...184 D2
Cocking Yd LA6 .....167 C7
Cockle St LA10 .....201 C5
Cockpit CA28 ....187 C7

Cockrig La LA8 ......144 C2
Cockshot La LA7 ....209 F4
Cockton Yd 4 CA13 .190 C4
Colby La CA6 ....194 B3
Colchester Pl 1 LA13 .207 C3
Cold Harbour La LA8 .143 C7
Cold Springs Pk CA11 .191 E6
Cold Well La CA7 ...209 F1
Coldbeck Barn CA17 .119 C3
Coldgill Ave CA14 ....63 E6
Coldkeld Rigg CA17 .105 E1
Coldmire Rd CA7 ....25 C1
Coledale Gdns CA12 ..80 E6
Coledale Hall CA2 ...176 C7
Coledale Mdws CA2 .176 C7
Coledale Mews CA2 .176 C7
Coleridge Cl LA13 ..207 D6
Coleridge Ct CA12 ..192 A4
Coleridge Dr CA22 ..189 D6
Coles Dr LA5 ....209 B1
Colesberg Ct LA5 ...209 B2
College Cl CA7 ......50 C8
College Ct CA12 ....198 E5
College Rd LA23 ....198 E5
College St
Grasmere LA22 .....194 B4
6 Whitehaven CA28 .186 C1
College View CA28 ...187 C6
Collier La CA1 ....214 B1
Collier's La LA6 ....212 E3
Collin Cl LA9 ....200 B2
Collin Croft LA9 ....200 B2
Collin Hill LA9 .....200 B2
Collin Pl CA2 ....176 D6
Collin Rd CA2 ......176 D6
Collinfield LA9 .....200 B2
Collingwood Cl LA21 .196 A4
Collingwood St
Barrow-In-F LA14 ...206 F4
Carlisle CA2 ....214 A1
Collins Terr CA15 ...182 C4
Colmore St CA2 ....176 C7
Colonnade The LA12 .141 D1
Colony Candles* LA12 .162 E6
Colt House La LA12 .141 D1
Colton Hill LA12 ....152 D8
Colville St CA2 .....214 A1
Colville St N CA2 ...214 A1
Colville Terr CA2 ...176 E5
Combe Cres LA17 ...151 C5
Combe View Bootle LA19 .137 B3
Haverigg LA18 .....149 F2
Walney Island LA14 .206 C5
Comely Bank CA7 ....50 C8
Commercial Row CA7 .53 C6
Commodore St CA28 .186 D2
Common La CA17 ..199 C2
Common The CA13 ..129 D6
Commonholme Rd CA10 .86 D7
Compston La LA8 ...156 B8
Compston Cnr LA22 .195 D6
Compston Rd LA22 .195 D5
Compston St LA22 ..195 D5
Compton St CA1 ...214 B3
Concle Terr LA13 ...171 E5
Conder Brow LA9 ...213 D4
Coney St CA2 ....177 A3
Coneygarth La
Tunstall LA6 ....168 D4
Whittington LA6 ...168 D6
Conisburgh Ct CA2 .214 A1
Conishead Priory*
LA12 ....163 D6
Coniston Ave
Dalton-In-F LA15 ...205 B3
Flimby CA15 ....183 C7
Seascale CA20 .....123 B8
Coniston CE Prim Sch
LA21 ....196 A4
Coniston Cl CA14 ..184 E3
Coniston Cres LA14 .184 E4
Coniston Dr
Cockermouth CA13 .190 F3
Kendal LA9 ....200 F6
Workington LA14 ..184 E4
Coniston Pk CA25 ..188 B8
Coniston Rd
Barrow-In-F LA14 ..207 B6
Carnforth LA5 .....213 D2
Whitehaven CA28 .187 C5
Coniston Way CA2 ..176 A5
Consett St 8 LA11 .207 B3
Constable St CA2 ..176 C7
Conway Gdns LA14 .206 A4
Conyers Ave LA14 .207 C8
Coogan Cl CA2 .....176 F8
Cook Rd LA18 ......202 D4
Cook St CA14 ......184 C4
Cook's Cnr LA23 ...198 D7
Cookson Ct CA11 ..191 A5
Coombe Height CA2 .176 C2
Cooper La LA12 ....163 D5
Cooper Way CA3 ...175 B6
Coopers Croft CA10 .85 D6
Coopers Garth CA11 ..55 B2
Coophouse La CA5 ..19 E1
Cop La LA22 ....195 D6
Copeland Ave
Egremont CA22 ....189 D7
Whitehaven CA28 .187 D4
Copperfield La LA9 .200 E6
Coppice Brow CA5 ..213 E4
Coppice Terr La LA12 .203 D3
Copshaw Pl TD9 ....1 B6
Corby Gates CA4 ...177 E2
Corker La LA12 .....140 F4
Corkickle Sta CA28 .187 D7

Corn Market CA11 ...191 D5
Cornbirthwaite Rd
LA23 ....198 D4
Cornerhouse Pk LA14 .206 E3
Corney Pl 2 CA11 ...191 C5
Cornwallis St LA14 ..206 F3
Coronation Ave CA14 .62 E4
Coronation Cotts LA11 .154 C3
Coronation Cres CA14 .185 D3
Coronation Dr
Dalton-In-F LA15 ...205 C3
Frizington CA26 .....92 D8
Whitehaven CA28 ..186 E3
Workington CA14 ..184 C1
Coronation Mount LA6 .169 C3
Coronation St CA15 .182 D4
Coronation Terr CA7 ..37 C2
Corporation Rd
Carlisle CA3 ....214 B3
Workington CA14 ..184 D5
Corporation Terr 9
LA14 ....207 B2
Cote Ley Cres LA14 .170 C6
Cote Lighthouse* CA7 .174 C6
Cotswold Cres LA14 .206 F5
Cottage Cvn Pk CA7 ..17 D3
Cottage Hospl CA13 .190 D5
Cottage Row
Braystones CA21 ...108 A5
Morland CA10 ......86 E4
Coulter Beck La LA6 .169 A7
Coulton St LA14 ...206 E5
Council Hos CA10 ...58 B4
Countess Rd CA28 .186 D2
Countess Terr CA28 .186 D2
County Mews LA9 ..200 C6
County Park Rd LA14 .206 E8
County Rd LA12 ....203 D5
Court Guards LA14 .170 C6
Court Sq CA1,CA3 ..214 B2
Court Square Brow CA1,
CA3 ....214 B2
Court The
8 Barrow-In-F LA14 .207 B3
Workington CA14 ..184 F5
Court Yard The CA11 ..71 F7
Court Yd The CA6 ...19 D4
Courtyard The
Broadwath CA8 ....178 E3
Kendal LA9 ....200 E6
Moorhouse CA5 .....29 A7
Thurstonfield CA5 ...28 F7
Cove Dr LA5 ....210 C4
Cove Ho LA14 .....206 F4
Cove Rd LA5 ......210 B4
Cowbound La CA10 .118 E3
Cowbrow Foot LA6 .156 E4
Cowlarns Rd LA14 .207 B8
Cowper Rd CA11 ...191 E6
Cows Tarn La LA14 .206 B4
Cox St LA12 ....203 D5
Cox's La CA8 ......179 B5
Crabtree La LA6 ...156 E4
Crag Bank Cres LA5 .213 B2
Crag Bank La LA5 .213 A3
Crag Bank Rd LA5 .213 B2
Crag Brow LA23 ...198 C3
Crag La Cartmel LA11 .153 F2
Gosforth CA19 ....109 E1
Hutton Roof LA6 ...156 F1
Crag Rd LA5 ......213 B7
Crag View Kendal LA9 .200 C6
Staveley LA8 .....130 C5
Cragg Brow LA12 ..152 F8
Cragg Gr LA11 ....208 C4
Cragg Rd CA25 ...188 C6
Cragg St LA14 ....207 A5
Craglands Pk LA12 .162 F5
Craig Dr CA28 ....186 E3
Craig Rd CA14 ....184 E4
Craig Wlk LA23 ...198 D3
Craignair Cl DG12 .172 F5
Craignair Gdns DG12 .172 F5
Craignair Pk DG12 .172 F5
Craigs Bank NE49 ..24 D3
Craika Rd CA15 ....49 A2
Crake Mount LA12 .152 D7
Crake Rd LA14 ....206 A4
Crakegarth CA5 ....40 A8
Crakegarth Cl CA5 ..40 A8
Craketrees CA5 .....29 D1
Cranbourne Rd CA2 .176 C6
Cranbourne St LA14 .184 C2
Craven Park La LA14 .206 E4
Craven Way LA10 ..159 D8
Craw Hall CA8 .....179 C4
Craw Pk CA8 ......179 C4
Creighton Ave CA2 ..176 B6
Crellin St LA14 ....207 A3
Crerar Cl CA15 ...182 B4
Crescent Cotts CA20 .123 A7
Crescent Gn LA9 ...200 C3
Crescent Rd LA23 ..198 E5
Crescent The
Barrow-In-F LA14 ..204 E1
Bransty CA28 .....186 D4
Carlisle CA1 ......214 B2
Cleator Moor CA25 .188 C8
Eastriggs DG12 ....17 D8
Egremont CA22 ....189 D7
Grange-Over-S LA11 .208 D3
High Cummersdale CA2 .176 D1
Holme LA6 ....156 B1
Keswick CA12 .....192 A3
Kirkby Lonsdale LA6 .212 E4
Kirkby Stephen CA17 .199 D5
Penrith CA11 ......191 C3
Seascale CA20 ....123 A7

Crescent The *continued*
Thornhill CA22 . . . . .189 E2
Wigton CA7 . . . . .180 E2
Workington CA14 . . . . .184 C1
Cresswell Ave CA1 . . . . . . .177 F4
Crest The Ulverston LA12 . . .203 D3
Whitehaven CA28 . . . . .187 F8
Creton Villas LA11 . . . . . . .208 C4
Criffel Ave CA15 . . . . .182 D7
Criffel Rd Carlisle CA2 . . . . .176 A6
Parton CA28 . . . . .186 E6
Criffel St CA7 . . . . .174 C4
Cringlethwaite Terr
CA22 . . . . .189 E5
Crinkledyke Cl CA6 . . . . . .175 A8
Crinkledyke Est CA6 . . . . .175 A8
Croadalla Ave CA28 . . . . . .189 D6
Croasdale Ave CA28 . . . . .187 E4
Croasdale Cl LA3 . . . . .213 B3
Croasdale Pl CA25 . . . . . . .188 E6
Croft Ave Penrith CA11 . . . .191 C6
Shap CA10 . . . . .101 C5
Croft Cl Brough CA17 . . . . . .105 B5
Lazonby CA10 . . . . .57 A6
Croft Cres CA15 . . . . .49 B2
Croft Ct High Hesket CA4 . . .41 F3
Wigton CA7 . . . . .180 C3
Croft Cttyd LA22 . . . . .195 B4
Croft End CA10 . . . . .85 D1
Croft Foot CA28 . . . . .187 A2
Croft Garth LA12 . . . . .152 B5
Croft Gdns LA15 . . . . .205 B5
Croft Head Rd CA20 . . . . . .123 B8
Croft Head View CA28 . . . .186 E8
Croft Park Gr LA13 . . . . . . .207 C2
Croft Pk CA4 . . . . .178 A1
Croft Pl Kirkoswald CA10 . . .57 B8
Temple Sowerby CA10 . . . . .72 E1
Croft Rd Brampton CA8 . . . . .
Carlisle CA3 . . . . .175 F1
Gretna DG16 . . . . .173 D3
Croft St CA17 . . . . .199 C6
Croft Terr Alston CA9 . . . . . .181 D4
Beckermet CA21 . . . . .108 C5
Braithwaite CA12 . . . . .80 F6
Carlisle CA1 . . . . .177 E6
Cleator CA23 . . . . .188 C3
Cockermouth CA13 . . . . . . .190 D4
Egremont CA22 . . . . .189 E6
Penrith CA11 . . . . .191 D6
Croft The Ambleside LA22 . .195 B4
Bothel CA7 . . . . .51 A6
Burton in L LA6 . . . . .169 C3
Flookburgh LA11 . . . . .164 D6
Grasmere LA22 . . . . .194 A5
Long Marton CA16 . . . . .88 A7
Stainton With A LA13 . . . . . .205 F1
Warcop CA16 . . . . .104 C6
Croft View
Long Marton CA16 . . . . .88 A7
Millburn CA10 . . . . .73 C4
Crofters Cres LA13 . . . . . . .207 F4
Croftfield Rd CA14 . . . . . . .183 B3
Croftlands Bigrigg CA22 . . .188 A2
Borwick LA6 . . . . .167 B3
Bothel CA7 . . . . .51 C6
Warton LA5 . . . . .213 D8
Croftlands Dr CA18 . . . . . .123 F3
Croftlands Inf & Jun Schs
LA12 . . . . .203 D2
Crofton Est CA7 . . . . .28 B2
Crofts The Crosby CA15 . . . .49 B5
Silloth CA7 . . . . .174 C2
St Bees CA27 . . . . .91 D2
Wigton CA7 . . . . .180 C2
Croftside CA13 . . . . .190 D4
Croglam La
Kirkby Stephen CA17 . . . . .199 B4
Kirkby Stephen CA17 . . . . .199 C5
Croglam Mdws CA17 . . . . .199 C4
Crompton Dr LA15 . . . . . . .205 B3
Cromwell Cres
Carlisle CA3 . . . . .214 A4
High Harrington CA14 . . . . .185 D7
Cromwell Rd CA15 . . . . . . .191 C5
Crook Brow LA8 . . . . .130 A2
Crook Rd Burneside LA9 . . .130 D2
Kendal LA8 . . . . .130 E1
Staveley LA8 . . . . .130 B4
Crookburn Cl CA3 . . . . .175 B2
Crooked Gate LA8 . . . . . . .143 D4
Crookey CA7 . . . . .50 C8
Crooklands CA14 . . . . .185 D5
Crooklands Brow LA15 . . . .205 D5
Crooklands Terr LA15 . . . . .205 D5
Crooklands View CA10 . . . .71 C1
Crosby on Eden CE Sch
CA6 . . . . .20 F2
Crosby Ravensworth CE Sch
CA10 . . . . .102 C5
Crosby St Carlisle CA1 . . . . .214 B4
Maryport CA15 . . . . .182 D6
Crosfield Rd CA14 . . . . . . .186 D2
Croslands Park Rd
LA13 . . . . .207 C7
Cross Bank LA6 . . . . .145 E4
Cross Cotts CA7 . . . . .50 F8
Cross Croft CA16 . . . . .193 E4
Cross Croft Ind Est
CA16 . . . . .193 F5
Cross Fell Dr CA16 . . . . . . .88 C6
Cross Garth CA10 . . . . .101 C6
Cross Gate CA11 . . . . .98 E4
Cross Gates CA13 . . . . .79 C8
Cross Gr Cleator CA23 . . . . .188 D5
Wigton CA7 . . . . .180 C5
Cross Hill St Bees CA27 . . . .91 D2
Workington CA14 . . . . .184 F5

Cross How CA10 . . . . .72 E5
Cross Howe
Broughton Cross CA13 . . . . .63 E5
Crosthwaite LA8 . . . . .142 E6
Cross La
Barrow-In-F LA14 . . . . .207 A8
Kendal LA9 . . . . .200 C4
🟧 Penrith CA11 . . . . .191 C6
Ulverston LA12 . . . . .163 D8
Whitehaven CA28 . . . . .187 E7
Wigton CA7 . . . . .180 C5
Cross Lane Workshops
CA20 . . . . .123 B8
Cross Lanes CA20 . . . . . . .123 B8
Cross Lonning CA7 . . . . . . .51 A6
Cross Moor LA12 . . . . .162 F7
Cross North St CA25 . . . . .188 D7
Cross Rd CA15 . . . . .183 C7
Cross Rigg CA26 . . . . .78 C1
Cross Side CA22 . . . . .189 E6
Cross St
Barrow-In-F LA14 . . . . .207 A2
Carlisle CA3 . . . . .175 D2
Grange-Over-S LA11 . . . . . .208 D4
Kendal LA9 . . . . .200 C6
Keswick CA12 . . . . .192 C3
🟧 Penrith CA11 . . . . .191 C5
Whitehaven CA28 . . . . .187 C8
Windermere LA23 . . . . .198 E6
Workington CA14 . . . . .184 C3
Crosscanonby St John's CE
Sch CA15 . . . . .49 B5
Crosscrake CE Prim Sch
LA8 . . . . .144 B1
Crossfell View
Alston CA9 . . . . .181 E3
Lowther CA10 . . . . .85 F6
Crossfield CA3 . . . . .175 D2
Crossfield Ct LA5 . . . . .209 A1
Crossfield Rd CA25 . . . . . . .188 C7
Crossgates CA14 . . . . .78 B4
Crossgates Rd CA8 . . . . . . .23 B2
Crosshaw Brow LA10 . . . . .146 F8
Crosshill Dr CA2 . . . . .176 C5
Crosshow Rd CA15 . . . . . . .49 A3
Crossings Cl CA25 . . . . . . .188 C7
Crosslands LA6 . . . . .168 D7
Crosslands Cl LA12 . . . . . . .203 A3
Crosslands Pk LA13 . . . . . .207 C2
Crossley St 🟧 LA16 . . . . . .162 A8
Crossrigg La LA6 . . . . .87 C6
Crossrigg La CA11 . . . . . . .177 E3
Crosthwaite CE Sch
LA8 . . . . .142 F6
Crosthwaite Ct CA14 . . . . .184 E3
Crosthwaite Gdns CA12 . .192 A5
Crosthwaite Rd CA12 . . . .192 A5
Crow Park Rd CA12 . . . . . .192 A3
Crow Park Way CA24 . . . . .91 F5
Crow Pk CA28 . . . . .186 D1
Crow Wood Field LA8 . . . .143 D4
Crowgarth Cl CA25 . . . . . . .188 D6
Crown Hill LA11 . . . . .208 D4
Crown Inn Fields CA10 . . . .86 F5
Crown Mews 🟧 LA15 . . . . .205 C5
Crown Rd CA2 . . . . .176 A6
Crown Rigg LA23 . . . . .198 C2
Crown Sq CA11 . . . . .191 D4
Crown St
Carlisle CA1,CA2 . . . . .214 B1
Cockermouth CA13 . . . . . . .190 C4
Millom LA18 . . . . .202 C5
Crown Terr 🟧 CA11 . . . . . .191 D5
Crummock Ave
Cockermouth CA13 . . . . . . .190 E4
Whitehaven CA28 . . . . .187 B5
Whitehaven CA28 . . . . .187 C5
Crummock Dr
Barrow-In-F LA14 . . . . .204 D1
Kendal LA9 . . . . .200 F2
Crummock Rd
Maryport CA15 . . . . .182 E3
Workington CA14 . . . . .184 D3
Crummock St CA2 . . . . . . .176 D5
Ctyd The CA10 . . . . .43 A1
Cuckoo Brow La LA22 . . . .128 E2
Cuddy Lonning
Wigton CA7 . . . . .180 A1
Wigton,Red Dial CA7 . . . . . .38 B5
Culgaith CE Sch CA10 . . . . .72 E5
Culgaith Rd CA10 . . . . .72 A8
Culgarth Ave CA13 . . . . . . .190 D3
Culgarth Cl CA13 . . . . .190 E3
Cumberland Bird of Prey
Ctr* CA5 . . . . .28 F7
Cumberland Cl
Clifton CA10 . . . . .71 C1
Millom LA18 . . . . .202 C4
Cumberland Ct
Barrow-In-F LA14 . . . . .206 E4
Carlisle CA2 . . . . .214 A1
Cumberland Dr LA9 . . . . . .200 E3
Cumberland Infmyl The
CA2 . . . . .176 D7
Cumberland Pencil Mus*
CA12 . . . . .192 A4
Cumberland Pl CA11 . . . . .191 E4
Cumberland Rd CA28 . . . . .187 E5
Cumberland St
Carlisle CA2 . . . . .214 A1
Workington CA14 . . . . .184 D5
Cumberland Terr DG12 . . .172 D4
Cumberland Toy & Model
Mus* CA13 . . . . .190 D4
Cumberland Way CA10 . . . .71 C1
Cumbria Ct 🟧 LA23 . . . . . .198 E5

Cumbria Inst of the Arts
CA3 . . . . .175 E1
Cumbria View LA14 . . . . . .170 B6
Cumbrian Hospl CA14 . . . . .62 E1
Cummersdale Rd CA2 . . . . .176 D1
Cumbrian Sch CA2 . . . . . . .176 D1
Cumrew Cl CA1 . . . . .177 F5
Cumwhinton Dr CA1 . . . . . .30 E4
Cumwhinton Rd CA1 . . . . .177 C2
Cumwhinton Sch CA4 . . . . .31 A3
Cardiff CA8 . . . . .23 A1
Curlew Cen CA16 . . . . .103 D7
Curlew Rise DG16 . . . . . . .173 D3
Curlew Wlk CA1 . . . . .177 D6
Currie St CA1 . . . . .214 C2
Currock Bank Rd CA2 . . . . .177 A2
Currock Mount CA2 . . . . . .177 A2
Currock Park Ave CA2 . . . .177 A2
Currock Rd CA2 . . . . .177 A2
Currock Road Trad Ctr
CA2 . . . . .214 B1
Curson Rise LA9 . . . . .200 F3
Curwen Gr 🟧 CA13 . . . . . .190 C4
Curwen Rd CA14 . . . . .184 C6
Curwen St CA14 . . . . .184 F6
Curwendale CA14 . . . . .62 E3
Curzon St CA15 . . . . .182 D5
Cusack Cres CA14 . . . . . . .184 D4
Custy Steps LA9 . . . . .200 C3
Cuthberts Cl CA10 . . . . . . .86 E7
Cypress Way CA11 . . . . . . .191 F5
Cypress Wlk LA13 . . . . . . .207 E4

D

Dacre Rd Brampton CA8 . . .179 B6
Carlisle CA3 . . . . .214 A3
Hethersgill CA6 . . . . .11 F2
Dairy Cotts CA8 . . . . .23 B5
Dale Ave LA9 . . . . .200 E6
Dale Bank LA8 . . . . .207 C4
Dale Cl CA13 . . . . .190 D2
Dale Ct CA2 . . . . .176 F4
Dale End Rd CA1 . . . . .177 D1
Dale St
🟧 Askam-In-F LA16 . . . . . .162 A8
Carlisle CA2 . . . . .214 B2
Ulverston LA12 . . . . .203 D5
Dale Street Inf Sch
LA12 . . . . .203 E5
Dale Terr LA12 . . . . .205 C5
Dale View Carlisle CA2 . . . .177 A2
Cockermouth CA13 . . . . . . .190 D2
Laversdale CA6 . . . . .21 C5
Dale View Cl CA22 . . . . . . .189 D5
Dale View Gdns CA22 . . . . .189 D5
Dalegarth LA12 . . . . .171 C8
Dalegarth Ave
Carlisle CA1 . . . . .177 E3
Whitehaven CA28 . . . . .187 D4
Dalegarth Cotts CA19 . . . .125 C7
Dalegarth Sta* CA19 . . . .125 C7
Dalehome Ho* CA11 . . . . .70 C2
Dalelands Rd CA28 . . . . . . .187 B2
Dalemain Ho* CA11 . . . . . .70 C2
Dalesman Dr CA7 . . . . .177 F2
Daley Beck 🟧 LA16 . . . . . .162 A8
Dalkeith St LA14 . . . . .206 F3
Dallam Chase LA7 . . . . . . .211 D4
Dallam Dr LA7 . . . . .209 F6
Dallam Sch
Heversham LA7 . . . . .211 D7
Milnthorpe LA7 . . . . .211 E4
Dallam View LA7 . . . . .211 D3
Dalmeny Rd CA3 . . . . .175 D1
Dalmore Ct LA13 . . . . .207 C7
Dalston Rd Carlisle CA2 . . .176 D6
Workington CA14 . . . . .184 E5
Dalston St CA2 . . . . .176 F4
Dalston Sta CA5 . . . . .29 D1
Dalton Ave CA2 . . . . .176 C5
Dalton Castle* LA15 . . . . .205 B4
Dalton Dr LA9 . . . . .200 F5
Dalton Fields La
Dalton-In-F LA15 . . . . .205 B3
🟧 Dalton-In-F LA15 . . . . . .205 B4
Dalton La
Barrow-In-F LA14 . . . . .207 B8
Burton-in-K LA6 . . . . .167 C7
Eaglesfield LA15 . . . . .64 A3
Dalton Rd
Askam-In-F LA16 . . . . .162 A8
🟧 Barrow-In-F LA14 . . . . . .206 F3
Kendal LA9 . . . . .200 F5
Dalton St LA13 . . . . .190 B3
Dalton St Mary's CE Prim
Sch LA15 . . . . .205 C3
Dalton Sta LA15 . . . . .205 C4
Daltongate LA12 . . . . .203 D5
Daltongate Bsns Ctr
LA12 . . . . .203 C5
Daltongate Ct 🟧 LA12 . . .203 C5
Dalzell Gdns LA14 . . . . . . .63 B4
Dalzell St CA22,CA24,
CA23 . . . . .188 B4
Damson Cotts LA12 . . . . . .171 C8
Dan Wilson Ave CA15 . . . .182 F4
Dane Ave LA14 . . . . .204 D1
Dane Ghyll Sch LA14 . . . . .204 C1
Danes Cres LA8 . . . . .130 B5
Danes Rd LA8 . . . . .130 B5
Danny Brow LA10 . . . . . . .147 A6
Darcy St CA14 . . . . .184 C7
Darent Ave LA14 . . . . .206 A4
Darley Dale Rd 🟧 LA14 . . .207 A6
Dartmouth St 🟧 LA14 . . . .206 C1

David St CA1 . . . . .214 C1
Davies Rd CA14 . . . . .184 D3
Davis Yd LA10 . . . . .201 C5
Dawson St CA25 . . . . .188 E7
Days Bank LA21 . . . . .196 A3
De Whelpdale 🔲 CA11 . . .191 D5
Deal Ave LA14 . . . . .206 C1
Dean Barwick Sch LA11 . .154 E7
Dean CE Sch CA14 . . . . . . .78 B8
Dean Cl CA26 . . . . .92 D8
Dean Gibson RC Prim Sch
LA9 . . . . .200 C2
Dean St CA14 . . . . .184 D6
Deardon Cl LA11 . . . . .208 D4
Dearham Bridge Rd
CA15 . . . . .49 A4
Dearham Prim Sch CA15 . .49 A3
Dee Cl CA2 . . . . .176 B4
Deep Dale CA2 . . . . .176 C2
Deepdale Cl LA7 . . . . .155 E1
Deepdale Rd LA10 . . . . . . .159 D8
Deer Orchard Cl CA12 . . . .191 D8
Deer Park Barn LA7 . . . . . .156 C7
Deer Park Rd CA3 . . . . .175 C2
Deerfield 🔲 LA12 . . . . .203 C5
Deerpark Rd CA7 . . . . .180 E1
Delagoa St CA1 . . . . .177 C5
Delanby's Terr CA7 . . . . . . .37 C2
Delhi Rd DG12 . . . . .17 D8
Delhi St LA14 . . . . .206 C1
Dell The CA8 . . . . .23 A1
Demainholm Forest Walks*
. . . . .1 A4
Dendron Cl LA15 . . . . .205 B2
Dene Ave CA14 . . . . .185 B7
Dene Cres CA3 . . . . .175 D2
Dent CE Prim Sch LA10 . . .147 B2
Dent Rd
Cleator Moor CA25 . . . . . . .188 F6
🔟 Moresby Parks CA28 . . . .76 F2
Thornhill CA22 . . . . .189 E3
Whitehaven CA28 . . . . .187 E3
Dent Sq CA25 . . . . .188 F6
Dent St LA10 . . . . .148 B2
Denton Cres CA8 . . . . .23 B6
Denton Hill CA2 . . . . .214 A2
Denton Holme Trad Ctr
CA2 . . . . .214 A2
Denton Mill Cl CA2 . . . . . .176 F4
Denton Mill La CA2 . . . . . .176 F4
Denton Park Ct CA20 . . . . .123 B8
Denton Pk CA20 . . . . .109 B2
Denton Rd 🟧 LA13 . . . . . . .207 C5
Denton St CA2 . . . . .176 F4
Derby Sq LA23 . . . . .198 E6
Derby St LA13 . . . . .207 B3
Derbyshire Rd LA14 . . . . . .207 A6
Derry St LA14 . . . . .207 A2
Dertern La LA15 . . . . .213 A1
Derwent Ave
Maryport CA15 . . . . .182 E5
Seaton CA14 . . . . .183 A1
Workington CA14 . . . . .184 D4
Derwent Bank
Seaton CA14 . . . . .183 B1
Walney Island LA14 . . . . . .206 B3
Derwent Bay Bears Craft
Ctr* CA12 . . . . .81 B4
Derwent Cl
🟧 Keswick CA12 . . . . .192 B3
Penrith CA11 . . . . .191 B4
Seaton CA14 . . . . .183 B1
Derwent Ct 🟨 CA13 . . . . . .190 C4
Derwent Dr Kendal LA9 . . .200 F2
Workington CA14 . . . . .184 C6
Derwent Howe Ind Est
CA14 . . . . .184 B6
Derwent Mdws CA14 . . . . .62 F4
Derwent Mills 🟧 CA14 . . . .190 C4
Derwent Mills Comm Pk
CA13 . . . . .190 C5
Derwent Pk CA13 . . . . .63 E5
Derwent Pl LA22 . . . . .203 E4
Derwent Rd CA14 . . . . .184 C3
Derwent Ridge CA14 . . . . .183 B1
Derwent Row CA13 . . . . . . .63 E5
Derwent St Carlisle CA2 . . .176 D5
Cockermouth CA13 . . . . . . .190 C4
🔟 Workington CA14 . . . . . .192 B3
Workington CA14 . . . . .184 E7
Derwent Vale Prim Sch
CA14 . . . . .63 B4
Derwent Water Cvn Site
CA12 . . . . .192 A3
Derwentside Gdns
CA13 . . . . .190 C5
Derwentwater Cl LA18 . . . .202 C4
Devoke Water Gdns 🟧
LA15 . . . . .205 B4
Devon Rd CA28 . . . . .187 F5
Devon St LA13 . . . . .207 B3
Devon Terr 🟧 LA13 . . . . . . .207 B3
Devonshire Bglws LA18 . .202 D4
Devonshire Cl LA18 . . . . . .202 D4
Devonshire Rd
Barrow-In-F LA14 . . . . .206 F5
Millom LA18 . . . . .202 D4
Ulverston LA12 . . . . .203 E5
Devonshire Road Est
LA18 . . . . .202 E4
Devonshire St
Carlisle CA3 . . . . .214 B1
🟧 Dalton-In-F LA15 . . . . . .205 C5
Penrith CA11 . . . . .191 D5

Cre – Duk 223

Devonshire St *continued*
Workington CA14 . . . . .184 E5
Devonshire Terr
Carlisle CA3 . . . . .214 A4
Kirkby-in-F LA17 . . . . .151 B5
Devonshire Wlk CA3 . . . . .214 A3
Dick Trod La CA7 . . . . .25 D7
Dickgate Rd LA8 . . . . .144 E8
Dickie Green Cotts
CA17 . . . . .120 A2
Dickinson Ct 🟧 CA28 . . . . .186 C1
Diggle Rd CA2 . . . . .176 E4
Distington Com Sch
CA14 . . . . .185 D4
Distington Pk CA14 . . . . . .185 D3
Dixon Ct CA2 . . . . .176 E6
Dixon Pl CA3 . . . . .175 C2
Dixon Rd CA3 . . . . .175 C2
Dixon St CA3 . . . . .214 A3
Dixon Wood Cl LA11 . . . . .154 C3
Dobbie Bank LA11 . . . . . . .164 D7
Dobby La LA8 . . . . .130 B1
Dobdale Rd LA8 . . . . .143 C4
Dobinson Rd CA2 . . . . .176 B5
Dock Mus The* LA14 . . . . .206 D3
Docker Brow LA8 . . . . .131 F3
Docker La Kendal LA8 . . . .131 F1
Whittington LA6 . . . . .168 C5
Docker Park Farm*
LA6 . . . . .168 A4
Dockray Hall Ind Est
LA9 . . . . .200 D7
Dockray Hall Rd LA9 . . . . .200 C7
Dockray Meadow Cvn Site
LA9 . . . . .200 D7
Dodd's La LA3 . . . . .129 C8
Dodding Holme LA8 . . . . . .131 C2
Dodds Howe LA8 . . . . .142 E6
Dodgson Croft LA6 . . . . . .212 B2
Dodgson Ct LA14 . . . . .212 C2
Dolholme Hill LA8 . . . . . . .130 B1
Dollywood La LA7 . . . . . . .209 F1
Dominion Rd DG16 . . . . . .173 C3
Dominion St LA14 . . . . . . .206 C1
Donald Rd CA14 . . . . .184 C6
Donaldson's Cotts 🟧
CA7 . . . . .180 D3
Doncaster Pl 🟧 LA13 . . . .207 C3
Doncaster Rd CA16 . . . . . .193 C5
Doomgate CA16 . . . . .193 C5
Dora Cres LA14 . . . . .184 D6
Dorcas Ave LA13 . . . . .207 C6
Dorcas Gdns LA13 . . . . . . .207 C6
Dorchester Cres LA12 . . . .203 C2
Doris St LA14 . . . . .206 C3
Dorset Cl LA14 . . . . .187 F5
Dorset St LA14 . . . . .206 F5
Douglas Gdns DG12 . . . . .172 D4
Douglas Pl DG16 . . . . .173 C2
Douglas Rd CA14 . . . . .184 D5
Douglas Sq TD9 . . . . .1 B6
Douglas St LA14 . . . . .206 C3
Dove Cottage & Wordsworth
Mus* LA22 . . . . .194 C3
Dove La CA14 . . . . .184 F6
Dove Nest La LA8 . . . . .156 D7
Dovehouses La LA6 . . . . . .156 D4
Dover St LA14 . . . . .206 C1
Dovers La LA13 . . . . .190 B5
Dowbeck Rd CA2 . . . . .176 E5
Dowbiggin La LA10 . . . . . .146 F7
Dowdales Sch LA15 . . . . . .205 B5
Dowker's La LA9 . . . . .200 D4
Downfield La CA22 . . . . . .188 A3
Downie's Wynd DG12 . . . .172 E3
Drake St LA14 . . . . .206 F4
Drawbriggs Ct CA16 . . . . .193 D6
Drawbriggs La CA16 . . . . .193 E5
Drawbriggs Mount
CA16 . . . . .193 D5
Drigg Dunes & Irt Estuary
Nature Reserve*
CA19 . . . . .123 D3
Drigg Rd CA20 . . . . .123 B7
Drigg Sta CA19 . . . . .123 D5
Drive The Carnforth LA5 . .213 A1
Newton Rigg CA11 . . . . . . .70 E5
Seascale CA20 . . . . .123 B8
Ulverston LA12 . . . . .203 C4
Droomer Dr LA23 . . . . .198 F5
Droomer La LA23 . . . . .198 F5
Drover La CA11 . . . . .191 C6
Drovers La Carlisle CA3 . . .214 B3
Penrith CA11 . . . . .191 C6
Drovers Mews CA11 . . . . .191 C6
Drovers Way LA6 . . . . .167 B7
Drumburgh Ave CA3 . . . . .175 E4
Drummermire LA22 . . . . . .195 C5
Drummond Rd DG12 . . . . .172 D4
Drury La CA10 . . . . .10 D6
Dry La LA8 . . . . .131 C4
Dryden St LA14 . . . . .206 F4
Dryden Way CA22 . . . . . . .189 D6
Dub Brow CA26 . . . . .77 D1
Dubbs Rd LA23 . . . . .129 D8
Dubdale Brow LA18 . . . . . .150 C8
Duchess Ave CA14 . . . . . . .184 D6
Duddon Ct CA18 . . . . .187 E6
Duddon Dr LA17 . . . . .206 B3
Duddon Rd LA16 . . . . .162 A8
Duddon View LA16 . . . . . . .162 A8
Dudley St LA14 . . . . .206 F6
Dugg Hill LA7 . . . . .211 D7
Duke St Askam-In-F LA16 . .162 A8
Barrow-In-F LA14 . . . . .206 F2

Duke St *continued*
Barrow-In-F LA14 ....206 F3
Burton in L LA6 ....169 C3
Carlisle CA2 ....176 E6
Cleator Moor CA25 ....188 D7
Dalton-In-F LA15 ....205 C5
Gleaston LA12 ....162 E1
Holme LA6 ....156 B1
Millom LA18 ....202 C5
Penrith CA11 ....191 C5
Whitehaven CA28 ....186 C1
7 Wigton CA7 ....180 D3
Workington CA14 ....184 D6
Duke's Rd CA1 ....214 B3
Dukes Dr CA6 ....175 A6
Dukes Mdw CA11 ....54 D2
Dukes Wood Rd CA6 ....10 C4
Dumb Tom's La LA2,LA6 ..169 E1
Dumfries St LA14 ....207 A3
Dunbar St LA14 ....206 F1
Duncan Sq 20 CA28 .....186 C1
Duncan St LA14 ....206 F3
Dundalk St LA14 ....206 F1
Dundas St LA14 ....206 F5
Dundee St LA14 ....206 F1
Dundonald St LA14 ......206 F4
Dunfell View CA10 ....87 D8
Dungeon Ghyll Force* LA22 ...112 F5
Dungeon La
Barrow-In-F LA13 ....207 F3
Bootle LA19 ....136 F4
Dunkirk Ave LA5 ....213 D2
Dunlin Dr LA15 ....205 C4
Dunmail Cres CA13 ......190 B3
Dunmail Dr Carlisle CA2 .176 D5
Kendal LA9 ....200 E2
Dunmail Park Sh Ctr CA14 ...62 C5
Dunmail Raise LA14 .....204 D1
Dunmallet Rigg CA2 .....176 C4
Dunnerdale LA17 ....151 B5
Dunoon St LA14 ....206 F1
Dunvegan St 8 LA14 .....206 F1
Durdar Rd CA2 ....30 B3
Durham St LA13 ....207 B3
Durranhill Ind Est CA1 ...177 D4
Durranhill Rd CA1 ......177 F5
Dyke Hall La LA10 ......159 D8
Dyke Nook St CA26 ....92 D8
Dyke St CA26 ....92 D8
Dykecrofts Visitor Ctr* TD9 ...1 D6
Dykes Ave DG12 ....172 D5
Dykes La LA5 ....166 F5
Dykes Terr CA3 ....175 F1

E

Eadie St CA14 ....185 A7
Eagles Way 2 CA28 ......76 F2
Eaglesfield St CA15 ....182 D6
Eaigle Terr CA15 ....183 A6
Eals Bank CA8 ....34 F6
Eamont Cl LA14 ....206 B3
Eamont Mews 13 CA11 ....191 E4
Eamont Pk CA10 ....191 E2
Earl Henry's Dr
Askham CA10 ....85 E8
Eamont Bridge CA10 ......191 E1
Penrith CA10 ....71 B2
Earl St Carlisle CA1 ....214 B2
Cleator Moor CA25 ....188 D6
Millom LA18 ....202 D5
Earl's Rd CA28 ....186 D2
Earle St LA14 ....206 E2
Earls La CA3 ....214 B2
Earls Way CA6 ....19 E2
Easdale Bank CA2 ....176 B3
Easedale Rd LA22 ....194 A5
East Ave CA14 ....185 B8
East Cres CA7 ....36 C1
East Croft Terr CA28 ...186 E8
East Ct LA12 ....203 A1
East Dale St CA2 ....176 F4
East Dr Swarthmoor LA12 .203 A1
Ulverston LA12 ....162 F6
East Hecklegirth DG12 ..172 E2
East La CA14 ....185 B8
East Lakes Bsns Pk CA11 ...191 A5
East Mount 6 LA13 .....207 B6
East Nelson St CA2 .....214 A1
East Norfolk St CA2 ....176 F4
East Pk CA5 ....39 B8
East Rd Egremont CA22 ..189 E7
Lowca CA28 ....186 E8
East Strand CA28 ....186 C1
East Terr CA7 ....50 F8
East Tower La CA3 ......214 B3
East Vale Ct CA2 ....176 F4
East View Kendal LA9 ...200 C4
Lindal in F LA12 ....162 E6
Prospect CA7 ....49 F7
East View Cotts CA12 ...199 C6
East View Ct 8 LA9 .....200 C4
East View Rd CA14 ......185 C3
Eastern Way CA1 ....177 E4
Eastgate LA9 ....200 E6
Eaves Lea LA6 ....212 B2
Eccle Riggs La LA20 ....139 A2
Eccleriggs Ave LA14 ....204 C1
Eccleston Mdw LA11 .....164 D6
Echo Bank LA9 ....200 B3
Echo Barn Hill LA9 .....200 C3
Eden Ave LA14 ....206 B3
Eden Cl Cargo CA6 ....19 D2
Great Salkeld CA11 ....57 B3
Wigton CA7 ....180 A3
Eden Cres CA3 ....175 D2
Eden Ct Carlisle CA3 ...175 D1
Crosby-On-E CA6 ....20 F2
Eden Dr 1 CA28 ....76 F2
Eden Garth CA10 ....71 F8
Eden Gr CA10 ....57 A6
Eden Grange CA4 ....178 D7
Eden Grove Sch CA16 ......87 D6
Eden Mdws CA10 ....72 E1
Eden Mount Carlisle CA3 .214 A4
Grange-Over-S LA11 ......208 C5
Penrith CA11 ....191 E5
Ulverston LA12 ....203 D2
Wetheral CA4 ....178 B1
Eden Mount Rd LA11 .....208 C4
Eden Mount Way LA5 .....213 E4
Eden Ostrich World* CA11 ...71 F8
Eden Park Cres CA1 .....177 E6
Eden Park Rd LA11 ......208 C5
Eden Pk CA10 ....57 B8
Eden Pl Annan DG12 .....172 E4
Carlisle CA3 ....175 D1
Eden St Carlisle CA3 ...175 D2
Silloth CA7 ....174 C3
Eden Straits CA10 ....71 F8
Eden View CA16 ....73 E2
Edenfold CA16 ....87 E6
Edentown Ct CA3 ....175 D2
Edge Brow CA10 ....86 C1
Edgecombe Ct 5 LA9 .....200 D5
Edgehill CA28 ....186 D2
Edgehill Rd CA1 ....177 F3
Edinboro LA22 ....195 E6
Edinburgh Ave CA14 .....184 E3
Edinburgh Rd CA15 ......182 D3
Edmonson St 3 LA12 .....203 E5
Ednam St DG12 ....172 C3
Edward Pl DG12 ....172 D5
Edward St Carlisle CA1 .214 C1
Carnforth LA5 ....213 C4
Egdale La CA17 ....120 C1
Egerton Bldgs 2 LA14 ...206 F1
Egerton Gr CA2 ....176 B5
Egerton Terr LA15 ......205 C6
Eggerslack Ho LA11 .....208 D6
Eggerslack Terr LA11 ...208 E5
Egremont Castle* CA22 ...189 D5
Egremont Gdns LA14 .....204 E1
Egremont Rd
Hensingham CA24 ....91 F5
St Bees CA27 ....91 D1
Egremont St LA18 ....202 D4
Ehen Ave CA28 ....187 D7
Ehen Court Rd CA22 .....189 E6
Ehen Ct CA22 ....189 E6
Ehen Garth CA23 ....93 A6
Ehen Hall Gdns CA23 ....188 C3
Ehen Pl CA25 ....188 F6
Ehen Rd
Cleator Moor CA25 ....188 F6
Thornhill CA22 ....189 E2
Ehenside Com Sch CA23 ...188 F6
Eight Acre La LA5 ......166 F6
Elbra Farm Cl CA15 .....182 F5
Eldon Dr CA1 ....177 F4
Eldred Rd CA14 ....184 E4
Eldred St CA1 ....177 C6
Eleventrees CA12 ....192 E4
Elim Gr LA23 ....198 D3
Elim Mews LA23 ....198 D3
Elizabeth Cotts CA10 ...102 C7
Elizabeth Cres CA28 ....186 F3
Elizabeth Smyth Bglws LA13 ...207 C4
Elizabeth St
8 Maryport CA15 ....182 E5
Workington CA14 ....184 F5
Elizabeth Terr 11 CA15 .182 E5
Elizabethan Way LA14 ...206 F5
Ellen Cl CA7 ....180 B3
Ellen Garth CA7 ....50 D8
Ellen Villas CA15 ......182 F4
Ellenborough & Ewanrigg Inf Sch CA15 ...182 E4
Ellenborough Old Rd CA15 ...182 E5
Ellenborough Pl CA15 ...182 C4
Ellenborough Rd CA15 ...182 E5
Ellenfoot Dr CA15 ......182 F4
Eller Bank CA14 ....185 A8
Eller Beck Raise CA2 ...176 C2
Eller Raise LA9 ....200 E6
Eller Riggs Brow LA12 ..152 A3
Elleray Gdns LA23 ......198 E6
Elleray Prep Sch LA23 ...198 E6
Elleray Rd LA23 ....198 E6
Ellerbeck Brow CA13 .....64 A5
Ellerbeck Cl CA14 ......184 F3
Ellerbeck La CA14 ......184 F3
Ellergreen LA9 ....130 E2
Ellerigg La LA6 ....157 F6
Ellerigg Rd LA22 ....195 D7
Ellers Brow LA22 ....113 E2
Ellers The LA12 ....203 D5
Ellerside 24 LA12 ......203 D5
Ellerslie Pk CA20 ......109 B2
Ellerslie Terr CA20 ....109 B2
Ellerthwaite Rd LA23 ...198 E5
Ellerthwaite Sq LA23 ...198 E5
Ellesmere Way CA2 ......176 B3
Elliot Pk CA12 ....192 A4
Ellis Wood LA12 ....152 D5
Elliscales Ave LA15 ....205 B5
Ellonby Rd CA11 ....55 B2
Elm Ave CA15 ....183 C7
Elm Cl Endmoor LA8 .....156 D8
High Hesket CA4 ....41 F3
Elm Ct Kendal LA9 ......200 C7
1 Keswick CA12 ....192 A4
11 Penrith CA11 ....191 C5
Workington CA14 ....184 E3
Elm Garth CA4 ....178 A3
Elm Rd Annan DG12 ......172 C2
Barrow-In-F LA14 ....206 F6
Elm St CA2 ....214 A1
Elm Terr CA11 ....191 C5
Elmfield CA8 ....179 B4
Elms The CA22 ....189 B6
Elmsfield Park Cotts LA6 ...156 A3
Elmslack Ct LA5 ....210 C4
Elmslack La LA5 ....210 C4
Elmvale Sch DG12 ....172 C3
Elph Howe La LA8 ....130 B6
Elterwater Ave CA14 ....184 D4
Elterwater Cres LA14 ...204 E1
Ely Cl CA14 ....184 E3
Embleton Rd CA2 ....177 B2
Emerald Cl CA14 ....184 D1
Emesgate La LA5 ....210 C3
Emlyn St LA14 ....206 F4
Emmanual Ct 5 LA14 .....207 A5
Emperor's Dr
Hackthorpe CA10 ....86 A4
Lowther CA10 ....85 E5
Empire Ct DG16 ....173 D2
Empire Rd CA2 ....176 E5
Empire Way DG16 ....173 C2
Empress Dr LA14 ....206 D1
Empsom Rd LA9 ....200 C7
Engine Lonning CA2 .....176 C7
Englethwaite Hall Cvn Pk CA4 ...31 D1
English Damside CA3 ....214 A2
English St Annan DG12 ..172 C4
Carlisle CA3 ....214 B2
Longtown CA6 ....10 C3
Ennerdale & Kinniside CE Prim Sch CA23 ...93 B6
Ennerdale Ave
Carlisle CA1 ....177 D5
Workington CA14 ....184 E4
Ennerdale Cl
Cockermouth CA13 ....190 F4
Dalton-In-F LA15 ....205 B3
Millom LA18 ....202 C4
Ennerdale Dr LA14 ......204 D1
Ennerdale Rd
Cleator Moor CA25 ....188 E6
Maryport CA15 ....182 E4
Ennerdale Terr CA28 ....187 B6
Ennerdale View CA14 ....185 D4
Enyeat Rd LA8 ....156 D7
Esk Ave CA28 ....187 D7
Esk Bank CA6 ....10 B3
Esk Pl DG12 ....172 E4
Esk Rd Carlisle CA3 ....175 C3
Gretna DG16 ....173 C2
Esk St Longtown CA6 .....10 B3
Silloth CA7 ....174 C4
Eskdale Ave
Barrow-In-F LA13 ....207 B3
Carlisle CA2 ....176 D5
Seascale CA20 ....123 B8
Eskdale Cl CA25 ....188 C8
Eskdale Cres CA14 ......184 D3
Eskdale Dr LA15 ....205 C3
Eskdale Green Forest Walks* CA19 ...124 F7
Eskdale Green Sta* CA19 ...124 F6
Eskdale Mill* CA19 ......125 C8
Eskett View CA26 ....77 E1
Eskin St CA12 ....192 B3
Eskrigg La LA8 ....144 C1
Esperanto Way CA16 .....193 F5
Esplanade The LA11 .....208 D4
Espland Cl CA11 ....70 C6
Essex St LA14 ....207 A5
Esther St CA2 ....177 B4
Esthwaite Ave LA9 ......200 F2
Esthwaite Gn LA9 ....200 F2
Estuary Pk 2 LA16 ......162 A8
Etterby Cl CA13 ....190 D3
Etterby Lea Cres CA3 ...175 D1
Etterby Lea Gr CA3 .....175 D1
Etterby Lea Rd CA3 .....175 D1
Etterby Rd CA3 ....175 B1
Etterby Scaur CA3 ......175 C1
Etterby St CA3 ....175 D1
Etterby Terr CA3 ....175 D1
Euryalus St LA14 ....206 C1
Evening Hill Dr CA13 ...190 B3
Eveninghill View CA13 ..190 B3
Everest Mount CA14 .....184 D2
Ewan Cl LA13 ....207 C5
Ewanrigg Brow CA15 .....182 F4
Ewanrigg Jun Sch CA15 ...182 E4
Ewanrigg Rd CA15 ....182 D4
Ewbank La LA8 ....144 F5
Ewebank Rd LA8 ....145 A5
Ewelock La CA5 ....39 E3
Exchange Ct LA9 ....200 C5
Exmouth St LA14 ....206 E4

F

Fair Haven 3 LA23 .....198 E5
Fair View
Dalton-In-F LA15 ....205 B5
Egremont CA22 ....189 C6
Fair View Rd LA22 ......195 D6
Fairbank LA6 ....212 B2
Fairfield
Bowness-On-W LA23 ....198 C2
Cark LA11 ....164 D7
Fairfield Cl Cark LA11 .164 D7
Carnforth LA5 ....213 D3
Staveley LA8 ....130 C5
Fairfield Gdns CA2 .....176 D5
Fairfield Inf & Jun Sch CA13 ...190 C3
Fairfield La
Barrow-In-F LA13 ....207 B5
Kendal LA9 ....200 B7
Fairfield Pl DG12 ......172 C4
Fairfield Rd Millom LA18 .202 C6
Windermere LA23 ....198 F4
Fairfield Row LA10 .....146 E6
Fairfield View CA13 ....190 C3
Fairgarth Dr LA6 ....212 B2
Fairhill Cl CA11 ....191 C7
Fairhill View CA9 ......181 E3
Fairholme LA10 ....201 C5
Fairmile Rd CA10,LA8 ...132 F6
Fairthorns Rd LA8 ......145 B6
Fairview LA6 ....212 B3
Fairview Gdns CA10 ......71 C1
Fairways The CA20 ......123 A8
Fairybead La CA11 ....70 D3
Fairybead Pk CA11 ....70 D3
Falcon Dr DG16 ....173 D3
Falcon Pl
Moresby Parks CA28 ....76 F2
Workington CA14 ....184 D6
Falcon St CA14 ....184 D6
Falkins Hill CA8 ....179 C5
Fall Beck Cotts LA8 ....144 D1
Fall Kirk LA2 ....167 F1
Fallbarrow Ct LA23 .....198 C3
Fallbarrow Cvn Pk LA23 .198 C3
Fallbarrow Rd LA23 .....198 C3
Fallowfield CA10 ....86 E8
Fallowfield Ave 3 LA12 .203 C5
Fallowfield Ct CA11 ....191 C4
Fallowfield Rd 24 LA16 ..162 A8
Fallows The 13 CA13 ....190 C4
Falls The LA22 ....195 D6
Falmouth St LA14 ....206 B1
Fangs Brow CA13 ....78 E5
Far Close Dr LA5 ....165 F8
Far Leases La CA17 .....120 C8
Far Moor CA22 ....188 A3
Far Moss CA14 ....184 E7
Faraday Rd CA17 ....199 C6
Farbrow Rd CA1 ....177 F1
Farish Cl CA8 ....179 B5
Farlam Dr CA1 ....177 F5
Farleigh Ct CA11 ....57 A4
Farleton Cl LA5 ....213 B7
Farleton View 4 LA6 ....156 B1
Farm St LA14 ....206 F1
Farriers Way CA4 ....41 E5
Faustin Hill CA4 ....178 A2
Fawn Cl 35 LA16 ....162 A8
Fell Brow 7 LA9 ....200 C5
Fell Cl
Grange-Over-S LA11 ......208 C4
Oxenholme LA9 ....144 B4
Sedbergh LA10 ....201 D5
Silloth CA7 ....174 C4
11 Ulverston LA12 ....203 E5
Fell Cotts LA11 ....208 C4
Fell Croft
Dalton-In-F LA15 ....205 B5
Pooley Bridge CA10 ....84 F7
Fell Dr LA11 ....208 C4
Fell End Cvn Pk LA7 ....166 F8
Fell Foot LA6 ....156 C4
Fell Foot Brow LA12 ....141 F2
Fell Foot Pk* LA12 ......141 F1
Fell La Hallthwaites LA18 .150 B8
Old Town LA6 ....157 D6
Penrith CA11 ....191 D6
Ravenglass CA18 ....124 B3
Waberthwaite LA19 ....137 C8
Warcop CA16 ....104 D7
Winton CA17 ....105 B1
Fell Rd LA6 ....158 C2
Fell Side CA12 ....82 C8
Fell St Barrow-In-F LA14 .206 F3
Ulverston LA12 ....203 E5
Fell View Anthorn CA7 ...16 F1
Bridgefoot CA14 ....63 C3
Browtop CA14 ....77 F7
Cockermouth CA13 ....190 D3
Milton CA8 ....22 E3
Silloth CA7 ....174 C4
Swarthmoor LA12 ....203 A2
Welton CA5 ....39 F3
Wigton CA7 ....180 B4
Fell View Ave CA28 .....187 C5
Fell View Dr CA22 ......189 D5
Fell View Pk CA20 ......109 B2
Fell View Rd CA20 ......123 B8
Fell View Trad Pk LA9 ...131 B1
Fell View Wlk CA14 .....184 D3
Fellfoot Cotts LA8 .....130 B6
Fellfoot Rd LA6 ....158 A3
Fellgate La LA10 ....147 A7
Fellside Allithwaite LA11 .164 F8
Windermere LA23 ....141 F6
Fellside Ct
Grange-Over-S LA11 ......208 C4
Kendal LA9 ....200 C6
Fellside Gr CA2 ....176 B5
Fellside Terr CA16 ....73 F2
Fellview Prim Sch CA7 ....53 C6
Fenman Cl LA14 ....207 B3
Fenton CA12 ....192 D3
Fenton Gate CA8 ....31 F8
Fenton La CA8 ....32 A6
Fenton St LA14 ....207 A3
Fergus Way CA2 ....176 C5
Ferguson Pl CA2 ....176 E4
Ferguson Rd CA2 ....176 E4
Fern Bank
Bowness-On-W LA23 ....198 C2
Carnforth LA5 ....213 C3
Cockermouth CA13 ....190 C3
Fern Croft LA6 ....212 E4
Fern Ct CA28 ....186 F1
Fern Gr CA28 ....186 E1
Fern Way CA28 ....186 E1
Fernbank La CA14 ....62 F4
Ferney Gn LA9 ....200 C6
Ferney Green Dr LA23 ...198 C1
Fernhill Rd LA11 ....208 C3
Fernlea Cres DG12 ......172 E5
Fernlea Way CA3 ....175 C2
Fernleigh Ave LA11 .....208 D4
Fernleigh Cl
Seaton CA14 ....183 C2
Tallentire CA13 ....49 E2
Fernleigh Dr CA14 ......183 C2
Fernleigh Rd LA11 ......208 C4
Ferns The CA22 ....189 C6
Fernwood Dr LA9 ....200 B3
Ferry Rd LA14 ....206 E2
Festival Cres CA15 .....182 E4
Festival Rd LA18 ....202 C6
Fiddler's Cswy LA8 .....143 D2
Fiddler's La CA10 ....57 A7
Fiddlergill LA8 ....131 F2
Field End LA8 ....131 E3
Field Foot LA22 ....194 B4
Field Hall LA18 ....202 B5
Field Head Pl LA11 .....164 D6
Field House Gdns CA11 ..191 C6
Field St LA14 ....207 A3
Field View CA7 ....17 D5
Fieldside Annan DG12 ....172 D5
Burnrigg CA8 ....178 D4
Fieldside Cl CA12 ......192 E4
Fife St LA13 ....207 B3
Fifkettle Brow CA14 .....63 F1
Finch Cl CA1 ....177 D6
Finch St LA18 ....202 C5
Findlay Pl 24 CA14 .....184 D6
Finglandrigg Wood National Nature Reserve* CA7 ...28 A7
Finkle St Carlisle CA3 ..214 A3
Kendal LA9 ....200 D5
Pooley Bridge CA10 ....84 F7
Sedbergh LA10 ....201 C5
St Bees CA27 ....91 D2
Workington CA14 ....184 E6
Finley Cl LA9 ....200 E7
Finley Dr LA9 ....200 D7
Finn Ave CA2 ....176 E6
Finsthwaite La LA12 ....153 C8
Fir Ends Prim Sch CA6 ....20 F8
Fir Garth
Chapel Stile LA22 ....113 B4
Cleator Moor CA25 ....188 C8
Fir Tree Cres LA23 .....198 C1
Fir Tree Rise LA13 .....207 F5
Firbank LA9 ....200 F5
Firlands CA3 ....175 E2
Firs Cl LA7 ....211 D3
Firs Flats LA7 ....211 D3
Firs Rd LA7 ....211 D3
Firs The CA9 ....181 D3
First Moss La LA8 ......143 C5
Firth Dr CA27 ....91 C2
Firth View CA28 ....186 E6
Firth View Wlk CA14 ....184 D3
Firtree La LA8 ....131 C5
Fish Cross DG12 ....172 C4
Fisher Beck Pk LA22 ....195 D4
Fisher Pl CA12 ....82 B1
Fisher St
4 Barrow-In-F LA14 ....206 F2
Carlisle CA3 ....214 A3
Workington CA14 ....184 D6
Fisher's Yd 13 LA14 ....206 F3
Fitz Rd CA13 ....190 C3
Fitz Stps LA22 ....113 B2
Fitz View CA13 ....190 C3
Five Lane Ends CA10 .....44 A1
Flag St LA22 ....197 E5
Flakebridge Cotts CA16 ..88 E5
Flan Cl LA12 ....203 D6
Flass La LA13 ....207 D4
Flass Mdws LA13 ....207 D4
Flat La Carlisle CA2 ...176 C6
Yealand Redmayne LA5 ....166 F6
Flats Cotts 9 CA11 .....191 D5
Flatt Walks CA28 ....187 D8
Fleet St CA14 ....184 D5
Fleming Dr CA21 ....108 B5
Fleming Pl CA15 ....182 D6
Fleming Sq CA15 ....182 D6
Fleming St CA15 ....182 D6
Fleswick Ave CA28 ......187 C5
Fletcher Cl
6 Cockermouth CA13 ......190 C4
Great Broughton CA13 .....63 E6
Fletcher Cres CA15 .....182 E4
Fletcher Hill Pk CA17 ..199 C5

Fletcher St
Cleator Moor CA25 . . . . . . .188 E6
7 Cockermouth CA13 . . . .190 C4
10 Workington CA14 . . . .184 D6
Fletcher Way CA3 . . . . . . .175 B6
Fletchers Croft CA13 . . . . . .63 E4
Flimby Brow CA15 . . . . . . .183 D7
Flimby Prim Sch CA15 . .182 A1
Flimby Sta CA15 . . . . . . .183 C8
Flintergill Cl CA10 . . . . . .147 B1
Flookburgh CE Prim Sch
LA11 . . . . .164 D6
Florence Mine Heritage Ctr*
CA22 . . . . .189 C5
Florence St LA14 . . . . . . .207 A3
Florence Terr 9 CA15 . . .182 E5
Flosh Cotts CA23 . . . . . . .188 D4
Flosh Mdws CA23 . . . . . . .188 D4
Flower St Carlisle CA1 . . . .214 C1
Leece LA12 . . . . .171 C8
Flowerden Ct LA7 . . . . . . .211 D4
Floyd St LA18 . . . . .150 A2
Flush Brow LA6 . . . . .212 F5
Fold Brow CA13 . . . . .190 E4
Fold The LA11 . . . . .164 D7
Folkestone Ave LA14 . . . . .206 C1
Folly La CA11 . . . . .191 E5
Footeran La LA5 . . . . .166 F6
Force La Ambleside LA22 .195 D4
Levens LA8 . . . . .143 F1
Force Mills Forest Wlk*
LA12 . . . . .141 B5
Ford La LA5 . . . . .210 E5
Ford Park Cres LA12 . . . . .203 E6
Ford Rd LA11 . . . . .153 E1
Ford Terr LA9 . . . . .200 D2
Forelands The CA7 . . . . . . .49 F4
Forest Hill CA1 . . . . .177 F2
Forest Houses CA23 . . . . . .93 A6
Forge Ct CA4 . . . . .41 E5
Forge La CA12 . . . . .192 D4
Forge The Coniston LA21 . .196 A4
Dalston CA5 . . . . .40 B7
Keswick CA12 . . . . .192 E4
Forgeholm DG14 . . . . .3 D3
Fort Putnam* CA11 . . . . . . .70 A5
Foster St Penrith CA11 . . . .191 C6
Shap CA10 . . . . .101 C6
Fothergills The CA15 . . . .182 A1
Foulney St LA13 . . . . .171 B3
Foulstep LA22 . . . . .113 E2
Foundarygdns LA5 . . . . . .213 C5
Foundry Rd CA20 . . . . . . .186 E7
Foundry St LA14 . . . . .207 B3
Fountain Brow 5 LA9 . . . .200 C5
Fountain St LA22 . . . . . . .203 D5
Fountains Ave CA14 . . . . .184 E3
Four Lane Ends
Burton in L LA2 . . . . .169 C1
Field Broughton LA11 . . . .154 A5
High Newton LA11 . . . . . .154 A4
Leece LA12 . . . . .171 C7
Fowl Ing La LA9 . . . . .200 E7
Fox La
10 Whitehaven CA28 . . . .186 C1
Workington CA14 . . . . . . .184 F6
Fox's St LA12 . . . . .203 A3
Fox's Pulpit* LA10 . . . . . .145 E8
Foxfield Cl 6 LA16 . . . . . .162 A8
Foxfield Rd
Broughton-In-F LA20 . . . . .139 A2
Walney Island LA14 . . . . .206 C5
Foxfield Sta LA20 . . . . . . .150 F8
Foxhills CA6 . . . . .21 E4
Foxhole Rigg La LA10 . . . .184 A2
Foxhouses Rd CA28 . . . . . .187 E7
Foxhowe 8 LA12 . . . . . . .203 D5
Frances Croft CA14 . . . . . .184 F5
Frank Coutts Ct TD9 . . . . . . .1 A8
Frankland Pk CA10 . . . . . .118 C6
Franklin St LA14 . . . . .206 E4
Fraser Gr CA3 . . . . .175 C2
Frazer St LA14 . . . . .184 D5
Frederick St
Barrow-In-F LA13 . . . . . . .207 C2
Carlisle CA2 . . . . .176 E4
Freer Ct CA2 . . . . .176 F4
Freer St CA2 . . . . .176 F4
French St LA14 . . . . .206 D2
Frenchfield Cotts CA11 . . .191 F4
Frenchfield Way CA11 . . . .191 F4
Freshfield Ct LA7 . . . . .57 A4
Friar Bottom La CA7 . . . . .119 F4
Friar Row CA7 . . . . .53 C6
Friar's Crag Nature Trail*
CA12 . . . . .192 A1
Friargate CA11 . . . . .191 D5
Friars Cl CA11 . . . . .191 E5
Friars Ct CA3 . . . . .214 B2
Friars Garth
Abbey Town CA7 . . . . .26 C1
Cartmel LA11 . . . . .153 F1
Friars La LA13 . . . . .207 D4
Friars Rd CA11 . . . . .191 D5
Friars Rise CA11 . . . . .191 E5
Friars Terr
Barrow-In-F LA13 . . . . . . .207 D4
Penrith CA11 . . . . .191 E5
Friars View LA13 . . . . .207 D4
Friary Fields CA16 . . . . . . .193 C6
Friary Pk CA16 . . . . .193 C6
Frith La CA16 . . . . .88 C6
Frizington Com Prim Sch
CA26 . . . . .92 D8
Frizington Rd
Cleator Moor CA25 . . . . . .188 F6
Frizington CA26 . . . . .92 D7
Frome Rd LA14 . . . . .206 A4

Front Corkickle CA28 . . .187 D8
Front St Alston CA9 . . . . . .181 D3
Armathwaite CA4 . . . . .42 C5
Brampton CA8 . . . . .79 B5
Cotehill CA4 . . . . .31 B1
Mealsgate CA7 . . . . .37 C1
Orton CA10 . . . . .118 C7
Front The LA18 . . . . .202 A2
Frostoms Rd CA14 . . . . . .184 D4
Frostrow La CA10 . . . . . . .201 F3
Fruids Park Ave DG12 . . . .172 C3
Fulford Wlk 9 CA3 . . . . . .175 B1
Fulmar Dr LA9 . . . . .200 F1
Furnace Cl CA15 . . . . . . .188 D7
Furnace La CA15 . . . . . . .182 D5
Furnace Pl LA16 . . . . .162 A7
Furnace Rd CA15 . . . . . . .182 D5
Furnace Row CA14 . . . . . .185 E5
Furness Abbey* LA13 . . .207 D8
Furness Bsns Pk LA14 . . .206 E4
Furness Coll LA14 . . . . . .206 D4
Furness General Hospl
LA14 . . . . .207 C8
Furness Park Rd LA14 . . . .207 B6
Furness St LA14 . . . . .184 E3
Furness St LA18 . . . . .202 D4
Furze Ct CA1 . . . . .177 C6
Fusehill St CA1 . . . . .214 C1
Fusethwaite La LA23 . . . .129 C8

G

Gable Ave CA13 . . . . .190 F4
Gable Rd CA28 . . . . .187 F3
Gainsborough Pl LA14 . . .206 F6
Gait Burrows Nature
Reserve* LA7 . . . . .166 D8
Gaitle Bridge CA6 . . . . .9 F3
Galabank Ave DG12 . . . . .172 C5
Galava Roman Fort*
LA22 . . . . .195 C3
Gale How Pk LA22 . . . . . .195 D5
Gale Pk LA22 . . . . .195 D5
Gale Rigg LA22 . . . . .195 D5
Gale Rigg Ho LA22 . . . . . .195 D5
Gale The LA22 . . . . .195 D5
Gallansay La CA17 . . . . . .104 A1
Gallery Ho CA1 . . . . .177 C3
Galloper Pk CA10 . . . . . . .118 B3
Galloway Cl CA15 . . . . . . .182 F4
Gallowbarrow
Cockermouth CA13 . . . . . .190 C3
Kendal LA9 . . . . .200 D1
Gallower La LA6 . . . . .157 B4
Gamblesmire La LA8 . . . . .143 E7
Gameriggs Rd CA28 . . . . .187 D4
Gandy St LA9 . . . . .200 E6
Gap La Sedbergh LA10 . . .156 F8
Winton CA17 . . . . .105 A1
Garborough Cl CA15 . . . . . .49 B5
Garbridge Ct CA16 . . . . . .193 E6
Garbridge La CA16 . . . . . .193 E6
Garburn Rd LA9 . . . . .200 D3
Garden Cl 7 LA11 . . . . . .191 C5
Garden Ct LA12 . . . . .162 F7
Garden Ct CA11 . . . . .35 C1
Garden Lea
6 Dalton-In-F LA15 . . . .205 B4
Ulverston LA12 . . . . .203 D4
Garden Mews LA9 . . . . . . .200 D3
Garden Pl LA6 . . . . .167 C7
Garden Rd LA9 . . . . .200 D3
Garden St Carlisle CA1 . . .214 C1
Carlisle,Edentown CA3 . . .175 D1
Kendal LA9 . . . . .200 D3
Garden Terr
Baycliff LA12 . . . . .163 B3
Dalton-In-F LA15 . . . . . . .205 B5
Ulverston LA12 . . . . .203 D6
Garden Village CA2 . . . . . .176 B2
Garden Villas CA28 . . . . . .187 F6
Garden Wlk CA4 . . . . .21 E1
Gardenia St CA2 . . . . .177 B2
Gardens The CA28 . . . . . .187 D8
Gardinar Bank LA9 . . . . . .200 C6
Gardner Hall CA20 . . . . . .123 A8
Gardner Rd LA5 . . . . .213 C7
Garfield St Carlisle CA2 . . .214 A1
Workington CA14 . . . . . . .184 E5
Garland La CA11 . . . . .57 A4
Garlands Rd CA1 . . . . .177 F2
Garner St CA15 . . . . .182 C4
Garnet Cres CA14 . . . . . . .184 C3
Garnett Bridge Rd LA8 . . .131 A4
Gars La CA17 . . . . .105 A4
Garsdale Rd LA10 . . . . . . .148 D6
Garth Bank LA9 . . . . .200 F6
Garth Brow LA9 . . . . .200 B7
Garth Heads Rd CA16 . . . .193 D5
Garth Heads Rise CA16 . . .193 D8
Garth Inf Sch LA9 . . . . . .200 E7
Garth Pk CA14 . . . . .31 B1
Garth Row La
Kendal LA8 . . . . .131 B3
Underbarrow LA8 . . . . . . .131 A3
Garth The Coniston LA21 . .196 B4
Crosby-On-E CA6 . . . . .20 F2
Garthside CA7 . . . . .180 B8
Gaskell Cl LA5 . . . . .210 C3
Gatacre St LA14 . . . . .206 C2
Gateacre Terr LA14 . . . . . .206 C2
Gatebeck La LA8 . . . . .156 D8
Gatebeck Rd LA8 . . . . . . .156 D8
Gatehead CA14 . . . . .63 A4

Gateheads Brow LA6 . . . .212 F3
Gatelands Cvn Site LA6 . .167 B4
Gatesbield LA23 . . . . .198 E5
Gateshead St LA13 . . . . . .207 B3
Gateway LA13 . . . . .207 D3
Gauber Rd LA6 . . . . .160 C1
Gavel St CA15 . . . . .182 D4
Gavels The CA14 . . . . .63 B4
Gawith Pl 4 LA9 . . . . . . .200 D5
Gayle Ave CA10 . . . . .101 C5
Gaythorne Terr CA14 . . . . .63 C3
Gelt Cl CA13 . . . . .175 C3
Gelt Rd CA8 . . . . .179 C4
Gelt Rise CA8 . . . . .179 B4
Geltsdale Ave CA1 . . . . . . .177 F5
Geltsdale Gdns CA1 . . . . .178 A3
Geltwood Ave CA14 . . . . . .185 D8
Geneva St 3 LA14 . . . . . .207 A2
George Hestwell Sch
LA14 . . . . .206 B2
George Moore Ave CA7 . . . .37 C2
George Moore Ind Est
CA7 . . . . .37 C1
George Romney Jun Sch The
LA15 . . . . .205 C5
George St Annan DG12 . . .172 C4
16 Keswick CA12 . . . . . .192 B3
Maryport CA15 . . . . .182 C5
Newcastleton TD9 . . . . .1 B6
Whitehaven CA28 . . . . . . .186 D1
Wigton CA7 . . . . .180 D3
George Terr 15 CA15 . . . .182 E5
Georgian Way CA1,CA3 . . .214 B3
Ghyll Bank Lowca CA28 . . .186 E8
Threlkeld CA12 . . . . .82 C8
Ghyll Br CA13 . . . . .63 E6
Ghyll Cl LA23 . . . . .198 F5
Ghyll Gr CA28 . . . . .186 A4
Ghyll Head Rd LA23 . . . . .142 B7
Ghyll Rd Scotby CA4 . . . . . .30 F5
Windermere LA23 . . . . . . .198 F5
Workington CA14 . . . . . . .184 C2
Ghyll Side 10 LA9 . . . . . .200 C4
Ghyllside Ambleside LA22 .195 E5
Dent LA10 . . . . .148 B1
Ghyllside Prim Sch LA9 . .200 C4
Gilbert Rd CA2 . . . . .176 D1
Gilgarran Pk CA14 . . . . . . .77 D5
Gilgarran View LA14 . . . . .185 D4
Gill Cl CA28 . . . . .187 F7
Gill La CA11 . . . . .154 C3
Gill The Ulverston LA12 . . .203 B8
Gillam Way CA11 . . . . .191 B3
Gillbank Cotts CA10 . . . . . .71 C1
Gillbeck Pk CA15 . . . . . . .182 F4
Gillfoot Ave CA22 . . . . . . .189 D7
Gillfoot Rd CA22 . . . . .189 D7
Gillford Cres CA1 . . . . . . .177 D2
Gillhead Brow LA2 . . . . . .169 D1
Gillinggate LA9 . . . . .200 C4
Gilmordend Brow
Aspatria CA7 . . . . .36 F4
Mealsgate CA7 . . . . .37 A4
Gilmore Cl CA9 . . . . .181 D4
Gilmour St CA15 . . . . .182 C4
Gilnockie Twr* DG14 . . . . .3 C5
Gilpin Wlk LA14 . . . . .206 B5
Gilshaw View DG14 . . . . . . .9 A7
Gilsland CE Prim Sch
CA8 . . . . .14 D1
Gilsland Rd CA1 . . . . .177 F5
Gilthwaiterigg La LA9 . . . .131 B1
Gilts La CA22 . . . . .102 C3
Gilwilly Back La 3
CA11 . . . . .191 C5
Gilwilly La CA11 . . . . .191 B5
Gilwilly Rd CA11 . . . . .191 B5
Ginns CA28 . . . . .187 C7
Ginns To Kells Rd CA28 . .187 C6
Gladstone St CA14 . . . . . .184 D6
Gladstone Terr LA14 . . . . .207 A8
Glamara Dr CA2 . . . . .176 B3
Glasgow Rd CA1 . . . . .173 D4
Glasgow St LA14 . . . . .207 A3
Glasson Ct CA11 . . . . .191 C6
Glasson Ind Est CA15 . . . .182 C4
Glave Hill CA5 . . . . .29 D1
Gleaston Ave LA13 . . . . . .207 D4
Gleaston Watermill*
LA12 . . . . .162 F1
Glebe Cl
Appleby-In-W CA16 . . . . . .193 C4
Burton-in-K LA6 . . . . .167 C7
Dalston CA5 . . . . .40 A8
Keswick CA12 . . . . .192 A5
Glebe Cres CA16 . . . . .193 C4
Glebe Ct Annan DG12 . . . .172 C3
Kirkby Lonsdale LA6 . . . . .212 B3
Glebe Fold LA23 . . . . .198 C1
Glebe Fold LA10 . . . . .147 B1
Glebe La CA11 . . . . .185 D4
Glebe Rd
Appleby-In-W CA16 . . . . . .193 C4
Bowness-On-W LA23 . . . . .198 B1
Distington CA14 . . . . .185 D4
Glebe La LA9 . . . . .200 C3
Glebe Terr CA14 . . . . .200 C6
Glebe The
Castle Carrock CA8 . . . . . .32 D6
Chapel Stile LA22 . . . . . . .113 C4
Great Corby CA4 . . . . . . .178 C1
Wetheral CA4 . . . . .178 C1
Glebeland Terr CA14 . . . . .185 B7
Glen Terr CA8 . . . . .31 E5
Glen The LA12 . . . . .153 C7
Glen View LA12 . . . . .153 C7
Glencoe Cl LA18 . . . . .150 A1

Glendale Cvn Pk CA7 . . . . .17 D3
Glendale Rise CA2 . . . . . .176 B3
Glenderamackin Terr
CA12 . . . . .82 C7
Glendowlin Lodges CA10 . .71 A1
Gleneagles Dr CA3 . . . . . .175 B1
Glenedyth LA11 . . . . .208 F5
Glenfield Pl CA14 . . . . .62 E4
Glenfield Rd 4 LA15 . . . .205 B4
Glenn Rd CA14 . . . . .184 D3
Glenridding Dr LA14 . . . . .204 E1
Glenwhelt Bank CA8 . . . . .24 D8
Globe La Alston CA9 . . . . .181 D3
Carlisle CA3 . . . . .214 B3
Gloucester Rd CA1 . . . . . .177 E5
Gloucester Sq 6 LA12 . . .203 C5
Gloucester St LA13 . . . . . .207 C3
Glynt View DG12 . . . . . . .172 D2
Glynt Wynd DG12 . . . . . . .172 D2
Goat Brow CA13 . . . . .190 B6
Golden Lion Ct 10 CA28 . .186 C1
Goldsmith Rd CA2 . . . . . .189 C6
Goldsmith St LA14 . . . . . .206 F4
Golf Terr LA14 . . . . .174 B2
Goodly Dale Cotts LA23 . .198 D6
Goodly Dale Prim Sch
LA23 . . . . .198 D4
Goodman Rd CA14 . . . . . .184 C2
Goodmickle La LA6 . . . . . .157 B5
Goodwin Cl CA2 . . . . .177 B4
Goodwin Pl CA1 . . . . .177 B4
Goose Gn 3 LA15 . . . . . .205 B4
Goosegarth CA14 . . . . . . .178 A1
Gooseland Head LA1 . . . . .177 E1
Gordon Dr CA28 . . . . .186 B4
Gordon Terr DG12 . . . . . .172 C1
Goschen Rd CA2 . . . . .176 E4
Gosforth CE Sch CA20 . .109 B2
Gosforth Cross* CA20 .109 B2
Gosforth Rd Carlisle CA2 . .29 C6
Seascale CA20 . . . . .123 B8
Gosling Dr CA3 . . . . .175 D3
Gosport St LA14 . . . . .206 F5
Gote Rd CA13 . . . . .190 C4
Gowan Cl LA8 . . . . .130 B5
Gowan Cres LA8 . . . . .130 C5
Gowan Terr LA8 . . . . .130 C5
Gowlands Cross LA10 . . . .147 A2
Grace St CA1 . . . . .177 C6
Gradwell Ct LA13 . . . . . . .207 A4
Graggs Rd CA13 . . . . .190 B8
Graham Ave DG12 . . . . . .172 D5
Graham St Carlisle CA2 . . .214 A1
Longtown CA6 . . . . .10 C3
Penrith CA11 . . . . .191 C6
Grahams Croft CA4 . . . . . .178 A5
Grahams Rigg CA16 . . . . . .87 D6
Graigmore Ct 1 CA7 . . . .180 E7
Granary The LA11 . . . . . . .208 D3
Granby Rd LA11 . . . . .208 B1
Grand Cl CA22 . . . . .194 A5
Grange Ave Flimby CA15 . .183 C7
Great Broughton CA13 . . . .63 E6
Grange CE Prim Sch
LA11 . . . . .208 C4
Grange Cl CA22 . . . . .189 E2
Grange Cres 4 LA14 . . . .206 F3
Grange Fell Rd LA11 . . . . .208 B4
Grange Field CA10 . . . . . . .85 E1
Grange Gdns CA7 . . . . . . .180 C5
Grange La CA23 . . . . .78 F5
Grange Mews LA11 . . . . . .208 E5
Grange Pk CA22 . . . . .189 D2
Grange Rd CA11 . . . . .177 D3
Grange The Arnside LA5 . .210 A8
Dalston CA5 . . . . .40 F1
Whitehaven CA28 . . . . . . .187 F8
Grange View LA5 . . . . . . .213 C5
Grange-Over-Sands Sta
LA11 . . . . .208 E3
Grantley Rd LA14 . . . . . . .207 A6
Granville Cl CA28 . . . . . . .187 F7
Granville Rd CA2 . . . . . . .176 D6
Granville St LA14 . . . . . . .206 F5
Grapes La CA3 . . . . .214 B2
Grasmere Ave
Whitehaven CA28 . . . . . . .187 B5
Workington CA14 . . . . . . .184 D3
Grasmere CE Prim Sch
LA22 . . . . .194 B3
Grasmere Cres LA9 . . . . . .200 F1
Grasmere Rd
Barrow-In-F LA14 . . . . . . .207 A6
Ulverston LA12 . . . . .203 E4
Grasmere St CA1 . . . . . . .177 B2
Grasmere Terr CA15 . . . . .182 E4
Grasmoor Rd CA14 . . . . . .184 C1
Grassgarth Cotts LA8 . . . .130 B5
Grasshill Cswy DL13 . . . . . .61 F4
Grasslot Inf Sch CA15 . . .182 D4
Grasslot St LA15 . . . . .182 C4
Grassmoor Ave CA10 . . . .190 C4
Graves Mill CA13 . . . . . . .190 D4
Gray St CA14 . . . . .184 E5
Grayson Dr CA11 . . . . .57 B3
Graythwaite Ct 1 LA15 . .205 C4
Graythwaite Hall Gdns*
LA12 . . . . .141 D6
Grearshill Rd CA3 . . . . . . .175 C5
Great Corby Prim Sch
CA4 . . . . .178 C1
Great Dockray 20 CA11 . .191 D5
Great Heads Rd LA11 . . . .208 B3

Great Orton Prim Sch
CA5 . . . . .28 F4
Great Tower Scout Camp
LA23 . . . . .142 A6
Greatcross Cotts LA22 . . .194 B5
Greaves Wood Rd LA11 . .165 A6
Grecian Cl CA3 . . . . .190 C4
Grecian Terr CA14 . . . . . .185 A7
Green Bank
Biennerhasset CA7 . . . . . . .50 F8
Ulverston LA12 . . . . .203 D6
Green Cl Caldbeck CA7 . . . .53 C7
Crosby CA5 . . . . .49 B5
Lupton LA6 . . . . .156 E3
Seascale CA20 . . . . .123 A8
Green Cotts LA21 . . . . . . .127 B1
Green Croft Askham CA10 . .85 D6
Brampton CA8 . . . . .179 B5
Green Garth
Great Clifton CA14 . . . . . . .63 A4
Holme LA6 . . . . .156 B1
Green Gate LA23 . . . . . . .114 F1
Green Gates CA14 . . . . . . .183 B2
Green Haume Cotts
LA15 . . . . .205 A7
Green Hill LA9 . . . . .200 C6
Bowness-On-W LA23 . . . . .129 C1
Cark LA11 . . . . .164 D7
Carlisle CA2 . . . . .176 A6
Clifton CA10 . . . . .71 D2
Crosby-On-E CA6 . . . . .20 B6
Dalton-In-F LA15 . . . . . . .205 B3
Great Salkeld LA7 . . . . . . .57 A3
High Newton LA11 . . . . . .154 A4
Houghton CA3 . . . . .20 C2
Old Town LA6 . . . . .157 A7
Penrith CA11 . . . . .191 C8
South Stainmore CA17 . . .106 B2
Storth LA7 . . . . .209 E5
Green Lane Cotts LA12 . . .162 F6
Green Mkt CA3 . . . . .214 B2
Green Moor Rd CA22 . . . .189 D7
Green Moss LA23 . . . . . . .198 E4
Green Rd LA9 . . . . .200 C6
Green Side LA6 . . . . .212 C1
Green St LA18 . . . . .212 C1
Green St LA18 . . . . .150 A1
Green The
Ambleside LA22 . . . . .195 D6
11 Barrow-In-F LA14 . . . .207 A3
Bassenthwaite CA12 . . . . . .66 C7
Bransty CA28 . . . . .186 D2
Cockermouth CA13 . . . . . .190 E4
Dalston CA5 . . . . .40 A8
Great Broughton CA13 . . . .63 E6
Kendal LA9 . . . . .200 C4
Kirksanton LA18 . . . . .149 F3
Lindal in F LA12 . . . . .162 E6
Lindal in F LA12 . . . . .205 F8
Natland LA9 . . . . .200 B3
Wetheral CA4 . . . . .178 B1
Green View LA9 . . . . .200 C6
Greenacres
Grange-Over-S LA11 . . . . .208 B2
Wetheral CA4 . . . . .178 A2
Wetheral CA4 . . . . .178 A3
Wigton CA7 . . . . .180 B3
Greenacres Pk CA11 . . . . . .56 C4
Greenbar La LA16 . . . . . . .113 B2
Greenbank Ave
Whitehaven CA28 . . . . . . .187 B5
Workington CA14 . . . . . . .184 D3
Greenbank Rd CA22 . . . . .195 C6
Greenber La LA16 . . . . . . .212 F5
Greencastle Brow CA13 . .63 E6
Greencroft CA10 . . . . .101 C5
Greendale La LA15 . . . . . .213 C5
Greenfield La CA8 . . . . . . .179 B5
Greengarth CA2 . . . . .177 B2
Greengate Kendal LA9 . . . .200 C3
Levens LA8 . . . . .143 D1
Greengate Cres LA8 . . . . .143 D1
Greengate Inf Sch LA23 . .207 B3
Greengate Jun Sch
LA14 . . . . .207 A3
Greengate La
Carnforth LA5 . . . . .213 B2
Kendal LA9 . . . . .200 C2
Greengate St LA14 . . . . . .207 A3
Greengill La Penrith CA10 .71 A8
Plumpton CA11 . . . . .56 D1
Greenhead CE Fst Sch
CA8 . . . . .24 D8
Greenhill CA8 . . . . .24 C8
Greenknowe Ave DG12 . . .172 D2
Greenlands Ave CA28 . . . .187 E7

Greenlands Cl CA28 .....187 F7
Greenlands Rd CA15 ....49 A2
Greenlea Rd DG12 .....172 D4
Greenmeadow Gdns
DG12 ....172 B3
Greenmill Rd CA6 ....9 F3
Greenmouth La CA8 .....23 A7
Greens Yd ❶ CA13 ....190 C4
Greenside LA9 ....200 B4
Greenside Ct LA7 ....156 A6
Greenside La CA17 .....119 F3
Greenside Rd
Carlisle CA2 ....176 D3
Glenridding LA11 ....98 C7
Greenstile Pk LA23 ....129 A1
Greenthwaite CA25 ....188 D6
Greenvale Ct CA26 .....142 D8
Greenways Dr LA8 .....144 C1
Greenwood LA9 ....200 B4
Greenwood Cl ❺ CA5 ...28 F1
Greenwood Garth ❹ CA5 .28 F1
Greenwood Terr LA15 ..182 E4
Gregg's La ❷ CA28 .....186 C1
Greta Ave CA2 ....176 D5
Greta Ct CA12 ....192 A3
Greta Grove Ho ❸
CA12 ....192 A4
Greta Hamlet CA12 .....192 B4
Greta Heath LA6 ....169 C3
Greta Side CA12 ....192 B4
Greta Side Ct CA12 ....192 B4
Greta St CA12 ....192 B4
Gretenhow DG16 ....173 B2
Gretna Gateway Outlet
Village DG16 ....173 E3
Gretna Ind Est DG16 ..173 D3
Gretna Loaning DG16 .173 C3
Gretna Prim Sch DG16 .173 C3
Gretna Sta DG16 ....173 C4
Grey St CA1 ....214 C2
Greyfriar Cl LA13 ......207 E5
Greyrigg Ave CA13 ....190 D2
Greyrigg CE Sch LA8 ..132 A4
Greyriggs Ct LA11 .....208 C4
Greystoke Gdns LA14 .204 D1
Greystoke Park Ave
CA11 ....191 B4
Greystoke Park Ct CA11 .191 B4
Greystoke Park Rd
CA11 ....191 B4
Greystoke Rd
Penrith CA11 ....191 B4
Penrith CA11 ....70 E4
Greystoke St CA15 .....69 E5
Greystone Ave CA25 ..188 E8
Greystone Cl CA28 ....187 E4
Greystone La LA13 .....162 C2
Greystone Mount LA15 .205 C4
Greystone Pl CA25 ....188 F6
Greystone Rd CA1 .....177 C6
Greystone Terr CA25 ..188 F6
Grierson Rd CA2 ....177 B3
Griffin Cl CA26 ....92 D8
Griffin St LA20 ....139 A2
Grigg Hall La LA8 ......143 B6
Grindal Pl CA27 ....91 D2
Grinsdale Ave CA2 .....176 A7
Grisedale Cl
Cleator Moor CA25 ....188 B8
Whitehaven CA28 .....187 E4
Grisedale La CA8 ....181 D3
Grisedale Pl CA13 .....190 F4
Grisenthwaite Yd ❼
CA11 ....191 D5
Grisleymires La LA7 ...211 D4
Grizebeck Brow LA7 ..151 D7
Grizebeck Gdns LA14 .206 C5
Grizedale Ave LA9 .....144 C7
Grizedale Cl LA12 .....192 C3
Grizedale Forest Pk*
LA22 ....128 B1
Grizedale Visitor Ctr*
LA22 ....128 A1
Grizedale Visitor Ctr Forest
Walks* LA22 ....128 A1
Grosvenor Ct
Carlisle CA3 ....175 D1
Carnforth LA5 ....213 B3
Grosvenor Ho
Carlisle CA1 ....214 C2
Carlisle,Newton CA2 ..176 C7
Grosvenor Pl
Carlisle CA3 ....175 D1
Carnforth LA5 ....213 B3
Grosvenor Rd LA5 .....213 C3
Grosvenor St LA14 ....206 E8
Grosvenor Terr LA23 .198 C3
Grove Ct CA11 ....191 C6
Grove St ❷ LA15 ......205 C4
Grove The Brampton CA8 .179 B4
Carnforth LA5 ....213 A3
Groves The CA28 ......187 F5
Grune Point Cl CA7 ....174 F8
Guard Hill La LA7 ......209 E4
Guard Ho CA7 ....26 C1
Guard St CA14 ....184 F5
Guards Rd LA12 ....205 F8
Guards The
Gleaston LA12 ....162 E1
Whitehaven CA26 ....36 B2
Guldrey LA10 ....201 B4
Guldrey Fold LA10 ....201 B4
Guldrey La LA10 ....201 B5

Guldrey Terr LA10 .....201 B5
Gulfs Rd LA9 ....200 D5
Gulley Flatts CA22 ....189 D5
Gummers Howe Wlk
LA5 ....213 D2
Gurnal Bridge La LA8 .131 B4
Guy La LA23 ....114 F2
Guysgill DG12 ....172 D5

H

Hackthorpe Hall Bsns Ctr
CA10 ....86 A5
Hacra La LA10 ....147 A3
Hadrian's Cres CA8 ....14 D1
Hadrian's Wall* CA8,
NE49 ....15 D1
Hadrians Ave CA7 ......16 F1
Hadrians Gdns CA3 ....20 C1
Hagget End CA22 .....189 D6
Hagget End Cl CA22 ..189 D6
Haggs La Allithwaite LA11 .164 F8
Cartmel LA11 ....153 F1
Haggy La CA10 ....71 C1
Haig Ave CA28 ....186 C1
Haig Colliery Mining Mus*
CA28 ....187 B8
Haig Ent Pk CA28 .....187 B8
Haig Rd CA1 ....177 D2
Haile Pk CA22 ....108 D7
Hale Green Farm LA7 .155 F1
Half Moon La ❽ CA7 ..180 D3
Halfey's La CA11 ......177 C6
Halhead Brow Crook Rd
LA8 ....130 D1
Haliburton La LA9 .....200 F1
Halier How La LA12 ...162 F6
Hall Bank NE49 ....24 E3
Hall Brow CA14 ....184 F6
Hall Garth LA13 ....171 C5
Hall Garth Gdns LA16 .167 B1
Hall House Ind Est LA8 .144 E6
Hall La Dent LA10 .....147 A2
Staveley LA8 ....130 C7
Hall Lodge La CA14 ....63 B4
Hall Moor Ct CA4 .....178 A2
Hall More Cvn Pk LA7 .166 F8
Hall Pk LA9 ....130 F2
Hall Rd Burneside LA9 .130 F2
Dent LA10 ....147 A2
Hall St Barrow-In-F LA14 .207 A4
Dalton-In-F LA15 ......205 C5
Hall Terr 64 A3
Halla Way CA3 ....175 C2
Hallbank LA10 ....146 F6
Hallbankgate Village Sch
CA8 ....23 A2
Hallbeck Pl CA20 .....109 A2
Hallfield LA22 ....203 C3
Hallgarth Circ LA9 ....200 B7
Hallin Cres CA2 ....176 C3
Hallin Croft LA11 ......191 E6
Halls Mead LA12 ......192 C3
Hallsenna La CA20 ....123 B8
Hallsenna Rd CA20 ...123 B8
Hallwood Rd LA14 ....185 E6
Halton Terr CA11 ....98 C8
Halvellyn Ct LA11 .....191 C3
Hamilton La CA28 .....186 C1
Hamilton Terr
❺ Dalton-In-F LA15 .205 B4
Whitehaven CA28 .....187 E8
Hammond Cl CA2 ......177 B3
Hampsfell Rd
Grange-Over-S LA11 .208 D5
Ulverston LA12 ....203 D2
Hampton Ho CA2 ......176 C7
Hangbridge La LA7 ....211 F1
Hannahmoor La CA28 ..91 B5
Hannay Cl ❶ LA14 ....207 A3
Hanover Ct Carlisle CA2 .176 B5
Penrith CA11 ....191 C5
Harberwain La CA10 ..102 B5
Harbour View CA26 ...186 B1
Harbourside ❶❾ CA28 .186 C1
Harcourt St ❷ CA14 ..184 D6
Hard Knott Rise LA5 ..213 D2
Hard Knotts La LA12 ..171 C8
Hardcragg Way LA11 .208 D4
Hardgates Rd CA22 ..108 D6
Hardingill CA20 ....109 A2
Hardknott Castle*
CA19 ....126 A8
Hardknott Gdns
Barrow-In-F LA14 .....204 D1
Kendal LA9 ....200 F1
Hardwick St LA14 .....206 F5
Hardwicke Ct CA14 ...214 B3
Hardy St ❷ LA14 .....206 F2
Hare Ghyll
Barrow-In-F LA13 .....207 C5
Dalton-In-F LA15 ......205 D5
Hare La Barrow-In-F LA13 .207 C5
Walney Island LA14 ..170 E2
Harecroft Hall Sch
CA19 ....109 B1
Haregate LA6 ....104 A7
Hargreaves Ct ❶❶ CA11 .191 E4
Harker Pk CA6 ....175 D8
Harley St ❾ LA14 .....207 A3
Harling Bank LA6 ......212 B2
Harold St CA2 ....177 B3
Harpers La CA12 ....63 D3
Harpur Pl CA22 ....189 E2
Harraby Gdns CA1 ....177 D3
Harraby Gr CA1 ....177 D3

Harraby Green Bsns Pk
CA1 ....177 C3
Harraby Green Hall
CA1 ....177 C3
Harraby Green Rd CA1 .177 C3
Harraby Grove Ct CA1 .177 D3
Harraby St CA1 ....177 C4
Harras Rd CA28 ....186 E1
Harrel La LA13 ....207 C5
Harrier Cl ❼ CA28 ......72 F2
Harringdale Rd CA14 .185 C7
Harrington Inf Sch
CA14 ....185 A8
Harrington Jun Sch
CA14 ....185 A7
Harrington Rd CA14 ..184 E5
Harrington Sta CA14 ..76 E8
Harris Brow CA13 ......63 E6
Harris Cres CA1 ....177 E2
Harris St LA16 ....162 A7
Harrison St
Barrow-In-F LA14 .....207 A3
Carlisle CA2 ....177 B4
❼ Penrith CA11 ....191 C6
Harriston CA7 ....50 E8
Harriston Rd CA7 ....50 D8
Harrogate St LA14 ....207 A5
Harrot Hill CA13 ....190 D3
Harrot Rd CA13 ....190 B3
Harrowbeck Edge CA10 .57 A6
Harry Brow LA7 ....155 F7
Hart St Carlisle CA1 ..214 C2
Ulverston LA12 ....203 D5
Hartington Pl CA1 ....214 A4
Hartington St
Barrow-In-F LA14 .....206 F4
Carlisle CA1 ....214 C3
Dalton-In-F LA15 ......205 C5
Workington CA14 .....184 E5
Hartland Rd LA14 .....207 B7
Hartley Ave CA3 ....175 B2
Hartley La
Kirkby Stephen,Hartley
CA17 ....199 E6
Kirkby Stephen,Nateby
CA17 ....199 C3
Hartley Rd CA1 ....177 A4
Hartley St LA12 ....203 D5
Hartness Rd CA11 ....191 A6
Hartside Rd LA9 ....200 C2
Harvey St CA2 ....176 C7
Haseli St CA2 ....177 B3
Hastings St LA14 .....206 C2
Hause The CA10 ....84 B2
Havelock Rd
Windermere LA23 ....198 E5
Workington CA14 .....184 C6
Havera LA10 ....201 B5
Haverflatts Flats LA7 .211 D4
Haverflatts La LA7 ....211 E5
Haverigg Gdns LA14 .206 C5
Haverigg Prim Sch
LA18 ....150 A1
Haverigg Rd LA18 ....202 B3
Haversham St Peter's CE
Prim Sch LA7 ....155 E7
Haverthwaite Sta*
LA12 ....153 B7
Haverwood LA7 ....156 A6
Haw Bk CA11 ....70 D3
Haw Lane Cnr LA8 ....130 C5
Hawcoat La CA14 .....207 A7
Hawes La LA9 ....144 A4
Hawes St CA2 ....176 D5
Hawesmead Ave LA9 .200 C3
Hawesmead Dr LA9 ..200 C2
Haweswater Cl CA28 ..72 F2
Haweswater Rd CA11 .191 B4
Hawick St CA2 ....176 E6
Hawk Pl ❹ CA28 ....76 F2
Hawk St LA5 ....213 D4
Hawke St LA14 ....206 F3
Hawker Marsh CA15 ..49 A4
Hawkeswood Terr LA15 .205 B5
Hawkrigg La LA8 ......144 E6
Hawksgarth LA22 .....197 E5
Hawkshead Ave CA14 .184 F4
Hawkshead Esthwaite Prim
Sch LA22 ....197 E4
Hawkshead Gdns LA14 .204 D1
Hawkshead Old Rd
LA21 ....196 A4
Hawksley Terr ❶❾ CA14 .184 D6
Haws Ave LA5 ....213 C3
Haws Hill LA5 ....213 C3
Haws La LA18 ....150 A1
Haws View Ind Est LA14 .204 A1
Hawthorn Ave
Maryport CA15 ....182 E5
Ulverston LA12 ....203 D3
Hawthorn Ct CA14 ....185 D3
Hawthorn Dr
Barrow-In-F LA13 .....207 F5
Clifton CA11 ....177 F5
Hawthorn Gdns LA9 ..200 C8
Hawthorn Gr CA2 .....176 B5
Hawthornes The CA25 .188 C8
Hawthorns The
Gretna DG16 ....173 B3
Wigton CA7 ....108 E1
Hawthwaite La
Dalton-In-F LA14 .....204 E6
Dalton-In-F LA15 ......205 B6
Hayber La CA16 ....104 C7
Hayclose Cres LA9 ...200 C2
Hayclose Ct LA9 ......200 C2
Hayclose La LA9 ......200 D1
Hayclose Rd LA9 .....200 F1

Haycock La CA2 ....176 B3
Hayescastle Rd CA14 .185 C1
Hayfell Ave LA9 ....200 E2
Hayfell Rise LA9 ....200 E3
Haygarth Cl ❸ LA9 ...200 C4
Hayton CE Prim Sch CA8 .31 F8
Hayton Rd CA2 ....177 D2
Hazel Bank Gdns CA10 ..71 A2
Hazel Cl CA14 ....206 F8
Hazel Dene CA1 ....177 E3
Hazel Gill LA14 ....206 F8
Hazelcroft Gdns ❻
LA12 ....203 C5
Hazelgarth LA11 ......164 F7
Hazelgrove CA14 .....183 A2
Hazelmount Ave LA5 .213 C5
Hazelmount Cres LA5 .213 C5
Hazelmount Dr LA5 ..213 B5
Hazelrigg La LA12 ....153 E7
Hazeltree Rd LA12 ...203 D2
Hazelwood Kendal LA9 .200 B3
Silverdale LA5 ....210 C2
Hazelwood South Cres
LA23 ....198 D5
Hazelwood Terr LA14 .208 F5
Head House Hill LA11 .154 A5
Head Rd CA13 ....190 C6
Head St CA13 ....190 C6
Headland Rise LA14 ..170 C6
Headland The ❺ LA16 .162 A8
Headlands Cl ❷ CA28 .187 A8
Headlands Dr CA28 ..187 E8
Headlands The
Glenridding CA11 ......98 C8
Keswick CA12 ....192 A3
Headless Cl LA11 .....153 E1
Headmeadow LA13 ..207 C4
Heads Dr LA11 ....208 C3
Heads La Carlisle CA3 .214 A2
❻ Keswick CA12 .....192 A4
Heads Mount CA12 ..192 A3
Heads Rd CA12 ....192 A3
Heads The
Grange-Over-S LA11 .208 C3
Keswick CA12 ....192 A3
Heath Cl LA9 ....200 B3
Heathcote Pk CA25 ..188 E7
Heather Bank
Barrow-In-F LA13 .....207 E5
Cleator Moor CA25 ...188 D7
Swarthmoor LA12 ....203 A2
Heather Cl LA9 ....200 B3
Heatherfields CA25 ....63 C8
Heathfield Cl CA1 ....177 F5
Heathwaite Cl LA7 ...209 E4
Heatley Ct DG12 .....172 B3
Hebblethwaite Hall La
LA10 ....146 F8
Hebden Ave CA2 ......176 C3
Hecklegirth Prim Sch
DG12 ....172 D3
Hector St LA13 ....207 C6
Hector Terr LA13 .....207 C6
Heddon Ho CA1 ....214 C2
Hedley Ct CA1 ....177 E2
Heggerscales La CA17 .105 E1
Height Ash La LA8 ....144 E6
Height Rd LA11 ....208 A3
Helbeck Rd CA17 .....105 B5
Helder St CA14 ....62 C6
Helena Thompson Mus*
CA14 ....184 F6
Hellens Ct LA21 ....196 A4
Hellwell La LA8 ....115 D3
Helm Cl LA23 ....198 D2
Helm La LA9 ....144 B3
Helm Rd
Bowness-On-W LA23 ..198 D2
Great Ormside CA16 .103 E6
Helm Rigg LA23 ....198 D2
Helm View LA9 ....200 F2
Helme Chase Gdns LA9 .200 E2
Helme Dr LA9 ....200 E1
Helme La LA8, LA9 ...131 C2
Helmside Cl LA14 .....144 C4
Helmside Gdns LA14 .144 C4
Helmside Rd LA9 .....144 B4
Helmsley Cl LA11 .....191 F5
Helmsley Dr LA14 ....206 F7
Helmsington La LA8 ..200 D1
Helsington Laithes LA9 .200 B1
Helsington Rd LA9 ...200 C2
Helton Rd CA10 ....85 D6
Helvellyn Cl CA13 ....190 F4
Helvellyn Rise CA2 ..176 B3
Helvellyn St LA12 ....192 C3
Helvellyn Wlk LA14 ..204 D1
Helvellyn YH* CA11 ..200 E1
Hempland Ave LA13 .207 C5
Hen Parrock La LA12 .163 A5
Henderson Gdns CA2 .177 B2
Henderson Rd CA2 ...177 A2
Henderson's Croft CA6 ..20 E7
Henry St
Cleator Moor CA25 ...188 E7
Cockermouth CA13 ...190 C3
Whitehaven CA28 .....187 D5
Hensingham Com Prim Sch
CA28 ....187 E2
Hensingham Rd CA28 .187 E2
Herbert Hill ❶ CA28 .186 B1
Herbert St CA2 ....177 C3
Hereby Bank Fst Sch
NE49 ....24 E5
Herdus Rd CA28 ......187 E4
Heron Cl LA9 ....200 F2

Heron Corn Mill & Mus of
Paper Making* LA7 .155 E2
Heron Dr CA1 ....177 D6
Heron Hill LA9 ....200 E2
Heron's Quay LA7 ....211 A2
Herschell Terr LA17 ..151 C5
Hertford St ❷ LA14 ..207 A5
Hervey Nature Reserve*
LA11 ....142 E2
Hesket Pk CA4 ....41 C4
Hespek Raise CA1 ...177 F5
Hest View Rd LA12 ...203 D2
Hether Dr CA3 ....175 C3
Heversham Cl LA12 ..203 D3
Heversham Gdns LA7 .211 D7
Hewetson Ct ❼ LA12 .192 A4
Hewson St CA2 ....214 B1
Hewson Street Workshops
CA2 ....214 B1
Hewthwaite La LA10 .146 D4
Heysham Park Ave CA2 .176 C8
Hibbert Rd LA14 ....206 F5
Hicks La ❸ CA28 .....186 C1
Higginson Mill CA2 ...176 F4
High Bank LA15 ....205 C6
High Bell Garth CA4 ...41 E5
High Bldgs CA4 ....178 D6
High Brigham CA13 ...63 F5
High Carley Villas LA12 .162 F7
High Castle Terr CA8 ..14 F1
High Cl CA14 ....185 B6
High Cleater St LA15 .205 C5
High Cliff LA14 ....204 B1
High Close Cvn Pk CA12 .66 D7
High Croft Dr LA11 ...164 F7
High Cross
Broughton-In-F LA17 .139 C1
Hawkshead LA22 .....197 A6
High Cross Brow LA20 .138 F2
High Cross St CA8 .....14 F1
High Duddon Cl ❶❷
LA16 ....162 A8
High Fell Gate Barns
LA11 ....208 A4
High Fellside ❶❶ LA9 .200 C5
High Gale LA22 ....195 D5
High Garth Kendal LA9 .200 B8
Penny Bridge LA12 ..152 E5
High Garth Mdws CA5 ..40 F2
High Gate LA22 ....153 C6
High Green Croft CA1 .177 F1
High Greenbank LA12 .195 F3
High Hasket CE Sch CA4 ..41 F3
High Hill CA12 ....192 A4
High House Rd CA27 ..91 D3
High Kepplewray LA20 .139 A2
High Knott Dr LA14 ..112 F4
High Knott Rd LA5 ...209 B1
High La Kentmere LA8 .115 E3
Newbiggin-on-L LA12 .119 E4
High Lea CA22 ....189 D6
High Lea Wlk LA14 ...204 B1
High Leases La CA17 .120 C8
High Mdw CA2 ....176 B6
High Mead LA9 ....200 C7
High Moor La CA4 ....188 A5
High Moor Rd ❶❶ CA28 ..76 F2
High Park Ho LA9 .....144 B4
High Portinscale CA12 ..81 A6
High Rd Blennerhasset CA7 .50 F8
Carlisle CA1 ....177 D3
Middleton LA6 ....157 F7
Thornhill CA22 ....189 E2
Wigton CA7 ....187 B5
High Ridge LA9 ....200 C2
High Ridley NE49 ......24 F2
High Rigg CA13 ....63 F5
High Row LA14 ....153 C7
High Sand La ❶ CA13 .190 D4
High School Ho LA9 ..200 C5
High Seaton CA14 ...183 C2
High Sparrowmire LA9 .200 C8
High St Annan DG12 .172 C4
Barrow-In-F LA14 .....206 F4
Bigrigg CA22 ....188 A3
Brough CA17 ....105 B5
Cleator Moor CA25 ...188 D7
Keswick CA12 ....192 B3
Kirkby Stephen CA17 .199 C5
Maryport CA15 ....102 D6
Morland CA10 ....86 F5
Pooley Bridge CA10 ...84 F7
Whitehaven CA28 .....186 D1
Windermere LA23 ....198 E6
Workington CA14 .....184 F5
High Style Cl CA28 ...187 E8
High Tenterfell LA9 ..200 C5
High Wield CA14 .....206 F8
High Wiend CA16 .....193 C5
High Winder La CA22,
CA23 ....92 E2
Highbank Cl LA11 ....177 D3
Highbeck La CA10 ...118 B4
Highbeck Rd LA9 .....200 F2
Highfield Cl CA10 ....118 B3
Highfield Ct CA20 ....123 B8
Highfield Ave CA2 ...176 C3
Highfield Ct
Whitehaven CA28 ....187 E8
Wigton CA7 ....180 D3
Highfield Gdns CA1 ..180 B5
Highfield Ho LA10 ...201 C5
Highfield Pk CA7 .....180 C4

Highfield Rd
Barrow-In-F LA14 . . . . .207 A6
Carnforth LA5 . . . . .213 D2
Cleator Moor CA25 . . . . . .188 D6
Cockermouth CA13 . . . . . .190 F4
Grange-Over-S LA11 . . . . .208 C4
Sedbergh LA10 . . . . .201 C5
Highfield Villas LA10 . . . .201 C5
Highfields Annan DG12 . . .172 E5
Whitehaven CA28 . . . . . . .187 F8
Highfieldside LA22 . . . . . .194 A5
Highgarth Ct CA2 . . . . . . .171 B5
Highgate LA9 . . . . .200 C4
Highgate Farm* CA10 . .87 A5
Highgate La LA9 . . . . .144 E3
Highland View CA28 . . . . .186 D2
Highlands Ave LA13 . . . . .207 D6
Highlands Gr LA13 . . . . . .207 D6
Highmoor CA7 . . . . .180 E2
Highmoor Bglws CA7 . . . .180 E2
Highmoor La CA16 . . . . . . .88 C5
Highmoor Mans CA7 . . . . .180 E2
Highmoor Pk CA7 . . . . . . .180 E1
Highpark Wood Forest Trail*
CA12 . . . . .97 B7
Highwood Cres CA1 . . . . .177 E2
Hilden Rd CA23 . . . . .188 D4
Hilderstone La LA5 . . . . . .167 A7
Hill Cl Kendal LA9 . . . . . . .200 C4
Sedgwick LA8 . . . . .144 A1
Hill Cotts CA14 . . . . .185 D4
Hill Cres CA13 . . . . .63 F5
Hill Crest
Distington CA14 . . . . .185 C2
Workington CA14 . . . . . . .184 E7
Hill Fall LA12 . . . . .203 E5
Hill Head CA4 . . . . .30 F6
Hill House La CA9 . . . . . . .181 E3
Hill La LA10 . . . . .147 A3
Hill Pl LA9 . . . . .144 C4
Hill Rd LA14 . . . . .207 B7
Hill Rise LA15 . . . . .205 C6
Hill St Carnforth LA5 . . . .213 C3
Cockermouth CA13 . . . . . .190 C3
Hill Terr CA19 . . . . .123 E6
Hill The Brigham CA13 . . . .63 F5
Eaglesfield CA13 . . . . .64 A1
Hill Top*
Hawkshead LA22 . . . . . .128 D2
Milnthorpe LA7 . . . . .211 D5
Warehouse LA23 . . . . . . .198 E3
Hill Top Ct LA5 . . . . .166 F6
Hill Top Rd LA22 . . . . .195 D6
Hillary Cl CA14 . . . . .184 C1
Hillary Gr CA1 . . . . .177 E2
Hillcrest LA7 . . . . .211 D4
Hillcrest Ave
Carlisle CA1 . . . . .177 D3
Whitehaven CA28 . . . . . . .187 E8
Hillcrest Ct CA1 . . . . .177 D3
Hillcrest Dr LA7 . . . . .155 E1
Hillcroft Cvn Pk CA10 . . . .84 F7
Hillend Gdns DG12 . . . . . .172 B2
Hillend Rd DG12 . . . . .172 C2
Hillersdon Terr CA9 . . . . . .47 A2
Hillgarth LA8 . . . . .143 B7
Hillside Holme LA6 . . . . . .156 B2
Laversdale CA6 . . . . .23 C5
St Bees CA27 . . . . .91 D2
Temple Sowerby CA10 . . . .72 E2
Hillside Cl CA15 . . . . .182 F4
Hillside Cotts LA11 . . . . . .154 C3
Hillside Rd LA12 . . . . .203 D3
Hillswood Ave LA9 . . . . . .200 B3
Hilltop Cotts CA9 . . . . .47 A2
Hilltop Ho [1] LA14 . . . . . .207 A6
Hilltop Rd CA28 . . . . .187 B7
Hillview Cres DG12 . . . . . .172 E4
Hillview Ct DG16 . . . . .173 E5
Hillview Terr DG12 . . . . . .172 E5
Hilton Terr CA28 . . . . .186 D2
Himalaya Ave LA14 . . . . . .170 C6
Hinnings Rd LA14 . . . . . . .206 F3
Hinnings Rd LA14 . . . . . . .185 C3
Hoad La LA12 . . . . .203 F6
Hoad Terr [2] LA12 . . . . . .203 D6
Hobson's La LA6 . . . . .167 C2
Hobsons La CA17 . . . . . . .199 C2
Hodbarrow Lake Nature
Reserve* LA18 . . . . . .202 C2
Hodden Ct CA7 . . . . .53 C6
Hodgehowe LA23 . . . . . . .198 C8
Hodgson Brow LA8 . . . . . .115 D3
Hodgson Gdns LA18 . . . . .202 B4
Hodgson Terr LA18 . . . . . .150 C6
Hodgsons Cl [2] CA7 . . . .180 D3
Hodgsons Ct CA3 . . . . . . .214 B3
Hog House La
Cartmell Fell LA11 . . . . . .142 C1
Hawkshead LA22 . . . . . . .128 D6
Hoggs La CA10 . . . . .87 C4
Hogue St LA14 . . . . .206 D1
Holbeck Cl LA23 . . . . .129 A8
Holbeck La LA23 . . . . .129 A8
Holbeck Park Ave LA7 . . .207 F5
Holborn Hill LA18 . . . . . . .202 B5
Holcroft Hill LA13 . . . . . . .207 C3
Holden Pl CA25 . . . . .188 C6
Holden Rd CA14 . . . . .185 A8
Holebeck Rd LA13 . . . . . . .207 E4
Holehird Gdns* LA23 . .129 B7
Holesmire La CA17 . . . . . .104 D1
Holgates Cvn Pk LA5 . . . .210 B5
Holker Cl CA15 . . . . .205 D4
Holker Hall* LA11 . . . .164 C8
Holker St LA14 . . . . .206 F5
Holliday Cres CA7 . . . . . . .174 C3

Hollies The
Egremont CA22 . . . . .189 C6
[15] Keswick CA12 . . . . . . .188 B3
Hollin Bank Hill LA8 . . . . .143 A6
Hollin La LA8 . . . . .115 D3
Hollinrigg La LA8 . . . . . . .115 D2
Hollins Cl
High Harrington CA14 . . .185 B7
Whitehaven CA28 . . . . . . .187 F4
Hollins La Arnside LA5 . . .209 C1
Burneside LA9 . . . . .130 E2
Hollins La
Barrow-In-F LA13 . . . . . . .207 B6
Dent LA10 . . . . .147 A3
Lindale LA11 . . . . .154 B3
Hollow W LA21 . . . . .140 A8
Hollowgate Rd LA16 . . . . .162 B8
Hollowrane LA16 . . . . .167 C7
Hollows DG14 . . . . .3 C5
Holly Bank
Ulverston LA12 . . . . .203 E3
Warton LA5 . . . . .213 C7
Holly Cl CA7 . . . . .211 D7
Holly Dr CA3 . . . . .175 E2
Holly Gate Rd LA15 . . . . .205 B4
Holly La LA7 . . . . .30 E4
Holly Rd LA23 . . . . .198 E5
Holm Cultram Abbey CE Sch
CA7 . . . . .146 D8
Holm Garth CA6 . . . . .19 D2
Holmacres Dr CA1 . . . . . .177 D2
Holme Cl CA4 . . . . .30 E6
Holme Cres CA14 . . . . . . .185 C3
Holme Croft CA5 . . . . .29 A2
Holme Ct CA16 . . . . .119 C3
Holme Farm Ct CA4 . . . . . .30 E3
Holme Fauld CA4 . . . . .30 E6
Holme Head Way CA2 . . .176 E3
Holme Houses LA9 . . . . . .130 F2
Holme La
Allithwaite LA11 . . . . .164 F7
Cark LA11 . . . . .164 E7
Kirkandrews-on-E CA5 . . . .19 C1
Scotby CA4 . . . . .30 E7
Holme Lo LA9 . . . . .200 E1
Holme Mdw CA4 . . . . .30 F3
Holme Mills LA6 . . . . .156 B2
Holme Mills Ind Est LA6 .167 B8
Holme Open Farm*
LA10 . . . . .146 A5
Holme Park Sch LA8 . . . .144 D6
Holme Pines Sch LA6 . . . .156 F1
Holme Rd LA11 . . . . .154 C6
Holme Riggs Ave CA11 . .191 C3
Holme St CA16 . . . . .193 C5
Holme St Cuthbert Sch
CA15 . . . . .35 E6
Holme Terr CA2 . . . . .214 A2
Holmefield [3] LA6 . . . . . .156 B1
Holmes Ave CA2 . . . . .177 A2
Holmes Rd LA8 . . . . .143 B4
Holmewood Ave LA13 . . .190 B3
Holmewood Paddock
CA13 . . . . .190 C3
Holmfoot TD9 . . . . .1 B6
Holmrook Rd CA2 . . . . . . .176 A5
Holy Family RC Prim Sch
LA13 . . . . .207 C6
Holy Well La LA11 . . . . . . .164 F5
Holyoake Ave LA13 . . . . . .207 C6
Holyoake Terr
Beckermet CA21 . . . . .108 C5
Penrith CA11 . . . . .191 B5
Holywell Cres CA1 . . . . . .177 A8
Homefield CA11 . . . . .98 C7
Homewood Dr CA28 . . . . .187 F4
Homewood Rd CA28 . . . . .187 F4
Homewood Terr
Cockermouth CA13 . . . . . .190 B3
Kendal LA9 . . . . .200 F2
Workington CA14 . . . . . . .184 D4
Honister Dr
Cockermouth CA13 . . . . . .190 B3
Kendal LA9 . . . . .200 F2
Workington CA14 . . . . . . .184 D4
Honister Hause YH*
CA12 . . . . .95 E4
Honister Pass CA13 . . . . . .95 B5
Honister Rd CA28 . . . . . . .187 F4
Hoo La The LA23 . . . . .198 D7
Hood St LA14 . . . . .206 E4
Hooks La LA12 . . . . .162 F5
Hooper Hill CA10 . . . . .97 A4
Hope St
[6] Barrow-In-F LA14 . . . .207 A2
Carlisle CA2 . . . . .176 F4
[1] Dalton-In-F LA15 . . . .205 C5
Millom LA18 . . . . .202 D4
Hopedene CA25 . . . . .188 C8
Hopes Hill Dr CA1 . . . . . . .177 E2
Hophouse La LA6 . . . . . . .157 C3
Horland Ct [4] LA14 . . . . .207 A2
Horn Hill LA11 . . . . .202 C5
Hornbeam Cres LA13 . . . .207 B5
Horncop La LA9 . . . . .200 C5
Hornedale Ave LA13 . . . . .207 B5
Horse Close La LA12 . . . . .162 F6
Horse Market LA6 . . . . . . .212 C2
Horsfield Ct CA28 . . . . . . .187 A6
Horsley Terr CA11 . . . . . . .191 B5
Horsman Ct [5] LA13 . . . .190 C4
Horsman St CA2 . . . . .176 E4
Hospital Rd DG12 . . . . . . .172 E6
Hosticle La LA6 . . . . .168 C7
Hotchberry Brow CA13 . . .63 F4
Hotchberry Rd CA13 . . . . . .63 F4
Hothfield La CA13 . . . . . . .193 D6
Hothfield Dr CA13 . . . . . . .193 D5
Houghton CE Sch CA3 . . .175 F5

Houghton Pk TD9 . . . . .1 B6
Houghton Rd CA3 . . . . . . .20 C1
Houghton Rd N CA3 . . . . .175 F6
Housesteads Rd CA2 . . . . .29 D6
Howard
Portinscale CA12 . . . . .81 A7
How La Heads Nook CA8 . .31 F7
Portinscale CA12 . . . . .81 A7
How St Castle Carrock CA8 .32 B8
Hayton CA8 . . . . .31 F8
Howard Arms La CA8 . . . .179 B5
Howard Gdns CA8 . . . . . . .179 B5
Howard Mews CA1 . . . . . .213 B3
Howard Pk CA11 . . . . .69 F6
Howard Pl CA1 . . . . .214 C2
Howard Rd CA8 . . . . .179 B6
Howard St
Barrow-In-F LA14 . . . . . . .206 E4
Carlisle CA2 . . . . .176 D5
Kendal LA9 . . . . .200 D2
Penrith CA11 . . . . .191 B5
Howarth Ave CA8 . . . . .23 C2
Hoobank Rd CA22 . . . . . .189 D7
Howe Bank Cl LA9 . . . . . .144 B5
Howe Bank View LA22 . . .113 B4
Howe Ct LA9 . . . . .144 B5
Howe Gdns LA9 . . . . .144 B5
Howe La Levens LA8 . . . . .143 A3
Portinscale CA12 . . . . .81 A6
Howe St
Barrow-In-F LA14 . . . . . . .206 F4
Carlisle CA1 . . . . .214 C1
Howgill Brae DG12 . . . . . .172 F4
Howgill Cl
Bolton Low Houses CA7 . . .37 F3
Burneside LA9 . . . . .130 F2
Howgill Houses LA9 . . . . .130 F2
Howgill La
Beck Foot LA10 . . . . .133 A2
Sedbergh LA10 . . . . .201 B5
Howgill St CA28 . . . . .187 C8
Howgillbridge DG12 . . . . .172 F3
Howrahs Ct CA12 . . . . . . .192 A4
Howrigg Bank CA7 . . . . . .180 E4
Howthorn Fields CA23 . . .188 D4
Huddleston Rd LA18 . . . . .202 C6
Hugh Little Garth CA2 . . .177 C2
Hugh St CA20 . . . . .186 D2
Humber Terr LA14 . . . . . . .206 A4
Hummer La LA11 . . . . .139 F8
Hunday Ct CA14 . . . . .184 F4
Hundith Hill Rd
Cockermouth CA13 . . . . . .190 A3
Embleton CA13 . . . . .65 A4
Hundreds Rd LA23 . . . . . .114 D1
Hungriggs La CA16 . . . . . .193 D7
Hunter Bank CA4 . . . . .30 E5
Hunter Hall Sch CA11 . . . .71 C4
Hunter Ho LA23 . . . . .198 D5
Hunter Rise CA21 . . . . . . .108 B5
Hunter St CA14 . . . . .184 E5
Workington CA14 . . . . . . .184 E5
Hunter Street Back LA5 . .213 C4
Hunter's Cl CA14 . . . . .183 B3
Hunter's Dr CA14 . . . . . . .183 B3
Hunter's La [2] CA1 . . . . .183 D5
Hunters Cres CA1 . . . . . . .177 F3
Hunting Hill Rd LA5 . . . . .213 A3
Hunting Lodge Cl CA7 . . . .51 A5
Huntington Pl CA14 . . . . .182 B2
Huntley Ave CA11 . . . . . . .191 D3
Huntley Ct CA11 . . . . .191 C3
Huntsman La CA1 . . . . .30 E5
Hurley Rd CA4 . . . . .178 D2
Hutton Cl LA6 . . . . .167 C2
Hutton Ct [8] CA11 . . . . . .191 D5
Hutton Gdns CA11 . . . . . .191 D5
Hutton Hill CA11 . . . . .191 E5
Hutton Pl CA11 . . . . .182 C5
Hutton Way CA1 . . . . .176 A5
Hutton-in-the-Forest*
CA11 . . . . .55 E2
Hycemoor Way LA14 . . . .136 F4
Hyde St CA14 . . . . .184 D6
Hylton Terr CA7 . . . . .174 C4
Hyndburn Cl LA5 . . . . . . .213 E4
Hyning La8 . . . . .143 E1
Hyning Brow LA8 . . . . . . .142 F5
Hyning Rd LA8 . . . . .143 D1
Hyning Rd LA5 . . . . .166 F4
Hyton Cvn Pk CA7 . . . . . .174 C3

Inglewood Rd
Carlisle CA2 . . . . .176 C5
Penrith CA11 . . . . .70 F7
Inglewood Terr
Broughton-In-Furness
LA20 . . . . .150 F8
Calthwaite CA11 . . . . .55 F7
Inglis Ct CA15 . . . . .182 E4
Ingmire Back La LA10 . . .146 A6
Ingman Lodge Rd BD24 . .160 C1
Ings Mill Cvn Pk LA8 . . . .129 F6
Ingwell Dr CA22 . . . . .91 F5
Inkerman Terr CA28 . . . . .187 E7
Innoor Rd CA10 . . . . .86 C5
Inner Long Rd CA14 . . . . .183 B2
Ireby CE Sch CA7 . . . . .51 F5
Ireby Rd LA6 . . . . .169 C3
Iredale Cres CA14 . . . . . . .184 D4
Ireleth Brow LA16 . . . . . . .162 A8
Ireleth Rd LA16 . . . . .162 A8
Ireleth St Peter's CE Prim
Sch LA16 . . . . .162 B8
Irish St Maryport CA15 . .182 C5
Whitehaven CA28 . . . . . . .187 C8
Ironworks Rd LA14 . . . . . .206 D4
Irt Ave CA28 . . . . .187 D7
Irthing Bsns Ctr CA8 . . . .179 B5
Irthing Pk Brampton CA8 .179 B5
Gilsland CA8 . . . . .14 D1
Irthing St CA1 . . . . .177 C6
Irthing Vale Cvn Pk
CA8 . . . . .179 A5
Irthing Wlk CA8 . . . . .179 A5
Irthington Village Sch
CA8 . . . . .21 E4
Irton Cross* CA19 . . . . .124 A7
Irton Pl CA2 . . . . .176 C3
Irton Road Sta* CA19 .124 E6
Irving Ct [12] CA11 . . . . . .191 E4
Irving St CA14 . . . . .184 E5
Irving Vale CA14 . . . . .63 B4
Irvings Pl CA2 . . . . .176 C2
Irvings Terr CA15 . . . . . . .182 C8
Irwell Rd LA14 . . . . .206 B4
Isabella Rd CA14 . . . . .184 B7
Isabella St CA2 . . . . .176 D6
Isel Rd CA13 . . . . .190 E5
Island Rd LA14 . . . . .206 F1
Island The CA7 . . . . .16 E1
Islay Pl CA14 . . . . .184 D4
Ismay Cres CA1 . . . . .177 F5
Ismay Wharf CA15 . . . . . .182 C6
Ivegill CE Sch CA4 . . . . . . .41 A2
Ivory Cl CA2 . . . . .176 C6
Ivy Ave LA14 . . . . .206 E2
Ivy Cl CA6 . . . . .19 D2
Ivy Cres LA9 . . . . .130 F2
Ivy Garth LA9 . . . . .200 E5

J

Jack Hill LA11 . . . . .164 F7
Jackson Croft
Morland CA10 . . . . .86 F5
Shap CA10 . . . . .101 C6
Jackson Rd Houghton CA3 .20 C2
Salterbeck CA14 . . . . .183 A8
Jackson St Carlisle CA1 . .177 C6
Seaton CA14 . . . . .183 B1
Jackson Terr LA5 . . . . .213 C5
Jackson's La CA10 . . . . . .101 C6
Jacktrees Cres CA25 . . . .188 C6
Jacktrees Rd CA25 . . . . . .188 D6
James Dr CA25 . . . . .188 C6
James Freel Cl LA14 . . . . .206 D4
James Pit Rd CA28 . . . . . .186 D2
James Rennie Sch CA3 . .175 D5
James St
[8] Askam-In-F LA16 . . . .162 A8
Barrow-In-F LA14 . . . . . . .207 A3
Carlisle CA2 . . . . .214 B1
Cleator Moor CA25 . . . . . .188 C6
[10] Maryport CA15 . . . .182 E5
Penrith CA11 . . . . .191 C5
Whitehaven CA28 . . . . . . .187 C8
Workington CA14 . . . . . . .184 E6
James St W [1] CA14 . . . .184 E6
James Street Workshops
CA2 . . . . .214 B1
James Terr [4] LA15 . . . . .205 C5
James Watt Terr LA14 . . .170 C6
Jane St Carlisle CA2 . . . . .176 E3
[13] Maryport CA15 . . . .182 E5
Jarrow St CA14 . . . . .184 E6
Jarrow St LA13 . . . . .207 B3
Jason St LA14 . . . . .170 C6
Jaysmith Ct CA13 . . . . . . .175 D3
Jefferson Dr LA12 . . . . . . .203 D3
Jefferson St CA2 . . . . .69 E5
Jenkin Gap CA13 . . . . .79 C4
Jenkin Rise LA9 . . . . .200 F6
Jennet Croft CA4 . . . . .178 A1
Jennings Brewery*
CA13 . . . . .190 D4
Jennings Terr LA9 . . . . . . .200 D4
Jeremy Hill LA11 . . . . .164 F7
Jericho Prim Sch CA28 . .187 F7
Jericho Rd CA28 . . . . .187 F7
Jesmond Ave LA13 . . . . . .207 B5
Jesmond St CA1 . . . . .177 C6
Jesson Way CA15 . . . . . . .213 B3
Jingling La LA6 . . . . .212 C2
Jinny Hill LA8 . . . . .143 B7
Jocks Hill CA8 . . . . .179 C5
Joe McBain Ave CA28 . . . .76 F1

John Colligan Dr CA25 . . .188 C8
John Colligan Wlk
CA25 . . . . .188 C8
John Gaskell Ct CA28 . . . .187 F5
John Johnston Ct CA1 . . .177 D2
John Ruskin Sch The
LA21 . . . . .196 A3
John St
[20] Askam-In-F LA16 . . .162 A8
Carlisle CA2 . . . . .176 E6
Carnforth LA5 . . . . .213 C4
Cockermouth CA13 . . . . . .190 D3
Maryport CA15 . . . . .182 D6
Moor Row CA24 . . . . .188 B5
Workington CA14 . . . . . . .184 E5
John's La [11] CA28 . . . . .186 C1
John's Pl CA2 . . . . .214 A2
Johnson Cl CA1 . . . . .213 B3
Johnson Mill CA2 . . . . . . .176 F4
Johnson St [20] CA14 . . .184 D6
Johnstone St DG12 . . . . . .172 C4
Jollybeard Gate CA9 . . . . .181 E3
Jollybeard La CA9 . . . . . . .181 E3
Jones's Yd LA6 . . . . .167 B7
Jordan La LA10 . . . . .146 A4
Joseph Noble Rd LA14 . . . .77 C3
Joseph Wilson Meml Homes
CA8 . . . . .22 E3
Joss La LA12 . . . . .201 C5
Jubilee Cl CA11 . . . . .191 E4
Jubilee Cotts CA14 . . . . . .184 C3
Jubilee Ct LA14 . . . . .188 A3
Jubilee Gdns CA22 . . . . . .188 A3
Jubilee La LA6 . . . . .156 E3
Jubilee Rd Carlisle CA2 . .183 A1
High Harrington CA14 . . .185 F7
Whitehaven CA28 . . . . . . .187 F8
Jubilee Terr CA15 . . . . . . .182 D4
Junction St CA2 . . . . .214 A2
Juniper Cl [8] LA15 . . . . .205 B4
Juniper Gr CA28 . . . . .186 E1
Juniper Way CA11 . . . . . .191 F5
Juno St LA14 . . . . .206 D1
Jutland Ave LA11 . . . . . . .164 D6

K

Kaber Cross CA17 . . . . . . .105 B2
Kates La CA9 . . . . .181 D3
Katharine St LA18 . . . . . . .202 D5
Kaye Cl CA2 . . . . .176 C4
Keasdale Ave LA7 . . . . . . .209 E3
Keasdale Rd LA7 . . . . .209 E3
Keats Ave LA14 . . . . .184 F4
Keekle Flats CA25 . . . . . . .188 B8
Keekle Terr CA25 . . . . .92 A7
Keer Holme La LA6 . . . . . .167 B6
Keets Cl LA13 . . . . .207 D6
Keir Hardie Ave CA25 . . . .188 B6
Keith St LA14 . . . . .206 F3
Keld Cl CA11 . . . . .70 D3
Keld Head CA11 . . . . .70 D3
Keld La CA10 . . . . .101 B5
Keldwith Dr LA23 . . . . . . .198 D8
Keldwyth Pk LA23 . . . . . .198 D6
Kell's Pl CA3 . . . . .175 E1
Kellet La LA6 . . . . .167 B3
Kellet Rd
Carnforth LA5,LA6 . . . . . .213 E3
Over Kellet LA6 . . . . .167 A1
Kellet Road Ind Est LA5 .213 E3
Kells Int Sch CA28 . . . . . .187 B6
Kelly St CA14 . . . . .184 E5
Kellybark La CA16 . . . . . .103 C4
Kelsick (St Martins Coll
Annexe) LA22 . . . . . . .195 E5
Kelsick Cotts LA22 . . . . . .195 D6
Kelsick La [4] CA28 . . . . .186 C1
Kelsick Rd LA22 . . . . .183 B1
Kelsick Rd LA22 . . . . .195 D5
Kelton Croft CA25 . . . . . . .78 B1
Kelvin Gr CA2 . . . . .176 D4
Kemplay Bank CA10 . . . . .191 E2
Kemplay Foot CA10 . . . . .191 E2
Kendal Bsns Pk LA9 . . . . .200 E6
Kendal Coll LA9 . . . . .200 C2
Kendal Gn LA9 . . . . .200 C2
Kendal Mus* LA9 . . . . . .200 D6
Kendal Parks Cres LA9 . .200 F1
Kendal Parks Rd LA9 . . . .200 F1
Kendal Rd
Bowness-On-W LA23 . . . .198 C1
Kirkby Lonsdale LA6 . . . .212 B2
Staveley LA8 . . . . .130 C4
Kendal St
Barrow-In-F LA14 . . . . . . .207 A5
Carlisle CA2 . . . . .177 A2
Kendal Village Her Ctr*
LA9 . . . . .200 D3
Kendall Croft LA13 . . . . . .207 C5
Kenmount Pl CA2 . . . . . . .176 C5
Kennedy Rd CA14 . . . . . . .183 B3
Kennedy St LA12 . . . . . . .203 D8
Kennels Rd DG12 . . . . . . .172 D5
Kennet Rd LA14 . . . . .206 A3
Kent Cl LA8 . . . . .130 E3
Kent Dr LA8 . . . . .130 C5
Kent Lea Kendal LA9 . . . .131 A1
Kendal LA9 . . . . .200 C8
Kent Park Ave LA9 . . . . . .200 C1

Kent Pl LA9 ....200 D4
Kent Sq 8 LA12 ......203 E5
Kent St Barrow-In-F LA13 207 B3
 Kendal LA9 ....200 D5
Kentdale Rd LA9 ......200 F6
Kentmere Brow LA4 ...200 F6
Kentmere Cres LA14 ..204 D1
Kentmere Gr CA2 .....176 D3
Kentrigg LA9 ....200 C8
Kentrigg Wlk LA9 ....200 C8
Kents Bank Ho LA11 ..165 A6
Kents Bank Rd LA11 ..165 A6
Kents Bank Sta LA11 .165 A6
Kents Ford Ho LA11 ..208 B1
Kentsford Rd LA11 ...208 B1
Kentsford Terr LA11 .165 A6
Kentwood Rd LA9 .....200 B1
Keppel St LA14 ....206 E4
Kepplewray Dr LA14 ..204 C1
Kepplewray Hill LA20 .139 A2
Kersey Rd CA2 ....189 D2
Kershope Rd LA5 ......175 C3
Kestrel Dr LA15 ......205 C4
Kestrel Gr 5 CA28 ...76 F2
Kestrel Hill Rd LA9 ..173 D3
Keswick Art Gal & Mus*
 CA12 ....192 B4
Keswick Ave LA14 .....204 D1
Keswick Bridge CA12 .192 C4
Keswick Sch CA12 .....192 A5
Kettlewell Rd LA9 ....200 B8
Keyes St LA14 ....206 F4
Keyhow CA19 ....124 E7
Kidside Cotts LA14 ...156 B5
Kilbride Pl CA26 .....92 D8
Killhope Lead Mining Ctr*
 CA9 ....47 E1
Killington Dr LA9 ....200 E2
Kilmidyke Dr LA11 ...208 B1
Kilmidyke Rd LA11 ...208 B1
Kiln Bank Cross LA20 .139 A8
Kiln Brow CA23 ....188 D3
Kiln Croft LA9 ....131 C2
Kiln Green Ave CA14 .185 C2
Kiln Hill CA15 ....183 C8
Kiln La LA12 ....171 C8
Kilner Cl LA9 ....200 F5
Kilnside CA14 ....185 D4
Kilnside Pl CA14 .....185 D4
Kimmeter Pl DG12 ....172 E4
Kimmeter Sq DG12 ....172 E5
Kimmeter Wynd DG12 .172 F4
King Alfred St LA14 ..206 C1
King Aurther's Round Table
 Henge* LA9 ....191 E1
King Garth CA6 ....19 D2
King George's Cl CA25 .188 E7
 Aspatria CA7 ....50 C8
 Carlisle CA1 ....214 C1
 Carnforth LA5 ....213 C3
 Cleator Moor CA25 ...188 F6
 Dalton-In-F LA15 ....205 E5
 Great Broughton CA13 .63 E6
 Maryport CA15 ....182 C6
 Millom LA18 ....202 D5
 Penrith CA11 ....191 D5
 Ulverston LA12 ......203 D5
 Whitehaven CA28 .....186 C1
 Wigton CA7 ....180 E4
 Workington CA14 .....184 F5
King's Arms La CA9 ...181 D4
King's Arms Yd CA7 ..180 C3
King's Ave LA14 ......62 E4
King's Dr Carnforth LA5 .213 D3
 Dalton-In-F LA15 ....205 B5
King's Rd LA11 ....203 D5
Kingfisher La CA9 ....200 F5
Kingmoor Bsns Pk CA6 .175 A7
Kingmoor Ind Est CA3 .175 B2
Kingmoor Jun Sch CA3 .175 C4
Kingmoor Nature Reserve*
 CA3 ....175 B3
Kingmoor Park Central
 CA6 ....175 A5
Kingmoor Park Harker Est
 CA6 ....175 B8
Kingmoor Park Heathlands
 Est CA6 ....19 E4
Kingmoor Park Rd CA6 .19 E2
Kingmoor Park Rockcliffe Est
 CA6 ....19 D3
Kingmoor Park S CA6 .175 A4
Kingmoor Rd CA3 .....175 B3
Kingmoor Sidings Nature
 Reserve* CA3 ....175 B2
Kingrigg CA2 ....176 C3
Kings Cl LA5 ....209 B1
Kings Ct LA10 ....201 C5
Kings Dr Carlisle CA6 .175 A4
 Egremont CA22 ....189 C5
Kings Mount LA15 ....205 B5
Kings Yd LA22 ....197 E5
Kingsland Rd LA18 ...202 B5
Kingsley Ave LA12 ...203 A3
Kingstown Broadway
 CA3 ....175 B5
Kingstown Ind Est CA3 .175 B4
Kingstown Rd CA3 ...175 D4
Kingsway Carlisle CA6 .175 A4
 Ulverston LA12 ......203 E5
Kingwater Cl CA8 ....179 B4
Kinn Rd LA8 ....144 F8
Kinniside Ave CA28 ..187 D4
Kinniside Pl CA25 ...188 E6

Kipling Ave CA14 .....185 D8
Kirk Flatt LA12 ......162 F5
Kirk Hey LA11 ....165 A6
Kirk La LA23 ....129 A8
Kirk The 4 CA28 .....186 D1
Kirkbampton CE Sch CA5 .28 E7
Kirkbank CA13 ....190 D3
Kirkbank La
Kirkby Stephen CA17 .199 D8
 Winton CA17 ....105 A1
Kirkbarrow LA9 ....200 D3
Kirkbarrow La LA9 ...200 D4
Kirkbeck Cl CA3 .....175 B2
Kirkbeck Dr CA11 ....108 B5
Kirkbie Gn LA9 ......200 E5
Kirkbie Kendal Sch LA9 .200 D3
Kirkbrae CA3 ....175 C2
Kirkbride Prim Sch CA7 .27 C7
Kirkby Cl 17 LA16 ...162 A8
Kirkby Gdns LA14 ....206 C5
Kirkby Lonsdale Rd LA6 .167 B1
Kirkby Slate Rd LA12 .151 F5
Kirkby St LA15 ......182 D6
Kirkby Stephen Gram Sch
 CA17 ....199 C6
Kirkby Stephen Ind Est
 CA17 ....199 C7
Kirkby Stephen Prim Sch
 CA17 ....199 D5
Kirkby Stephen Sta
 CA17 ....199 C6
Kirkby Thore Sch CA10 .73 A1
Kirkby-in-Furness Sta
 LA17 ....151 B5
Kirkcroft CA8 ....31 F3
Kirkfell Ave CA13 ...190 E3
Kirkfield Dr LA15 ...195 D6
Kirkfield Rise LA22 .195 D6
Kirkgate Bolton CA16 .87 D7
 Cockermouth CA13 ...190 D4
 Milnthorpe LA7 ......211 D5
Kirkgate Ctr LA13 ...190 D4
Kirkgate La Borwick LA6 .167 B4
 Milnthorpe LA7 ......211 E5
Kirkhaugh Sta CA9 ..45 D8
Kirkhead Cl CA2 .....211 D4
Kirkhead Cotts LA11 .165 A6
Kirkhead Rd LA11 ...165 A6
Kirkland Ave CA7 ...180 C4
Kirkland Cl CA7 ....180 E4
Kirkland Mdws CA7 ..180 E4
Kirkland Rd CA7 .....211 D4
Kirklands CA13 ....190 C3
Kirklands Rd CA2 ....177 B2
Kirkside LA13 ....63 E6
Kirkoswald CE Sch CA10 .57 B8
Kirkstall CI LA13 ...207 C6
Kirkstead Cl CA14 ...29 D6
Kirkstead Rd CA2 ....29 D7
Kirkstone Ave CA13 ..190 B3
Kirkstone Cl LA22 ..195 D6
Kirkstone Cres
 Barrow-In-F LA14 ....204 C1
 Carlisle CA2 ....176 D5
Kirkstone Pass
 Ambleside LA22 ......114 D5
 Hartsop LA11 ....98 E1
Kirkstone Rd
 Ambleside LA22 ......195 E6
 Whitehaven CA28 .....187 F4
Kirriemuir Way 10 CA3 .175 B1
Kirstall Rd 4 LA13 ..207 C5
Kirtle Pl DG16 ......173 C3
Kitchener St LA14 ..206 C1
Kittygill La LA6 ....212 A1
Kittyson La LA13 ...190 D3
Knights Dr CA6 .....175 A5
Knoll The CA7 ......189 E2
Knott Hill Cvn Site CA11 .84 B4
Knott La Arnside LA5 .210 A8
 Broughton-In-F LA20 .139 A2
 Orton CA10 ....118 D5
Knott St LA22 ....198 C5
Knowe Park Ave CA3 .175 E1
Knowe Terr 1 CA3 ...175 E1
Knowefield Ave CA3 .175 C2
Knowefield Cl CA3 ...175 E2
Knox St LA14 ....206 D2
Kylbarrow La CA9 ...166 F5

L

Laburnum Cres LA14 .206 F6
Laburnum Ct LA14 ...175 E2
Laburnum Gr LA15 ...182 F5
Laburnum Pk LA6 ....213 B2
Laburnum Way CA11 .191 F5
Ladies' Wlk CA14 ...184 E6
Lady Ct CA14 ....184 E3
Lady Hall La LA18 ..138 E1
Lady Ing La CA17 ...105 A2
Lady St DG12 ....172 C4
Lady's Well DG12 ...172 C4
Ladybank CA7 ....175 D5
Ladylands La CA5 ...19 C1
Ladypit Terr CA28 ..186 D2
Ladysteps CA4 ......30 F5
Laithwaite CE CA13 .190 C3
Lake District Bsns Pk
 LA9 ....200 D8
Lake District Visitor Ctr
 (Brockhole)* LA23 .129 A7

Lake Gdns LA23 ......198 C1
Lake Rd Ambleside LA22 .195 D4
 Coniston LA21 ......196 B3
 Keswick CA12 ....192 A2
 Keswick CA12 ....192 B3
 Windermere LA23 ....198 D4
Lake View CA26 .....93 A8
Lake View Dr LA22 ..194 B3
Lakeland Ave
 Barrow-In-F LA13 ...207 D4
 Whitehaven CA28 ....187 B6
Lakeland Bird of Prey Ctr*
 CA10 ....85 F6
Lakeland Bsns Pk CA13 .190 B2
Lakeland Ct CA12 ...82 C8
Lakeland Pk CA12 ...192 D2
Lakeland Sheep & Wool Ctr*
 CA13 ....190 C1
Lakeland Workshops
 LA21 ....196 B3
Lakelands The LA22 .195 D5
Lakes Coll LA14 ....185 E6
Lakes Glass Ctr The*
 LA12 ....203 F6
Lakes Par LA14 .....207 B8
Lakes Rd LA14 ......184 B4
Lakes Sch The LA23 .129 B7
Lakeside & Haverthwaite
 Rly* LA12 ....153 C7
Lakeside Cvn Pk CA12 .192 A3
Lakeside Sta* LA12 .141 E2
Lakeview Ave CA2 ...177 C1
Lamb Croft LA13 ....207 C4
Lamb La CA22 ....189 E6
Lamb Lea CA10 .....57 A6
Lamb St CA2 ....177 C1
Lambfoot Rake CA13 .45 D6
Lambhowe Cvn Pk LA8 .142 D6
Lamley Gdns CA11 ..191 C6
Lamplugh CE Sch CA26 .78 A1
Lamplugh Rd CA13 ..190 C3
Lamport St CA14 ....184 E5
Lancashire Rd LA18 .202 C5
Lancaster Pl CA13 ..190 B3
Lancaster Rd LA5 ...213 B2
Lancaster St 9 LA12 .203 E5
Lancaster St
 Barrow-In-F LA14 ...207 A5
 Carlisle CA1 ....214 B1
 2 Dalton-In-F LA15 ..205 C5
Landing Cl LA12 ....141 E2
Landing Rd CA12 ....141 E2
Lands Cl LA12 ......171 E8
Landsdown Cl LA9 ..200 F3
Lane Ends LA11 .....164 F7
Lane Head
 Spark Bridge LA12 ..152 D7
 Windermere LA23 ...198 F4
Lane Terr CA8 ......24 C1
Lanercost CE Prim Sch
 CA8 ....22 E6
Lanercost Priory* CA8 .22 E6
Lanes The CA1 .....214 B3
Laneside Rd LA18 ..208 B1
Langber End La LA6 .169 F1
Langdale CA7 ....180 B3
Langdale Ave CA2 ..176 E5
Langdale Camp Site
 LA22 ....112 E4
Langdale CE Sch LA22 .113 C4
Langdale Cl Millom LA18 .202 C4
 Whitehaven CA28 ....187 D4
Langdale Cres
 Dalton-In-F LA15 ...205 B3
 Kendal LA9 ....200 F6
 Windermere LA23 ....198 E3
Langdale Crest LA7 .203 D5
Langdale Dr CA13 ..190 F4
Langdale Gr 2 LA1 .207 B3
Langdale Rd Carlisle CA2 .176 E5
 Carnforth LA5 ......213 D2
 Workington CA14 ...184 D4
Langholm St TD9 ...1 B6
Langley Gdns CA4 ..178 E7
Langrigg Rd CA2 ...176 E4
Langrigge Dr LA23 .198 D2
Langrigg Howe CA12 .198 C2
Langrigg Pk LA23 ..198 C2
Langton Ct LA15 ...191 D4
Langton St LA15 ...191 D4
Langwathby CE Prim Sch
 CA10 ....71 F8
Langwathby Sta CA10 .72 A8
Laning (A10) 147 B2
Lansbury Pl CA25 ..188 F6
Lansdowne Cl CA3 ..175 E3
Lansdowne Cres CA3 .175 D2
Lansdowne Rd CA3 ..175 D3
Lansdowne Sch CA28 .187 F8
Lantern Moss Cvn Pk
 CA23 ....108 A4
Lanty Cl CA13 ......63 F5
Lapstone Rd LA18 ..202 C5
Larch Cl CA11 .....191 F5
Larch Dr CA3 ......175 E2
Larch Gr Kendal LA9 .200 F4
 Keswick CA12 ......192 E4
 Ulverston LA12 .....203 E2
Larch Rise LA13 ...207 C6
Larches The CA2 ...189 C6
Lark La CA11 ......191 C6
Larkfield CA11 ....191 B6
Latimer Rd DG12 ...172 D4
Latona St LA14 ....206 C3
Latrigg Cl CA12 ...192 D4
Latrigg Rd CA28 ...187 E4
Lattrig St CA7 ....174 C4

Launchy Gill Forest Trail*
 CA12 ....97 A6
Laundry Hill LA11 ..208 D4
Laundry St 7 LA14 .206 F3
Laurel & Hardy Mus The*
 LA12 ....203 D5
Laurel Bank
 Seascale CA20 ......123 A8
 Whitehaven CA28 ....186 E1
Laurel Ct CA28 .....186 E1
Laurel Dr LA13 .....207 F5
Laurel Gdns LA9 ....200 C8
Laurel Terr CA7 ....180 D3
Laurels The CA22 ..189 B6
Lawrence Ave LA13 .134 C6
Lawson Cl CA28 ...187 B6
Lawson Garth CA13 .63 F5
Lawson Rd LA14 ...206 F3
Lawson St Aspatria CA7 .36 D1
 Carlisle CA2 ....176 D7
 Maryport CA15 .....182 D5
 Workington CA14 ...184 C7
Layburn Ho CA14 ..184 F3
Layfield La CA25 ..188 D8
Lazonby CE Sch CA10 .57 B6
Lazonby Hall Cotts CA10 .56 F7
Lazonby Row CA7 ..17 E3
Lazonby Sta CA10 .57 A6
Lazonby Terr CA2 ..177 C1
Lea The CA11 ......70 B8
Lea Yeat Brow LA10 .148 B2
Leabank Rd CA3 ...175 C5
Leabourne Rd CA2 .177 A2
Leacett La LA17 ...105 B4
Leagarth La CA16 ..89 B3
Leagate Brow CA20 .109 C3
Leas Cl CA25 ......24 C1
Leatham St CA2 ...176 E6
Leather La 1 LA12 .203 D5
Leathwaite CA28 ..187 E8
Leck St Peter's CE Prim Sch
 LA6 ....169 B7
Leconfield Ind Est CA25 .188 D7
Leconfield St CA25 .188 D7
Lediard Ave CA7 ..177 A3
Leece Dr LA15 ....205 B3
Leece La LA13 ....207 F4
Leeches Ct CA15 ..183 A6
Leeds Ave LA14 ...206 F7
Leeming La LA6 ...169 C3
Lees The CA7 .....27 B7
Leicester St
 Barrow-In-F LA13 ..207 B3
 Carlisle CA2 ......176 F4
Leighton Cl LA7 ..155 D1
Leighton Dr
 Slack Head LA7 ...155 D1
 Walney Island LA14 .206 C4
Leighton Hall* LA5 .166 E5
Leighton Moss Nature
 Reserve* LA5 ......210 F2
Leith Beck Fold LA10 .86 B8
Leith Flat Brow LA13 .207 C8
Leonard St LA12 ..192 B3
Leopard St LA14 ..206 C4
Lesh La LA13 .....207 D7
Leskew Cotts CA20 .109 B2
Level The
 Cockermouth CA13 .190 C3
 High Newton LA11 ..154 A4
Leven Valley CE Prim Sch
 LA12 ....153 C7
Levens CE Sch LA8 .155 D8
Levens Cl
 Dalton-In-F LA15 ..205 D4
 Kendal LA9 ....200 D2
Levens Hall* LA8 .155 E8
Levens La LA8 ....155 E8
Levens Terr 10 LA14 .207 A4
Levens Way LA5 ..210 C3
Levensgarth LA12 .153 B8
Lewis Cl CA2 .....214 A1
Leyfield Cl LA18 .202 C5
Leyfield Ct LA6 ...212 C1
Leythey La LA12 ..163 B3
Leywell Dr CA1 ..177 F3
Library Rd LA9 ...200 C5
Lichen Gr CA2 ....189 C6
Lichfield Cl CA14 .207 A6
Lickbarrow Cl LA23 .198 F3
Lickbarrow Rd
 Windermere LA23 ..198 E4
 Windermere LA23 ..198 F3
Liddel Rd CA6 ....10 C4
Liddell St CA7 ...174 C4
Liddesdale Heritage Ctr*
 TD9 ....1 B6
Liddle Cl
 Barrow-In-F LA14 ..207 C2
 Carlisle CA3 ......175 C4
Lido Village The CA7 .174 D5
Lightburn Ave LA12 .203 D4
Lightburn Rd LA12 .203 D5
Lightburn Trad Est
 LA12 ....203 C4
Lightfoot Dr CA1 ..177 D2
Lilac Sq CA14 .....30 E6
Lilacs The CA2 ...189 B6
Lillyhall Bsns Ctr CA14 .185 F8

Lillyhall Bsns Pk CA14 .185 F7
Lillyhall Ind Est CA14 .77 C8
Lime Gr Carlisle CA2 .176 B5
 Maryport CA15 .....182 F5
Lime House Sch CA4 .40 B6
Lime Kiln Wlk LA14 .206 F8
Lime La CA16 ......88 C5
Lime Rd CA14 .....185 A7
Lime St Barrow-In-F LA14 .206 F6
 Carlisle CA2 ......214 A1
 Shap CA10 ....101 C5
Lime Tree Rd LA12 .203 D3
Limekiln La CA22 ..92 C1
Limepots Rd LA12 .192 A5
Limes The CA22 ...189 B6
Limethwaite Rd LA23 .198 F4
Limetree Cres LA13 .190 C5
Limetree Gr CA7 ..180 C5
Lincoln Rd CA28 ..187 F6
Lincoln St
 Barrow-In-F LA14 ..207 A5
 Millom LA18 ....202 D4
Lindal & Marton Prim Sch
 LA12 ....162 D7
Lindal Bsns Pk LA12 .162 E6
Lindal Cl LA15 ....205 B3
Lindal St 4 LA14 ..207 A3
Lindale Brow LA11 .165 C8
Lindale CE Prim Sch
 LA11 ....154 C3
Lindale Cl LA6 ....209 B2
Lindale Rd LA11 ..208 F6
Linden Fold LA11 .208 C2
Linden Pk CA10 ...72 E2
Linden Terr CA1 ..177 E3
Linden Wlk CA14 .62 F3
Lindeth Cl LA5 ...210 C2
Lindeth La LA23 .129 C2
Lindeth Rd LA5 ..210 C2
Lindisfarne Ct LA1 .177 C5
Lindisfarne St CA1 .177 C5
Lindow St CA26 ...92 D8
Ling Beck Cres LA4 .183 A2
Ling Beck Pk CA14 .183 A2
Ling Beck View CA14 .183 A2
Ling Cl CA14 .....184 E8
Ling La CA5 ......39 E4
Ling Rd Egremont CA22 .189 B6
 Seaton CA14 ......183 B2
Lingarth LA11 ....154 C3
Lingfell Ave CA13 .190 E4
Lingholm Gdns* CA12 .81 B5
Lingla Bank CA26 .92 C7
Lingley Fields CA26 .92 D8
Lingley Rd CA26 ..92 D8
Lingmell Cl CA28 .187 D3
Lingmell Cres CA20 .123 B8
Lingmell Ctyd CA20 .123 B8
Lingmell Wood CA20 .123 B8
Lingmoor Rise LA9 .200 F3
Lingmoor Way LA12 .113 B4
Lingmoor Way CA1 .177 D3
Lingside Cres LA1 .207 B3
Lingy Cl CA5 .....29 E3
Link Rd CA28 .....187 E4
Links Cl CA7 .....174 B3
Links Cres CA20 .123 A8
Linne View LA14 ..85
Linnet Gr LA9 ....200 F1
Linstock Ave CA14 .190 D2
Linsty Gn LA12 ..153 C8
Linton St CA1 ....177 C5
Lismore Pl Carlisle CA1 .214 C3
 Workington CA14 .184 E6
Lismore St CA1 ..214 C2
Lister Ct CA2 ....176 C6
Listers Cotts LA14 .63 E6
Litchmead Gr LA13 .207 B6
Litt Pl CA25 .....188 D8
Little Aynam LA9 .200 D5
Little Brow CA13 .63 F6
Little Camp St CA5 .182 D6
Little Corby Rd CA4 .177 F7
Little Croft
 Barrow-In-F LA14 ..207 D4
 Cleator Moor CA25 .188 C7
 High Harrington CA14 .185 B7
Little Dockray 10 CA11 .191 C6
Little Heads LA11 .208 C5
Little Hills 14 CA12 .192 B3
Little Mill CA21 ..189 E5
Little Mill CA13 ..63 F6
Little Moss Cl LA21 .196 A4
Little Salkeld Watermill*
 CA10 ....57 C3
Little Sandhill CA10 .57 B8
Little Union St 10 LA13 .203 D5
Littlebeck La CA10 .87 C3
Littledale La LA9 ..200 F3
Liverpool St 3 LA14 .206 F6
Loaning The CA4 ..181 E5
Loanthwaite La LA22 .197 F7
Loanwath Rd DG16 .173 C2
Lochinvar Cl CA3 .10 C3
Lochinvar Sch CA6 .175 E1
Locka La CA4 .....167 F3
Locker La LA11 ...164 F7
Lodge Cl
 Cockermouth CA13 .190 D3
 Holme LA6 ....156 B6
Lodge La LA2,LA6 .168 D1
Lodge Terr LA20 ..139 A2
Lodore Dr CA2 ...29 D6
Lodore Fells* CA12 .81 C1
Loftus Hill LA10 .201 C4
Logan Rd CA6 ....175 C8
London Rd Carlisle CA1 .177 D3

London Rd continued
Lindal in F LA12 . . . . .162 E6
London Road Terr CA1 .177 C4
Long Acre CI LA5 . . . . . . .213 B2
Long Bank LA14 . . . . .170 C6
Long CI LA9 . . . . .200 C3
Long Croft
Barrow-In-F LA14 . . . . . . .204 B1
Egremont CA22 . . . . .189 D7
Long Cswy DL11,CA17 . . .122 E7
Long Island Pk CA2 . . . . .214 B1
Long La Blawith LA12 . . . .140 A2
Carlisle CA3 . . . . .214 A3
Newbiggin LA12 . . . . .171 D7
Sedbergh LA10 . . . . .201 D5
Stainton With A LA13 . . . .205 D2
Long Level LA6 . . . . .168 F8
Long Marton Rd CA16 . . .193 C7
Long Marton Sch CA16 . . .88 A7
Long Meg Cotts CA10 . . .57 C3
Long Row
Kirkby-in-F LA17 . . . . .151 C6
Swarthmoor LA12 . . . . . . .203 A2
Longbarrow CA25 . . . . . . .188 D6
Longber La 169 B3
Longburgh Fauld CA5 . . . .18 E1
Longcroft
Braithwaite LA22 . . . . .80 F6
Cockermouth CA13 . . . . . .190 E3
Longdyke Dr CA1 . . . . . . .177 E7
Longfield Dr LA5 . . . . .213 B2
Longholme Rd CA1 . . . . . .177 F2
Longlands Ave LA13 . . . . .207 D5
Longlands CI CA3 . . . . . . .175 F1
Longlands Lake Nature
Reserve* CA23,CA25 . .188 C2
Longlands Rd
Bowness-on-W LA23 . . . . .198 C3
Carlisle CA3 . . . . .175 F1
Longlands View LA9 . . . . .200 E2
Longmeadow Ave DG12 .172 B2
Longmeadow La LA9 . . . .144 B4
Longmere Cres LA5 . . . . .213 B2
Longmire Rd
Troutbeck LA23 . . . . .114 F1
Windermere LA23 . . . . . . .129 C8
Longmynd Ave LA14 . . . . .206 F5
Longpool LA9 . . . . .200 E6
Longreins Rd LA14 . . . . . .207 A4
Longsowerby Rd CA2 . . . .176 D4
Longtail Brow LA8 . . . . . .132 A4
Longtail Hill LA23 . . . . . . .129 B2
Longthwaite Cres CA7 . . .180 C2
Longthwaite Farm Ct
CA4 . . . . .178 D6
Longthwaite Rd CA7 . . . . .180 C2
Longton Rigg LA5 . . . . .39 F2
Longton's Cotts LA6 . . . . .167 B1
Longtown Ind Est CA6 . . . .10 C3
Longtown Prim Sch CA6 . . .10 C3
Longtown Rd CA8 . . . . . . .179 B5
Longway LA13 . . . . .207 D2
Longwood LA8 . . . . .156 D8
Lonning Foot CA6 . . . . .19 D4
Lonning Head CA8 . . . . . . .179 B4
Lonscale View CA12 . . . . .192 E4
Lonsdale CI CA15 . . . . .49 D5
Lonsdale Ct
Bransty CA28 . . . . .186 E3
6 Penrith CA11 . . . . .191 E4
Lonsdale Ho Carlisle CA2 .176 C7
2 Keswick CA12 . . . . . . .192 A4
Lonsdale Pl CA28 . . . . . . .186 E3
Lonsdale Rd LA18 . . . . . . .202 D5
Lonsdale St
Barrow-In-F LA14 . . . . . . .207 A2
Carlisle CA1 . . . . .214 B2
Whitehaven CA28 . . . . . . .186 D2
Workington CA14 . . . . . . .184 D6
Lonsdale Terr
Cockermouth CA13 . . . . . .190 B3
Crosby Villa CA15 . . . . .49 D6
Dearham CA15 . . . . .49 A2
Millom LA18 . . . . .202 D5
3 Penrith CA11 . . . . .191 D5
St Bees CA27 . . . . .91 D2
Lonsdale View CA15 . . . . .49 A2
Lonsties CA12 . . . . .192 D3
Loop Rd N CA28 . . . . .186 D3
Loop Rd S CA28 . . . . .186 D1
Lord Roberts St LA14 . . . .206 C2
Lord St
22 Askam-In-F LA16 . . . .162 A8
Barrow-In-F LA14 . . . . . . .207 A3
Carlisle CA1 . . . . .214 C1
Dalton-In-F LA15 . . . . . . .205 D5
Millom LA18 . . . . .202 D5
Lord's Lot Rd
Over Kellet LA6 . . . . .167 C1
Over Kellet LA6 . . . . .167 D1
Lord's Plain Cswy LA8 .143 D1
Lords Way CA6 . . . . .175 A4
Loreburn Ct DG12 . . . . . .172 E4
Lorne Cres CA14 . . . . .214 A1
Lorne Rd LA13 . . . . .207 A6
Lorne St CA2 . . . . .214 A1
Lorne Terr CA8 . . . . .179 B5
Lorne Villas LA14 . . . . . . .184 F5
Lorton Ave CA14 . . . . .184 F4
Lorton CI CA28 . . . . .187 D4
Lorton Rd CA13 . . . . .190 D3
Lorton Sch LA10 . . . . .79 D8
Lorton St CA13 . . . . .190 D3
Lots Rd LA16 . . . . .162 A7
Loughrigg Ave
Ambleside LA22 . . . . .195 D4
Kendal LA9 . . . . .200 E2

Loughrigg Brow LA22 . . .195 B5
Loughrigg Mdw LA22 . . .195 C4
Loughrigg Terr CA2 . . . . .176 C3
Lound Rd LA9 . . . . .200 D3
Lound Sq LA9 . . . . .200 D3
Lound St LA9 . . . . .200 D3
Lovers La CA6 . . . . .10 C4
Lovers' La CA5 . . . . .179 C5
Lovers' Wlk DG12 . . . . . . .172 C2
Low Brow Edge LA12 . . . .153 C7
Low Castle Terr CA8 . . . . .14 F1
Low Cliff LA14 . . . . .206 F8
Low Corkickle CA28 . . . . .187 D8
Low Cotts LA8 . . . . .156 D7
Low Croft CA20 . . . . .108 E4
Low Cross St CA8 . . . . . . .179 B5
Low Farm CA10 . . . . .71 F8
Low Farm CI LA12 . . . . . . .162 E6
Low Fellside LA9 . . . . .200 C5
Low Fold LA23 . . . . .198 C2
Low Furness CE Prim Sch
LA12 . . . . .162 F5
Low Gale LA22 . . . . .195 D5
Low Garth LA9 . . . . .200 B8
Low Gate LA12 . . . . .153 A8
Low House Gdns LA12 . . .162 F4
Low Ibbotsholme LA23 . .129 B7
Low Kepplewray LA20 . . .139 A2
Low Kiln Ct CA12 . . . . .66 A7
Low La Leck LA6 . . . . .169 B7
Levens LA8 . . . . .143 C4
Middleton LA6 . . . . .157 E8
Ravenstonedale CA17 . . . .120 B2
Tebay CA10 . . . . .118 B3
Low Langstaffe LA10 . . . .201 C5
Low Leases La CA17 . . . . .120 C8
Low Lonnin CA20 . . . . .109 D2
Low Mdw Carlisle CA2 . . .176 B6
Old Hutton LA8 . . . . .144 F3
Low Mead CA8 . . . . .200 C8
Low Mill Langwathby CA10 . .71 F8
Thornhill CA22 . . . . .189 D2
Low Moor Ave CA2 . . . . . . .30 B3
Low Moor Terr LA14 . . . . .206 F8
Low Moorlands CA5 . . . . . .29 D1
Low Park La LA8 . . . . .144 D1
Low Plains Ct CA11 . . . . . .56 B8
Low Rd Brigham CA13 . . . . .63 F5
Cockermouth CA13 . . . . . .190 B4
Whitehaven CA28 . . . . . . .187 D6
Low Row
Backbarrow LA12 . . . . . . .153 C7
Cark LA11 . . . . .164 D7
Low Sand La CA13 . . . . . .190 C4
Low Seaton CA14 . . . . . . .183 B1
Low Sleights Rd
Ribblehead LA6 . . . . .159 F1
Ribblehead LA6 . . . . .160 A1
Low St Burton in L LA6 . . .169 C3
Milburn CA10 . . . . .73 C4
Low White CI LA14 . . . . . .206 F8
Low Wiend CA16 . . . . .193 C5
Low Winder La CA22 . . . . .92 D2
Low Wood Water Sport &
Activity Ctr* LA23 . .128 F8
Lowbyer Pk CA9 . . . . .181 D5
Lowca Com Sch CA14 . . . .76 E5
Lowca La CA14 . . . . .183 A3
Lower Abbotsgate LA6 . .212 B2
Lower Brook St 14 LA12 .203 D5
Lower Castle Pk LA9 . . . . .200 E5
Lower Gale LA22 . . . . .195 D5
Lower Gate CA10 . . . . .87 A5
Lower Haverflatts LA7 . . .211 E6
Lower Stonecroft LA12 . .195 D4
Loweswater Ave
Whitehaven CA28 . . . . . . .187 C5
Workington CA14 . . . . . . .184 E4
Loweswater CI CA5 . . . . . .190 F3
Loweswater Terr LA15 . . .205 B4
Lowfield LA22 . . . . .195 D4
Lowfield La LA8 . . . . .115 D2
Lowfields La LA6 . . . . . . .212 D7
Lowgate LA8 . . . . .143 D1
Lowick CE Sch LA12 . . . . .152 B8
Lowkirkbarrow La LA9 . . .200 D4
Lowmoor Rd CA2 . . . . . . .180 E2
Lowmoor Row CA10 . . . . . .72 F1
Lowrey CI CA21 . . . . .108 B5
Lowry CI CA13 . . . . .101 C5
Lowry Hill Rd CA3 . . . . . . .175 B4
Lowry St CA7 . . . . .177 A1
Lowscales Dr CA13 . . . . . .190 E2
Lowside CA17 . . . . .141 D2
Lowther CA10 . . . . .85 F6
Lowther Arc CA3 . . . . .214 B2
Lowther Browns Lonning
CA2 . . . . .176 C3
Lowther Cres LA14 . . . . . .206 C4
Lowther Ct 4 CA11 . . . . .191 C6
Lowther Endowed Sch
CA10 . . . . .85 F6
Lowther Gdns LA11 . . . . .208 D4
Lowther Glen CA10 . . . . . .181 C6
Lowther Leisure & Wildlife
Pk* CA10 . . . . .85 F5
Lowther Pk LA9 . . . . .200 F4
Lowther Rd Millom LA18 . .202 C4
Workington CA14 . . . . . . .184 C5
Lowther St Carlisle CA3 . . .214 B2
Flimby CA15 . . . . .183 C8
Great Clifton CA14 . . . . . . .63 A4
Kendal LA9 . . . . .200 E6
Penrith CA11 . . . . .191 D6
Waberthwaite LA19 . . . . .137 C8
Whitehaven CA28 . . . . . . .186 C1

Lowther View CA10 . . . . . .71 C1
Loyne Pk LA6 . . . . .168 D2
Ludgate Hill CA5 . . . . .18 F1
Ludgate Terr CA7 . . . . .180 C4
Lumley Rd LA9 . . . . .200 B2
Lumley St 1 LA14 . . . . . . .207 B2
Lund Cres CA2 . . . . .176 F3
Lund Rd LA12 . . . . .203 E5
Lund Terr LA12 . . . . .203 E5
Lune CI LA6 . . . . .212 C3
Lune Valley Ct LA6 . . . . . .118 B2
Lunefield Dr LA6 . . . . .212 C1
Lunefield Gdns LA6 . . . . .212 C2
Lupton Ct 4 LA23 . . . . . . .198 E5
Lyalls' Pl 5 CA15 . . . . . . .182 E5
Lydia's Cotts CA2 . . . . . . .192 D4
Lynchetts The CA10 . . . . . .101 C6
Lyndale Ave LA13 . . . . . . .207 B5
Lyndale La 1 LA14 . . . . . .208 F8
Lyndhurst Gdns CA2 . . . . .176 B3
Lyndhurst Pk LA12 . . . . . .203 D4
Lyne CI Carlisle CA3 . . . . . .175 C4
Walney Island LA14 . . . . .206 B3
Lyne Riggs Est LA5 . . . . . .213 C3
Lyngarth CA1 . . . . .177 F4
Lynngarth Dr LA9 . . . . . . .200 C4
Lynsiack Terr LA5 . . . . . . .210 B8
Lynter CI 1 LA14 . . . . . . .207 B6
Lyon St LA14 . . . . .206 E4
Lytham CI CA2 . . . . .176 B5

M

Macadam Gdns CA11 . . . .191 C6
Macadam St LA14 . . . . . . .207 B2
Macadam Way CA11 . . . . .191 C6
Macan St CA15 . . . . .182 D7
Machell CI 4 LA12 . . . . . .203 C5
Mackies Dr DG16 . . . . . . .173 C3
Mackreth Row 8 CA13 . . .190 D4
Macnish Dr DG12 . . . . . . .172 D5
Madam Banks Rd CA5 . . . .40 A8
Mafeking Pl DG12 . . . . . . .172 D4
Maiden Way CA10 . . . . .73 B2
Maidenhill Rd CA11 . . . . . .71 C7
Maidenlands Cres LA15 . .205 C4
Main Rd Flimby CA15 . . . . .183 B7
Great Clifton CA14 . . . . . . .63 B4
High Harrington CA14 . . . .185 C7
Maryport CA15 . . . . .183 B1
Seaton CA14 . . . . .183 B1
Swarthmoor LA12 . . . . . . .203 A2
Ulverston LA12 . . . . .162 F7
Windermere LA23 . . . . . . .198 E5
Main St Abbey Town CA7 . .26 C1
Allonby CA15 . . . . .35 C1
Bootle LA19 . . . . .151 A6
Brampton CA8 . . . . .79 B3
Brough CA17 . . . . .105 B5
Burton-in-K LA6 . . . . .169 C3
Cleator CA23 . . . . .188 D4
Cockermouth CA13 . . . . . .190 D4
Dearham CA15 . . . . .49 B3
Dent LA10 . . . . .147 B1
Distington LA14 . . . . .185 C2
Egremont CA22 . . . . .189 C5
Elterwater LA22 . . . . .113 C3
Endmoor LA8 . . . . .156 C7
Flimby CA15 . . . . .183 C8
Flookburgh LA11 . . . . . . .164 D6
Frizington CA26 . . . . .92 D8
Grange-Over-S LA11 . . . . .208 D5
Great Broughton CA13 . . . .63 E6
Gretna DG16 . . . . .173 E5
Greysouthen CA13 . . . . . . .63 E4
Haverigg LA18 . . . . .201 D5
Hawkshead LA22 . . . . . . .197 E5
Hensingham CA28 . . . . . . .187 F6
Keswick CA12 . . . . .192 A4
Kirkby Lonsdale LA6 . . . . .212 C2
Kirkby Thore CA10 . . . . . . .87 D8
Levens LA8 . . . . .143 D1
Maryport CA15 . . . . .182 E5
Milnthorpe LA7 . . . . .211 D4
Newbiggin-on-L CA17 . . . .119 F7
Parton CA28 . . . . .186 D5
Pennington LA12 . . . . .162 E8
Ravenglass CA18 . . . . . . .123 F3
Sandwith CA28 . . . . .187 A2
Sedbergh LA10 . . . . .201 D5
Shap CA10 . . . . .101 C5
Silecroft LA18 . . . . .148 A4
St Bees CA27 . . . . .91 D2
Staveley LA8 . . . . .134 C5
Warton LA5 . . . . .213 C7
Whittington LA6 . . . . .168 B5
Mains Brow LA8 . . . . .150 C8
Mains Fauld CA5 . . . . .29 A5
Mains The Beetham LA7 . .155 E2
Stainton LA11 . . . . .170 D3
Mainsgate Rd LA18 . . . . . .202 C4
Maitland St CA2 . . . . .177 A3
Mall The 10 LA14 . . . . . . .206 F3
Mallard Dr LA14 . . . . .206 B1
Mallard Rd DG16 . . . . .173 D3
Mallings The 15 LA12 . . . .203 D6
Mallsknowe CA16 . . . . .10 B3
Mallyclose Dr CA1 . . . . . . .176 F4
Malor Pk DG16 . . . . .173 B3
Malt Kiln Rd LA12 . . . . . . .171 E8
Maltings The LA6 . . . . . . .168 D7
Malton Cres 5 LA14 . . . . .206 B7
Manchester St LA14 . . . . .206 F4
Mande Terr
Crosby Villa CA15 . . . . .49 D6
7 Maryport CA15 . . . . . . .182 E5
Manesty Rise CA2 . . . . .76 F3

Manesty View CA12 . . . . .192 C3
Manor CI LA6 . . . . .169 C3
Manor Croft CA4 . . . . .30 F7
Manor Ct
Cockermouth CA13 . . . . . .190 C4
Kirkby Stephen CA17 . . . .199 C5
Wigton CA7 . . . . .180 C3
Manor Farm LA6 . . . . .168 D7
Manor Gdns CA8 . . . . .179 B5
Manor House Wynd
CA17 . . . . .105 A1
Manor Pk
Barrow-In-F LA13 . . . . . . .207 C7
Keswick CA12 . . . . .192 C3
Manor Pl CA2 . . . . .177 C2
Manor Rd
Barrow-In-F LA13 . . . . . . .207 D8
Carlisle CA2 . . . . .177 C2
Mansride LA11 . . . . .164 D6
Mansergh High La LA6 . .157 D6
Mansfield Ho DG16 . . . . . .173 C3
Manx View 4 LA16 . . . . . .162 A8
Maple Ave LA12 . . . . .203 D2
Maple CI Greystoke CA11 . . .69 E5
Maryport CA15 . . . . .182 E9
Workington CA14 . . . . . . .184 C1
Maple Ct LA23 . . . . .198 E6
Maple Dr Kendal LA9 . . . .200 B3
Penrith CA11 . . . . .191 F4
Maple Gr Carlisle CA3 . . . .175 E2
Whitehaven CA28 . . . . . . .187 E7
Maple St LA14 . . . . .206 F6
Marconi Rd CA2 . . . . .176 F7
Mardale CA7 . . . . .180 B3
Mardale CI CA11 . . . . .191 B4
Mardale Gr LA13 . . . . .207 B3
Mardale Rd Carlisle CA2 .176 D4
Penrith CA11 . . . . .191 B4
Margaret Creighton Gdns
CA1 . . . . .177 C6
Margaret St CA15 . . . . . . .183 C8
Margaret's Way CA16 . . . .193 B4
Margate St LA14 . . . . .206 C2
Margery St CA1 . . . . .177 C6
Margery Terr CA2 . . . . . . .176 D1
Margrats Croft CA10 . . . . .86 F4
Marina Cres CA2 . . . . .177 A2
Marina The LA23 . . . . .129 A2
Marina View LA18 . . . . . . .202 A2
Marine Rd CA15 . . . . .182 C5
Marine Terr
Roa Island LA13 . . . . .171 B3
Silloth CA7 . . . . .174 C4
Whitehaven CA28 . . . . . . .186 D2
Market Arc CA3 . . . . .214 B3
Market Cross LA22 . . . . . .195 D6
Market Hall CA7 . . . . .180 C3
Market Hill CA7 . . . . .180 D4
Market Pl Alston CA9 . . . . .181 D3
Ambleside LA22 . . . . .195 D7
Cleator Moor CA25 . . . . . .188 D7
Cockermouth CA13 . . . . . .190 D4
2 Dalton-In-F LA15 . . . . .205 B4
Egremont CA22 . . . . .189 E6
1 Kendal LA9 . . . . .200 D5
3 Keswick CA12 . . . . .192 B3
17 Ulverston LA12 . . . . . .203 D5
Wigton CA7 . . . . .180 C3
Workington CA14 . . . . . . .184 F6
Market Sq Aspatria CA7 . . .50 C8
8 Brampton CA8 . . . . .79 C5
Cleator Moor CA25 . . . . . .188 D7
Market St
Barrow-In-F LA14 . . . . . . .206 F3
Broughton-In-F LA20 . . . .139 A2
Cockermouth CA13 . . . . . .190 C4
Carnforth LA5 . . . . .213 C4
Cleator Moor CA25 . . . . . .188 D7
Dalton-In-F LA15 . . . . . . .205 B4
Egremont CA22 . . . . .189 E6
Flookburgh LA11 . . . . . . .164 D6
Kirkby Lonsdale LA6 . . . . .212 C2
Kirkby Stephen CA17 . . . .199 D6
Millom LA18 . . . . .202 D5
Ulverston LA12 . . . . .203 D5
Marks Ave CA2 . . . . .176 B6
Marlborough Ave CA3 . . . .175 C3
Marlborough Gdns CA3 . .214 A4
Marlborough St CA28 . . . .186 C1
Marne Ave LA11 . . . . .164 D6
Marron La CA14 . . . . .63 D4
Marsden St LA14 . . . . .207 B3
Marsh Garth LA17 . . . . . . .151 C6
Marsh Gdns LA11 . . . . . . .164 D6
Marsh House Gdns CA5 . .18 F1
Marsh La
6 Askam-In-F LA16 . . . .162 A8
Carlisle CA1 . . . . .134 A1
Marsh Rd LA7 . . . . .211 B5
Marsh Side LA17 . . . . .151 C6
Marsh St
1 Askam-In-F LA16 . . . .162 A8
Barrow-In-F LA14 . . . . . . .207 B3
Barrow-In-F LA14 . . . . . . .207 B3
Marsh Terr CA15 . . . . .182 F4
Marshall Terr CA10 . . . . . .101 C5
Martinagga La CA10 . . . . . .41 E4
Martindale CI CA2 . . . . .91 F7
Martindale View CA16 . . .104 C6

Marton CI LA15 . . . . .205 C2
Marvejols Pk CA13 . . . . . .190 B3
Marvic Yard The 2 LA6 .200 C4
Mary Hannah Cotts 4
CA3 . . . . .175 B1
Mary Hewetson Cottage
Hospl CA12 . . . . .192 A5
Mary Jane Way CA11 . . . .191 E4
Mary St Carlisle CA1 . . . . .214 B2
Longtown CA6 . . . . .10 C3
Silloth CA7 . . . . .174 C4
Maryfell LA10 . . . . .201 D4
Maryland CA15 . . . . .210 D2
Maryport Aquarium*
CA15 . . . . .182 C6
Maryport CE Jun Sch
CA15 . . . . .182 E7
Maryport Cotts CA2 . . . . .176 F3
Maryport Ct CA2 . . . . .176 F3
Maryport Inf Sch CA15 . .182 D7
Maryport Maritime Mus*
CA15 . . . . .182 C6
Maryport Rd CA13 . . . . . . .49 A2
Maryport Sta CA15 . . . . . .182 D5
Mask Rd
Crosby Garrett CA17 . . . .104 B3
Great Asby CA16 . . . . .103 F5
Mason St CA14 . . . . .184 E4
Mason Terr CA15 . . . . .183 C8
Masongill Fell La LA6 . . . .169 E7
Matheson Terr DG12 . . . . .172 D5
Matlock Rd LA14 . . . . .207 A6
Matty Lonning CA5 . . . . . . .28 F1
Maude St LA9 . . . . .200 C6
Maudy Lonning CA10 . . . . .86 B5
Mawflat La LA14 . . . . .170 D3
Maxwell Dr Carlisle CA3 . .191 D3
Mayburgh CI CA10 . . . . . .191 E1
Mayburgh Henge*
CA10 . . . . .191 D1
Maychells Orch LA11 . . . .164 F7
Mayfair Ave LA13 . . . . . . .207 B5
Mayfield CA2 . . . . .30 B3
Mayfield Ave
Carlisle CA1 . . . . .177 D3
Holme LA6 . . . . .156 B1
Mayfield Rd Kendal LA9 . .200 F2
Ulverston LA12 . . . . .203 C4
Mayfield Specl Sch CA28 .37 F1
Mayfield Terr LA11 . . . . . .208 C3
Maylands Ave LA13 . . . . . .207 D6
Maylands Gr LA13 . . . . . . .207 D6
Mayo St CA14 . . . . .190 B3
Mayo St CA13 . . . . .190 B3
Mayor's Dr CA3 . . . . .214 A4
Mayson St CA2 . . . . .177 A3
MC Gowan St CA14 . . . . . .62 D6
MCcarron CI CA15 . . . . . . .182 F4
MClintock St LA14 . . . . . .206 E4
McIver CI LA22 . . . . .195 D3
McIver La LA22 . . . . .195 D3
MClean CI 3 LA14 . . . . . .207 A3
McMurdo Rd DG12 . . . . . .172 C3
Meade Rd CA1 . . . . .177 D2
Meadley Pl CA25 . . . . .188 E6
Meadow Bank
Beetham LA7 . . . . .155 E2
Prospect CA7 . . . . .49 F7
Cleator Moor CA25 . . . . . .190 D3
Meadow CI
Appleby-In-W CA16 . . . . .193 D6
Aspatria CA7 . . . . .50 C8
Bowston LA8 . . . . .130 E3
Gosforth CA20 . . . . .109 A2
Maryport CA15 . . . . .182 F5
Meadow Croft
Appleby-In-W CA16 . . . . .193 D6
Langwathby CA10 . . . . . . .57 C1
Egremont CA22 . . . . .62 E4
Meadow Gr
Cockermouth CA13 . . . . . .190 D3
Dalton-In-F LA15 . . . . . . .205 C5
Grange-Over-S LA11 . . . . .208 B1
Meadow Rd Kendal LA9 . . .171 D6
Whitehaven CA28 . . . . . . .187 D4
Meadow Vale CA14 . . . . . .183 A2
Meadow View Cark LA11 .164 D7
Carlisle CA1 . . . . .177 F3
Lowca CA28 . . . . .186 F8
Whitehaven CA28 . . . . . . .187 C7
Meadow Way
Arkholme LA6 . . . . .168 B3
Maryport CA15 . . . . .182 F5
Meadowbank Fold LA11 . .208 B4
Meadowbank La LA11 . . . .208 B4
Meadowcroft
Bowness-on-W LA23 . . . . .129 A2
Holme LA6 . . . . .156 B2
Meadowcroft Cotts
Dalton-In-F LA15 . . . . . . .129 A2
Windermere LA8 . . . . .129 F5
Meadowcroft Rd CA26 . . . .92 D7
Meadowfield
Gosforth CA20 . . . . .109 A2
Meadowfield Gr CA20 . . . .109 A2

Meadowlands Ave LA13 .207 D6
Meadows Cl LA5 ......166 F6
Meadows The
Arnside LA5 ....210 C8
Langwathby CA10 ....57 C1
Southwaite CA4 ....41 C4
Yealand Redmayne LA5 ..166 F6
Meadowside
Chapel Stile LA22 ....113 C4
Swarthmoor LA12 ....203 A2
Meadowside Cl LA8 ....144 C1
Mealbank Mill Trad Est
LA8 ....131 D2
Mealbank Rd LA9 ......131 C1
Mealrigg La LA6 ....168 A7
Means Brow CA11 ....83 D5
Mearness Dr LA12 .....166 F6
Meathop Grange LA11 .154 E3
Meathop Rd
Grange-Over-S LA11 ...208 F5
Lindale LA11 ....154 E2
Medway Rd LA14 ......206 B2
Meeting House La
Great Broughton CA13 ...63 E6
Penrith CA11 ....191 D5
Tirril CA10 ....70 F1
Ulverston LA12 ....203 C2
Meetinghouse La CA7 .180 C3
Meetings View LA14 ..204 B1
Meggy Loaning CA8 ....32 D1
Melampus St LA14 ....206 C3
Melbourne Ave DG12 ..17 D8
Melbourne Rd CA1 ....177 C5
Melbourne St LA14 ....206 E4
Melbourne Terr CA14 .185 B7
Melbreak Ave
Cleator Moor CA25 ....188 D6
Cockermouth CA13 .....190 E4
Maryport CA15 ....182 E4
Melbreak Cl CA28 .....187 E3
Mell Fell View CA11 ....69 D2
Mell Wood CA17 ....199 C5
Mellbecks CA17 ....199 D6
Mellbutts CA12 ....82 C8
Melling Brow LA6 .....168 C2
Melling St Wilfred CE Prim
Sch LA6 ....168 D2
Melrose Terr CA1 .....177 C5
Mendip Gdns LA14 ....206 F5
Mercer St LA14 ....207 A3
Merchant's Dr CA13 ..175 B6
Merewood Lodge LA23 .129 A8
Merith Ave CA1 ....177 C5
Merle Bank CA12 ....82 B8
Merlin Dr
Dalton-In-F LA15 ......205 C4
Moresby Parks CA28 ...76 F2
Mersey Rd LA14 ......206 B3
Metcalfe St CA2 ......214 A1
Methuen St LA14 .....206 C2
Methven Cl LA11 .....208 C3
Methven Rd LA11 ....208 C3
Mews Cotts CA16 .....193 D5
Mews The CA10 ....85 D1
Michael St CA28 .....186 D1
Michaelson Rd
Barrow-In-F LA14 .....206 F2
Kendal LA9 ....200 B2
Micklam Cotts CA14 ...76 E5
Mid Liddle St TD9 ......1 B6
Mid St CA28 ....187 B6
Mid Town Cott CA14 ..185 B7
Middle Barrow La LA12 .162 E5
Middle Cl CA16 ....193 D6
Middle Cliff LA14 ....204 B1
Middle Entrance Dr
LA23 ....129 A1
Middle Hill LA12 .....207 C4
Middle La Haverigg LA18 .149 F1
Kendal LA9 ....200 C5
Middle Pk CA9 ....181 C3
Middle White Cl LA14 .206 F8
Middlefield LA14 .....204 B1
Middlegate
· Great Clifton CA14 ....63 B4
Penrith CA11 ....191 C5
Middlerigg CA2 ......176 C3
Middleshaw Cres LA8 .144 E4
Middleton Ave LA13 ..207 C5
Middleton Gr CA13 .....49 E2
Midfield Mews CA16 ..193 D6
Midland Terr LA5 ....213 C5
Midland Units LA5 ...213 D5
Midtown Cl CA14 ....185 D4
Mikasa St LA14 ......206 D1
Milbourne Cres CA2 ..214 A2
Milbourne St CA2 ....214 A2
Milburn Croft CA14 ..183 B1
Milburn Ct CA8 ......179 B5
Milburn Rd Milburn CA10 .73 A3
Temple Sowerby CA10 ..72 F3
Milburn St CA14 .....184 D6
Mile La LA11 ....70 E4
Miles MacInnes Ct CA14 .214 B4
Milestone Ho LA6 ....212 C2
Mill Bank
Barrow-In-F LA14 .....206 F4
Low Hesket CA4 ....41 E5
Mill Bank Cotts CA12 .129 C4
Mill Brow CA22 ......129 D4
Mill Brow
Armathwaite CA4 ....42 C4
Droomer LA23 ....198 F5
Kirkby Lonsdale LA6 ..212 C2

Mill Cl LA11 ....164 D7
Mill Cotts LA8 ....130 E4
Mill Ct Carlisle CA1 ..177 C3
8 Wigton CA7 ....180 D3
Egremont CA22 ....189 E5
Mill Dam **4** LA12 ....203 D6
Mill Fields The CA21 .108 B5
Mill Gate CA10,CA11 ...57 B4
Mill Gr CA13 ....190 D3
Mill Hill
Appleby-In-W CA16 ...193 D4
Cleator Moor CA25 ...188 C8
Mill La Beckermet CA21 .108 C6
Beetham LA7 ....155 E2
Crosthwaite LA8 .....142 F5
Glasson CA7 ....17 E3
Great Asby CA16 .....103 B6
Great Ormside CA16 ..103 D7
Hutton Roof LA6 .....157 A1
Kirkby Stephen CA17 .199 D6
Milburn CA10 ....73 B4
Sedbergh LA10 ....146 E7
Sedbergh,Lenacre LA10 .146 C4
Soulby LA17 ....104 C1
Underbarrow LA8 .....143 B7
Warton LA5 ....213 C6
Mill Pk LA18 ....150 C7
Mill Race View CA2 ..176 F3
Mill Rd CA7 ....17 E3
Mill Rise LA23 ....198 F5
Mill Row LA22 ....113 C3
Mill St Barrow-In-F LA14 .207 A4
Bootle LA19 ....150 C8
Cleator CA23 ....188 D4
Frizington CA26 ....92 D8
Longtown CA6 ....10 C3
Maryport CA15 ....182 D5
Penrith CA11 ....191 C5
Ravenstonedale CA17 .120 A3
Ulverston LA12 ....203 D5
Whitehaven CA28 .....187 C6
Mill Terr LA11 ....191 C5
Mill Vale CA5 ....40 B8
Mill Yd LA9 ....200 D1
Millans Pk LA22 .....195 D6
Millars Wlk CA23 ....188 D3
Millbank Ct
Bridgefoot CA14 ....63 C4
Carlisle CA2 ....177 B3
Millbeck Carlisle CA2 .176 C2
Kendal LA8 ....144 F5
Millbecks CA12 ....80 E6
Millbeckstock LA23 ..198 C4
Millbrook Cvn Pk LA6 .156 D8
Millbrook Rd CA3 ....175 C5
Millburn Terr CA8 .....24 C8
Millcroft CA3 ....175 B4
Milldikes La LA5 ....19 B2
Miller Bridge Ho LA22 .195 C5
Miller Cl LA13 ....162 C2
Miller Pk CA7 ....180 C4
Millerstone Rise CA10 ..87 E8
Millfield Brampton CA8 .179 C4
3 Ulverston LA12 ..203 D6
Millfield Gdns CA12 ..192 C3
Millfield Terr LA8 ....130 C5
Millholme Ave CA7 ...177 A3
Millicent Cl CA14 ....185 D8
Millness La LA7 .....156 F6
Millom Folk Mus*
LA18 ....202 C5
Millom Hospl LA18 ..202 C4
Mill In Sch LA18 .....202 C4
Millom Rd LA18 ......202 D5
Millom St CA15 ......202 C5
Millpark Cres DG12 ..172 C4
Millrace Cl **4** CA7 ..180 D3
Millrace Rd CA7 .....176 E7
Millrigg St LA14 .....184 E4
Millriggs CA4 ....178 E2
Millstone Ave CA7 ...206 F8
Millstream Ct LA11 ..164 D7
Millview Terr LA22 ..195 C5
Millwood La LA14 ...204 F2
Milner Mount CA11 ..191 E5
Milnthorpe Prim Sch
LA7 ....211 D3
Milnthorpe Rd
Holme LA6 ....156 B1
Kendal LA9 ....200 C2
Milton Dr CA14 ......184 E6
Milton La Burgh-By-S CA5 ..18 F2
Millness LA7 ....156 C6
Milton Rd CA22 .....189 C7
Milton Terr
Barrow-In-F LA14 .....206 F4
Penrith CA11 ....191 C6
Milton Terr
Grange-Over-S LA11 ..208 C4
Milton CA8 ....22 E3
Minster Cl CA14 .....184 E3
Minster La LA13 .....207 D4
Mint Bridge Rd LA9 ..200 E8
Mint Cl LA9 ....200 D7
Mint Dale LA9 ....200 D7
Mint St LA9 ....200 E7
Mintsfeet Rd LA9 ....200 D7
Mintsfeet Rd N LA9 ..200 D7
Mintsfeet Rd S LA9 ..200 D8
Mirehouse* CA12 .....66 C3
Mirk La CA13 ....60 A6
Mislet Brow LA23 ...129 E6
Mitchelgate LA6 .....212 B2
Mitchell Ave CA14 ...184 E8
Miterdale Cl CA28 ..187 F8

Moat CA6 ....10 F8
Moat Hill Ho CA8 ....179 B4
Moat Rd DG12 ....172 C4
Moat Side CA8 ......179 C5
Moat St CA8 ....179 C5
Moffat Terr CA26 .....92 D8
Mona Rd Bransty CA28 .186 D3
Workington CA14 ....184 C1
Mona St CA26 ....77 F1
Monk Castle Bglws CA4 .41 A4
Monk Moors LA19 ...137 A7
Monk St LA14 ....206 F4
Monkhill Rd CA5 ....29 A7
Monkhouse Rd CA14 .184 C2
Monks Brow LA13 ...207 C3
Monks Cl CA11 ......191 C7
Monks Close Rd CA2 .176 E6
Monks Croft Ave LA14 .207 C8
Monks Hill CA27 ....91 C3
Monksvale Gr LA13 ..207 C6
Monkwray Brow CA28 .187 C7
Monkwray Cotts CA28 .187 C7
Monkwray Jun Sch
CA28 ....187 C7
Monkwray Rd CA28 ..187 B6
Monnington Way CA1 .191 C7
Montagu St TD9 ....1 A6
Montague St **3** LA11 .206 F3
Montgomery Ct CA1 ..177 F6
Montgomery St CA1 ..177 F6
Montgomery Way CA1 .177 F6
Montreal Ave CA25 ..188 D6
Montreal CE Prim Sch
CA25 ....188 C6
Montreal Cl CA25 ...188 D6
Montreal Pl CA24 ...188 B6
Montreal St Carlisle CA2 .177 A3
Cleator Moor CA25 ...188 D7
Moor Cl CA5 ....28 F4
Moor Close La LA6 ..167 B1
Moor Cres CA6 ....10 C3
Moor House National Nature
Reserve* LA6 ....74 D8
Moor La Beetham LA7 .211 F1
Clifton CA10 ....71 D3
Flookburgh LA11 ....164 D6
Melkinthorpe CA10 ...86 A8
Satterthwaite LA12 ..141 A7
Moor Park Ave CA2 ..176 A7
Moor Pk LA18 ....202 B5
Moor Pl Carlisle CA3 .175 B2
Moor Rd
Askam-In-F LA12 ....151 C1
Great Broughton CA13 ..63 E6
Great Clifton CA14 ....63 A2
Great Clifton CA14 ....63 B4
Longtown CA6 ....10 C4
Millom LA18 ....202 B5
Stainburn CA14 ....63 F3
Moor Row Com Prim Sch
CA24 ....188 A5
Moor Tarn La CA14 ..206 B2
Moor Terr LA8 ....202 B4
Moorbanks Rd CA14 .184 D4
Moorclose Croft CA14 .184 D3
Moorclose Rd
Salterbeck CA14 .....185 A8
Workington CA14 ....184 D2
Moorcock Cotts LA10 .148 E7
Moordale Cvn Pk CA4 ..25 B2
Moore Field Cl CA28 .200 B8
Moore Way CA14 ....185 D7
Moorfield Ave CA14 ..184 F4
Moorfield Bank CA13 ..63 D6
Moorfield Cotts **12** LA14 .207 B2
Moorfield St CA13 ...207 C3
Moorfields CA5 ....63 C8
Moorgarth LA12 .....203 A3
Moorhouse Rd CA2 ..176 A7
Moorhowe Rd LA23 .129 D7
Moorlands Dr CA14 ..184 E6
Moorside
Flookburgh LA11 ....164 D6
Hunsonby CA10 ....57 E2
Melling LA6 ....168 D2
Prospect CA7 ....49 F7
Yanwath CA10 ....71 A2
Moorside Cl LA46 ...168 D2
Moorside Dr Carlisle CA1 ..30 E5
Maryport CA15 ......182 D7
Moorside Rd LA8 ...144 C1
Moorthwaite La LA6 .157 F5
Moorview Cl LA14 ..185 C8
Moorville Dr CA3 ...175 D3
Moorville Dr N CA3 .175 D3
Moorville Dr S CA3 .175 D3
Moorville Way CA3 ..175 D4
Moorwood Cl CA1 ...177 F5
Morass Rd CA21,CA22 .108 B6
Morecambe Bank LA11 .208 D4
Morecambe Bay Nature
Reserve* LA5 ....165 F6
Morecambe Cres LA14 .206 F8
Morecambe Rd LA12 .203 E4
Moresby Parks Rd CA28 .76 F2
Moresby Prim Sch CA28 .76 F2
Moresby Rd CA28 .....91 F8
Moresby Terr CA28 ..186 E6
Morewood Dr LA14 ..167 C7
Moricambe Cres CA7 ..16 F1
Moricambe Pk CA7 ..174 D8
Morland Area CE Sch
CA10 ....86 F5
Morland Pl CA13 ....190 C3
Morley St Carlisle CA2 .214 A1
Workington CA14 ....184 C5
Morningside Rd DG12 .172 E5
Morpeth Cl CA8 .....179 C6

Morton Ct CA2 ......176 C4
Morton Park Prim Sch
CA2 ....176 C3
Morton Sch The CA2 .176 B4
Morton St CA2 ....176 E6
Mortonrigg CA2 .....176 C4
Mosedale Cres CA15 .182 D4
Mosedale Rd CA14 ..184 E4
Moser Hill Brow LA10 .201 C1
Mosley St LA14 .....207 B3
Moss End La LA7 ....156 E5
Moss Force* CA13 .....95 B8
Moss Ghyll LA9 .....200 C8
Moss Gr CA10 ....101 C5
Moss La Allonby CA15 ..35 C2
Burton-in-K LA5 .....167 A8
Holme LA6 ....156 A1
Leece LA12 ....171 C7
Silverdale LA5 ......210 F5
Moss Lea LA8 ....144 D1
Moss Lonning CA7 ....37 A7
Moss Pl Gretna DG16 .173 C2
Newcastleton TD9 .....1 B6
Moss Rd Cliburn CA10 .86 E8
Newcastleton TD9 .....1 B6
Moss Side CA15 ....35 C2
Moss Side Rd LA7 ..211 B7
Mossbay Rd CA14 ...184 C3
Mosser Ave CA13 ...190 E3
Mossrigg CA2 ......176 C3
Mosswell Terr CA28 ..186 D2
Mothercroft CA28 .....86 F5
Mount Barnard View
LA12 ....203 D2
Mount Pleasant
Arnside LA5 ....210 C8
12 Barrow-In-F LA14 ..207 A3
6 Holme LA6 ....156 B1
13 Kendal LA9 ......200 C5
Lindal in F LA12 .....162 E7
Mount Pleasant Gdns
CA7 ....180 C2
Mount Pleasant Rd CA2 .177 A2
Mount St **6** LA9 ...200 C4
Mount The
Camerton CA14 ......183 F3
Cockermouth CA13 ..190 B5
Mountain View
Carlisle CA3 ....175 D3
Cockermouth CA14 ..184 E4
High Hesket CA4 ......41 F3
Kendal LA9 ....200 C6
Moresby Parks CA28 ..76 F2
Sedbergh LA10 ......201 C4
Mountbarrow Rd LA12 .203 C2
Mountbarrow Way
LA12 ....203 D2
Mountbatten Way LA18 .202 A5
Mountjoy Brow LA8 ..143 B7
Mounts Meadow Cl
LA12 ....162 E1
Mouzell Bank LA15 ..205 D6
Mowbray Dr LA6 ....167 C7
Mowing's La LA12 ..203 C6
Muirbeck Rd DG12 ..172 A1
Muirfield Cl CA2 ....175 B1
Muirfield Gdns DG12 .172 A4
Mulberry Way LA13 .207 F5
Mulcaster Cres CA4 .175 E1
Mulgrew Cl CA15 ...182 F4
Muncaster Castle*
CA18 ....124 B3
Muncaster Cl CA28 ...91 F7
Muncaster Hall* CA8 .124 A4
Muncaster Rd
Walney Island LA14 .206 C5
Whitehaven CA28 .....91 F7
Muncaster Water Mill*
CA18 ....124 A4
Munroe Ave LA18 ...202 C6
Murley Moss LA9 ...200 E1
Murley Moss Bsns Pk
LA9 ....200 E1
Murley Moss La LA9 .200 E2
Murray Rd CA14 ....184 E6
Murray St DG12 .....172 A4
Murraydale Terr CA14 .184 E6
Murrayfield Terr CA18 .123 F3
Murrell Hill LA11 ...208 C4
Murreyfield Cotts DG12 .172 D3
Murton Cl CA16 ....193 D4
Murton Ct CA26 ......77 E2
Murton Pk CA26 .....77 E2
Murton View CA10 ...69 D2
Mus of Lakeland Life*
LA9 ....200 D4
Museum Sq CA12 ...192 A3
Musgrave Cl CA28 ..191 E5
Musgrave St
Brough CA16 ....105 A5
Brough CA17 ....105 A5
Kendal LA9 ....200 D5
Muslins The CA7 ......50 C5
Myddleton St CA1 ...214 C2
Myers La CA11 ......191 C4
Myers St CA15 ....192 B3
Myerscough St **5** LA14 .207 B2
Myerscroft LA12 ....163 B3
Mylnbeck St LA23 ..198 D3
Mylnegarth Gdns LA23 .198 E5
Myrtle Gr LA14 .....207 A4
Myrtle Terr LA15 ...205 B5
Myrtle Villas CA12 ..192 B4

Naiad St LA14 ......206 D1
Nairn St CA15 ......183 C8
Nairn St CA2 ....176 C5
Nannycatch Rd CA23 ..92 D5
Nannypie La CA2 ...143 F2
Napier St
Barrow-In-F LA14 ...206 F4
Dalton-In-F LA15 ...205 C5
Workington CA14 ...184 D5
Natal Rd LA14 ......206 D1
Nateby Rd CA17 ....199 C4
Natland Mill Beck La
LA9 ....200 D1
Natland Rd LA9 ....200 D1
Naworth Castle* CA8 .22 E5
Naworth Dr CA3 ....175 C4
Neals Row LA12 ....162 F5
Near Field Wlk LA14 .204 B1
Near Moss CA2 ....30 E6
Neaum Crag Chalet Pk
LA22 ....113 C2
Neddy Hill LA6 .....167 B7
Needham Dr CA14 ..184 D2
Nelson Bridge CA2 ..214 A1
Nelson Bridge Ct CA2 .214 A1
Nelson Rd LA23 ....198 F4
Nelson Sq
Egremont CA22 .....189 D6
Levens LA8 ....155 D8
Nelson St
Barrow-In-F LA14 ...206 F4
Carlisle CA1 ....214 A1
Dalton-In-F LA15 ...205 B5
Maryport CA15 ......182 C6
Maryport CA15 ......182 D7
Millom LA18 ....202 C5
Nelson Thomlinson Sch The
CA7 ....180 D3
Nent Ct CA9 ....47 A2
Nenthead Mines Heritage
Ctr* CA9 ....47 A2
Nent St Dent Sch CA9 .46 F2
Nepgill CA14 ....63 D4
NER Cottage Homes
CA4 ....178 C2
Ness Way CA2 .....176 B4
Nest Brow CA12 ....192 F2
Nether Beck LA6 ...213 F5
Nether St LA9 ......200 D3
Nether View
Maryport CA15 ......182 F5
Melling LA62 ....168 C1
Netherby Dr CA3 ...175 C4
Netherby Rd CA6 .....10 B3
Netherend Rd CA11 .191 D3
Netherfield CA6 ......11 E1
Netherfield
Hensingham CA28 ...188 A8
Walney Island LA14 .170 C6
Netherhall Sch CA15 .182 E6
Netherleigh Ct LA11 .208 C4
Netherton Inf Sch CA15 .182 E6
Nethertown Rd CA27 ..91 D2
Nethertown Sta CA22 .107 E6
Netherwood Gdns LA11 .208 B5
Neville Ave CA11 ...191 C4
Neville Ct **26** LA12 ..203 D5
Neville St LA12 .....203 D5
Neville Terr 27 LA12 .203 D5
New Acres LA14 ....213 E4
New Barns Cl LA5 ...165 F8
New Barns Rd LA5 ..154 F1
New Bldgs **7** CA11 ..191 C6
New Bridge Rd CA14 .184 D7
New Bridge St CA15 .182 D4
New Church La **7** LA12 .203 C5
New Cl
Eskdale Green CA19 ..124 F7
Newbiggin LA10 .....171 E8
New Cotts LA11 ....154 C3
New Croft CA7 ....180 C3
New England Cvn Pk
LA6 ....167 B2
New Gr LA14 ....206 C1
New La Burton-in-K LA6 .167 B7
Carlisle CA3 ....214 B2
New Leys LA13 .....207 C4
New Lowther St CA28 .186 C1
New Market St 21 LA12 .203 D5
New Midland Cotts
CA17 ....199 A2
New Path DG12 ....172 D5
New Prom CA15 ....182 D8
New Rd Askam-In-F LA16 .162 A7
Askham CA10 ....85 F7
Beck Foot LA10 .....133 A1
Brough CA17 ....107 C7
Burneside LA9 ....50 D2
Cockermouth CA13 ..190 D3
Great Asby CA16 .....103 F5
Kendal LA9 ....200 D5
New Shables **5** LA9 .200 D5
New South Watt St
CA14 ....184 D6
New St Barrow-In-F LA14 .207 B2
Bolton Low Houses CA7 ..37 F3
Broughton-In-F LA20 ..139 A2

New St *continued*
Burneside LA9 130 F2
Carnforth LA5 213 C4
Cockermouth CA13 190 C4
6 Keswick CA12 192 B3
Sedbergh LA10 201 C5
Silloth CA7 174 C3
Whitehaven CA28 186 C1
Wigton CA7 180 D4
New Town CA28 187 C8
New Villas CA14 62 D6
New Yd CA14 184 C4
Newark Terr CA1 214 B3
Newbarns Ct 3 LA13 207 C5
Newbarns Prim Sch LA13 207 C5
Newbarns Rd LA13 207 C3
Newbiebarns DG12 16 C7
Newbiggin LA9 200 C8
Newbiggin Cotts LA19 124 A1
Newbiggin La LA6 156 E2
Newbiggin Rd CA4,CA5 30 C2
Newby Bridge Halt* LA12 141 D1
Newby Ct CA10 86 F4
Newby Terr LA14 207 A6
Newcastle St
6 Barrow-In-F LA13 207 B3
Carlisle CA2 176 E6
Newcastleton Prim Sch TD9 1 B6
Newclose La CA16,CA17 119 F8
Newcroft LA5 213 D8
Newfield Dr CA3 175 D4
Newfield Pk CA3 175 D4
Newington Ave DG12 172 D4
Newington Prim Sch DG12 172 E5
Newington Rd DG12 172 D5
Newlaithes Ave CA2 176 C3
Newlaithes Inf Sch CA2 176 C4
Newlaithes Jun Sch CA2 176 C4
Newland Rd LA12 203 F6
Newlands Ave CA28 187 D4
Newlands Gdns CA14 184 E4
Newlands La CA14 184 E4
Newlands La S CA14 184 D3
Newlands Pk
Dearham CA15 49 A2
Workington CA14 184 F5
Newlands Pl CA11 191 B4
Newlands Rd
Carlisle CA2 177 B3
Cockermouth CA13 190 C3
Crosby Garrett CA17 104 A2
Newlands Rise DG12 172 E5
Newlands Terr 6 CA11 191 C5
Newman RC Sch CA1 214 C3
Newmarket Rd CA1 214 B3
Newport St LA14 206 F6
Newry St LA14 206 E2
Newton Brow LA13 207 D3
Newton Com Prim Sch CA2 176 B5
Newton Cross Rd
Askam-In-F LA13 162 C2
Dalton-In-F LA13 205 D1
Newton Mdws CA11 70 C6
Newton Rd
Barrow-In-F LA13 207 F8
Dalton-In-F LA13,LA15 205 B2
Penrith CA11 70 E5
Newton Rigg Coll CA11 70 E6
Newton Sq DG16 173 D5
Newton St Millom LA18 202 D4
Ulverston LA12 203 E5
Newton Terr LA18 202 B5
Newtown CA26 92 D8
Newtown Cl CA2 176 C6
Newtown Ind Est CA2 176 C7
Newtown Rd CA2 176 C6
Next Ness Cotts LA12 152 D1
Next Ness La LA12 203 F6
Nichol Hill 8 CA11 191 C6
Nicholson Cl LA18 202 B4
Nicholson La CA11 191 D6
Nicholson Pl DG12 172 B3
Nicholson St
Annan DG12 172 B3
Carlisle CA2 177 B4
Niger St LA14 206 D1
Nightingale Ct CA4 30 F5
Nilsson Dr CA14 184 D2
Nine Rigg CA5 29 D1
Nineteen Acre La LA5 166 F6
Niobe St LA14 206 C3
Nittyholm DG14 3 B6
Noble Croft CA7 50 D8
Noble Knott Forest Wlks CA12 80 E7
Noble's Rest LA9 200 C5
Nook La Ambleside LA22 195 D7
Dalston CA5 40 A8
Farleton LA6 156 D4
Underbarrow LA8 143 B7
Nook Lane Cl CA5 40 A8
Nook St Carlisle CA1 177 C6
Frizington CA26 92 D8
Workington CA14 184 F5
Nook The Brampton CA8 179 C5
Carlisle CA3 175 D2
Finsthwaite LA12 141 D2
Great Broughton CA13 63 E6
Irthington CA6 21 E4
Silecroft LA18 149 E4
Wigton CA7 28 A4
Nookdales Cotts LA6 169 F1
Norbeck Pk CA25 188 C7
Norfolk Ct CA2 176 F4
Norfolk Pl CA11 191 B4
Norfolk Rd Carlisle CA2 176 E4
Penrith CA11 191 B5
Norfolk St
Barrow-In-F LA14 207 A6
Carlisle CA2 176 F4
Norfolk Terr CA2 176 F4
Norland Ave LA14 207 B8
Norman St CA1 177 C6
Norman Street Prim Sch CA1 177 C6
North Cl CA13 190 B3
North Cotts LA23 198 D3
North Craig LA23 198 D3
North Cumbria Tech Coll CA1 177 F3
North Dr CA20 108 D4
North End CA16 87 D6
North Gn LA12 162 F7
North Hermitage Sq TD9 1 B6
North Hermitage St TD9 1 B6
North La LA18 150 A2
North Liddle St TD9 1 B6
North Lonsdale Rd LA12 203 F5
North Lonsdale Terr LA12 203 E5
North Park Cotts CA4 30 D2
North Quay CA15 182 C6
North Range The CA10 86 A5
North Rd Ambleside LA22 195 D6
Aspatria CA7 36 C1
Barrow-In-F LA14 206 E3
Bransty CA28 186 D3
Carnforth LA5 213 D4
Egremont CA22 189 D7
Holme LA6 156 B2
Kirkby Stephen CA17 199 C6
North Road Prim Sch LA5 213 C3
North Row
Barrow-In-F LA13 207 E3
Whitehaven CA28 187 B7
North Scale LA14 206 C4
North Shore Rd CA28 186 C2
North Shore St CA14 185 A7
North St Annan DG12 172 C5
Barrow-In-F LA13 207 C2
Carlisle CA2 176 F4
Cleator Moor CA25 188 D7
Maryport CA15 182 D6
Mealsgate CA7 37 C2
North Terr
Bowness-On-W LA23 198 D3
Tebay CA10 118 B2
North View Aspatria CA7 36 C1
Carlisle CA3 175 E1
Crosby CA15 49 B5
Great Asby CA16 103 B3
North Walney Nature Reserve* LA14 161 C3
North Walney Prim Sch LA14 206 B3
North Watt St 4 CA14 184 D6
Northcote St CA14 184 C3
Northern Terr LA5 210 F5
Northfield Ave CA14 185 C8
Northfield Pk DG12 172 D6
Northgate Annan DG12 172 C5
Kendal LA9 200 E6
Northside Prim Sch CA14 184 D8
Northside Rd CA14 184 E7
Northumberland St
Carlisle CA2 214 A1
Workington CA14 184 E5
Northwood Cres CA3 175 E2
Norwood Dr CA13 190 D3
Nuns Ave LA7 209 E3
Nurseries The CA6 20 D1
Nursery Fold LA11 164 E6
Nursery Gdns LA15 205 C5
Nursery Pl Annan DG12 172 C4
Whitehaven CA28 187 F6
Nursery Rd
Beckermet CA21 108 C5
Carlisle CA2 177 B2
Nutberry Pl DG16 173 C2
Nutting Hall La LA7 156 C7
Nutwood Cres LA11 208 E5
Nweton Prim Sch LA13 162 C2

O

Oak Bank Houghton CA3 175 F5
Stainton CA11 70 B4
Oak Cres CA28 186 E4
Oak Dr CA6 21 E5
Oak Head Rd LA14 170 C6
Oak La Carlisle CA1 30 E4
Crosthwaite LA8 142 F6
Oak Lea Rd LA14 204 D5
Oak Pk CA8 179 D4
Oak Rd Barrow-In-F LA14 206 F6
Penrith CA11 191 E5
Oak St LA23 198 E5
Oak Tree Cl CA10 101 C5
Oak Tree Rd LA9 200 F5
Oak Vale LA12 152 D5
Oakbank Kendal LA8 131 A3
Whitehaven CA28 186 D2
Oakbank Ave CA28 186 D3
Oakfield Ct CA28 187 F8
Oakfield Ho CA12 66 E1
Oakland LA23 198 D7
Oakland Ave CA15 182 F4
Oakland Dr LA23 198 D7
Oakland View CA6 20 F5
Oaklands Ambleside LA22 195 C6
Egremont CA22 108 B6
Oaklands Dr CA2 177 B1
Oakleigh Way CA1 177 E5
Oakley Ave CA14 185 D8
Oakmoss LA12 153 B6
Oakroyd Cl LA5 209 B2
Oaks Field LA22 195 D6
Oaks La CA5 28 D7
Oaks The CA22 189 C6
Oakshaw Cl CA3 175 B3
Oakthwaite Rd LA23 198 E4
Oaktree Cres CA13 190 E5
Oakwood LA9 200 B4
Oakwood Cl LA8 143 D1
Oakwood Crest LA12 203 D2
Oakwood Dr
Barrow-In-F LA13 207 F4
Ulverston LA12 203 D2
Oakwrea Bank CA15 49 D6
Oasis Wildlife Ctr* LA7 166 F8
Ocean Rd LA14 170 C6
Oddfellows Terr CA22 189 D7
Old Auction Mart LA6 212 C2
Old Brewery Yd CA8 179 C4
Old Bridge CA22 189 E5
Old Chapel La LA8 143 D1
Old Chapel The CA4 178 B6
Old Church La CA8 22 A4
Old College La LA23 198 E5
Old College Pk LA23 198 D6
Old Farm Cl LA14 207 A8
Old Farmhouse Mews The CA12 80 F6
Old Fire Station The 8 LA9 200 D5
Old Furness Rd LA21 196 A3
Old Graitney Rd DG16 173 B2
Old Hall CA23 188 C3
Old Hall Dr LA12 203 D7
Old Hall Park Cvn Site LA6 167 C1
Old Hall Rd
Troutbeck Bridge LA23 198 C8
Ulverston LA12 203 C7
Old Hall Went 6 CA13 190 D4
Old Harker Cotts CA6 175 B8
Old Hutton CE Sch LA8 144 E3
Old Kells CA28 187 B6
Old Lake Rd LA22 195 D4
Old London Rd CA11 191 D4
Old Lound LA9 200 D3
Old Midland Cotts CA17 199 A2
Old Mill Cres LA23 129 A1
Old Mill Ct DG12 172 B3
Old Moor Gdns LA18 202 B4
Old Myse The LA7 209 F5
Old Nurseries The LA11 208 C2
Old Park La LA14 170 E1
Old Police Station The LA22 197 E5
Old Powleys CA10 71 F8
Old Raffles Par CA2 176 C5
Old Rake LA21 139 F8
Old Rampside Rd LA13 207 E3
Old Rd Crosby CA15 49 B5
Garsdale Head LA10 148 C6
Kendal LA8 131 B5
Levens LA8 155 C8
Longtown CA6 10 C3
Old Roose LA13 207 E4
Old Row Greenhead CA8 24 D7
Sedgwick LA8 144 A2
Old Scotch Rd
Beck Foot LA8 132 D3
Killington LA8 145 C4
Old Town LA6 157 C7
Old Shambles LA9 200 C5
Old Shore Rd CA19 123 D6
Old Smithy Visitor Ctr* DG16 173 D5
Old Tannery The
Kirkby Lonsdale LA6 212 C2
Scotby CA4 30 E6
Old Town Hill LA11 154 A4
Old Woodyard The 15 LA9 200 C5
Oldfield Ct LA23 198 E5
Oldfield Rd LA23 198 E4
Oldham St 8 LA14 207 A3
Olive Cl 7 LA15 205 B4
Oliver Pl Carnforth LA5 213 D4
Newcastleton TD9 1 B6
Onchan View LA14 206 B1
Orcades Gn LA14 170 C6
Orchard Ave LA13 207 B6
Orchard Beck CA8 179 B5
Orchard Cl Bardsea LA12 163 C5
Burgh-By-S CA5 18 F1
Cartmel LA11 153 F1
Long Marton CA16 88 A7
Seaton CA14 183 B2
Sedgwick LA8 144 A2
Silverdale LA5 210 B2
Orchard Garth CA4 30 E1
Orchard Gdns CA3 175 F5
Orchard Gr CA11 70 C6
Orchard La CA3 175 F5
Orchard Paddock CA7 49 C6
Orchard Pl CA25 188 E6
Orchard Rd Arnside LA5 209 B2
Bardsea LA12 163 C5
Wigton CA7 180 E4
Orchard St CA1 214 C1
Orchard The
Bassenthwaite CA12 66 B7
Orchard The *continued*
Grange-Over-S LA11 208 C2
Great Corby CA4 178 C1
Lindale LA11 154 C3
Milnthorpe LA7 211 E4
Orepit Cotts CA22 188 A2
Orest Drive Flats LA23 198 E6
Orfeur St CA1 214 C2
Orgill Prim Sch CA22 189 C6
Oriana Mews LA14 206 C2
Orion Terr LA14 170 C6
Ormsgill La
Barrow-In-F LA14 206 E7
Barrow-In-F LA14 206 F8
Ormsgill Prim Sch LA14 206 F8
Oronsay Gdns LA14 170 C6
Orontes Ave LA14 170 C6
Orrest Dr LA23 198 E5
Orsova Gdns LA14 170 C6
Orton CE Sch CA10 118 C7
Orton Pl CA2 176 B5
Orton Rd Carlisle CA2 176 B5
Tebay CA10 118 B3
Osborne Ave CA2 176 E6
Osborne Pl CA7 49 F7
Osborne St LA14 206 F5
Osprey Dr LA14 206 B1
Osprey Gdns CA28 76 F2
Ostley Bank LA13 207 C6
Ostley Gdns LA14 207 B7
Oswald St CA1 177 C5
Otley Rd CA12 192 B4
Oulton Terr CA8 179 C4
Our Lady of Lourdes RC Prim Sch LA5 213 D3
Our Lady of the Rosary RC Prim Sch LA15 205 D5
Our lady's Chetwynde Sch LA13 207 C7
Out Rigg CA27 91 D2
Outfield Lonning CA7 37 A7
Outgang Rd CA7 36 C1
Oval The
High Cummersdale CA2 176 D1
Whitehaven CA28 187 E3
Overbeck Dr LA13 207 F3
Overburn CA9 181 E3
Overdale Cl LA9 200 B8
Overend Rd
Greysouthen CA13 63 E4
Whitehaven CA28 91 F7
Owlet Ash Fields LA7 211 E4
Oxen Croft LA13 207 C4
Oxenholme Junc LA8 144 C5
Oxenholme La LA9 144 B4
Oxenholme Rd LA9 200 F1
Oxford Cl CA28 187 F5
Oxford Pl 2 LA14 207 B6
Oxford Rd LA14 207 B6
Oxford St
Barrow-In-F LA14 207 A6
Carnforth LA5 213 C3
Millom LA18 202 D4
Ulverston LA12 203 D5
Workington CA14 184 E6
Oxlands LA6 156 B1

P

Pack Horse Ct 5 CA12 192 B3
Pack The CA5 18 F2
Paddle CE Prim Sch CA13 64 B2
Paddock Cl CA7 36 D1
Paddock The
Sedbergh LA10 201 D5
Threlkeld CA12 82 C8
Paddock Way LA7 209 F4
Paddocks The
Great Broughton CA13 63 E6
Thursby CA5 28 F1
Paddy La LA9 144 D7
Page Bank La LA13 171 C6
Palace La LA11,LA12 153 E6
Palmer Rd CA2 176 A7
Palmer's Ct CA23 188 D3
Palmers La LA18 202 B5
Pannatt Hill LA18 202 B5
Parade St LA14 206 F3
Parade The LA5 213 A3
Paradise La LA7 211 E2
Paradise St LA14 207 A3
Parham Dr CA2 176 B6
Parham Gr CA2 176 B6
Park Ave
27 Askam-In-F LA16 162 A8
Barrow-In-F LA13 207 A4
Kendal LA9 200 D3
Seaton CA14 183 B1
Swarthmoor LA12 203 A2
Swarthmoor LA12 203 A3
Windermere LA23 198 E4
Park Brow CA11 83 D3
Park Cl Natland LA9 144 A4
Penrith CA11 191 E5
Scotby CA4 30 E6
Windermere LA23 198 E4
Park Dr Barrow-In-F LA13 207 B4
Stainburn CA14 62 E3
Ulverston LA12 203 E4
Whitehaven CA28 187 D8
Park End Rd CA14 184 F5
Park Field LA12 203 A2
Park Foot Cvn Site CA10 84 F6
Park Garth LA12 162 F4
Park Head Brampton CA8 179 B6
1 Workington CA14 184 D6
Park Holme CA12 192 B5
Park House Animal Farm* LA13 207 E7
Park House Dr LA7 211 D7
Park La Alston CA9 181 C3
Holme LA6 156 B2
Orton CA10 118 B7
Walney Island LA14 206 C2
Workington CA14 184 D6
Park Rd Aspatria CA7 36 D1
Barrow-In-F LA14 204 B3
Bothel CA7 51 A5
Carlisle CA2 176 D4
Grange-Over-S LA11 208 D3
Greystoke CA11 69 E5
Millom LA18 202 D4
Milnthorpe LA7 211 B3
Scotby CA4 30 E6
Silverdale LA5 210 D4
Swarthmoor LA12 203 A2
Wigton CA7 180 B3
Windermere LA23 198 F4
Park Road Est
Barrow-In-F LA14 204 B2
Bothel CA7 51 A5
Park Side LA12 203 A2
Park Side Rd Kendal LA9 200 E3
Kendal LA9 200 F4
Park Sq CA7 180 C3
Park St Ambleside LA22 195 D6
Frizington CA26 92 D7
Kendal LA9 200 D3
Park Terr
Hallbankgate CA8 23 B2
Kirkby Stephen CA17 199 C4
Maryport CA15 182 D6
Silloth CA7 174 C4
Workington CA14 184 F6
Park The Old Hutton LA8 144 E3
Scotby CA4 30 E6
1 Thursby CA5 28 F1
Park View Arnside LA5 209 B1
Bassenthwaite CA12 66 B7
Egremont CA22 189 D6
Great Asby CA16 103 C4
Whitehaven CA28 186 D2
Park View La CA9 181 E3
Park View Sch LA13 207 B5
Parkend La LA8 143 D3
Parker St LA14 206 F4
Parkers Croft CA10 101 C6
Parkett Hill CA4 30 E6
Parkfields Rd CA28 76 F2
Parkhead Rd
Brampton CA8 179 B5
Ulverston LA12 203 D1
Parkhill Rd CA3 175 C5
Parkhouse Rd
Barrow-In-F LA13 207 E7
Carlisle CA3 175 C6
Dalton-In-F LA13 205 B1
Parkin Hill CA16 193 C4
Parkland Ave CA1 30 E4
Parkland Mews CA1 30 E4
Parklands Cres CA11 191 F5
Parklands Dr
Askam-In-F LA16 162 A8
Egremont CA22 189 D5
Parklands The
Cockermouth CA13 190 B3
Penrith CA11 191 F5
Parklands View CA11 191 F5
Parklands Way CA11 191 F5
Parkside Carlisle CA3 175 C2
Crosby CA15 49 B5
Parkside Ave CA13 190 C3
Parkside Bsns Pk LA9 200 E3
Parkside Cl LA12 162 D7
Parkside Dr LA5 209 A1
Parkside Mdw LA9 200 E4
Parkside Rd CA25 92 D6
Parr St LA9 200 D4
Parrock Gn LA14 204 B1
Parrock Mews LA22 194 B4
Parry St LA14 206 F4
Parson's Way LA7 155 F7
Parsonage Fold LA7 155 E2
Parsonby Brow CA7 50 C5
Parton Brow CA28 186 D5
Parton Sta CA28 186 D6
Partridge Pl CA2 176 C5
Pascway Terr LA14 204 B1
Pass Of Dunmail Raise LA22 97 C2
Pasture Houses CA9 60 C8
Pasture La CA7 53 E4
Pasture Rd CA26 77 F1
Pasture The LA7 209 E5
Pasture Wlk CA1 177 F5
Pategill Ct 3 CA11 191 E4
Pategill Farm 2 CA11 191 E4
Pategill Hamlet 4 CA11 191 E4
Pategill Pk CA11 191 E3
Pategill Rd CA11 191 E4
Pategill Sq 9 CA11 191 E4
Pategill Wlk CA11 191 E3
Paternoster Row CA3 214 A2
Patten Garth CA7 49 F8
Patterdale Ave CA28 91 F7
Patterdale CE Sch CA11 98 D7
Patterdale Cl CA28 91 F7
Patterdale Dr LA14 204 D1
Patterdale Rd LA23 198 D8

Pattinson Cl CA10 ....85 F6
Pavilion The CA11 ....70 D3
Paving Brow CA8 ......179 C3
Paxton St LA14 ....206 F3
Pear Tree Gdns CA13 ....63 E6
Pear Tree Pk LA6 .....156 B2
Pear Tree Way CA11 ....71 C5
Pearl Rd CA14 ....184 C1
Pearson Cl CA24 ......188 B5
Pearson Ct CA11 ......191 C3
Pearson La CA16 ....88 B6
Pearson St CA14 ......184 D5
Peart Rd Maryport CA15 .182 D4
   Workington CA14 ....184 C4
Peartree Bank LA13 ....207 E5
Peascod La CA3 ....214 B3
Pease Close La LA11 ...153 F5
Peasholmes La LA13 ...171 C6
Peat La LA9 ....200 F6
Peatfield Rd CA14 ....183 B3
Pecklewell La CA15 ...182 F4
Pecklewell Terr CA15 .182 E4
Peckmill CA27 ....91 C2
Peddar Cotts LA11 ....164 D7
Peel St CA2 ....176 D6
Peel Tower (Clifton Hall)*
   CA10 ....71 C2
Pegbank La LA6 ....168 A8
Peggy Hill LA22 ......195 D6
Peggy Nut Croft CA10 .101 C6
Pelham Dr CA20 ....108 E4
Pembroke Cl LA9 .....200 C2
Pembroke Pl CA11 ....191 C7
Pembroke St CA16 ....193 D6
Penarth St 9 LA14 ...207 A2
Pendle Dr CA28 ......187 D8
Pendragon Castle*
   CA17 ....121 A1
Pennine Cl Lowther CA10 .85 F6
   Silloth CA7 ....174 C4
Pennine Gdns
   Barrow-In-F LA14 ...206 F5
   Carlisle CA1 ......177 E4
Pennine Rd CA16 ......24 C1
Pennine Terr CA10 ....57 E2
Pennine-View
   Appleby-In-W LA6 ..193 C1
   Armathwaite CA4 ....42 C5
   Blencarn CA10 ......73 A6
   Carlisle CA1 ....30 E5
   Silloth CA7 ....174 C4
   Skelton CA11 ....55 B2
   Stainton CA11 ......70 B4
Pennine View Cl CA1 ...30 E5
Pennine Way
   Calthwaite CA11 ....55 E7
   Carlisle CA1 ......177 F4
   Penrith CA11 ......191 E5
Pennine Way Prim Sch
   CA1 ....177 F4
Pennington CE Sch
   LA12 ....162 F8
Pennington Cl LA15 ...205 B2
Pennington Dr CA3 ...175 E3
Pennington La LA12 ...162 E7
Penny Bridge CE Sch
   LA12 ....152 E5
Pennyhill Pk CA11 ....191 B7
Penrith Castle* CA11 ..191 C4
Penrith Hospl CA11 ...191 E3
Penrith Ind Est CA11 .191 B4
Penrith Mus* CA11 ...191 C5
Penrith Pl CA14 ......207 A3
Penrith Rd Keswick CA12 .192 C4
   Keswick CA12 ......192 E4
Penrith St 16 CA14 ...207 A3
Penrith Sta CA11 .....191 C4
Penruddock Prim Sch
   CA11 ....69 D2
Penton Cl CA3 ....175 C3
Penzance St CA24 ....188 A5
Pepper Hall Wlk LA18 .202 A2
Peppercoats Brow CA14 .78 D8
Peppercorn La LA9 ...200 D4
Percy Rd CA2 ....176 E4
Percyrig Cl 3 CA28 ..187 F5
Peter Gate CA4 ....31 A2
Peter La Carlisle CA2 .176 B1
   Yealand Conyers LA5 .166 E5
Peter St Carlisle CA3 .214 B3
   Whitehaven CA28 ...186 D1
   Workington CA14 ...184 E5
Peter's Dr LA18 .....202 B6
Peterfield Rd CA3 ...175 C5
Petrel Bank LA14 ....170 C6
Petteril Bank Rd CA1 .177 D2
Petteril Bank Sch CA1 .177 D1
Petteril Rd CA1 .....191 C6
Petteril St Carlisle CA1 .177 C6
   Silloth CA7 ....174 C4
Petteril Terr
   Carlisle CA1 ......177 D4
   Plumpton CA11 ......56 A3
   Silloth CA7 ....174 C4
Petton Pl CA20 ......109 A2
Pheasants Rise CA26 ..77 F1
Philpin La LA6 ......159 F1
Phoenix Ct LA14 .....206 D5
Phoenix Pk CA11 .....207 A8
Phoenix Rd LA14 ....206 D5
Phoenix Way LA23 ...198 E6
Pica CA14 ....77 C5
Pickles Field LA7 ...211 D4
Piel Castle* LA13 ...171 B2
Piel St LA13 ....171 B3

Piel View Gr LA13 .....207 D3
Pier La LA5 ....209 B2
Pig La LA11 ....208 D4
Pikeingthorne LA19 ...137 B3
Pikestone La CA10 ....118 A3
Pilgrim St CA14 ......184 D5
Pillar Rd CA28 ....187 E4
Pinders La LA6 ....156 B1
Pine Cl
   Grange-Over-S LA11 .208 C3
   Kendal LA9 ....200 F2
Pine Gr CA10 ....57 A6
Pine Lake* LA6 ....213 F7
Pine Rd LA14 ....206 F7
Pinecroft CA3 ....175 D5
Pinetree Rd LA12 ....203 D3
Pinewood Dr CA15 ...182 F5
Pinewoods LA14 ....77 D6
Pinfold Cl CA13 .....190 E4
Pinfold Cvn Site LA10 .201 E4
Pinfold St CA14 .....184 F5
Piper La CA10 ....87 D8
Piper's La
   Burton-in-K LA6 ...167 C8
   Holme LA6 ....156 C1
Pipers Cl LA7 ....209 E4
Pipers Ct 3 CA28 ....186 D1
Pit La Kirkby Lonsdale LA6 .157 C1
   Lindal in F LA12 ..162 D7
Pitcairn Cres CA15 ..182 E4
Pitt Garth LA11 .....153 F1
Pittwood Rd CA14 ...185 F6
Plains Rd CA4 ....178 A3
Plamers Hill LA10 ...201 C5
Plantation Ave LA5 ..210 C8
Plantation Gr LA5 ...210 C8
Plaskett's La CA7 ...180 D4
Players Ct LA11 .....191 C5
Pleasant View CA4 ...178 A2
Pleaslands Lonning CA7 .37 A6
Plimsoll Cl 2 CA11 ..191 C6
Ploughlands La CA14 .104 D4
Plover Cl LA6 ....161 F8
Plumbland CE Sch CA7 ..50 C6
Plumdon Park Ave
   DG12 ....172 D2
Plumpton Sch LA11 ...56 B4
Plymouth St LA14 ...206 C1
Police Court Yd 2
   CA12 ....192 B3
Police Sq LA7 ....211 D4
Pond St LA5 ....213 C4
Pond Terr LA14 .....213 C4
Pool Darkin La LA7 ..211 E1
Poole Cl LA14 ....184 C2
Poole St LA14 ......206 F5
Pooles Cl CA28 .....186 D1
Poolside LA18 ......202 A2
Poplar Bank LA13 ...207 F5
Poplar Gr LA12 .....203 E6
Poplar Pl 1 LA11 ...191 C6
Poplar St LA14 .....192 B3
Poplar Terr LA12 ...105 B2
Popplemire La LA8 ..144 E3
Port Haverigg Holiday Village
   LA18 ....202 A2
Port Rd CA2 ....176 E6
Port Road Ind Est CA2 .176 D7
Port St DG12 ....172 B3
Porter St 9 LA15 ...205 C5
Porthouse Rd CA11 ..191 C3
Portland Cres LA14 .207 B8
Portland Pl Carlisle CA1 .214 B4
   Workington CA14 ...191 C5
Portland Sq Carlisle CA1 .214 C2
   Workington CA14 ...184 F6
Portland Wlk LA14 ..206 F3
Portsmouth St LA14 .206 C1
Post Office Row
   Gleaston LA12 .....162 E1
   Tunstall LA6 ......168 D4
   Westhouse LA6 .....169 E4
Post Office Terr CA8 ..23 E2
Potter Fell Rd
   Bowston LA8 ....130 F4
   Kendal LA8 ....131 A5
Potter's Pl CA2 ....176 E6
Potter's Bank
   Kirkoswald CA10 ...57 B8
   Staffield CA10 ....43 B1
Potters La CA9 ......181 F2
Pottery La CA15 .....49 A2
Pottery Rd CA28 ....187 C7
Pottery St 5 LA14 ..207 B2
Pow Ave CA28 ......187 D7
Pow Beck Ct CA28 ...102 D6
Pow St CA14 ....101 C6
Pow St LA14 ....184 E6
Powdrake Cres CA6 ...10 C4
Powerful St LA14 ...206 C3
Powleys Garth CA10 ..72 A8
Powsy Sike CA4 .....42 F5
Preedy Rd CA4 .....184 D5
Prescott Rd CA2 ...176 E4
Preston Rd LA12 ...172 E6
Preston St
   Barrow-In-F LA14 ...206 F3
   Carnforth LA5 .....213 C4
   Whitehaven CA28 ...187 C8
Prestonfield Rd
   Annan DG12 ....172 D5
   Annan DG12 ....172 E6
Priest Hill Forest Trail*
   TD9 ....1 D7
Priest La Cartmel LA11 .153 F1
   Milburn CA10 ......73 A1
   Temple Sowerby CA10 .72 F1

Priestclose La CA10 ...86 B5
Priests Mill* CA7 ....53 C6
Primrose Bank
   Crosby-On-E CA6 ...20 F2
   1 Holme LA6 ......156 B1
   Wigton CA7 ....180 D1
Primrose Cres CA14 ..185 A8
Prince Ave LA5 .....213 D3
Prince Charles Cl CA11 .191 E4
Prince St LA15 .....205 C5
Prince's Ct CA11 ...177 D2
Prince's Rd LA23 ...198 E4
Prince's St
   Broughton-In-F LA20 .139 A2
   Ulverston LA12 ...203 D5
Prince's Way CA14 ..184 B5
Princes Ave DG12 ...172 D4
Princes Rd CA13 ...190 C3
Princes St
   Cleator Moor CA23 .188 F6
   Penrith CA11 .....191 D4
Princes Way LA7 ...211 D7
Princess Ave CA14 ..62 E4
Princess Dr CA15 ...182 D3
Princess Park Way CA6 .19 E2
Princess St
   5 Barrow-In-F LA14 .207 A6
   Carlisle CA1 .....214 C1
   Workington CA14 ...184 D5
Princewood Dr LA12 .207 F5
Pringle CA7 ....50 C8
Pringle Bank LA5 ...213 C4
Printing House Mus The*
   CA13 ....190 C4
Prior Ave DG14 ......3 D3
Priors Lea LA12 ....207 C4
Priors Path LA13 ...207 C4
Priors Wlk 16 LA16 .162 A8
Priorwood Cl CA2 ...29 D6
Priory Cl CA26 .....92 D8
Priory Cres LA11 ...165 A6
Priory Ct LA12 .....203 E4
Priory Dr CA25 .....188 E6
Priory Gdns LA23 ...198 D7
Priory Grange LA23 .198 D7
Priory La LA6 ......165 A6
Priory Manor LA23 ..198 D7
Priory Rd Carlisle CA2 .176 E6
   St Bees CA27 ......91 C2
   Ulverston LA12 ...203 E2
Priory The CA14 ....78 B8
Proctor's Row CA7 ..180 D3
Proctor's Sq 18 CA7 .180 D3
Promenade
   Bowness-On-W LA23 .198 C2
   Walney Island LA14 .206 C3
   Walney Island LA14 .206 D1
Promenade The
   Arnside LA5 ....209 B2
   Maryport CA15 ....182 D7
Prospect Ave LA14 ..207 B6
Prospect Rd LA13 ...207 B6
Prospect Row CA13 .188 C4
Prospect View CA14 .185 D3
Provincial St LA13 .207 C3
Puddlemire La LA6 ..156 D3
Pugin St CA2 ....176 E4
Pump Sq CA17 ......105 B5
Punton Rd CA3 .....175 E1
Purser Rd CA14 ....185 A8
Pye La LA22 ....194 E4
Pye's Bridge La
   Beetham LA7 ......155 F1
   Holme LA6,LA7 ....156 A2
Pypers Croft LA13 ..207 C4

Q

Quaggs Rd LA8 ......143 D2
Quaker Fold LA12 ...203 C3
Quakers Cl CA10 ....70 D1
Quakers La CA10 ....70 F1
Quality Cnr LA14 ...183 B2
Quantock Gn LA14 ...206 F5
Quarry Brow
   Barrow-In-F LA14 ...207 A8
   Bowness-On-W LA23 .198 C3
Quarry Cl CA17 .....199 C4
Quarry La
   Allithwaite LA11 ..164 F7
   Bolton CA16 ......87 D4
Quarry Rigg LA23 ...198 C3
Quarry St CA7 ....37 C1
Quay St Harrington CA14 .76 E8
   Ulverston LA12 ...203 E5
   Whitehaven CA28 ..186 C1
Quaysiders LA22 ...195 D3
Quebec Ave LA22 ...177 A3
Quebec St LA12 ....203 E5
Queen Elizabeth Gram Sch
   CA11 ....191 C4
Queen Elizabeth Sch
   LA6 ....212 B2
Queen Katherine Sch The
   LA9 ....200 D4
Queen Katherine St
   LA9 ....200 D4
Queen Katherines Ave
   LA9 ....200 D8
Queen St Aspatria CA7 ..50 C8
   Barrow-In-F LA14 ..207 A6
   Carlisle CA2 ......214 B2
   Carnforth LA5 ....213 C4
   Cleator Moor CA25 .188 D7

Queen St continued
   Dalton-In-F LA15 ...205 C5
   5 Kendal LA9 ......200 C4
   Maryport CA15 ....182 D5
   Millom LA18 ......202 D5
   5 Penrith CA11 ...191 D5
   Ulverston LA12 ...203 D5
   Whitehaven CA28 ..186 C1
   Whitehaven CA28 ..187 C8
   Workington CA14 .184 D5
Queen's Ave CA14 ...62 E4
Queen's Dr Carnforth LA5 .213 D3
   Sedbergh LA10 ....201 B4
   Windermere LA23 .198 E4
Queen's Pk LA18 ...202 B5
Queen's Sq
   Bowness-On-W LA23 .198 C2
   Kirkby Lonsdale LA6 .212 C2
   Whitehaven CA28 ..186 C1
Queen's Terr LA6 ..156 B2
Queens Ave CA15 ..182 D3
Queens Cl CA28 .....91 F8
Queens Cres CA26 ..92 D8
Queens Ct 8 LA12 ..203 D5
Queens Dr Arnside LA5 .209 B1
   Carlisle CA3,CA6 ..175 A4
   Egremont CA22 ....189 C4
Queens Pk CA7 ......36 D1
Queens Rd CA14 ...185 C7
Queensberry St LA12 .162 E6
Queensberry St DG12 .172 C4
Queensway Annan DG12 .172 D4
   Whitehaven CA28 ..187 A8
Quillet The LA5 ....210 F3
Quintin Pl DG16 ...173 D5

R

Race Gr LA18 ....150 C7
Rachael's Ct 22 LA12 .203 D5
Raeburn Cres DG16 ..173 C2
Raefield CA6 ....10 C3
Raffles Ave CA2 ...176 C6
Raglan Ct 8 LA14 ..207 B2
Raglan St 7 LA14 ..207 B2
Raglan's Ct CA7 ...174 C4
Railton Gdns CA2 ..176 C6
Railway Cotts
   Crosby Garrett CA17 .120 A8
   Dalston CA5 ......29 D1
   Langwathby CA10 ..72 A8
   Long Marton CA16 ..88 A7
   Newby Bridge LA12 .141 E1
Railway Terr
   Askam-In-F LA16 ...207 B8
   Blennerhasset CA7 ..50 F8
   Cockermouth CA13 .190 D3
   4 Dalton-In-F LA15 .205 C4
   Garsdale Head LA10 .148 D6
   Lindal in F LA12 ..162 E6
   1 Maryport CA15 ..182 E5
   Moor Row CA24 ....188 B6
   Seascale CA20 ....123 A7
Raise Bank CA14 ...181 C3
Raise Hamlets CA9 .181 C3
Raiselands Croft CA11 .191 B7
Raiselands Rd CA2 ..176 C6
Raisthwaite La LA12 .140 B2
Rake La Leece LA12 .171 C7
   Ulverston LA12 ...203 D3
Rake The
   Bassenthwaite CA12 .66 B7
   Penny Bridge LA12 .152 D5
Rakehead Cl LA12 ..203 C3
Rakes La Marton LA15 .162 C7
   Walney Island LA14 .170 D4
Rakesmoor La LA14 ..204 D3
Raleigh St LA14 ....206 F4
Raffland View CA14 .184 B5
Rampkin Pastures CA16 .193 C4
Rampside Rd
   Barrow-In-F LA13 ..207 E2
   Roosebeck LA13 ...171 B7
Ramsay Brow CA14 ..184 E6
Ramsden Dock Rd LA14 .170 D6
Ramsden Inf Sch LA13 .207 A4
Ramsden St
   Barrow-In-F LA14 ..207 A3
   Carnforth LA5 ....213 C4
Ramsey Dr CA28 ....186 E5
Ramsey Pk LA13 ...207 A4
Ramsgate Cres LA14 .207 A4
Randall St CA2 .....214 A1
Ranneydale Cl CA28 .186 E4
Rashdall Rd CA2 ...176 D3
Ratcliffe Pl 17 CA12 .192 B3
Ratherheath La LA12 .130 D2
Ratherheath Lane Camping
   &Cvn Site LA12 ...130 C2
Rating La LA13 .....207 D4
Rattlingate La
   Kirkandrews-on-E CA5 ..19 C1
   Moorhouse CA5 ....29 C8
Raughton Head CE Sch
   CA5 ....29 E4
Ravelands Brow CA16 .104 B5
Raven Garth LA8 ...150 D8
Raven Cl CA14 .....192 A6
Raven Nook LA14 ...177 C5
Raven Pl DG16 ....173 D3
Raven St CA1 ......177 C5
Ravenghyll LA14 ...187 F6
Ravenglass & Eskdale Rly*
   CA19 ....124 C6

Ravenglass Railway Mus*
   CA18 ....123 F3
Ravenglass Rd LA14 .204 D1
Ravenglass Roman Bath Ho*
   CA18 ....123 F2
Ravenglass Sta CA18 .123 F3
Ravenhall Rd CA28 .187 B7
Ravenhill Rd CA28 .187 B7
Ravens Close Brow LA2 .168 F1
Ravenstone Way CA2 .176 A5
Ravenstonedale Endowed
   Sch CA17 ....120 A3
Rawes Garth LA8 ...130 B5
Rawlinson Pl LA15 .205 B5
Rawlinson St
   Barrow-In-F LA14 ..205 B5
Rawthey Gdns LA10 .201 B4
Rayend La LA18 ....149 C4
Raygarth La LA6 ...212 B3
Rayrigg Gdns LA23 .198 E5
Rayrigg Rd LA23 ...198 C3
Rayrigg Rise LA23 .198 C3
Rd CA28 ....186 E3
Rectory Dene CA10 ..86 E7
Rectory Pl CA14 ...185 D4
Rectory Rd
   Bowness-On-W LA23 .198 C1
   Castle Carrock CA8 ..32 D6
Rectory Sq CA14 ...185 D4
Red Bank LA28 ....113 D4
Red Bank Sq CA2 ...177 A4
Red Bank Terr CA2 .177 A4
Red Beck Pk CA25 .188 F6
Red Bridge La LA5 .210 F4
Red Dial Cotts CA7 ..38 B5
Red Gate La LA11 ..154 D4
Red Hills Bsns Pk LA5 .191 A2
Red Hills Rd LA5 ..209 A1
Red La Bardsea LA12 .163 C6
   Ulverston LA12 ...163 C6
Red Ley La LA14 ...206 B5
Red Lion Yd LA22 ..197 C5
Red Lonning CA28 ..91 F8
Red Lonning Ind Est
   CA28 ....186 F1
Red Peth NE49 ....11 A6
Red Pike Cl CA28 ..76 F1
Red River Wlk LA13 .207 D4
Red Tarn Rd LA9 ..200 F1
Red Terr CA7 ....50 F8
Red Wood Dr CA3 ..175 C2
Redding Brow LA11 .164 E7
Redgate La CA17 ...105 C2
Redmayne Ave LA14 .207 B8
Redmayne Cl CA7 ...180 D4
Redmayne Dr LA5 ..213 E4
Redmayne Rd LA17 .199 C6
Redoak Ave LA13 ..207 E4
Redruth Dr LA5 ....213 B3
Redshaw Ave LA13 .207 E4
Redwater Gdns LA13 .207 A4
Reeth Rd CA2 ......176 A5
Redlands Rd LA14 ..184 C4
Reeth Rd CA2 ......176 A5
Regent Ho CA2 ....176 A5
Regent St CA2 .....177 B4
Regent The LA14 ...208 D4
Reiver Pl CA3 ......175 D3
Reservoir Rd LA8 ..145 B5
Reservoir St 1 LA14 .207 A3
Reston Cotts LA8 ..130 A5
Retreat The CA28 ..187 E7
Reynolds Pl LA14 ..206 F6
Rheda Cl CA28 .....92 C7
Rheda Pk CA28 ....92 C7
Rheda Terr CA28 ..92 C7
Rheged Exhibition &
   Discovery Ctr* CA11 .70 E3
Ribble Gdns LA14 ..206 B3
Ribblehead Sta LA6 .160 B3
Ribblehead Viaduct*
   LA6 ....160 A2
Ribton Moor Side CA13 .187 B6
Richard Thornton's CE Prim
   Sch LA6 ....169 B3
Richardson St CA2 .176 A5
Richmond Cl CA14 ..62 E2
Richmond Cres CA27 .91 C2
Richmond Croft CA14 .184 C2
Richmond Gdns LA18 .150 A1
Richmond Gn CA2 ..176 B5
Richmond Hill Rd CA28 .91 F7
Richmond Rd LA14 .184 D2
Richmond St LA18 ..202 D4
Richmond Terr
   Barrow-In-F LA14 ..207 B6
   Ulverston LA12 ...203 D4
   Whitehaven CA28 .187 C8
Rickerby Gdns CA3 ..30 C8
Rickergate LA12 ...203 E4
Rickerby La CA2 ....81 A6
Rickertgate CA12 ..142 D7
Rickettrae LA8 .....142 D7
Riddings La LA12 ..162 F1
Ridge The DG12 ....17 D8
Ridgemount Rd CA14 .177 D2
Ridgevale Terr LA18 .179 C5
Ridgeway LA11 .....164 F7
Ridley Pl CA2 ......177 A3
Ridley Rd CA2 .....176 A5
Rifle Terr CA21 ....105 C5
Rigg St CA2 ....176 E6
Riggs Cl LA11 .....208 E5
Riggside CA11 .....191 E4
Rigmaden Ct LA6 ...157 E8

Rigney Bank LA7 . . . . .211 D3
Rimington Way CA11 . . . . .191 F4
Rinkfield LA9 . . . . .200 D2
Rise The CA28 . . . . .187 C7
Risedale Fold LA11 . . . . . .208 B2
Risedale Rd LA13 . . . . . . .207 B3
Risehow Ind Est LA15 . . . .182 B1
Risingside LA13 . . . . .207 C5
Ritson CI CA3 . . . . .175 D4
Ritson Row CA7 . . . . .49 C6
Ritson St CA14 . . . . .184 E5
Ritson Wharf CA15 . . . . . .182 C5
Ritz Sh Ctr CA14 . . . . .184 E6
River Bank Rd LA9 . . . . . .200 C1
River Pk DG12 . . . . .172 B4
River St CA1 . . . . .177 C6
River View Stainburn CA14 .62 E4
Carlisle CA2 . . . . .176 F3
Riverbank Ct CA3 . . . . . . .175 B1
Riverdale Ct LA9 . . . . .200 E2
Riverdale Dr CA13 . . . . . .190 D2
Riverside Caldbeck CA7 . . .53 C6
Dalston CA5 . . . . .40 B8
Great Clifton CA14 . . . . . . .63 A4
Kirkby Stephen CA17 . . . . .199 D6
Riverside Cotts
Ambleside LA22 . . . . .195 C4
Skelwith Bridge LA22 . . . .113 E2
Riverside Ct CA12 . . . . . . .192 A4
Riverside Dr CA22 . . . . . .189 E8
Riverside Flats CA12 . . . .192 B4
Riverside Gdns LA13 . . . .207 D3
Riverside Pk CA4 . . . . .3 D3
Riverside Terr 2 CA14 . . .190 C4
Riverside View CA16 . . . .103 B4
Riverside Way CA1 . . . . . .177 D6
Roa Island Rd LA13 . . . . .171 B4
Roachburn Cotts CA 23 E2
Roadend DG14 . . . . .4 A5
Roanhead La LA14 . . . . . .207 A8
Roanlands Brow LA18 . . . .150 D8
Robby Lea Dr LA9 . . . . . . .144 B4
Robert Chance Gdns
CA2 . . . . .176 C3
Robert Ferguson Prim Sch
CA2 . . . . .176 C3
Robert Owen Ave CA25 . . .188 F6
Robert Owen Pl CA25 . . . .188 F6
Robert St
Barrow-In-F LA14 . . . . . . .207 A3
Carlisle CA1 . . . . .214 B1
Robertlands La LA10 . . . . .58 A7
Roberts Ct LA5 . . . . .213 C8
Robin Croft LA2 . . . . .168 A1
Robin La Burton in L LA2 .169 D1
Troutbeck LA23 . . . . .114 E1
Robins Wood CA3 . . . . . . .175 E2
Robinson Ave CA2 . . . . . .177 B3
Robinson Pl LA23 . . . . . . .198 D2
Robinson Row LA18 . . . . .202 B5
Robinson St Carlisle CA2 .177 B4
3 Penrith CA11 . . . . .191 C6
Workington CA14 . . . . . . .184 D5
Robinson's Terr CA15 . . . .182 F4
Robraine LA6 . . . . .212 C1
Rochester Pl 4 LA13 . . . .207 C3
Rock Terr LA5 . . . . .209 B2
Rock View LA9 . . . . .200 C4
Rockcliffe CE Sch CA6 . . .19 C4
Rockery Terr LA11 . . . . . . .208 C4
Rockland Rd LA11 . . . . . . .208 C4
Rockwell Gdns LA11 . . . . .208 C5
Roding La LA14 . . . . .206 B3
Rodney St LA14 . . . . .206 D6
Roger Row LA9 . . . . .130 F2
Rogerfield LA12 . . . . .192 C2
Roman Rd LA11 . . . . .191 E5
Roman Way 3 CA3 . . . . . .175 E1
Romanby Cl CA3 . . . . .175 E1
Romany Way CA16 . . . . . .193 C7
Rome St CA2 . . . . .214 B1
Romely Pl CA13 . . . . .190 C3
Romney Rd
Dalton-In-F LA15 . . . . . . .205 A5
Kendal LA9 . . . . .200 D2
Romney Ct LA9 . . . . .200 D2
Romney Gdns LA9 . . . . . .200 D3
Romney Grange LA22 . . . .195 B4
Romney Pk LA15 . . . . .205 A5
Romney Rd
Barrow-In-F LA14 . . . . . . .206 F6
Dalton-In-F LA15 . . . . . . .205 C4
Kendal LA9 . . . . .200 D3
Roods Ct CA10 . . . . .57 B8
Roods Dr CA10 . . . . .57 B8
Roods Pl CA10 . . . . .57 B8
Roods The LA5 . . . . .213 D8
Roose Cotts LA13 . . . . . . .207 E3
Roose Farm La LA13 . . . .207 E3
Roose Prim Sch LA13 . . . .207 E3
Roose Rd LA13 . . . . .207 D3
Roose Sta LA13 . . . . .207 E3
Roosecote Terr LA13 . . . .207 E3
Roper St
Cleator Moor CA23 . . . . . .188 F5
Maryport CA15 . . . . .182 C4
Penrith CA11 . . . . .191 D4
Whitehaven CA28 . . . . . . .186 C1
Workington CA14 . . . . . . .184 E6
Roper Terr CA14 . . . . .185 A8
Ropery St LA15 . . . . .182 C4
Rose Acre La LA5 . . . . . . .166 F5
Rose Cswy CA5 . . . . .40 B5
Rose Ct LA9 . . . . .200 C4
Rose Gate CA4 . . . . .30 F7
Rose Gdns CA14 . . . . .77 D5

Rose Hill Gilsland CA8 . . . .14 D1
Harrington CA14 . . . . .76 E8
Rose Hill Gr LA7 . . . . .209 F6
Rose La CA14 . . . . .190 E2
Rose Paddock CA8 . . . . . . .31 E6
Rose St Annan DG12 . . . . .172 D4
Carlisle CA2 . . . . .177 B4
Rose Terr CA2 . . . . .192 C4
Rosebank
Hensingham CA28 . . . . . . .187 F6
Stainton CA11 . . . . .70 D3
Rosebank Ct CA4 . . . . . . .178 D7
Rosebank Cotts CA5 . . . . .40 A5
Rosebank Ct DG16 . . . . . .173 D4
Roseberry Rd CA14 . . . . .184 E5
Rosebery Rd CA3 . . . . . . .175 D1
Rosehill CA8 . . . . .14 D1
Rosehill Dr CA2 . . . . .176 D3
Rosehill Ind Est LA7 . . . . .177 F6
Rosemary La CA28 . . . . . .186 F3
Rosemary La
Carlisle CA2 . . . . .214 B3
Great Clifton CA14 . . . . . . .63 B4
4 Kendal LA9 . . . . .200 C5
Whitehaven CA28 . . . . . . .186 C1
Workington CA14 . . . . . . .184 F5
Rosemede Ave LA9 . . . . . .200 D7
Rosemount Cres DG12 . . .172 E5
Rosetrees La CA6 . . . . .9 E2
Rosevale CA2 . . . . .177 F4
Rosevine Terr DG12 . . . . .172 C1
Rosley CE Sch CA7 . . . . . .39 B6
Rosmomond Ct DG16 . . . .173 D2
Ross View CA28 . . . . .186 E6
Rosse Field LA13 . . . . . . .207 D3
Rosside LA12 . . . . .203 A6
Rothay Rd LA22 . . . . .195 C5
Rothay Holme Ind Est
LA22 . . . . .195 C5
Rother Gn LA14 . . . . .206 B4
Rothesay St LA14 . . . . . . .206 F1
Rottington Gn LA18 . . . . .202 D4
Rottington Rd
Millom LA18 . . . . .202 D4
Sandwith CA28 . . . . .187 A1
Round Cl 3 CA28 . . . . . . .76 E7
Round Close Pk CA28 . . . .76 F2
Row Brow Pk CA15 . . . . . . .49 B3
Row La LA8 . . . . .143 A4
Row Rd LA8 . . . . .143 A4
Row The Silverdale LA5 . . .210 E3
Spark Bridge LA12 . . . . . .152 D7
Rowan Ave LA12 . . . . . . .203 D3
Rowan Cl CA14 . . . . .184 E3
Rowan Ct CA11 . . . . .191 E5
Rowan Dr LA13 . . . . .207 E4
Rowan Garth LA6 . . . . . . .212 C2
Rowan Side LA11 . . . . . . .208 B2
Rowan Tree Cres LA9 . . . .144 F3
Rowanburn DG14 . . . . .3 E3
Rowcliffe La 28 CA11 . . . .191 D5
Rowe Head Farm LA2 . . . .162 F8
Rowe Terr CA14 . . . . .184 C3
Rowell La LA7 . . . . .156 A5
Rowgate CA17 . . . . .199 C4
Rowntree Cres 6 CA28 . . .76 F1
Royal Arc CA17 . . . . .199 D6
Royal Dr CA22 . . . . .189 D4
Rubbybanks Rd CA13 . . . .190 D3
Ruby Rd CA14 . . . . .184 D1
Rudchester Cl CA2 . . . . . .176 A6
Rudds Ct 18 CA28 . . . . . . .186 C1
Rueberry Dr CA20 . . . . . . .123 B7
Rufford Dr LA11 . . . . .208 C4
Rufus Ho CA3 . . . . .214 A3
Rufus La LA12 . . . . .203 A3
Rupert St LA5 . . . . .213 C5
Ruskin Ave
Coniston LA21 . . . . .196 A4
Dalton-In-F LA15 . . . . . . .205 B3
Ruskin Cl
High Harrington CA14 . . . .185 D8
Kendal LA9 . . . . .200 E2
Millom LA18 . . . . .202 B4
Ruskin Dr
Kirkby Lonsdale LA6 . . . . .212 C2
Workington CA14 . . . . . . .184 F4
Ruskin Mus* LA21 . . . . . .196 A4
Ruskin Pl CA25 . . . . .188 B8
Ruskin Terr 14 LA14 . . . .207 B2
Rusland Ave LA14 . . . . . . .207 A7
Rusland Cres LA12 . . . . . .203 C2
Rusland Dr LA15 . . . . .205 C4
Rusland Pk LA9 . . . . .200 F5
Russell Rd LA5 . . . . .213 D3
Ruth Lancaster James
Cottage Hospl GY9 . . . . .181 D3
Ruthella St LA7 . . . . .176 D7
Rutland Ave CA28 . . . . . . .187 F4
Rutland St LA14 . . . . .206 F1
Rutter Force* CA16 . . . . .103 C6
Rydal Ave
Barrow-In-F LA14 . . . . . . .204 D1
Maryport CA15 . . . . .182 E5
Whitehaven CA28 . . . . .76 D8
Rydal Cl Dalton-In-F LA15 .205 B4
Millom LA18 . . . . .202 C4
Wigton CA7 . . . . .180 A3
Rydal Cres CA11 . . . . .191 D3
Rydal Ct CA11 . . . . .191 D3
Rydal Dr CA13 . . . . .190 C3
Rydal Mount*
Ambleside LA22 . . . . .114 A5
Kendal LA9 . . . . .200 C6

Rydal Pl CA1 . . . . .214 C1
Rydal Rd Ambleside LA22 .195 C6
Kendal LA9 . . . . .200 F6
Ulverston LA12 . . . . .203 E4
Rydal St Carlisle CA1 . . . .214 C1
Frizington CA26 . . . . .92 D8
Workington CA14 . . . . . . .184 D6
Rye Cl CA2 . . . . .30 B3
Rye Hill Cres CA15 . . . . . .183 C8
Ryehill Pk CA6 . . . . .19 C8
Ryehill Rd CA15 . . . . .183 C8
Ryehills Rd CA7 . . . . .174 E8
Ryley Field Rd LA7 . . . . . .211 D4

S

Sacred Heart RC Prim Sch
CA14 . . . . .207 B2
Saddleback View CA12 . . .82 C7
Saddler Nook La LA6 . . . .168 C8
St Aidan's Sch
Specialist Sports Coll
CA1 . . . . .214 C2
St Aidan's Rd CA1 . . . . . . .177 C7
St Albans Row CA3 . . . . . .214 B2
St Andrew's Churchyard 16
CA11 . . . . .191 D5
St Andrew's Rd DG16 . . . .173 C2
St Andrew's Pl 17
CA11 . . . . .191 D5
St Andrew's St 5 LA14 . . .206 F1
St Andrew's View 14
CA11 . . . . .191 D5
St Andrews Cl CA1 . . . . . .177 E6
St Andrews Rd CA14 . . . . .62 F3
St Ann's Cres CA3 . . . . . .175 C2
St Ann's St CA3 . . . . .175 B1
St Ann's Rd CA3 . . . . .175 B1
St Anne's Cl LA22 . . . . . . .195 C6
St Anne's Hospl CA16 . . .193 C5
St Anne's Sch LA23 . . . . .129 B7
St Annes St 3 CA3 . . . . . .175 B1
St Anthony's Cl LA7 . . . . .211 D4
St Anthony's Hill LA7 . . . .211 D4
St Augusta View CA3 . . . .175 B1
St Austell Pl LA5 . . . . .213 B2
St Bede's RC Prim Sch
CA2 . . . . .176 D5
St Bee's Sta CA27 . . . . . . .91 D2
St Bees Rd CA13 . . . . . . .187 D3
St Bees Sch CA27 . . . . . . .91 D3
St Bees Sch (Abbots Ct)
CA27 . . . . .91 C3
St Bees Vill Prim Sch
CA27 . . . . .91 D2
St Bega's CE Prim Sch
CA19 . . . . .124 E7
St Begh's RC Jun Sch
CA28 . . . . .187 D8
St Benedict's RC High Sch
CA2 . . . . .91 F8
St Bernard's RC Prim Sch
CA14 . . . . .207 D7
St Bridget's CE Sch
Broughton Cross CA13 . . .63 E5
Parton CA28 . . . . .186 D5
St Bridget's La CA22 . . . .189 D6
St Bridget's Sch CA22 . . .189 D6

St Catherin's Ct 11
CA1 . . . . .191 C6
St Catherin's RC Prim Sch
CA11 . . . . .191 C6
St Columba's RC Sch
CA14 . . . . .206 C2
St Columba's RC Sch
DG12 . . . . .172 E4
St Cuthbert's La CA3 . . . .214 B2
St Cuthbert's RC Prim Sch
CA7 . . . . .180 D4
St Cuthbert's RC Prim Sch
LA23 . . . . .198 A4
St David's Rd LA12 . . . . . .203 D6
St Edmunds Pk CA2 . . . . .176 A4
St Francis Gdns LA14 . . . .206 F7
St Gabrel's Ct CA1 . . . . . .214 C3
St George's CE Sch
CA14 . . . . .207 A2
St George's Cres CA3 . . . .214 A4
St George's Rd LA18 . . . .202 C5
St George's Sq 8 LA14 . . .207 A2
St George's Terr
Millom LA18 . . . . .202 C5
Whitehaven CA28 . . . . . . .186 D2
St George's Wlk LA9 . . . .200 C5
St Gregory's & St Patrick's RC
Inf Sch CA28 . . . . .187 E6
St Gregory's RC Prim Sch
CA14 . . . . .184 E3
St Helen's LA14,LA15 . . .204 F6
St Helen's Bsns Pk
CA14 . . . . .62 C5
St Helens Ave CA3 . . . . . .183 C8
St Helens Cl LA15 . . . . . .190 E4
St Helens Rd LA15 . . . . . .183 A6
St Helens St CA15 . . . . . .190 E4
St Herbert St CA12 . . . . . .192 C3
St James RC Prim Sch
LA18 . . . . .202 D5
St James' Ave CA2 . . . . . .176 E5
St James' CE Inf Sch
CA28 . . . . .186 D1

St James' CE Jun Sch
CA28 . . . . .186 D1
St James' Rd CA2 . . . . . . .176 E5
St James's CE Jun Sch
LA14 . . . . .206 E4
St James's Ct 2 CA28 . . .186 D1
St James's Dr LA6 . . . . . .167 B7
St John's Arc CA14 . . . . . .184 E6
St John's Ave LA5 . . . . . . .210 C3
St John's Ct Carlisle CA2 .177 B2
Cleator Moor CA25 . . . . . .188 D7
St John's Cres CA11 . . . . .70 D3
St John's Ct
Carlisle CA1 . . . . .214 C1
Stainton CA11 . . . . .70 D3
St John's Ct
Whitehaven CA28 . . . . . . .187 F6
Workington CA14 . . . . . . .184 E6
St John's Rd
Annan DG12 . . . . .172 C3
Stainton CA11 . . . . .70 D3
Thornhill CA22 . . . . .189 E2
St John's St CA12 . . . . . . .192 B3
St John's Terr CA24 . . . . . .94 F3
St John's View LA11 . . . . .208 C4
St Johns Cl CA14 . . . . .31 B1
St Joseph's RC High Sch
CA14 . . . . .184 E5
St Joseph's RC Prim Sch
Cockermouth CA13 . . . . . .190 C3
Frizington CA26 . . . . .92 D8
St Josephs Ct CA1 . . . . . .177 E6
St Kentigern's CE Prim Sch
CA12 . . . . .144 B4
St Kentigerns Cl CA12 . . .192 A5
St Kentigerns Ct CA7 . . . .50 C8
St Kentigerns Way CA7 . .50 C8
St Leonard's St LA13 . . . .190 C4
St Leonard's La CA13 . . . .190 C3
St Luke's Ave LA13 . . . . . .207 C2
St Luke's St LA13 . . . . . . .150 A1
St Luke's St LA13 . . . . . . .207 C3
St Margaret Mary RC Prim
Sch CA2 . . . . .177 B2
St Mark's CE Prim Sch
LA9 . . . . .144 B4
St Marks Fold LA9 . . . . . .144 B3
St Martin's Cl CA3 . . . . . .179 B4
St Martin's Coll
Ambleside LA22 . . . . .195 D6
Carlisle CA1 . . . . .214 C2
St Martin's Dr CA3 . . . . . .179 B4
St Martin's Pl CA3 . . . . . .179 B4
St Martin's Pl LA23 . . . . . .198 C2
St Martins Ct LA21 . . . . . .196 A4
St Mary's CE Inf Sch
LA23 . . . . .198 E4
St Mary's Ct CA14 . . . . . .206 D8
St Mary's Garth LA12 . . . .162 F5
St Mary's Gate CA12 . . . .214 A2
St Mary's Gn LA8 . . . . . . .142 F6
St Mary's La LA12 . . . . . .162 F5
St Mary's Mews 8
LA12 . . . . .203 D6
St Mary's Pk LA23 . . . . . .198 D6
St Mary's RC Prim Sch
CA14 . . . . .185 A8
St Mary's Rd CA28 . . . . . .187 B6
St Mary's Rd LA13 . . . . . .207 D5
St Marys CE Prim Sch
LA6 . . . . .212 B2
St Matthew's CE Sch
CA3 . . . . .36 B3
St Mattthew's Mews 3
LA14 . . . . .207 A6
St Mellion Cl 2 CA3 . . . . .175 B1
St Michael's CE Prim Sch
CA7 . . . . .51 A6
St Michael's Cl 3
CA14 . . . . .184 D6
St Michael's Inf Sch
CA14 . . . . .184 D6
St Michael's Rd CA14 . . . .184 D6
St Michaels La CA16 . . . . .193 D5
St Michaels Rd CA15 . . . .181 D5
St Monica's Prep Sch Ltd
CA3 . . . . .175 C1
St Mungo's Pk CA7 . . . . . .36 C1
St Nicholas Ave CA15 . . .183 C8
St Nicholas Bridges
CA2 . . . . .177 B4
St Nicholas Gate Trad Est
CA1 . . . . .214 C1
St Nicholas St CA1 . . . . . .214 C1
St Ninian's Ave CA2 . . . . .177 C1
St Ninian's Rd CA2 . . . . . .177 C2
St Oswald's View LA9 . . . .130 F2
St Oswalds Dr CA28 . . . . .76 D8
St Patrick's CE Sch
LA8 . . . . .156 D8
St Patrick's RC Prim Sch
CA25 . . . . .188 E5
St Patrick's CE Sch
CA15 . . . . .182 C4
St Patrick's Rd LA14 . . . . .206 E6
St Patricks RC Sch
CA14 . . . . .184 E7
St Paul's Ave CA26 . . . . . .92 D7

Rig – Sav 233

St Paul's Ave CA14 . . . . . .183 B2
St Paul's CE Jun Sch
LA14 . . . . .207 B7
St Paul's Sq CA1 . . . . .214 B2
St Pauls Pl 3 LA14 . . . . . .207 B6
St Peters Cl CA3 . . . . .175 D4
St Peters Dr CA3 . . . . .175 D4
St Pierre Ave CA3 . . . . . . .175 B1
St Pius X RC Prim Sch
CA14 . . . . .206 E7
St Quintin Ave LA13 . . . . .207 C5
St Stephen's St CA2 . . . . .214 B1
St Thomas's CE Prim Sch
CA2 . . . . .189 F5
St Thomas's Cross
CA2 . . . . .189 F5
St Ursula's Convent High
Sch CA7 . . . . .180 D4
St Vincent St 9 LA14 . . . .206 F3
Salisbury Cl CA14 . . . . . . .184 C3
Salisbury Pl 5 LA23 . . . . .198 E5
Salisbury Rd CA2 . . . . . . .177 B4
Salisbury St CA14 . . . . . . .184 C3
Salkeld Rd
Great Salkeld CA11 . . . . . .57 A3
Langwathby CA10 . . . . . . .71 F8
Penrith CA11 . . . . .191 D8
Plumpton CA11 . . . . .56 F2
Sally Scot's Cnr CA5 . . . . .28 F1
Salmoor Way CA15 . . . . .182 E5
Salt Marsh Cvn Pk LA14 .170 C5
Salt Pie La LA6 . . . . .212 C2
Salter Lonning CA7 . . . . . .54 A4
Salterbeck Dr CA14 . . . . .185 A8
Salterbeck Rd CA14 . . . . .184 C1
Salterbeck Terr CA14 . . . .184 B1
Salterbeck Trad Est
CA14 . . . . .184 D1
Salthouse Gdns LA13 . . . .207 D3
Salthouse Mills Bsns Ctr
LA13 . . . . .207 D3
Salthouse Rd
Barrow-In-F LA13 . . . . . . .207 C2
Barrow-In-F LA14 . . . . . . .207 B2
Millom LA18 . . . . .202 C6
Saltom Rd CA28 . . . . .187 B7
Saltpie La CA10 . . . . .113 B6
Sampool La LA8 . . . . .155 D7
Samuel King's Sch
CA9 . . . . .181 D3
Sand Croft CA11 . . . . .191 D6
Sand La Flimby CA15 . . . .183 C8
Warton LA5 . . . . .213 B6
Sandalwood Ct LA13 . . . .207 F4
Sanderling La LA15 . . . . .205 C4
Sanderson Cl CA3 . . . . . . .175 C4
Sanderson Pk CA25 . . . . .188 D8
Sandersons Croft CA10 . . .87 E8
Sandes Ave LA9 . . . . .200 C6
Sandes' Hospital Cotts 12
LA9 . . . . .200 C5
Sandford Fold CA16 . . . . .104 B7
Sandgate Kendal LA9 . . . .200 E6
11 Penrith CA11 . . . . . . .191 D5
Sandgate Ct
Long Marton CA16 . . . . . . .88 A7
6 Penrith CA11 . . . . .191 D5
Sandgate Sch LA9 . . . . . .200 E6
Sandhall LA13 . . . . .163 D8
Sandhall Cotts LA12 . . . . .163 D7
Sandham La LA14 . . . . . . .150 A1
Sandhills Cl 6 CA28 . . . . .186 C1
Sandhills La 5 CA28 . . . . .186 D1
Sandhurst Dr CA28 . . . . . .187 F8
Sandpiper Cl 34 LA16 . . .162 A8
Sandringham Ave LA14 . .207 A6
Sandringham Cl LA14 . . . .207 A6
Sandi Cl LA12 . . . . .203 D2
Sands Cotts LA9 . . . . .179 C5
Sands Rd LA12 . . . . .203 E2
Sands The CA16 . . . . .193 D5
Sandscale Cotts LA14 . . . .204 B8
Sandscale Haws Nature
Reserve* LA14 . . . . .161 C6
Sandscale Terr LA14 . . . .204 B1
Sandsfield Rd CA2 . . . . . . .29 D6
Sandside LA12 . . . . .163 D8
Sandside Lodge Sch
LA12 . . . . .163 D8
Sandside Rd LA5,LA7 . . .209 D3
Sandy Gap La LA14 . . . . . .206 B1
Sandy Gr CA2 . . . . .189 D6
Sandy La
22 Askam-In-F LA16 . . . .162 A8
Broadwath CA8 . . . . .178 D3
Great Corby CA4 . . . . .178 D2
Shap CA10 . . . . .101 C6
Sandy Lonning CA15 . . . .182 C4
Sandylands La LA13 . . . . .207 C6
Sandylands Rd LA9 . . . . .200 E6
Santon CA13 . . . . .124 A8
Santon Way CA20 . . . . . . .123 B8
Sark Cl CA3 . . . . .175 C4
Sarkfoot Cl DG16 . . . . . . .173 D3
Sarkfoot Rd DG16 . . . . . . .173 D3
Sarkside DG16 . . . . .173 D5
Sarsfield Rd LA14 . . . . . . .184 C2
Satterthwaite & Rusland CE
Sch LA12 . . . . .141 A6
Sattery La LA11 . . . . .140 B8
Saul's Dr LA5 . . . . .210 A8
Saunders Ct LA14 . . . . . .206 A4
Savenoaks Terr CA7 . . . . .180 B5
Saves La LA16 . . . . .162 A8

Savinhill Rd Levens LA8 ..143 A4
Levens LA8 ....143 B3
Savoy Gdns LA12 ....203 C2
Sawmill Cl LA9 ....200 F5
Sawmill La
Brampton CA8 ....179 C5
Kendal LA9 ....200 E5
Sawrey Ct LA20 ....139 A2
Sayle La CA16 ....103 B3
Scafell Cl
Cockermouth CA13 ....190 F4
Whitehaven CA28 ....187 E6
Scafell Dr LA9 ....200 F5
Scale Force* CA13 ....94 D8
Scale Hill CA2 ....176 C2
Scale Villas CA20 ....123 A8
Scalebarrow CA27,CA22 ...97 F3
Scalebeck Ct CA14 ....184 E5
Scaleber La LA6 ....212 D8
Scaleby Cl CA2 ....177 B2
Scalegate Rd CA2 ....177 B2
Scalegill Pl CA24 ....91 F5
Scalegill Rd CA24 ....188 A5
Scales Cl LA15 ....205 B2
Scales View LA18 ....202 A5
Scalesceugh Gdns CA4 ...41 C8
Scar House La LA22 ......197 F6
Scar View Rd LA9 ....144 B4
Scarbarrow La LA21 .....171 C8
Scarrows La CA10 ....57 A7
Scarth Rd LA14 ....204 C3
Scattergate CA16 ....193 C4
Scattergate Cl CA16 ....193 C4
Scattergate Cres CA16 ..193 C4
Scattergate Gn CA16 ....193 C4
Scaur Cl CA10 ....57 A6
Scaur La CA10 ....57 A6
Scaur Terr CA10 ....118 B3
Scaur The CA6 ....10 B3
Scaurbank Rd CA3 ....175 B1
Scaurbank Terr **5** CA3 .175 B1
Scaw Rd LA14 ....185 D8
Scawfell Ave CA14 ....184 E4
Scawfell Cres CA20 .....123 B8
Scawfell Rd CA2 ....176 E5
Scawfield CA14 ....185 C8
Scaws Dr CA11 ....191 E6
Schneider Rd LA14 ......206 F7
Schneider Sq **11** LA14 ..206 F3
Scholars Gn CA7 ....180 E2
School Brow
Appleby-In-W CA16 ....193 D6
Brigham CA13 ....63 F5
Moresby Parks CA28 ......76 F2
School Cl
Broughton Moor CA15 ....63 C8
Maryport CA15 ....182 D4
School Dr CA15 ....182 A1
School Hill LA11 ....154 C3
School Hos LA7 ....156 C6
School Knott Cl LA23 ...198 F4
School Knott Dr LA23 ...198 F4
School La Bothel CA7 ....51 A6
Kirkby Stephen CA17 ....120 C6
Rockcliffe CA6 ....19 C4
Silloth CA7 ....174 C5
Staveley LA8 ....130 B5
School Rd Carlisle CA1 ..177 E3
2 Thursby CA5 ....28 F1
School St
2B Askam-In-F LA16 ...162 A8
1C Barrow-In-F LA14 ...207 A3
Carlisle CA1 ....177 C5
Moor Row CA24 ....188 A5
School Terr
Lindal in F LA12 ....162 D7
Parton CA28 ....186 D6
Schoolhouse Ct **8**
CA28 ....186 D1
Schoolhouse La **9**
CA28 ....186 C1
Schoolhouse The **8**
CA12 ....192 A4
Schooner St LA14 ....206 F1
Scot Brow LA23 ....114 F2
Scotby Cl St CA4 ....30 E6
Scotby Gdns CA1 ....177 E5
Scotby Green Steading
CA4 ....30 F6
Scotby Rd (Ho Pq) CA4 ..30 E6
Scotby Rd CA4 ....30 F6
Scotch Jeans LA10 ......145 E6
Scotch St Carlisle CA3 ..214 B3
Port Carlisle CA7 ....17 D5
Whitehaven CA28 ....187 C8
Scotgate Cvn Pk CA12 ...80 F6
Scotland Rd Carlisle CA3 .175 D2
Carnforth LA5 ....213 D5
Penrith CA11 ....191 C6
Scotraby Brow CA7 ......36 C4
Scots Croft CA14 ....63 C4
Scott St Barrow-In-F LA14 .206 F3
Newcastleton TD9 ....1 B6
Scott's St DG12 ....172 D3
Screel View CA28 ....186 D5
Scroggie Mdw DG12 .....172 C2
Scroggs Cl LA18 ....202 A5
Scroggs La LA9 ....200 C1
Scurgill Terr CA22 ......189 F4
Sea La CA22 ....107 E7
Sea Mill La CA22 ....91 D2
Sea View Haverigg LA18 .202 A2
Millom LA18 ....202 B5
Prospect CA7 ....49 F7

Sea View continued
7 Ulverston LA12 ....203 D8
Workington CA14 ....184 C7
Sea View La CA4 ....188 E6
Sea View Rd CA28 ....186 D2
Sea View Terr CA27 .....91 D2
Seacote Cvn Pk CA7 ....174 E7
Seacroft Dr CA27 ....91 D2
Seadown Dr CA14 ....185 D8
Seafield Rd DG12 ....172 F2
Seaforth Ave DG12 ......172 D3
Seaforth Pk DG12 ......172 D3
Seaford La
Hutton Roof LA6 ....157 A2
Lupton LA6 ....156 F2
Seams The **16** CA12 ....192 B3
Seascale Pk CA20 ......123 B8
Seascale Prim Sch
CA20 ....123 B8
Seascale Sta CA20 .....123 A8
Seat Hill LA10 ....57 A6
Seathwaite Ave CA28 ...187 D4
Seathwaite Cl LA18 ....202 C7
Seathwaite La LA12 ....195 E6
Seathwaite Rd LA14 ....204 D1
Seatle La LA11 ....153 E6
Seatoller Cl CA2 ....176 C3
Seaton CE Jun Sch
CA14 ....183 A1
Seaton Inf Sch CA14 ...183 A2
Seaton Pk CA14 ....183 A1
Seaton Rd
Broughton Moor CA15 ...63 B8
Seaton CA14 ....62 E4
Seaview Dr CA28 ....187 F8
Second Moss La LA8 ...143 C5
Sedbergh Dr LA9 ....200 F5
Sedbergh Prim Sch
LA10 ....201 D4
Sedbergh Rd LA9 ....200 E5
Sedbergh Sch LA10 ....201 C4
Sedgefield Rd LA13 ....207 E4
Sedgwick Cl
Grange-Over-S LA11 ....208 C2
Kendal LA9 ....200 C2
Sedgwick Ho LA8 ....144 A2
Sedgwick Mews LA8 ...144 A1
Seed Howe LA8 ....130 B5
Seedfield LA8 ....130 C4
Seg La LA12 ....162 F7
Selby Terr
Maryport CA15 ....182 D5
Whitehaven CA28 ....187 F6
Selford Terr CA22 .....189 E6
Selina Terr LA15 ....182 F4
Sella Brow LA20 ....138 E7
Sellafield Sta CA20 ....108 C2
Selside CE Prim Sch
LA8 ....131 C5
Semple Rd CA1 ....177 E2
Senhouse Ct LA14 .....184 D6
Senhouse Roman Mus*
CA15 ....182 D7
Senhouse St
Maryport CA15 ....182 D5
5 Whitehaven CA28 ...186 C1
Workington CA14 ....184 D6
Workington,Siddick CA14 .62 D6
Senhouse Terr **8** CA14 .184 D6
Senhouse Wlk **2C** CA14 .184 D6
Sentinal St LA14 ....206 C3
Sepulchre La
Endmoor LA8 ....144 C1
Kendal LA9 ....144 C1
Serpentine Rd LA9 .....200 C5
Settle St
Millom LA18 ....202 C5
Settlebeck High Sch
LA10 ....201 D4
Seven Acres CA28 .....186 D5
Seven Acres Cvn Pk
CA19 ....123 E8
Severn Rd LA14 ....206 A3
Sewell Pl CA2 ....177 A2
Sewell Rd CA2 ....177 A2
Seymour Ct LA14 ......206 F4
Shacklabank La LA10 ..145 F6
Shaddongate CA2 ......176 E6
Shady Grove La CA2 ...176 C6
Shady Grove Rd CA2 ..176 C6
Shakespeare Ave CA22 .189 C6
Shakespeare St **8** LA14 .206 F4
Shamhill CE Prim Sch
CA6 ....11 F6
Shankly Rd CA2 ....176 F4
Shanny La LA9 ....144 B4
Shap Abbey (rems of)*
CA10 ....101 A6
Shap CE Prim Sch CA10 .101 C6
Shap Gr CA2 ....176 D4
Shap Rd LA9 ....200 E7
Sharp St LA14 ....162 A8
Sharps La LA9 ....130 E2
Shaw Gn LA7 ....209 F5
Shaw La LA7 ....209 F5
Shaw St Maryport CA15 .182 D5
Workington CA14 ....184 D5
Shaw's Hill CA6 ....4 B1
Shaw's Wiend CA16 ....193 C4
Shawbank Brow CA15 ...78 B8
Shawfield Rd LA12 ....163 B3
Shawhill Ct DG12 ......172 F5
Shawhill Rd DG12 .....172 E4
Shawk Cres **3** CA5 ...28 F1
Shearwater Cres LA14 .206 B1

Sheehan Cres CA2 ......176 B5
Sheepbarrow Cl LA11 ..154 C3
Sheeplands Gr LA13 ...207 D6
Sheernest **5** LA6 .....156 B1
Sheernest La LA6 ......156 B1
Sheffield St CA2 ....214 A1
Shelley Cl CA14 ....184 C1
Shelley Dr LA13 ....207 D6
Shepherd Cl CA2 ......176 E4
Sheriff Bank LA12 .....152 E5
Sheriff Well Cl LA12 ..152 E5
Sheriff's Gate CA26 ...93 A8
Sherman's Terr CA22 ..189 F5
Sherwin St LA13 ....207 C2
Ship St LA14 ....206 F1
Shore Cl LA5 ....210 B2
Shore Gn LA5 ....210 B2
Shore Rd Drigg CA19 ...123 C5
Silverdale LA5 ....210 B2
Workington CA14 ......184 B2
Shore Side LA14 ....62 C6
Shore St LA14 ....204 A2
Shore Terr LA14 ....184 C2
Shoregill CA16 ....104 C6
Shorley La CA12 ....192 B3
Short Acres CA15 .....182 E5
Short St LA11 ....177 C6
Shortbutts La LA14 ...157 A1
Showfield CA8 ....179 B4
Shu-le-Crow Gdns **9**
CA12 ....192 B3
Shuts La CA10 ....66 B8
Shuttle St LA20 ....139 B5
Shyreakes LA8 ....144 B2
Shyreakes La LA8 .....144 B2
Side Gates LA12 ......112 C6
Sidney St LA14 ....206 F3
Siemen's St **3** LA14 .206 F1
Sikemeadow LA14 .....204 B1
Sikeside La CA17 .....104 C2
Silecroft CA13 ....63 E3
Silecroft Gdns LA14 ..206 C5
Silecroft Sta LA18 ...149 F5
Silloth Cres LA14 ....206 B4
Silloth Ind Est CA7 ..174 C5
Silloth St CA2 ....176 E6
Silver Band Villas CA16 .73 E2
Silver Howe Cl LA9 ...200 E2
Silver La LA12 ....152 C7
Silver St Bolton CA16 .87 D6
Crosby Ravensworth CA10 .102 C5
Kirkby Stephen CA17 ..199 C6
Marton LA12 ....162 D7
Staveley LA8 ....130 C5
Silverdale Moss Rd LA5 .210 D7
Silverdale Rd
Arnside LA5 ....209 B1
Carlisle CA1 ....177 A4
Yealand Redmayne LA5 .166 F7
Silverdale St
6 Barrow-In-F LA14 ..207 A3
Haverigg LA18 ....150 A3
Silverdale St John's CE Prim
Sch LA5 ....210 C3
Silverdale Sta LA5 ...210 F3
Silverhill DG12 ......172 D5
Silverhill Pl DG16 ....173 C2
Silverlaw DG12 ......172 D5
Silverlaw Cres DG12 .172 D5
Silverlaw Ind Est DG12 .172 D5
Silvermount DG12 ...172 D5
Silverwalk DG12 .....172 D5
Sim Court Ho **8** CA11 .191 E4
Sim Ct DG12 ....191 E4
Simmerson Dr CA2 ...176 C3
Simonscales La CA13 .190 D2
Simpson Ground Rd
LA11 ....154 B8
Sinclair Ct CA1 ......177 E6
Singleton Park Rd LA9 .144 C6
Singleton Pk LA8 .....144 C6
Sir John Barrow Sch
LA12 ....203 E5
Siskin Ave **6** LA15 ..205 C4
Sizergh Castle & Gdn*
LA8 ....143 E2
Skeldene Cl LA15 .....205 B5
Skelgate LA15 ....205 B5
Skelghyll La
Ambleside LA22 ......195 D3
Ambleside LA23 .....195 E1
Windermere LA23 ....129 A8
Skelgillside Workshops
CA6 ....181 F3
Skellands Ride CA10 ..85 E7
Skelsceugh Rd
Arlecdon CA26 ....77 E1
Frizington CA26 .....59 E8
Skelton Sch CA11 ....55 B2
Skelwith Cl CA2 .....176 C3
Skelwith Dr
Barrow-In-F LA14 ...204 E1
Dalton-In-F LA15 ....205 C3
Skelwith Fold Cvan Pk
LA22 ....113 F1
Skelwith Force* LA22 .113 E2
Skiddaw Ave CA15 ...182 D7
Skiddaw Cl CA7 ......174 C4
Skiddaw Cres LA14 ..185 D5
Skiddaw Gdns LA14 ..204 D1
Skiddaw Rd Keswick CA12 .176 D5
Whitehaven CA28 ....187 E3
Skiddaw St
Keswick CA12 ....192 C3
Silloth CA7 ....174 C5
Skiddaw Terr CA7 ....37 C1

Skiddaw View
Cockermouth CA13 ...190 C3
Penrith CA11 ....191 A5
Wigton CA7 ....180 D3
Skinburness Cres CA7 .174 D6
Skinburness Dr CA7 ..174 D7
Skinburness Rd CA7 ..174 D7
Skinner How La LA22 .197 C7
Skinner St CA13 .....190 D3
Skipton Gate LA6 ....156 E2
Skirsgill Bsns Pk CA11 .191 B2
Skirsgill Cl CA11 ....191 C3
Skirsgill Gdns CA11 .191 C3
Skirsgill La CA10 ....191 D2
Skitby Rd CA6 ....20 F8
Skye The **8** LA9 ....200 C5
Slack Randy CA10 ...102 B4
Slack The LA22 ......195 D5
Slackbury La LA8 ....143 A7
Slackgap La CA17 ....199 E8
Slacks La LA10 ......146 A7
Slackwood La LA5 ...210 E2
Slape La LA6 ....167 C8
Slapestones CA11 ....70 E3
Slatefell CA13 ....190 F3
Slatefell Dr CA13 ...190 E4
Slater St
Barrow-In-F LA14 ...206 F3
Dalton-In-F LA15 ...205 C5
Slattery Lonnin CA27 .91 D3
Sleastonhow La CA10 .87 E8
Sleetbeck Rd CA6 ...5 C3
Sloan Cl CA14 ......185 D7
Sloop St LA14 ......206 F1
Slop La LA13 ......205 D7
Smardale Gill Nature
Reserve* CA17 ......120 B6
Smeaton St LA14 ....207 A2
Smith Rd CA14 ......184 C2
Smith's Ct **1C** LA12 ..203 D5
Smithfield Dalston CA5 .29 D1
Egremont CA22 ......189 C6
Smithfield Rd CA22 ..189 D7
Smithy Banks CA19 ..123 E6
Smithy Brow
Ambleside LA22 .....195 D6
Coniston LA21 ......127 F8
Smithy Croft CA3 ...175 F5
Smithy Garth CA7 ...26 F6
Smithy Hill LA11 ...154 C3
Smithy How LA6 ....212 E3
Smithy La
Bowland Bridge LA11 .142 C4
Bowness-On-W LA23 .198 C1
Broughton-In-F LA20 .138 E3
Caldbeck CA7 ....53 C6
Clifton CA10 ....71 C1
Westhouse LA6 ......169 E4
Smithybrow La CA10 .124 F7
Smityh St LA14 .....69 E5
Snaefell View LA14 ..206 B1
Snape La LA5 ....166 F5
Snape Rd LA14 .....184 C5
Snebro Rd CA28 ....187 E6
Sneckyeat Ct CA28 ..187 F5
Sneckyeat Gr CA22 ..91 F7
Sneckyeat Rd
Whitehaven CA28 ...187 F5
Whitehaven CA28 ...91 F7
Snowdon Ave CA25 ..188 C8
Sockbridge Dr CA10 .70 F1
Solomon Ct CA28 ...186 D1
Solway Ave CA15 ...183 C7
Solway Aviation Mus*
CA6 ....21 D4
Solway Com Sch CA7 .174 C4
Solway Cres DG12 ..172 D3
Solway Ct LA15 .....182 D6
Solway Dr Anthorn CA7 .16 E1
Walney Island LA14 ..206 B4
Solway Pk LA14 ....182 C4
Solway Rd Annan DG12 .172 D2
Carlisle CA2 ....176 B5
Solway Rd Gretna DG16 .173 C3
Lowca CA28 ....186 E8
6 Moresby Parks CA28 .76 F2
Whitehaven CA28 ...187 B7
Workington CA14 ...184 C4
Solway Rise CA27 ..91 C2
Solway St Annan DG12 .172 D2
Silloth CA7 ....174 C4
Workington CA14 ...184 C7
Solway Terr CA15 ..182 D6
Solway View
Bolton Low Houses CA7 .37 F3
Kirkbampton CA5 ...28 E7
Whitehaven CA28 ...186 D2
Somerwood Cl CA16 ..88 A7
Somme Ave LA11 ....164 D6
Sorotergate LA12 ...203 D6
Soutersykes CA13 ...65 A4
South Bank Cl CA7 ..180 D1
South Craig LA23 ...198 D3
South Croft CA3 ....175 F5
South End Bolton CA16 .87 E5
Wigton CA7 ....180 D2
South End Cvn Site
LA14 ....170 C1
South George St CA2 .214 B1
South Gn LA12 ......162 F6
South Henry St
Carlisle CA1 ....214 C1
Whitehaven CA28 ...187 C7
South Hermitage Sq TD9 .1 B6
South Hermitage St TD9 .1 B6
South John St
Workshops CA2 .....214 B1

South Lakes Wild Animal
Pk* LA15 ....205 D7
South Liddle St TD9 ..1 B6
South Par CA20 .....123 A7
South Quay CA15 ...182 C6
South Rd Kendal LA9 .200 D3
Kirkby Stephen CA17 .199 C4
South Row
Barrow-In-F LA13 ...207 E3
Whitehaven CA28 ...187 B6
South St Carlisle CA1 .214 C1
Cockermouth CA13 ..190 D4
Egremont CA22 .....189 E5
Mealsgate CA7 .....37 C2
South Terr
Bowness-On-W LA23 .198 D3
Great Broughton CA13 .63 D6
Tebay CA10 ....118 B2
South Tynedale Rly*
CA9 ....181 C6
South Vale CA7 .....176 F4
South View Aspatria CA7 .50 D8
Barrow-In-F LA14 ...207 A6
Mealsgate CA7 .....37 A1
South View La LA9 ..200 C6
South View Rd
Bransty CA28 ......186 D3
Distington CA14 ...185 C3
South View Terr
Carlisle CA1 ....214 C1
Wigton CA7 ....180 B4
South Wakefield Cl
CA3 ....175 C3
South Walney Inf Sch
LA14 ....206 C1
South Walney Jun Sch
LA14 ....206 C1
South Walney Nature
Reserve* CA14 .....171 A1
South Walney Nature Trails*
LA14 ....170 F1
South Watt St **7** CA14 .184 D6
South Western Terr
CA2 ....177 A4
South William St LA14 .184 E6
Southampton St LA14 .206 C2
Southdale St CA2 ...177 B3
Southend Rd CA11 ..191 D4
Southesk CA10 .....72 D4
Southey Ave CA22 ..189 C6
Southey Hill Trad Pk
CA12 ....192 A4
Southey St CA12 ...192 B3
Southey Wlk CA25 ..189 C6
Southfield CA5 ....18 F1
Southfield Rd LA10 .201 B4
Southfield Technology Coll
CA28 ....184 D2
Southport Dr LA14 ..206 B2
Southwaite Barns CA4 .41 D4
Southwaite Rd CA4 ..41 E4
Sow How La LA11 ...142 A2
Sowerby Ave LA14 ..204 B1
Sowerby Ct CA2 ....176 E4
Sowerby Woods Bsns Pk
CA14 ....204 C3
Sparrowmire La LA9 .200 C7
Speedwell La CA14 ..184 E6
Spencer Ho CA1 ....214 B2
Spenser Cl CA22 ...189 C6
Spicka La LA22 .....128 C7
Spindrift Cl **3** LA16 .162 A8
Spinney La LA5 .....210 C5
Spinney The Arnside LA5 .210 C8
Bowness-On-W LA23 .198 C1
Spital Ing La CA13 ..190 C5
Spital Pk LA9 ......200 D3
Spital View **3** LA12 .200 C5
Spittal Farm CA7 ...180 C5
Spooner Sale CA23 ..198 D6
Spoonygreen La CA12 .192 B5
Spout Force (waterfall)*
CA13 ....65 D1
Spout Force Forest Wlk*
CA13 ....80 A8
Spout La Ulverston LA12 .203 E6
Wrayton LA2 ....168 F1
Spring Bank
Silverdale LA5 .....210 C3
Whitehaven CA28 ...187 E7
Spring Bank Rd LA11 .208 B5
Spring Croft Cl CA13 .63 F5
Spring Field Rd CA15 .182 E5
Spring Gardens La CA3 .214 B3
Spring Gdns
1 Kendal LA9 .....200 C5
Kirkby-in-F LA17 ...151 C7
Spring Gr LA14 ....207 B6
Spring St **1** LA12 ..207 A2
Spring Vale LA12 ..203 A2
Spring Wood LA12 ..197 E4
Springbells DG12 ..172 E5
Springbells Rd DG12 .172 E5
Springbells Workshops
DG12 ....172 E5
Springfield Arnside LA5 .209 B2
Holme LA6 ....156 B1
Springfield Ave
High Harrington CA14 .185 C7
Ulverston LA12 ....203 D4
Whitehaven CA28 ...187 E7
Springfield Cl LA14 ..206 C5
Springfield Gdns CA22 .188 A3
Springfield Gr CA28 ..187 F7
Springfield Park Rd
LA12 ....203 D3

Springfield Prim Sch DG16 173 D6
Springfield Rd
Bigrigg CA22 188 A3
Carlisle CA1 177 F3
Ulverston LA12 203 D4
Windermere LA23 198 E4
Springfields CA7 180 D1
Springkell CA7 36 D1
Springs Garth CA12 192 C2
Springs Rd CA12 192 C2
Sprint Holme LA9 130 F2
Spruce Gr CA28 186 F1
Spruce Rise LA13 207 F4
Square The
Allithwaite LA11 164 F7
Allonby CA15 35 C2
Brough CA17 105 B5
Broughton-In-F LA20 139 A2
Burton-in-K LA6 167 B7
Cartmel LA11 153 E1
Dalston CA5 29 D1
Gosforth CA20 109 A2
Hawkshead LA22 197 E5
High Cummersdale CA2 176 E1
Longtown CA6 10 C4
Milnthorpe LA7 211 D3
Orton CA10 118 C7
Parton CA28 186 D6
Sandford CA16 104 A7
Storth LA7 209 F5
Whitehaven CA28 186 D2
Stable Yd 11 CA12 192 B3
Stables Ct 9 CA13 190 C4
Stack Yd The CA16 88 A5
Stackbraes Rd CA6 10 C4
Stackwood Ave LA13 207 C5
Stafford Ct CA25 188 D6
Stafford St
Askam-In-F LA16 162 A7
Barrow-In-F LA14 207 A5
Dalton-In-F LA15 205 C6
Stagshaw Gdns* LA22 195 D2
Stagstones Farm CA11 71 C6
Stagstones Rd CA11 71 C6
Stainbank Rd LA9 200 B3
Stainburn Rd CA14 62 E4
Stainburn Sch CA14 62 E3
Stainton CE Prim Sch CA11 70 D3
Stainton Cross LA8 156 B8
Stainton Ct LA8 156 B8
Stainton Dr LA15 205 B3
Stainton La LA13 162 E3
Stainton Rd Carlisle CA3 175 A1
Stainton CA3 176 D8
Stalker Rd CA11 191 B5
Stamford Hill Ave CA28 186 F8
Stampery The CA7 180 D4
Stan Lonning CA13 63 F5
Stanah Cotts CA12 82 B2
Stanah La CA12 82 B1
Stanbeck Mdws CA14 184 F5
Standalane DG12 172 D4
Standalane Ct DG12 172 E4
Standings Rise CA28 187 E8
Standish St CA12 192 B3
Stanegate CA6 21 E4
Stanger St CA12 192 B4
Stanhope Rd CA2 176 E6
Stank La LA13 162 C1
Stankelt Rd LA5 210 C2
Stanley Cres CA8 14 D1
Stanley Rd
Barrow-In-F LA14 206 E2
Brampton CA8 179 C6
Stanley St Beetham LA7 155 E2
Carnforth LA5 213 C3
Ulverston LA12 203 D6
Workington CA14 184 C6
Stanley View CA28 187 E3
Stanwix Bank CA3 214 A4
Stanwix Pk Holiday Ctr CA7 174 B2
Stanwix Prim Sch CA3 175 E1
Stapleton Rd DG12 172 F4
Stapleton Road Ind Est DG12 172 E4
Star St LA12 203 C6
Stark St LA14 207 A2
Starnthwaite Ghyll LA8 142 E7
Station App Cark LA11 164 D7
Dalton-In-F LA15 205 C4
Station Ave CA12 192 B4
Station Bldgs LA8 144 C5
Station Bsns Pk CA2 214 B1
Station Cl 3 LA15 205 C4
Station Cotts CA8 24 C8
Station Cres CA21 108 B5
Station Hill
Ravenglass CA18 123 F3
Wigton CA7 180 B4
Station La
Burton-in-K LA6 167 B7
Staveley LA8 130 B5
Station Rd Alston CA9 181 D4
Annan DG12 172 C3
Appleby-In-W CA16 193 D6
Armathwaite CA4 42 C5
Arnside LA5 209 C2
Aspatria CA7 50 C8
Brampton CA8 179 D5
Broughton-In-F LA20 139 A2
Burgh-By-S CA5 18 F1
Cark LA11 164 D7
Cockermouth CA13 190 D3
Coniston LA21 196 A4
Crosby Garrett CA17 120 A8
Station Rd *continued*
Culgaith CA10 72 E4
Dalton-In-F LA15 205 C4
Drigg CA19 123 D5
Flimby CA15 183 C8
Holme LA6 156 B1
Kendal LA9 200 D6
Keswick CA12 192 B4
Kirkby Stephen CA17 199 C4
Millom LA18 202 C5
Penruddock CA11 69 D3
Sedbergh LA10 201 B4
Shap CA10 101 C5
Silloth CA7 174 B3
St Bees CA27 91 C2
Staveley LA8 130 B5
Temple Sowerby CA10 72 F3
Threlkeld CA12 82 B7
Whitehaven CA28 187 D8
Wigton CA7 180 C4
Workington CA14 184 D6
Station St
Cockermouth CA13 190 D4
Keswick CA12 192 B3
Maryport CA15 182 D5
Station Terr
Bridgefoot CA14 63 C4
1 Dalton-In-F LA15 205 C4
Embleton CA13 65 B5
Lindal in F LA12 162 E6
Station View CA15 49 D5
Station Yard Ind Est LA11 208 E5
Station Yd
10 Askam-In-F LA16 162 A8
Wigton CA7 180 C4
Staunton St LA5 213 C5
Staveley CE Sch LA8 130 B5
Staveley Mill Yard Ind Est LA8 130 C5
Staveley Sta LA8 130 B5
Steamer St LA14 206 F1
Steel Brow CA26 77 C2
Steel St Askam-In-F LA16 162 A8
Barrow-In-F LA14 206 E4
Ulverston LA12 163 D8
Steele's Bank CA4 178 B1
Steele's Row LA9 130 F2
Steeple Cl CA28 187 E5
Steer Ave CA15 182 D4
Stephen St LA14 206 F3
Stephenson Croft CA16 87 D6
Stephenson Rd CA1 177 D4
Stevenson Pl DG12 172 B3
Stewart Cl LA5 210 B8
Stewart St LA14 206 E2
Stile Brow LA23 129 D1
Stock Hill Kennels CA7 50 E8
Stock La LA22 194 B3
Stockbeck LA9 200 E6
Stockbridge La LA12 203 C6
Stockdale Farm LA11 164 D6
Stockgate LA9 200 E6
Stockghyll Brow LA22 195 D5
Stockghyll Ct LA22 195 E5
Stockghyll Force* LA22 195 E6
Stockghyll La LA22 195 E6
Stocks Hill Cl CA14 185 B7
Stocks Hill Rise CA14 185 B7
Stockwell Rd CA2 30 B3
Stokoe Ct CA2 176 F4
Stone Barrow La LA15, LA13 162 E4
Stone Cl LA13 205 F2
Stone Croft LA22 195 D5
Stone Dike La LA12 162 F5
Stone Dyke LA13 207 F4
Stone How Lonning CA7 37 A7
Stone Lands LA8 155 D8
Stone Rigg Outrake LA10 146 F1
Stone Terr LA11 208 C4
Stonebank Gn LA9 200 A3
Stonebeck Cotts LA11 154 C3
Stonecross Gdns
Kendal LA9 200 C2
Ulverston LA12 203 C5
Stonecross Gn LA9 200 C2
Stonecross Rd LA9 200 B2
Stonedross La LA6 212 E8
Stonedyke La LA13 207 F4
Stonegarth Carlisle CA2 176 C4
Greystoke CA11 69 E5
Stonehall La LA10 201 F6
Stoneham Cl LA13 207 E3
Stonehill Mill CA17 199 D6
Stonehouse Pk CA5 29 A1
Stoneleigh Cl LA13 207 C6
Stoneleigh Ct LA5 210 C3
Stoneraise Sch CA5 40 E8
Stones La LA22 128 E2
Stonesdale La DL11 122 E1
Stoneshot CA17 199 D6
Stoney Croft Dr LA5 213 D8
Stoney La
Ambleside LA22 195 C6
2 Kendal LA9 200 C5
Kendal,Kentrigg LA9 200 B8
Stoneycroft CA14 63 B4
Stoneycroft Dr LA5 209 B1
Stony Banks CA7 180 D3
Stonydale LA12 203 D2
Stonyhurst Dr CA28 187 D8
Stopford St TD9 1 B6
Storey Bank CA10 72 A8
Storey Sq
Barrow-In-F LA14 207 A3
Storey Sq *continued*
15 Dalton-In-F LA15 205 C5
Stormont Cres DG16 173 D2
Storrs La LA5 166 D6
Storth Brow CA7 37 A5
Storth CE Sch LA7 209 F5
Storth Rd LA7 209 F3
Stott Park Bobbin Mill* LA12 141 E3
Strait Loaning CA10 43 A1
Straits 10 CA7 180 D3
Stramongate LA9 200 D5
Stramongate Prim Sch LA9 200 D5
Strand LA14 207 A2
Strand Ct LA11 208 D4
Strand Rd CA1 214 C3
Strand St Maryport CA15 182 C6
Whitehaven CA28 186 C1
Strand Terr CA7 180 D4
Strand The CA4 30 F7
Strands The
Milnthorpe LA7 211 C3
Milnthorpe LA7 211 D3
Strathaird Ave LA14 206 C1
Strathclyde Ave CA2 176 C6
Strathmore Ave LA14 206 C1
Strathnaver Ave LA14 206 C1
Strawberry How Bsns Ctr CA13 190 E2
Strawberry Howe Rd CA13 64 E4
Strawberry Terr CA3 175 C1
Street CA10 86 D6
Street La CA10 118 D8
Street The CA7 53 C5
Strickland Ct LA9 200 C6
Strickland Terr 10 CA11 191 C6
Stricklandgate
Kendal LA9 200 C5
Penrith CA11 191 C6
Stripes La CA16 104 C6
Stubshead La CA19,CA20 109 B1
Sty Gate CA14 78 C4
Stylecroft CA7 180 C8
Suffolk Cl CA28 187 F5
Suffolk St LA13 207 B3
Sullart St CA13 190 C3
Summer Hill Bootle LA19 137 B3
Carlisle CA1 177 C4
Summer Hill Cvn Pk LA23 142 A6
Summerfields CA5 29 D1
Summergate Cres DG12 172 D3
Summergate Rd DG12 172 D2
Summergrove Pk CA28 188 A8
Summerhill Gdns LA14 207 B8
Summerhow LA9 131 B1
Summersty Bank LA23 142 A6
Summervale Ave DG12 172 D2
Summervale Pl DG12 172 D2
Summerville Rd LA7 211 D4
Summit Ave LA13 207 B6
Sun Croft CA7 51 F5
Sun St Askam-In-F LA16 162 B8
Ulverston LA12 203 C6
Sunbrick La LA12 163 B4
Suncroft CA15 49 B5
Sunderland Terr LA12 203 E5
Sunningdale Cl CA3 175 B1
Sunningdale Gdns 8 CA3 175 B1
Sunny Bank Cark LA11 164 D7
Lindal in F LA12 162 D7
Stainton CA11 70 D3
Stainton With A LA13 205 F2
Sunny Bank Rd LA23 198 E4
Sunnybank CA12 82 B8
Sunnymeade CA2 177 C1
Sunnyside
9 Cockermouth CA13 190 D4
Egremont CA22 189 D6
Seaton CA14 183 C3
Kendal LA9 200 D4
Sunray Terr CA10 57 A6
Sunscales Ave CA13 190 E2
Surrey St LA18 202 D4
Surrone Ct DG16 173 C3
Surrone Gdns DG16 173 C3
Surrone Rd DG16 173 C3
Sutherland St LA14 207 A3
Sutherland Terr DG12 172 C1
Suttle Cl CA2 176 B4
Sutton Ct CA4 30 F5
Swallow Cl LA9 200 F2
Swan Ave CA17 105 B5
Swan La LA22 194 B5
Swan St Longtown CA6 10 C3
Ulverston LA12 203 E5
Swarthdale Ave LA12 203 D3
Swarthmoor Hall* LA12 203 C3
Swarthmoor Hall La LA12 203 B3
Swartle The CA8 179 D6
Sweden Bridge La LA22 195 D7
Sweden Pk LA22 195 D6
Swillings La CA17 104 E4
Swinate Rd LA5 209 C1
Swinburn Dr CA3 175 C3
Swindale La CA10 100 D4
Swinestead La LA12 163 C3
Swingpump La 18 CA28 186 C1
Swinside Cl CA13 190 F3
Sybil St CA1 177 C5
Sycamore Ave
Sedbergh LA10 201 B5
Sycamore Ave *continued*
Ulverston LA12 203 D3
Sycamore Cl
Endmoor LA8 156 C8
Whitehaven CA28 186 E3
Sycamore Ct CA14 184 E3
Sycamore Dr CA11 191 F5
Sycamore Gr
Barrow-In-F LA14 206 F6
Milnthorpe LA7 211 E4
Sycamore La CA1 30 E4
Sycamore Rd CA15 182 E5
Syke Bsns Pk CA7 180 E1
Syke Pk CA7 180 E1
Syke Rd CA7 180 E1

T

Tail Bank Lonning LA20 138 E3
Tait St CA1 214 C2
Talbot Rd CA2 176 E5
Talisman Cl 4 LA14 207 B3
Talkin Cl CA1 177 F5
Talkin Tarn Ctry Pk* CA8 179 F1
Tallow Whins CA10 57 A6
Tallythwaite Garth LA8 143 C6
Tamar Gdns LA14 206 A4
Tangier Bldgs 1 CA28 186 C1
Tangier St CA28 186 C1
Tannery Court Flats CA1 177 C3
Tannery Ct Carlisle CA1 177 C3
12 Wigton CA7 180 D3
Tanpits La LA6 167 B7
Tantabank Rd LA15 205 C4
Tarn Cl Kendal LA9 200 E2
Storth LA7 209 F5
Ulverston LA12 203 B6
Tarn Flatt LA12 162 C7
Tarn Green Rd LA11 154 C7
Tarn How La CA20 109 A1
Tarn Hows* LA21 196 F8
Tarn La
Burton-in-K LA5,LA6 167 B6
Crosby Garrett CA17 120 B8
Tarn Rd CA8 179 D3
Tarn Side 3 LA12 203 D5
Tarn St CA14 184 E5
Tarnbrook Cl LA5 213 B3
Tarnhead LA18 150 A2
Tarnhead La LA18 150 A2
Tarnside CA2 177 B1
Tarnside Cvn Pk CA21 108 A5
Tarraby La CA3 175 E1
Tay Ct LA14 206 E4
Teal Beck LA9 200 F2
Teal Cl LA16 161 F8
Teasdale Rd Carlisle CA3 175 C3
Walney Island LA14 206 C5
Tebay Comm Prim Sch CA10 118 B3
Tebay La LA12 203 F7
Tees Gdns LA14 206 B2
Telford Rd CA1 177 D4
Telford St 2 LA14 207 B2
Templand Gate LA11 164 F7
Templand Pk LA11 164 F7
Temple Ct LA5 166 E7
Temple Sowerby CE Prim Sch CA10 72 E2
Temple Terr Aspatria CA7 50 D8
Whitehaven CA28 186 D1
Tennyson Ave LA13 207 D6
Tennyson Dr CA22 189 C6
Tenterfell Ct 14 LA9 200 C5
Tenters CA7 180 D3
Terrace The LA23 198 E6
Tewfittmire La CA10 86 A8
Tewthwaite Hill Rd CA17 104 A3
Thacka La CA11 191 B6
Thames Rd LA14 206 B3
Thanet Terr CA16 193 D6
Theatre St 17 LA12 203 D5
Third Moss La LA8 143 C5
Thirlemere Rd CA15 182 E4
Thirlmere Ave
Cockermouth CA13 190 E3
Workington CA14 184 F4
Thirlmere Cl
Dalton-In-F LA15 205 C3
Millom LA18 202 C4
Thirlmere Pk CA11 191 C3
Thirlmere Rd LA9 200 F6
Thirlmere St CA2 177 A4
Thirlwell Ave CA1 177 D6
Thirlwell Gdns CA1 177 D6
Thirnby Ct LA6 212 C2
Thistle Cl CA28 186 E1
Thomas La CA2 176 B7
Thomas Rd CA14 184 C2
Thomas St Annan DG12 172 C4
Carlisle CA2 214 A1
Thomlinson Ave CA2 176 C6
Thomlinson Jun Sch CA7 180 D3
Thompson Cl CA25 188 D7
Thompson St 7 LA14 207 A3
Thompson's Yd CA14 63 B4
Thompsons Terr CA15 183 C8
Thomson St CA1 177 C5
Thorburn Cres DG12 172 D5
Thornbarrow Rd LA23 198 E4
Thorncliffe Rd LA14 207 A7
Thorncliffe Sch LA14 207 A7
Thorncroft Gdns CA14 184 F5
Thornfield Cl CA25 188 D6
Thornfield Pk LA14 207 A7
Thornfield Pl LA11 208 C3
Thornfield Rd LA11 208 C3
Thornhill LA23 198 E4
Thornhill Prim Sch CA22 189 E2
Thornleigh Dr LA6 167 C7
Thornleigh Rd LA9 200 C2
Thorns La Sedbergh LA10 201 D5
Underbarrow LA8 143 C6
Thornsbank LA10 201 D5
Thornship La CA10 101 B5
Thornthwaite Forest Walks* CA12 66 C3
Thornthwaite Rd LA23 198 F4
Thornton La
Dent LA6,LA10 159 C3
Thornton in L LA6 169 F5
Thornton Pk LA15 205 B3
Thornton Rd
Carlisle CA3 175 D1
Whitehaven CA28 187 F7
Thorntrees Dr CA22 189 E2
Thorny Hills LA9 200 E5
Thorny La
Newbiggin-on-L CA17 119 E4
Thornhill CA22 189 E3
Thorny Nook La LA14 170 C5
Thorny Rd CA22 189 E2
Thoroughfare The LA5 213 C7
Thorpe Field CA10 70 E1
Thrang Brow LA22 113 B4
Thrang Brow La LA5 166 E7
Threagill La LA5 213 E7
Threaplands CA25 188 C8
Threave Ct CA1 177 D6
Three Bridges LA12 203 B4
Three Trees Rd DG12 16 C7
Threlkeld CE Prim Sch CA12 82 B8
Threlkeld Gdns LA14 204 E1
Threlkeld Quarry Mus* CA12 82 C7
Throstle Ave CA7 180 B3
Throughs La LA7 209 F5
Thrums St LA13 207 D3
Thurlow Way LA14 207 A6
Thursby Prim Sch CA5 28 F1
Thurston Bank LA21 127 C4
Thwaite Bank CA14 184 E8
Thwaite Brow La LA5 213 A1
Thwaite Flat Cotts LA14 204 F5
Thwaite Flat Rd LA14 204 F5
Thwaite St LA14 207 A4
Thwaites La LA23 198 F5
Thwaites Sch LA18 150 C8
Tideway Dr LA14 170 C6
Tiffin La CA14 184 E6
Tilberthwaite Ave LA21 196 A4
Tilbury Rd CA1 177 E6
Timber Hill LA20 139 A2
Tindale Dr CA1 177 F4
Tindale Terr CA8 23 E2
Tinkler's La Askham CA10 85 F8
Clifton CA10 71 C1
Tippin's La LA16,LA17 151 B2
Titchfield St LA14 206 F5
Tithebarn Cotts 9 LA9 200 C4
Tithebarn Ct 4 CA12 192 A4
Tithebarn St Carlisle CA2 177 B4
5 Keswick CA12 192 A4
Todholes Rd CA25 188 E6
Toft La CA20 109 C1
Toll Bar Ct LA6 167 C7
Toll Bar Est LA10 201 A4
Tollbar Hos CA14 185 E5
Tom Fold LA22 195 D6
Tomlin Ave CA28 187 E5
Tommy Rd CA17 120 E2
Topaz Terr CA14 184 C1
Tor Scar Rd LA6 169 F6
Torduff Rd DG16 173 C3
Toronto St CA2 177 B3
Torridge Dr LA14 206 A4
Totter Bank LA8 142 E6
Tow Top Rd LA11 154 B6
Tower Cotts CA12 81 B6
Tower Ct CA3 214 A3
Tower Hill CA28 187 E7
Tower St LA13 171 B3
Tower View CA22 189 D6
Towers La CA13 190 E2
Towers St LA12 203 E5
Towerson St CA23 188 F6
Town Bank Rd LA12 203 D7
Town Bank Terr 1 LA12 203 D6
Town Cross CA12 82 C8
Town End Cl LA11 154 F6
Town End Ct LA8 144 B4
Town End Farm CA7 28 C4
Town End Mdw LA11 153 F1
Town Foot CA11 55 B2
Town Head
Haverigg LA18 150 A1
Sleagill CA10 86 E1
Town Head Cl CA10 86 B5
Town Head Garth CA10 87 E8
Town Quay CA14 184 C7
Town St LA12 203 D6
Town View LA9 200 C6
Town View Rd LA12 203 D6
Towncroft CA15 49 B3
Townend* LA23 114 E1

Townfield Cl CA18 ......123 F3
Townfoot Ct CA8 ......179 A4
Townfoot Ind Est CA8 ...179 A5
Townfoot Pk CA8 ......179 A5
Towngate CA17 ......120 B7
Townhead Brow CA23 ....114 F2
Townhead Ct CA4 ......31 A3
Townhead La
  Cliburn CA10 ....86 E8
  Ravenstonedale CA17 ...120 B2
Townhead Rd Cotehill CA4 .31 B1
  Dalston CA5 ....29 D1
Townsfield LA5 ......210 C4
Towpath Wlk LA5 ......213 C3
Tows Bank NE49 ......34 F7
Trafalgar Ct LA15 ....205 B5
Trafalgar Sq CA26 ......92 D8
Trafalgar St CA2 ......214 A1
Tram La LA6 ......212 C2
Tram The LA9 ......200 C5
Tranthwaite La LA8 ....143 C7
Tree Gdns CA8 ......179 D4
Tree Rd CA8 ......179 D4
Tree Terr CA8 ......179 D4
Trent Vale LA14 ......206 B2
Trevor St CA1 ......177 C4
Tribune Dr LA3 ......20 C2
Trinity CE Sch CA22 ....192 D4
Trinity Ct ⑤ LA12 ....203 C5
Trinity Dr Holme LA6 ..156 B1
  Workington CA14 ......184 E8
Trinity Ent Ctr LA14 ...206 D4
Trinity Gdns ⑧ LA12 ..203 C5
Trinity Rd LA18 ......202 C6
Trinity Sch CA1 ......214 B3
Trinity St LA14 ......206 F1
Trinity Way CA12 ......192 D4
Trinkeld Ave LA12 ....203 A2
Troon Cl CA3 ......175 C3
Trotter's World of Animals*
  CA12 ....65 F7
Troutbeck Dr CA2 ....176 A5
Troutbeck Gdns LA14 ..204 D1
Troy Gdns LA13 ......207 C6
Trumpet Rd CA23 ....188 E5
Trumpet Terr CA8 ....188 E5
Tubal Cnr CA7 ......36 F8
Tuchwud LA23 ......198 E6
Tudor Sq ⑫ LA15 ....205 C5
Tullie House Mus & Art Gall*
  CA3 ....214 A3
Tullie St CA1 ......177 C6
Turbary Rd LA6 ......169 E7
Turnberry Cres DG12 ..172 F5
Turnberry Rd DG12 ....172 F5
Turnberry Way CA3 ....175 D3
Turners Cl LA6 ......156 B2
Turning Course Lonning
  CA8 ....179 C6
Turnmain Dell DG12 ...172 F4
Turnstone Cres LA16 ..161 F8
Tweed Mill La CA13 ....190 D3
Tweed Rise LA14 ......206 B2
Tweedie Terr DG12 ....172 F5
Twentyman Ct ⑧ CA12 .192 B3
Twine Wlk
  Burton in L LA6 ......169 C3
  Millthorpe LA7 ......211 D4
Tyne Close Ave LA11 ...191 C4
Tyne Close Terr LA11 ..191 C4
Tyne Field Ct CA11 ....191 D4
Tyne Rd LA14 ......206 B2
Tyne St CA1 ......177 C4
Tynefield Dr CA11 ....191 E3
Tyson Sq ⑩ LA12 ....203 E5

U

Udale Ct CA14 ......184 F3
Udale St CA14 ......184 E6
Uldale Rd Carlisle CA2 ..177 F3
  Stainburn CA14 ......62 E3
Ullcoats CA28 ......187 D5
Uldale View CA22 ....199 D4
Ullcoats Ind Est CA22 ..92 C1
Ullswater Ave
  Whitehaven CA28 ......91 F7
  Workington CA14 ....184 E4
Ullswater Cl
  Dalton-In-F LA15 ....205 C3
  Ullswater LA12 ......203 E4
Ullswater Com Coll
  CA11 ....191 D4
Ullswater Cres LA5 ...213 D2
Ullswater Ct CA11 ....98 C8
Ullswater Rd
  Carlisle CA2 ......176 D5
  Kendal LA9 ......144 C8
  Maryport CA15 ......182 D4
  Penrith CA11 ......191 C4
Ullverston LA12 ......203 C4
Ullverston CE Inf Sch
  LA12 ....203 D6
Ullverston Hospl LA12 .203 C6
Ullverston Rd
  Dalton-In-F LA15 ....205 D5
  Gleaston LA12 ......162 E2
  Lindal in F LA12 ....203 B4
  Swarthmoor LA12 ....203 A3
Ullverston Sta LA12 ...203 C4

Ullverston Victoria High Sch
  LA12 ....203 D4
Underbarrow Rd
  Kendal LA9 ......200 A4
  Underbarrow LA8 ....143 E7
Undercliff Rd LA9 ....200 B5
Underfell LA11 ......164 F8
Undergreens Rd LA14 ..207 A8
Underhill LA3 ......143 D1
Underley Ave LA9 ....200 C7
Underley Hall Sch LA6 .212 C5
Underley Hill LA9 ....200 B7
Underley Rd LA9 ....200 B7
Underwood LA9 ......200 B3
Underwood Rd LA12 ...203 D3
Underwood Terr LA15 ..205 A4
Union Ct CA8 ......179 C5
Union La Brampton CA8 .179 C5
  Penrith CA11 ......191 B5
  Ulverston LA12 ......203 C6
Union Pl ⑧ LA12 ....203 D5
Union Rd DG16 ......173 C3
Union St
  Cleator Moor CA25 ...188 E7
  Dalton-In-F LA15 ....205 C5
  Kendal LA9 ......200 C6
  Newcastleton TD9 .....1 B6
  Ulverston LA12 ......203 D5
  Wigton CA7 ......180 C3
Union Terr CA11 ......191 B5
Uninn Ho CA12 ......173 D3
Uplin Cres LA11 ......164 F7
Upper Brook St LA12 ..203 D5
Upper Oak St LA23 ...198 E5
Upperby Ct CA2 ......177 C2
Upperby Prim Sch CA2 .177 B2
Upperby Rd CA2 ......177 B2
Upphall La LA6 ......167 C4
Upton Cotts CA7 ......53 C6
Upton St CA14 ......184 E6
Urswick Gn LA13 ....207 D3
Urswick Rd
  Dalton-In-F LA15 ....205 E5
  Ulverston LA12 ......203 C2

V

Vale Cl CA13 ......190 B2
Vale Side Gdns LA13 ..207 C4
Vale View
  Camerton CA14 ......183 F3
  Lowca CA28 ......186 F8
  St Bees CA27 ......91 D2
Valley Dr
  Barrow-In-F LA13 ....207 B6
  Carlisle CA1 ......30 E5
  Kendal LA9 ......200 F2
Valley Inf Sch CA28 ...187 E4
Valley Jun Sch CA28 ...187 E4
Valley Pk CA8 ......187 E7
Valley View CA14 ....184 D3
Valley View Rd CA28 ..187 C4
Vallum Cl CA3 ......175 F1
Vallum Pl CA5 ......19 B1
Vancouver Dr DG12 ....17 E8
Vancouver Pl DG12 ....17 D8
Vancouver Rd DG12 ....17 E8
Vasey Cres CA11 ......177 C6
Vengeance St LA14 ...206 C1
Verdun Ave LA11 ....206 C1
Vernon St LA14 ......206 F4
Vestaneum CA6 ......20 F2
Viaduct CA14 ......184 D6
Viaduct Estate Rd CA2,
  CA3 ....214 A2
Vicarage Cl
  Burton-in-K LA6 ....167 C7
  Grange-Over-S LA11 ..208 C4
Vicarage Dr Brough CA17 .105 B4
  Kendal LA9 ......200 C3
Vicarage Hill
  Frizington CA26 ......92 D7
  Keswick CA12 ......192 A5
Vicarage La
  Allithwaite LA11 ....164 F7
  Burton-in-K LA6 ....167 C7
  Cockermouth CA13 ...190 E3
  Ennerdale Bridge CA23 ..93 A6
  Hawkshead LA22 ....197 D5
  Kirkby Lonsdale LA6 ..212 C2
  Sedbergh LA10 ......201 D5
  Temple Sowerby CA10 ..72 E1
  Vicarage Mount LA14 ..206 B2
Vicarage Park CE Prim Sch
  LA9 ....200 C3
Vicarage Rd
  Ambleside LA22 ....195 C5
  Levens LA8 ......143 D1
Vicarage Terr
  Nenthead CA9 ......47 A2
  Roan LA10 ......118 B3
Vicars Fields LA9 ....200 C3
Vicars Garth LA9 ....200 C3
Vicars Hill LA9 ......200 C3
Vicars Wlk LA9 ......200 C3
Vickerstown Sch LA14 .206 C3
Victoria Ave Annan DG12 .172 C3
  Barrow-In-F LA14 ...207 A6
Victoria Cnr CA17 ....199 D5
Victoria Cottage Hospl
  CA15 ....182 D4
Victoria Ct ② CA13 ...190 D4
Victoria Inf Sch
  Barrow-In-F LA14 ...207 A6
  Workington CA14 ...184 D4
Victoria Jun Sch
  Barrow-In-F LA14 ...207 A6

Victoria Jun Sch continued
  Workington CA14 ....184 D5
Victoria Mews ④ LA14 .207 A5
Victoria Pl Carlisle CA1 .214 C3
  Whitehaven CA28 ....186 D2
  Workington CA14 ...184 E5
Victoria Rd Annan DG12 .172 C3
  Barrow-In-F LA14 ...207 A6
  Carlisle CA1 ......177 E6
  Cockermouth CA13 ...190 D3
  Penrith CA11 ......191 D4
  Ulverston LA12 ......203 D4
  Whitehaven CA28 ....186 E3
  Workington CA14 ...184 E5
Victoria Rd W LA23 ...198 F4
Victoria Sq Alston CA9 .181 D3
  Kirkby Stephen CA17 ..199 D5
Victoria St
  Askam-In-F LA16 ....162 A7
  Carnforth LA5 ......213 C3
  Cleator Moor CA25 ...188 E7
  Frizington CA26 ......92 D7
  Hawkshead LA22 ....197 E5
  Keswick CA12 ......192 B4
  Millom LA18 ......202 C5
  Ulverston LA12 ......203 C5
  Windermere LA23 ....198 E6
Victoria Terr
  Dalton-In-F LA15 ....205 C5
  ② Maryport CA15 ...182 E5
Victoria Viaduct CA3 ..214 B2
Victoria Villas CA28 ..187 F6
Victory Ave DG16 ....173 C3
Victory Cres CA15 ....182 E5
Villas The CA22 ......189 E5
Vine Rd LA9 ......200 E6
Violet Bank CA13 ....190 F1
Viver La LA7,LA8 ....156 A7
Vulcan Cl ② LA16 ....162 A8
Vulcan Rd LA14 ......207 B2
Vulcan's La CA14 ....184 E6

W

Waberthwaitw CE Prim Sch
  LA19 ....137 B8
Wadsworth Pk CA14 ...77 F7
Wadsworth Rd CA2 ...176 F4
Wain Gate CA11 ......57 A4
Waingap La CA10 ....118 F4
Waingatebridge Cotts
  LA18 ....150 A2
Waitholme La LA8 ....167 A7
Wakefield Mdw LA8 ..144 A2
Wakefield Rd
  Carlisle CA3 ......175 D4
  Cockermouth CA13 ...190 C4
Wakefield St ⑬ LA16 .162 A8
Waldegrave Rd CA2 ...176 E4
Walden Gr CA3 ......175 D2
Walk Mill Community
  Woodland * CA8 ....77 A1
Walker Brow CA14 ....185 A8
Walker Croft CA13 ....190 C3
Walker Rd LA14 ......184 C2
Walker Rise CA11 ....191 C7
Walker St
  ⑨ Askam-In-F LA16 .162 A8
  Cockermouth CA13 ...190 C3
Walkmill Cl ⑫ CA8 ...76 F2
Walkmill Cres CA1 ...177 D6
Wall St ⑭ CA14 ......184 D6
Wallace Cres DG12 ...172 C5
Wallace La
  Kirkandrews-on-E CA5 ..19 B3
  Thursby CA5 ......182 C6
Wallace St ⑭ LA14 ..206 F3
Walled Gdn The LA8 ..144 A1
Waller St LA11 ......177 D6
Walling's La LA5 ....210 B4
Walls Cotts CA18 ....123 F3
Walls Cvn Pk CA18 ...123 F3
Walls Dr CA18 ......123 F3
Walls Rd CA18 ......123 F3
Walna Scar Rd LA12 ..126 C3
Walney Rd LA14 ......206 E6
Walney Road Ind Est
  LA14 ....206 E4
Walney St LA14 ......206 B1
Walnut Hill LA13 ....207 A4
Walter St TD9 ......1 B6
Walthwaite Terr LA22 ..113 C4
Walton La LA13 ......207 C3
Walton Quarry Trail*
  CA8 ....24 D8
Wampool Pl CA7 ......180 B3
Wampool St CA7 ......174 C4
Wandales La
  High Casterton LA6 ...212 F2
  Natland LA9 ......144 B4
Wandsworth Gdns
  CA10 ....101 C5
Wansfell Ave LA14 ...176 D4
Wansfell Dr LA9 ....200 E2
Wansfell Holme LA22 .195 E2
Wansfell Rd LA22 ....195 D4
Wansfell Terr LA22 ...195 D4
Wansfell Tower Ct
  LA22 ....195 D5
Warcop CE Prim Sch
  CA16 ....104 C6
Ward St Longtown CA6 ..10 C3
  ④ Maryport CA15 ...182 E5
Wardhall Cotts CA7 ...50 A5
Wardway The CA9 ....181 C3

Warnell Dr CA1 ......177 E3
Warren Hill CA8 ......31 F6
Warren St LA14 ......206 D3
Wart Barrow La LA11 ..164 F8
Warth La LA6 ......169 F2
Warton Archbishop Hutton's
  Prim Sch LA5 ......213 C7
Warton Old Rectory*
  LA5 ....213 C7
Warton Rd LA5 ......213 C4
Wartonwood View LA5 .213 C3
Warwick Bridge Sch
  CA4 ....178 C6
Warwick Cres CA4 ....178 C6
Warwick Farm CA4 ...178 A5
Warwick Mill Bsns Ctr
  CA4 ....178 C6
Warwick Pl Penrith CA11 .191 C4
  Workington CA14 ...184 E6
Warwick Rd CA4 ....177 E6
Warwick Sq CA1 ....214 C2
Warwick St
  Barrow-In-F LA14 ...207 A5
  Carlisle CA3 ......214 B3
Wasdale Shap CA10 ...101 C6
  Wigton CA7 ......180 B3
Wasdale Cl
  Cockermouth CA13 ...190 F4
  Kendal LA9 ......200 E3
Wasdale Gdns LA14 ...187 E4
Wasdale Gr LA13 ....207 B3
Wasdale Pk CA20 ....123 A7
Wasdale Rd
  Gosforth CA20 ......109 B2
  Millom LA18 ......202 D4
Washington Dr LA5 ...213 D8
Washington St LA14 ..184 E6
Waste La CA13 ......190 E4
Wastwater Ave CA14 .184 D3
Wastwater Cl
  Carlisle CA2 ......176 D5
  Cleator Moor CA25 ..188 C8
Wastwater Rd CA28 ...187 C5
Wastwater Rise CA20 .123 B8
Watchhill Pk DG14 ....3 D3
Watchhill Rd DG14 ....3 D3
Water Bank CA7 ......52 C8
Water Cl LA12 ......153 C4
Water Garth LA14 ....170 C6
Water St
  ④ Barrow-In-F LA14 .207 A6
  Carlisle CA2 ......214 B1
  Glasson CA7 ......17 E3
  Morland CA10 ......86 F5
  Wigton CA7 ......180 D3
Watercrook Farm LA9 .200 C1
Waterfalls Rd LA9 ....86 B7
Waterfoot Cvn Pk CA11 ..84 E7
Waterfoot Rd DG12 ...172 B2
Watergap La CA17 ...199 D4
Watergates Lonning CA7 .37 D7
Waterhead Cotts LA22 .195 D3
Waterhouse Mill* LA7 .155 E2
Waterloo St CA13 ....190 D4
Waterloo Terr CA20 ...77 E1
Waters Edge
  Milnthorpe LA7 ....211 A3
  Seaton LA14 ......62 E4
Waters Meet CA4 ....178 D6
Waterside
  ⑧ Askam-In-F LA16 .162 A8
  Kendal LA9 ......200 D2
Waterside Pottery LA6 .169 C2
Waterslack Rd LA5 ...210 E6
Watery La Barbon LA6 .157 F5
  Crosthwaite LA8 ....142 E5
  Endmoor LA8 ......200 D2
  Millness LA6,LA7 ....156 B4
  Ulverston LA12 ......203 E4
Wath La CA17 ......119 C4
Watson St CA7 ......177 C5
Watson Terr CA11 ....191 C5
Watsons Terr CA7 ....49 F7
Wattsfield Ave LA9 ...200 D2
Wattsfield La LA9 ....200 D2
Wattsfield Rd LA9 ...200 D2
Wawell Dr CA1 ......177 F6
Waver La CA7 ......180 A3
Waver Rd CA7 ......16 F1
Waver St CA7 ......174 C4
Waverley Gdns CA7 ..175 D2
Waverley Rd CA3 ....175 D2
Wayside Terr CA11 ....55 E6
Weaddale Rd CA7 ...176 E5
Weathercock La LA10 .166 A6
Weaver Gn LA14 ....206 A4
Weaver Terr CA7 ....26 C1
Weavers Bank CA3 ...214 A3
Weavers Ct LA9 ....200 D3
Webster Cres CA2 ...177 A3
Webster St LA14 ....206 B1
Webstrey Cl LA14 ....170 C6
Weddicar Gdns CA25 .188 C8
Wedgwood Rd CA15 ..183 C8
Weint ⑪ LA12 ......203 D5
Weint La LA12 ......163 A6
Well Bank CA2 ......176 E4
Well Bank Pl CA2 ...200 D3
Well Beck Cl LA13 ...207 C6
Well Heads La
  Hincaster LA7,LA8 ..155 E4
  Sedgwick LA8 ......144 A1
Well House Rd CA8 ..193 F5
Well Ings LA9 ......200 C3
Well La Barrow-In-F LA13 .207 E3
  Carlisle CA3 ......175 E1
  Egremont CA22 ......189 C2
  High Casterton LA6 ..212 F2

Well La continued
  Hutton Roof LA6 ....157 B2
  Maryport CA15 ......182 C6
  Morland CA10 ......87 A5
  Ulverston LA12 ......203 E4
  Yealand Redmayne LA5 .166 F6
Well Lonning Cl CA8 ..179 B4
Well St ⑫ LA12 ......203 D5
Wellgate CA4 ......30 F5
Wellhead ② LA12 ....203 D5
Wellhead Cotts CA7 ...50 D6
Wellington Pl LA15 ..205 B5
Wellington Row CA28 .186 D1
Wellington St
  Annan DG12 ......172 C4
  Dalton-In-F LA15 ...205 B5
  Millom LA18 ......202 D5
Wellmead CA8 ......179 C5
Wells Cl CA14 ......184 E3
Wells Cotts CA10 ....71 F8
Wells Wlk CA1 ......30 E5
Welltree Brow CA10 ...87 A5
Welsh Rd CA1 ......177 E2
Welton Sch CA5 ......39 F2
Wennington Hall Sch
  LA2 ....168 E1
Wensum Lea LA14 ...206 B3
Went Mdws CA13 .....63 D4
West Ave
  Barrow-In-F LA13 ...207 B5
  Wigton CA7 ......180 D2
West Cl CA10 ......101 C6
West Cres LA23 ......198 D5
West Croft CA14 ......183 B1
West Croft Terr CA28 .186 E8
West Ct CA7 ......52 B8
West Cumberland Hospl
  CA28 ....187 F5
West End CA13 ......63 E6
West End Cl Flimby CA15 .183 C7
  Oulton CA7 ......180 B8
West End Croft CA5 ...18 E1
West End La LA12 ...203 F3
West End Rd CA10 ...118 B7
West Gate Rd LA14 ..206 F5
West Gr Kendal LA9 ..200 C4
  Workington CA14 ...184 E5
West Hall La LA6 ....168 C6
West Hills Dr LA12 ..203 C1
West La Flimby CA15 .183 C7
  Kirkbride CA7 ......27 B7
  Kirkoswald CA10 ....191 C4
  Shap CA10 ......101 C6
West Mount LA14 ....207 B6
West Pk CA5 ......39 B8
West Rd Kirkland CA26 ..78 B1
  Wigton CA7 ......180 B3
West Row
  Barrow-In-F LA13 ...207 E3
  Whitehaven CA28 ...187 B6
West Shore Pk LA14 .206 A5
West Shore Rd LA14 .206 A5
West Spur CA24 ......188 A5
West St Aspatria CA7 ..50 C8
  Kendal LA9 ......200 D3
  Maryport CA15 ......182 C6
  Mealsgate CA7 ......37 D2
West Strand CA28 ....186 B1
West Terr CA7 ......50 F8
West Tower St CA3 ...214 B3
West View
  Allithwaite LA11 ....164 F7
  Carnforth LA5 ......213 C5
  Cumwhinton CA4 ......31 A3
  Hensingham CA28 ...187 F6
  Kirkby-in-F LA17 ....151 B5
  Whitehaven CA28 ...186 D2
West View Rd
  Barrow-In-F LA13 ...207 B5
  Distington LA14 ....185 C3
West View Wlk CA14 .184 C2
West Walls CA3 ......214 A2
Westbourne Cres LA13 .207 B5
Westbourne Rd LA5 ..213 B6
Westbrook Fields CA7 .199 C5
Westcliffe Gdns LA11 .208 C4
Western Bank Ind Est
  CA7 ....199 C5
Westfield Bridge Ct
  LA14 ....184 D3
Westfield Dr
  Egremont CA22 ......189 D5
  Workington CA14 ...184 D2
Westfield Nature Trail*
  LA13 ....171 B5
Westfield Prim Sch
  CA14 ....184 D2
Westfield Terr ⑬ LA14 .207 B2
Westfield View CA13 .183 C8
Westgarth Ave CA17 ..199 C5
Westgarth Cl CA17 ...199 C5
Westgarth Gr CA17 ...199 C5
Westgate CA5 ......200 E6
Westgate La CA5 ....169 E5
Westgill Rd DG16 ....173 C5

Westgill Sq DG12 ....172 E5
Westhaven CA5 ....28 F1
Westhill Pl DG16 ......173 C2
Westlakes Science Pk
  CA24 ....91 F5
Westminster Ave LA14 ..170 C6
Westmoor Rd CA3 ......175 B4
Westmore Cl LA12 ......171 E8
Westmorland Bsns Pk
  LA9 ....131 A1
Westmorland Ct CA2 ...214 A1
Westmorland General Hospl
  LA8 ....144 B5
Westmorland Rd CA28 ..187 F5
Westmorland Sh Ctr The ⊞
  LA9 ....200 D5
Westmorland St
  Barrow-In-F LA14 ....206 F5
  Carlisle CA2 ....214 A1
Weston Ave LA12 ......203 C2
Weston Hos LA8 ......156 D7
Westover Ave LA5 .....213 D7
Westover Gr LA5 ......213 D7
Westover Rd LA5 ......213 D7
Westrigg Rd CA2 ......176 C3
Westvale Ct CA2 ......176 F4
Westville CA1 ....177 E4
Westway LA13 ....207 D3
Westwood CA2 ....176 B3
Westwood Ave LA9 ....200 C3
Wether Riggs Rd LA14 ..184 C1
Wetheral Pasture CA4 ..31 B4
Wetheral Priory Gatehouse*
  CA4 ....178 B1
Wetheral St CA2 ......176 E6
Wetheral Sta CA4 .....178 B2
Wetheriggs Jun Sch
  CA11 ....191 D3
Wetheriggs La CA11 ...191 D3
Wetheriggs Pottery*
  CA10 ....71 E1
Wetheriggs Rise CA11 ..191 C4
Weymouth St LA14 ....206 B2
Whalley Dr CA28 ......187 E8
Wharton La CA17 .....120 C4
Wheatclose Rd LA14 ...207 B7
Wheatlands CA2 ......176 D5
Wheatsheaf Gdns CA4 ..178 A1
Wheatsheaf La CA7 ....180 C3
Wheelbarrow Ct CA4 ...30 E7
Whelpdale Ho CA11 ...191 D4
Whernside CA2 ....176 A5
Wherside Gr LA5 .....213 E4
Whetstone La LA8 ....143 E4
Whicham Terr LA18 ....149 E4
Whimbrel Dr CA1 .....177 D6
Whinbarrow La CA7 ...36 C1
Whinfell Ave CA13 ....190 E4
Whinfell Dr LA9 ......200 F4
Whinfell Rd CA16 ......87 D5
Whinfell Terr CA10 ....118 B2
Whinfield Pl ⑩ LA16 ..162 A8
Whinfield Rd
  Ulverston LA12 ......203 D6
  Windermere LA23 ....198 E4
Whinlatter Cl LA18 ....202 B4
Whinlatter Dr
  Barrow-In-F LA14 ....204 D1
  Kendal LA9 ....200 D6
Whinlatter Forest Pk*
  CA12 ....80 D8
Whinlatter Forest Wlk*
  CA12 ....80 D7
Whinlatter Pass CA12,
  CA11 ....80 C7
Whinlatter Rd CA28 ...187 E5
Whinlatter Visitor Ctr*
  CA12 ....80 C7
Whinlatter Visitor Ctr Forest
  Wlk* CA12 ....80 C7
Whinlatter Way CA2 ...176 E5
Whinney Ends LA13 ...207 C4
Whinnie House Pk CA2 .176 B5
Whinnie House Rd CA2 .176 B5
Whinrigg CA2 ....176 C3
Whinrigg Dr CA28 ....76 F1
Whins The CA8 ....31 E6
Whinsfield Ave LA14 ...204 B1
Whinsmoor Dr CA1 ....177 E3
Whitbarrow Cl LA9 ....144 C8
Whitbarrow Gr LA8 ...143 D1
Whitbarrow Rd LA8 ...142 F4
Whitbarrow View LA8 ..155 D8
Whitber La CA17 ......119 E4

Whitberry Ct CA6 ......5 D2
Whitchester La TD9 ....1 B6
Whitchester St TD9 ....1 B6
White Croft CA15 .....182 C4
White Croft Ct CA15 ..182 C3
White Cross Bay Holiday Pk
  LA23 ....129 A7
White Gate CA4 ......178 A2
White Gill Cl LA12 ....163 C5
White Gill La LA12 ....163 B5
White Hall Cvn Pk LA12,
  LA13 ....171 D6
White Hart Yd ⑨ CA11 .191 C5
White House Gdns
  CA11 ....191 D4
White La LA7 ....156 A6
White Moss Ct LA9 ...200 B6
White Ox Way CA11 ...191 C7
White Pk CA28 ....186 D1
White Row CA5 ....18 F2
White School Cl CA28 ..187 B6
White St LA14 ....206 D3
White Star Way CA15 ..182 C5
White Stiles CA11 ....200 D7
Whitebarrow Hall Cvn Pk
  CA11 ....69 B3
Whitebarrow Village*
  CA11 ....69 B3
Whitebeam Gdns LA13 .207 E5
Whitebeck La LA6 .....167 B4
Whiteclosegate
  Carlisle CA3 ....30 C8
  Houghton CA3 ....20 C1
Whitecroft CA20 .....109 B2
Whitegate
  Egremont CA22 ......189 D6
  Levens LA8 ....143 E1
Whitehaven Castle
  CA28 ....187 D8
Whitehaven Commercial Pk
  CA28 ....76 F1
Whitehaven Sch CA28 ..91 F8
Whitehead Cl LA14 ...207 A4
Whitehead St LA14 ...207 A4
Whitehouse CA8 ......22 B7
Whites Yd CA15 ......183 D7
Whiteside Ave CA13 ..190 E3
Whiteside Cotts LA12 ..153 C7
Whitestiles CA14 .....183 C3
Whitfell Ave CA2 .....176 B3
Whitfield Ct ⑩ LA14 ..184 D6
Whitriggs Cl LA18 ....202 A3
Whittaker St ① LA14 ..206 F3
Whitthorn Terr LA9 ...200 D4
Whole House Rd CA20 .123 B8
Whooff Ho CA4 ......30 F7
Whyber La CA16 ......87 D4
Wickham Ct ⑩ CA12 ..192 B3
Wiggonby CE Sch CA7 .28 C4
Wigton Hospl CA7 ....180 B5
Wigton Inf Sch CA7 ...180 C2
Wigton Rd Allonby CA15 .35 C1
  Silloth CA7 ....174 C4
Wigton Sta CA7 ......180 C4
Wild Rose Cvn Pk CA16 .103 D7
Wildman St LA9 ......200 D6
Wilfred St CA1 ....214 B2
William Cl LA15 ......205 C6
William Fletcher Ct CA7 .37 C1
William Howard Sch
  CA8 ....179 B5
William Morris Ave
  CA25 ....188 E6
William Pitt Ind Est
  CA28 ....186 C3
William St
  ⑥ Barrow-In-F LA14 ..206 F3
  Carlisle CA1 ....214 C1
  Carnforth LA5 ....213 C5
  Cotehill CA4 ....31 B1
  Great Clifton CA14 ...63 A4
  Haverigg LA18 ......150 A1
  Maryport CA15 ......182 D6
  ⑥ Penrith CA11 .....191 D5
  Ulverston LA12 ......203 E5
  Wigton CA7 ....180 D3
  Workington CA14 ....184 D7
Williamson La CA28 ...186 C1
Williamson's La CA28 ..187 F6
Willow Bank CA7 .....176 E7
Willow Cl CA11 ......191 F4

Willow Ct
  Backbarrow LA12 .....153 C7
  Swarthmoor LA12 ....203 A3
  Workington CA14 ....184 E3
Willow Dr Kendal LA9 .200 F4
  Whitehaven CA28 ....187 E7
Willow Holme Ind Est
  CA2 ....176 E7
Willow Holme Rd CA2 .176 E7
Willow La
  Cockermouth CA13 ...190 E2
  Flookburgh LA11 ....164 E6
Willow Pk CA1 ......177 D6
Willow Rd LA14 .....206 F7
Willowdene Gdns LA12 .203 C7
Willowholme Gdns CA2 .176 E7
Willows The Durdar CA2 .30 B2
  Egremont CA22 .....189 B6
  Milnthorpe LA7 .....211 D3
Willowside Pk LA18 ...202 A3
Wilson Ave LA18 .....150 A2
Wilson Homes Milton CA8 .22 E3
  Walton CA8 ....22 B7
Wilson Meml Homes
  CA8 ....179 D5
Wilson Pit Rd CA28 ..187 C3
Wilson Pl LA8 ......143 F2
Wilson St Carlisle CA2 ..176 D4
  Kendal LA9 ....200 D3
Wilson's Terr CA15 ...63 C8
Winchester Dr CA28 ...91 F8
Winchester St LA13 ..207 C3
Windebrowe Ave CA12 .192 C3
Winder Farm Cl CA15 ..49 B3
Winder Garth LA6 ....167 B1
Winder Gate CA26 ....92 E8
Winder La LA11 ......164 C6
Winder Lonning CA13 .63 E6
Windermere Ave
  Barrow-In-F LA14 ...204 D1
  Maryport CA15 .....182 D4
Windermere CE Jun Sch
  LA23 ....198 E4
Windermere Gdns LA18 .202 C4
Windermere Pk LA23 ..198 E3
Windermere Rd
  Burneside LA9 ......130 E1
  Carlisle CA2 ....176 D1
  Carnforth LA5 ......213 D2
  Grange-Over-S LA11 ..208 E7
  Kendal LA9 ....200 B7
  Staveley LA8 ....130 B5
  Whitehaven CA28 ...187 C4
Windermere Sta LA23 .198 E6
Windermere Steamboat
  Mus* LA23 ....198 E3
Windmill Brow ⑤ CA28 .186 D1
Windmill Cl LA13 ....190 E3
Windmill La CA11 ....190 E3
Windrigg Cl CA22 ...189 E7
Windrush Cres LA14 ..206 A4
Windsor Cres LA12 ...203 C2
Windsor Ct
  ⑦ Penrith CA11 ....191 E4
  Whitehaven CA28 ...187 F7
Windsor Dr CA11 ....191 B4
Windsor Ho CA2 ....176 C2
Windsor Rd CA14 ....184 C2
Windsor St
  Barrow-In-F LA14 ...207 A5
  Millom LA18 ....202 D4
Windsor Terr CA28 ...186 F1
Windsor Way CA3 ....175 D3
Windy Hall Rd LA23 ..129 B2
Windy Hill LA7 ......211 D4
Winfield Rd LA10 ....201 C5
Winscale Dr CA28 ...187 F7
Winscale Way CA14 ..185 E5
Winscales Rd LA14 ...63 A1
Winstanley Pl LA8 ...130 E3
Winster Dr CA28 .....187 F7
Winter La LA8 ......130 E3
Winter's Pk CA11 ....191 F4
Winterhope Rd DG12 ..172 E3
Winton Cres CA1 ....177 E3
Winton Manor Ct CA17 .105 A1
Witham Wlk LA14 ...206 B3
Witherslack Hall Sch
  LA11 ....142 E1
Wiza Ave CA7 ....180 B3

Woburn St ⑧ CA3 ....175 B1
Wodow Rd CA22 .....189 D2
Wolsty Cl CA3 ......175 E3
Wood Ave DG12 .....172 C3
Wood Broughton LA11 .153 F4
Wood Close Cvan Pk
  LA6 ....212 D1
Wood Close Gdns LA5 .209 B2
Wood La
  Appleby-In-W CA16 ...88 C7
  St Bees CA27 ....91 D3
Wood St Carlisle CA1 ..177 E6
  Carlisle,Newton CA2 ..176 D6
  Maryport CA15 .....182 D6
Wood View LA6 .....169 C3
Woodbank
  Egremont CA22 .....189 E5
  Endmoor LA8 ......156 D8
Woodend Dr CA2 ...176 D4
Woodend Terr CA10 ..118 B3
Woodgate LA9 ......200 E6
Woodhall Brow CA14 ..78 B8
Woodhayes CA2 .....30 B2
Woodhead Terr LA11 ..208 C4
Woodhill Cres LA13 ..171 B5
Woodhouse La LA7 ...211 D7
Woodhouse Rd CA28 .187 C5
Woodland Cl LA23 ...198 E5
Woodland Pk LA14 ...207 A6
Woodland Rd
  Ulverston LA12 ......203 C4
  Windermere LA23 ...198 E5
Woodland Vale LA12 ..141 E2
Woodlands
  Gosforth CA20 ......109 A2
  Great Corby CA4 ....178 C2
  Haverigg LA18 .....187 F8
Woodlands Cl
  Carlisle CA3 ....175 E2
  Endmoor LA8 ......156 D7
  Lakeside LA12 ......141 E2
  Lowther CA10 ......85 F6
  Storth LA7 ....209 F4
Woodlands Dr
  Ulleskelf LA11 ......164 F7
  Maryport CA15 ......182 E5
  Silverdale LA5 ......210 C4
Woodlands Grange CA13 .64 A8
Woodlea Gr CA25 ....188 A8
Woodleigh CA8 .....22 B7
Woodman Ave DG12 ..172 E3
Woodman La LA6 ....168 F6
Woodrouffe Terr CA1 ..214 C1
Woodsghyll Dr CA1 ..177 D1
Woodside Endmoor LA8 .156 D8
  Longtown CA6 ......10 B1
  Workington CA14 ...184 D4
Woodside Ave
  Cockermouth CA13 ..190 E3
  Sedbergh LA10 .....201 B5
Woodside Cl
  Endmoor LA8 ......156 D8
  Whitehaven CA28 ...187 F8
Woodside Cotts LA13 .153 C8
Woodside La LA8 ...156 D8
Woodside N CA2 ....177 C1
Woodside Rd
  Bowland Bridge LA11 .142 D4
  Endmoor LA8 ......156 D8
  Gretna DG16 ....173 C3
Woodville Terr CA10 ..101 C5
Woodville Way CA11 ..185 D8
Woodward Ave LA3 ..207 C5
Woodwell La LA5 ....210 C1
Woollenscroft CA14 ..62 E3
Wootton Way CA2 ...176 B4
Worcester St LA13 ...207 C3
Wordsworth Cl CA22 .189 C6
Wordsworth Ct
  Bowness-On-W LA23 .198 C2
  ⑭ Penrith CA11 ....191 D6
Wordsworth Dr LA9 ..200 E2
Wordsworth House Mus*
  CA13 ....190 C4
Wordsworth St
  Barrow-In-F LA14 ...206 F4
  Hawkshead LA22 ...197 E5
  Keswick CA12 ......192 C3
  Penrith CA11 ....191 D6
  Workington CA14 ...184 D5
Wordsworth Terr CA11 .190 C1
Wordsworth View CA14 .184 C1

Workington Bridge
  CA14 ....184 F7
Workington Hall* CA14 184 F6
Workington Infmy CA14 .184 E4
Workington Rd
  Seaton CA14 ....183 A1
  St Helens CA25 .....183 A6
Workington Sixth Form Ctr
  CA14 ....184 D2
Workington Sta CA14 .184 C6
World of Beatrix Potter
  Visitor Ctr* LA23 ...198 C3
Wrae Pl DG14 ....9 B8
Wray Cres LA9 ......200 F2
Wray Head CA19 ....123 D6
Wraysholme La LA11 ..164 F6
Wreay CE Prim Sch CA4 .41 B7
Wreay Gdns CA4 ....1 B7
Wreay Mans CA10 ...84 C6
Wybrow Terr CA14 ..184 E6
Wyddleton Terr CA1 ..214 C2
Wynd The DG14 .....3 D3
Wyndam Terr CA22 ..189 E7
Wyndham Ct CA25 ...188 D7
Wyndham Row
  Broughton Moor CA15 .63 C8
  ⑧ Cockermouth CA13 .190 D4
Wyndham St CA22 ...189 D6
Wyndham St CA25 ...188 E7
Wyndham Way CA22 .189 E6
Wyndsore Ave LA7 ...211 D4
Wynlass Pk LA23 ....198 D7
Wyre Gn LA14 ......206 B3
Wythburn Cl CA28 ...91 F7
Wythburn Rd CA14 ...91 F7
Wythop Mill* CA13 ..65 C4
Wyvern Cl CA2 .....176 C5

Y

Yans La LA7 ....209 F5
Yanwath Prim Sch CA10 .71 A2
Yarl Mdw LA13 .....207 D3
Yarl Well LA15 .....205 D5
Yarlside Cres LA13 ..207 E5
Yarlside Prim Sch LA13 .207 E5
Yarlside Rd LA13 ...207 E5
Yealand CE Prim Sch
  LA5 ....166 F6
Yealand Dr
  Barrow-In-F LA14 ...207 B8
  Kendal LA9 ....200 F3
  Ulverston LA12 .....203 D3
Yealand Gr LA5 .....213 D4
Yealand Rd LA5 ....166 F5
Yearl Rise CA14 ....62 E4
Yeathouse Rd CA26 ..92 D8
Yeats Cl LA9 ....200 C2
Yeorton Brow CA22 ..108 C6
Yeowartville ⑥ CA14 .184 D6
Yetlands CA5 ....29 D1
Yew Cl CA2 ....176 C4
Yew Tree LA6 ......157 F5
Yew Tree Cl LA14 ...207 C5
Yew Tree Gdns LA13 ..207 C5
Yew Tree Rd LA11 ...208 C2
Yew Tree Terr LA13 ..207 C5
Yew Tree Wlk ① LA11 ..207 C5
Yewbank La CA28 ...187 F7
Yewbarrow Cl CA28 ..187 F4
Yewbarrow St LA11 ..208 D5
Yewbarrow Lodge LA11 .208 C5
Yewbarrow Rd LA12 ..203 D2
Yewbarrow Terr LA11 ..208 E5
Yewdale Ave LA14 ...204 E1
Yewdale Rd Carlisle CA2 .176 A5
  Coniston LA21 .....196 A4
  Yewdale Sch CA2 ...176 A5
York Gdns CA2 .....177 B3
York Rd Carlisle CA3 ..175 D1
  Whitehaven CA28 ...187 B7
York Sq ⑦ LA12 ....203 E5
York St Barrow-In-F LA14 .207 A5
  Carlisle CA2 ....176 E6
  Penrith CA11 ....191 C5
  ⑨ Workington CA14 ..184 D6
York Terr CA28 .....186 D2

PHILIP'S MAPS

the Gold Standard for drivers